Life Skills

PERSONAL AND HOME MANAGEMENT

Connie Sasse
Anne Hagy
Tybe Kahn
Jeanne Brinkley

GLENCOE
Macmillan/McGraw-Hill
Lake Forest, Illinois Columbus, Ohio Mission Hills, California Peoria, Illinois

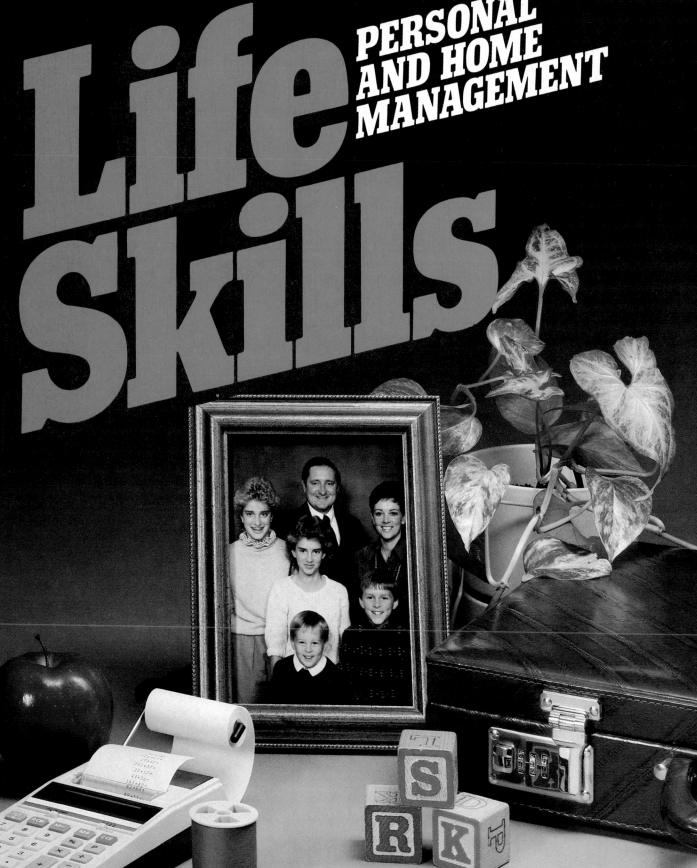

Life Skills
PERSONAL AND HOME MANAGEMENT

Special Contributing Writers:
Anne Marie Soto
Celia Snyder
Teresa Farney

Send all inquiries to:
GLENCOE DIVISION
Macmillan/McGraw-Hill
3008 W. Willow Knolls Drive
Peoria, IL 61615

ISBN 0-02-668460-8 (Text)

Printed in the United States of America.

5 6 7 8 9 10 11 12 13 14 15 99 98 97 96 95 94 93 92 91

Contents

UNIT II
PLANNING YOUR FUTURE 68

UNIT IV CLOTHING AND TEXTILES 194

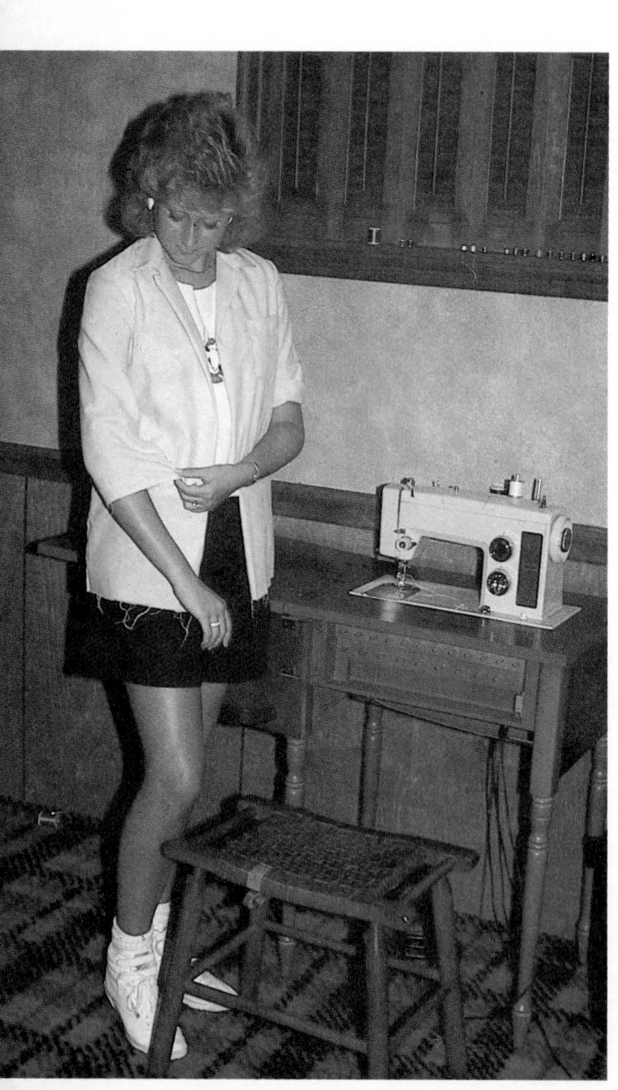

UNIT V FOOD AND NUTRITION

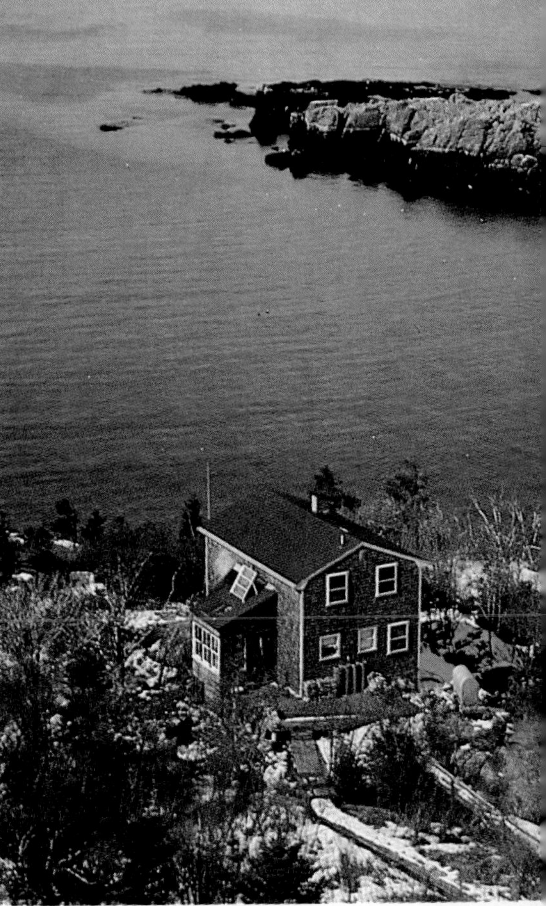

Unit 1

MAKING THE MOST OF YOUR WORLD

Everyone has dreams and ideas of what a perfect life would be like. This unit is designed to help you make the most of your present world.

Learning to use what you have to get what you want is the central theme of this book. Unit I looks at the relationships you have with others and how they can help you reach your goals.

Understanding yourself, the management process, and what makes good relationships are basic to making the most of life. Building better relationships with your friends, your peer group, dating partner, and family can help you live a more satisfying life now and in the future.

Chapter 1
MANAGEMENT BEGINS WITH YOU

Has this ever happened to you?

Bob and Teresa were talking as they walked to the bus after school. Teresa said, "The thing that really bothers me is I can't figure out what I'm going to do when I graduate."

"But I thought you wanted to go to college," answered Bob.

"Well, I did," said Teresa. "My mom is really pushing it too. But I just don't know. I keep thinking I'd like to do something besides go to school for a while. Besides, going away to college will cost a lot, and my folks don't have much money."

"Have you ever thought about going to the community college?" asked Bob. "You could live at home and save lots of money."

"Yes, that is one idea." said Teresa. "But I keep thinking I might like to learn to repair computers. I'd have to go to a technical school for that. Sometimes I think it would be simpler just to get a job—but I don't know if I'd like the kind of job I'd get without any training. I just don't know what I want out of life."

Have you ever felt like you do not know where you are going with your life?

Have you ever had trouble making decisions about problems you face?

After reading this chapter, you will be able to

- identify areas of growth in adolescence;
- explain the major developmental tasks of adolescence;
- recognize the importance of a good self-concept;
- understand the management process.

Adolescence is one of the most important periods of your life. It is a time when you change from a dependent child to an independent adult. As a teen, you work to become the kind of person you will be as an adult. The habits and patterns you learn now form a base for life as an adult. How you manage the pleasures and problems of the teen years will influence your ability to cope with them during your adult life.

The first step in becoming the person you want to be is to look at the person you are now, the kind of life you live, and how you feel about yourself and your life.

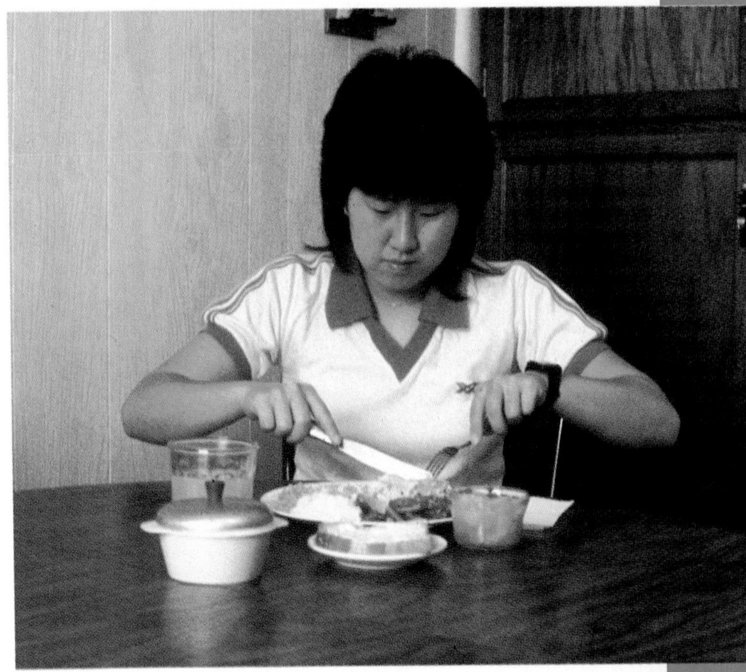

By eating well-balanced meals, following a regular exercise program and getting enough rest, you can promote healthy, normal growth.

A TIME OF GROWTH

Sometimes it may be hard to know exactly who you are now because the teen years are a time of rapid growth. You have changed physically, mentally, emotionally, and socially. The changes brought about by growth are not always easy to see or handle.

PHYSICAL GROWTH

During the teen years the body changes from that of a child to that of an adult. This physical growth may be early or late. You may have completed your physical growth several years ago. Or you may still have a small, childlike body in your late teen years.

Growth is affected by several factors. A well-balanced, nutritious diet and regular exercise promote normal growth. Illness can hinder growth. If you have had a long-term illness or are often sick, you may grow more slowly than your friends. Growth patterns tend to be the same within families. Your adult height and weight and the timing of your growth spurt will be similar to others in your family.

Growth, whenever it happens, is rapid and uneven. You may not feel comfortable in your changing body. The feet that were surefooted and swift last year may seem long, awkward, and clumsy this year. If your growth has not occurred at the same time as classmates or friends, you may feel left out or out of place.

MENTAL GROWTH

During the teen years, rapid mental growth also takes place. Your school work may seem more meaningful as you prepare for a career or further education. You learn to be objective. You use logic and reason to analyze situations as you develop higher thinking skills.

During this time, most people establish a lifelong approach to learning. You will discover those subjects of most interest to you and find the means of learning more about them. Taking school courses about subjects that appeal to you is a way to learn more about many topics. Books from the library, instructional video tapes, and television specials are sources of information. You may join a special club in your school or community to learn more about a topic that interests you.

Intellectual interests come and go and may frequently change in the teen years. You may have taken a course and joined a club only to find you are not really interested in the subject. However, sooner or later, teenagers are usually attracted to the subject areas they want to pursue as careers.

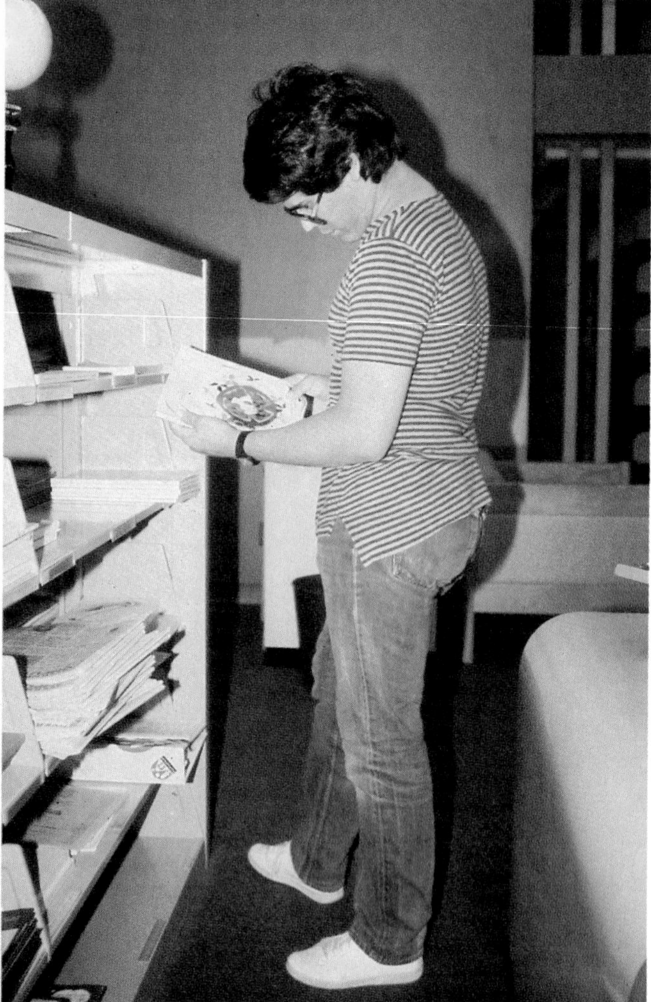

Use the teen years as a time to stretch your mind. Books, instructional videotapes, and television specials can help you learn more about topics that interest you.

EMOTIONAL GROWTH

One of the major influences on teenage life is the roller coaster of emotions. **Hormones,** which are chemicals that are produced by the body and that cause it to grow and mature, can also cause your emotional feelings to swing wildly. You may be on top of the world one minute and then sink into dark despair the next.

Learning to control and handle these changing feelings may not be easy for you. Being able to control wild emotional states and to express emotion appropriately are steps toward adult maturity.

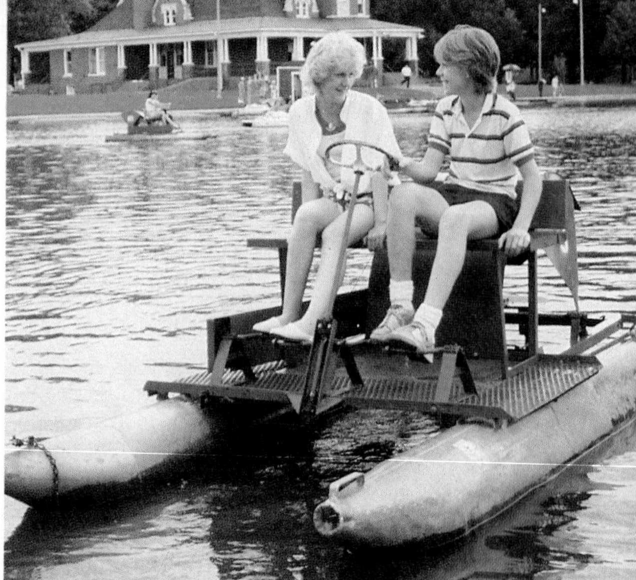

Learning to relate to persons of the opposite sex is an important developmental task of the teen years.

SOCIAL GROWTH

The teen years are a time of intense social growth. During these years, you learn to get along with a wide variety of people. You may make new friends and begin to form relationships with persons of the opposite sex. You also begin to learn to get along with others on the job as you enter the labor market.

ADOLESCENCE

Part of being an adolescent is learning to cope with the changes and growth described above. In addition, each stage of life has certain tasks or jobs, called **developmental tasks,** which must be accomplished as a part of growing older. These tasks are the skills, knowledge, and attitudes you need to succeed in that stage of life. Your most important task during the teen years is to find and form an identity for yourself.

There are several aspects of this task. During your teen years, you will work toward

1. accepting your changing body and your role as a man or woman;
2. growing socially to establish relations with peers of both sexes;
3. controlling your emotions as you become independent of parents and other adults;
4. developing intellectual skills and concepts;
5. preparing for and reaching economic independence;
6. becoming a responsible citizen.

By mastering these tasks, you prepare for responsible adult behavior, which may include marriage and family life.

SELF-CONCEPT

As you proceed through the teen years and cope with rapid growth and changes in yourself, you will also further develop and refine your self-concept. **Self-concept** is basically how you feel about yourself. It is an overall sense of how much you like yourself. *Self-concept* is also called *self-image* or *self-esteem*.

If you have a strong self-concept, you can see your good features and accept your bad. You know that no one is perfect. You feel able to handle the changes that occur and the problems you must face. A strong self-concept helps you accomplish your developmental tasks.

On the other hand, if you have a poor self-concept, you are not sure about your abilities. You tend to focus on your weaknesses and downplay your strengths and talents. You may feel overwhelmed by changes in your life and believe you will not be able to handle what happens.

Actually, self-concept is not a single good or bad feeling about yourself. Instead, your self-concept is made up of good and bad feelings. For example, you may feel good about your physical appearance but uncertain about your athletic ability. Your feelings about these and other parts of your life all help to form your overall self-concept.

However, your overall self-concept is not fixed or set. It can be changed by activities and relationships. After you experience a success, your self-confidence rises. A good test score, making a new friend, or winning a part in the school play can all help to raise self-esteem. In contrast, being fired from a job, getting cut from a sports team, or breaking up with a dating partner can damage self-image.

Your self-concept is actually based on two related concepts. The first concept is what you feel your ideal self should be. This is your idea of what you should be like. The second concept is what you see your real self to be. This concept reflects what you think you really are. If the gap between your ideal self and real self is too wide, your self-concept will be poor. Low self-esteem is often caused by impossible demands placed on the self.

On the other hand, if there is a small gap between your ideal and real selves, your self-esteem will be high. However, if there is no gap, you may feel there is little reason to try to improve yourself.

Success in areas of your life, such as a good test score, can raise your self-esteem. What have you accomplished recently that bolstered your self-concept?

ORIGIN OF SELF-CONCEPT

Your overall self-concept began to develop early in your life. The initial parts of your self-concept arose from **heredity,** those traits you inherited from your parents. You were born with certain physical, mental, and emotional qualities. These formed the basis of your first self-concept—the first information in your judgment of yourself.

However, the experiences you have had since you were born have probably been more important in forming what you think about yourself. These experiences have shaped what you believe about your ideal self and your real self.

If you were born with red hair, what you think about that color depends on what you have learned about red hair since then. If you believe red hair is ugly, having it may have a negative effect on your self-concept. If you have learned that red hair is attractive, having it will probably have a good effect on your self-image.

The emotional parts of your self-concept are more complex than your feelings about your physical self. Some people are born with outgoing personalities. Others are more inward looking. However, life experiences can influence your basic personality traits and change them.

Lively, bouncing, confident babies can become withdrawn if their parents constantly punish or abuse them. Quiet, shy children can become more confident and outgoing with love, attention, praise, and help. Children who are always interrupted when speaking are not apt to grow up feeling free to express themselves.

IMPORTANCE OF SELF-CONCEPT

Self-concept is an important part of your adult personality. It forms the core of your self and determines how you will use your talents and skills to achieve what you want.

A person with a good self-concept usually has good relationships with others. A good self-concept is important for success in your family life, work life, and friendships. If you are not sure of your abilities, you may worry about whether or not others will accept you. You may find it hard to build good relationships because you are defensive in your attitudes. Often people treat others badly because they do not feel good about themselves.

A strong self-concept is often related to achievement. If you are confident in your abilities, you may be more willing to try new activities. In addition, your self-confidence means you are more apt to make a success of what you attempt. People who do not believe in themselves may find their lack of confidence leads to a lack of success.

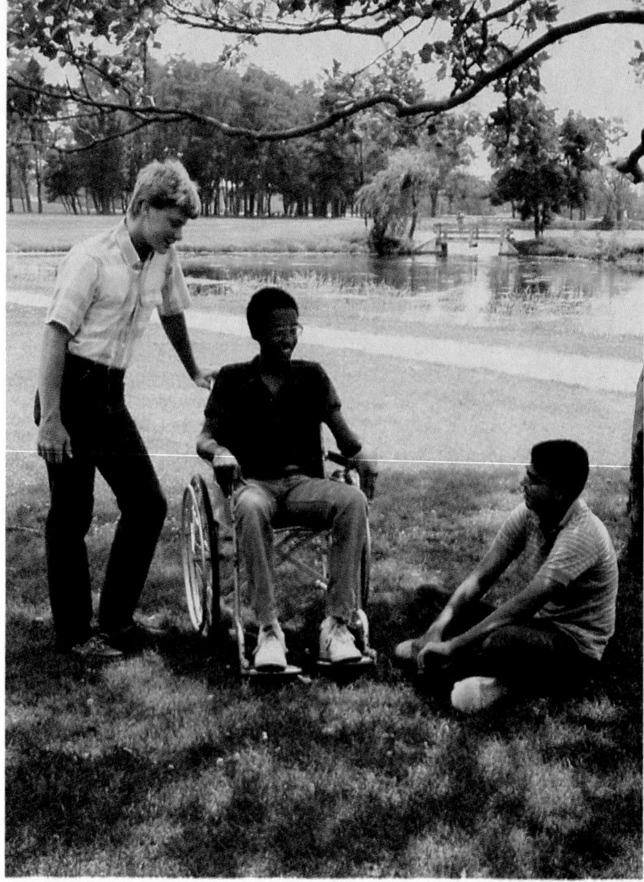

People who have good self-concepts usually relate well to others. What are other advantages of a good self-concept?

LEARNING FROM YOUR MISTAKES

Because human beings are not perfect, they all make mistakes at times. Students may make mistakes at school, work, or in their relationships with others. Many people who make mistakes are so miserable about them that they give up. Students with poor grades may drop out of school as soon as they are old enough. They want to get away from the source of their failures.

Such a reaction is natural. If you have made mistakes or failed, why stay in a place where the same thing may happen again? In one sense, this protects your self-concept. You can focus on what you do well and avoid those activities in which you lack skill.

However, for some people, mistakes are simply a challenge to do better. Most people can do anything they want to. It may take lots of effort to return to school after dropping out or to earn enough money to replace the car damaged in an accident. However, with hard work and effort, you can overcome most obstacles. Mistakes and failure do not have to be the end of the line; instead, they can be the beginning of new successes.

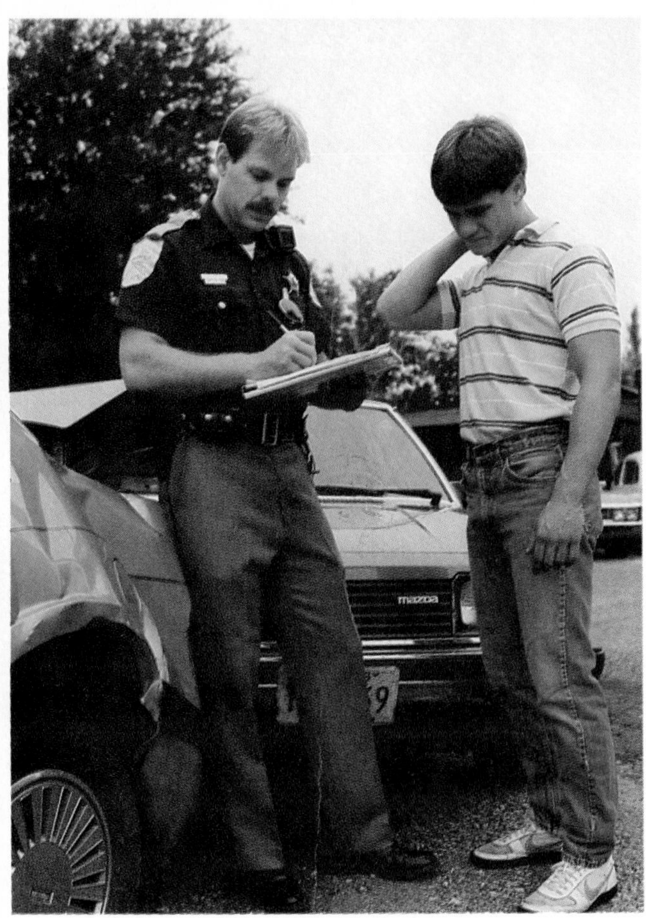

When you make a mistake do not consider yourself a failure. Instead learn from the mistake and plan how to avoid making the same one in the future.

TAKING RESPONSIBILITY FOR YOURSELF

A self-concept develops over the years through your experiences in life. But whether you have a strong or a weak self-concept, you are responsible for it. To become fully adult, you must take responsibility for yourself. You alone can do your developmental tasks. You must discover your own identity. You can influence how you feel about yourself.

THE MANAGEMENT PROCESS

You have learned about the growth you have experienced during your teen years, and you have looked at how you feel about your traits and qualities. The next step is to consider where you want to go in the future and how you can get there.

One skill that is valuable in coping with life is management. **Management** is the process of reaching your goals through the good use of human and material resources. Using good management skills can help you control and direct change in your life. As you learn to manage yourself, your self-concept can improve.

SETTING YOUR GOALS

The first step in the management process is setting your goals. **Goals** are what you want from life. They are objectives for which you are willing to make an effort to achieve. The management process is designed to help you reach your goals.

Some goals are short-term, that is, they can be reached in a short period of time. You may wish to buy the newly released cassette tape of your favorite recording star. That goal is easy to accomplish once you have money to buy the tape and are able to go shopping.

Some short-term goals take more effort to achieve. Reading an eight-hundred-page book for an English report means saving time for reading. It may take a lot of planning to visit a friend who has moved across the state. If you would like to lose five pounds in the next month, you will have to eat low calorie meals and increase the amount of exercise you get.

Other goals require much more time and effort to accomplish. These goals are called long-term. Perhaps your goal is to become an accountant, a profession which requires a college degree. To reach your goal, you would need to plan on four or more years of education after you graduate from high school. Your goal may be to own a brand new car or to travel abroad. Perhaps you want to have children or your own business someday. Long-term goals are very satisfying to achieve, but they are not accomplished overnight.

Sometimes, long-term goals seem more reachable if they are broken down into a series of short-term goals. It may take many years for you to reach the long-term goal of owning your own business. In the meantime, your short-term goals may include taking business-related courses at the community college and working full- or part-time at a job in a business like you want to own. You may also work to save money for your business, as well as establish a good credit rating so you can borrow needed funds. As you accomplish each of these short-term goals, you will have taken a step toward achieving your long-term goal—owning your own business.

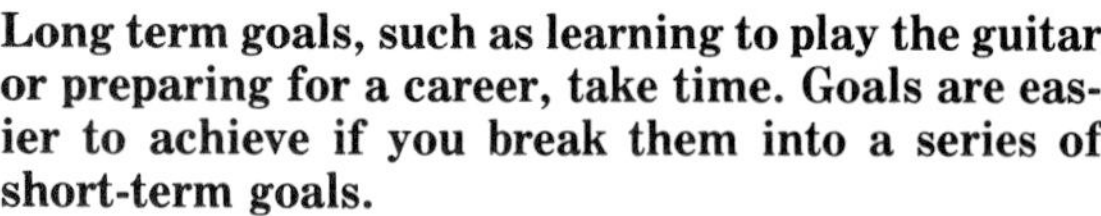

Long term goals, such as learning to play the guitar or preparing for a career, take time. Goals are easier to achieve if you break them into a series of short-term goals.

Close relationships with family and friends fulfill one's need for affection, love, and a feeling of belonging.

NEEDS AND WANTS

You probably can think of a variety of items and experiences you would like to have. Maybe you would like to buy a new winter coat, to attend a concert, or to make some new friends. All people have needs and wants that they believe would make their lives better. **Needs** are things that are essential for survival. **Wants** are things you desire to make life more enjoyable.

You need certain things to be physically and mentally healthy. Food, water, clothing, exercise, and shelter are needed for survival and good health. A feeling of being safe is important in being comfortable in your world. As a child, you probably believed your parents kept you safe and secure. As an adult, you will develop your own ways to protect yourself.

People need other people. You need to feel affection, love, and a feeling of belonging. Most people meet this need through relationships with family and friends.

One part of being mentally healthy is feeling good about yourself. A strong self-concept is important. Finally, people need to use their skills and talents to make something of themselves. Those who stretch themselves to fulfill their potential find life richer and more satisfying.

Besides filling these general needs, most people have additional wants. You may need transportation to your job from school. This need may be met by walking or taking the bus. However, you may want a car of your own to drive to work.

Beyond a certain minimum level, most needs become wants. You *need* clothing for protection from the weather, but you *want* several new outfits of the latest style. You *need* food to satisfy your hunger, but you *want* a steak rather than a hamburger.

You probably have goals that concern both your needs and wants. However, good managers are able to identify which of their needs and wants are more important than the others. Then they work to accomplish those goals that are of the highest priority.

IDENTIFYING VALUES

Underlying the goals you set and the needs and wants you believe important are the values you hold. **Values** are personal ideals and principles about what makes life important and worthwhile to you.

You developed your values from your experiences and from what you have been taught is important in life. Values include the standards of excellence you live by. They are a personal code of right and wrong.

Your values are almost a plan for life. The ideals you decide are important are those that guide you in choosing what you will do with your life. Well-thought-out values help you deal with both good times and bad.

People value many ideals and principles. These differ for different people. For example, in a recent poll, 82 percent of those polled said having a good family life was important. Thus, for those people, a close-knit family life is an important value.

Sixty-one percent of those polled said following God's will was important to them. Therefore, their values focused strongly on the religious aspects of their lives.

Almost 40 percent of the people felt a nice home, car, and other belongings were important. Having a certain amount of material goods was a part of their outlook on life.

Where do people get their ideas about what is important? How will you choose those values that will be important in your future? The largest influence on your values is the family setting in which you are being raised. As you were growing up, you saw what was important to your parents or to those with whom you lived. You evaluated activities on the basis of the rewards they brought to your home. If you enjoyed the family activities fostered by your parents, you will probably promote similiar activities as an adult.

As you grew up, you became more aware of how other people lived. You were able to compare and contrast different approaches to life. You probably found some more attractive than others. As you become an adult, you will use your experiences to decide what kind of life you want.

Identifying your values is not a simple, easy, quick task. It means considering what really is important to you and how you can live according to your ideals. However, when you have developed your values, they can be a guideline for your life.

Returning a lost wallet or not cheating on an exam are examples of personal values. These values influence your behavior and the type of goals that you set for yourself.

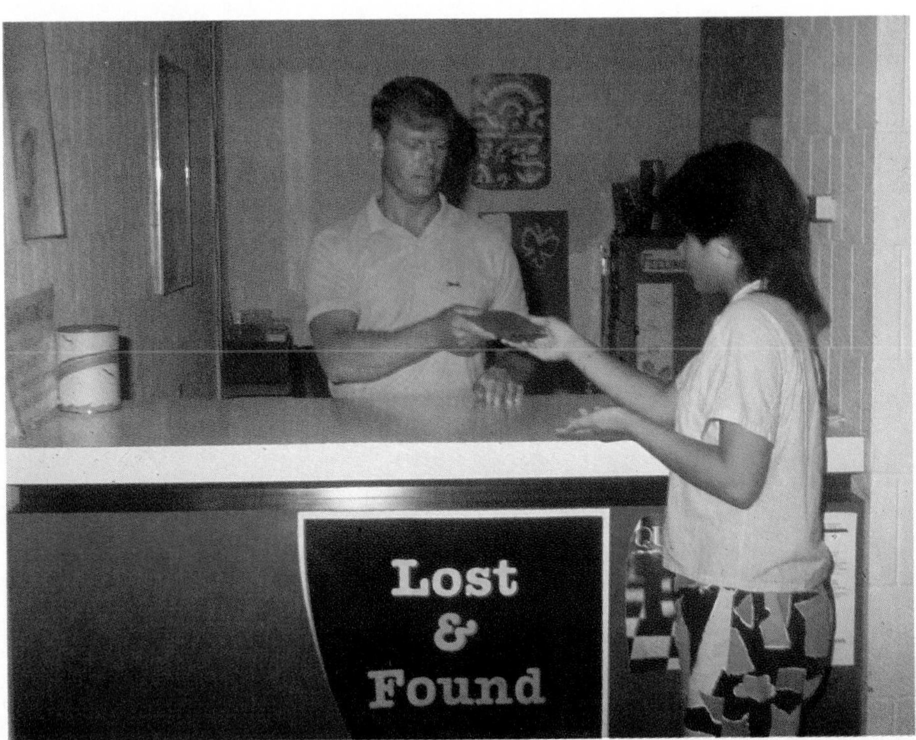

DISCOVERING YOUR RESOURCES

Once you have identified your goals, based on your needs, wants, and values, the next step in the management process is to discover what resources you have to use in working toward your goals. In management, **resources** are human and material sources of support or supply that can be used to accomplish a goal. Human resources include time, knowledge, skills and talents, energy level, and relationships. Material resources are money, possessions, and community facilities and agencies.

Human resources involve the qualities and characteristics of people. Time is a very important human resource. Knowledge is another major human resource. When you want to earn the most interest on your savings for college, knowing about investment options will help you choose the one that will keep your savings safe and growing.

Your skills and talents are another resource that can make a big difference in how you reach your goals. If your goal is to give your car a tune up and oil change, how you accomplish this goal may depend on whether you have the skill to do the jobs yourself.

Energy level is a human resource that varies from person to person. You may have the energy and related good health to work part-time, go to school, and participate in several school activities. Others may find they have to give up outside activities to have the energy for both work and school.

Relationships with others are a major human resource. Other people can give you advice and emotional support, as well as share their time, knowledge, skills, and energy.

Money is a material resource. It buys goods and services that can be used to reach goals. Getting a haircut and buying a new outfit before a school dance are ways that money can help you reach your goal of looking attractive.

Possessions are another resource. You are able to use what you own to help in reaching your goals. Owning your own instrument is a necessary part of the goal of being a professional musician.

Finally, community facilities and agencies are resources. Parks, libraries, and shopping facilities are resources you can use. Agencies, such as social service groups, can provide help and support as a resource for those who need them.

Once you have identified your goals you can use resources to help you achieve them. How can the resources below help you? Identify the human and the material resources.

DECISION MAKING

The heart of the management process is making decisions about how to use your resources to reach your goals. **Decision making** is the process of making choices from among options.

In normal day-to-day living, you make decisions all the time. These are based on your past experiences, your outlook on life, and what you value. Most of the time, these decisions are easy and not about major life issues.

Once in a while, however, a major decision faces you that cannot be solved quickly and easily. Sometimes the choice is so difficult that there is no good answer. At other times, the choice may be vital to your future. In these cases, you want to be sure you have thought about all the possible outcomes of your decision.

The decision-making process will help you be more conscious that your choice has been made according to your goals and values. The steps in the decision-making process are listed below.

1. *What is your problem?* First, consider just what the decision is you must make. Is it which courses to sign up for next year? Is it whether to attend college or a technical training program? Is it where to live after you graduate from high school and get a job? All of these decisions have a long-range influence on your life. Thus, they should be made with more care and thought than a decision about what to wear to a party.

2. *What are your options?* What are the different choices you could make? List as many options as you can for the problem you face. The more choices you list, the more apt you are to make a good decision.

3. *Think about your choices.* What would be the results of each option? What are the pros and cons of each choice? How would each possibility influence your relationships with others, your financial situation, your long-range plans, your self-concept? How would each alternative fit with your ideals and values?

4. *Make your decision.* Base your choice on what you have considered, what you think is important, and the probable outcome of each option. Once the choice is made, carry it out.

5. *Be responsible for your choice.* Was your choice a good one? Have you been happy with the results? If not, what could you do now that would make it a better decision? Whether the decision was a good one for you or not, you are responsible for the choice and must accept the consequences.

Each day you are faced with some tough decisions. The ones you make today–regarding classes to take, friendships, and how to handle peer pressure–can affect your entire life.

HOW TO FEEL GOOD ABOUT YOURSELF

How can you learn to feel good about yourself? What are some practical ways you can raise your self-concept?

- *Emphasize your strengths.* Any skill, talent, ability, or personal trait that helps you function well as a person is a strength. Feel proud of your strengths, talents, and skills, whatever they may be. You may have a talent in making friends or you may organize and manage your life well. You may have special ability in music, mechanics, homemaking, or in getting along with helping others. Making the most of your strengths helps you feel good about yourself.
- *Look carefully at your ideal and real selves.* Is your ideal self realistic for you? Do you really have the talents to get straight As, be a professional athlete, a world famous surgeon, or a beauty contest winner? If your ideal self is unrealistically high, would lowering or changing your ideal help you feel better about yourself?
- *Improve your real self.* Would more study, a greater effort, or more education make your real self more like your ideal self? Think of those talents you have but have not worked on. What abilities do you have within you that you have not yet developed?
- *Use imagination to forecast success.* Imagine yourself in some situation that is coming to you soon, but is not here yet. Imagine yourself carrying out your responsibilities well. Think of how successfully you can do the job. Imagine your feeling of satisfaction when everything goes well. If you believe you can handle a situation well, you are more apt to be a success.
- *Keep a "Success Journal."* Each day, in a notebook, jot down the successes you have had. Count all your successes—large or small. Keep your journal for several weeks. You will be amazed at the number of successes you record.

EVALUATION

Evaluation is the final stage of each step of the management process. **Evaluation** is the process of judging or measuring performance. Are the goals you have set really the ones you want for your life? Have you identified your wants and needs based on your values? Are the values you are living by the ones on which you want to base your life?

How well are you using your resources? Are you able to be efficient in using them to reach your goals? Do you reflect your values in your use of resources?

Goals, values, and decisions can and do change over time as people grow and develop. Through evaluation in your use of the management process, you will know when and how to change to reflect your growth as a person. Through management of your resources to meet your goals, you can control your own destiny and look forward to a happy and successful future.

WORDS TO REMEMBER

decision making	goal	management	self-concept
developmental task	heredity	needs	wants
evaluation	hormones	resources	

CHECKING YOUR UNDERSTANDING

1. Why are the teen years so important in life since they span only seven or eight years?
2. Brainstorm to make a list of all the features or traits people have that could relate to their self-concepts. How does your list show that each person has many self-concepts?
3. Describe specific examples of how people's ideal selves might be different from their real selves.
4. Define goals, values, wants, and needs and describe the relationships between the terms.
5. Outline the steps in the management process and identify two areas of your life where it could be used to help you solve problems.

APPLYING YOUR UNDERSTANDING

1. Draw a line down the center of a piece of paper. On one side of the line, list your strengths. On the other, list your weaknesses. When you are finished, look at your lists. Which list is longer? Which list was easier to make? What does this tell you about your self-concept?
2. Research and report on at least three opportunities available in your school or community that could lead to an improved self-image. Why would these activities raise self-esteem?
3. Analyze your own behavior in the last three days. Identify situations in which your actions had a good influence on other people's self-concepts. Did any of your actions have a poor effect on the self-concepts of others? What could you do to increase your positive influence on others?
4. Think of a character you like on a television show or in a book. Write a brief summary of what you believe are his or her goals and values. Are these goals and values similar to or different from yours? Are the character's goals and values part of what attracts you?
5. Consider some problem you are facing or will face in the next few months. On a separate piece of paper, write down the decision you must make. Using the decision-making process described in this chapter, make your choice, writing each step on the paper. If possible, put your decision into action. Do you feel that using a formal written process led to a different choice than you might otherwise have made? How did (or will) this decision help you use your resources to reach your goals?

Chapter 2
GETTING ALONG WITH OTHERS

Has this ever happened to you?

Carrie slammed her lunch tray down on the cafeteria table. "That's just the last straw," she muttered as she sat down.

Megan looked at her angry face and asked, "What's the matter, Carrie?"

"There is something wrong with me," Carrie replied. "I can't get along with anyone today. First thing this morning, my mom scolded me because I drove the car last night and hadn't put gas in it. Tonight I'm supposed to be playing the piano for choir practice, but last night my boss told me I have to come in to work tonight."

"It sounds like this hasn't been your day," said Megan.

"Oh, you haven't heard the half of it," said Carrie. "Mr. Barkley kicked me out of class this morning for being disrespectful. All I was trying to do was stick up for my ideas. The final blow was when I asked Beth if she was going to sit with me at lunch and she said she'd rather not—that I was so moody anymore I wasn't fun to be with. What more could possibly go wrong today?"

Have you ever felt that you could not get along with anyone and that all your relationships were strained?

What kind of advice would you give a friend who had Carrie's problems?

After reading this chapter, you will be able to

- explain the importance of satisfying relationships in a happy and productive life;
- identify qualities of good relationships;
- recognize the importance of roles in relating to others;
- understand the role of communication in strong relationships;
- describe ways of managing conflict and stress.

Satisfying **relationships,** or special bonds with other people, are important for both your physical and mental health. If you have strong, caring relationships with others, you are more apt to be healthy and live longer. Having friendly relationships with family and friends can help you be more successful in your career. Learning to manage your relationships well will make life more satisfying. Good relationships can help you be productive and happy with yourself. Poor relationships can cause depression, drug abuse, and other mental health problems.

Learning certain skills can help you make the most of your relationships with others. Good relationships require management, effort, and attention. They do not just happen. In fact, relationship skills are like any other skills. To master them requires practice, effort, some self-sacrifice, and determination.

KINDS OF RELATIONSHIPS

Your life is made up of many relationships. Some are close and caring, while others are distant and less important. Your family and best friends form your closest relationships. These are the ones that need the most effort to manage and maintain. These are also the ones that bring you the most joy and satisfaction.

Next in importance are other friends and colleagues. These include people with whom you interact on a daily basis, such as fellow students, teachers, or co-workers. Good relationships with these people are vital because of their constant presence in your life.

You probably have a lot of acquaintances. These are people with whom you get together once in a while. Because you do not see or work with these people daily, relationships with them are less important.

Since you live in a family group and learn, work and play with others, good relationship skills are an important asset in life.

QUALITIES OF GOOD RELATIONSHIPS

Strong relationships share many qualities. Some of these qualities can be seen as soon as you meet someone new. They help the relationship grow. Other traits develop with the relationship and help keep it strong and stable.

In a good relationship, you have rapport with the other person. **Rapport** means you are comfortable and at ease together. You may have met a friend with whom you "clicked," that is, you felt rapport immediately. Some of your other relationships may take more time to have rapport. Sooner or later, however, building a strong relationship means you and your partner will have rapport.

Good rapport is partly based on empathy. **Empathy** is the ability to see the world through the other person's eyes. It is "putting yourself in the other's shoes" and understanding his or her feelings and actions.

When you and another person have some rapport and empathy, you begin to build trust and respect for each other. **Trust** means you can rely and depend on the other person. To trust another person is to expect acceptance and support. **Respect** is accepting and appreciating the other person in his or her own right. These two qualities are important if your relationship is to grow.

Two people with a good relationship depend on each other. You rely on the other to be there when needed. You each know you can depend on support from the other in activities and feelings.

As a relationship grows, it is important that you and your partner have the same or **mutual expectations** for it. You should each expect the relationship to head in the same way or toward the same purpose. You and your parents may have different expectations for your relationship. These differences may lead to conflict if you want independence from your parents when they still want to provide guidance and discipline for you.

Finally, good relationships are flexible, meaning they can adapt and change. Because of the demands of life, you cannot always do and be everything another person wants. You sometimes have to compromise to help and please each other.

The closer and more personal your relationships, the more important it is that they have these qualities. A close relationship without these traits is not going to be satisfying to either partner.

When friends feel at ease with one another, they relax and are able to enjoy their time together.

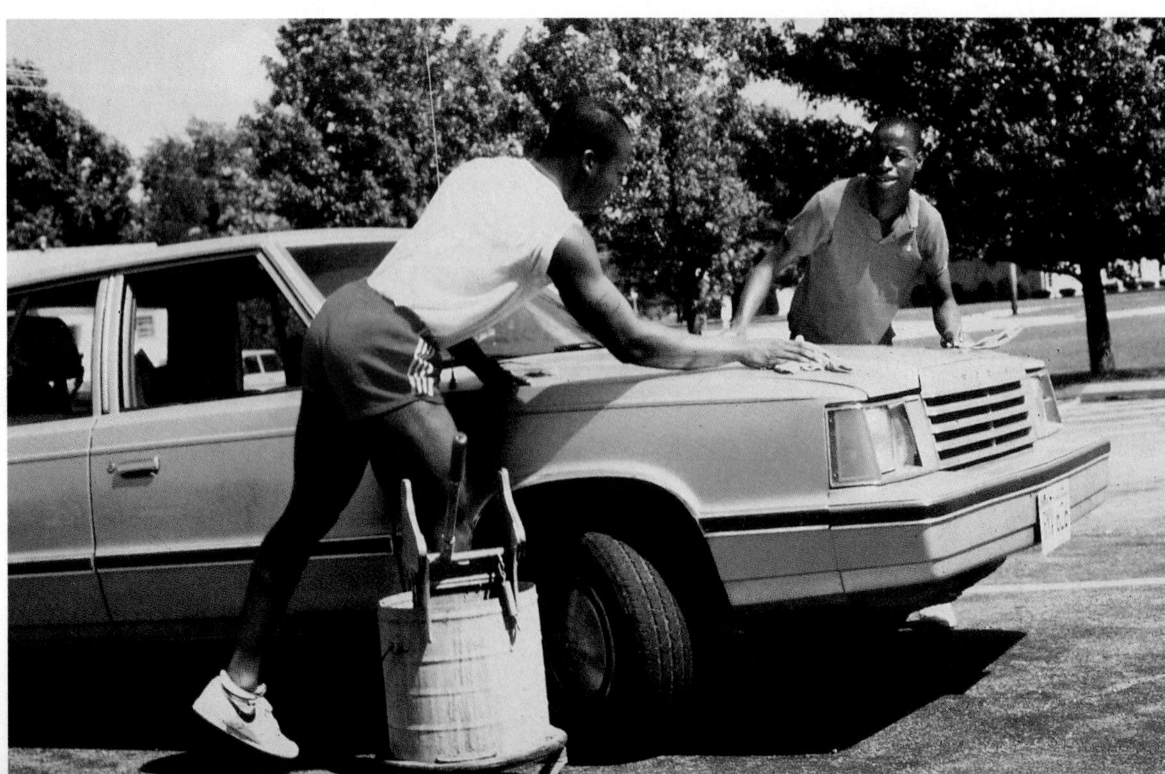

ROLE RELATIONSHIPS

One aspect of a relationship is the **role** or part you play in that relationship. You have, or play, many roles in your life. You are a student, a son or daughter, a friend, and a consumer.

When you interact with someone on the basis of your role, you have a role relationship. If you have a job, you are an employee and you have an employer. You may be a grandchild to your grandparent. Perhaps you share the role with others of being a member on the volleyball team.

Roles change throughout life. When you finish school, you will no longer be a student, although you may continue to be a learner. You may become a husband or wife and a parent. You may become a tennis player and give up being a member of the basketball team. As you grow and mature, your goals and values change as do the roles you play.

Roles can often make life easier. You have ideas about roles and how you should manage them. For example, you know that employees are supposed to be prompt, respectful, honest, and productive. Your idea of the role of an employee gives you a guideline to follow when you get a job.

Sometimes roles can be bad if or when they keep you from seeing others as people. Perhaps you see your teachers only through their roles in the classroom. The labels *teacher* and *student* make it hard for you to see each other as unique individuals.

Roles can also cause conflict. Your roles may interfere with each other. Perhaps you are supposed to be on the job an evening when you need to study for a big test. Or maybe your mother wants you to go with her to visit your grandfather in a nursing home when your friends are having a party. In both these cases, your different roles are in conflict.

Sometimes role conflict can result when two people have different ideas about how to play their roles. Perhaps you and your dating partner differ about what your relationship means. One of you might expect a commitment that the other is not ready to make.

Managing your roles, role relationships, and role conflicts is not always easy. Your ability to use the management process in getting along with others can help make your role relationships positive parts of your life.

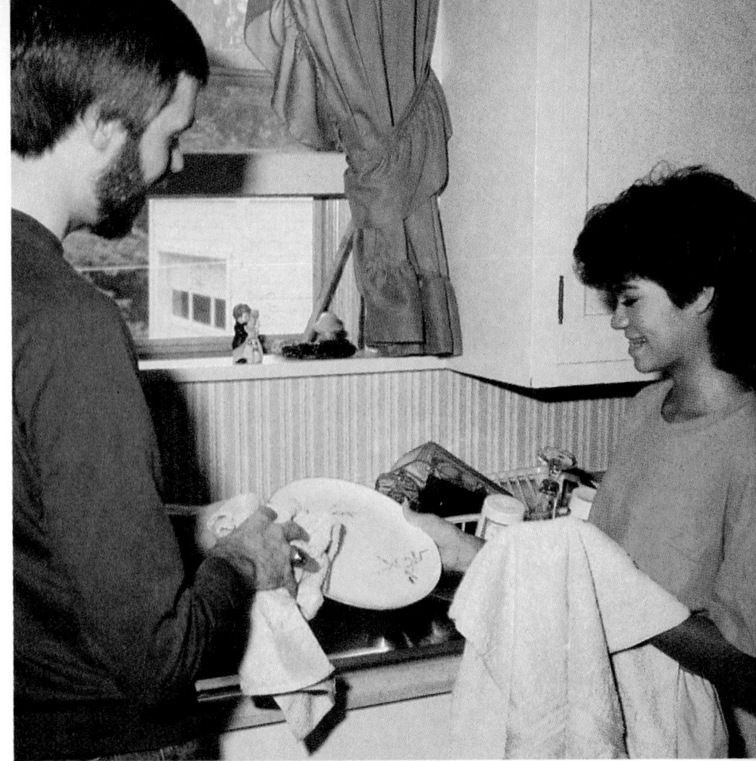

Everyday you fill many roles as student, employee, son or daughter. Conflict among these roles can be avoided if you know which roles are most important to you.

COMMUNICATING WITH OTHERS

The basis for building strong relationships is being able to communicate with others. **Communication** involves sharing messages or ideas with other people. It can be compared to a chain that links you with others. You have good communication when the message, or chain links, reflects what you meant and when the message is received and understood by your listeners.

Unfortunately, there is lots of room for error in the process of communicating. You may not really have sent the message you intended. Your message may not be clear. Your listeners may be involved in their own thoughts, so they may not hear your message correctly. Even if your message is heard, it may not be understood.

Being aware of how well you communicate can be vital in building your relationships with others. Learning to send and receive messages accurately is the key to good communication.

You can develop good communication skills when you make a conscious effort to send and receive accurate messages.

An important, but often overlooked, aspect of good communication is the ability to listen. What are some ways that a listener can help create better understanding?

VERBAL COMMUNICATION

One of the main ways you communicate with others is through words, that is, verbal communication. This is a main communication channel—one that is often broken.

When you are the message sender, you originate the message or speak first. The initial step in the communication chain is whether or not the message accurately reflects your intent. Does the message give both the content and emotional feeling you want to express? Sometimes the content is muddled if you are not quite sure what to say.

Other times, your content is clear but your emotional tone is not clear. The message sent may not really reflect your feelings. As a child, you may have shouted, "I hate you," to a friend who chose to play with someone else. What you really may have meant, but were unable to say, was, "I'm hurt because I wanted you to play with me." The more accurately your messages reflect your intent, the better your first step in communication.

The next step in the communication chain is the receiver, or listener. When you are the listener, do you hear what is being said? Sometimes you may get lost in your own thoughts and concerns and "tune out" someone talking to you. For example, your brother or sister might tell some long involved story about what happened at school. You find your thoughts drifting, but manage to respond, "Yes," "Oh really," or "Wow," at the correct times. You are not truly listening, however, and the communication chain is not strong.

Listening for messages sent is probably the most crucial link in the communication chain. However, listening is a neglected skill. You may think that because you are hearing the messages from others, you are listening. Sometimes hearing has nothing to do with listening.

When you are really listening, you are thinking about the words being received and trying to decode, or figure out, what the words mean. Is the sender giving a clear message? If not, how can you figure out what is meant? What does the message mean in terms of the content and emotional tone? What is the speaker really trying to say to you?

When you are a good listener, you try to hear and understand the message. If it is not clear, you ask questions and try to discover the real meaning of the message being passed. You ask questions that begin with "what," "how," and "could you" to help create better understanding.

Sometimes you may block communication by judging the messages you hear. You evaluate the other person instead of feeling empathy for him or her.

Listening is not easy to do and it takes time to learn. It means you have to be willing to "dig" for the real meaning of the messages received. It means paying close attention to the other person to try to understand. However, the effort will help you to understand the sender better. Your relationship is made stronger by strengthening the communication chain.

When verbal and non-verbal messages do not agree, people tend to believe the non-verbal ones. What strong non-verbal message is being sent by this person's facial expression.

NONVERBAL COMMUNICATION

Although words are the main way you communicate with others, they are not the only way. Another major means of communication is "body language," or nonverbal communication. Nonverbal communication is related to how you speak words and the way you look and act. It can involve how you dress. Your tone of voice is a powerful means of sending nonverbal messages. Even walking and posture are examples of nonverbal communication.

The way you use your body tells others how you feel about what is happening. When you are involved and excited, you are more apt to open your body to others. You relax and sit back, have a wide smile, and appear at ease. On the other hand, when you are nervous or anxious, you probably tend to close in, almost as if you are protecting yourself. You may sit straight and stiff in your chair. Your face muscles may be tight, and you may have your arms and legs crossed.

People have their own special nonverbal languages. As you get to know others better, you learn their specific habits. A friend may pull his ear when he gets excited. Another may clear her throat when nervous. As a child, you soon learned what tone of voice meant your parent was pleased or angry.

Learning to receive and decode nonverbal messages is an important part of the communication chain. Nonverbal messages are often a true reflection of the feelings of the person sending the message. It is easier to say something you do not mean than it is for your body to pass along a misleading message.

This means if you are not being open and honest in your messages, your body is apt to tell others. You will be sending conflicting messages. When verbal and nonverbal messages do not agree, people tend to believe the nonverbal ones.

SPACE NEEDS

Closely related to nonverbal communication is your need for personal space. The distance you keep between yourself and others reflects your personality and the closeness of your relationships. In general, the closer the relationship, the less space you will keep between yourself and the other person.

People differ in the amount of space they need. You may like to be close to others, to touch them, and to be hugged and cuddled. You feel lonely when others keep their distance.

On the other hand, you may want more space. You may feel crowded and upset when someone comes too close. You may not enjoy touching or being close to others.

Understanding your and others' space needs can be important in building relationships. Most people indicate their need for space through nonverbal messages. If you can discover how much space a friend or family member needs and give them that space, your relationship will improve.

Do you shake hands, embrace or keep your distance when meeting people? This can be one clue to a person's preference for space.

MANAGING CONFLICT

Because you are an individual with your own thoughts and ideas, you probably do not always agree with others. These disagreements can lead to quarrels and conflict.

Conflict is simply a normal part of daily life. In fact, differences are to be expected and can help make your life interesting. However, sometimes another person may try to block your actions or ideas. This results in an open struggle between the two of you. Such conflict is not necessarily bad. The crucial question is how you manage the conflict.

Conflict can be especially strong in close relationships. The more emotional energy you put into a relationship, the more powerful conflict in it will be. Therefore, your family and friends will usually be those with whom you have the most intense quarrels and fights. Disagreements with them may bring pain and frustration. This is because they are the people most important to you, those with whom you have the greatest interaction.

CONSTRUCTIVE AND DESTRUCTIVE CONFLICT

Conflict can be either helpful or harmful to a relationship. Helpful, or constructive conflict, occurs when you solve your conflict and come to a better understanding of the other person. You may have more respect for each other and more empathy as a result of resolving your differences. For example, when dating partners resolve a "lovers' quarrel," they develop a higher level of closeness and intimacy.

Harmful, or destructive conflict, occurs when it causes your relationship to weaken or even end. Quarrels in which people try to tear each other down are especially harmful to a relationship. For example, if you are quarreling and call another person names, with little or no basis in reality, you are trying to harm or destroy, not help, the other person and your relationship.

One of the main differences in the two types of conflict is the focus of the disagreement. Quarrels begin when you and another person feel differently about some action or belief. If the quarrel stays focused on the one disagreement until it is solved, the conflict is apt to be helpful to your relationship. However, if the quarrel involves name calling or pointing out another's faults, real or imagined, it is apt to be harmful to the relationship. Such verbal battles can only end with resentment and bad feelings.

Another difference in the types of quarrels is in the emotional level involved. Quarrels can be more constructively solved when you keep the emotional level low, or cool. You may be angry and violently upset, but if you can control these emotions, you will be able to work "logically" on the disagreement. If you want a constructive solution to conflict, you do not give in to the feelings that are boiling within you.

On the other hand, if you lose control of your emotions, conflict becomes heated and often spiteful. A person without control of the emotions is not apt to think logically or find a constructive solution to the quarrel.

When couples stay focused on the disagreement and avoid name calling and personal attacks, they have taken the most important step in solving conflict.

NEGOTIATING SKILLS

Resolving conflict peacefully means making compromises and concessions. You must be ready to accept something less than what you wanted. Or you must be willing to accept some variation of your original plan. If you are good in managing conflict and can see solutions to problems that will suit everyone involved, you probably have good negotiating skills. This means you are able to compromise, to give something in order to get something else. As a negotiator, you also may help others see how give and take can benefit them.

A successful means of solving conflict is to discuss and examine both sides of the issue involved. There is usually more than one or two ways to solve a problem. Perhaps some other option could be agreed on. A solution that pleases both sides in a conflict is more likely to be carried out.

RESOLVING CONFLICT

If you are like most people, you want to resolve your conflicts constructively. Unfortunately, you may not know how or may not be willing to try. Resolving conflicts constructively involves controlling your emotions, which is not easy. It may mean you will have to compromise and negotiate. But the benefits of learning to resolve conflict are many.

Some suggestions for learning to manage conflict successfully are listed in the following box.

1. Keep the quarrel focused on the disagreement involved. The other person's faults are not the issue to be settled.
2. Keep the emotional level low, or cool. Anger and spiteful hate are emotions that need to be controlled in order to work toward a solution. When emotions heat up, take a "time out" to cool down.
3. Listen for the other person's ideas and feelings. Avoid thinking of what you will say next while he or she is talking.
4. Remember that the other person is a unique and important individual, not merely a stumbling block in your way. The partner's point of view may not make much sense to you, but you can try to appreciate it.
5. In most quarrels, there are issues where it is possible to compromise. Discover what these issues are. Analyze the problem in your mind and decide what you can "give" in order to "get."
6. Avoid quarrels at mealtime or bedtime. Being hungry or tired means you are less apt to have self-control.
7. Settle the disagreement yourselves. Do not rely on a third party to make peace between you.
8. Do not take physical action against the other person.

RELAX!

When you face stress, your body reacts. Your pupils become larger and your hearing is sharpened. Your muscles tense, your heart beats faster, and your rate of breathing increases. Blood drains from your arms and legs, pooling in your trunk and brain. This leaves your hands and feet cold and sweaty. Once the threat or stress is past, your body should return to normal. However, sometimes knowing how to relax can speed the process. In addition, relaxing can help reduce the severity of your response to stress.

• *Breathing.* Anxiety often brings short, fast, shallow breaths. Taking deep, long breaths can help you relax. Expand your chest and abdomen as you feel the air going to the very bottom of your lungs. Inhale through your nose and exhale gently through your mouth.

Sighing and yawning can be symptoms that your body is not getting enough oxygen through normal breathing. A sigh releases a bit of tension and can help you relax. Sit or stand up straight. Sigh deeply, letting the air rush out of your lungs. Repeat the sigh several times to help you relax.

• *Muscle Relaxing.* Because your muscles tighten up when you are stressed, learning to relax the muscles will help you feel less tense. Lie down or sit with your head supported. Identify which muscles are tense. Further tighten the muscle or muscle group for five to seven seconds. Relax the muscles for about twenty to thirty seconds. Repeat if your muscles do not feel completely relaxed. Be aware of the difference in how the muscles feel when they are tensed and relaxed.

• *Imagining.* Your imagination can help you relax when you are feeling anxious and tense. Close your eyes and imagine you are alone outdoors at a favorite place—the beach, the mountains, a park, or a field. Visualize the scenery and then imagine the quietness and stillness of being alone in such a place. Think of the smells and sounds you might experience there. Relax and enjoy the peace of your imagined haven.

• *Exercise.* Exercise is one of the simplest and most effective means of reducing stress. Aerobic exercises involve the large muscle groups, especially the legs. During aerobic exercises, the body uses lots of oxygen. Your heart and breathing rates increase. Brisk walking, jogging, running, swimming, dancing, and bicycling are examples of aerobic exercising.

Low intensity exercises are used to increase muscle strength and flexibility. They include calisthenics, which are stretching exercises to improve muscle flexibility. Lifting weights, walking, house cleaning, and gardening are other examples of low intensity exercise.

Learning to relax is not easy. However, when you can relax your body during stressful times, you will feel powerful and in control.

COPING WITH STRESS

Life can be complex at any age. It is never possible to be all you want to be, do all you want to do, and have all you want to have. Learning to cope with the stress and tension of the teen years will make your life easier to manage.

Many of the stresses of adolescence involve fears about change. If you are like most teenagers, you are concerned about

1. the physical and emotional changes in yourself;
2. being rejected or unpopular;
3. not living up to your own or your parents' ideals;
4. whether or not you can cope with new experiences and situations;
5. handling the responsibilities of growing up.

These are normal fears. However, living with these fears causes stress and tension. Too much stress can cause you to become ill. However, avoiding stress altogether is no solution, because it is a part of everyday life. There are ways, though, that stress and tension can be reduced or managed.

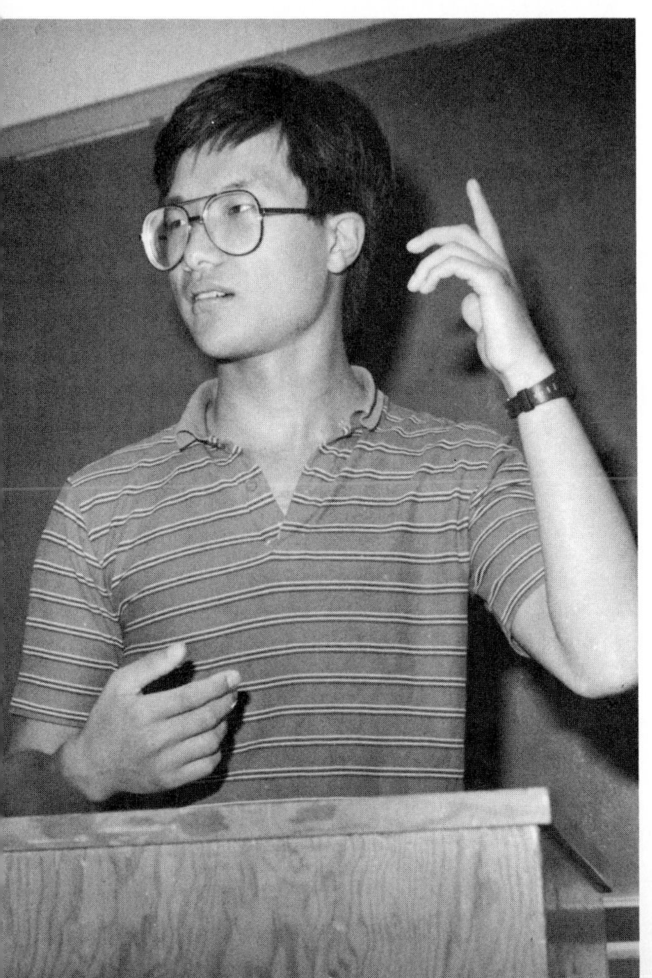

TALKING IT OUT

Many people brood and worry about their fears and tensions. Often this causes problems to seem more important than they are. One of the best ways of coping with the stresses of life is to talk to someone you trust, such as your parents, friends, minister, priest or rabbi, or a counselor at school. A psychologist or psychiatrist may be helpful if you are deeply troubled.

Talking over your problems with others can help in several ways. First, you do not feel as alone when you share your troubles. There is someone else who knows your problems and who may have similar ones. Second, often the very fact of talking may help you see the problem in perspective. Talking can help you get your thoughts in order and see things as they really are. Third, sharing troubles may help you release your pent up emotions. Finally, you may be able to see one or even several ways to manage the problem.

ESCAPE

Perhaps you face stress and fears by escaping. You may choose reading, watching television, "hanging around," or videos as a means to avoid frustration. Once in a while, you need a means of escape from the grind of daily life. Escape can give you a chance to settle down and regain your poise and calm.

Unfortunately, escape will not solve your problems. A problem is solved only when you face it. A troubled relationship may be causing you anxiety or stress. The solution is to try to work out the problem, not to avoid the other person altogether. Escape may ease the pain a problem or stress is causing you, but it will not take away the stress until the problem is solved.

Some people use drugs, alcohol, cigarettes, or even overeating, to escape their problems. They feel that these quick-and-easy solutions will help eliminate their problems. In fact, many times these temporary solutions create a whole new set of problems. Take a few moments to analyze the escape methods that you use. Are you turning to harmful substances in an attempt to escape, only to find that these methods cause additional stress and tension and do nothing to solve your problems?

Delivering a speech in class may be a stressful situation to some people. To others, it is a challenge and an opportunity.

RECREATION

Recreation is an important part of life. During the teen years you spend more time on recreation than at any other time of life. You spend time with friends, go out, and have school activities in which to participate. By breaking monotony and giving you a change of pace, recreation can help dissolve the stresses that life can produce.

Involvement in an active game can help reduce tensions and stresses of daily life.

DISPEL YOUR ANGER

A stressful life usually produces anger in an individual. If you are having conflict with parents, you may be full of anger. Frustration with athletics or school work may cause you to become angry or unhappy with yourself. You need some means to get rid of, or dispel, anger so you can face the problem rather than spend your time dealing with the anger inside. Sulking or throwing a temper tantrum is not a constructive way to face a problem.

You need to find your own ways of dealing with anger. You may find being alone and thinking about the problem helps. You may prefer the stimulation of many people around you. Perhaps hard physical work or exercise helps to get rid of your anger. When you get rid of anger, you can start to work toward easing the stress that caused it.

TAKE LIFE ONE DAY AT A TIME

Often when problems or stress become major facts of life, you get weighed down and feel there is no way to manage or cope. One way to help live with this feeling is to take life one day at a time. You do not have to live your whole life in fear of what is ahead. Look at tomorrow and plan what you can do. You *can* get through that day without your sweetheart, who has found someone else. You *can* manage one day of classes and homework. You *can* get the costume done for the school play. By taking one day at a time, you minimize the problems you face.

You can also gain control over your life and reduce tension by learning to manage your time more efficiently. By keeping schedules, making lists, and prioritizing activities you can eliminate much of the stress that is caused from unfinished business. Good time management techniques can help you achieve your goals. You will have time left over to relax or do the activities you really enjoy doing. In chapter 10, you will learn more about effective techniques.

DO SOMETHING FOR OTHERS

When pain and stress overwhelm people, they tend to become very self-centered and worried about themselves. One method of raising spirits and improving self-concept is to do something for others.

Everyone has problems and needs. By doing something nice for other persons, you take the focus off yourself. You help them solve their problems and, thus, take your mind off yours. Sometimes, just filling your time so you will not think about your problems can be helpful. You get double the benefit if you fill that time doing something for others. Offering to run errands for an elderly person, fixing dinner for your family, or visiting a friend who is ill can make you feel better and take your mind off of your problems.

Lend a hand or offer support to someone else when you become stressed. It will make you feel better and take your mind off of your worries.

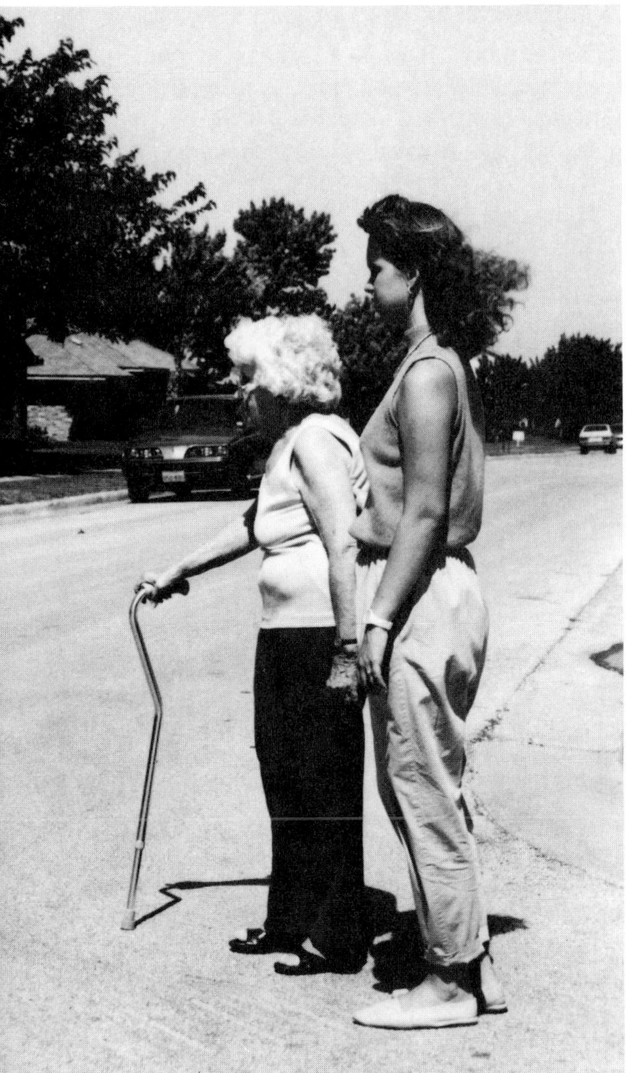

MANAGING RELATIONSHIPS

Learning to get along with others is one of the most important skills you need in life. You probably spend most of your time with people. You live in a family group and learn, work, play and worship with others.

Good relationships are not just something "nice" to have. As you progress through life, you will find that your relationships become more complicated. They are a basic resource to help manage or make a happy and satisfying life for yourself.

How you get along with others is vital in all facets of life. Your skills in managing your roles, communicating, resolving conflict, and lessening stress will affect how much joy and pleasure you get from your relationships. They are built from shared experiences and a willingness to give of yourself. You can work to improve your relationship skills so that your involvement and interaction with others is a source of joy, satisfaction, and personal rewards.

WORDS TO REMEMBER

communication	mutual expectations	relationships	role
empathy	rapport	respect	trust

CHECKING YOUR UNDERSTANDING

1. Explain the importance of good relationships in people's lives. How does the quality of your relationships affect your life?
2. Define and describe the following relationship qualities in your own words: rapport, empathy, trust, respect, interdependence, mutual expectations, and flexibility. Which of these qualities seems most important to you in having good relationships with others? Least important? Explain your answers.
3. Explain why questions that begin with "what," "how," and "could you" can help improve communication. Give examples of questions starting with each word or phrase.
4. Describe what is meant by negotiating skills. Why are these skills so important in resolving conflict?
5. List specific stresses that teenagers face in everyday life. Give appropriate suggestions for overcoming the stresses you listed.

APPLYING YOUR UNDERSTANDING

1. Read a book or watch several television programs looking for examples of poor communication between characters. What problems kept the characters from communicating well? What suggestions could you make to help them communicate more effectively?
2. Observe the space needs of students at your school when they are in the halls between classes. Can you identify people who need lots of personal space? Are there some who seem to enjoy the closeness of others? What conclusions can you draw from your observations?
3. Think of some recent conflict you have been involved in. Was it constructive or destructive? Why? If it was destructive, how could you have worked to make it constructive? If it was constructive, could you have made it more so? What specific improvements could you work on to help you do a better job of solving conflict with others?
4. Doing something for others helps reduce stress and tension. Imagine you are a reporter for your local newspaper and your assignment is to write an article featuring teenagers who are involved in helping others. Do research to learn about activities in your community where teenagers are helping others. Write the article, stressing the benefits to the teenagers as well as to those they help. If possible, submit your article to your school or local newspaper.

Chapter 3
MAXIMIZING RELATIONSHIPS

Has this ever happened to you?

Sandy gulped nervously as she reached for the handle on the door of her new high school. She thought to herself that after attending three high schools, she should be used to enrolling in a new school. But somehow, the older she got, the harder she found getting settled in a new town.

This school was bigger than any she had ever gone to before. Sandy wondered to herself how she was going to make new friends. She had never been good at meeting people. At each new school she went to, it seemed harder to find others who shared her interests. And just when she had made a few friends, her family would move on.

As Sandy slid into a seat in her first class, the girl in front of her smiled and said, "Hey, are you a new student here? My name is Marty. Do you have your enrollment form for the teacher? What's your name?"

Sandy smiled back, took a deep breath, and said, "I'm Sandy. We just moved here last week. What's this class like?"

Have you ever been in a situation where you did not know anyone? How did you begin to make friends?

What are some ways you could help make new students at your school feel welcome and at home?

After reading this chapter, you will be able to

- identify qualities of friendship and ways of making and keeping friends;
- recognize the responsibilities and opportunities in group relationships;
- understand the importance of peers and the peer group during the teen years;
- describe and compare dating for companionship and recreation with dating for courtship.

Some of life's greatest pleasures are the relationships you have with others. These relationships also can become major resources that you can use in managing your life to reach your goals. Whether you are relating to friends, others in a group, a dating partner, family members, or work colleagues, you can use your skills to maximize these relationships for yourself and others.

BUILDING FRIENDSHIPS

A **friend** is someone with whom you are on familiar and good terms. Friends provide opportunities for emotional closeness. They are supportive and accepting when you need them. Friends are important throughout life, but they are an especially vital resource during your teen years as you work to become independent of your family.

For many teenagers, friendships add pleasure to an active, full life.

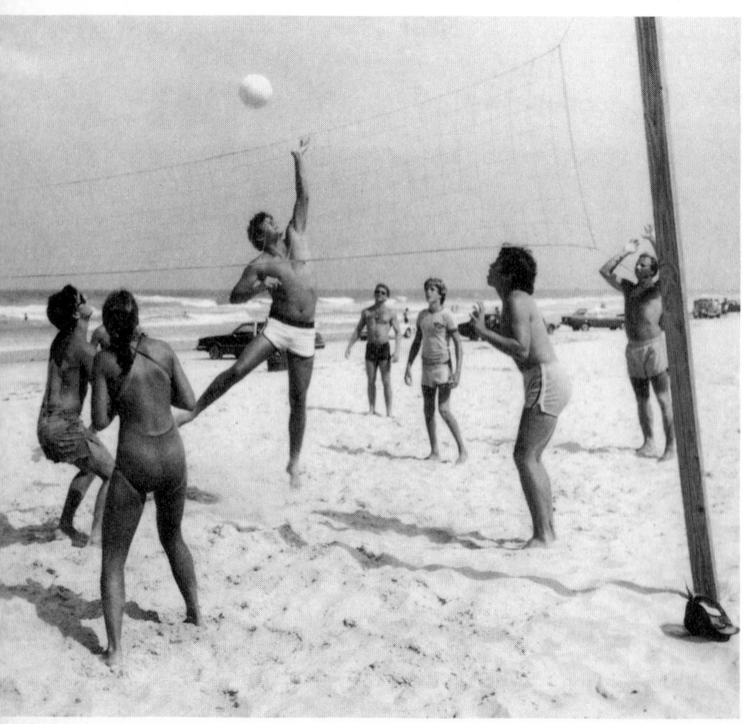

Satisfying friendships are built through personal attraction and shared experiences. You meet someone, are interested in knowing the person better, and begin to spend some time together. As a friendship begins to grow, you work to make your relationship meaningful and enjoyable.

The meaning of friendship in your life varies with your personality and circumstances. For some people, friendships with others are just one part of a full and active life. For others, friendships are the most vital relationships a person can have. The more important your relationships with friends are to you, the more time and effort you need to put into keeping them strong.

MAKING FRIENDS

Making friends is not easy for all people. If you are assertive and outgoing, you probably make friends easily. You are confident of your ability to attract others and are able to draw them into your activities.

On the other hand, you may have more difficulty making friends. You may be shy and afraid to approach other people for fear of being rejected. It is not easy to cope with being scorned or ignored if you have made a gesture of friendship to another person.

Having few or no friends is often an unhappy experience for people. The way out of this situation is to take the initiative. Set a goal for yourself to develop new friendships. Use your resources to make plans and decisions that will help you reach your goal.

You can promote growth of friendship through your actions. Treating other people as you would like to be treated is one way to build friendships. A kind word and a friendly smile should bring the same in return to you. Join a club or group where there are people you would enjoy knowing. Doing volunteer work at your school or in the community is another way to meet new people and make friends as you work together with others.

If you are trying to make friends, organize an activity other people would enjoy. Invite someone to your home or to share a recreational activity with you. Many people are lonely and would be pleased to be sought out by you. Enjoy being yourself and you will have the best chance of finding a friend who likes what you are.

Building friendships means thinking of others and working to become involved with them. Be friendly and interested in other people, and you will make friends. Organize and enjoy having a good time, and others will want to be with you. Show that you like people and will accept them in an open, friendly manner.

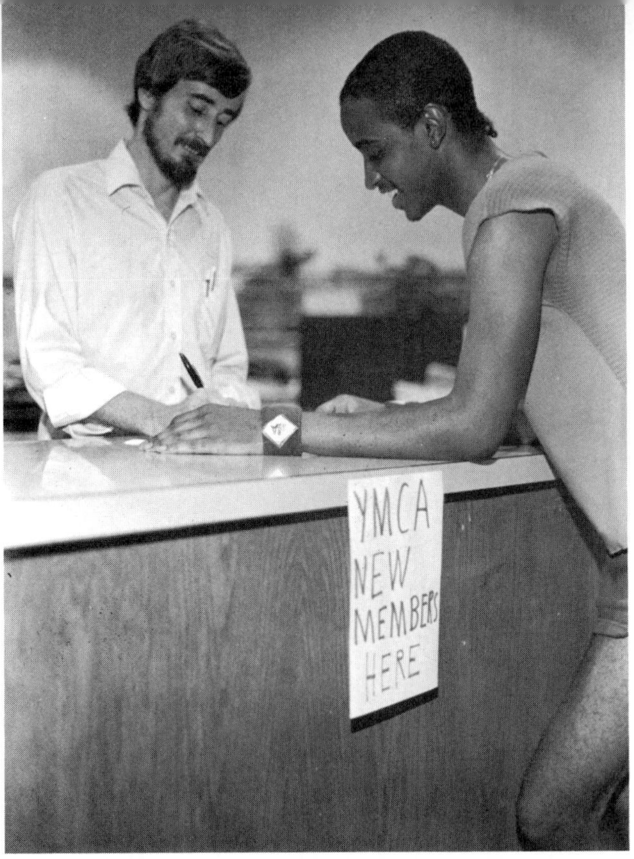

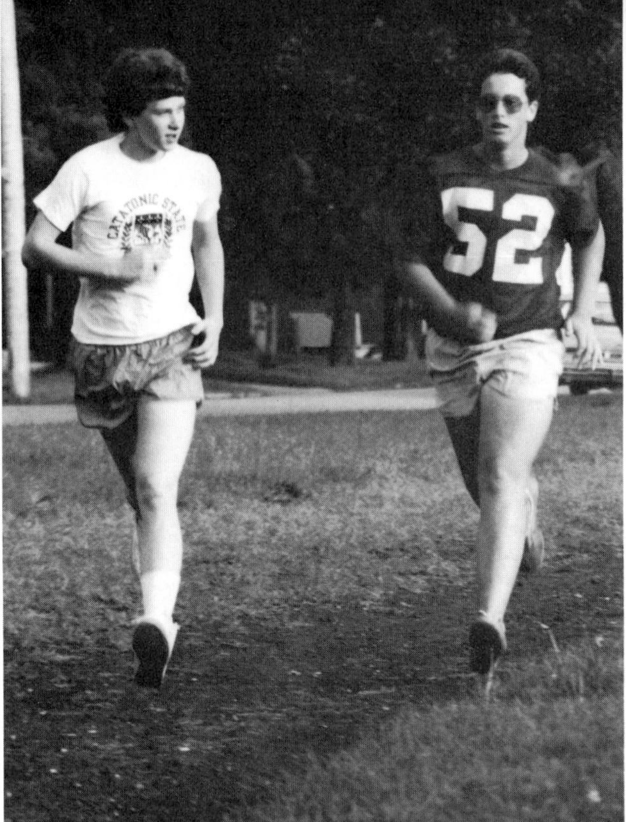

Get involved in school, recreational or community activities. In that way you can meet people who enjoy doing similar activities as you.

Riding bikes, shopping, jogging or playing video games are common interests that friends share. What activities do you share with your friends?

QUALITIES OF FRIENDSHIP

A strong friendship has the traits of a good relationship described in chapter 2. You will find your friendships that are strong and well built very satisfying. You and your friends share rapport, empathy, trust, and respect with each other. You are interdependent, yet flexible in your relationships. Able to communicate well with your friends, you have learned to resolve the conflicts that always arise in close friendships.

But in addition, friendships have some other qualities. As friends, you are tolerant and accepting of each other. You are able to see each other as you are, but can live with each other's faults and shortcomings. You have learned from your friends' differences.

Friends have common interests and experiences. You may share an interest in athletics, chess, dance, or drama. Your shared interests give you topics to discuss and activities in which to participate. Friendships are frequently born because two people share an interest in an unusual subject.

Finally, friends usually share attitudes and beliefs. Your goals and values are often like those of your friends.

BREAKDOWN OF FRIENDSHIP

Unfortunately, friendships, like all relationships, often break down. The closer the friendship, the more painful such a separation can be.

Sometimes the cause of the breakup is unresolved conflict. You can use conflict management skills and sometimes prevent such a serious result. However, it takes two people working together to resolve conflict. If your friend will not cooperate, you cannot solve the problem alone.

Changing tastes and interests can also cause you and a friend to grow apart. If you have a friendship that has been based on a mutual enjoyment of computer games, it may not last long if you develop a new enthusiasm. Changes in beliefs and attitudes may cause a similar growing apart between friends. Sometimes people just become bored with a relationship.

When a painful separation between you and a friend occurs, it is best to get involved in activities with others and seek new friends. Dwelling on your loss will only make the pain more acute and bring feelings of depression and sadness. Involvement with others will help take your mind off your feelings and may build new relationships that will partly take the place of the old one.

FRIENDSHIPS THROUGHOUT LIFE

You may have had the same friends all your life. Friendships that last through the years can bring you a great deal of pleasure and satisfaction.

On the other hand, you may have had several different sets of friends. Perhaps you have lived in different places and attended a number of schools. Or maybe your friendships have changed as your interests have grown and developed.

Most people continue to make friends as they grow older. A new job, going to college, a move to a different home or town, or a new hobby can bring you opportunities to meet people. From these new acquaintances, you can build friendships.

These opportunities may mean you will have to leave old friends behind. As you attend college or become involved in a new job after graduation, you may find you see your high school friends less frequently. Because good friends are a valuable resource, you may want to work to maintain your old ties.

Even if you live across the country from a friend, you can maintain your relationship across miles and years. However, it takes time and effort to keep a friendship alive when you do not see the other person often. You can write letters, tele phone, and send cards on birthdays and anniversaries. You may have a chance to visit each other once in a while.

Keeping up with old friends adds depth and richness to your life. On the other hand, new friends can expand your horizons and help you grow and mature as a person. The goals you have and the decisions you make about your life will affect your friendships. Using some of your resources to maintain old ties and to build new ones ensures that you will continue to enjoy friendships throughout your life.

GROUP RELATIONSHIPS

One-to-one relationships are the most important ones you have. On the other hand, you are probably also deeply involved in group relationships. You live in a family, attend classes in school, share recreation with friends, and work in groups of people. Being able to relate well in groups is an important life skill.

The type and intensity of relationships change throughout a person's life. You can keep a distant relationship alive by writing letters, telephoning and remembering special occasions.

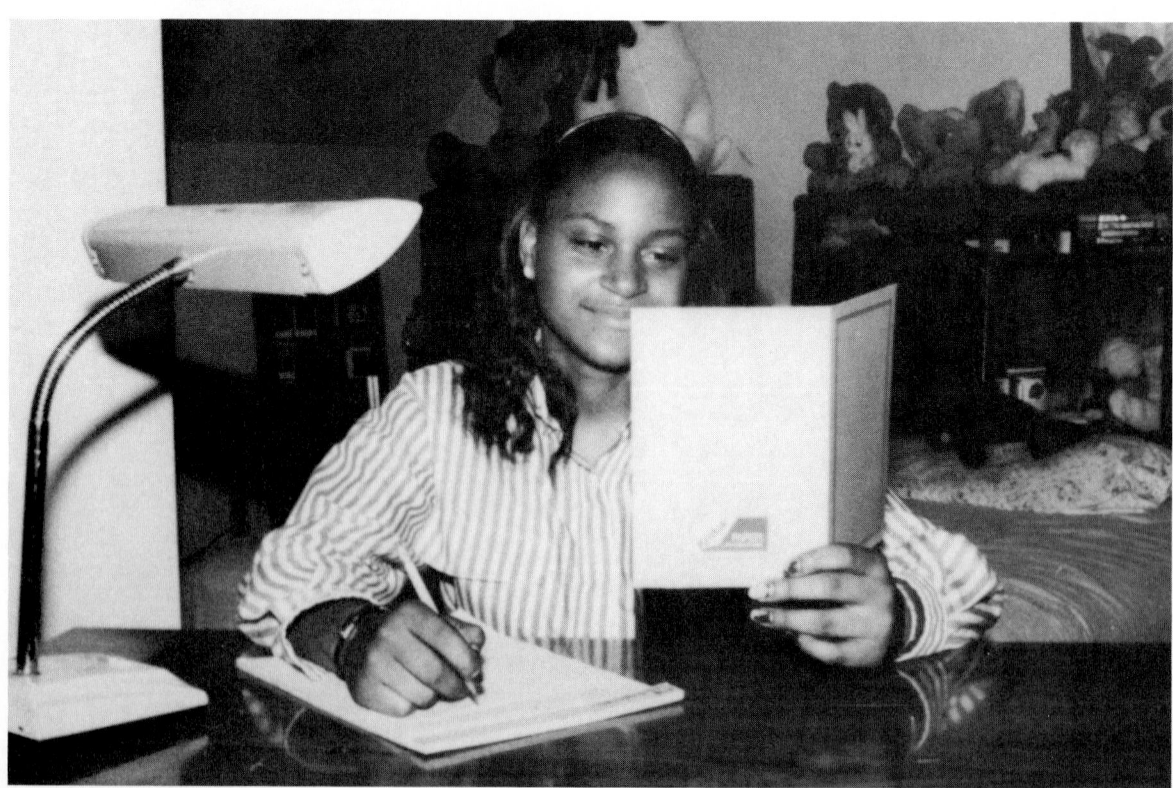

Careers
A BRIEF LOOK

MAKING THE MOST OF YOUR WORLD

Many people who enjoy people want a job that will let them work with others. If you like and respect most people, like to help others, can speak well, and have good conflict management skills, you may want to pursue one of the careers listed below. Experience in working in groups and as a leader are also important if you want a career working with others. To succeed in one of the jobs below would require working well with others. However, most of the jobs also involve some knowledge and skills in a specific job area.

Entry Level Jobs
Food service worker
Hospital attendant
Nursing aide
Nursing home aide/attendant
Orderly
Recreation assistant
Sales clerk

Jobs That Require More Training
Airline flight attendant
Dental assistant
Dental hygienist
Food service manager
Hotel/motel manager
Library clerk
Management in business or government
Minister
Nurse
Personnel work
Police officer
Social service worker
Teacher's aide
Teacher in continuing education

Jobs That Require a Degree
Counselor
Dentist
Family therapist
Home economist
Lawyer
Librarian
Occupational therapist
Physical therapist
Physician
Psychologist
Recreation leader
School administrator
Social worker
Teacher

For more information, see your guidance counselor, or write to:

American Physical Therapy Association
1111 N. Fairfax St.
Alexandria, Virginia 22314

American Psychiatric Association
1400 K. St., N.W.
Washington, D.C. 20005

GROUP PARTICIPATION

Being a member of a group means you have a responsibility to others in the group. There are many ways you can help develop good relationships in your group.

Groups are formed for various purposes. You and the others at work have tasks to do for your employer. You may belong to a club in which you get together with others to work or play. Friendship groups are usually formed for the pleasure and personal support the members get from each other.

When a group has a job to do, group members can help get the task done. You may be able to give information needed to do the work. Others may provide motivation and get the action started in the group. Someone else may summarize ideas and help people see what is needed and where the group is going. People who give directions or coordinate activities help the group do its work. A leader may do some of these tasks, but often it is group members who are crucial in helping the group produce.

Group members also can help build up the group. Each member in the group is important and needs recognition from the others. Often one person in the group is needed to help others communicate. You may be able to relieve tension by joking or suggesting interesting activities. A negotiator who can help solve problems is useful because all groups have some conflict. Every member of the group is needed to build up a positive group feeling.

LEADERSHIP

All groups have a **leader,** someone who guides or influences the group. In some groups, such as clubs, there may be a formal leader, such as a president or advisor. In other groups, like friendship groups, there is usually one person the others look up to as the leader.

BECOMING A GROUP LEADER

How can you become a group leader? Good leaders have a number of qualities and traits you can practice and learn.

A leader is well prepared. Leadership takes practice and work. If you are prepared, you are a step ahead of the others. In preparation, set goals for yourself and for the group. Gather the facts to present to group members. Help the others analyze the facts before drawing conclusions. Develop a plan of how you and the group can reach your goals. Arrange activities that will help all members learn and grow.

Leaders are group minded. You may be the leader, but think of yourself as a part of the group. Say "we" instead of "I." Provide leadership but be guided by the group's wishes. Your liking for the group and the people in it should be shown by your understanding and friendliness.

Leaders are also responsible workers. Do not ask other group members to do something you would not be willing to do yourself. You have the responsibility to live up to your word and duties. Through your actions, you can set an example for other group members. Show the others how to work and that you enjoy working with them.

As a leader, you set the example for others. The words "please" and "thank you" pay dividends. Use them often as you work with group members. Being appropriately dressed with a good personal appearance helps establish your credibility with others.

As a leader, you can be open minded and honest. Be willing to admit to others that you do not know everything. Get advice and help from others, but do not be afraid to do your own thinking.

Leaders need good communication skills. State your positions openly, clearly, and effectively. Let each group member do the same. When disagreements occur, use conflict management skills to solve them.

Group members have important tasks to help the group achieve its goals. Your role in a group may be to be the leader, negotiator or organizer.

Leadership Styles

There are three general leadership styles. These are democratic, autocratic, and laissez-faire (pronounced *lay say fair*). Each of these types of leadership is appropriate in some circumstances. There is no one "right" kind of leadership for all situations. Some groups are more effective with each. In addition, people differ in the kind of leader with whom they wish to work.

If you are a democratic leader, you want to get everyone in the group involved. You work to discover everyone's ideas and wishes and to have all participate. In a working group, a democratic leader spreads the authority around to others. People usually like working in a group with a democratic leader because they feel involved and important. However, such groups do not always produce much work and often are inefficient in their achievements.

An autocratic leader is more apt to be "the boss." If you are this type of leader, you look at the the group, decide what it should do or accomplish, and organize the work. A group led by an autocratic leader usually can accomplish a lot without much hassle. However, members of the group may not enjoy their participation. They see themselves as "taking orders" rather than being actively involved in decisions.

It is the leader's responsibility to promote positive group feelings and to provide direction and motivation. How do the leaders that you know do this?

If you are a laissez-faire leader, you have a casual attitude about leadership and let the group go as it will. Laissez-faire literally means "hands off." You would not give orders or seek suggestions from other group members. Instead, you would serve as a resource person, helping and guiding only as needed. Laissez-faire leadership lets people work on their own and does not try to interfere too much.

Leadership skills are needed by all people. Certainly, no one can be a leader all the time. On the other hand, there are occasions when everyone needs to be a leader. Learning about leadership will help you to be able to show it when needed.

PEER GROUPS

One type of group that is very important during the teen years is the peer group. **Peers** are those of the same age, so **peer groups** are groups of people of the same or similar age.

Your contact with peer groups probably started as a preschooler with a circle of friends and has continued ever since. When you become an adult, your peer group relationships may change, but they will still exist. Your peer group may take many forms throughout your life. But whatever the form, the peer group is an important resource. Managing your peer relationships is one way to reach the goal of enjoying friendships.

As a teen you become more independent of your parents and look to your peers for support and encouragement.

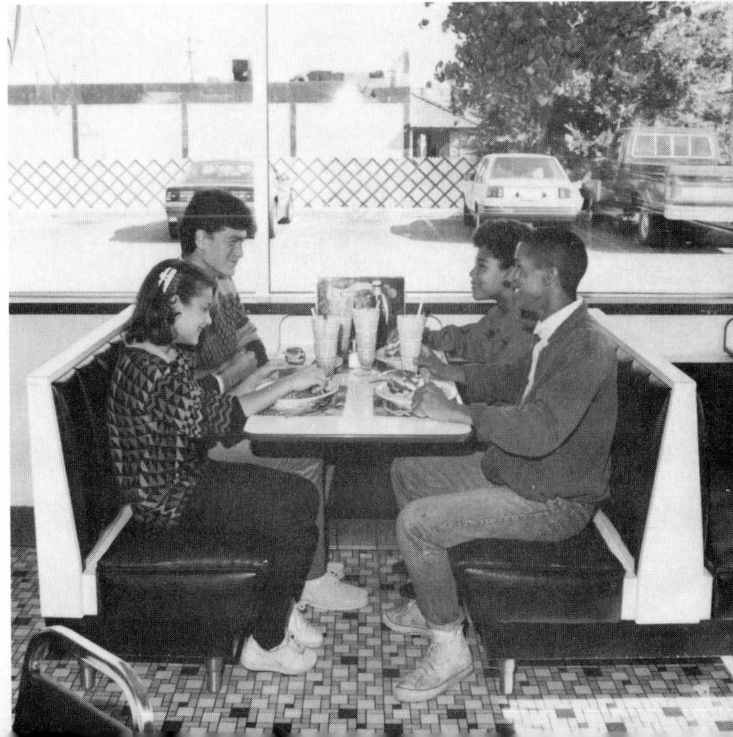

IMPORTANCE OF PEER GROUPS

Although you may have friends of many ages, your peers share your developmental tasks and the fears and concerns you have about the future. Therefore, the peer group provides a setting where you can feel free to relax among others like yourself.

Your need for closeness to others can be met by the peer group. The teen years are a time when you are beginning to loosen the bonds to your family as you learn to become independent. Your friends in the peer group can provide a sense of closeness and involvement for you as you move into the larger world.

The peer group gives you a feeling of belonging. As you begin to establish your own identity, the peer group provides support and friendship. It also gives you experience in group relations. You can learn how you appear to others and learn about leading and following in the group.

Finally, the peer group provides an opportunity for you to talk about and think through what is important in life. You can compare the goals of the group with those of your family. You have the chance to talk about your values and what you believe is important. The peer group provides a setting where you are exposed to a wide range of options for decision making. You can take a long look at yourself before deciding what kind of adult you wish to be.

When cliques are formed, people are excluded who may feel hurt, rejected or upset.

KINDS OF PEER GROUPS

There are several kinds of peer groups. Some are more important to young people, while others last through the years.

When you were a young child, you formed loose ties, or associations, with others. You learned about the give and take of relationships and were able to practice social skills in these groups.

As you grew older, you discovered friendship and the value of having a special "someone" with whom to share interests and problems. Friendships with peers are important throughout life.

Somewhere between the fourth and sixth grades, **cliques** start to form. These are small groups of three-to-eight people who exclude others from the group. At this age, males and females are involved in separate cliques. If you were in a clique, you probably did not mean to be deliberately exclusive. The result, however, was that many people were left out of the group.

As a teenager, you probably belong to a **crowd,** which is a loosely knit group of peers. A crowd begins to form when male and female cliques start to interact with each other. At this time, there are few, if any, paired-off couples. As the crowd develops, it is usually made up of several cliques, which are formed of both males and females for the first time.

The larger number of members in a crowd helps you to become familiar with many types of people. The crowd is also an important setting in which young men and women learn to relate to each other. Dating usually begins among members of the same crowd.

Finally, usually near the end of high school, the crowd begins to break up. Participation in the group becomes less important to its members. During this time, individual male-female couples and dating become more important.

PERSPECTIVES ON THE PEER GROUP

Although peer groups are important throughout life, they are probably most meaningful during the teen years. Your peer group may then have its most influence on you, for good or bad, than at any other time in your life.

PEER GROUP POSITIVES

- *Gives support for changes.* Your peers can help you adjust to the changes in your life and give you support as you grow to independence. As you move from being dependent on parents, the peer group gives you encouragement while you practice your new role.
- *Provides opportunities to learn appropriate behavior.* You may not always be certain of what is appropriate behavior for new situations. The peer group gives you an opportunity to practice behaviors and discover how acceptable they are.
- *Builds self-concept.* The peer group may help you to build a good self-concept. Being accepted as part of the group helps build good feelings about yourself.

PEER GROUP NEGATIVES

Although the peer group provides you many supports, it also has a negative side. The group may pressure you to *conform,* to act as all the others do. Conformity in dress is usually harmless, though it may cause conflict with your parents. However, your conformity in other activities, such as the use of drugs or in a prank that breaks the law, can be very harmful.

There may be situations in which you feel peer pressure to behave against your better judgment. You may be encouraged to smoke cigarettes, shoplift, cheat at school, drink, take part in sex, take illegal drugs, or break the law. It is not easy to say no to others in your crowd. If you do not want to take part, you may find it hard to be laughed at or excluded. Such feelings may lead you to take the easy route and conform even when you would rather not.

RESISTING PEER PRESSURE

The challenge of the peer group is to take advantage of its positives and avoid its negatives. You can do this by having a firm sense of your own values and goals and the courage to live by them. The key to resisting peer pressure is to be strong enough to say no. You may have to practice saying no many times before you feel secure in going against peer pressure. Here are some simple ways of saying no and meaning it.

- "NO, but thanks."
- "I don't drink."
- "Thanks, but I'm not in the mood."
- "I'm driving tonight. It wouldn't be safe for me to drink and drive."
- "I don't care if you do, but I don't want to."
- "I made a pact with my parents not to."

DATING

As described above, dating grows out of the crowd peer group. It is a new phase of friendship—between a male and a female. Members of the crowd begin to pair off and take part in activities as couples. If their relationship grows, they may soon begin to plan activities of their own.

You and a dating partner develop and build your relationship just as friends do. In fact, most relationships between dating couples are very much like those of friends. Your relationship grows as you come to accept each other. Having common interests and similar attitudes and beliefs helps your relationship grow stronger. The experiences you share as members of the crowd or as a dating couple tie you closer together.

Dating during the teen years helps pave the way for mature, loving relationships later on.

DATING FOR COMPANIONSHIP AND RECREATION

Dating begins as entertainment and recreation. It is an opportunity for you to get to know someone of the opposite sex in an atmosphere of fun and relaxation. You can have fun as you take part in activities you enjoy.

You can share companionship and closeness with a dating partner. Being able to share feelings and thoughts with each other helps to prevent loneliness. In the beginning, dating provides affection and closeness without long-term ties.

Dating is one way you can learn new social skills. You may learn to talk easily with others. As you plan activities with a partner, you can learn to cooperate and to be considerate of the other.

Through dating, you can gain confidence and poise. Knowing you are attractive to someone else helps you feel good about yourself.

Dating gives you valuable experience in getting along with someone of the opposite sex. It can help you learn what qualities you value in a dating relationship. Through dating, you learn more about sex roles, that is, what kind of man or woman you want to be.

Because dating is primarily recreation, you probably look for dating partners who are attractive and fun to be with. Because you usually see each other when you are relaxing and having fun, you may have a one-sided view of each other. You may idealize each other, seeing only your partner's best traits and overlooking the worst.

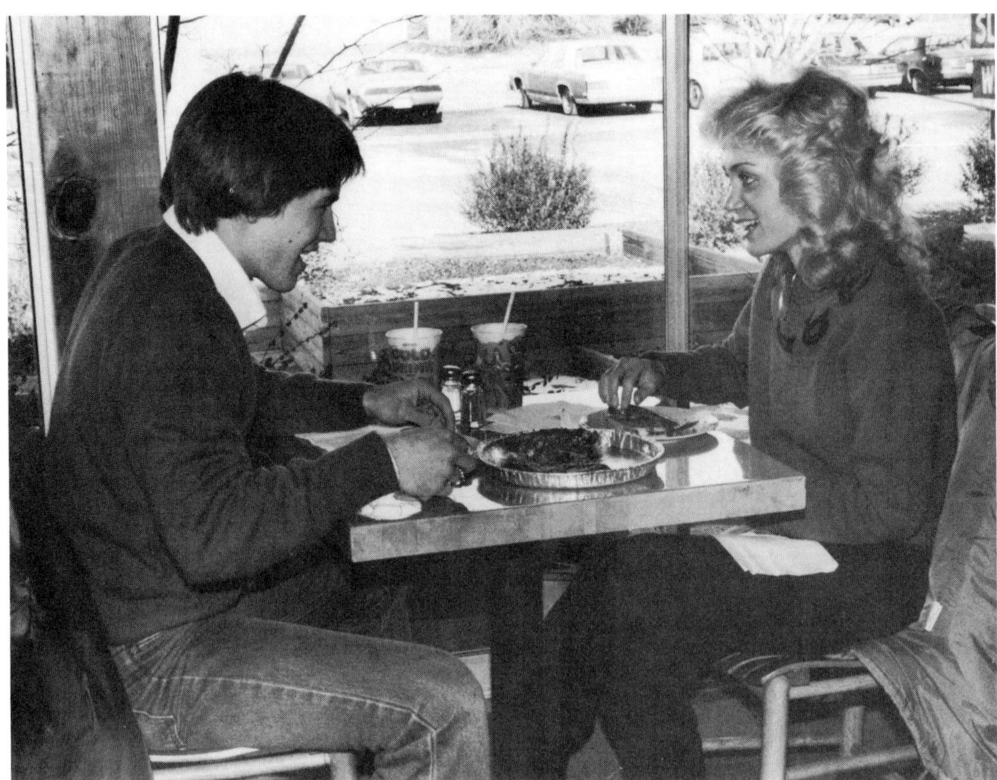

Dating gives couples the chance to get to know each other without the responsibility of long term ties.

DATING AS COURTSHIP

At some point, dating ceases to be strictly recreation and becomes dating for courtship. In **courtship** the couple becomes more serious about each other and begins to think of the future and the chances that they may be building a long-term relationship.

Sometimes courtship begins when a couple who have been dating discover that their feelings have become stronger and more loving. In other cases, a person may feel that it is time to "settle down" and begins to look at dating partners as potential mates. This may be before a serious relationship develops.

For whatever reason, the couple begins to focus on the likelihood of a future together. Their relationship becomes more meaningful. They discover that they share goals and values, and they begin to assess each other's outlook on life.

Couples who are looking to the future become concerned about the personal qualities of the partner rather than focusing on physical attractiveness. They may find they want different traits in a mate than they did in a dating partner.

Personal qualities, such as honesty, sincerity and sensitivity become more meaningful to couples who enter the courtship stage of a relationship.

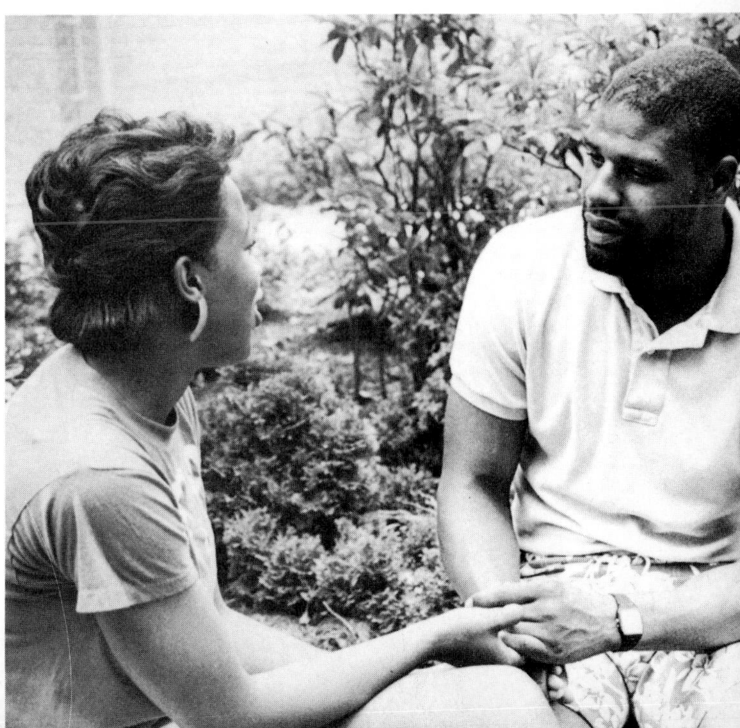

DATING PROBLEMS

The dating relationship, like all relationships, can be a source of problems and conflict. Some problems can be solved if you and your partner work together. Others may lead to the end of the relationship.

Personality faults and immaturity are the basis of some problems. Some people are immature or unstable. A bad temper, jealousy, possessiveness, or being self-centered may be traits that harm a good dating relationship.

Sometimes couples are incompatible. You and your partner may quarrel all the time and do not share goals and values. Unless you have some common interests, your relationship is not apt to last long.

Parents can be the cause of some problems in dating relationships, especially if the parents do not approve of the person their teenager is dating. Parental rules about dating may also cause conflict.

Many dating couples disagree over friends. You may not like the friends your dating partner has. You may also disagree over how much time you will spend together and how much time you will spend with your other friends.

Another major issue for many dating couples is premarital sexual behavior. The partners have to decide what their behavior will be on the basis of their values.

Sometimes, you may not be able to solve your problems with a dating partner. You may decide your wisest course is to break off the relationship and try again with someone new. The more serious your relationship has been, the more painful this will be.

On the other hand, many problems in dating partnerships can be solved through good communication and conflict management. If you have built a good relationship with your dating partner, you can work together to overcome your problems. This is apt to bring you closer together and make your relationship even more satisfying to both of you.

Parental approval and acceptance can play a major influence in the development of a relationship.

WORDS TO REMEMBER

cliques
courtship
crowd
friend
leader
peers
peer group

CHECKING YOUR UNDERSTANDING

1. Which of the qualities described in the chapter do you feel are most important in a friend? What qualities, if any, do you seek in a friend or friendship that are not included in the chapter? Why are these important to you?
2. Outline some actions you could take to strengthen or mend a failing friendship.
3. Describe qualities of a leader. Which quality seems most important to you for a club president? A leader in a group of friends? A sports team captain? A work supervisor?
4. Describe some of the functions of a teen peer group. Which functions seem most and least important to you?
5. Explain why crowds usually break up as members approach high school graduation.
6. What are the similarities and differences between dating as companionship and recreation and dating as courtship? Describe problems that can occur in both types of relationships.

APPLYING YOUR UNDERSTANDING

1. Imagine it is your first day on a new job in a department store. You walk into the store where you know no one. With a partner, act out what you might do to start making friends with the other employees.
2. Observe children at play with each other. What qualities do their friendships seem to have? Compare the children's friendships to your friendships. Do they seem to have the same qualities as your friendships or are they different? Now compare your friendships to those of some adults you know. What conclusions can you draw about how friendships change through the years?
3. Interview your friends and others to see how they manage peer pressure to conform. Write a short report outlining your findings and listing actions that teenagers can take to avoid being pressured to conform against their wills.
4. Write a report explaining how you feel about dating at this time of your life. Do you look upon dating as simply recreation? Or are you more interested in courtship? What goals and values do you hold that affect the role of dating in your life?

Chapter 4

ENJOYING FAMILY LIFE

Has this ever happened to you?

Suzie slid into her seat a couple of minutes before the bell rang to start the school day. She turned to the boy seated behind her. "Hi Jeremy," she said. "How was Thanksgiving?"

"Oh, great!" he replied. "We went to my grandmother's house and she fixed a big dinner with turkey, dressing, and pie. All the family was there and we stuffed ourselves as usual! I've got seven cousins, so it was pretty noisy and crazy. How about you?"

"Well," said Suzie, "it was really different this year. My parents got divorced last spring and my dad's remarried and moved away. So it was just mom, Dale, and me for Thanksgiving. We decided to try starting a new tradition this year. So we went out for Thanksgiving dinner and had steak instead of turkey! Then we went to a movie and finished up with ice cream sundaes afterwards. It was really fun."

"So you didn't see your dad at all?" asked Jeremy.

"No," replied Suzie. "But Dale and I are going down there at Christmas. I miss dad and it will be good to see him again."

What kind of family do you live in?

What kinds of families do your friends have? How much variation in family type are you familiar with?

How does the kind of family you live in influence your daily life?

After reading this chapter, you will be able to

- identify types and functions of families;
- recognize different management needs during the family life cycle;
- describe qualities of strong families;
- understand characteristics and traits of relationships between family members;
- appreciate the importance of community services and supports for families.

You probably are growing up in a family. Your family life is one of the most important factors affecting you. It affects your personality and your way of life. If you are like most people, your family can bring frustration and pain, as well as joy and pleasure. Managing family life to make it enjoyable and rewarding is one of the best ways of making the most of your world.

A **family** is two or more people related to each other by blood, marriage, or adoption. Family members share goals, values, and resources. They share responsibility for decisions. Being a part of your family means having a commitment to the others over time.

Families can be formed in three ways. The most common method is through marriage. In addition, families are formed through childbirth or adoption. Once a family is established, new members can be added in the same way.

TYPES OF FAMILIES

The family is the most basic of all human groups. However, families are not all alike. The type of family you live in may be very different from the families of your friends.

The definition of the family given above does not indicate that family members must live together. In fact, you probably do not live with all the relatives you consider part of your family. However, the term *family* is also used in another way to identify relatives who live in the same household. The different types of families described below are those people related by blood or other means who live in one household.

The joys and satisfactions of a strong, healthy family are universal. A family can be formed in three ways: marriage, childbirth, and adoption.

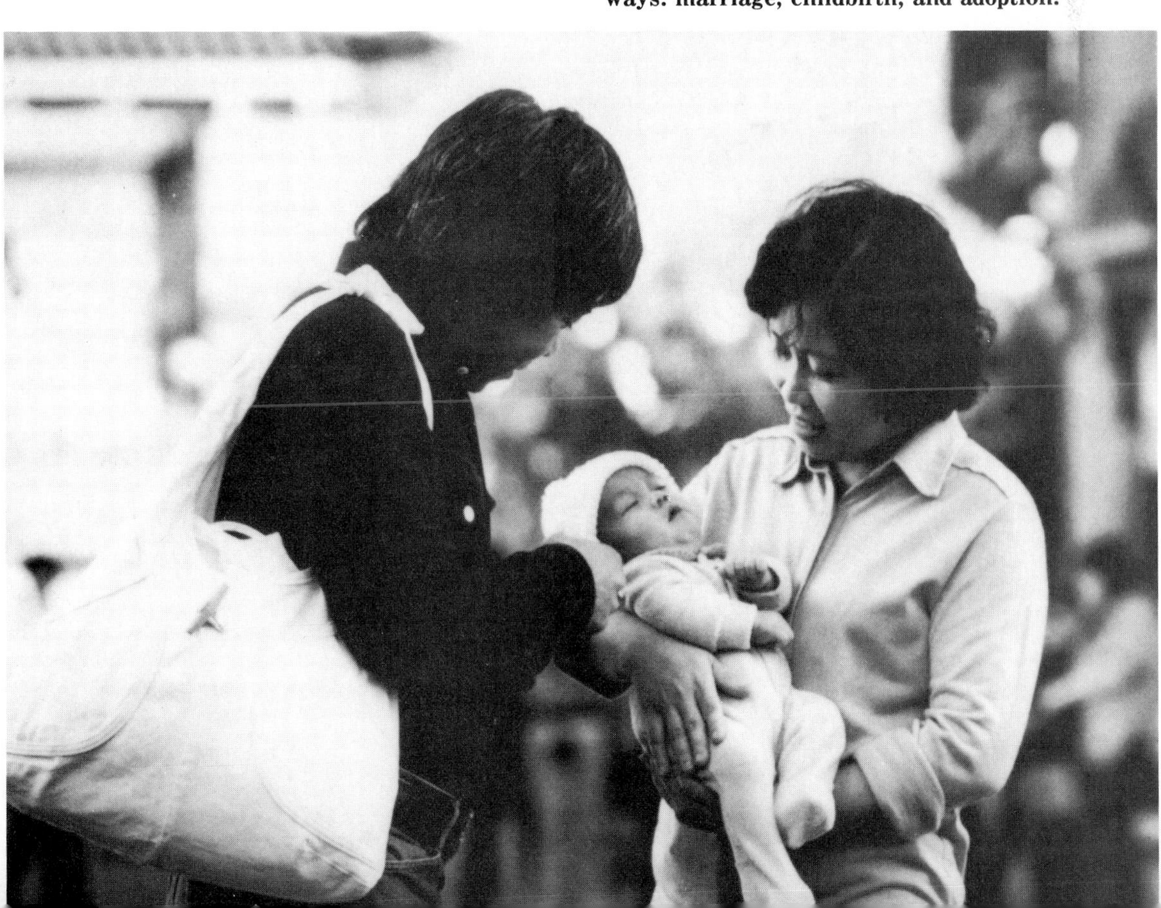

NUCLEAR FAMILY

The **nuclear family** is made up of two parents and their children who live together. You may think of the nuclear family as the most common type of family. However, only a fraction of Americans live in a nuclear family.

The children in nuclear families can be related by either birth or adoption. Some nuclear families have children added to the family by both means.

SINGLE-PARENT FAMILY

One of the fastest growing types of families is the **single-parent family.** In this kind of family, children live with only one parent. Over one-fourth of the families with children are headed by a single parent.

If you live in a single-parent family, you are most apt to live with your mother. However, more fathers are gaining custody of their children after divorce. Therefore, the percentage of single-parent families led by fathers is increasing.

Whether you are in a nuclear family, single-parent family or blended family, the primary purpose of the family remains the same—to provide love, support and care for its members.

BLENDED FAMILY

A **blended family** is formed when a couple with children from previous families marry. Sometimes only one of the married couple has a child or children. Often, both partners are parents.

Many couples in a blended family have children of their own. If you live in a blended family, you may have brothers and sisters from your original nuclear family. You may have stepbrothers and sisters from your stepparent's former marriage. In addition, you may also have halfbrothers and sisters. Blended-family relationships can be very complex.

COUPLE FAMILY

The majority of families do not have children living in the home. Instead, these families, **couple families,** are made up of only the couple. Some couple families never have children. They may choose a childless life-style based on their goals and values. On the other hand, some couples are not able to have children and do not adopt.

Couple families may have grown children who no longer live with them. These couples can be middle-aged or in their retirement years. A couple family may consist of remarried people whose children live with the former spouse.

EXTENDED FAMILY

An **extended family** consists of several generations of relatives living together. Usually extended families are formed when a grandparent moves in with a son's or daughter's family. However, you may know extended families who include aunts, uncles, or other relatives.

Sometimes, extended families skip a generation. For example, you may live with a grandparent or some other relative without your parents. There can be a great variety in who makes up an extended family.

Learn more about your ancestors and family history by spending time with extended family members.

OTHER FAMILY VARIATIONS

There are other kinds of families and familylike groups. Foster children live in a family setting and are considered part of the family while they are there.

Sometimes children live with family friends during emergencies or when they wish to finish a school year after their parents have moved from the community. A child whose parents are deceased may live with a guardian who is not related by blood, marriage, or adoption.

In addition, sometimes relatives live together in patterns that do not fit the types of families described above. Brothers and sisters, who are also called **siblings,** may live together. Two sisters may share an apartment after leaving the nuclear family.

It would be impossible to list all the various family types that exist. Each type is formed because it meets a need for those people who live in it. Whatever type of family you live in, you can work to maximize the satisfactions you get from it.

FAMILY FUNCTIONS

Families are the basic living pattern in our society because they serve so many functions, or purposes. The important functions served by the family make it a major source of life satisfaction for most people.

PHYSICAL NEEDS

The family is the setting where most people meet their physical needs. Your family shares housing that provides shelter from the elements. Your family also supplies food and clothing.

Family members protect each other. They provide care and security in times of illness, injury, old age, and unemployment. Protection is an especially important family function when there are young children who are unable to care for themselves.

The physical needs of the individual—food, clothing and shelter are met by the family.

EMOTIONAL DEVELOPMENT

The family promotes the emotional development of its members. Your family gives you a sense of belonging. Each member of your family has a place and a role to fill. This sense of belonging helps you feel accepted and secure. You know that your family is a partner in your life.

The family gives a sense of intimacy to member's lives. Your family members probably know you better than anyone else. They provide emotional support through their interest in your life.

The family is the place where you can get help with your problems and have someone to share your joys. It is a retreat when the stress and pressure of the outside world become too heavy.

The family also promotes the development of positive self-concepts in its members. Love and support from family members help you feel good about yourself.

PERSONAL GROWTH

The family is the setting where members are encouraged to develop themselves personally. You learn social skills through your interaction with family members. As you move into relationships with others, you are supported by the family. Your family may encourage you to ask friends to your home or suggest activities you may do with others.

The family teaches its members many things. It provides a climate for learning. Each member of your family can learn from the others. When you were small, your parents were your first teachers. They helped you learn to talk, to manage yourself, and to get along with people. The family also encourages its members to learn from others. This can be done through schooling and in informal ways.

Personal development of family members is also fostered. Each member has skills and talents that can be expanded and refined. Training and opportunities to use these skills are provided through the family.

COMMON INTERESTS AND GOALS

Family members work toward goals they share as a family. Your family may be saving money for a special vacation next summer. Many family goals relate to educating and training children to be productive citizens.

Common interests often provide enjoyment for family members. Your family may like playing games, attending sporting events, or working for your church. These shared activities help strengthen the bonds that tie family members together.

Family bonds can be strengthened by sharing common interests and activities such as fishing, bowling, jogging, tennis or attending cultural events.

ADAPTING TO CHANGE

Life today changes at a rapid pace. The family is important. It helps its members adapt to change. New ways of behaving can be learned in the family so members can adjust to the changing world.

Your family might move to a new home in a different town. There you would have to adjust to many changes. If you were able to work together and help each other, family members would probably be able to settle comfortably into new lives.

The family itself is changing. Your nuclear family may have turned into an extended family or a single-parent family. When these changes occur, family members help each other adapt to the new way of life. Whatever the form of your family, you can rely on the others as a resource in adjusting to change.

MAKING MEMORIES

Family traditions and rituals are important parts of life in a strong family. The memories of a rich, full family life can sustain you through problems and troubles. How can you make family memories?

• *Assemble a family photo album.* Identify the people in each photo and the occasion. The pictures in the album will allow you to remember important as well as trivial events in your family life.

• *Make a videotape of a family occasion.* This may be a family dinner, holiday celebration, birthday or anniversary, or a reunion. Play the tape to relive the special occasion.

• *Start working on a family tree.* Discover the names, birth dates, and death dates (when applicable) of as many past generations as you can. You may have to write to distant relatives to discover some of this information. Libraries sometimes have information on genealogy that can help you develop a family tree.

• *Take a family history trip.* Go back to the area where your parents were raised and ask them to show you places from their pasts. Find out where they lived and went to school, and what they did for fun.

• *Make a list of your family traditions.* If you would like, ask other family members to make similar lists and compare them. Your traditions may include simple things such as celebrating the cat's birthday, leaving notes on the refrigerator, hiding the family valentines, having leftovers on Monday night, celebrating a good report card by eating out, or going to a fireworks show together on the Fourth of July.

• *Develop a family trivia game.* Write questions about people and events in your family. For example, in what year were your parents married (or divorced)? What were your great grandparents' names? In what countries were they born? Who is Aunt Mamie and how is she related to you? How many second cousins do you have? Play the game on important family days such as holidays, birthdays, or anniversaries.

• *Discover traditions from your family's ethnic background.* Whether your heritage is Dutch, German, American Indian, Japanese, Russian, Cuban, Mexican, African, or French, there are customs that you could discover to enrich family life. What foods are traditional? Are there symbols that have meaning in those cultures? Are there special rituals or traditions you could adopt that come from your ethnic background?

• Plan and arrange a family reunion. A small family reunion might be just your grandparents, aunts and uncles, and cousins. Or you may try to organize a larger reunion, using your family tree to invite people. Such a reunion will help you see where you fit into your family and can help cement generations together.

MANAGING THE FAMILY LIFE CYCLE

Most families change and develop over the years. These changes are called the **family life cycle.** During this cycle, the family's goals, needs, wants, and values may change. New decisions and choices are needed.

Families who decide to have children go through four general stages in the life cycle—the beginning stage, the parental stage, the middle-aged stage, and the retirement stage. Each family stage has developmental tasks, just as individuals do. Refer to the Family Life Cycle Stages Chart.

LIFE CYCLE VARIATIONS

The life cycle is a useful way of thinking about the changing and developing family throughout life. It also provides a framework to use when you are looking ahead and planning your future. However, there are many variations in people's lives that do not fit the four general stages described above.

Some people never marry. Others marry but do not have children. Divorce and single parenthood will change the way a family moves through the life cycle. Remarriage may mean people go through some stages more than once.

No matter what particular life cycle pattern you choose to live, good management of your resources can help make it satisfying and enjoyable for you.

FAMILY LIFE CYCLE STAGES

Stages	Developmental Tasks
1. Beginning Stage	The couple works to establish their home and to build a satisfying marriage relationship.
2. Parental Stage	The parents raise children to become productive, independent adults. This stage lasts until the children are financially on their own.
3. Middle Age Stage, Launching Stage, or Empty Nest Stage	The couple renews the marriage relationship, keeps ties with children and their families, helps aged parents if necessary, and plans for retirement.
4. Retirement Stage	The couple adjusts to retirement and to the aging process.

Understanding the stages of the family life cycle can help you anticipate and prepare for the changes that can occur during your lifetime.

QUALITIES OF STRONG FAMILIES

There are some traits that researchers have found related to strong families. Families who have these qualities tend to be more satisfied in their home lives than those that do not.

Happy families show appreciation for all members. They build each other up and help make each other feel good about themselves. They look for the good qualities and strengths in others and express their satisfaction in having these qualities in family members.

A second trait of strong families is that members spend time together. They enjoy being together. They make a special effort to plan activities in which all members can participate.

Strong families have good communication patterns. They talk to each other. Family members tend to be good listeners. Because of their good communication habits, they also have good conflict management skills. They bring disagreements into the open and work to resolve them.

Commitment to each other is another trait of strong families. Members work to promote each others' happiness and welfare. The best relationships are ones in which there is commitment to each other and to the family group. Families with commitment tend to show it by putting time and effort in the family.

Another trait of strong families is the sharing of values and goals. These families also build traditions and customs that reflect their values and are meaningful to all family members. Such families may have strong religious values.

Finally, strong families know how to use the management process to make decisions that will help them reach their goals. They are able to deal positively with problems and crises. Working together, they manage life's difficulties. By helping each other, they come through problems with stronger relationships.

UNDERSTANDING YOUR FAMILY

Family relationships are based on the same principles as other relationships. Good family relations show rapport, empathy, trust, respect, interdependence, and flexibility. Members of families need to communicate well and know how to solve differences.

However, getting along with your family is not always as easy as getting along with others. The strong bonds you have with other family members may mean strong friction and conflict. Understanding your family is not always an easy task.

When difficulties or crisis situations occur, strong families pull together to help solve the problem and offer support.

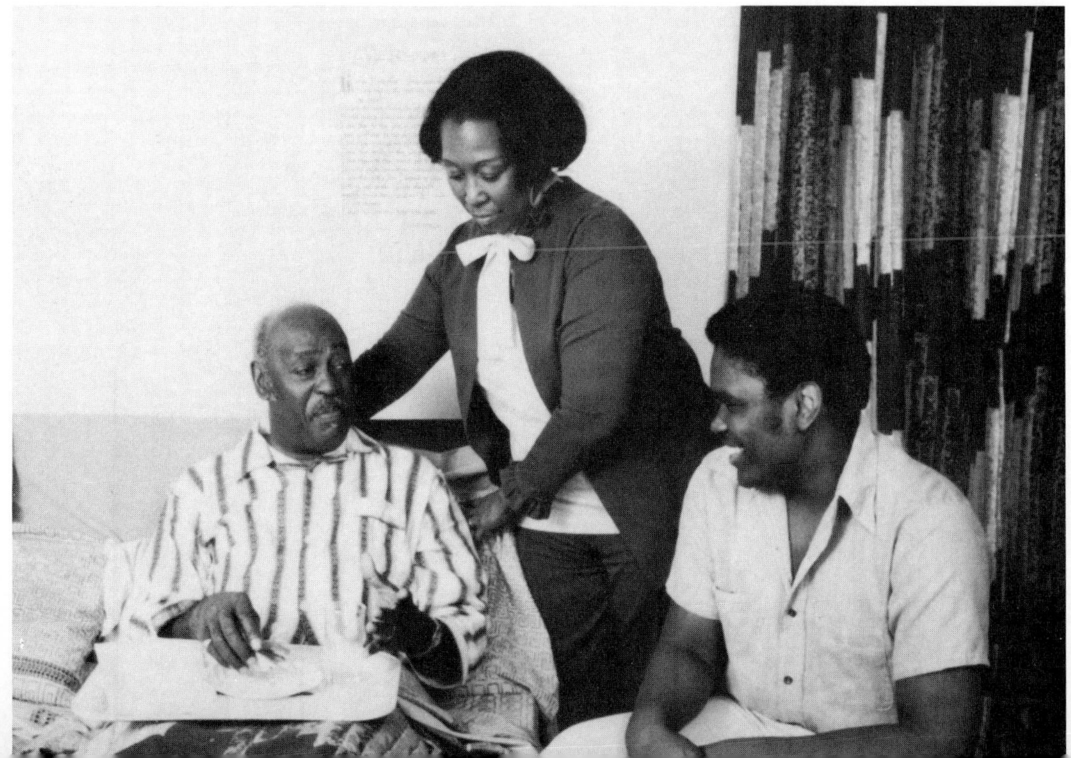

PARENT-TEENAGER RELATIONSHIPS

The parent-child tie is one of the strongest in human experience. Love and shared lives create a powerful bond. However, during the teen years, the bond begins to loosen as teenagers search for their own identities. During this time, parents have mixed feelings. They want their teenagers to grow to be happy, independent adults. However, they are very aware of and afraid of the problems of the teen years. They know a wrong choice may harm the teenager's whole life.

Good parent-teenager relationships are a two-way street. Your parents' behavior influences you. In turn, your behavior affects your parents and your relationship with them.

The main key to good relationships between parents and their children is whether they are able to see and respect each other as people. Your parents have strengths and weaknesses just as you do. Sometimes they make good decisions and, at other times, mistakes. Learning to see your parents as they really are and respecting them as individuals is part of growing up.

You can try to help your parents or stepparents understand you as a person at the same time you work to understand them. Talk about your goals and values and how you feel about issues. Listen when they talk about things that matter to them.

Understanding your parents' points of view does not mean you have to agree with them. Your parents probably understand your point of view better than you realize because they can remember their teen years. But their experiences of life overlay that understanding with a layer of caution.

Therefore, building a better relationship with your parents means understanding their caution. You can realize how their viewpoints have developed. You know they want what is best for you even if you do not agree on how to accomplish that. As you reach such understanding, you will be in a better position to negotiate changes that are a compromise between your view of life and theirs.

The closeness of family ties may mean that family members feel they do not have to be polite or consider others' feelings. So some families are characterized by rudeness and a lack of courtesy for others.

Instead, because family ties are so close, it is even more important that you treat family members as well or better than you treat others. When you consider your parents as individuals and respect them, you can begin to relate to them as you would a friend. If you treat your parents in such a way, it is easier for them to see you as a person and to begin relating to you in the same way.

If the relationship with your parents has appeared to falter, don't be surprised. The teen years are a difficult time as teens reach for power and parents try to maintain control.

Skillful communication and respect helps a teenager and parent view each other as individuals, thus developing a good relationship.

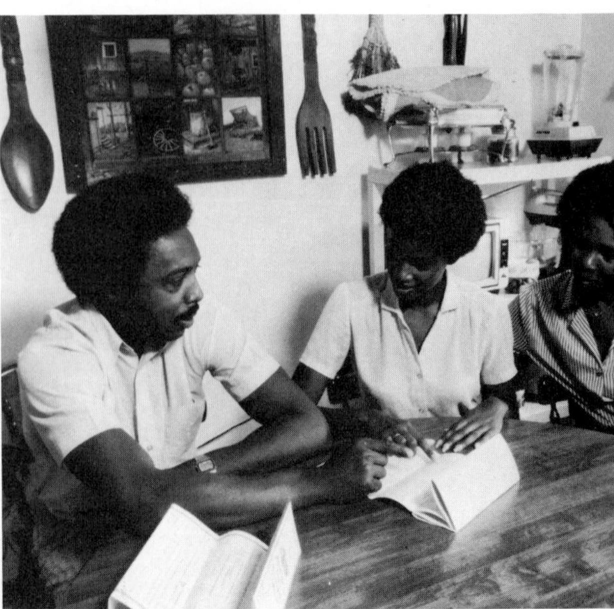

SIBLING RELATIONSHIPS

The relationship between siblings are an important part of family ties. If you have siblings, they have had a strong affect on the development of your personality. You have also influenced their development.

In many families, sibling relationships are not good. Siblings are often in conflict with each other. One main source of conflict is the competition for the attention and love of the parent. A parent only has so much time and energy. Children may believe that the only way to get their fair share of the parent is to compete with their siblings.

Children choose a variety of ways to compete for attention. Sometimes they try to outachieve each other. One child may excel in school, another in sports, and a third in music. In other families, children may compete in negative ways. They may misbehave to attract the parents' attention.

Sibling relationships can also be a challenge in blended families. Because stepsiblings come from different families, they sometimes find they have little in common with each other.

Stepsiblings in a blended family are not immediately going to have the same kind of relationship as siblings in a nuclear family. It takes time to build a family bond among stepsiblings who have never lived together before and who may not know each other well.

Getting along with your siblings and stepsiblings is good experience for learning to get along with others. If you can adjust to the traits and values of brothers and sisters, you may be more able to get along with others outside the family. Thus, sibling relationships are a practice ground for building relationship skills.

If you apply the conflict management skills described in chapter 2 to sibling relationships, your family life can be more pleasant.

Getting along with your brothers or sisters can be good practice for building positive, lasting relationships with others.

SPECIAL NEEDS

Some families have special needs for understanding beyond parent-teenager and sibling relationships. Understanding extended families and families with handicapped or other exceptional members can sometimes be a special challenge.

Every person that is added to a family makes family relationships more complicated. An extended family usually has a member of a third generation involved. The combination of the extra person in a different life stage sometimes causes problems.

Although grandparents may love their grandchildren dearly, they often are not used to living with the commotion and noise of children. They may be uncertain of their role in the household. Being patient and giving your love and support can help them adjust to life in your family.

On the other hand, the extended family can be a special support to its members. Children may find a grandparent has more time, patience, and understanding than a busy parent. The extra family member can share the responsibilities of the household, making each person's tasks easier.

Sometimes grandparents do not live in your household, but still require many resources from your family. They may be unable to manage living independently. Your parents may have to provide meals and transportation for them. If they are ill or in a hospital or nursing home, there may be further demands on you. Your home life may be disrupted while their more pressing needs are taken care of.

Others may live with your family. A foster child, an aunt or uncle, or nephew or niece may be a member of your household. Each of these people has his or her own values and needs, which may not mesh with your family's. Feeling empathy for the other person is one of the best ways to build a relationship that makes life together satisfying.

Families with a handicapped member have many adjustments to make. The more severe the handicap, the more changes will have to be made in daily living.

Handicaps in a parent may mean children have to take more responsibility for family life. Income may be reduced and the parent may be unable to handle some household chores. In these cases, children can make a valuable contribution to family life.

Handicapped people usually need extra support from their families. They may need help to manage simple, everyday routines and chores. Adjustments may be needed to accomodate a wheel chair. It may seem that family life revolves around the handicapped person as family members work to make the handicapped member's life easier and manageable.

Having a handicapped member in the family can be challenging. Handling it well means having the maturity to accept that person's limitations and helping in whatever way you can to help meet that person's needs as well as your own.

Living areas can be redesigned to create a pleasing, efficient use of space for family members who are physically handicapped.

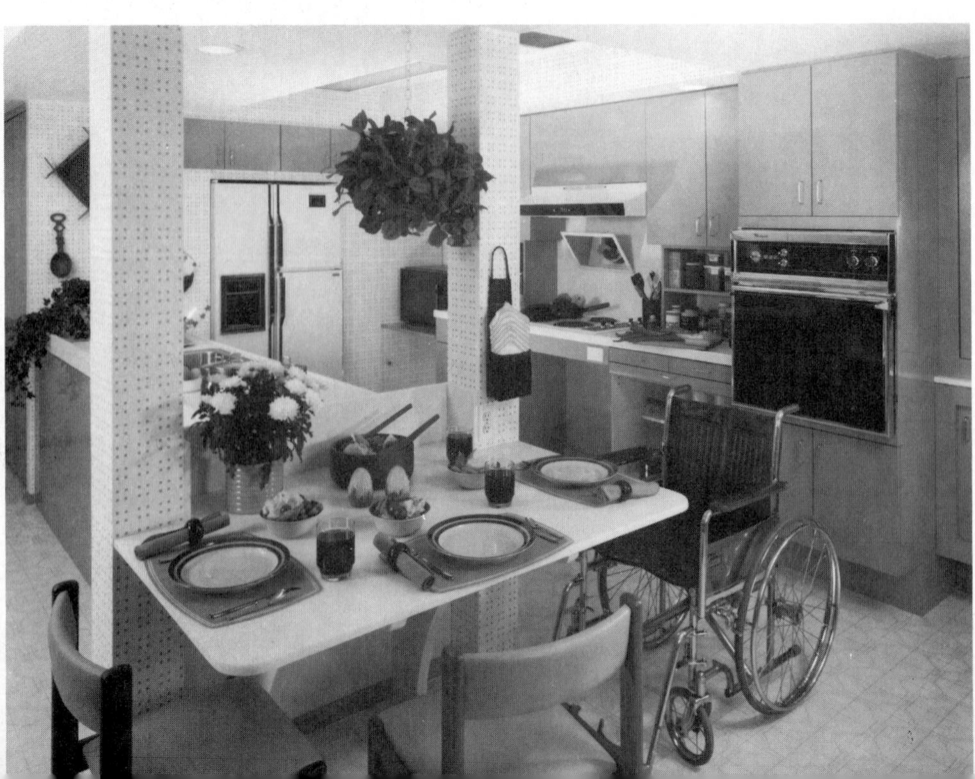

COMMUNITY SUPPORTS AND SERVICES

Sometimes families cannot fill all their needs well because of lack of resources, misfortune, or mistakes. When this happens, community supports can help keep the family together. Sometimes finding aid for your specific problem may be hard. But finding the help you need can enable you to get past the bad times and on to a brighter future.

Sometimes community services provide enrichment to family life. For example, your family may enjoy using the swimming pools, parks, and libraries provided by your city or county. Courses sponsored by schools or other community groups can help families.

Other community supports and services are designed to help families in need. Your community may have hot meals at noon for the elderly who find cooking a problem. There may be drug and alcohol abuse programs for families who need them. Counseling services are often available on a sliding fee scale, which requires people to pay only what they can afford.

Families with financial problems may find assistance in several places. Food stamps can help with grocery bills. Governmental or charitable agencies may have funds to pay utility bills. Cash assistance is available to some families under some circumstances.

It is sometimes hard to know where to find the help you need. Your school counselor or social worker may be a good starting point. The counselor should be familiar with community services and know where to direct you to get help.

Another source of help is your local church or temple. Ministers, priests, and rabbis are trained in counseling. If they are not able to give help themselves, they can refer you to other community resources.

Some governments have a special supplement in the yellow pages listing agencies that offer help and support to those in need. In some communities, there is a special phone number that people can call to find out more about community services. Special suicide or drug "hot lines" can give immediate help in an emergency and suggest other alternatives.

This center is one type of community service that is available to families. What other community supports and services are available to families in your area?

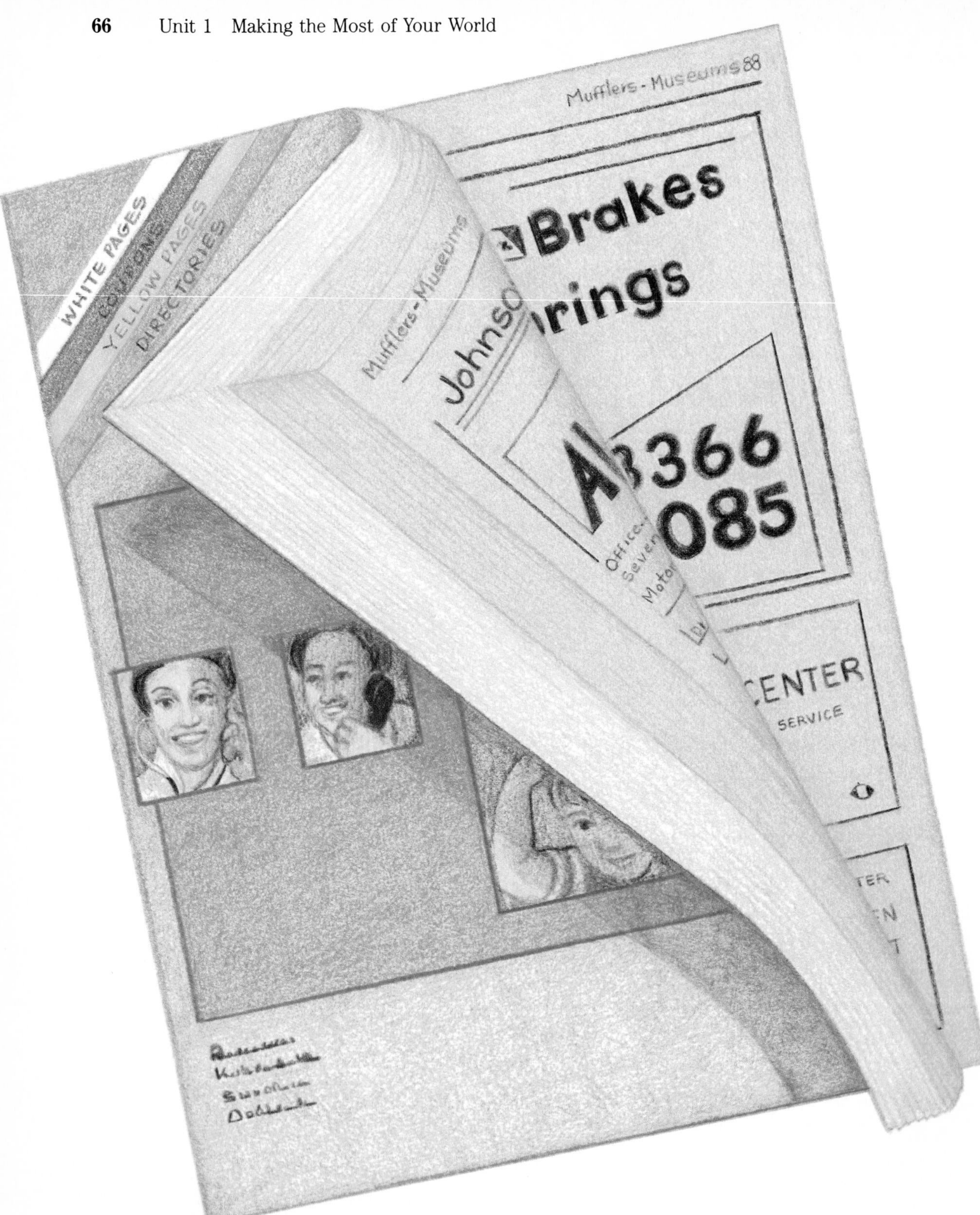

The telephone yellow pages can be a good resource to help you find listings of agencies that can provide help and support. Sometimes telephone numbers listed under the county will also list valuable services.

WORDS TO REMEMBER

blended family
couple family
extended family
family
family life cycle
nuclear family
siblings
single-parent family

CHECKING YOUR UNDERSTANDING

1. Define a family. What is *your* definition of a family? What makes a family different from other groups?
2. Compare and contrast the types of families discussed in this chapter.
3. Describe some functions of the family. How do these relate to family members' needs and wants?
4. How does the management process vary over the family life cycle?
5. Identify the qualities of strong families outlined in this chapter. Which trait do you think most important? Why? Which trait do you think least important? Why?
6. Give suggestions for improving understanding between teenagers and parents, siblings, and members of families with special needs.

APPLYING YOUR UNDERSTANDING

1. Because of the increasing number of single-parent and blended families, many articles about them appear in newspapers and magazines. Locate an article about a single-parent or blended family. Give a brief oral report to the class summarizing what the article has to say about the satisfactions and frustrations of these kinds of families.
2. If possible, interview four people, one from each of the four general stages of the family life cycle. Explain the management process to them and ask how it applies to their stage of life. How does life stage affect their goals? Needs? Values? Resources? Decision making?
3. Research the facilities and agencies in your community that support and service families. First, identify those that offer opportunities and enrichment for families. Then list those that help families. Discover whom each agency helps and what kind of help it provides. Compile your findings with those of other class members and prepare a report. Try to get your report published in the school or community newspaper.

Unit 2

PLANNING YOUR FUTURE

Unit 2 will help you to think about three important aspects of your future: career, life-style, and children. How you manage your career, your choice of life-style, and whether you choose to become a parent will all affect how happy and satisfying your adult life will be.

Choosing a career involves the management process. Your goals, values, wants, needs, and resources will all affect your choice of a career. Careful decision making will help you to find and to prepare for a career that is right for you.

Your goals and values will also affect the kind of life you will lead as an adult. There are many options you will face—a single life, marriage, parenthood, divorce, and remarriage. Because parenthood is a lifetime role, it is very important that you look at all the responsibilities and opportunities it brings when you think about becoming a parent. Weighing all your options will help you make decisions that will let you live the life you desire.

Chapter 5
THE RIGHT CAREER FOR YOU

Has this ever happened to you?

Jeff and Barbara were walking home from school one sunny April afternoon. Barbara said, "I've got to start thinking about what I'm going to do this summer. I'm finally old enough to get a job, but I've never had one before and I really don't know how to get one."

"I've heard it's pretty hard to find a summer job around here," said Jeff. "Are you looking for something specific?"

"What I would really like is a job in a bank," replied Barbara. "I want to be a financial advisor, so that would be good experience."

"You probably need to start looking now," said Jeff. "It might be an advantage if you could begin work before the end of the school year. Do you know anybody who works at a bank?"

"No," answered Barbara.

"Maybe you could make a list of the banks in the phone book and go around to talk to the managers."

"That's a good idea!" Barbara exclaimed. "I think I'll work on it as soon as I get home. Thanks for your help, Jeff."

Have you ever wanted to find a job, but did not know how to go about it?

What opportunities for summer employment are available in your community?

After reading this chapter, you will be able to

- understand factors to be considered in choosing a career;
- describe the process of looking and applying for a job;
- identify qualities needed to be an entrepreneur or a good employee.

What is the most important decision you will make during your life? Will it be a decision on whether or whom to marry? A choice of where to live? Or, as for most people, will your most important choice be selecting a career that is right for you?

Work will be a central part of your adult life. If you start work at age eighteen or twenty-one, you will probably work forty to fifty years before you retire. Even parents who leave the job market to care for their children work twenty-five to thirty years of their lives.

The job or career you choose will affect all parts of your adult life. It will affect the amount of schooling you need and the money you will earn. Your job will dictate where you live and the hours you work. A decision that has so much effect on your life needs to be made thoughtfully and carefully.

Because people spend about one-third of their lives at work, the choice of a job or career is an important one.

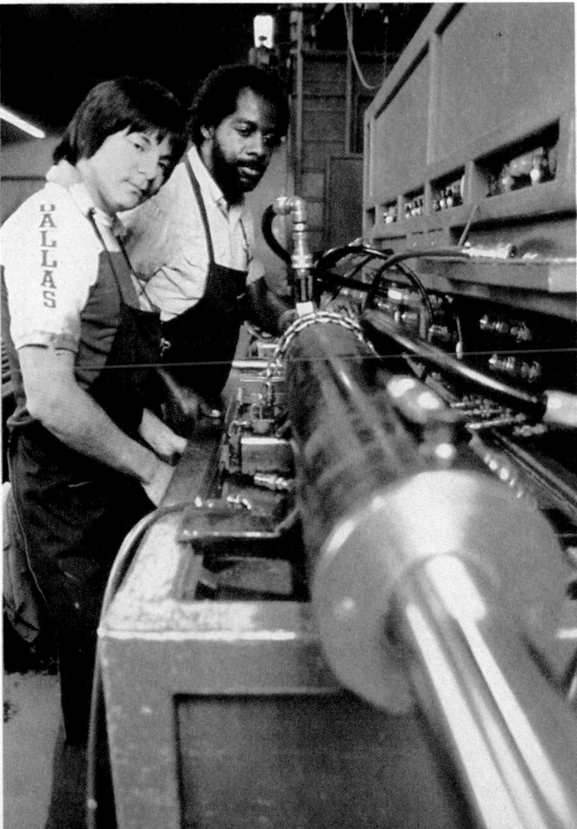

You are at a point in life where you will soon be making a major career decision. But as important as your first career choice is, it probably will not be your only one. Most people make major career decisions three to five times during their lives. Career decision making is a lifelong process rather than a single event.

Some people actively seek career changes and new career fields. They use such changes to maintain their interest and enthusiasm for the job. Others find the changing job market or technology has eliminated their jobs. These people have decisions to make as they search for new work or choose new training for different careers. Other people are given or find opportunities to change career paths during their work lives.

Knowing what makes a good career choice can help you face the major career decisions of your life. The basis for good career choices is matching your talents and goals with those needed by a given field of work. Because of changing economic conditions and the complex nature of people, this process is not always easy or foolproof.

Changing technology has affected the outlook of the job market and created new types of jobs.

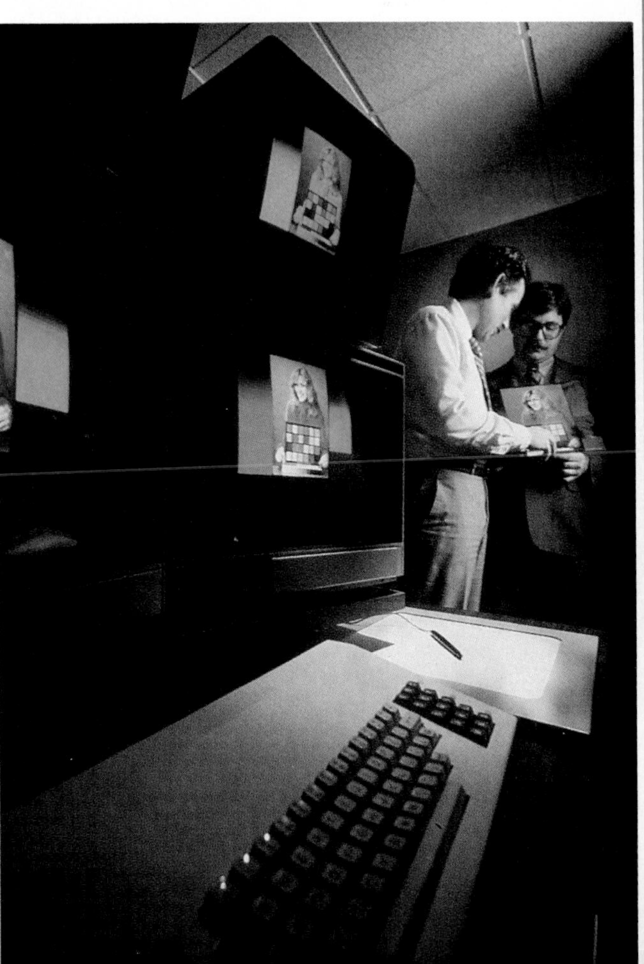

CHOOSING A CAREER

Throughout history, people's definitions of themselves have been closely bound up with their work. The jobs people choose still play a major part in how they present themselves to others. The work role you choose will affect how you see yourself and how others will see you.

The first step in thinking about a career is to consider your goals and values. What career will allow you to accomplish your goals and express your values? Values and goals related to career choices could include concern for the environment, family life, creativity, fame, wealth, power, leadership, friendship, religion, outdoor living, and helping others. Identifying your goals and values can help you see possible career areas and the type of job setting you would enjoy.

Besides goals and values, there are other factors to consider in choosing a career. These include your interests and abilities, the amount of schooling needed for the career, the long-term outlook of the job market, and how you plan to combine and manage a career and family life.

INTERESTS AND ABILITIES

Probably the most important factor for being happy at work is matching your interests and skills with those required by the job. Of course, it is not always easy to know for sure whether you will enjoy a particular job. Many people choose a career only to discover they do not really like the tasks involved in the work. However, it is possible to narrow your choices based on your interests and talents. It is important to look at both your interests and skills. You may be considering a field where you have few abilities. Or you may have talent in a career area that does not appeal to you.

In thinking about your career, consider what you enjoy. Do you have a hobby that might become a career? What is your best subject in school? Do you enjoy reading books or watching television programs on a certain topic? Do you like to work with your hands or do you enjoy planning, organizing, or calculating better? What do you prefer—working with ideas, objects, people, or data?

The next step is to identify your specific skills and talents. You have many abilities that could be used in pursuing a career. Refer to the Skills and Talent Inventory Chart.

The desire to help others is the basis or motivation for some peoples' career choice.

SKILLS AND TALENT INVENTORY

Manual Ability:	Are you good at running machinery, vehicles, or equipment? Do you enjoy working with your hands?
Athletic and Outdoor Skills:	Are you physically coordinated and good at sports? Do you enjoy working outdoors or with animals?
Analytical and Mathematical Skills:	Are you good with data and numbers? Do you enjoy calculating, managing money, budgeting and keeping reports? Are you good at research or investigating?
Relationship Skills:	Are you able to influence others? Do you enjoy working with people, negotiating, motivating others, and solving problems? Do you like to teach people, or help and serve others?
Performing Skills:	Are you talented in music, art, drama, or dance? Do you enjoy performing before a group, explaining products, playing music, singing or making people laugh?
Management and Leadership Skills:	Are you able to problem solve, make decisions, guide and inspire others? Do you meet people easily? Can you develop programs, organize tasks, or set standards?

Some skills are useful in many kinds of jobs. For example, if you are willing to learn, have good verbal skills, can write well, relate well to others, and are a good manager, you can use these skills in a wide range of careers.

All of the talents, skills, and abilities listed above are useful in some jobs or careers. Your task is to match them with your interests, skills, values, and goals in order to find the right job or career for yourself.

There are several tests that can help you make this match. Some tests survey your interests and point out career areas you would probably like. Other tests learn what your talents and skills are. Your school counselor can arrange for you to take these tests. They will help in finding a career that is right for you.

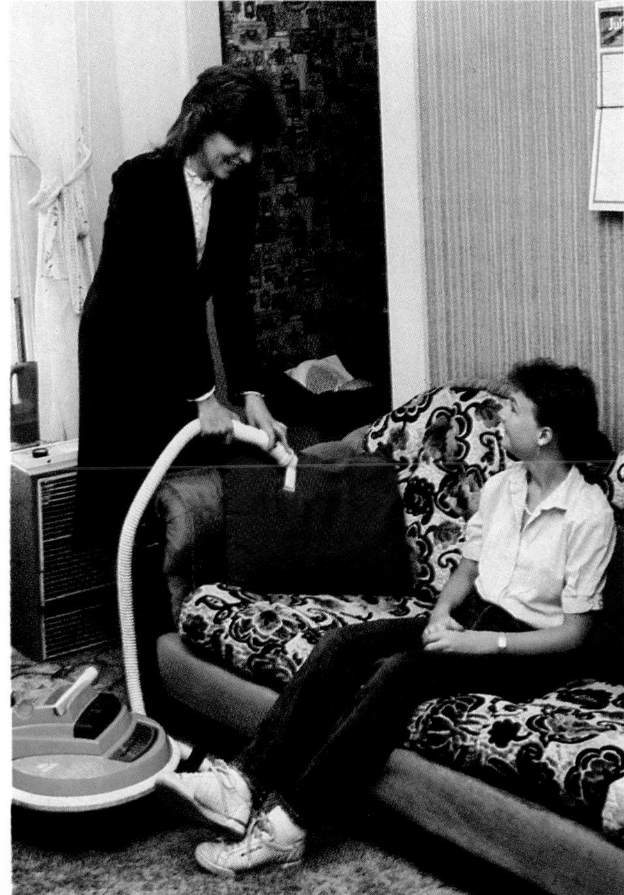

Strong oral and written communication skills are valuable in all jobs and can be transferred from one job to another.

EDUCATION NEEDED

Many jobs require certain schooling or training. In general, there are three levels of jobs or careers. An **entry level job** is one that requires little, if any, skill, schooling, or experience to do. Workers in these jobs do not need special talents or training. If you have a high school degree or less, you would qualify for an entry level job. You may find these types of jobs in food service, retail shops, maintenance, wholesale business, and many other career fields. Many part-time employment opportunities are available in entry level positions.

The next job level requires training. These jobs require less than a college degree, but more than a high school diploma. An associate degree from a community college will qualify you for some jobs. For example, you might choose to study computer programming or dental hygiene at such a college.

Vocational schools provide training for some jobs. You might enroll in an auto mechanics or child-care program there. Technical schools offer specialized training for specific careers. Perhaps you are interested in going to an electronics school, a secretarial school, a truck drivers' school, or a beauty or barber school. This further training will qualify you for a better job.

The third level of careers are those that require a college degree. You may go to a four-year college to qualify to be a teacher, chemist, engineer, or accountant. Some careers need even more schooling than a college degree. For example, lawyers, doctors, psychiatrists, and veterinarians go to college for more than four years.

For most jobs, the amount of training required is rewarded by the job itself. To some extent, the more training or schooling needed, the higher the salary a job pays. Interesting and challenging jobs often require more education than jobs that are boring or easy to learn.

Entry level positions are generally lower in pay but provide needed background, experience, and training.

Programs offered at technical schools offer training for specialized skills such as: carpentry, fashion merchandising or electronics.

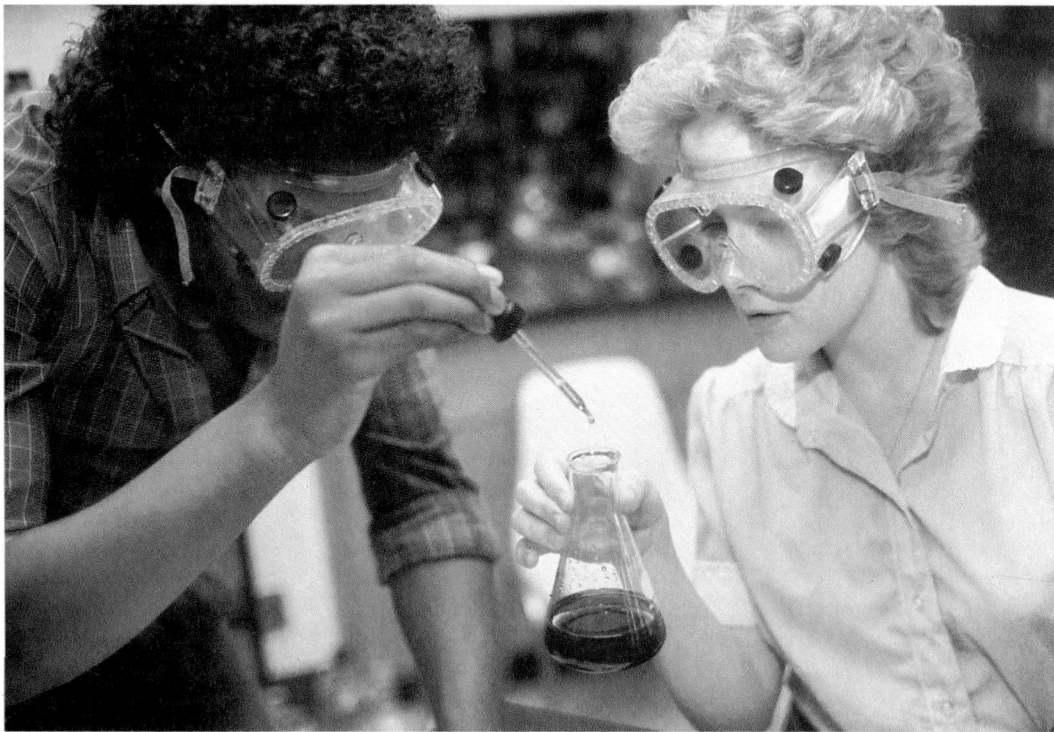

A minimum of a four year college degree is required for professional careers such as lawyers, engineers, nutritionists, and accountants.

LONG-TERM OUTLOOK

The jobs in the United States are undergoing many changes. The major shift is from an industrial economy to an information-oriented service one. See management feature, "The Changing Working World," page 80.

Career choices can be made on the basis of these changes. Consider the future and whether the career you want holds long-term promise. A career field where jobs are growing offers you more than a field where the job market is shrinking.

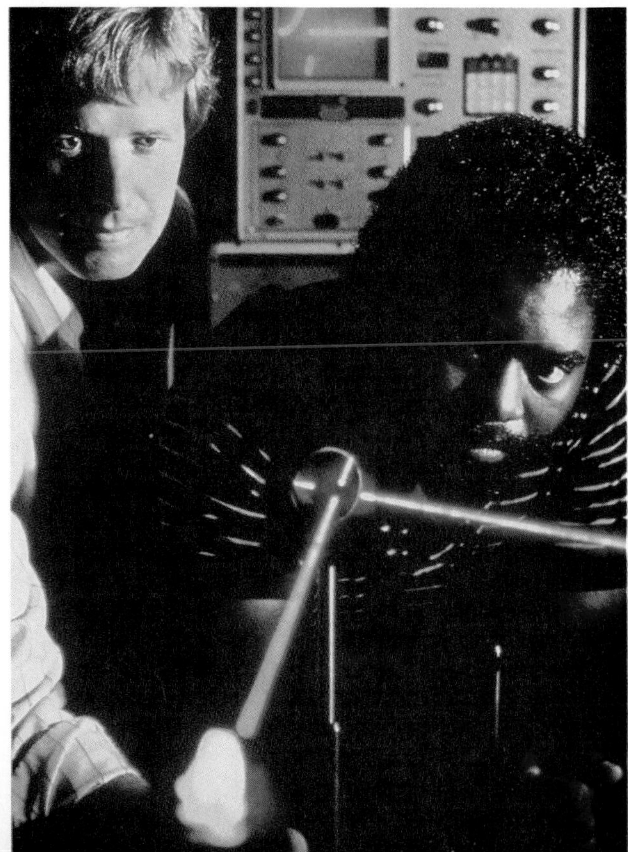

The job outlook for careers related to the health industry, computers and service industry hold promising futures and growth potential for aspiring individuals.

MANAGING A CAREER AND FAMILY

Family and work are the two major areas in which people look for life satisfaction. It is not easy to combine these two and be successful in both areas. You may find the needs and demands of the job often conflict with the needs and demands of family life.

Today, men and women are learning to share work and family life. As this sharing grows and continues, both men and women will consider their family responsibilities and how to manage them in making career choices.

It can be a challenge to balance the demands of family and work life.

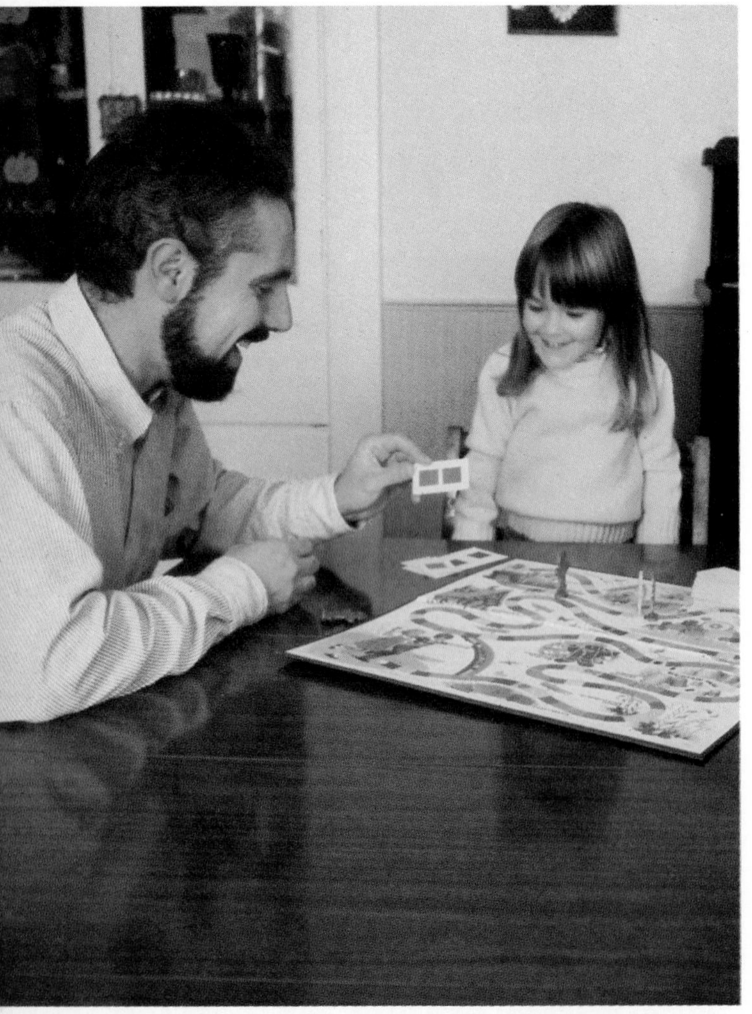

INFORMATION SOURCES

Because of the many factors to weigh in choosing a career, it is vital to have enough information when making a choice.

Your school counselors are a good place to start your search for career information. They have material on thousands of careers and jobs. Besides, they know where to find or get information that is not easily found.

One of the best sources of information about a special career is someone in the career now. Such a person can give you details about life on the job as well as information about the schooling needed, salary, and job outlook.

The United States government prints many publications about jobs and the labor market. One of the most useful is the *Occupational Outlook Handbook.* This book has information for jobs in more than three hundred fields. It is printed by the United States Department of Labor and is updated every two years. Most libraries have the *Handbook* in their reference section.

There is much information around about jobs. However, you may have to hunt to find the exact material you need for the job in which you are interested. Use the resources in your school and community. The more information you have about your chosen career, the more apt you are to be happy with your decision and your job.

FINDING A JOB

Choosing and getting ready for the job that you think you will enjoy are only the first steps in the process of finding a job. Once you have decided what field you wish to work in and have gotten the training you need, you must find someone to hire you.

LOOKING FOR WORK

For most people, looking for a job is stressful. It is not always easy to find who has jobs available. You may spend much time, energy, and money only to discover that a company has no openings.

One of the best places to look for work is in the classified ads of the local newspaper. Many businesses who need workers advertise in the want ads. The jobs available are described very briefly. Information about where you can call or write is given. Most jobs listed in the want ads are filled quickly so you will need to act as soon as the ads are printed.

Job hunters may find jobs by visiting the businesses in which they are interested. Retail stores or shops sometimes post "Help Wanted" signs in their windows. Larger companies that hire workers for many types of jobs often have a personnel office. The job seeker can go to the office, find out what types of jobs are open, and leave an application on file.

Jobs listed in the classified ads are usually filled quickly so the job hunter should apply immediately.

Most state governments run local job service centers with the United States Employment Service. Employers list job openings, and the agency makes the information public. There is no charge for using the government agency.

There are also many private employment agencies. A private agency will charge a fee if it places a person in a job. Depending on the agreement contract signed, either the person or the new employer may take care of the fee. If you use such an agency, be sure you know what the agency will do, how much you will pay, and for what. Find out about its charges, if any, if it is not able to find you a job.

Some schools offer job placement services to students. Most colleges post job opportunities for students so they can find jobs in their fields. Many companies send recruiters to schools to talk to students about jobs. Some community colleges also have career and job information for all people in the community.

One of the best sources of information about jobs is your personal network. A **network** is a system of relationships in which you are involved. **Networking** means working with others in the network to achieve your goals. In networking, you talk to your friends, family, and others about the kind of job you are seeking. If the people in your network know you are job hunting, they may be able to help you find openings.

By networking with friends, family and acquaintances you may find out about job opportunities available in your community.

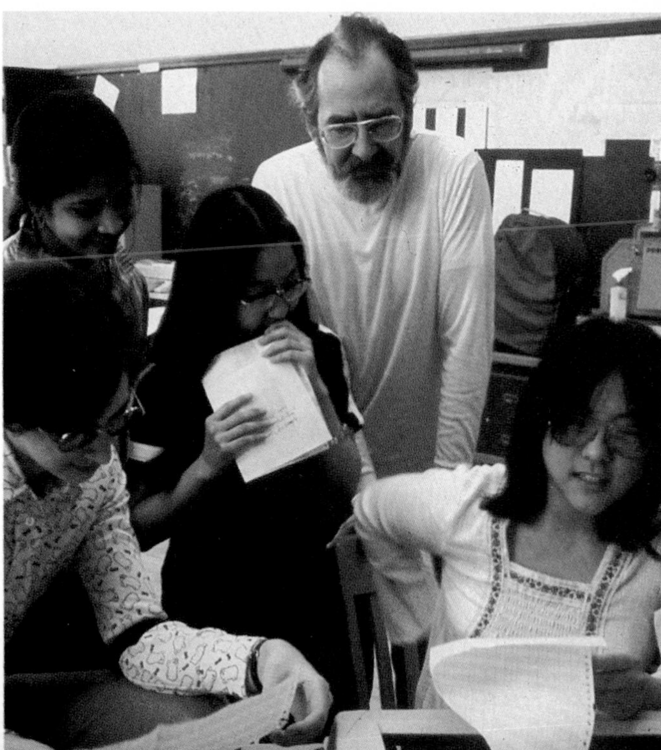

APPLYING FOR A JOB

After you have found a job opening, the next step is to convince the employer you are the right person for the job. The employer will want to know about your training and experience in the job area, your willingness to work, personality, health, and character.

For many jobs, you will have to fill out an application blank. These forms usually ask for personal information, such as your name, social security number, address, and telephone number. Your school record and job experience will be listed. Sometimes, you will need to give the names of people who can give you a reference. Be sure to get permission from these people before you list them on an application.

The application form will let the employer learn about you and your qualifications. To make a good impression, fill in all of the form neatly. Be sure all blanks are filled in accurately.

Sometimes instead of an application blank, you will apply for a job through a letter. In your letter, you can highlight why you think you could do the job better than anyone else.

Often a **resume** will be needed with the letter of application. This is a listing of your personal information, your school record, and work experience. A resume often has about the same information as an application blank, but you can organize it however you wish. Both an application letter and resume should by typewritten.

Usually the final step in applying for a job is an interview. The employer wants to learn what type of person you are. It is important to give as good an impression as possible in an interview. If you dress neatly, are honest and sincere in your answers, and show your enthusiasm for the work, you will have a better chance of getting the job.

While the employer uses the interview to learn more about you, you can also use it to ask questions about the job. The following questions, as well as others you may have, will give you valuable information about the job you are seeking:

1. What is the job description?
2. What duties and responsibilities are involved in doing the job?
3. What type of training and schooling are required?
4. What chances will there be for getting ahead?
5. What will the work place be like?
6. What are the salary and fringe benefits for the job?

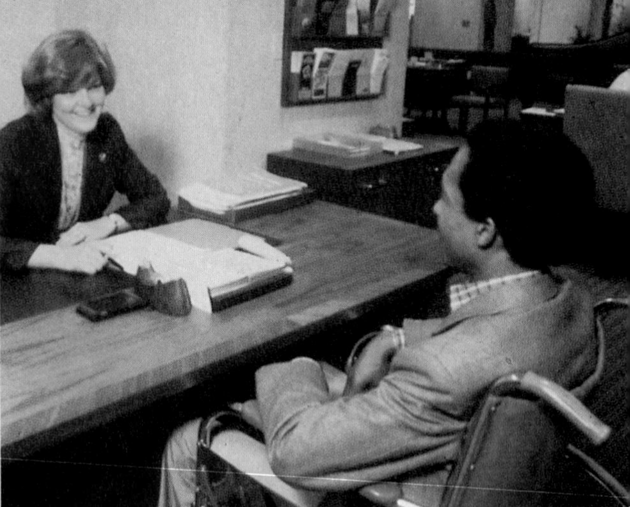

The job interview is a time for the employer to find out about your qualifications and for you to ask questions about the job.

Fringe benefits include things such as paid vacation, personal holidays, life or health insurance, and sick leave. Because the value of fringe benefits can be about one-fourth of the job's salary, it is important to know what fringe benefits are offered.

MAKING A JOB FOR YOURSELF

Many people like to work for themselves. They want to own their own businesses. Such people are called **entrepreneurs.** Most new jobs in the United States are offered by small businesses. However, as many as 80 percent of the fifty thousand new businesses started each year will fail. This is because their owners did not know how to run the business to make a profit or lacked the know-how to run a business.

Many home economics skills can be used as the basis of a business. Catering, sewing, child care, elder care, interior design, drapery making, and upholstery are good ideas for small businesses.

Not everyone makes a good entrepreneur. To be successful at your own business means long hours and hard work. You would need to have self-confidence and discipline and be able to organize your work well. You must be a self-starter and have lots of energy and enthusiasm.

To be successful, you must also have some basic knowledge of business. Courses in accounting, marketing, inventory control, pricing, and other business activities are useful. The Small Business Administration, a government agency, offers publications and workshops for owners of small businesses. Many community colleges offer courses to help business owners become successful.

QUALITIES OF SUCCESSFUL WORKERS

Successful workers are those who enjoy and find satisfaction in their work and who are able to please their employers. They carry out their duties promptly and well and do good quality work. The chart on Job Survival Skills lists twenty-one job survival skills that help employees be successful workers.

JOB SURVIVAL SKILLS*

1. Be dependable.
2. Follow directions.
3. Know what an employer expects.
4. Manage time and materials efficiently.
5. Get along with a variety of people.
6. Maintain good health.
7. Be punctual.
8. Adapt to varying work situations.
9. Work without close supervision.
10. Be loyal to employer.
11. Work as a team member.
12. Work under tension and pressure.
13. Use initiative and imagination.
14. Make decisions on your own.
15. Be neat and clean in appearance.
16. Follow safety regulations.
17. Use information, materials, and equipment.
18. Have basic speaking skills.
19. Have basic arithmetic skills.
20. Have basic writing skills.
21. Organize work activities of others.

*Note: From Hazel Taylor Spitze, "A New Look at the Basics: Leadership through Home Economics," *Illinois Teacher* (September/October 1978): 4. Used with permission.

Which of these twenty-one skills do you have? Which can you learn? Why are these skills needed to survive on the job?

The most important quality you can have as an employee is a good attitude toward work. If you believe your job is important and worthwhile, you will work hard to do the job to the best of your ability.

Good workers are reliable. If the boss gives them a task, they will do the task well and when it is due. Following rules and directions will make you a valued employee.

Finally, good workers get along and work well with others. They have good relationship skills and know how to use them to have good relations with co-workers.

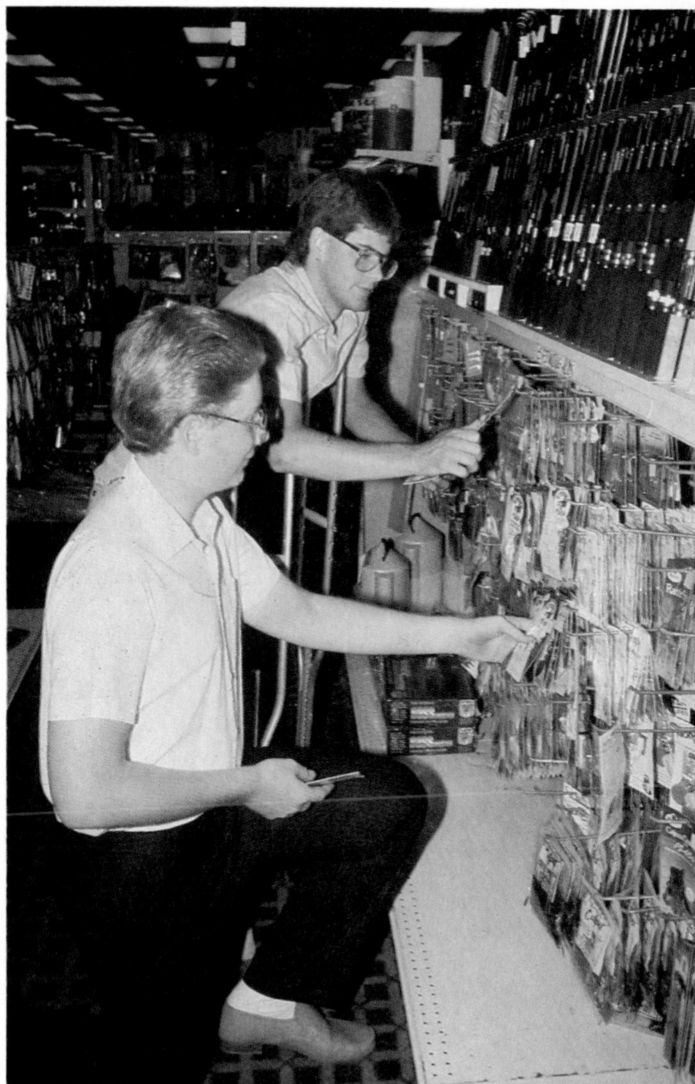

Workers who build good relationships with co-workers are more apt to be happy with their work and do it well.

THE CHANGING WORKING WORLD

The working world is undergoing many changes. Being aware of these changes can help you take advantage of them as you plan your work life.

• *The computerization of the work world.* Computers are playing an ever-larger role in all kinds of jobs. Word processing, data processing and management, and financial analysis are three major things that computers do in business. There are specialized computer programs for hospitals, banks, retail stores, and most other types of companies.

This growth in the use of computers has opened up many new career opportunities. People are needed to run computers—to run the programs used in business. Those who can program computers are in great demand. There are job openings in computer sales and repair.

• *Opportunities at the work place.* Many employers are recognizing that happy, healthy, satisfied workers do more work. Some firms have weight rooms or exercise equipment, which employees can use during the lunch break or before or after work.

Since many parents work when their children are small, some companies are beginning to help arrange child care for their workers. A few firms run child-care centers on the job site. Others may keep a listing of group or family child-care centers, which parents can use to find care. Some firms help pay for child care for workers with young children

Flextime is another opportunity offered by some businesses. Workers are given the chance to set their own hours. Usually, all employees must work certain core hours, often 10:00 A.M. to 2:00 P.M. The rest of the day can be scheduled to suit the employee as long as a certain number of hours are worked. Some people may work from 6:00 A.M. to 3:00 P.M. Others may choose 10:00 A.M. to 7:00 P.M. or some other hours that suit their needs.

• *"Cafeteria" benefit plans.* In the past, all employees who worked for a firm had the same benefit plan. Perhaps they received vacation, sick leave, life and health insurance, and a pension plan. However, because not all employees have the same needs, some companies now offer "cafeteria" benefit plans—so named because workers can choose among options. Some options might include child-care benefits, extra sick leave or vacation, more insurance, or money for more schooling.

For example, a mother with a preschool child whose husband has health insurance through his job might choose child care and extra sick leave (for days when the child was ill) instead of health insurance. Employees who are given benefit options are better able to manage their resources to meet their needs and goals.

WORDS TO REMEMBER

entrepreneurs
entry level job
network
networking
resume

CHECKING YOUR UNDERSTANDING

1. Explain why your goals, values, interests, and abilities are important in the process of choosing a career or job.
2. List three general levels of jobs. Compare the benefits and costs of jobs on each level.
3. Describe various sources of job and career information in your school and community. Which sources would you be most apt to use?
4. Compare the use of the application form with an application letter. How can you make either approach *sell* yourself to an employer.
5. How do qualities needed for an entrepreneur differ from those of an employee? Why is being a self-starter important for an entrepreneur?
6. Explain the importance of getting along with others to being a success on the job.

APPLYING YOUR UNDERSTANDING

1. Brainstorm with classmates to make a list of the many ways that a job or career might affect other aspects of your life. Is the list longer or shorter than you thought it might be? What conclusions can you draw from this activity?
2. Talk with someone who recently changed jobs. Why did the person decide to change? Has the change been a happy one? How many different jobs has the person held over a lifetime? Share your findings with your classmates.
3. Get the want ads section of a newspaper and find at least three jobs that interest you. What do you like about the jobs? Are you qualified for them? List the strong and weak points of the want ads as a source of job information.
4. With your classmates, role play job interviews for entry level work for which students in your class might apply. Have one student be the job applicant and another be the employer. Role play several interviews for different jobs to give all class members a chance to take part.

Chapter 6
CHOOSING A WAY OF LIFE

Will this happen to you?

Lisa gave Betsy a big hug. "Betsy, it's been so long!" she exclaimed. "I don't think I've seen you since the summer after we graduated from high school."

"It's hard to believe that this is our five-year class reunion!" said Betsy. "What have you been doing since then?"

Lisa said, "Let's sit down and catch up on the news. I'm an accountant—I graduated from Great State University a year ago. I'm not married and really don't intend to be for several years at least. How about you?"

"Well, I went to the community college and studied business management for a while," replied Betsy. Brian and I have been married for three years. We have a two-year-old daughter named Sasha and I'm pregnant again."

"I always knew you and Brian would stay together," said Lisa. "I'm really happy for you! What about some of our other friends?"

"Did you know Francie's already on her second marriage?" asked Betsy. "Bob married an older divorced woman with three children and Tom's a confirmed bachelor like you."

"It's really amazing what different paths we've all taken," said Lisa.

What do you plan to do after high school?

How do the plans for your future differ from those of your friends?

After reading this chapter, you will be able to

- understand some of the benefits and disadvantages of being single;
- describe the purposes of engagement and the wedding;
- analyze some of the adjustments a newly married couple must make;
- describe the process of divorce, getting use to divorce, and how divorce affects children.

When you think about your future, what do you imagine life will be like? What kind of personal life do you dream about having in five years or in twenty-five years?

You can use your management skills to help you reach your personal dreams for the future. First, you will need to look ahead to think about all the possibilities in choosing a way of life. On the basis of your goals and values, you can make a plan for the future that seems right for you.

However, life is full of unexpected events. You might not be able to live out detailed plans. On the other hand, if you never plan, you will have little, if any, control over your life.

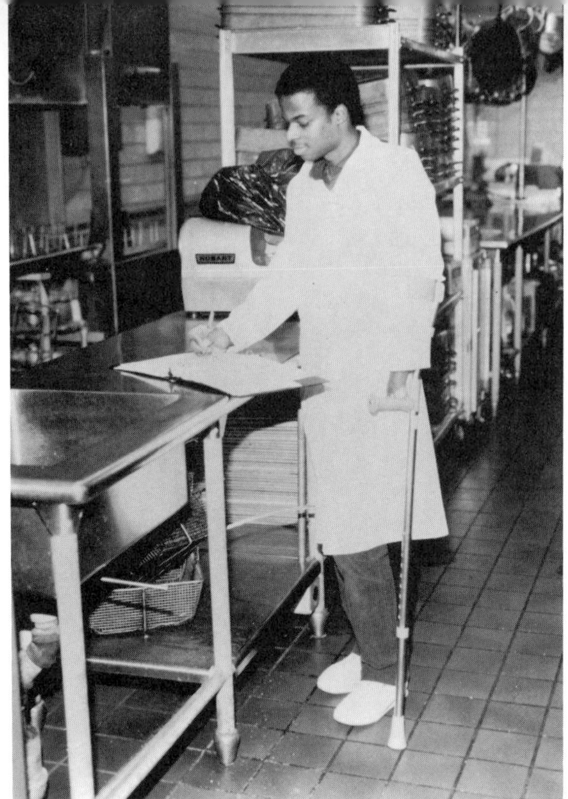

Although some circumstances occur that are beyond your control, you can work to guide and control your future.

Planning a future based on your values and goals can help you fulfill your personal dreams.

SINGLES

Most people begin their adult lives as singles. After high school graduation, you will have the chance to learn to live independently. You may be planning to attend college or a technical school, to join the armed services, or to find a job and move to your own apartment.

As a single, you will learn to take care of yourself. You will handle your own resources, identify your own needs and wants, and work toward your own goals and values. Setting up a life of your own lets you become self-sufficient.

The single life-style holds many attractions for some people. They like the freedom of not having to care for a spouse and/or children. Most singles can go where they please, do what they wish, and spend their money as they want. Singles tend to like privacy and being alone.

Although most people will marry, more and more are staying single. You may choose never to marry or decide to put off marriage for a while. You may have family obligations that keep you from marrying. Many people are single because of divorce or the death of their spouses.

If you stay single, you will miss the warmth and closeness of living in a family. Instead, you will probably have a close circle of friends or keep regular contact with your parents or siblings.

After graduation, friends may choose different paths. What are your plans after graduation?

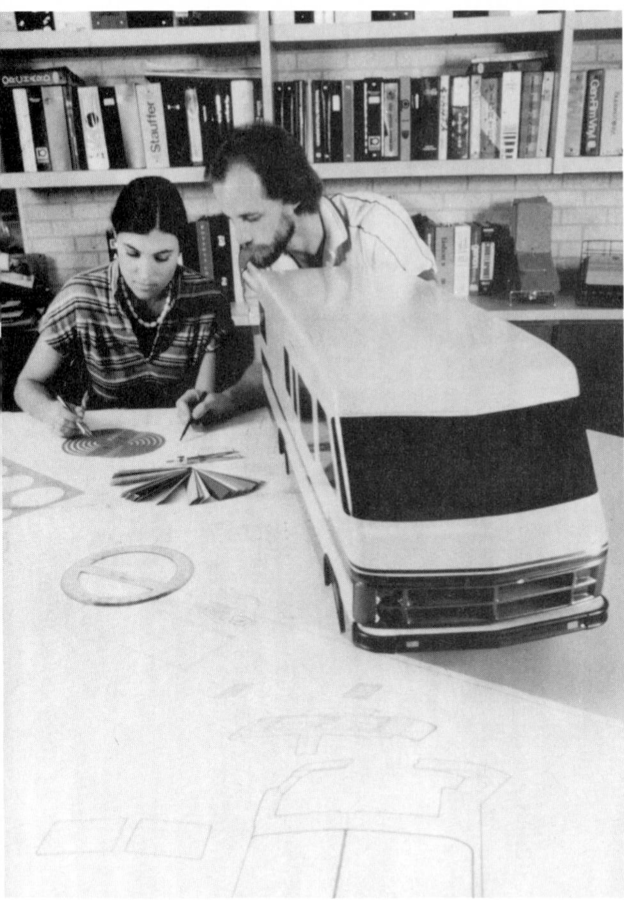

Ambitious young men and women may prefer to postpone a serious relationship until they have established their career.

ENGAGEMENT

If you and your dating partner have built a strong love relationship during courtship, you may begin to think about marriage. You decide if you want to pledge yourselves to each other over the years. When you commit yourselves to marry, you enter an **engagement.**

The engagement is a time for you and your future spouse to learn more about each other and plan for the future. You have a chance to think about how and where you will live. Decisions about if and when to have children can be discussed.

Many engaged couples have premarital counseling. You may talk with a minister, priest, or rabbi or take classes for engaged couples. This provides a structured chance to talk about many of the issues you will face during marriage such as, money, household chores, children, or job decisions. Talking these things through with help from a minister, priest, rabbi, or another counselor can give a strong base for your coming marriage. Facing such problems before marriage will help you meet them more successfully later.

The length of your engagement may rest on how long you have known each other before the engagement. Marriage after the partners have known each other for two or more years tends to be most successful.

FINDING A LIFE'S PARTNER

Most people choose marriage as a way of life. Americans are the world's most married people, with between 90 and 95 percent choosing to marry sometime during their lives.

Marriage is a setting where you can share your life with another. You and your **spouse,** your husband or wife, can give each other help, closeness, and companionship. Most people's emotional needs are met through marriage.

The engagement period is a time for a couple to plan realistically for the future. Topics including money, children, household chores and career decisions should be discussed.

THE WEDDING

Most people look forward to and back on their wedding day as a high point in their lives. The **wedding** is the public commitment of two people to each other. They promise to live and work together as husband and wife. The wedding marks the start of a new family.

Weddings range from simple civil ceremonies to elaborate religious rites. The type of wedding you will choose rests on many factors. In general, you and your future spouse will plan your wedding to reflect your personalities, resources, and values.

During the engagement period, a great deal of effort is often spent on planning the wedding. However special a wedding day is, it is no guarantee of a good marriage. The relationship built during dating and engagement has more to do with the success of the marriage than does an elaborate and costly wedding.

ADJUSTMENTS TO MARRIAGE

No matter how well you have known your spouse before the wedding, there are always adjustments to make in a marriage. Some of them are simply those of being in a new home and living with a new person. If you and your spouse move to another city or begin new jobs after marriage, there will be more changes to adapt to.

In addition, you have to adjust psychologically to your new married state. You and your spouse are now dependent on each other and must find a way of life that is pleasing to you both. You must learn to function as a family, cooperating and compromising as needed.

Financial Adjustments

Many couples find sharing decisions about money hard to make. You may be used to handling your own funds. As a single person living alone, you probably are not responsible to anyone else for how you spend your money.

Married couples often pool their incomes and spend money as a unit. They may not agree on who should spend how much money. If both partners work, should each of them have their *own* money? Who will pay what bills? Who decides how much money should be spent on running the household? Who keeps the checkbook and writes the checks? Will the couple have a budget? A savings account?

There are many issues involved in managing family funds that have to be settled for this part of the marriage to run well. Failure to deal with money problems is one of the chief causes of conflict in marriage. Satisfactory joint-spending patterns are the goal of newly married couples.

Newly married couples must learn to cooperate and compromise as they adjust to their life together.

Role Decisions

In chapter 2, you learned about roles. When you get married, you and your spouse will have to figure out how you want to play the roles of husband and wife. You will try to work out roles that satisfy both of you.

In the traditional family of the past, the husband was the wage earner and the wife was the homemaker. He earned the money and she managed the household and children.

Over the last few decades, fewer and fewer families have lived in the traditional style. Economic conditions and personal satisfaction have caused many women to become wage earners. This has left less time for home management. As a result, some families have taken on a more equal life-style. The marriage partners share the roles of the traditional family. Both are wage earners and share household jobs. If there are children, they share parenting tasks.

The roles you choose in your marriage will depend on many factors. You probably know the type of roles you think are ideal for you, whether traditional or equal. If your spouse agrees and you are able to live that life-style, there should be few conflicts. However, spouses often do not agree on ideal roles. Besides, life sometimes prevents the filling of ideal roles. Therefore, you may have to make compromises and negotiate to find the roles that are right for you and your spouse as well as your life circumstances.

Family and Friends

Another adjustment is learning to become part of the spouse's family and circle of friends. When you marry, you suddenly have new relatives. You may have parents-in-law, brothers-in-law and/or sisters-in-law. There may be grandparents, aunts, uncles, cousins, nieces, and nephews with whom to build new relationships.

As a married couple, you will also develop a circle of friends. You may easily fit into each other's friendship groups. However, you and your spouse may not like each other's friends. You may need to build a new group of friends that you both enjoy. Working out relations with new and old friends requires some give and take.

Good relations with parents can help a young couple build a strong marriage.

Couples who choose an equal life style share in the wage earning responsibilities.

ARE YOU READY FOR MARRIAGE?

Being ready for marriage is more than finding the right person. It also means looking at your personal qualities to find out if you have the background and skills needed to be a good marriage partner.

- *How old are you?* Age at marriage is strongly related to the success of marriage. Age brings experience and maturity to newlyweds. In general, the older you are when you marry, the stronger and more stable your marriage will be.
- *How much schooling have you had?* The more schooling you have, the better chance you have of having a good marriage. Education level is related to age. Those who marry young often do not have the money or time to get more schooling. Many people put off marriage until they have finished their schooling.
- *Can you earn a living and be financially responsible for yourself?* If you are self-sufficient, you will be able to help support a family. Money problems are often a major cause of marital conflict, so being ready for a good job through school or training is important for a strong marriage.
- *Do you have good relationship skills?* Marriage is the closest of all human ties. If you can talk to others well, solve conflict, and manage stress, you have skills that are vital to a good marriage.

Are you able to get along with other family members? Couples who have good relationships with parents and siblings usually have good marriages. This is because they have learned to use their relationship skills in the family setting. If you did not get along with your parents and siblings, it does not mean you cannot build a strong marriage. However, you may have to work harder to build a good marital relationship.

- *How mature are you?* Are you in control of your life? How well do you manage responsibilities? Are you dependable? Are you ready to be responsible for a child, whether the pregnancy is planned or otherwise? Can you give up some of your dreams if that is needed to build a partnership where you and your spouse can grow together?
- *Do you have good management skills?* Marriage means setting up mutual goals, values, wants, and needs. It means managing your money well and making decisions together. If you have good management skills, you are in a better position to build a strong marriage based on what you want from life.

There is no sure way to know whether you are ready for the responsibilities of marriage. However, your chances for a good marriage are better when you look at yourself to see if you have the qualities needed to make a success of marriage.

DIVORCE

Sometimes, a married couple decides they are better off apart than they are together. While you may not plan a divorce as part of your way of life, you may have to cope with the break up your marriage. A **divorce** is a legal end or dissolution of a marriage. It changes the legal rights and duties between a man and woman.

Divorce has become commonplace in our society. Almost one out of every two marriages will end in divorce. About half of all divorces occur in the first six years of marriage.

All types and kinds of people divorce. However, some people are more apt to divorce than others. Marriages in which the partners are teens have a high rate of failure, especially if the bride is pregnant. Divorce often occurs when couples have less education. A low-income level causes stress in a marriage as partners try to make ends meet. Couples in this situation often divorce. Finally, partners with no religious ties are more apt to have a broken marriage than those with strong beliefs.

THE PROCESS OF DIVORCE

Divorce is basically a legal procedure. The state licenses couples to marry and decrees the end of the marriage.

Divorce laws are governed by each state. Therefore, the laws in your state may be quite different from those in neighboring states. In general, there are two types of divorce: no-fault and adversarial. Most states have laws that allow both types of divorce.

In a **no-fault divorce,** the couple asks the court to dissolve the marriage. Neither partner is found to be "at fault," or to blame, for the end of the marriage. The couple agrees to divide their possessions, which is called a **property settlement.** They show evidence that the marriage has indeed broken down and the judge hands down the divorce decree.

On the other hand, in **adversarial divorce,** one partner is considered "at fault" and is blamed by the other for the end of the marriage. One partner charges the other with a marital "crime," such as desertion, adultery, or cruelty. These are called **grounds for divorce.** The judge makes the property settlement and child custody decision on the basis of who is at fault in the marriage. This type of divorce is usually a painful and a bitter experience to the people involved. The former spouses are often hostile and resentful toward each other.

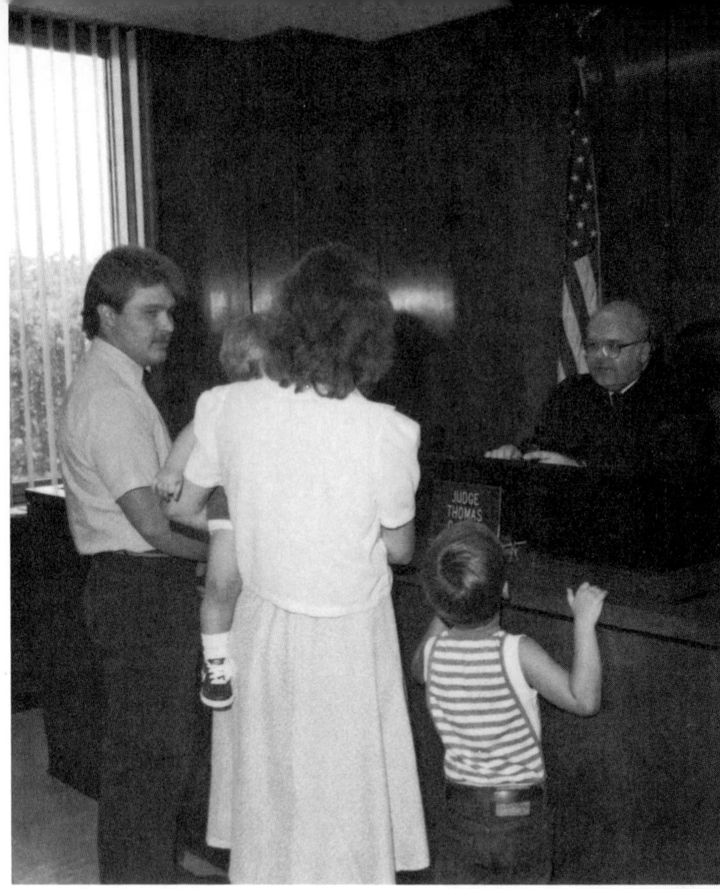

Child custody is often an area of confict in an adversarial divorce.

LEARNING TO BE SINGLE AGAIN

Although divorce is a legal process, many emotional and social consequences occur when couples divorce. If you divorce, you will have to learn to be single again. You will no longer have a spouse to rely on, to be close to, and to receive support from. You may find this a lonely time as you come to realize you have only yourself to depend on.

If you had an active social life as a couple, you may find your friends are no longer as interested in you. Many divorcees find it hard to adjust to the need to make new friends and develop a new single life-style.

Some couples have money problems after a divorce. The same money that supported the married couple may not stretch to pay for two households.

Even if you are happy to be divorced and know your life will be better, you may still find it hard to get used to single life. In general, the longer the couple has been married, the more adjustments there are to make.

DIVORCE AND CHILDREN

Much controversy exists over the effect of divorce on children. Some people feel that divorce is always bad for children. Many parents stay together "for the sake of the children."

Other people believe the circumstances of the divorce influence the effect it has on the children. Children may prefer divorce to living with conflict-prone parents who fight often and loudly. Children who are aware that their parents have problems are often able to handle a divorce better than those who are not aware of their parents' conflicts.

Most children accept the divorce in the same manner their parents do. The breakup of a family is always a painful experience. However, if parents try to make the divorce as friendly and peaceful as possible, children usually have a better attitude toward it. Parents who are bitter often have bitter children. Children who are caught between warring parents often have the worst time handling the divorce situation.

Divorce usually means children will live in a single-parent family. In fact, almost half of all children will live with a single parent at some time in their lives.

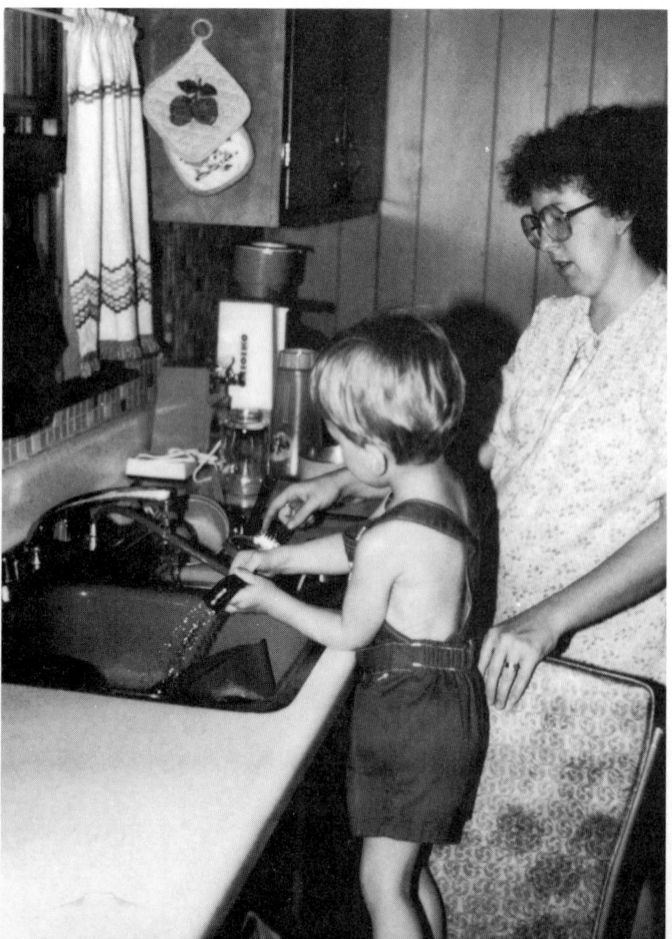

Single parenthood is often a very hard way of life. The parent usually juggles a job, home duties, and parenthood. Such heavy responsibilities can often seem overwhelming.

In addition, many single mothers have low-paying jobs, and not having enough money is a problem for the family. About half of single-parent families headed by women live in poverty. Most single men who care for their children have better-paying jobs. But even having enough money does not make being a single parent easy. It takes much time and effort to make a loving, comfortable home for children. Single parents usually are tired and rarely have much time for themselves.

REMARRIAGE

Most divorced people end up remarrying. They are not soured on marriage, just the one they were in. While some remain single, almost 80 percent of divorced people remarry.

Most people who look to the future do not expect divorce, remarriage, or a blended family. They dream of marriage or single life and living "happily ever after." However, life does not always work out that way. You may choose a way of life only to find the choice was not right for you. You may need to make a new decision about life-style. In the end, you must choose a way of life based on what you know about yourself and those who are important to you. Then you can do your best to make that way of life a happy and satisfying one.

Even young children can learn to cooperate to help a single parent with household tasks.

WORDS TO REMEMBER

adversarial divorce
divorce
engagement
grounds for divorce
no fault divorce
property settlement
spouse
wedding

CHECKING YOUR UNDERSTANDING

1. List the good and bad points you see in single life. Compare your list with those of your classmates. What does the class see as the main pros and cons of being single?
2. What are some ways a couple can focus their engagement on getting ready for marriage rather than on getting ready for the wedding?
3. Describe some of the common adjustments to marriage. How can problems in these areas be solved?
4. Discuss some of the things that lead couples to divorce. Why do you think these traits are related to the divorce rate?
5. Describe factors that make a divorce easier for a child to understand and accept. What factors might make it harder for the child to accept the parents' divorce?

APPLYING YOUR UNDERSTANDING

1. Interview a person who is single. Ask about the pros and cons of being single. What responsibilities to others does he or she have? How does the single person fill the need for companionship and intimacy? Is the person lonely? Does the person expect or want to remain single? Why or why not?
2. Find out about the legal requirements for marriage in your state. At what age can couples marry with or without a parents' consent? What are the state health requirements? Is there a waiting period after the license is issued before the couple can marry?
3. Research the legal requirements for divorce in your state. Does the state have a no-fault or adversarial system or both? How long is the waiting period between filing for divorce and the decree?
4. Invite several divorced persons to serve on a panel discussion for your class. Ask them to describe the adjustments they made to divorce and how their children, if any, were affected. What changes in their financial status did divorce bring? What type of divorce did they get? What were their reactions to the divorce? If any are single parents, ask them to discuss the pros and cons of single parenthood. If any have remarried, what adjustments have they faced in the new marriage?

Chapter 7
BECOMING A PARENT

Has this ever happened to you?

"I never worked so hard for so little!" exclaimed Ted. "In my child development class this morning, I was trying to teach Sammy how to tie his shoes."

"Sounds like you had trouble," commented Julie.

"I sure did," said Ted. "First of all, he's left-handed and I'm right-handed, so I had to figure out how to reverse the steps, which wasn't easy. We worked and worked and just never got the job done."

"I remember learning to tie my shoes," said Julie. "My parents both worked full-time, and I stayed with this retired lady, Mrs. Collier, when I was small. She was the perfect grandmother type. I think I was about five when I decided it was time to learn to tie shoes. She made me a little shoelike workboard that had shoe laces nailed on it so I could practice. She was so patient in teaching me."

"It sounds like you really loved Mrs. Collier," said Ted.

"Oh, I did!" said Julie. "I still go see her once in a while. I was really lucky to have her as a baby-sitter."

Do you have someone who took care of you when you were younger that you fondly remember?

What are some qualities of people who are successful in building good relationships with children?

After reading this chapter you will be able to

- list and discuss some of the responsibilities of parenthood;
- recognize factors to consider in deciding to become a parent;
- identify some ways children and parents interact with and influence each other;
- describe various options for parents who need alternative care for children.

An important part of your life plan may be becoming a parent. You may be looking forward to the joy of having your own child or children.

You enter **parenthood** by having your own children or by adopting children. Choosing parenthood requires a mature and honest evaluation of yourself, your income, and your life plans. This is because being a parent is a lifelong commitment. Once you become a parent, it is a role you have for the length of your life or that of your children.

Being a good parent is more than being the natural mother or father of children. Parents also care for their children and help them to grow and develop. These skills are called **parenting** skills. Parenting can be done by many people, not just natural parents. Relatives, friends, neighbors, siblings, baby-sitters, and child-care employees may all be care givers. They serve in parent roles to children. However, as the parent, you are entirely responsible for your children's physical, emotional, social, and intellectual needs.

RESPONSIBILITIES OF PARENTHOOD

While being a parent is a source of pleasure and joy for most people, it is also a large responsibility. You will be responsible for your children—twenty-four hours a day, 365 days a year—for many years. Such a heavy task is not always easy to carry out. People who have thought about their responsibilities before parenthood often find carrying them out easier to manage.

ECONOMIC RESPONSIBILITIES

Parents are responsible for meeting the needs of their children. They feed, clothe, house, educate, and entertain them. It is estimated that it takes at least two and one-half to three times the family's annual income when a child is born to raise the child to eighteen.

Obviously, raising a child is not cheap. Responsible parents plan ahead so they can be sure they will be able to provide for the child's needs. Parents who have gotten more schooling and better-paying jobs can better meet money needs of their families.

Relatives, friends, neighbors, siblings, babysitters and child care employees all use parenting skills when they interact with chilren.

Raising a child is expensive and can put a strain on the family's financial resources. Identify the costs involved with the birth of a newborn.

Parents need to provide constant supervision for infants and toddlers. What potential danger is this toddler heading toward?

PHYSICAL CARE

Parents are responsible for the physical care of their children. This includes keeping them safe, well-fed, and healthy. Infants and toddlers need to be watched all the time to ensure their safety. You will need large amounts of time to watch your young children. If you are not able to provide such time, because of work or other reasons, you will have to find someone else to be a care giver.

Parents arrange visits to doctors and dentists as needed. As children get older, parents teach the value of exercise and personal hygiene.

Young children thrive on routine. Their bodies need regular healthful meals, sleep, and care. You may have to alter your way of life to provide a good life-style for the children.

SOCIAL AND EMOTIONAL DEVELOPMENT

Children's social and emotional growth and development is based on the love and nurturing provided by parents. Nurturing, or to **nurture,** means to aid or guide development or growth. When parents provide a loving, nurturing environment, children are able to develop good self-concepts. They learn to feel good about themselves and their skills and abilities.

You will be your children's first teacher. You will teach them how to react to and get along with others. Children learn about people with different personalities in their families. They learn how to talk to others and to solve conflicts from parents and other family members.

Everyone has strong emotions. Some parents let their feelings control them. Others have learned to control their emotions. Children learn to manage emotions by watching their parents.

INTELLECTUAL DEVELOPMENT

In addition to affecting children's social and emotional growth, parents also play a major role in children's intellectual growth. Your children will learn early in life whether you value learning and school. They will probably reflect the same values as you.

Babies and toddlers learn about their world from play and their exposure to books, toys, and music. Parents who want to help their children to do well in school provide such stimulation.

Parents can help children become happy, healthy people by providing a loving nurturing environment where children are able to develop a good self-concept.

DECISION MAKING ABOUT PARENTHOOD

Having a child influences all parts of the parents' lives. Because parents now have responsibility for another, they take on a new life-style and new goals for their lives.

OPPORTUNITIES AND RESTRICTIONS

The tasks of parenthood bring many opportunities to parents. The pleasures and joys of being a parent provide many chances for personal growth in the parenting role. The chance to watch your children grow and develop is exciting because you will see their personalities unfold. Helping children to learn and cope with the world gives much satisfaction to parents.

On the other hand, being a parent can be very restricting. Just the presence of another person in the home requires an adjustment. When that person is a newborn infant who eats every three-to-four hours, sleeps only two-to-three hours at a time, and cries a couple of hours a day, the adjustments are even greater. The need for physical care and supervision places a heavy time and energy demand on parents.

As a parent, you will no longer be able to do many things on the spur of the moment. Instead, you will have to arrange for child care or choose an activity in which the children can be included. Not having enough time for their own interests and activities is one of the biggest complaints of parents with young children. This is even more true when both parents work.

Parents can work with their children to develop skills needed for math.

CHOOSING PARENTHOOD

Because of the changes that being parents brings, many couples wish to plan and control the timing of the births of their children.

Some people simply feel they are not ready for the duties of parenthood. They wish to retain the freedom they have to work, relax, and enjoy life.

Many couples are aware of the money needs of parenthood and decide to finish their schooling or become settled in their jobs before having children.

Decision making about parenting means facing the responsibilities of raising children and choosing how you and your spouse can best handle them. Your values, religious beliefs, and goals will guide you in making choices about parenting that are right for you.

Many couples postpone having children until they have established a secure financial basis.

ADOPTION

Some people's decisions on parenting involve adoption. Couples may not be able to bear their own children. Their desire to have a child may lead them to adoption. Other people may wish to give a home to children who do not have one and adopt children even when able to bear their own.

Adoption is a civil process in which an adult becomes legally responsible for a child who is not biologically related. This parent assumes all the duties of raising and supporting the child.

The choice to adopt a child may not be an easy one, especially if the couple has wanted to bear their own children. However, once the couple decides to adopt a child, they usually come to love and care for the child in the same way they would their own biological child.

The other side of the adoption process is whether to give up a child for adoption. Every child who is born has a right to be loved, cared for, and nurtured. Not every person who has mothered or fathered a child can provide for the child's needs. This is even more true when parents are very young.

It takes a great deal of courage for a parent to give up a child for adoption by others. Such a decision is hard to reach. Parents who make it have a great deal of pain, grief, and guilt. However, they usually feel that the child will be better off in an adopted family.

Adoption agencies carefully screen potential parents to be sure that the couple will be able to give the child good, loving care, in a positive environment.

CREATING A SAFE AND STIMULATING ENVIRONMENT

Children need a safe and stimulating environment for the best growth and development. Given below are some ways parents and other care givers can create such a setting for children.

A Safe Environment

A safe environment for small children requires *child-proofing* a home. Children need protection from common household dangers.

• Remove all breakable objects from the reach of toddlers. Children need to be able to explore without the threat of breaking items or being constantly told "Don't touch." As children grow older and become more responsible, you can replace these items.

• Lock up cleaning supplies and other household poisons. You can buy cupboard locks or move supplies to a locked cabinet. Moving supplies to a high shelf is not a safe solution, because many toddlers are often expert climbers.

• Lock up medicines, drugs, vitamins, and other similar items. Children may like candy-flavored aspirin, cold medicines, or laxatives. An overdose of these or other substances can cause severe illness or death in a small child.

• Place gates across stairways or steps. Protecting toddlers from falls until they learn to climb stairs is a must.

A Stimulating Environment

A stimulating environment is one in which children learn about themselves and their world. Young children learn easily and quickly. You can help prepare children for school through encouraging reading and math skills. It is not important actually to teach children to read or do computation. But there are underlying reading and math concepts you can teach.

• Read stories to children. This shows you think reading is important. Libraries have story and picture books to help children appreciate the value of reading and books.

• Encourage children to begin to learn sounds and letters. Some television programs teach reading readiness skills. You can watch these programs with children and reinforce what has been presented. When such programs treat learning as a game, children think learning is fun.

• Teach basic number skills early in life. Math concepts such as more than, less than, larger, and smaller are important. You can teach ideas such as first, second, and last. Easy counting books can be used to help children learn these ideas. Sometimes a casual talk is the best way to introduce number concepts. For example, you might say, "There are two apples in the bowl. If we share one for a snack, that will leave one for us tomorrow."

PARENT-CHILD INTERACTION

The interaction between parent and child is a two-way street. The child's personality affects the parent, and the parent's personality and approach to child rearing affects the child. Learning to adapt to each other is the heart of the parent-child relationship.

Adjusting well to being a parent involves several specific skills and strengths. Parents need to know about child growth and development, and child care and rearing. Besides, they need to be emotionally mature. Those who do not have these strengths and skills will find it harder to adapt to parenthood.

A CHILD'S INFLUENCE ON PARENTS

Through their care and routine, parents work to have an immediate impact on the child's development. But the child also has an impact on the parents' lives.

As mentioned earlier, the task of giving care to a helpless infant twenty-four hours a day can be a taxing one. Parents have to plan room in their lives for children. Good management skills are essential in this busy time of life.

The child's personality also has an immediate impact on the parents. Some babies have calm, placid personalities, and parents find them easy to love. Such babies are often easy to train to a schedule convenient to parents.

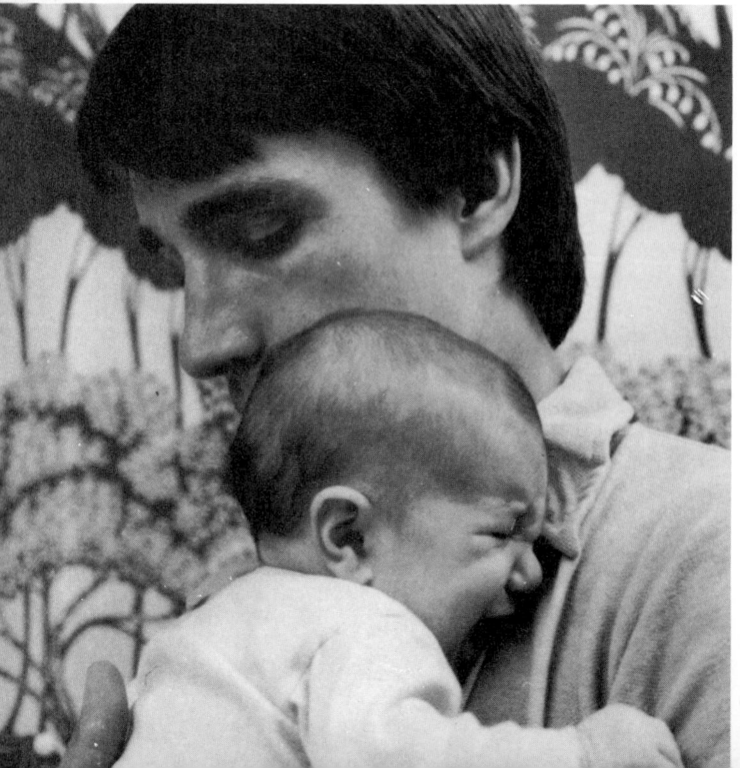

Other children are harder to handle. Some babies have colic and other upsets during their first few months. They may cry several hours a day, which most parents find upsetting and frustrating. Such babies may resist schedules set by the parents and want to set their own eating and sleeping times.

Thus, even those people who had planned for parenthood and learned about caring for babies may have problems. It is not always easy to cope with or foresee the impact your children will have on you.

PARENTING STYLES

Most parents develop an approach to their children, called a style of parenting, that fits their personalities. Parenting is really a form of leadership, as the parent leads or guides the child through life. In chapter 3, three leadership styles were described. Most people use one of these three approaches to parenting.

Parents who are autocratic feel they know what is best for their children. They mold infants and toddlers to their way of life as fast as they can. Children are allowed very little chance to show their individuality. The autocratic parent is the boss of the home.

Democratic parents share their power and allow the children to help make some decisions. Such parents want the children to have experience in decision making and accepting the consequences of their choices. But the parents keep final control and discipline over the children. The older the children, the more freedom or choice they are given within the limits set by the parents.

In the laissez-faire parenting style, parents tend to let their children do as they please. Children receive very little discipline and training from the parents.

Most people tend to lean toward one of the three leadership/parenting styles. But often, one style or combination of styles evolves from the parent-child interaction. It takes time to learn the best way to handle each child. Parents may find they need to use a different style for each child.

The personality of the baby has an impact on the adjustments parents must make.

New parents must develop a parenting style that is fair, consistent and suitable to the personalities involved.

CHOOSING ALTERNATE CAREGIVERS

Parents often need someone else to care for their children. For parents who work, child care is needed during working hours. Even when one parent stays at home to care for children, there are many times when parents have things to do that require child care. Parents also need time away from children to enjoy their personal relationships.

BABY-SITTERS

Babysitting is having another person look after your children. Babysitters should be responsible persons who will give the child good care. Teenagers often babysit during nonschool hours. Sometimes a relative, such as a grandparent, may take care of the children. Other adults can be hired to care for children. A baby-sitter usually sits with only the children of one family at a time.

Parents need to brief the sitter on the child's habits and schedule before they leave. The babysitter should know what to do in an emergency and be able to reach the parents if necessary.

CHILD CARE

Child care is having someone else look after your children in a group setting. One or more adults give care to several children. Some parents feel that children benefit from the chance to be with and learn to get along with other youngsters.

Many child-care settings are in private homes. An adult cares for several families' children. Parents will want to be sure that the main care giver is a person who likes and enjoys children and will give them good care.

Child care provides children with a chance to get along with other adults and children. What other benefits do child care situations provide?

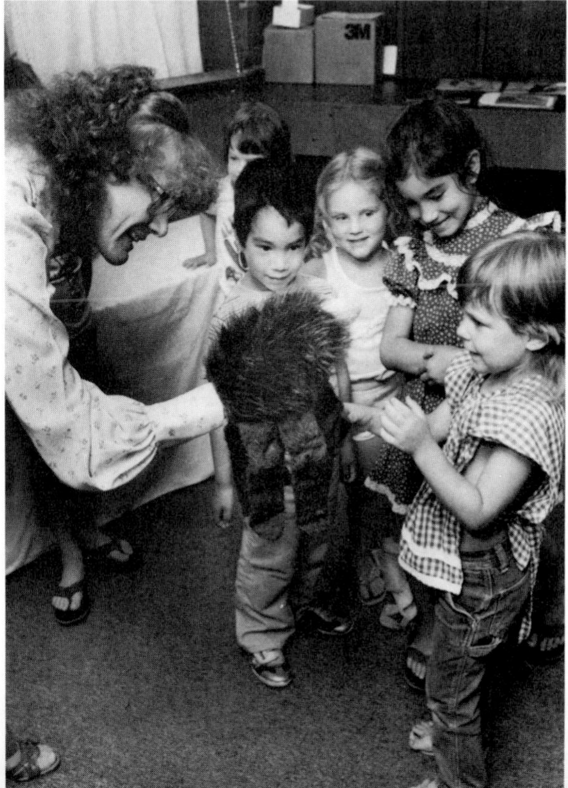

Each state makes rules for private child-care homes. In most states, such homes have to be licensed. If the child-care home has a license, you can have more confidence that it meets basic safety and care standards.

There are also organized child-care centers. These centers are nonhome settings where several teachers care for groups of children. Some child-care centers have programs that promote the children's physical, social, and intellectual growth. These are called **developmental child-care** programs. Others centers simply provide safe physical care and have no planned activities. These are called **custodial child care.** See the chart "Checklist for Choosing Child Care", for evaluating the quality of care for a child care center.

OTHER CAREGIVERS

Parents sometimes are able to make other arrangements for their children. Some parents belong to a babysitting cooperative in which they trade babysitting with other parents.

Parents may enroll their children in nursery school. This is usually for the educational benefits the children will receive.

Children need adult supervision until they are in their early teens. Infants and toddlers need the most care, but older children need the guidance and care of adults, too. Knowing how you will meet child-care needs is one part of becoming a parent.

CHECKLIST FOR CHOOSING CHILD CARE

The following checklist will help you identify qualities of good child care whether it is in a private home or an organized center.

Teacher-Child Interaction

Yes	No	
____	____	Do teachers and care givers seem to like and enjoy being around children?
____	____	Are the adults actively involved with the children rather than simply looking on?
____	____	Is the ratio of adults to toddlers at least one to six and the ratio of adults to infants at least one to three?
____	____	Are children able to work and play both in groups and individually?
____	____	Do children do the majority of talking in the room?

Space and Equipment

Yes	No	
____	____	Is there a variety of safe toys?
____	____	Is there space and equipment both inside and outside?
____	____	Are the toys stored so children can get them out and put them away?
____	____	Are materials on the walls hung at a child's eye level?
____	____	Will the child be exposed to books, music, and art?
____	____	Will the television be on a minimum amount of time each day?

The Physical Setting

Yes	No	
____	____	Is the physical setting attractive, bright, and cheery?
____	____	Is the environment safe for children?
____	____	Are meals healthful, well-balanced, and appetizing to children?
____	____	Are snacks provided during the morning and afternoon?
____	____	Is there a separate place where a sick child can rest?

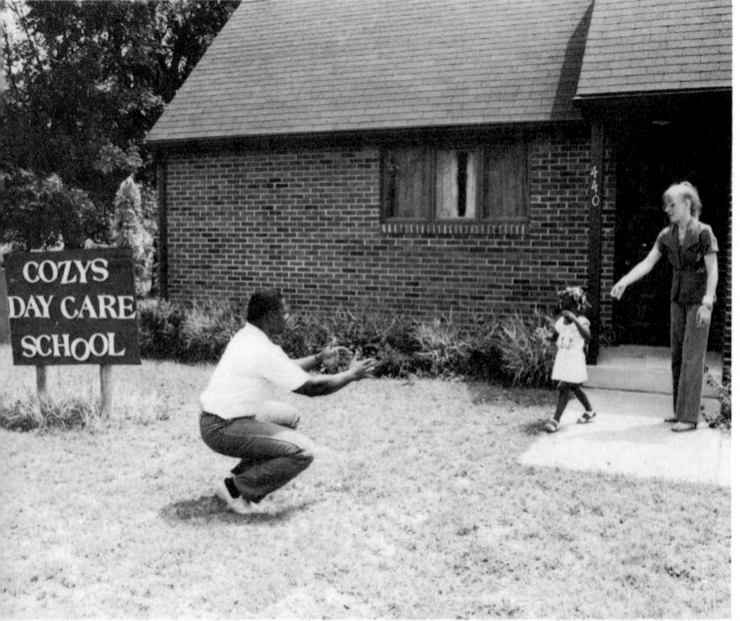

When parents work outside the home, good day care for the child is very important. The day care employees should be loving, reliable and trustworthy. They should provide treatment that maintains the child's health and safety.

WORDS TO REMEMBER

adoption
custodial child care
developmental child care
nurture
parenthood
parenting

CHECKING YOUR UNDERSTANDING

1. Children learn social and emotional development by watching their parents. Give examples of the ways children might imitate a parent's behavior in these areas.
2. Discuss the issues involved in adoption, being adopted, and giving up a child for adoption. What factors would lead people to adopt a child?
3. There is an old cliché, "Two's company, three's a crowd." How does this apply to the birth of a new baby?
4. Describe the three general parenting styles. What affect do you think each style would have on children? Which style would children like most? Which style would produce the most responsible, mature adults?
5. Discuss the pros and cons of the various kinds of alternate care givers.

APPLYING YOUR UNDERSTANDING

1. Brainstorm with your classmates to develop a detailed list of all the skills, personal qualities, and resources an *ideal* parent would have. How many items on the list do you have now? How could you develop more before you become a parent?
2. What are some of the costs involved in pregnancy and childbirth? With your classmates, develop a childbirth budget and get estimated costs for each item. Is the total higher or lower than you thought it would be?
3. Being a parent is a combination of satisfactions and sacrifices. Make two lists—one of the satisfactions and one of the sacrifices you think parenthood would bring. Which satisfaction would give you the most pleasure? Which sacrifice do you think would be the hardest to make? The easiest?
4. Visit a group child-care program. Find out whether it is a developmental or a custodial program. What are the program's fees? Use the checklist in this chapter to judge the program. Do you think you would like to place a child of yours in the program? Why or why not?

Chapter 8

UNDERSTANDING CHILDREN'S GROWTH AND DEVELOPMENT

Have you ever witnessed a scene like this one?

"You can't imagine how glad I am to be here for Mike's first birthday," said his grandmother, Mrs. Glenn. "I haven't seen him since he was six weeks old! He's changed so much; I'd never recognize him if you hadn't been sending me pictures, Tom."

"He's grown like a weed," said Mike's father, Tom. "It's really amazing the difference a year has made. When you were here last year, neither Nancy nor I were getting any sleep, Mike had colic and cried at suppertime every night, and he was losing weight. When we found out he was allergic to milk, it made all the difference in the world. He began to gain weight almost immediately after we started him on the soy milk."

"It's so cute to see him crawl around and pull himself up to stand by the furniture," said Mrs. Glenn. "He'll be walking soon. He'd just learned to lift his head up when I was here before."

Have you had the chance to observe the many changes that occur in a child in the first year of life?

At what ages do the most rapid physical growth and development occur in a child?

After reading this chapter, you will be able to

- recognize patterns of growth and development;
- describe various influences on development;
- understanding the importance of prenatal care and development;
- identify various traits and characteristics of the infant, toddler, the preschool child, and the school-age child.

If you decide to become a parent, you will witness one of nature's most gratifying events—the growth and development of your child. The event begins with pregnancy, which is a time of great physical growth. A single cell at conception develops into an independent human being made up of billions of cells.

This chapter will focus mainly on the child's physical growth and development.

PATTERNS OF DEVELOPMENT

Although children grow up at their own rates, they follow the same general patterns of growth and development.

Growth is considered a change in body size or weight. For example, a child may grow two inches and gain three pounds. **Development** is a change in body function or skill. For example, newborns wave their arms and hands randomly. As they develop, they learn to control their limbs and begin to use their hands as tools for grasping items. Growth and development are normal and occur together. A child's body becomes larger and more skilled at the same time.

Growth and development follow orderly patterns. A child will develop from head to foot, or from the top down. Thus children gain control of their heads before they sit, and they sit before they walk. Development also moves from the center of the body to the outside. For example, children will roll over before they can manipulate small objects in their hands.

A child's development goes from the simple to the complex. A baby first reaches clumsily for a toy, then learns to scoop it up with the whole hand. Later both hands begin to work together, and finally, the baby, using the thumb and index finger, learns to pick up small objects.

Children's growth and development will be continuous, though not constant. Sometimes children appear to be stalled in their growth. At other times, they spurt ahead. Children move at their own pace through the changes in their bodies and personalities.

Even though children grow at their own rates, averages or norms have been noted for each age level. Thus stages of growth and development occur at about the same time in most children.

Growth and development influence each other. Children who do not grow at the normal rate will be slower to develop. For example, children's leg muscles have to be large and strong enough to support their weight (growth) before they can learn to walk (development).

Physical growth and development will also affect other parts of a child's life. Each child is a total person. Physical changes and stages can affect social and emotional development. For example, a child who is ahead or behind the age norms in size may feel different and have a hard time relating to peers. Coping with physical change is a vital part of growing up.

By recording the child's height and weight, parents chart the *growth* of the child. By describing the child's skills and abilities, parents explain the *developmental* progress of the child.

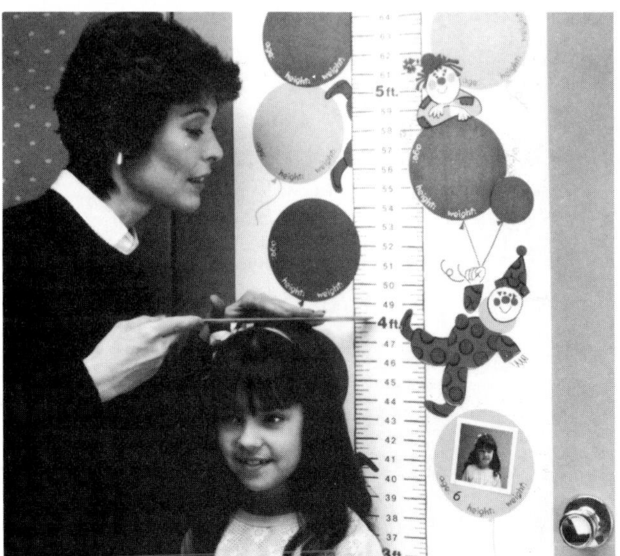

INFLUENCES ON DEVELOPMENT

All persons grow and develop as they become older. However, each change can be affected by a number of factors.

HEREDITY

Heredity includes the qualities or traits passed on from generation to generation through genetics. The part of a body cell that sets and passes on these traits is called a **chromosome.** Each chromosome has many genes. A **gene** is found in a definite location on the chromosome and holds the specific message for one inherited trait. For example, a gene may give a child the potential for a certain height, the color of eyes, or curly hair.

Heredity sets the outer limits of physical growth and development. A child thus inherits a potential for growth. Whether the child can fulfill that potential depends on other factors given below.

Children need a stimulating environment that promotes safe exploration.

Children in the same family may resemble one another because they have inherited physical characteristics from their parents.

ENVIRONMENT

The physical surroundings are called the *environment.* It affects how well children will grow and develop. For example, children need practice in crawling and walking. They need to handle small objects to learn to use their hands. Surroundings that provide interest, materials, and the chance to move and explore help children grow and develop to their fullest potential.

NUTRITION

Proper nutrition is essential for the best growth and development. All children need a balanced, adequate diet to provide nutrients and energy for growth. Children with poor diets are listless and grow more slowly than others. A good diet provides the basis for a healthy, active child whose growth and development are not curbed. Chapter 22 will discuss the dietary needs of young children.

HEALTH PRACTICES

The child's health will affect growth. Sickness saps the body's strengths so there is little energy left for growth and development. Children who are healthy can continue to grow without having to fight illness.

SPECIAL NEEDS

A major effect on development is the special needs of some children. Those who are physically or mentally handicapped do not develop at the same pace as other children. In some cases, all development is slowed. A child may be late in physical growth as well as in social, emotional, and mental development.

In other cases, development may be slow in only one area. For example, a child confined to a wheelchair because of physical problems may be advanced in social and intellectual growth. Or a child who is slow mentally may be tall and muscular, with advanced athletic skills.

Being aware of and accepting the specific problems of a child with special needs can be challenging. Parents can provide a safe setting where the child is encouraged to use his or her abilities. With patience, love, and care, the child can be helped to develop a good self-concept and to feel proud of talents and skills.

Children can be encouraged to eat nutritious food by cutting the food in interesting shapes. What other ideas can you think of for decorating a sandwich?

Children who are handicapped can overcome their disabilities and participate in competitive events, such as the Special Olympics.

MANAGING A SAFE AND HEALTHY PREGNANCY

One of the most important parts of prenatal development is managing the health and well-being of the mother. Her condition directly affects that of the child.

• *Nutrition.* If the mother is well fed and eats balanced meals each day, she can provide better nutrition for the fetus. A poorly fed mother does not have as many nutrients to pass along to her child, so it is apt to be smaller and less healthy.

• *Medical care.* Most pregnant women visit the doctor at least once a month. These visits allow the doctor to keep track of the health of the mother and whether the child seems healthy and normal. The doctor can advise the mother about rest, exercise, weight gain, and any problems that arise.

When problems do occur, the doctor may use amniocentesis. **Amniocentesis** is a medical procedure during which the doctor removes and analyzes a sample of the fluid from the amniotic sac. From the analysis, the doctor can identify pregnancy-related problems.

• *Keeping healthy.* A pregnant woman should avoid contact with persons who are ill. Some diseases caught by the mother can cause birth defects in the unborn child. For example, German measles can cause blindness, deafness, or other defects in the fetus.

Use of Drugs

• *Smoking.* Babies born to smokers tend to have low birth weights, be less healthy, and run a higher risk of dying due to Sudden Infant Death Syndrome (SIDS). Smokers have more problems conceiving and are more apt to have miscarriages than nonsmokers.

• *Drinking.* Alcohol, whether beer, wine, or hard liquor, has a direct affect on the fetus. Too much alcohol during pregnancy is a major cause of birth defects. Any alcohol drunk by the woman passes through the placenta and circulates in the fetus's bloodstream.

A child whose mother drinks heavily can be born with alcohol addiction, called Fetal Alcohol Syndrome (FAS). Such a child may suffer mental retardation, problems in learning, and heart defects. A child with FAS is rarely able to overcome its slow start in life.

• *Hard drugs.* Mothers who are addicted to hard drugs, such as heroin, methadone, or cocaine, often have babies who are also addicted. Soon after birth, these babies suffer withdrawal symptoms, such as vomiting and body tremors. Such a poor beginning means these infants are not apt to grow and develop normally.

• *Medication.* All medication for pregnant women should be prescribed by the doctor. Many common drugs can be harmful to the fetus. Laxatives, aspirin, and diet, sleeping, and pain pills should be avoided. In the past, some medication given for morning sickness caused birth defects. If there is some doubt, the mother is better off not taking any kind of drugs.

PRENATAL DEVELOPMENT

All expectant parents hope for a normal, healthy baby. The development of the child before birth, or in the **prenatal** stage, affects its health when it is born. Although heredity has a large effect on prenatal growth, the environment and the mother's diet and health practices also affect the baby's growth.

In the first two weeks of pregnancy, the organs to nourish, protect, and support the fetus are formed. The **fetus** is the unborn young. The **placenta** is the organ which nourishes the fetus during pregnancy. The **umbilical cord** attaches the fetus to the placenta. The fetus is surrounded by a fluid-filled membrane, called the **amniotic sac,** which holds and supports the fetus and allows it to move.

From about the second to the tenth week of pregnancy, the fetus's cells are dividing rapidly. They also begin to specialize, some cells becoming bone cells, others forming muscles, organs, and hair.

In the third month of pregnancy, the fetus has the major body parts. The breathing, digestive, and circulatory systems develop. All body parts and systems grow, develop, and mature during the last months of pregnancy.

The health practices and nutrition of the pregnant mother greatly influences the child during prenatal development.

THE INFANT

A newborn infant is totally helpless but is able to learn and respond to the environment. Newborns are capable of seeing, hearing, feeling, tasting, smelling, and sensing movement.

The first year of life brings a great amount of growth and development as the child learns to move about and cope with the world. At first, the baby sleeps close to twenty hours a day. Gradually, the child stays awake for longer periods. The newborn needs to be fed often, usually every three to four hours, and kept clean, dry, and warm. Infants have little, if any, control over their bodies.

Tremendous physical growth occurs during the first year of life. The newborn will double in size and triple in weight by her first birthday.

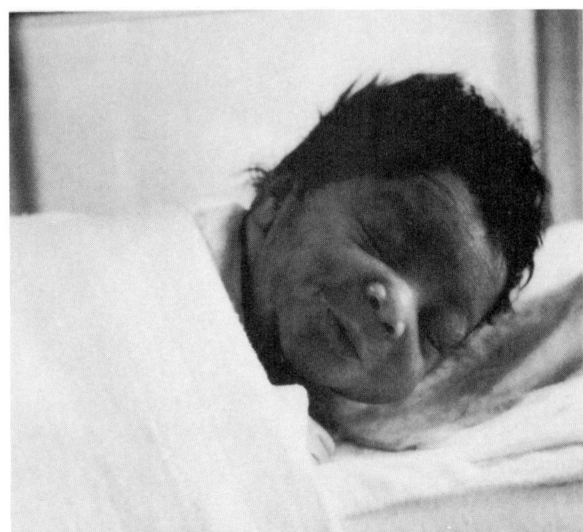

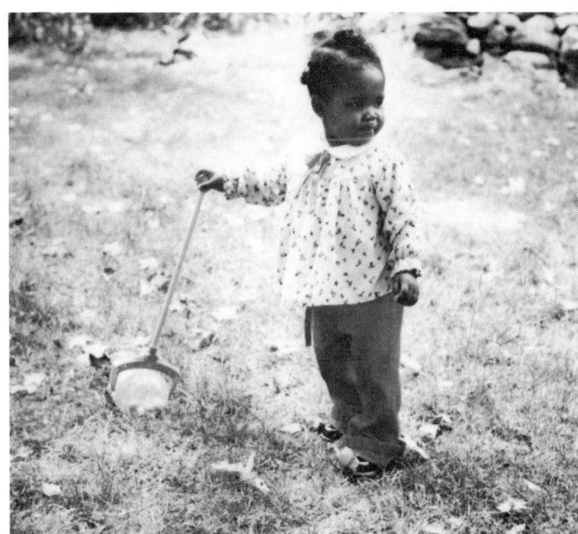

During the infant's second and third months, personality and physical control start to emerge. The baby may turn its head, learn to smile, and begin to reach for items, which later will often be put in the mouth as coordination increases.

As children approach six months of age, they can hold their heads up, turn over, and begin to learn to sit with support. Most children are sleeping through the night at this age. During this time, if not before, children start eating soft foods from a spoon.

Between six and nine months, children learn to sit alone and begin to crawl. Eye-hand coordination improves at this age so that children can hold two objects at a time and can pick up tiny objects with their thumbs and forefingers.

Many children begin to cut teeth during this stage. Children also begin to learn to chew at this age. They enjoy feeding themselves with soft, easy-to-chew, finger foods. Such foods need to be cut in bite-sized pieces.

Finally, as children near their first birthdays, they are on the brink of the stand-walk-run sequence. Crawling is still the method of getting around when the child is in a hurry. Children walk when their bodies are ready, usually between twelve and eighteen months.

During the first year, children begin receiving their immunizations against disease. Children are usually given a DPT shot first, which protects them against diptheria, whooping cough, and tetanus. Measles and polio vaccines are also given in the first year. Other immunizations and booster shots are given later.

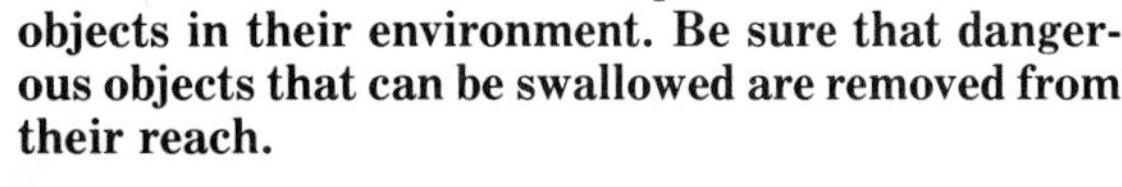

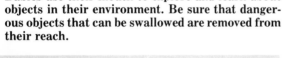

Babies use their mouth to explore and learn about objects in their environment. Be sure that dangerous objects that can be swallowed are removed from their reach.

Children receive immunizations at a doctor's office or health clinic to protect them from diseases.

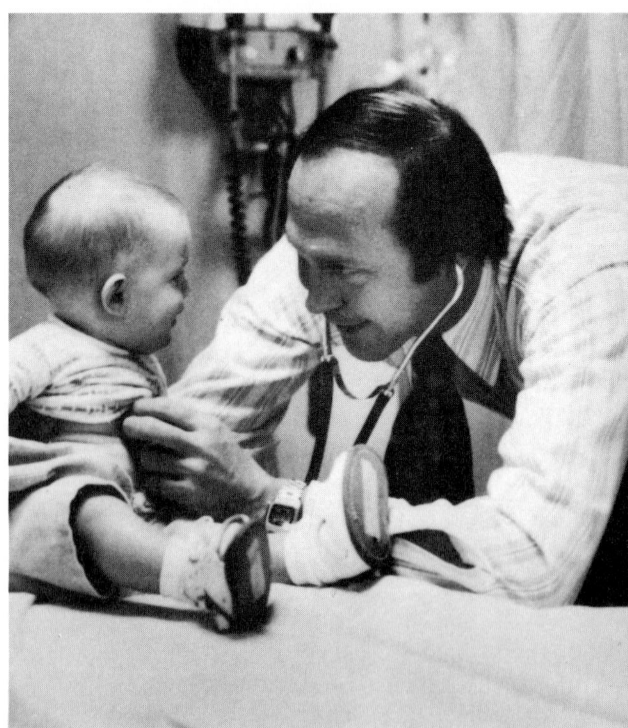

Careers
A BRIEF LOOK

PLANNING YOUR FUTURE

If you enjoy being with and helping children and find it easy to build relationships with them, you may wish to think about a career in child care or child development. Such a career would be right for you if you have a special concern for children, value young children, and see childhood as an important part of life. Working with children could bring you much satisfaction and pleasure. The need for people to work with children will increase as more parents are employed. Working with children requires a great deal from people who choose a career in this area. It also holds great rewards for those who enjoy helping children to grow and to develop to their fullest potential.

Entry Level Jobs
Child care aide
Park/playground supervisor
Camp worker
Baby-sitter

Jobs with Training
Child care paraprofessional
Child care assistant teacher
Teacher's aide
Pediatric nurse
Children's clothing designer
Homemaker's aide
Writer of children's books
Bus driver
Toy designer
Photographer
Children's television programmer

Jobs That Require a College Degree
Child care group teacher
Nursery school teacher
Elementary school teacher
Pediatrician
Children's dentist
Child psychologist
Children's librarian
4-H extension specialist
Recreation leader
Camp administrator
Social worker
Probation officer
Administrator of child care center
Religious educator
Pediatrics dietitian

For more information, write to:

National Association for the Education of Young Children
1834 Connecticut Avenue, N.W.
Washington, D.C. 20009

American Library Association
50 E. Huron St.
Chicago, Illinois 60611

American Federation of Teachers
555 New Jersey Avenue, N.W.
Washington, D.C. 20001

THE TODDLER

As children enter the toddler stage, from age one to three, they begin a period of less rapid growth. The slower increases in height and weight gains allow children more chances for mental, social, and emotional development.

Physically, children learn to walk, run, and climb early in this stage. They begin to become able to dress themselves. Eye-hand coordination increases, and skills such as catching and throwing a ball, stringing beads, and turning pages are learned.

Probably the biggest physical challenge during this time is toilet training. Children are ready to be trained at their own pace. Wise parents will allow children to progress in this area at their own speed.

Toddlers start to eat meals similar to those of the adults in the family. They begin to drink from a cup and eat with spoons and forks.

THE PRESCHOOL CHILD

Preschool children, ages three to six, continue their refinement and development of physical skills. They are still growing, though more slowly than before.

Many preschoolers are in constant motion. They run everywhere and are very active. They generally have mastered control of both large and small muscles. They roller skate and ride tricycles. They can manage buttons and zippers and are learning to control crayons and pencils. By the end of this stage, most children have good finger skills. Such skills are needed as the child begins school.

THE SCHOOL-AGE CHILD

Most development in the school-age years occurs in areas other than the physical. Although children's bodies continue to grow and develop, the most striking changes occur in other realms. As children attend school, the mental and social aspects of development become more important.

The pace of growth and development, which has been relatively slow and steady in the school-age child, begins to quicken again as the child reaches adolescence. Changes during the teen years will be dramatic and visible just as they were in the infant and toddler stages. In contrast, the preschool child and school-age child experience years of subtle but steady changes. Knowing how growth and development occur throughout childhood can help you understand and appreciate the changes in children that you care for.

The physical development of a child slows down during the school age years but the child continues to grow in the areas of social, emotional and intellectual growth.

Review CHAPTER 8

WORDS TO REMEMBER

amniocentesis, amniotic sac, chromosome, development, fetus, gene, growth, placenta, prenatal, umbilical cord

CHECKING YOUR UNDERSTANDING

1. Explain the difference between growth and development. Why are the two terms often linked together?
2. Give two examples of patterns of development.
3. Explain the influences that heredity, environment, nutrition, health practices, and special needs have on children's growth and development. Which of these do you consider most important? Why?
4. Why is it important to let children set their own pace in toilet training?
5. Why does physical development become less important in preschool and school-age children?

APPLYING YOUR UNDERSTANDING

1. Take a survey of several friends and have them identify at least one physical trait they inherited from a parent. With other class members, compile a joint list of inherited traits. How many different inherited traits were mentioned? What was the most common one?
2. Check a nutrition handbook to find out how the dietary needs of a woman change when she becomes pregnant. What foods should be added to her diet? Should any be eliminated? Does it make a difference if she is a teenager?
3. Interview a doctor or invite a doctor to speak to your class. Ask the doctor to discuss the importance of prenatal care, describe good health practices, and explain how things that happen during pregnancy can affect the child after birth.
4. Make a chart showing physical growth and development from birth to school age. To make the chart, first list the stages of growth (infant, toddler, preschool, and school-age) down the left-hand side of a sheet of paper. Across the top of the paper, write the following: eating habits, need for sleep, locomotion, and body control. Draw lines across the paper between the categories on the top and side of the paper. In the boxes you have drawn, describe the changes that occur in each category as the child ages.

Chapter 9

EDUCATING AND GUIDING CHILDREN

Have you ever witnessed a scene like this one?

David paused in the process of washing dishes and listened. His three-year-old daughter, Marnie, was in the next room and David had not heard a sound in several minutes. Drying his hands, he went to check on her. He saw Marnie trying to pull her favorite book out from under a stack of other books. "Do you need some help?" he asked.

"No!" said Marnie. "I'm a big girl." She gave another tug and spilled the entire stack of books. "I got it!" she crowed proudly.

Later that evening, David started to get Marnie ready for bed. Throughout the entire bedtime routine, Marnie insisted on doing things herself. However, when she squirted toothpaste on the bathroom mirror while trying to put some on her toothbrush, David stepped in. As he put the toothpaste on her brush, she began to cry, wailing, "But daddy, I could do it. I'm all grown up. I can take care of myself."

Have you ever cared for toddlers who insisted on doing things themselves?

How can children be helped and encouraged to develop the skills to become independent?

After reading this chapter, you will be able to

- identify two methods parents use in teaching their children;
- understand the important things that children learn;
- recognize the role of discipline in guiding and teaching children;
- describe the influence of play in children's learning and development.

Good physical care of your children will be a major duty if you decide to become a parent. However, even more vital will be the responsibility for your children's mental, social, and emotional growth.

This chapter will focus on how parents and other adults can help children grow and develop mentally, socially, and emotionally.

PARENTS AS TEACHERS

You will be your children's first teacher. You will have the most contact with your children and the most chance to teach them about life and coping with the world. Other family members and care givers also serve as teachers. But because parents are the most important people in their children's lives, they are the most important teachers.

Experts say that children's most active growth takes place between birth and age four. Thus the basic and most important learning years are those before children reach school age. By then, a child's general intelligence level is fairly well set.

The surroundings that parents give their children affect learning. Activities, materials, and people in the home make it exciting for children. They can learn from being exposed to nature, science, music, art, books, sports, or community life. A less-stimulating home environment can slow down children's learning.

Parents are the most important teachers and primary role models for a child.

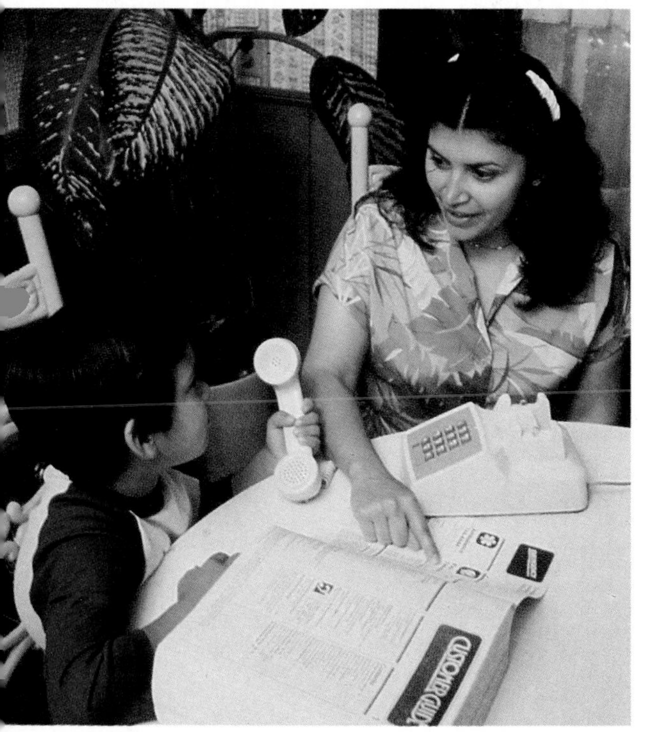

Children do not need elaborate toys and games. Old pots and pans, blocks, balls, book, and puzzles are excellent toys that provide stimulation and teach important concepts.

MODELING

The most important way you will teach your children is through modeling. **Modeling** means demonstrating actions or being an example for others to follow. Children are keen observers of their parents and other family members. They imitate and identify with their parents. They learn about parents' interests, attitudes, prejudices, and values. What they learn can be either positive or negative, good or bad, or helpful or harmful.

The power of modeling as a way of teaching means that a parent should set a good example for the children. Children are quick to pick up differences between parents' actions and words. For example, parents may talk about the importance of healthful food, but eat many sweets and few fruits and vegetables. Children are more apt to follow the actions than the words.

Children are most likely to model those who treat them with kindness and love. Therefore, warm, loving relationships between you and your children are more likely to produce children who will model your behavior.

USING ENCOURAGEMENT

In order to learn, children must feel good about themselves and their abilities. They must have courage to try new activities and skills. When they lose confidence, they become discouraged and lose the will to try to learn.

One of the most important aids to use in teaching children is encouragement. Parents must believe in children's ability to learn and help them have faith in that ability. When children's efforts are met with encouragement and pride, their self-concepts grow and they feel a sense of achievement.

Using encouragement with children means avoiding name calling, sarcasm, or ridicule as they learn. Making fun of or laughing at children tears down their self-esteem and willingness to try again.

Never ridicule or call a child names. Instead, always offer praise and encouragement so that the child will develop confidence to try again.

LEARNING IN CHILDHOOD

There are many things for children to learn. They learn to get along socially with others and they learn to control their emotions. Skills picked up in childhood form the basis of later learning.

IMPORTANT CONCEPTS

During the infant and toddler stages, children learn many important ideas or **concepts.** One of the first is that of cause and effect. A baby learns early in life that crying usually brings attention to satisfy hunger. When an infant bangs a rattle on the floor, it makes a noise. Children must learn about cause and effect because many other learnings are based on it.

Another important early learning is that of **object permanance.** For infants, only those objects or people they can see are real to them. Without memory, they cannot understand that objects exist out of sight. About nine months of age, an infant's memory is good enough to hold images in mind.

Another early learning skill is problem solving. Children learn to think to do a task. They need the chance to handle and manipulate objects as a base for learning problem solving. This skill starts to develop at about one year of age. During the preschool and early school-age periods, there are other ideas that children learn.

Children learn **classification,** or arranging items or ideas by their traits. For example, children group objects by color, size, or shape. They do this when they divide the toy cars into big and little ones.

Seriation means putting items in order. Children learn to order items by size, shape, or amount. This concept will be vital to learning math later.

Children have to learn spatial relationships—how they fit in spaces and how objects relate to each other in space. For example, children enjoy getting into boxes or under tables. They learn spatial relationships from puzzles and pegboard toys.

Children have very few notions about the concept of time. They have to learn to relate the passage of time to what is going on in their worlds. This is not learned well until children are six to seven years old.

While children are able to learn a great deal themselves, they will learn more if parents take an active role in teaching. For example, children ask many questions as they learn about cause and effect, problem solving, seriation, and the meaning of time. If you are a parent who wants to help your children grow mentally, you will answer these questions as best you can. Answering a question with a question can prompt children to think further. Asking "What do you think?" can help children to learn thinking skills.

A baby learns that by shaking a rattle it makes a noise. This is called cause and effect. What other examples can you think of that represent cause and effect?

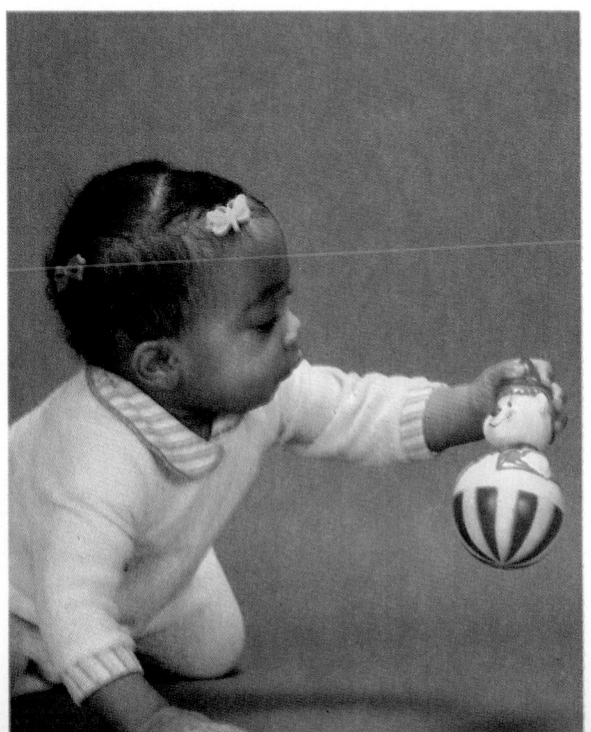

When a child divides all the toy cars into groups of big and little cars, he is learning classification.

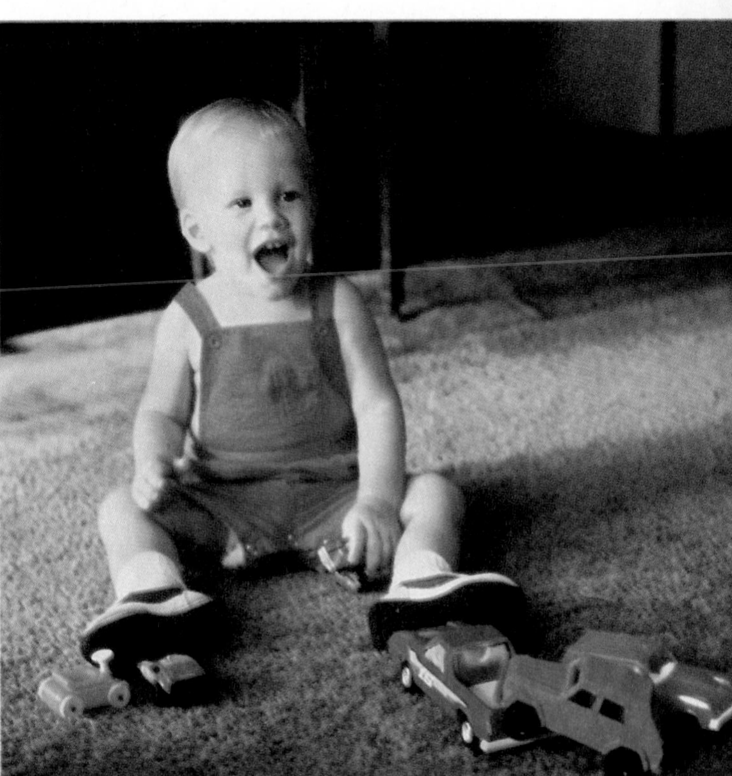

LANGUAGE

Language is another area where parents teach their children. The ability to learn and speak helps children to reason and put thoughts together. Language development often affects how well children will read.

You will first teach your children language by modeling. Children must hear speech to learn it. They will imitate the grammar and vocabulary of their parents.

A child's ability to speak follows a general pattern, though children differ in how fast they move through the pattern. Up to about two months of age, a child communicates through crying. Parents are usually quick to learn the differences in the quality of the cries. One cry may mean "I'm hungry," while another simply results from boredom or a desire for attention.

From two months to about a year, children learn to control the sounds they make. Children first learn to coo, then they start babbling or repeating vowel and consonant sounds. At seven or eight months, they begin to put syllables together in a way that imitates speech.

Somewhere between a year and eighteen months, children begin to talk. At two years of age, most children can speak about fifty words and use two-word sentences. Children have a vocabulary of about one thousand words by age three. Language growth is rapid in the third year as children learn more about grammar and sentence structure.

One important way you can teach children language is through **elaboration.** You repeat what the child has said, adding to it or elaborating on it. For example, suppose a young toddler said, "See doggy!" You could elaborate by replying, "Yes, I see the little white dog."

Young children understand better when parents speak slowly in simple sentences. Parents can encourage children's vocabulary growth by using new words. Explaining new words and their meanings is also important.

Elaboration helps to improve a child's language development. How would you elaborate if the toddler was pointing to the cat?

BECOMING INDEPENDENT

Your job as a parent is to raise children who will become independent adults. The drive for independence starts early when a toddler says, "Me do it!" As children grow, they learn to take responsibility and make decisions as a basis for independence. Becoming independent involves both social skills and emotional control.

You can help children learn and use the skills needed for independence. First, you can give children choices appropriate to their age and understanding. Children may be given a chance to make decisions about foods, play, clothes, or activities. However, you should offer a choice only when you are willing to let their decisions stand.

Once children have made choices, you can help them accept the consequences of their decisions. Not all decisions are good ones, and some have bad results. As a parent, you should not rescue the child from the results of a poor choice unless serious bodily harm may occur. Accepting the consequences of their actions helps children learn.

Although it takes more patience, a parent should encourage a child's independence. Allow the child to make decisions, to dress and feed herself, and to help in routine chores around the house.

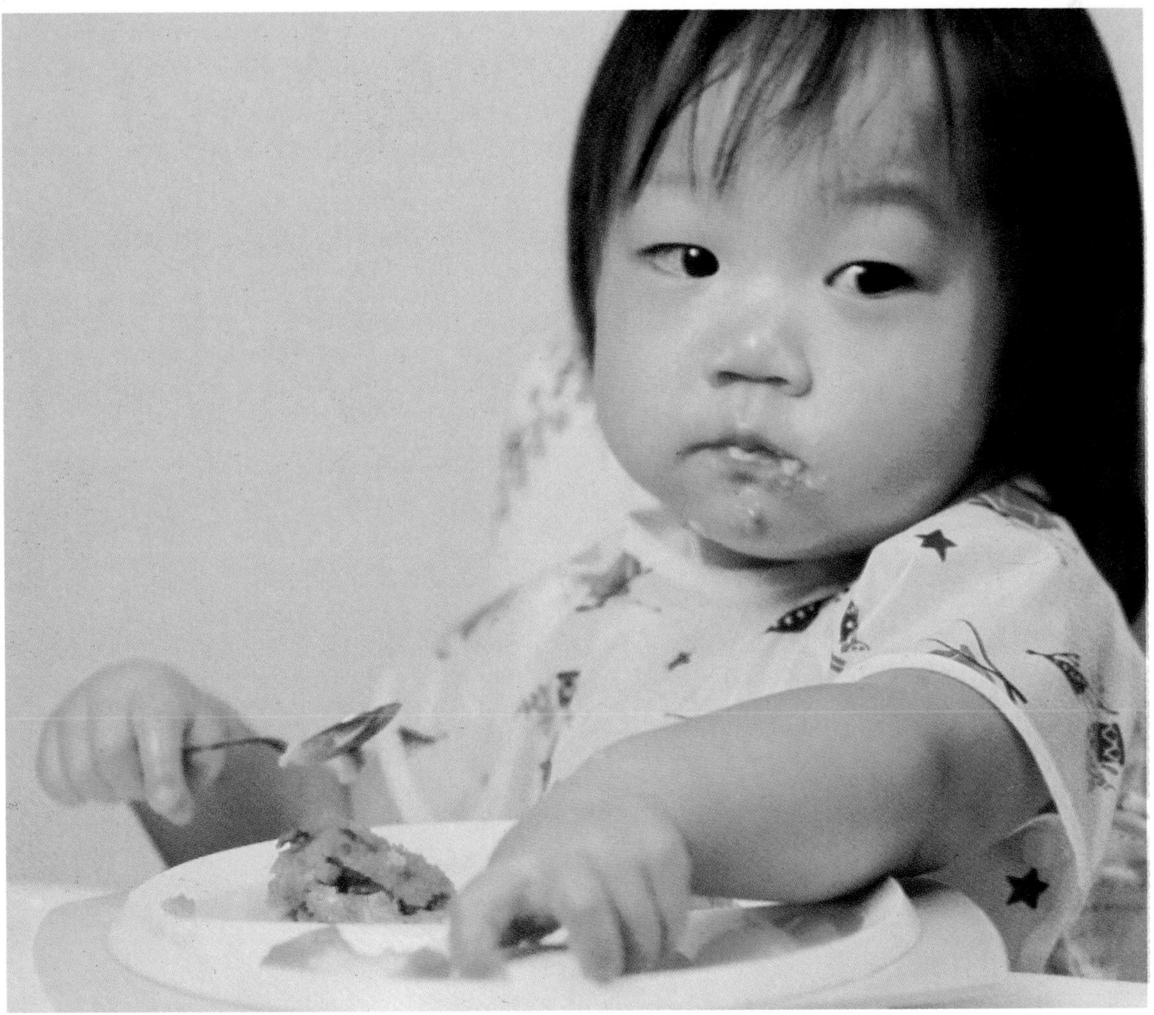

Managing Your Life

TOYS FOR LEARNING AND DEVELOPMENT

The toys children use in play are a resource, which can help them to learn and develop. They need a variety of toys to manipulate and work with.

• *Choosing toys.* Toys need to be appropriate to the age of the child. An infant needs toys that can be dangled, pulled, squeezed, rolled, or pushed. These types of toys help the child learn to control the body.

Older children need toys suitable for their levels of development. For example, puzzles help children develop spatial relationships. However, a three-year-old may only be able to master a seven-piece large wooden puzzle, while a six-year-old can put together a fifty or a hundred piece jigsaw puzzle.

Children need toys for use both indoors and outdoors. Outdoor toys, such as balls, jump ropes, swings, and bicycles, tend to help promote physical activity and the use of large-muscle skills. Indoor toys usually promote the use of small muscles, eye-hand coordination, and imagination and creativity.

Some of the best toys may be household materials like bowls, jar lids, boxes, wooden spoons, buckets, nuts and bolts, or hair curlers. Outside, children can play with rocks, leaves, sticks, and flowers. The cost of a toy is irrelevant to its usefulness to the child.

• *Versatility of toys.* Toys are more useful when they are versatile, that is, they can be used in different stages and types of play. Sand, water, dolls, blocks, balls, or vehicles such as cars or trucks, can be used in solitary, parallel, group, or cooperative play. They can be used in play that promotes several areas of development. Simple toys are best for developing a child's imagination.

Many commercial toys are not very versatile. A toy that does the same thing every time a string is pulled soon becomes boring. Simple, adaptable toys provide the most opportunities to learn and develop.

• *Toy safety.* Toys should be safe for the child. There should be no small parts that could be swallowed. Edges should be smooth and have no rough spots. Toys should not be brittle, poisonous, or flammable (burn easily). If painted, the paint should be lead free.

• *Care of toys.* Toys should be kept in good working order. A broken toy is frustrating to the child and should be fixed or thrown out. Toys that can be cleaned when dirty are practical for small children.

Children can learn to take care of their own toys. They can put them away when play is done. Neatness is encouraged when there is toy storage that is easy for the child to use.

GUIDANCE THROUGH DISCIPLINE

All children need discipline. The problem is that many parents feel that discipline means punishment. However, **discipline** means to train or develop through teaching and guidance. Good discipline teaches children to use desirable behavior and to avoid unwanted behavior.

The goal of discipline is self-control by the children rather than control by the parents. In other words, parents work toward self-discipline in the children.

Discipline will give children a feeling of security. They will feel at ease with the rules that have been set. These rules let the children know the beliefs and attitudes thought to be important.

Parental guidance can be either direct or not direct. Direct guidance is what parents say and do. It can be verbal or physical. Parents may tell children what to do or what they may touch. Or parents can physically restrain or lead the children in meaningful ways.

As a parent or other care giver, you should give direct verbal guidance in a positive, encouraging way. Tell the child what to do rather than what not to do. State directions in a clear simple manner that will be understood. For example, say, "Hold your glass steady and walk slowly," rather than "Be careful! You'll spill your juice."

Indirect guidance involves the type of setting parents create for their children. Orderly, warm, accepting surroundings provide different messages about behavior than do settings that are loud and untidy or sterile and rejecting.

SETTING LIMITS

It is important for parents to set limits or rules for their children's behavior. Children need a clear idea of conduct that is acceptable and not acceptable. Limits give a pattern and predictability to children's lives.

Too much freedom for children is as harmful as not enough. If they are not ready to make choices on their own, children may find freedom confusing. It may make them feel insecure.

Limits should be appropriate to the age of the child. A rule has no meaning until the child becomes about ten months old. The child can only begin to understand rules as he or she learns to think and reason. As a parent, you can enforce limits for a young child by distracting him or her from the forbidden activity.

The main challenge to parents in setting limits is to be consistent in enforcing them. Children need to know that the rules are real and parents mean what they say about the limits.

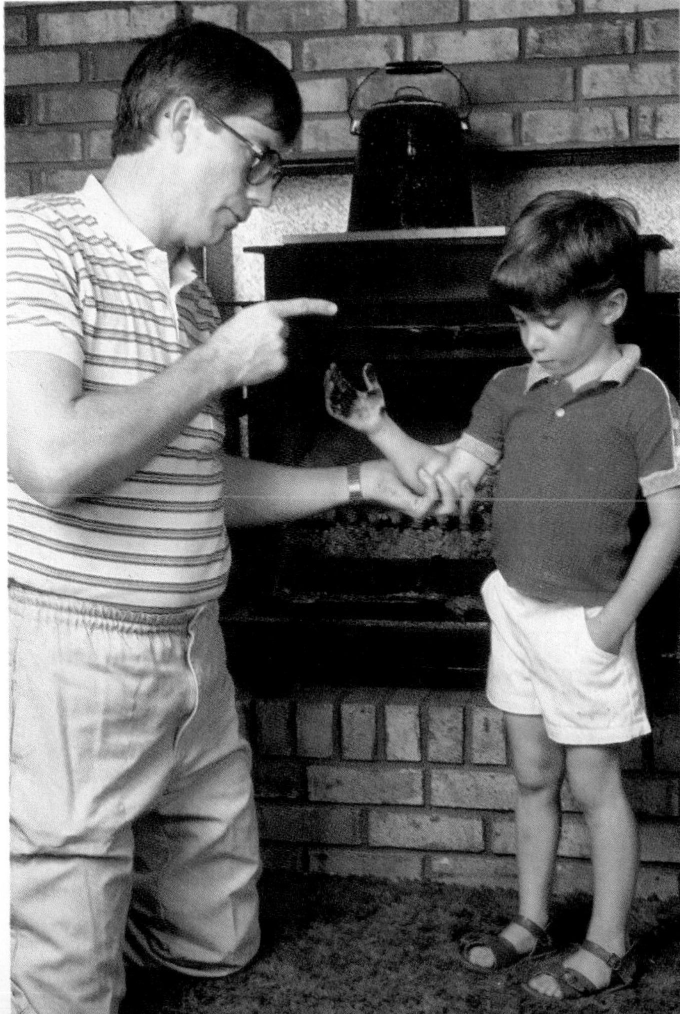

If a parent wants a well behaved child, the child must be taught discipline. By setting rules and teaching the child right from wrong, the parents can work toward self-discipline in the children.

Sometimes children receive special snacks as part of a positive reward system. Smaller children are usually satisfied with love rewards, including praises, kisses, hugs and affection.

POSITIVE REWARDS

Parental discipline and limit setting are most successful when parents use a positive reward system. With such a system, parents make a reward or payoff for desirable behavior. There is no payoff for behavior that is not desirable. When an action is followed by a reward or payoff, that action is likely to be repeated. The reward follows the action.

There are two basic kinds of rewards. "Love" rewards include praise, kisses, hugs, and verbal or physical affection. "Material" rewards can be candy, ice cream, the chance to stay up late, have a friend come to play, or earn points on a chart toward a large prize. Small children usually are happy with love rewards. However, older children may need the added bonus of a material reward to be motivated toward desired behavior.

When praise is the reward given a child, it is important that praise should be descriptive, not judgmental. For example, you might say, "I really was proud of the way you sat so still during the play we saw today." This praises the child's behavior. If you say, "You were a really good boy today," the child does not know what behavior was appreciated and may not know what you wanted.

Many people feel spanking is an essential part of disciplining children. They feel when children have been naughty, they deserve punishment. One problem with spanking is the lesson it promotes. Most parents spank their children while they are angry. Children learn that when they get angry, it is all right to hit someone else. Spanking teaches children a poor way to handle frustration and anger.

PLAY

Children learn mentally, socially, and emotionally through imitating their parents or other adults. But they also learn a great deal through their play.

IMPORTANCE OF PLAY

The child first learns through the senses in play. An infant learns to use eyes, ears, hands, and body while playing. The child can learn to solve problems through play—to think and exercise the memory. Play helps develop a child's attention span.

Play encourages children to explore and express themselves. During play, they explore new and old ways to use objects. They can show negative emotions such as worry, fear, or anger. Play can serve as a way of releasing tensions. In the same way, it serves as an outlet for positive emotions. Happiness and high spirits can emerge during play.

Play can involve all areas of development. Physical development of large muscles can take place during running games. Small-muscle development is helped by puzzles or matching games. Sand, clay, or dough allows children to manipulate materials. They can use their imaginations during dramatic or fantasy play. Music, dance, and art allow for the outlet of creative talent. Experience in all kinds of play helps provide balanced development of the child.

STAGES OF PLAY

The parents are a child's first playmates. The infant is limited to parents, care givers, and other family members for play. Because the infant is so helpless, the others must initiate the play.

Infants also learn to play alone. They play with objects, such as toys, or use their bodies for amusement. Some children are better at amusing themselves than others.

When they are about two years of age, children will begin parallel play. Children will play near other children, but they will play alone. If there is any interaction between the children, it is only for a few seconds at a time.

One-on-one play begins about age three. Children begin to play with one other playmate. The next stage is group play. Three or four children will play together doing the same activity. Finally, in cooperative play, children combine their efforts to work on projects and activities.

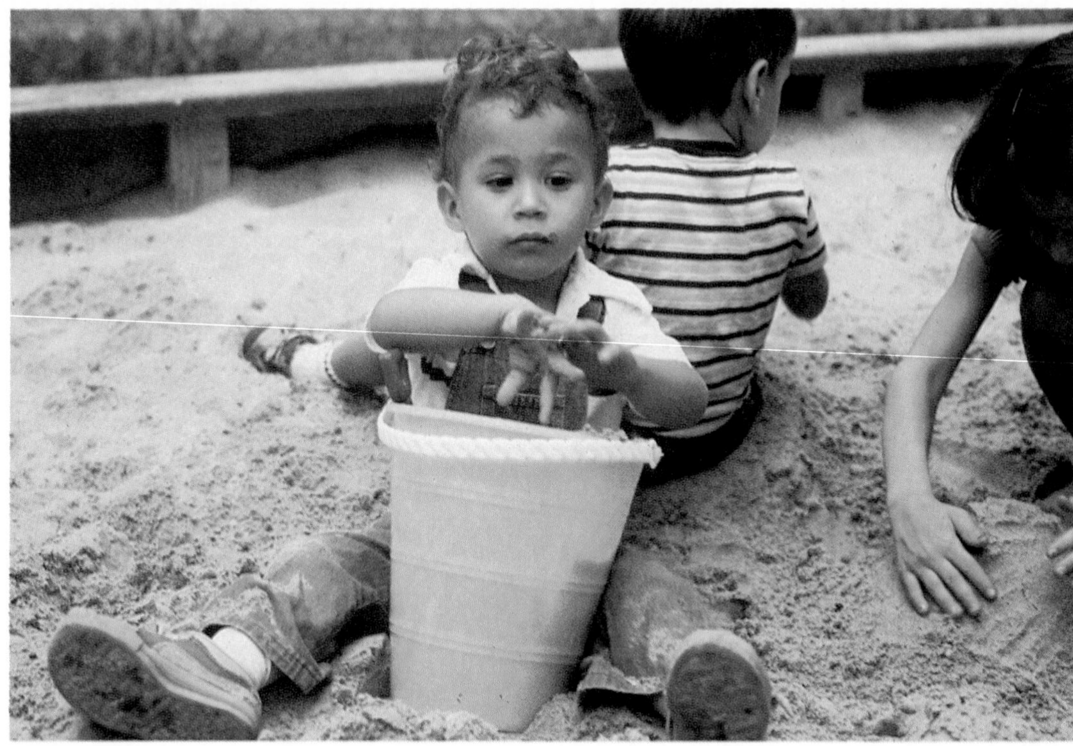

Observe two year olds at play. They engage in parallel play which means that they will play near others, but will still play alone.

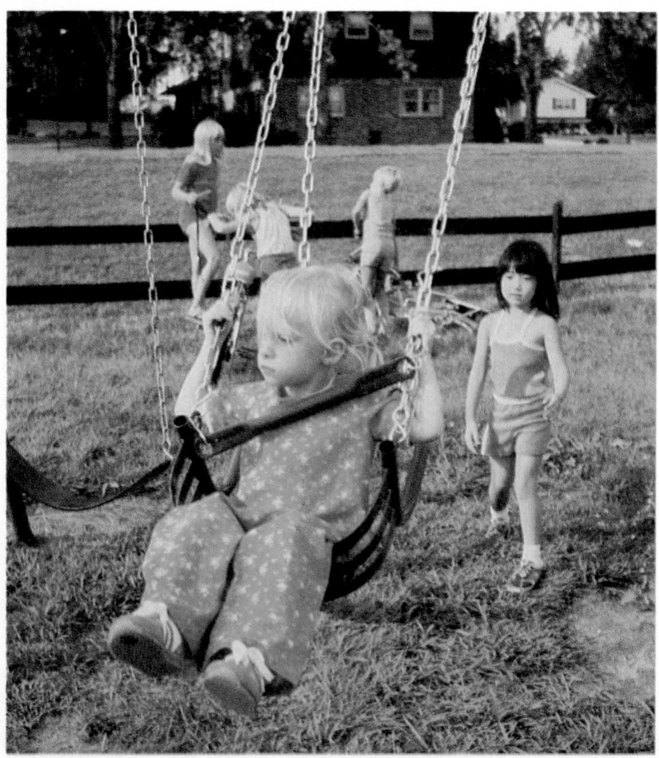

Children go through the stages of play at their own pace. One child with good social skills may advance faster, while another child who is withdrawn may need more time.

WORDS TO REMEMBER

classification
concepts
discipline
elaboration
modeling
object permanance
seriation

CHECKING YOUR UNDERSTANDING

1. It has been said that parents learn who and what they are from watching their children. Explain what this statement means.
2. Define object permanance, classification, and seriation. Why are these important concepts for children to learn?
3. How are decision making and learning to take responsibility related to becoming independent?
4. What is meant by discipline? How does discipline differ from guidance, encouragement, or punishment?
5. What are the advantages to the child when parents set and consistently enforce limits or rules?
6. Why is play so important in a child's life? What can parents do to help children get the most out of play?

APPLYING YOUR UNDERSTANDING

1. With your classmates, act out the following parent-child roles. When you role play the parent, use encouragement as much as possible. *(a)* The child has spilled a glass of milk all over the dinner table. *(b)* Your son has dressed himself but has his shirt buttoned incorrectly, his pants are on inside out, and his shoes are on the wrong feet. *(c)* The parent has asked the child to put away toys that are scattered all over the room and the child refuses.
2. Imagine you are caring for a toddler who is just beginning to talk. How might you elaborate on the following statements by the child? *(a)* Me want drink. *(b)* Give me. *(c)* Want that. *(d)* Read story?
3. Bring a toy to class. Evaluate it for its ability to promote the child's development, its safety, and its versatility.

Unit 3
MANAGING YOUR RESOURCES

A big step toward becoming independent and in control of your life is the ability to manage your resources effectively. By using your resources wisely, you can make your dreams come true.

In Unit 3, you will explore the many types of resources that are available to you. You will see how you can use and/or trade resources to meet personal goals and fulfill basic needs.

In this unit you will become acquainted with the basic principles of money management and financial planning. You also will learn more about money management techniques that can be used by you both now and in the future.

These money management skills, along with the shopping skills discussed in the unit, can help you become a more satisfied consumer who knows and understands the long-term benefits of comparing goods and services before buying them.

Chapter 10
RESOURCE MANAGEMENT BASICS

Has this ever happened to you?

Bill is looking forward to going to work today. He will receive his first paycheck since starting his summer job. Therefore, when he got home that evening with less than a happy face, his father was puzzled.

"For someone who just got a paycheck, you look real grim," Bill's father stated.

"I know dad, I am so disappointed," Bill replied. "I figured I would be getting more money on my paycheck. Actually, my paycheck is for about a third less than I expected. I wonder if a mistake was made?"

"Son, if an error was made, you should report it first thing on Monday morning," said Bill's father. "Let me take a look at it."

Bill's father looked closely at the check and then gave it back to Bill saying, "Your check is for the right amount, Bill. If you add the amount of your check and the deductions for Social Security and income tax, this figure is the same as your total earnings."

"Oh, I forgot to deduct those amounts!" exclaimed Bill. "No wonder the paycheck is for less than I thought it should be. Thanks Dad, I won't make that mistake again!"

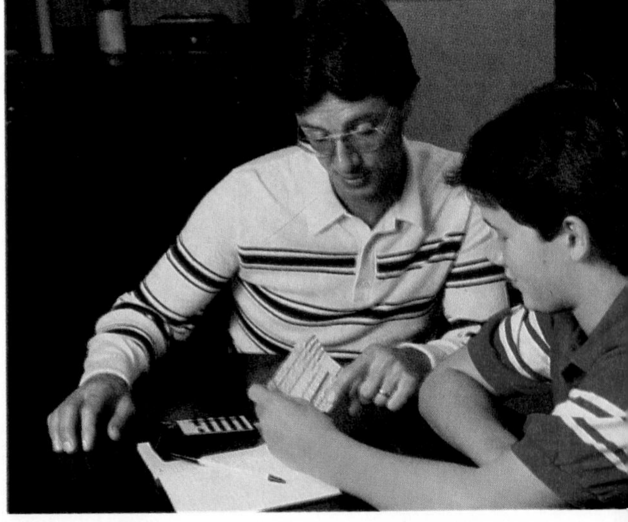

Have you ever received a pay check for less money than you expected?

Do you know that your employer is required by law to make deductions from your earned income?

After reading this chapter, you will be able to

- identify both human and material resources;
- understand the benefits of good time management;
- prepare a basic financial plan;
- recognize the value of keeping your financial records organized.

Resource management basics. What does that mean? Why should you study and understand them? How can they benefit you?

As you practice the good management of your resources, you will feel good about yourself because you get more done. Other people will learn that they can depend on you because you are responsible. You will be more confident about what you can do and learn the importance of thinking of others as well as yourself when making decisions. And the better you manage your resources, the more relaxed and happier you will be.

When you learn and practice the good use of resources, you are taking a big step toward being in control of your life and moving towards independence.

Resources can be used to help you solve problems, handle day-to-day situations and achieve your goals.

TYPES OF RESOURCES

Resources can be divided into two kinds, human and material. Human resources are personal qualities that each of us has. They include energy, attitudes, knowledge, skills/abilities, relationships, and time. Material resources, which are things that can be used to help you reach your goals, are money, possessions, community facilities, agencies, and services.

Resources vary. Some, like time and money, are limited. Some are interchangeable, that is, one can be used for another. For example, your brother may rake the lawn for you if you give him a ride to the basketball game. Or you may pay money in exchange for guitar lessons.

Others, like attitude, skills, and knowledge, can improve as you use them. Resources can also be shared. Perhaps, you lent your skate board to a friend or took part in a fund raiser for needy families.

ENERGY

One of your most vital resources is your personal energy. Energy gives you the go power to do things. Your mind and body are your best resources. They should be fed, rested, and cared for to keep them in good working order.

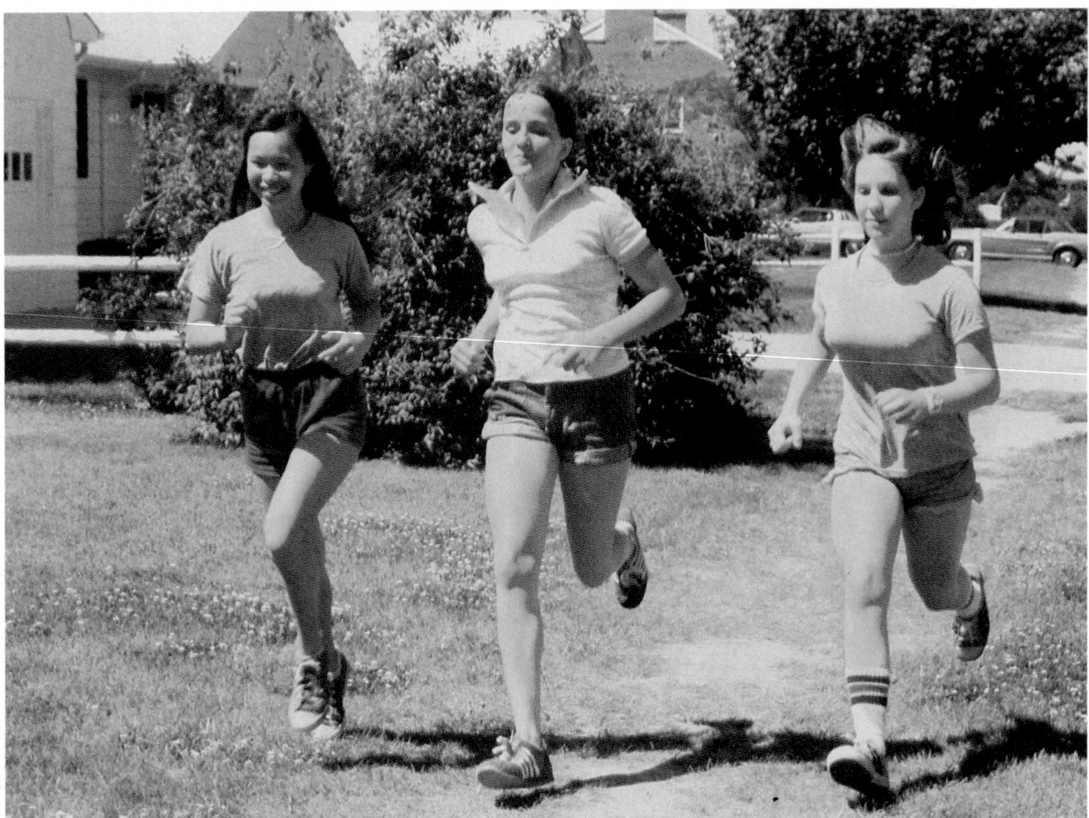

A routine exercise program can increase your physical stamina and keep your body in top condition.

ATTITUDES

What attitude do you show to your friends? Are you positive about life? Or do you find yourself griping and feeling sorry for yourself?

Your attitude includes your feelings, and opinions. Your words and actions reveal your attitude to others. Your daily outlook—good or bad—has a great deal to do with how others perceive you as a person.

But what is a good attitude? If you are a positive person, you look at the bright side rather than the dark side of life. People with positive outlooks still make mistakes and have setbacks, but they know that these things are only short-term. They learn and profit from their mistakes.

In contrast, people with bad or poor attitudes feel sorry for themselves and seldom learn from their mistakes. They focus on their misfortunes and do not try to avoid such events.

Remember that the type of attitude you choose to have is your choice. You can change your outlook and your goals. It is not always easy. It may take self-discipline, endurance, and time.

KNOWLEDGE

Knowledge is another resource. It is the wealth of information that you have, and it keeps growing as long as you live. As you learn and grow with each new experience, you gain knowledge. You gain knowledge not only in the classroom, but also through your relations with others and learning on your own.

Sometimes just knowing where to look for the information you need can be a great help. Places to look include school, your family and friends, community services, government agencies, business and professional organizations, newspapers, magazines, TV, and computer programs.

Today the average student is exposed to more information than anytime prior in history. Learn to take advantage of all your learning opportunities.

SKILLS/ABILITIES

A skill is the ability to do something well. The development of a skill requires talent, knowledge, and practice. A strong interest in an activity or career can motivate you to develop a skill.

Ann, for example, was interested in clothes and sewing as a young girl. Now a high school student, she has become a skilled seamstress. This skill has helped her to cut the cost and upkeep of her wardrobe. It has also let her use her creativity and earn some spending money.

A skill can help you with your tasks at home and school, improve your self-image, gain recognition, find jobs, and save time, energy, and money.

RELATIONSHIPS

The relationships that you form with others are vital for a happy life at home, school, and work. People are a source of knowledge and skills. You can get information when you associate with people who have different interests than you do. Sometimes friends introduce you to a new hobby or topic that you will enjoy. Relationships with family, friends, and with those you work, study, and play with can give you emotional support and encouragement.

TIME

Time is a limited resource. In spite of who, what, or where you are, you have only twenty-four hours a day to eat, sleep, go to school, work, shop, and play. Why then do some people get so much more done than others? The answer is good time management.

You cannot change the amount of time you have, but you can change the way you use it. Later in this chapter you will learn about time management and how to practice it daily.

POSSESSIONS

The word possession means ownership. Your possessions—the things you own—are your clothes, jewelry, gifts, sports equipment, records and cassette tapes, and the things you buy or are given to use.

These and other family possessions can be thought of as resources. For example, the family lawn mower can be a resource if you use it to earn money. A microwave oven is a resource that saves time for a parent. A car is a resource. It provides a way to get to and from school and/or work.

COMMUNITY FACILITIES

Community facilities can also be used as a source of knowledge and a place to develop skills. Perhaps, you have thought of the library as only a place that has books. But did you know that a library offers many more services? Some of these services are films, filmstrips, video cassettes, framed art, records, magazines and newspapers, a phone reference service, and a trained staff who can help you find what you need.

Classes are also offered by schools, hospitals, the YWCA, the YMCA, and museums. Sometimes businesses also sponser field trips, tours, and classes.

AGENCIES AND SERVICES

Other good sources of information are agencies and services. Some of them print newsletters, brochures, and pamphlets. Some even offer help by way of a toll free number.

Service agencies include the Better Business Bureau, Consumer Credit Counseling Service, youth services, medical support groups, the Food and Drug Administration, and the home economics extension service.

Government publications, ranging in topics from home security, gardening, to shopping for loans, are available free or at a minimal charge.

MONEY

Money is a medium of exchange for goods and services. As a consumer, you use money to buy goods and services. Food, clothes, a place to live, a car, health care, vacations, and entertainment—the vital and fun things in life—all usually require money. As an employee, you receive money in exchange for your work. Money will be one of the main resources you will use throughout your life. It is used to reach many goals. It is, then, vital, for you to know how to use your money wisely. This will be discussed later in this chapter.

TIME MANAGEMENT

There are many advantages of good time management. It can help you to get more done and to reach your goals. It can also help you plan for your future.

To manage your time, you first need to evaluate how you now "spend" your time. Do you put off starting a task? Do you forget deadlines? Or do you find that you do not have enough time to sit and relax? If any of these things are true, you have a need to plan and manage your time better than you do now.

KEEP A RECORD

To learn how you spend your time, keep a daily record for one week. Write down the types and length of your activities. Include the time you spend on school, study, home tasks, hobbies, appointments, watching TV, and so forth. The more detailed your records are, the more they will help you.

At the end of the week, evaluate how you used your time. Take special note of how often you were distracted from completing a task. Take note of needless trips, long phone calls, poor plans, or wasted time.

MAKE A TO DO LIST

For each day of the second week make a list of "things to do." Such a list for each day can help you gain control of your time. To make up a list, record all the things that you hope to do in one day. Then prioritize as A, B, C, and so on.

The As are your top priority tasks—what you must get done today. These are the ones that you work on first. The Bs are second in importance and will be taken on as soon as you finish the A tasks. The Cs are least important. Their not being done today will not create a problem.

Time management authorities stress the importance of making a daily list of things to do and keeping a monthly calendar of scheduled activities.

KEEP A MONTHLY CALENDAR

If you keep a monthly calendar, it will help you to see at a glance which tasks need to be done and which appointments need to be kept. Include test dates, term paper due dates, school functions, tasks at home, part-time job hours, doctor appointments, and concert dates.

Your calendar will be most helpful if you keep it where you can see it daily. This will help you not to forget to do something. It will help you not to plan to do two things at the same time. It, also, will help you make your "to do" list.

MONEY MANAGEMENT

How well you use your money will have a big impact on your total well-being. **Money management** is being in control of your money. This includes the money you earn; the money you get as a gift or inherit; and the money you spend, save, borrow, and invest.

Money management is a skill you can learn. The list below will help you to learn how to use your money wisely.

1. The amount of money you earn is important. But what you do with your money is more important. If you use your money wisely, you will do better than a friend who earns twice as much as you, but who has poor management skills.
2. Time is your best asset. As a young person, you have many years ahead of you. You have the time to develop the skills and talents that can help you earn money. You have the time to control your money and make it work for you.
3. Develop a savings plan. Make yourself save money from each pay check. If you do, you will have money for emergencies as well as for the opportunities of life.
4. Know what interest rates you get on savings and investments and those you pay when you borrow.
5. Learn what compound interest on your savings can earn for you. Over a period of years, it will make your dollars grow quickly. (This will be covered in more detail in chapter 11)
6. Review the changing financial picture. The financial decision that you make today may not be the best one three years from now. Stay flexible and make a change when you need to.
7. Your money skills will improve with practice. Learn from your mistakes as well as your successes. You will find that taking the time to learn all you can about money management and working at it will be a wise use of your time.

Put your finances in focus. Begin to practice money management skills.

Managing Your Life

TIME MANAGEMENT TIPS

Have you ever felt jealous of those who seem to do all they set out to do? Do you wonder how they take control of the time in their life? Would you like to end the day and not feel frazzled? Why not begin to follow some of these time management tips in your life? You may be surprised with the results!

• *Break big tasks into smaller tasks.* The next time you are faced with a big task—such as writing a term paper, cleaning your room, or organizing a school event—break the task into smaller tasks. For instance, if you are overwhelmed with a term paper, break it into four parts: research, writing, rewriting, and typing the final copy. Determine the number of days that can be spent on each phase of the paper. Complete each phase on time, and before you know it, it will be done!

• *Be aware of your efficiency peaks.* Are you a morning person or do your friends call you a "night owl"? You work better at different times of the day and night. Find out when these times are. When possible, plan to work on your hardest tasks when you work the best.

• *Be aware of the time wasters.* It is easy to let minutes slip away without realizing the amount of time that has been lost. Talking on the phone, daydreaming, or staring at the TV are the big culprits. Become aware of the time wasters. For one week, keep track of the time that you waste. The following week, work to improve your schedule. Begin by cutting down on your phone calls. Keep the TV turned off so that it does not distract you. And make yourself stay on a task rather than daydreaming about something else.

• *Use downtime.* If you are like most people, you waste minutes and sometimes hours just waiting. The next time you are waiting for a doctor or dentist, riding a bus or subway, or waiting for other people, be prepared. Always have something you can do. Use this time to organize your notebook, read a book, write a letter, or balance your checkbook.

• *Group trips together.* Make a list of all the errands that you need to do and keep the list in plain view. When it is time to go to a certain location, the dry cleaners for instance, cluster all the stops that need to be made in that area and do them at one time.

• *Make a list of things to do and prioritize them.* Time management experts agree that a "to do list" is a must for those who want to stay on task and reach their goals. Get into the habit of making a realistic "to do list" each day. Prioritize each activity and try to do all *A* and *B* tasks.

• *Stay organized.* An organized room, closet, desk, or study area makes your life more orderly. Keep your personal and family supplies and belongings organized. Develop a storage space for all items and put things back where they belong when you are done with them. This will help you save time so that you do not have to waste precious minutes looking for these items when you need them.

• *Stay fit.* Take time on a daily basis to enjoy an exercise program. Exercise releases stress and allows you to direct your energies into productive behavior. It not only improves your health, but it improves your attitude and makes you feel more energetic.

MAKING A FINANCIAL PLAN

A **financial plan** is more than a budget. It is a personal financial road map, a guide to show you where you are and help you to get where you want to go. Each of us can profit from a financial plan, not just people with lots of money.

Learning how to develop and use a basic financial plan is a tool to help you control your future. Now, while your income is low and your expenses are few, is the best time to develop your first plan.

When you spend money, you do more than buy clothes, food, furnishings, a car, or a vacation. You set up a pattern for your way of life. Your dollar decisions bring you closer to or take you farther away from what is important to you.

It takes planning to direct your life the way you want it to go. To find out where you are now, you need to make a detailed list of what you do with your money. To plan where you want to go, think about what you want to do. In other words, make a list of your goals.

A changing society and economic climate makes it vital that every young person develops a personal financial plan.

YOUR GOALS

Before you can budget your money well, you need to list your goals. Think about your goals, both short- and long-term. Try to estimate the dollar value of each, and list them in the order of their value to you. This is a priority list. It will help keep your goals from slipping away from you.

When you are on your own, your basic monetary goals will be to pay for necessities—rent or house payments, utility bills, food, clothes, and a car. You may be able to save only a small amount. However, as your income grows, more money can go towards your goals.

Over a period of time your needs, interests, and responsibilities change. Thus, it is wise to review and revise your goals from time to time.

Set clear, concise short term and long term goals. Estimate the costs and set a concrete date for achieving your goals.

BASIC FINANCIAL PLAN WORKSHEET
Three Month Trial Period

Income	**Month** ________		**Month** ________		**Month** ________	
	Est.	Actual	Est.	Actual	Est.	Actual
Total Income						
Expenses	**Month** ________		**Month** ________		**Month** ________	
Fixed/Periodic Fixed	Est.	Actual	Est.	Actual	Est.	Actual
	Month ________		**Month** ________		**Month** ________	
Flexible	Est.	Actual	Est.	Actual	Est.	Actual
Total Expenses						

Total Income $ ________________

Total Expenses ________________

$ ________________

Est. = estimated

A three month financial plan will help you keep track of your income and expenses.

INCOME AND EXPENSES

To reach your goals, you need to get a handle on your expenses. Make yourself keep records. This will help you as you start to implement your financial plan. Keep a small notebook with you to jot down how much you spend and for what. Keep cash register and sales receipts. Then regularly organize them into types of expenses, and you will know how much you spent and why.

If you organize your material so it is easy to use, working with your financial plan will not be a chore. Keep your plan simple. Most plans are made for a twelve-month period. For your first one, though, use a three-month trial period to see how it works. Then you can make changes before you make a plan for a longer period of time.

As you make your plan, round off numbers to even dollar amounts. If an amount includes 50 to 99 cents, round up to the next whole dollar. A $5.95 expense would be listed as $6. If the cents amount is less than 50, use the dollar figure as is. A $5.45 item would become a $5 item.

The heart of a financial plan is a record of income and expenses. **Income** is the money you have to work with to pay expenses, save, and invest. It does not include payroll deductions. List all sources of your income. Refer to the figure at the right.

To help you plan for expenses, divide them into two groups, fixed and flexible. A **fixed expense**, such as rent, utilities, and car payments, is a fixed amount of money paid each week, month, quarter, or year. A **flexible expense**, varies in amount and can occur irregularly. Food, clothes, gifts, dry cleaning, car repairs, and recreation are all flexible expenses. When you make your first financial plan, be sure to jot down flexible expenses like magazines, chewing gum, and snack foods.

Plan for emergencies and opportunities. Perhaps the best way is to save a certain amount from each pay check. Then, when the car will not start or you need a doctor or dentist, you can handle the cost with ease.

INCOME SOURCES

Though wages or salary are usually the main source of income, during a lifetime you can have many possible income sources.

In-school
Allowance
Part-time job
Neighborhood and/or family "odd" jobs
Money gifts

First Full-time Job
Wages or salary
Money gifts

Lifetime
Wages or salary
Money gifts
Fees, commissions, tips, bonuses
Inheritance
Insurance beneficiary payment(s)
Interest: savings accounts, money market funds, bonds
Dividends: mutual funds, stocks
Rent
Profits from sale of assets
Royalties
Pension, profit-sharing plan
Annuities
Social Security benefits
Public assistance
Child support, alimony

If you need to reduce your expenses, look first at the flexible ones. Because they are flexible, you can learn to spend less on them. You can even learn to do without some of them. For example, reduce food costs by buying sale items. Also you can reduce costs by giving up a movie, malt, or some other extra.

EVALUATE AND ADJUST YOUR PLAN

At this point, you have listed your goals and have worked with your income and expenses. The next step is to see how you are doing. To do this, check your expenses against your income. Are your expenses more, less, or about the same as your income? Will your spending and savings plan let you do what you want to do? Do not give up if your plan is not 100 percent successful. Very few are. With practice you will learn to balance your expenses and income better, and to make a plan you can live with.

YOUR NET WORTH

Your three-month trial period is over, you have looked at your income and expenses, and you made the needed changes. The last step, an essential part of a financial plan, is to find out how much you are worth. Your **net worth** is the total current cash value of your **assets** (what you own) less your **liabilities** (what you owe).

What you own – What you owe = Your net worth
or
Assets – Liabilities = Net worth

FLEXIBLE EXPENSES

Food
- Meals at home
- Meals eaten out

Clothing
- New clothes and accessories
- Laundry
- Dry cleaning
- Repairs and alterations

Household Equipment
- Appliances
- Furniture
- Repairs

Home Improvement
- Maintenance
- Remodeling
- Expansion

Household Supplies
- Cleaning supplies
- Small items for the home
- First-aid supplies

Household Help
- Babysitter
- Yard care
- Window washing
- Housecleaning

Gifts
- Birthdays
- Weddings and anniversaries
- Religious celebration
- Showers
- Illness
- Graduation

Transportation
- Gasoline
- Repairs and upkeep
- Taxi
- Bus or train

Contributions
- Religious
- Charities
- Service groups
- Professional groups
- Fraternal groups
- Social clubs
- Schools and colleges

Health
(not covered by insurance)
- Medical
- Dental
- Eye care/glasses
- Prescription drugs
- Medications

Personal Care
- Grooming aids
- Barber shop
- Beauty parlor

Entertainment
- Extra food
- Theater tickets
- Sports events

Recreation
- Hobbies
- Vacation
- Sports equipment

Miscellaneous
- Papers
- Magazines
- Stationery, postage
- Tobacco
- Others

Others
- ____________________
- ____________________
- ____________________
- ____________________
- ____________________
- ____________________

FIXED/PERIODIC FIXED EXPENSES

Housing
- Rent
- Mortgage payments
- Maintenance fee

Taxes
- Federal income tax*
- State income tax*
- Local taxes
- Property taxes

Utilities and Home Services
- Telephone
- Gas
- Water
- Fuel
- Sewage
- Garbage pickup
- Cable TV

Installment Payments
- Automobile
- Furniture or appliances
- Personal loans

*Estimate any additional payment beyond amount withheld from wages.

Insurance
- Life
- Automobile
- Health and accident
- Hospitalization
- Fire and theft
- Personal property
- Social Security
- Other

Fees for Education
- Tuition
- Room and Board
- Books
- Other

Transportation
- Automobile
- Vehicle sticker
- Commuting fare
- Parking
- Garage metal

Personal Allowances
- Husband
- Wife
- Children

Personal Improvement
- Music lessons
- Dancing lessons
- Books
- Other

Membership Dues
- Union
- Professional associations
- Clubs

Contributions
- Religious
- Charity

Savings
- Emergency fund
- For goals

Subscriptions
- Newspapers
- Magazines

Others
- ____________________
- ____________________
- ____________________
- ____________________
- ____________________

It may surprise you, but even now you have a net worth. Your clothes, jewelry, record player, books, records, bike, gifts, cash on hand, plus a checking and/or savings account are all assets.

You should check your net worth at least once a year to see how you are doing financially. Doing it the first time is very important because it gives you a figure for future comparison. Your net worth should increase over time. If it stays about the same or decreases, this alerts you to review and revise the money you spend and save.

YOUR NET WORTH WORKSHEET

Assets − Liabilities = Net Worth

Assets (What you *own*)

Cash
- On hand $ ________
- Checking account ________
- Savings account ________

Personal Property (Cash value)
- Car or other vehicle (motorcycle, motor bike) ________
- Furniture ________
- Appliances ________

Other assets
- ________ ________

Total assets $ ________

Liabilities (What you *owe*)

Current bills
- ________ $ ________
- ________ ________
- ________ ________

Installment debt(s)
- Car or other vehicle ________
- Furniture and/or appliances ________

Personal loans
- ________ ________

Other liabilities
- ________ ________

Total liabilities $ ________

Total assets $ ________
Total liabilities $ ________
Net worth $ ________
Date ________

If your net worth does not improve over time, you need to review your spending and saving pattern.

UNDERSTANDING YOUR PAYCHECK

Getting your first paycheck is a big event and gives you a good feeling. The money you earn will be the biggest part of the money you will have to control. Thus, it is vital that you learn and understand what paycheck terminology and deductions are.

You may already know the amount of your check will be less than the amount you earned. This is because your employer is required by law to make deductions from your pay.

A paycheck has two parts. The first part is made payable to you for the amount of your **net earnings,** or take-home pay. Net earnings are your total earnings less all deductions. The second part is a **statement of earnings,** an explanation of earnings and both required and optional deductions. It is wise to keep these statements as a record of your earnings (see page 138).

KEEPING ORGANIZED RECORDS

Keeping good records is the most important thing you can do to make your financial planning easy. Organized records also are good to have when you do your income tax.

To start, break the information into two kinds—current and "dead." The current file has material you use or may need within three years. The "dead" file is the place for records older than three years.

This information is usually kept at one or two places—at home and/or in a **safe deposit box.** A safe deposit box is one of a group of locked, metal boxes in a vault at your bank. They are different sizes and can be rented on a yearly basis. The keys you get for your box should be kept in a safe place.

SAFE DEPOSIT BOX

Personal papers: birth, baptismal, marriage and death certificates, military service record, adoption papers, citizenship records, passport, copy of will, Social Security card, separation agreement, divorce papers

Car title or bill of sale

Household or personal property inventory including receipts for major purchases and photographs

Property documents: titles, deeds, mortgage papers

Bonds, certificates of deposit, stock certificates

Important contracts

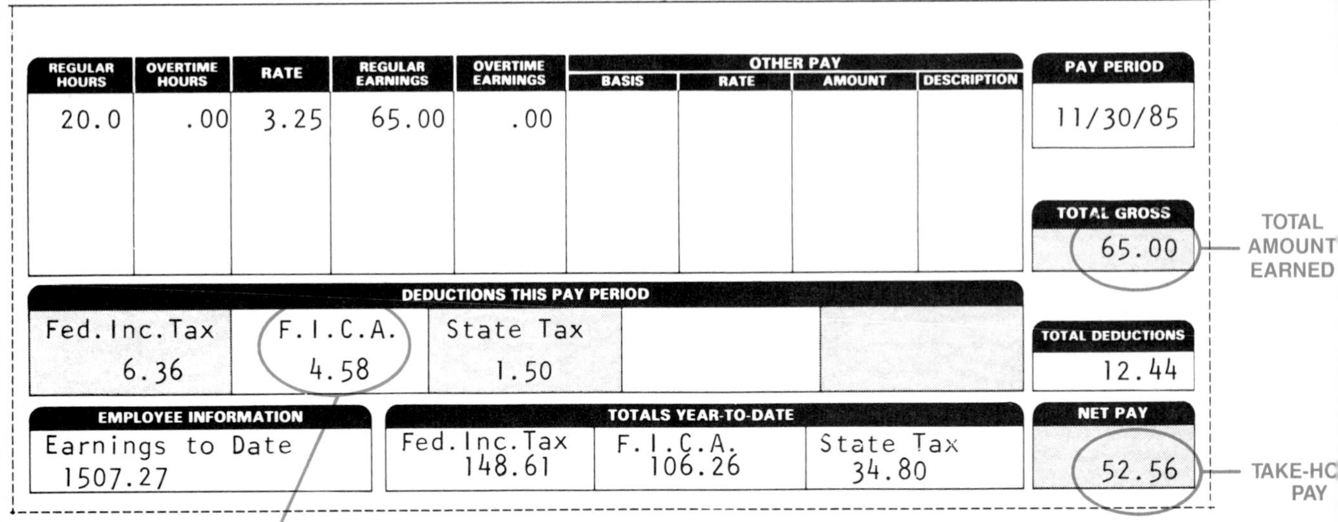

REGULAR HOURS	OVERTIME HOURS	RATE	REGULAR EARNINGS	OVERTIME EARNINGS	OTHER PAY BASIS	OTHER PAY RATE	OTHER PAY AMOUNT	OTHER PAY DESCRIPTION	PAY PERIOD
20.0	.00	3.25	65.00	.00					11/30/85

TOTAL GROSS: 65.00

DEDUCTIONS THIS PAY PERIOD

Fed. Inc. Tax	F.I.C.A.	State Tax		
6.36	4.58	1.50		

TOTAL DEDUCTIONS: 12.44

EMPLOYEE INFORMATION: Earnings to Date 1507.27

TOTALS YEAR-TO-DATE

Fed. Inc. Tax	F.I.C.A.	State Tax
148.61	106.26	34.80

NET PAY: 52.56

Study your paycheck to be sure you understand everything on it. If any figures puzzle you, ask a qualified person to explain them to you.

To make your record keeping at home easy to do and use, organize current material in one place. A clean, strong carton with file folders or envelopes can be used. When you set up your files, remember to label folders or envelopes clearly and to allow extra space for your file needs as they grow over a period of time.

INCOME TAX

When you work full-time, you need to think about income tax. The money used to run our government and its programs comes largely from this income tax.

On most jobs the tax is automatically withheld from each paycheck. The amount withheld is based on your earnings and the number of dependents you claim. A dependent is a person you support—including yourself. When you are first hired (and with each job change), you will be asked to fill out a form declaring how many dependents you have.

If you earn more than a certain amount in one calendar year, you must file an income tax return with the IRS. Your completed return is due by April 15 the following year. Figuring your tax lets you know if the amount withheld from your pay is correct.

If you owe more tax, you will include a check for that amount with your return. If you paid too much tax, the government will send you a refund check. Also, if your total earnings do not require you to pay tax, you still need to file a return to get a refund of the money withheld from your pay.

Each January your employer has to give you two copies of the **W-2 form.** This form has your total earnings for the prior year, the amount held out for taxes, and the amount held out for your Social Security payment. If you work for more than one employer during the year, you will receive W-2 forms from each one. Keep one copy of each W-2 form for your records and send the second copy with your completed tax return to the IRS.

To prepare your tax return, you need to use the right tax form and your W-2 for information. Most people use either the short forms, 1040EZ and 1040A, or the long form 1040. These can be found at the local IRS office and at some post offices. Get two copies of the form you will use—one for a worksheet to figure your tax, the other for the IRS.

You can sometimes reduce the amount of your tax by listing certain expenses. These include the interest charges paid during the year for loans on homes, cars, and credit cards. Part of high medical or dental expenses, not covered by insurance, may also be used as a deduction.

If you need help to prepare your form, you can get free general help at the local IRS office. If you need answers to only a few questions, the IRS has a toll free number to use.

The year after you file your first return, the IRS will mail the same form(s) to you in a booklet. This booklet has instructions for preparing your return, tax tables, and changes in tax legislation. It also has lists of free IRS publications and an order blank.

WORDS TO REMEMBER

assets	money management
financial plan	net earnings
fixed expense	net worth
flexible expense	safe deposit box
income	statement of earnings
liabilities	W-2 form

CHECKING YOUR UNDERSTANDING

1. Identify two groups of resources and give examples of each type. Briefly explain how you can benefit from each type.
2. What money management skills do you have? Name three more things that you could do to improve your money management skills.
3. Explain the purpose of setting up a basic financial plan. Why is it necessary to prioritize your goals before preparing a financial plan?
4. What are the benefits of keeping good financial records? Why would this be helpful when you are doing your income tax?
5. What do you need to prepare your first income tax return? How or where do you get the information and/or material?

APPLYING YOUR UNDERSTANDING

1. Prepare a pamphlet or brochure that lists facilities, agencies, or services found in your community. Write a short description of the purpose of each organization.
2. List three short-term and three long-term goals that you have. Estimate the cost of each. List the goals in their order of importance and outline a plan for completing each one.
3. For one week keep a daily record of how you used your time. List the goals in their order of importance and outline a plan for completing each one. Evaluate your record. What improvements can you make?
4. Outline how to develop and use a basic financial plan. Briefly explain the purpose of each step.
5. Define assets, liabilities, and net worth. Explain the relationship between the three terms and estimate your net worth.

Chapter 11

BANKING BASICS

Has this ever happened to you?

It is right before summer vacation and Meg and Claire are talking about their summer jobs. They both realize that they need to open a savings account so that they can save money to buy school clothes and supplies for next fall.

"Claire, did you see the neat duffle bag or exercise mat that you can get if you open an account at First National?" said Meg. "I think I will open my savings account today!"

"What is the minimum deposit required to open an account?" questioned Claire.

Meg replied, "Oh, I am not really sure. Don't all banks require the same amount?"

"No, banks differ in their services and that's an important question you will want to ask. I plan to open a savings account at Citizens Central. They require a minimum opening deposit of $100 for minors, and they have a twenty-four-hour teller service," stated Claire.

"That would be convenient," said Meg. "Plus First National is on the other side of town! Maybe the free gift is not worth it if I consider the inconvenience of getting to the bank each time I want to make a deposit. Now I don't know what to do."

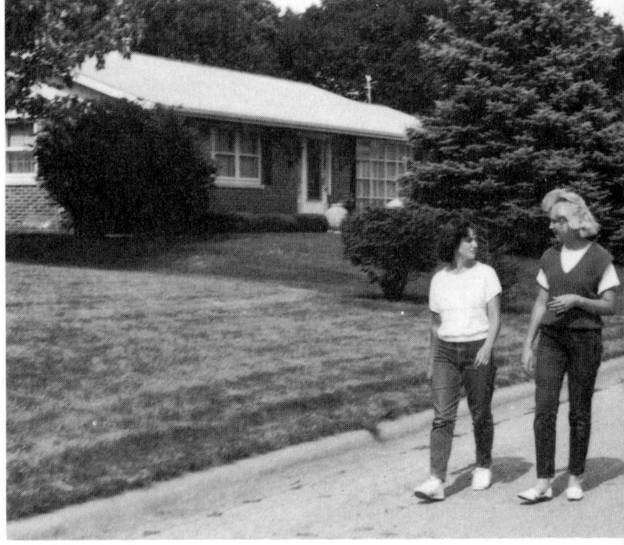

"Maybe you should compare the different banks before you make a decision," said Claire. "After all, you want to make it easy to save money."

"That's probably a good idea," agreed Meg. "I will let you know what I find out."

Have you ever been influenced by a "free" offer?

What services would you find important if you were opening a savings account?

After reading this chapter, you will be able to

- understand the difference between simple and compound interest and realize the productive power of compound interest on your savings;
- realize the importance of comparing service charges and interest rates at banks and savings and loan firms;
- evaluate banks and financial firms in your area to decide which one can best serve you;
- know how to use a checking account;
- identify the choice of savings accounts and plans available to you.

Once in a while you read or hear about someone who puts money in a mattress, in a cookie jar, or in a teapot for "safe keeping" or "a rainy day." Such news makes colorful talk or reading, but it is not a responsible way to save money. Other than cash you need for daily expenses, your money should be kept where it is safe and, whenever possible, earning interest.

FINANCIAL INSTITUTIONS

You can safeguard your money if you use the services of a financial firm. The major ones are commercial banks, savings and loan associations, mutual savings banks, and credit unions.

A financial firm makes loans and/or investments to make a profit. If you have an interest-earning account, the firm pays you interest for the use of your funds. If you get a loan from the firm, you pay interest for the time span you use their funds. In other words, you pay interest until you pay off the loan in full.

Such a firm uses the profits from its loans and investments to pay dividends to its stockholders, to pay for operating costs, and to keep the required reserves. Reserves may be vault cash (cash on hand) plus reserves held at the Federal Reserve Bank or in another depository institution.

In a financial firm your money is safe, may "work" for you by earning interest, and is generally easy to take out if you need it. A mattress, cookie jar, or teapot offers only easy access.

Financial institutions come in several shapes and sizes. Each one plays an important role in our society and together they offer a broad range of financial services.

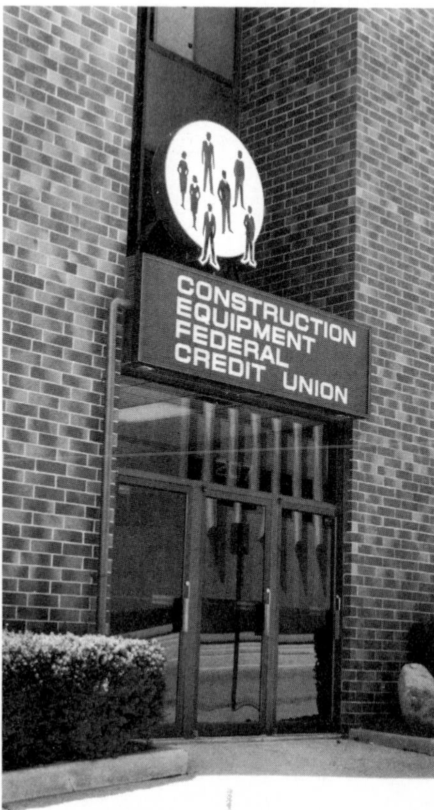

COMMERCIAL BANKS

Commercial banks are often referred to as "full service banks" because of the many services they offer. They include checking and savings accounts, loans, safe deposit boxes, sale and redemption of U.S. savings bonds, travelers checks, electronic fund transfers, and financial counseling. Banks serve individuals, families, businesses, industry, and governments.

SAVINGS AND LOAN ASSOCIATIONS

Savings and loan firms are sometimes called building and loan, homestead, or savings associations. Generally, they are mutually owned by shareholders. You are a member and shareholder when you open an account. Their services stress savings and loans for home building, buying, and remodeling. Other services include safe deposit boxes, sale and redemption of U.S. savings bonds, personal loans, money orders, traveler's checks, and others.

Mutual Savings Banks

Mutual savings banks are nonprofit specialized savings firms set up and run for their depositors. Their main service is to take savings and to invest this money in home mortgage and home improvement loans. Other services include safe deposit boxes, money orders, sale and redemption of U.S. savings bonds, and at some banks, checking accounts.

In these firms (savings and loan associations and mutual savings banks), your account earns dividends, not interest, as in a full-service or commercial bank.

Credit Unions

Credit unions are nonprofit cooperative firms owned and run by depositors. All members have a common tie—the same employer, the same union, or the same occupational group such as teachers or members of the armed forces. Each member is a shareholder, not a depositor, and has shares rather than deposits.

A credit union's main function is to use members' savings to make low cost loans to them. Other services include payroll deductions, credit counseling, credit cards, money orders, traveler's checks, and the sale and redemption of U.S. savings bonds.

From a credit union's income, operating costs are paid and the legal reserve set aside. The unused income is shared with members in the form of an extra dividend paid on savings or as a rebate of loan interest.

Savings and loan associations specialize in long-term mortgage loans on houses and other real estate.

Credit unions serve people who have a common bond, such as people working for the same company, attending the same church, or belonging to the same labor union.

KEEP UP-TO-DATE ABOUT SERVICES

In the past, the main services offered by the four firms above stayed largely the same. However, the differences are fading. The main services offered by all four types of firms may soon be more alike than not alike due to deregulation in the banking industry.

To help you keep up-to-date about the banking services in your area, look and listen for information. Sources are the newspapers, radio, TV, and pamphlets and signs at the institutions.

INTEREST

Interest rates make a difference in how fast your savings and investment dollars increase as well as in the cost of a loan or buying on credit. In order for you to get the most use of the dollars you save, spend, or invest, you need to learn what simple and compound interest are.

SIMPLE INTEREST

Simple interest is figured only on the principal, or the amount of money involved. To compute simple interest, you need to know:

1. the principal, or amount of money involved;
2. the interest rate;
3. the period of time the money is used.

For example, if a financial firm loans you \$700 for one year at 11 percent simple interest with the total amount due at the end of twelve months, you would owe \$777.

$$\text{Interest (I)} = \text{Principal (P)} \times \text{Rate (R)} \times \text{Time (T)}$$
$$\$77(\text{I}) = \$700(\text{P}) \times .11(\text{R}) \times 1(\text{T})$$

If the loan was for two years, the total due would be \$854:

$$\$154 = \$700 \times .11 \times 2$$
$$\$854 = \$700 + \$154$$

It is important to note that simple interest is figured on the principal only—not on the principal plus accumulated interest. In the second example above, interest for the second year was figured only on the \$700, not the \$777 (principal plus interest for the first year).

COMPOUND INTEREST

Compound interest, figured on the principal and accumulated interest, is not as easy to work with as simple interest. Although you may not fully understand all the details of how to figure it, you will want to be aware of the productive power of compound interest on your savings. And if compound interest is charged on a loan, the total amount owed is more with compound than with simple interest.

For example, if the total amount of your savings is $700 and the financial firm pays you an 11 percent compound interest computed annually, at the end of the year the $700 will earn an interest of $77. Your savings account now totals $777.

If you leave the money in your account for another year, at the end of the second year both the principal ($700) and the accumulated interest for the first year ($77) earn interest.

Principal	$700.00
Interest for first year on principal	77.00
Total savings, first year	777.00
Interest for second year on principal	77.00
Interest for second year on interest for first year	8.47
Total savings second year	$862.47

This is why compound interest is sometimes described as "earning interest with interest."

Compound interest also may be figured semiannually (twice a year), quarterly (four times a year), monthly (twelve times a year), or daily. The more often compound interest is figured and added to the principal, the faster the total grows—whether it is savings or money you owe on a loan.

Do you understand the multiplying effect of compound interest?

CHOOSING THE RIGHT FINANCIAL INSTITUTION FOR YOU

The selection of the place to do your banking business merits your doing some "homework." Many people shop and compare before they decide to buy a car, a microwave oven, or furniture. It is wise to give equal time to shop and compare "storehouses" for your money. Base your comparison on safety, services, charges, interest rates, and convenience.

Before deciding upon a financial institution, shop and compare safety, services, charges, interest rates and convenience of each firm.

Your savings insured to $100,000

NCUA

National Credit Union Administration, a U.S. Government Agency

Each depositor insured to $100,000

When selecting banking institutions, look for one of these symbols. They guarantee that your deposits will be insured up to $100,000.

SAFETY

At a good financial firm, the total of all deposits in your name is currently insured up to $100,000. Commercial banks operate under the Federal Deposit Insurance Corporation (FDIC), savings and loan associations under the Federal Savings and Loan Insurance Corporation (FSLIC), and the credit unions under the National Credit Union Association (NCUA).

Look for the emblem which tells you that the firm is protected with this insurance. The emblem is usually displayed on windows and counters. If you do not see it, ask if the firm has such insurance. The emblem "tells" you that if the firm has money problems, the insurance company guarantees to pay you the amount of your total deposits up to $100,000.

SERVICES OFFERED

It will help you to choose the right firm if you review your responsibilities and goals. At first, perhaps, you will need only a checking account. However, over a period of time, you may need to use other services. You may need a loan to buy a sofa, stove, or car, or to go to college. You may want to earn higher interest on your savings.

CHARGES AND EARNINGS

The charges for checking accounts and the interest you pay on loans vary. Check to see which rates are best for you. Earnings (interest or dividends) paid on savings accounts also vary. Look for the best return on your money. In other words, make your money work for you. These charges and earnings will be discussed later in this chapter and in chapter 12.

CONVENIENCE

Is the financial firm located near your home or place of work? What are the bank's hours? Does the bank have drive-in windows? Twenty-four-hour automated teller service? Bank-by-mail service?

ELECTRONIC FUND TRANSFER

Computers have made possible electronic fund transfer (EFT) systems. Each system is designed to hold down the growing cost and amount of paperwork involved in banking. When using EFT systems, carefully review your monthly statements. Federal law requires that all machine transactions be itemized on your statement.

The parts of an EFT system are computer terminals, automated tellers, access cards, push-button phones, and a main frame computer.

AUTOMATED TELLER MACHINE (ATM)

Many people do some of their routine banking on EFT systems. One often used part is the automated teller machine (ATM). An ATM lets you bank twenty-four hours a day, seven days a week. You can get cash, transfer funds, borrow money from your bank card account, check your bank balance, and put money in your account.

To use an ATM, you first insert your specially encoded plastic card. Then you punch in your personal identity number (PIN) or personal identity code (PIC). The last step is to choose the type of transaction. An ATM gives you a receipt for each transaction.

• Only you, the bank that issues your access card, and the ATM know your PIN or PIC. It is suggested that you memorize this number. Never write it on your card. Why? If your card is lost or stolen, anyone can take money from your account.

Your liability for unauthorized withdrawl is limited to $50, if you report a lost or stolen card within two business days after you learn it is missing. If you wait longer, your loss can soar.

POINT OF SALE (POS) TERMINAL

With a point-of-sale (POS) system, a business, such as a gasoline station or a supermarket, can withdraw money electronically from your account when you make a purchase. You use your ATM access card to activate the POS terminal. A POS purchase is the same as cash, because the money is transferred immediately from your, the buyer's, to the seller's account.

When you use a POS system, your identity is confirmed, and your transaction is accepted or rejected. The basis for a rejection might be that your purchase exceeds the amount of your daily withdrawl limit.

PREAUTHORIZED TRANSFERS

A preauthorized transfer is a method that automatically deposits or withdraws funds to or from your account. You must authorize your bank or employer to do so. For example you can authorize the direct electronic deposit of wages, Social Security, or dividend payments. Or you can instruct a financial institution to make regular payments of your insurance, mortgage, or utility bills.

CHECKING ACCOUNTS

The first banking service you probably will use is a checking account. It is the most often used bank service. Payment by check is easy, safe, and provides a record of how you spend money. A canceled check has the added advantage of being a legal receipt, a proof of purchase for your records. A **canceled check** shows that the bank made payment with money from your checking account.

The cost of having a checking account depends on the type you choose. Take the time to study and understand the charges made by the different banks. Usually, you are charged a small fee for each check you write plus a monthly service fee if you do not maintain the required minimum balance.

MINIMUM BALANCE CHECKING ACCOUNT

If you keep a required minimum balance at all times, you pay no charges other than the cost of personalized checks. This is a **minimum balance checking account.** The bank uses the interest your money (minimum balance) earns for them to cover the costs of your account (processing checks and making up and mailing monthly statements).

NOW ACCOUNT (NEGOTIABLE ORDERS OF WITHDRAWAL)

In 1981 the negotiable orders of withdrawal or NOW account became available in all states. With this account you write checks on the money you have in your savings account. A withdrawal order serves as a check, but the money for its payment comes out of your savings account. It combines the convenience of a checking account with the earning power of a savings account.

However, you do need to keep a minimum balance if you do not want to pay service charges. The required minimum balance varies between firms. As with a regular minimum balance checking account, it is wise to shop and compare for a NOW account.

SHARE DRAFT ACCOUNT

More and more credit unions offer share draft accounts. As a member, you write a checklike draft against your account. Until the draft clears your account, your money earns interest.

USING A CHECKING ACCOUNT

With the increased use of bank credit cards and electronic fund transfer systems, there may be fewer checks used in the future. Nonetheless, today checks are still the most used way to transfer funds.

When you open a checking account, you will find the prodecure a simple one. Take the money for your first deposit to the financial firm of your choice. You will be asked to sign a signature card. Sign your name as you will sign your checks. The bank will refer to this card to confirm your signature in future transactions, if it needs to.

The bank gives you a small number of checks and deposit slips to use until you get your printed personalized checks. It is wise to order these checks at the same time you open an account. The checks will include your name, address, phone number (if you choose to include it), your account number, and a check number. Each book of checks has several deposit slips with the same information, except for the check numbers. The bank orders the checks for you, deducts the cost from your account balance, and lists the charge on your monthly statement. You fill out a deposit slip or statement of transaction each time you put money in your account.

HOW TO WRITE A CHECK

Follow the steps below to write checks:

1. Check number. To help keep good records, number checks consecutively. Personalized checks are printed in numbered sequence.
2. Date check the day it is written. Checks are valid if dated on a Sunday or holiday.
3. Payee's name. Fill in the name of the person or firm to whom money is to be paid.
4. Amount in numbers. Write the amount close to the dollar sign.
5. Amount in words. Start writing at the far left and keep the words close together. This will stop someone from inserting a word and thus changing the amount. For example, changing two to twenty-two by writing the word twenty. After the dollars amount, write the word followed by the cents written as a fraction. Twenty cents is written 20/100. Fill in the rest of the space with a line. Be sure the numbers and words state the same amount.
6. Signature. Sign your name like you did on the signature card when you opened your account.

DEPOSIT TICKET

NAME Lynn Smith

DATE May 1, 19 87

CASH	CURRENCY		
	COIN		
LIST CHECKS SINGLY		150	00
TOTAL FROM OTHER SIDE			
TOTAL		150	00
LESS CASH RECEIVED		25	00
NET DEPOSIT		125	00

70-7275/2711

USE OTHER SIDE FOR ADDITIONAL LISTING

BE SURE EACH ITEM IS PROPERLY ENDORSED

1 FIRST NATIONAL BANK
City, U.S.A. 00000

:271172754: 9"006 240"' 7"' 0187

CHECKS AND OTHER ITEMS ARE RECEIVED FOR DEPOSIT SUBJECT TO THE PROVISIONS OF THE UNIFORM COMMERCIAL CODE OR ANY APPLICABLE COLLECTION AGREEMENT.

Fill out a deposit slip each time you put money into your account.

CHECK WRITING TIPS

Below are five check writing tips:

1. A checkbook register or stub is the second part of a checkbook. Always make an entry when you write a check. Do not trust your memory. The register or stub is a record of the date, amount, and purpose of the check. An up-to-date register or stub, also, is a current record of your account balance or how much money is in your checking account.

2. If you make a mistake when writing a check, or decide not to use it, write or print the word VOID across the check before you discard it. To keep your checkbook register or stub current, write the check number and mark it VOID.

Immediately after writing a check, record the date, number and amount of check in the checkbook register or stub.

3. Do not write a check unless you have enough funds in your account to cover the payment. An overdrawn account will cause your check to "bounce." The bank returns the check to the payee marked "insufficient funds." This is an inconvenience for the person to whom the check is written, it embarrasses you, and the bank charges you a service charge for an overdrawn account. A retail business will also charge you for an overdrawn check.

4. If you need money, you can write yourself a check. Make it payable to yourself and endorse it only after you are where you will cash it. To make a check payable to "Cash" is risky. Anyone can endorse it and get the money.

5. Never sign a blank check (no payee's name). Anyone can fill in a name, date, and amount of money and then cash the check.

RECORD ALL CHARGES OR CREDITS THAT AFFECT YOUR ACCOUNT

NUMBER	DATE	DESCRIPTION OF TRANSACTION	PAYMENT/DEBIT (−)		√ T	FEE (IF ANY) (−)	DEPOSIT/CREDIT (+)		BALANCE	
									$ 1277	—
452	9/14	State-Wide Tele. Co. Telephone Services	$ 32	—		$	$		1245	—
453	9/15	First National Bank Car Loan Payment	95	—					1150	—
454	9/21	Woodrow Medical Lab Medical Services	58	—					1092	—
455	9/25	Western Electric Electric Service	35	58					1056	42
456	9/27	Mid-West Gas Co. Natural Gas	36	50					1019	92
457	10/1	Martin Walsh Rent	300	—					719	92

HOW TO ENDORSE A CHECK

Before you can cash or deposit a check made payable to you, you need to endorse it. To do this, sign your name on the back of the check at the left end. Your signature should be exactly as your name appears on the check. If your name is spelled wrong as payee, endorse it the same way with a second endorsement, spelled the right way, below it.

There are three types of endorsements—blank, special, and restrictive. The payee's signature by itself is a blank endorsement, which makes the check as good as money. If you lose a check with a blank endorsement, the finder can cash it after endorsing the check below your name. The safe way is to sign a blank endorsement only after you are where you will cash or deposit the check.

A restrictive endorsement states what is to be done with the check. A common use of this type is to write "For deposit only" and then sign your name.

A special endorsement names the person who will next endorse the check. You write "Pay to the order of" plus the person's name. Then sign your name below it. No one but the person you name can cash or deposit the check.

HOW TO BALANCE YOUR CHECKBOOK AND BANK STATEMENT

You will get a monthly statement from the bank describing the activity in your checking account for the time span of the statement. The canceled checks (checks for which payment was made) will be enclosed. Each check is listed on the statement plus your deposits and service charges.

It is best to "balance your checkbook" promptly. You want to be sure you and the bank agree on how much money is in your account. At the same time you can check your statement and register (or stubs) for possible errors made by you or the bank. Usually, the statement has a step-by-step procedure form on the back for your use. It is wise to double check your math before thinking there is an error in the statement. A hand calculator is a big help.

To start, put the canceled checks in numerical order by check number. Then check off each one in your checkbook register (or stubs) and on the statement. Make sure the amount of each check is the same at both places. As you do this, also make a list of all outstanding checks. These are checks for which money was not taken out of your account for payment at the time the statement was prepared.

Next, compare your deposit receipts with the deposits listed on your statement and in your checkbook. Total any new deposits. These are deposits you made but which are not on the statement.

Now deduct the total amount of the service charges listed on your statement from your checkbook balance.

To find out if you and the bank agree on how much money is in your account (the account balance), fill in the form on the back of a monthly bank statement, and you will have the answer.

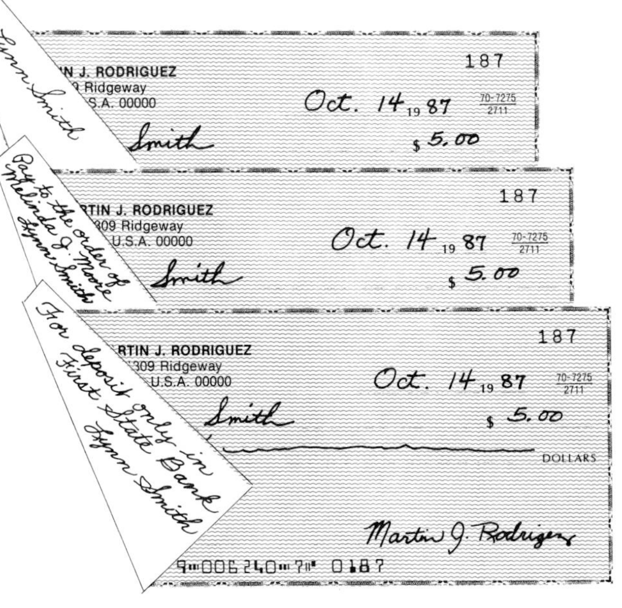

You must endorse a check before it can be cashed or deposited.

When you balance your checkbook, or reconcile your bank statement, you compare your record of your checking account with the bank's record of your account.

By saving regularly you can plan for major expenses (such as travel, tuition, a car) and you can provide for unforeseen expenses (such as a car or home repair bill)

SAVINGS ACCOUNTS AND PLANS

Each of us wants financial security or to have enough money when we need it. The safest and best way to build this security is to pay yourself first by saving each payday. How quickly these dollars multiply depends on you. Saving regularly is not always easy to do—especially at first. Many times you must make yourself save. If you can manage yourself, you can manage your money.

As with a checking account, it is wise to shop and compare the various savings plans before you make a decision.

REGULAR SAVINGS ACCOUNT

A regular savings account is the one most often chosen by first-time savers at banks, savings and loans, and credit unions. You can deposit or take out cash at any time. For each transaction you fill out a deposit or withdrawal slip. This account earns the lowest rate of interest paid on savings, but the money is liquid. **Liquidity** is the ease and speed with which you can take cash out of your account. This might be important if you need cash in a hurry. It also is important to know what minimum daily balance is required and the service charge made if your account is less than this amount.

You will get a savings account statement that lists your deposits, withdrawals, service charges and the interest earned for the time span of the statement.

There are several ways financial firms figure the interest paid on a regular savings account. They range from the use of an account's minimum or low balance to interest compounded daily for each dollar from day of deposit to the day it is taken out.

AN OVERALL VIEW OF BANKING SERVICES

Before you choose the financial institution where you will do business, it will be helpful if you are familiar with the most frequently used banking services.

- A **checking account** enables you to transfer money, by check, from your account to another person, company, or institution for the payment of bills and other expenses.
- A **savings account** enables you to accumulate money (deposits plus interest or earnings) for future use.
- **Credit (loan)** is an arrangement by which you receive money, merchandise, or a service now and pay for it later.
- A certified check is guaranteed to be negotiable or good by a bank. The bank issues the check on money taken from your account. Many businesses prefer certified checks for payment of "big ticket" items to be sure your funds are sufficient for payment.
- A cashier's check is used by a person who does not have an account. You give the bank your money, and the bank issues the check on money from its account.
- A money order is another way to make payment if you do not have a checking account. Banks, savings and loan associations, mutual savings banks, credit unions and the post office issue money orders. The sender pays the full amount of the order plus a small fee. The recipient can cash the order at any post office or bank.
- Travelers checks are used primarily by people who travel and prefer to carry little cash. The checks are available in different denominations, are generally accepted world-wide as readily as cash, and have no time limit on their use.

TIME OR TERM DEPOSITS

Time or term deposits are what the name states. You agree to leave a certain amount of money with a firm for a required time period. Usually, the larger the deposit and the longer the time period, the higher the rate of interest your savings earn.

Before you "tie up" money in a time deposit, be sure you will not need to take it out before the maturity date (the end of the required time period). If you take it out early, there is a large interest penalty.

U.S. SAVINGS BONDS

When you buy a U.S. savings bond, you loan your money to the U.S. government. In return, the government pays you interest for the use of your money. Series EE bonds are available in amounts starting at $50.

For an EE bond you pay one-half of the face value. The face value is the bond's cash value if held until the maturity date. A $50 bond costs $25. If you hold a bond beyond its maturity date, the government will continue to pay interest.

Interest is compounded every six months or semiannually. The rate is set in May and November. The total interest a bond earns is the difference between what you paid for the bond and the cash you get when you redeem the bond.

About half of all bond buyers obtain them through payroll savings programs operating at workplaces nationwide.

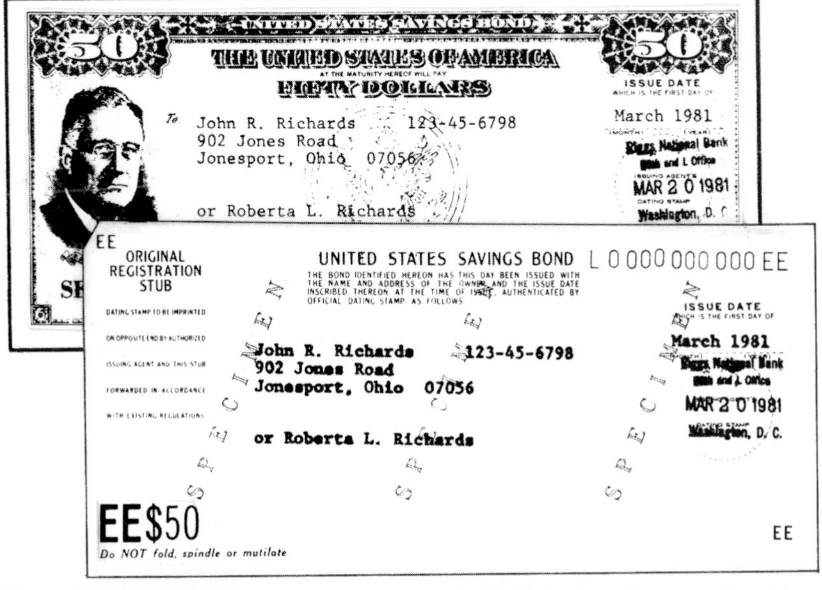

PAYROLL DEDUCTION PLANS

Good opportunities to save and/or invest are often found at your place of work. Many people save money by taking part in a **payroll deduction plan.** A signed agreement between you and the firm for which you work allows the company to deduct a set amount from your paycheck. These deductions are put into the savings/investment plan(s) of your choice and are usually listed on your paycheck's statement of earnings.

Some plans may be long-term. Some firms have a stock purchase program that lets you buy shares of company stock. Others let you buy mutual fund shares or U.S. savings bonds. Putting money in a firm's credit union, where it is always available, is a common choice. If you can take part in a payroll deduction plan, you should give it careful thought.

SAVINGS SAVVY

1. When you open your first savings account, how much you save each month is your choice. Your earnings, responsibilities, goals, and needs vary. A rule of thumb that many financial advisors suggest is to save 3 to 8 percent of your income after taxes. The important thing is that you pay yourself first. Make yourself save on a regular basis, even if, at first, the amount is less than 3 percent.

2. To help shop for and compare financial firms, check their **annual percentage yield (APY).** This yield is the number of dollars each $100 will earn if left in an account for one year. Usually, a higher yield is a plus.

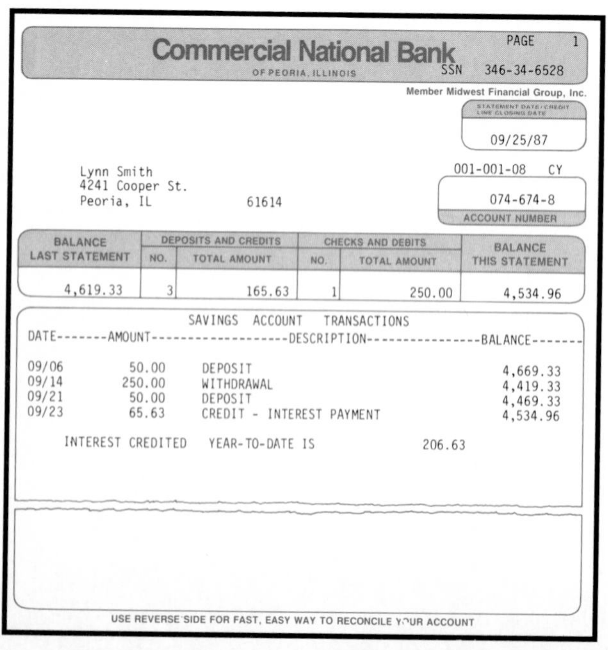

Commercial National Bank
OF PEORIA, ILLINOIS
PAGE 1
SSN 346-34-6528
Member Midwest Financial Group, Inc.

STATEMENT DATE/CREDIT LINE CLOSING DATE: 09/25/87

Lynn Smith
4241 Cooper St.
Peoria, IL 61614

001-001-08 CY
074-674-8
ACCOUNT NUMBER

BALANCE LAST STATEMENT	DEPOSITS AND CREDITS		CHECKS AND DEBITS		BALANCE THIS STATEMENT
	NO.	TOTAL AMOUNT	NO.	TOTAL AMOUNT	
4,619.33	3	165.63	1	250.00	4,534.96

SAVINGS ACCOUNT TRANSACTIONS

DATE	AMOUNT	DESCRIPTION	BALANCE
09/06	50.00	DEPOSIT	4,669.33
09/14	250.00	WITHDRAWAL	4,419.33
09/21	50.00	DEPOSIT	4,469.33
09/23	65.63	CREDIT - INTEREST PAYMENT	4,534.96

INTEREST CREDITED YEAR-TO-DATE IS 206.63

USE REVERSE SIDE FOR FAST, EASY WAY TO RECONCILE YOUR ACCOUNT

3. An emergency fund is a savings must. Its goal is to protect against emergencies—unplanned hospital bills, big car repairs, or a job layoff. Put this money in an account or plan where you can get it out quickly. How much you need in such an account depends on your situation. Do you have children? Are your parents willing and in a position to loan you money? Do you have health and life insurance and/or benefits that include unemployment insurance? Insurance and/or work benefits are an income source that can help you handle emergencies with ease. Insurance will be discussed in chapter 13.

4. Learn when interest is credited to your account. What are the interest payment dates? Even if interest is figured daily (day of deposit to day of withdrawal), it may be credited to your account once a month, every three or six months, or once a year. If you withdraw funds before the payment date, you may lose interest on the money for the whole interest time span. Unless it is an emergency, plan to take out money only after the payment dates.

5. To help you learn how fast your long-term savings and investments will grow, use the **Rule of 72.** Divide 72 by the rate of compound interest your savings and/or investments earn. The answer is roughly the number of years it will take your money to double. The rule does not apply to simple interest.

$$72 \div \text{Rate of compound interest} = \text{Approximate number of years for money to double}$$

Learn how interest is credited to your account. Compounded daily interest will accumulate faster than simple interest.

WORDS TO REMEMBER

annual percentage yield (APY)
canceled check
checking account
compound interest
credit
interest
liquidity
minimum balance
checking account
payroll deduction plan
rule of 72
savings account
simple interest

CHECKING YOUR UNDERSTANDING

1. What is the difference between simple and compound interest? Which one makes your savings produce more dollars? Briefly explain why.
2. You do not have a checking account and need to make a no-cash payment by mail. Explain how you can make the payment.
3. There are three types of endorsements to use when cashing a check. Name the three types and explain when to use each one.
4. What is a canceled check? An outstanding check?
5. What does the annual percentage yield (APY) tell you?
6. What is the Rule of 72, and what does it tell you?

APPLYING YOUR UNDERSTANDING

1. Assume you need to decide where to open a checking account. Choose and compare two to four financial firms (depending on how many are in your local area).

   Base your comparison on safety, services, charges, interest rates, and convenience. Limit your comparison of service charges and interest rates to only those that apply to checking accounts, including interest-earning checking accounts.

   Report your findings in chart form and make your choice.
2. Briefly, explain why it is important to learn when interest is credited to your savings account.
3. The saving and investing opportunities of a payroll deduction plan deserve your careful thought. Explain why.

Chapter 12
UNDERSTANDING AND USING CREDIT

Has this ever happened to you?

Mike was ecstatic when he heard the news. His parents told him that he may buy a car.

After reviewing his financial status, Mike decided that he will use 60 percent of his savings as a down payment. The balance will be paid with credit.

"Dad," Mike said, "I think I will compare the finance charges at the bank where I have my savings account with those of the dealer where I will buy the car. That will give me an idea what the installment loan will cost."

"That's good," replied Mike's father. "However, there is a lot more information that you will need to find out when you shop for your loan."

"What would that be?" asked Mike.

"Well, besides the finance charges, you will want to know what happens if you miss a payment. Also find out the time period of the contract."

"Good idea, Dad. Anything else?" Mike asked.

"Oh yes, check the contract to see what it states about repossession rights. Plus, if the car dealer is going to be the lender, find out if he will hold the contract or sell it to a finance bank," added Mike's father.

"There sure is a lot more to shopping for installment credit than a finance charge!" Mike sighed. "I am glad that you are going with me when I sign the contract!"

Have you ever shopped for an installment loan? What questions did you ask?

Why is it important to shop around for loans?

After reading this chapter, you will be able to

- identify types of consumer credit;
- evaluate the finance charge of a financial transaction involving credit;
- know what to do to establish good credit;
- explain how your credit history, good or bad, follows you wherever you go;
- know what indicators alert you to your overextending yourself or using too much credit.

You have probably heard or seen the statement *Buy now, pay later.* If you have taken advantage of this concept, you have used credit. When you use credit, you spend future income, dollars not yet earned. As defined in chapter 11, credit (loan) is an arrangement by which you get money, goods, or service now and pay for it later.

If used right, credit helps you reach your most important goals. It can help you continue your schooling, make big purchases, and handle big emergencies with ease. However, the abuse of credit creates problems and can lead to financial ruin.

The word credit comes from the Latin word *creditum,* which means trust. When you use credit, the other party trusts you and has confidence in your intention to make payment(s) when due.

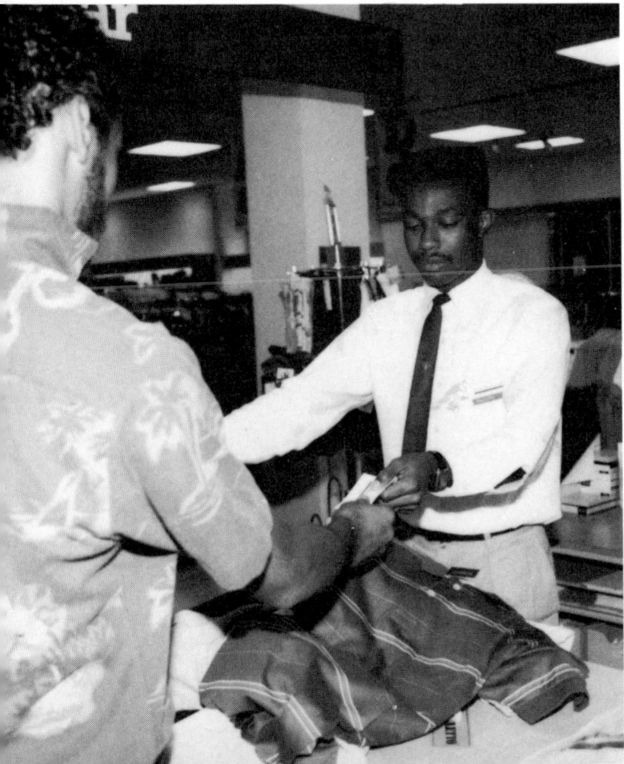

When you use credit, you are promising to pay with dollars not yet earned.

COMPARING CREDIT COSTS

In 1968, Congress passed the Truth in Lending Act. The purpose of this act is to state in understandable terms the cost of using **consumer credit,** the type of credit used by individuals and families. Prior to this legislation, firms could deceive you about the cost of using credit.

The Truth in Lending Act says that a credit contract must clearly state the **finance charge** in dollars. This charge must list the interest to be charged plus the other costs for a loan, such as, a credit investigation fee, life insurance (if wanted), service fees, and handling charges. Only mortgages are exempt from the law that requires the lender to state the finance charge in dollars.

The Truth in Lending Act requires lenders to tell consumers what the **annual percentage rate (APR)** of the loan will be. The APR is the finance charge stated as a percentage. It is the key figure to use to compare different lenders' credit costs. The higher the percentage rate, the more interest you will pay. For instance, a loan with an 18 percent APR has a higher interest rate than a loan with a 15 percent APR.

TYPES OF CREDIT

Consumer credit usually consists of sales and cash. Sales credit is usd to buy goods and services. Cash credit is money made available for your use. In the latter case you buy the use of money instead of goods or services.

SALES CREDIT

When you turn on the light, use the phone, or go to the dentist, you buy services with credit. In other words, you use or get the service before you pay for it. There is no charge for service credit if you pay the bill before its due date.

When you buy clothes, gas, a sofa, or a gas stove and "charge it," you buy goods with credit. Most people pay for large items, such as a car, stove, or stereo with credit.

You choose one of several payment plans when you pay for goods bought with credit. The most often used plans are the regular or single payment, the revolving or open-end, and the installment contract or closed-end.

Credit is often used to pay for large purchases such as a stereo, VCR, or television.

Regular or Single Payment Charge Account

A **single payment charge account** is what the name implies. You pay the bill in full within a certain time span, usually ten to thirty days after the billing date. Usually, there is no finance charge. Thus, the cost of the goods is the same as a cash sale.

You get a monthly bill listing your purchases and payments. It is wise to keep the charge receipts given to you at the time of the sale so you can check the accuracy of your bill.

Revolving or Open-end Charge Account

When you get a **revolving charge account,** the store sets a limit as to the maximum amount of credit you may use. You agree to make a required minimum monthly payment plus a finance charge on the unpaid balance. After you make your monthly payment, you may again charge goods up to the set dollar limit. The word open-end means that you can buy more goods so long as you do not exceed the set dollar limits.

A retailer, by law, must state both the monthly and annual percentage rates you pay on the unpaid balance. A 1½ percent monthly rate is an 18 percent annual (yearly) rate or 12 × 1½ or 1.5 percent = 18 percent. A 2 percent monthly rate is a 24 percent annual rate or 12 × 2. percent = 24 percent.

Retailers figure the finance charge in different ways. The monthly rate may be figured on the average daily balance, the opening unpaid balance, or the opening balance less payments made during the month.

With a revolving charge account, you may pay the bill in full within ten to thirty days as with the single payment account. If you do this, you pay no finance charge because there is no unpaid balance.

Some creditors let a single payment charge account become a revolving charge account if the bill is not paid in full within the ten to thirty days.

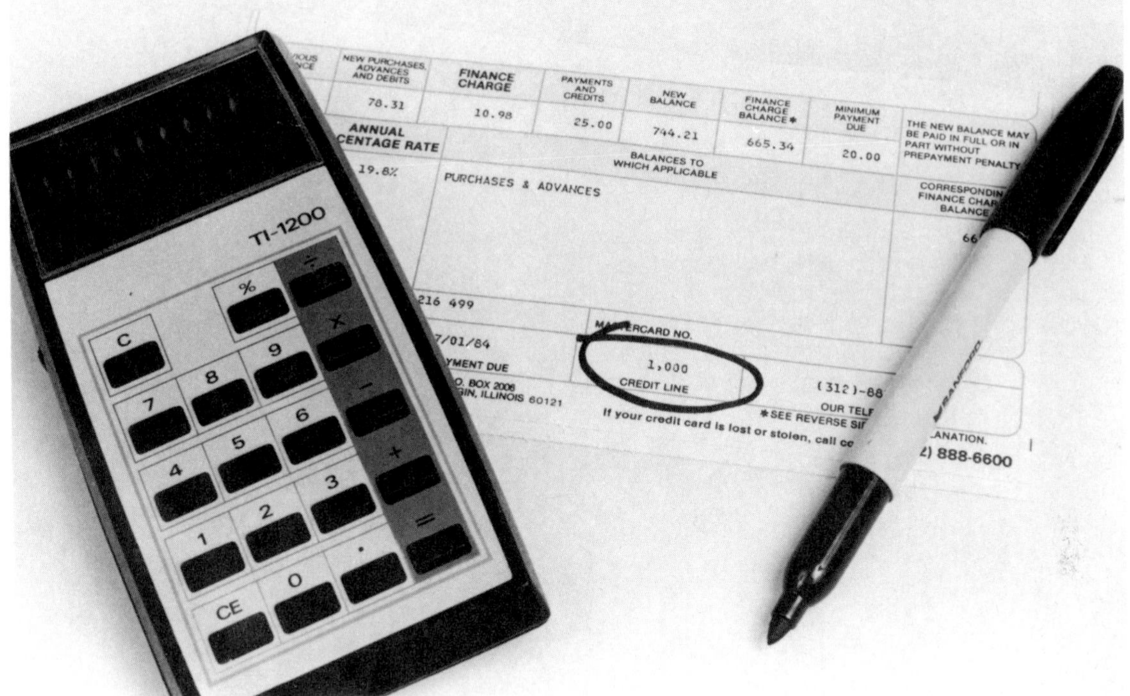

Many department stores offer their own revolving charge account. The store sets a limit as to the maximum amount of credit an individual may use.

Installment Credit or Closed-end Payment Plan

Installment credit usually involves a printed contract, or agreement, may need a down payment or trade-in, and requires the balance to paid in equal payments in a certain period of time. The finance charge is determined by the amount of money financed and the length of the payment period. The phrase closed-end means that the contract covers one purchase. This type of credit is used most often to buy things like a car, stove, TV set, stereo, or home computer.

The finance charge, when given as the annual percentage rate, can vary a lot. You do not own the goods until the contract is paid in full. If you do not keep the terms of the contract, the seller can take back or repossess the goods.

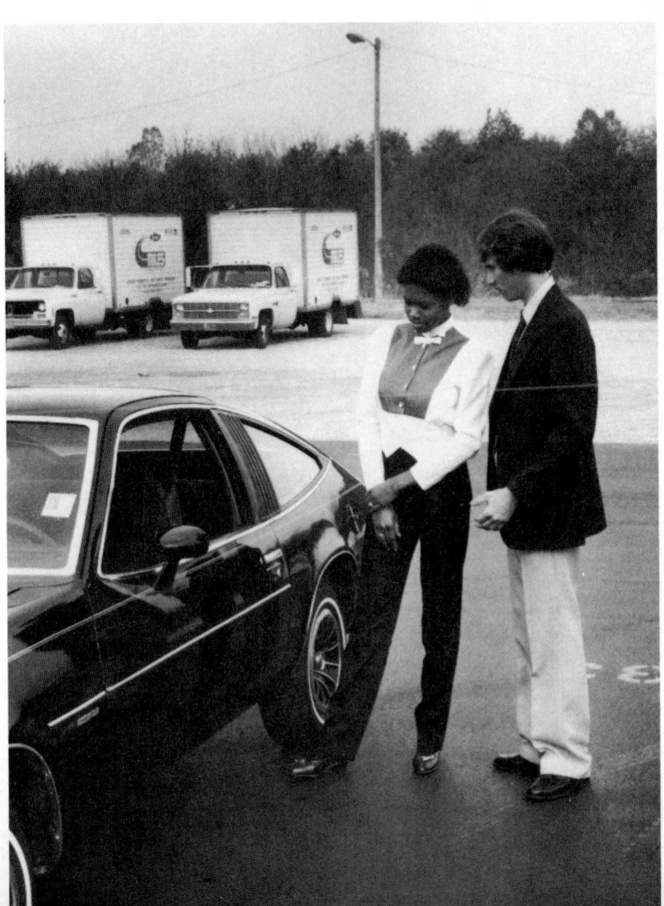

Major ticket items such as a car, computer, or membership to a health club offer installment credit. You sign a contract and agree to pay the balance in equal payments in a certain period of time.

Below is a list of Dos and Don'ts to consider before you sign any contract:

1. For your protection, do not sign a contract until you have read it with care and understand its terms.
2. Do not sign a contract with blank spaces. Details added after you sign it can change the terms of the contract.
3. Before you sign a credit contract, be sure the APR you talked about with the sales person is the same as the APR in the contract.
4. Check the contract to be sure the last payment is not too much higher (a "balloon payment") than the other payments. A balloon payment must be disclosed as part of the payment schedule. The cost for refinancing a balloon payment, if you cannot pay it when due, must also be disclosed.
5. If the lender will not give you a copy of the contract, take your business elsewhere.
6. Do not take on monthly payments that you cannot make with ease. Be honest with yourself about the size of payment you can afford to make.
7. Take the time to shop for and compare credit. A retailer's price for goods or services may be a "good deal," but the credit terms may be costly. Ask about the cost of the retailer's sales credit and two or three other lenders before you sign a contract. The finance for cash credit (loan) may be less than that for sales credit.

Credit Cards

A **credit card** identifies you as approved for a set amount of credit by the issuer of the card. Cards are usually one of two types, single purpose (one company) cards or multipurpose cards.

Single Purpose (One Company) Credit Cards

A single purpose or one company credit card is issued by firms—airlines, oil and phone companies, car rental agencies, motel and hotel chains, and retail stores. The card's use is limited to the goods and services offered by the firm or store.

If you use the card, you will get a monthly bill listing the goods you bought, the payment, and a due date. You will pay interest for a late payment. Extended payment (revolving charge account) is possible with some retail store credit cards.

Before you buy on credit consider the finance charge that you must pay for the use of the money.

Multipurpose Credit Cards

Many kinds of goods and services are available to you worldwide with a multipurpose credit card. These cards are issued by banks and companies. Company cards, often called travel and entertainment cards, are American Express, Diners Club and Carte Blanche. Widely used bank cards are VISA and MasterCard. The card issuer gives you information about the retailers who accept their cards.

You pay a yearly membership charge for a company card. The monthly bill lists the goods and services bought and includes a receipt for each. The company expects payment by the due date. If you fail to do this, you will make a late payment and may be denied credit in the future.

The billing procedure for the bank cards is much like that for company cards. However, the method of payment is more flexible with a bank card. If you pay the bill in full by the due date there is no additional charge. If you like, you can use a bank card like a retail store revolving charge card. You have a minimum monthly payment, a limit on how much you may charge, and a finance charge you pay on the unpaid balance. Many times banks charge a yearly fee for VISA and MasterCard.

Guidelines for Credit Card Use

1. It is wise to choose and use only credit cards that meet certain needs and that help you to manage money better. Credit counselors suggest that you use only two or three cards. A good mix of cards might be a multipurpose card for traveling and unplanned expenses, a gas credit card, and a card from the store where you buy most often.
2. Sign a credit card as soon as you get it in the mail.
3. Handle a credit card as though it were cash. Do not leave a card "sitting out" at home or in a hotel or motel room. Do not leave a credit card in the glove box of your car.
4. Keep a good record of your credit card spending. This will help you not to be shocked when you get a high bill.
5. Plan for the payment of an item with credit before you buy it.
6. Look at your monthly statement with care, especially after travel or holiday shopping.
7. Do not give a credit card number to someone who asks for it by phone. It is alright to use a credit card number to buy goods by phone if you know the retailer and ask to make an order.
8. Make a list of your cards and account numbers in case you lose the cards or they are stolen. Include, also, the name and phone number of each issuer. Keep this list in your current file.
9. Cut a credit card in half before you throw it out.
10. Report a lost or stolen card promptly by phone. Then confirm your call with a follow-up letter. Be sure to keep a copy in your file. If you do this, you may avoid paying $50 to a company or bank, which is their charge to you if someone wrongfully uses your card.

CASH CREDIT

Cash credit is a loan, money made available for your use. You pay a finance charge for the use of the money. The cost of a loan varies between lenders. Thus, it is best to shop around before you choose the lender that is best for you.

Sources of cash credit include commercial banks, savings and loans, mutual savings banks, credit unions, some credit cards, licensed loan or finance companies, the cash value of life insurance policies, your family and friends, and pawnshops.

Borrowers' credit ratings and lenders' terms of loans vary. Thus, one type lender is not the best source of a loan for everyone.

Commercial Banks

Commercial banks are the largest source of consumer credit. A bank is where most people first look to borrow money. If the bank thinks you are a good credit risk (able to pay back the money), it will loan you money.

Most borrowers pay back bank loans with monthly payments. It is much like buying goods or services with installment sales credit. The type of loan determines the length of the payment period.

The bank will approve your loan request more quickly and may charge you less if you have **collateral** to back or secure the payment of your loan. Collateral is something of value such as a savings account, stocks, bonds, a car, a home, or other real estate. The bank holds title to your collateral until you pay back the loan in full and then gives it back to you. If you do not pay back the loan within the stated time period, the bank takes possession of your collateral in the amount of the loan not paid plus the finance charge.

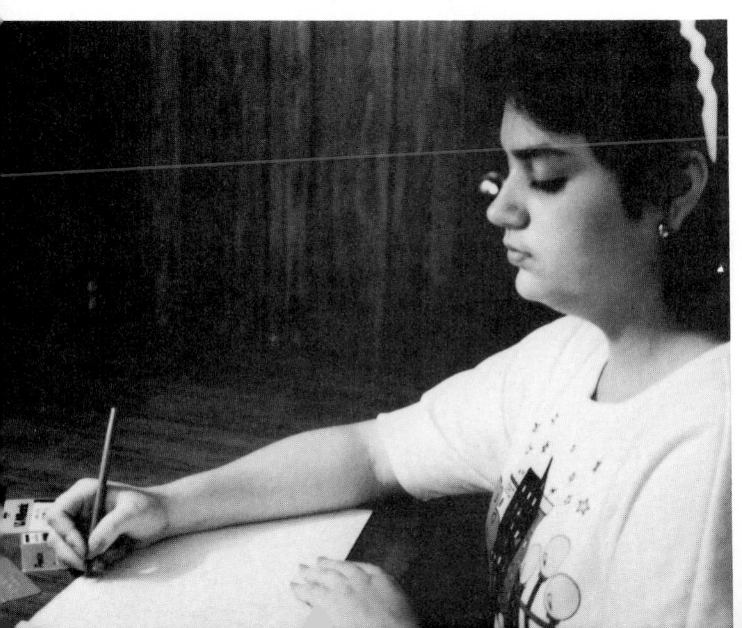

Make a list of your credit cards, expiration date and account numbers in case you lose the cards or they are stolen.

Savings and Loan Associations and Mutual Savings Banks

These financial firms specialize in loans for home mortgages and home improvement. They also make school loans and loans to customers who have saving accounts.

Credit Unions

If you are a member of a credit union, it is probably the best place to get a loan. Usually, interest rates are lower than those of other lenders. Free credit life insurance is usually part of the loan "package."

Licensed Loan and Finance Companies

These companies make small to moderate loans. Usually, the requirements for credit are not as strict as with other lenders. Because of this fact, the finance charge is higher than at most other credit sources.

Cash Value of Life Insurance

Some life insurance policies have a surrender cash value with a cash loan benefit. Each year the policy is in force, the cash value rises. The amount of cash value varies between types of insurance. Chapter 13 will discuss this at length.

Family and Friends

Only you know if you can ask a family member or friend to loan you money. Mutual feelings of respect and trust and how "well off" a person is financially are involved. Negotiate the loan on a businesslike basis. Be sure there is complete agreement on the terms of payment by both of you. This will lessen the chance for undue concern and possible friction.

Credit Cards

Usually, if you have a bank credit card (VISA and MasterCard), you can get a $500 to $1,000 loan. Before you ask for a loan, check the finance charge. You may pay an initial fee, a yearly interest rate of 12 to 18 percent on the unpaid balance, and a late fee if you miss a monthly payment.

The travel and entertainment card companies may offer loans (cash) in limited amounts at travel service offices, hotels and motels, airline counters, and at travelers' check dispensers.

Pawnbrokers

A pawnbroker loans you less than 50 percent of the value of your property—jewelry, an instrument, camera, and so forth. The pawnbroker sets the value, keeps your property, and sets the date by which you are to pay back the loan plus a finance charge, which is high. If you fail to meet the terms set, the pawnbroker keeps your property and will probably sell it.

Loan Sharks

A loan shark is someone who loans money at an excessive rate of interest. The loan shark is included for only one reason, which is to advise you never to use a loan shark as a lender. The finance charge is so high it is illegal. These high rates make it impossible for most people to pay back their loans. The result is that these people only go further into debt.

Credit Bureau

To make a credit check on each consumer takes time and is costly. Usually, granters of sales and cash credit cannot afford to make such checks. Thus, a credit bureau meets the need.

A **credit bureau** is a center for consumer information. It collects and keeps facts about your financial transactions. A credit bureau will know where you have loans and credit accounts, their dollar limits, balances due, and how promptly you pay bills. Your report also has your address, Social Security number, and sometimes the name of your employer. All this information is your **credit history.**

If you are denied credit, you are entitled by law to look at your files in a credit bureau.

When you apply for credit, the lender checks with the credit bureau. The bureau does not decide if you get credit nor does it give you a credit rating. A **credit rating** is how a potential lender of sales or cash credit rates you as a risk. This rating can range from "a prompt payer of debts" to "an always late payee." After getting the credit bureau's report and looking it over, the lender decides whether or not to give you credit.

Local bureaus are part of a national network of bureaus. This network helps local bureaus keep current files on a highly mobile population. Good or bad, your credit follows you wherever you go. Consumers have access by law to their files in a credit bureau.

A FAVORABLE CREDIT HISTORY

You create your own credit history and credit rating. Together, they are important financial assets and should be developed with care. Do not let the idea of setting up a good credit history scare you. It is not hard to do. If you follow several steps, you can be well on your way to becoming a good credit risk.

First, open a checking and savings account and keep the accounts active. Pay your bills by check and do not overdraw the account. Make small savings deposits on a regular basis.

The next step is to apply for a charge account at a department store or other retail business. If you drive, apply for an oil company credit card. Use your bank accounts as references. Pay the monthly bill(s) promptly.

Then, in the future, when you need more sales or cash credit, you can use the bank, store, and/or oil company as credit references.

The stronger your credit history and rating are, the more sales and cash credit will be available to you.

USING CREDIT

When used in a responsible way—with care, control, and judgement—credit helps you manage your finances with success. Remember though, that the use of credit is not free. The price of what you buy goes up by the amount of the finance charge.

Before you buy goods or services, plan for the payment. Credit counselors say that you should not let your monthly payments due on credit accounts and installment loans (excluding a home mortgage) be more than 20 percent of your monthly net pay.

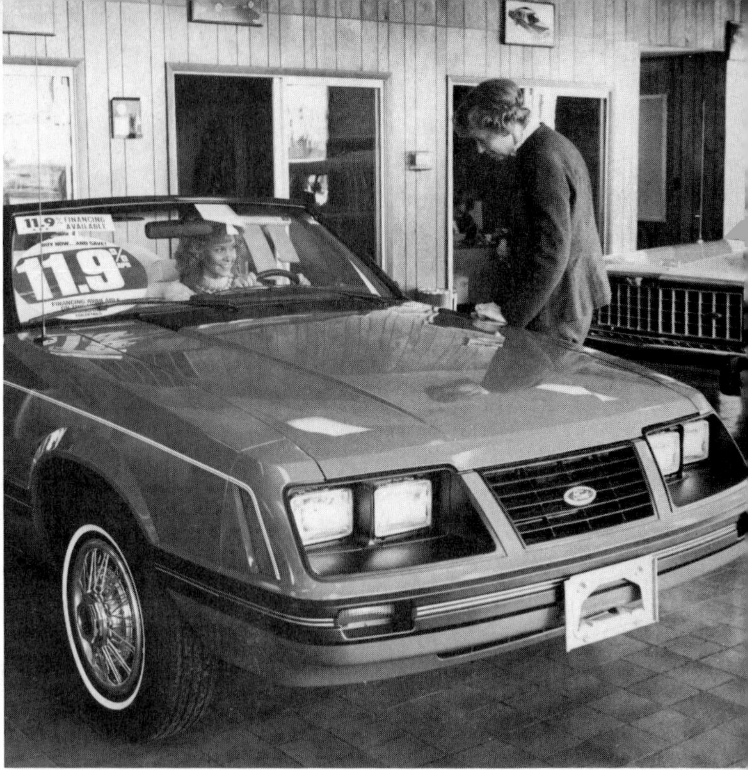

When making a large purchase, such as a car, shop for your loan. Compare interest rates and services from the various lending institutions.

ADVANTAGES OF USING CREDIT

The advantages of using credit are as follows:

1. The use of a credit or charge card is a convenience. You need to carry only a small amount of cash, and you can order goods by phone and mail.
2. If you have a problem with or want to return goods, service is often better if the goods were charged rather than paid for with cash.
3. You can save money on things you really need or want by buying them during sales.
4. A loan for school expenses is an investment in your future.
5. Combined, your canceled checks and the detailed monthly bills are a good record of your spending.
6. You can use credit for emergencies when savings are insufficient to pay for all the expenses.
7. When you unexpectedly find something you need but do not have enough cash with you to pay for it, you can use your credit.
8. When you set up a household, buy a home, and/or raise a family, costs are high. Knowing how to use credit wisely is helpful during these high-cost years.

DISADVANTAGES OF USING CREDIT

As in most cases, there are "two sides to the story." There are disadvantages to weigh before you use credit.

1. You are spending future income. This lessens your financial flexibility in the future. Are the goods or service worth this loss?
2. Easy credit makes it too easy to spend money. If you tend to buy on impulse, this weakness and easy credit could be disastrous.
3. The use of credit costs money. You need to decide whether or not the goods are worth the additional expense.
4. If you do not make all the payments scheduled in your contract, you may lose the goods and payments already made.

WHAT TO DO IF YOU NEED HELP

Hopefully, you will never be caught in a credit crunch. Hopefully, the size of your total debt will not overwhelm you. If you see that this is happening to you, though, do not panic and do not be embarrassed to ask for help.

Make an appointment at a nonprofit, consumer credit counseling service for help. Their one goal is to help people in financial trouble. For the name of the service located in your area, write to:

National Foundation for Consumer Credit
1819 H Street N.W.
Washington, D.C. 20006

You know you are in or heading for a credit crunch if you

1. pay more than 20 percent of your monthly net income on credit accounts and installment loans (excluding a home mortgage);
2. use savings account money to pay bills;
3. pay bills after due dates;
4. rely on credit card cash advances to pay bills;
5. choose stores for their easy credit;
6. argue with your spouse about money;
7. consider a second mortgage to consolidate debts.

To avoid trouble with debt, do not let your credit accounts and installment loans be more than twenty percent of your monthly net pay.

MANAGING YOUR RESOURCES

Do you like a challenge? Do you like to meet deadlines and solve problems? Are you the type of person who likes to set plans into action and evaluate the results? If so, a career in the consumer- and management-related areas may be for you.

Whether you manipulate numbers or data, give directions to workers, or show and sell goods or services, employees in this area need strong math, oral, and writing skills. While you are still in school, take the opportunity to enroll in courses, such as math, speech, and English, which can help you develop and polish your skills in these areas. In addition, get business experience by taking a part-time job in a retail store. Or get involved in a school club or a home economics related work program. These activities can give you the training and preparation required for many of the jobs in the consumer and management area.

Entry Level Jobs
Account executive
Bank teller
Cashier/clerk, sales
Consumer service representative
Interviewer
Manufacturer's representative
Sales representative

Jobs Requiring Additional Training
Administrative analyst
Advertising specialist
Bookkeeper
Computer programmer
Customer representative
Demonstrator
Financial consultant
Insurance salesperson
Magazine writer
Office manager
Publicity director

Jobs Requiring a Degree
Consumer information specialist
Data center director
Economist
Family service center director
Home economist
Marketing manager
Public relations coordinator
Teacher
Test kitchen home economist

For additional information you may want to check newspaper employment listings, check the career section at the local library, and write to:

Institute of Life Insurance
277 Park Avenue
New York, New York 10017

American Bankers Association
1120 Connecticut Avenue, N.W.
Washington, D.C. 20036

THE LAW AND CREDIT

Today, there are laws that help to protect you, the consumer. This is important because there has been an increase in the use of credit in our society, and because of the differences that exist between the types and charges for credit.

Familiarize yourself with the credit legislation in the chart "U.S. Credit Legislation in Brief." These laws help to inform and protect you.

U.S. CREDIT LEGISLATION IN BRIEF

ACT (date effective)	MAJOR PROVISIONS
TRUTH IN LENDING (July 1, 1969)	• Provides specific cost disclosure requirements for the annual percentage rate and the finance charge as a dollar amount • Requires disclosure of other loan terms and conditions • Regulates the advertising of credit terms • Provides the right to cancel a contract when certain real estate is used as security
(January 25, 1971)	• Prohibits credit card issuers from sending unrequested cards • Limits a cardholder's liability for unauthorized use of a card to $50
FAIR CREDIT REPORTING ACT (April 24, 1971)	• Requires disclosure to consumers of the name and address of any consumer reporting agency which supplied reports used to deny credit, insurance, or employment • Gives a consumer the right to know what is in his/her file, have incorrect information reinvestigated and removed, and includes his/her version of a disputed item in the file • Requires credit reporting agencies to send the consumer's version of a disputed item to certain businesses or creditors • Sets forth identification requirements for consumers wishing to inspect their files • Requires that consumers be notified when an investigative report is being made • Limits the time certain information can be kept in a credit file
FAIR CREDIT BILLING ACT (October 28, 1975)	• Establishes procedures for consumers and creditors to follow when billing errors occur on periodic statements for revolving credit accounts • Requires creditors to send a statement setting forth these procedures to consumers periodically • Allows consumers to withhold payment for faulty or defective goods or services (within certain limitations) when purchased with a credit card • Requires creditor to promptly credit customers' accounts and to return overpayments if requested
EQUAL CREDIT OPPORTUNITY ACT (October 28, 1975)	• Prohibits credit discrimination based on sex and marital status • Prohibits creditors from requiring women to reapply for credit upon a change in marital status • Requires creditors to inform applicants of acceptance or rejection of their credit application within 30 days of receiving a completed application • Requires creditors to provide a written statement of the reasons for adverse action
(March 23, 1977)	• Prohibits credit discrimination based on race, national origin, religion, age, or the receipt of public assistance
(June 1, 1977)	• Requires creditors to report information on an account to credit bureaus in the names of both husband and wife if both use the account and both are liable for it
FAIR DEBT COLLECTION PRACTICES ACT (March 20, 1978)	• Prohibits abusive, deceptive, and unfair practices by debt collectors • Establishes procedures for debt collectors contacting a credit user • Restricts debt collector contacts with a third party • Specifies that payment for several debts be applied as the consumer wishes and that no monies be applied to a debt in dispute

THE COST OF CREDIT

Consumer credit is a convenience that can be costly. Learn to ask questions, read contracts, and compare the costs and terms involved. In that way, you can be a wise manager of your money. Below is a list of facts to think about when you shop for credit.

• Often you have a choice about the length of the payment period. In order to make a wise decision, you need to consider two things: (1) the amount of the monthly payment you can make without hardship; (2) the cost of the credit. Often a person thinks only about the monthly payment. This can be costly. If you choose three years instead of one and a half years to pay back a loan, the total interest paid can increase more than 100 percent.

• If you use a revolving charge account, keep a record of the monthly finance charge you pay on the unpaid balance. This charge appears on your monthly bill. If you pay only the required minimum monthly payment over a long period of time and continue to charge goods and services, the cost of this credit may shock you.

• All lenders must figure the annual percentage rate (APR) the same way. Thus, you can use the percentages charged to compare the costs of credit.

However, even with the same APR, the cost of a revolving charge account can vary. Stores use different methods to figure the finance charge. One store may compute the charge for your account on the first day of the month. Another store may deduct your monthly payment before it figures the charge. The charge is less at the second store.

Usually, you pay the finance charge on the average daily balance with a bank card. Thus, if you are able, make your payment as promptly as you can to reduce your unpaid balance. This results in a lower average daily balance than if you delay payment.

• If you qualify for a loan from a financial firm (cash credit), the cost usually is less than retail installment credit (sales credit).

• During a period of inflation (prices rise) or projected inflation, ads will often encourage you to "buy now to avoid a price increase." This is not as simple as it sounds.

You first need to know the total finance charge in dollars for the credit you need to buy now. Then you need to compare this amount with the price increase (in dollars) of the goods or services you want to buy. You cannot predict the price increase accurately.

• The nation's general economy can affect how available money is for consumer loans. If creditors (lenders) can get money at low interest rates, money for consumer loans is quite available. However, when the government restricts the nation's money supply, there is less money available. When this happens, money for consumers becomes scarce, and consumer loans are harder to negotiate. Even if you are a good credit risk, you may be denied a loan. When this happens, it is due to economic conditions, not your credit rating.

Review CHAPTER 12

WORDS TO REMEMBER

annual percentage rate (APR)
collateral
consumer credit
credit bureau
credit card
credit history
credit rating
finance charge
installment credit
regular or single payment charge account
revolving charge account

CHECKING YOUR UNDERSTANDING

1. What is the key figure to use when comparing different lenders' credit costs? Define it.
2. Consumer credit is generally of two types. What are they? Define each one.
3. When you buy goods and charge them, you can choose one of three payment plans: (1) a regular or single payment charge account; (2) a revolving or open-end charge account; (3) installment credit or closed-end payment plan. Briefly explain each one and list the pros and cons of each.
4. It is wise to choose and use only credit cards that meet a certain need and that help you to manage money with success. Credit counselors suggest you use only two or three credit cards. Which three types of cards are they?
5. Using credit has pros and cons. List four advantages and give examples of two disadvantages.

APPLYING YOUR UNDERSTANDING

1. Assume you bought a sofa bed for your apartment. If you decide to use an installment contract for payment, list four to six *DOs* and *DON'Ts* you should check before you sign the contract.
2. Pretend you have just received your first credit card. List six to eight guidelines that you should follow for responsible credit card use.
3. Assume you are a good credit risk and need to make a $350 purchase at a department store. Compare the finance charge involved for each of the following three methods of payment: (A) a department store revolving charge account; (B) a department store installment contract; (C) a cash loan of $350. Get the finance charge information at a local department store, bank, and credit union. Summarize this information with a chart, choose one method of payment, and explain your choice.
4. You realize you use too much credit and need help to learn how to use less with control and judgment. Whom can you contact for help?

Chapter 13
INSURANCE AND INVESTMENTS

Has this ever happened to you?

On the way home from school one afternoon, Gini and her friend Mark are eagerly talking about their birthdays next month when both of them will be able to apply for a driver license.

"I can hardly wait to get my driver license," said Gini. "It will be nice to be able to go to the store or volleyball practice without having to rely on someone else for a ride."

"I know what you mean," replied Mark. "But have you shopped around for car insurance? For a teenage driver it is very expensive."

"Oh I know," stated Gini. "It is a good thing that we took the driver education course that was offered last summer. Plus, with our good grade point averages, we will be able to get a student discount."

"Is that right?" questioned Mark.

"Sure," replied Gini, "plus, some insurance companies give discounts to nonsmokers too."

"This is great news," exclaimed Mark. "As soon as I get home, I am going to call my insurance agent to see how these discounts will affect my premium. I sure could use a reduction in the cost of my insurance!"

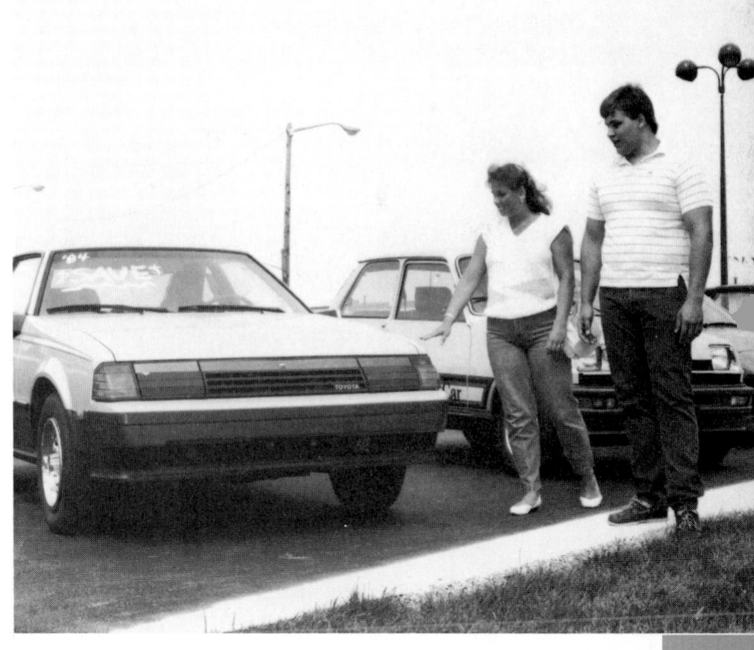

Have you ever experienced that doing something well proved beneficial at a later date?

Have you been in a situation where you learned that you could have saved money if you had prepared yourself to qualify for possible discounts or reductions?

After reading this chapter, you will be able to

- explain why insurance (life, health, auto, and household) is an essential part of a financial plan;
- understand how an automobile insurance firm sets a policy premium;
- identify investment opportunities;
- explain the advantages of an Individual Retirement Account (IRA).

Probably you or a member of your family has bought some type of insurance. Whether it was for car or life, health, or disability, insurance became a part of a financial plan.

The main reason to have **insurance** is to have financial protection against the risks, mishaps, and/or uncertainties of life. These include an illness, accident, disability, an early death, theft, or natural disaster. If one or more of these occur, money problems and the loss of life can result. Thus, an insurance plan can give security and financial help.

Different types of insurance plans can be bought—life, car, health, household, disability or income protection, and Social Security. With these types of insurance an individual, couple, or family can develop an insurance plan to meet their needs.

Before you read about the different types of insurance, it will help you if you learn a few insurance terms. The chart on this page lists the most common terms used.

INSURANCE TERMS

Beneficiary: The person the policyholder names to get the money (face value) after his or her death. More than one beneficiary may be named.

Cash value or cash surrender: The value of a policy a policyholder gets if he or she stops premium payments before the policy's maturity date. It is also the loan value of a policy and usually referred to as the savings.

Face value: The amount paid to a beneficiary after the policyholder's death. It is also the amount paid to the policyholder when a policy matures (the end of a certain time period).

Insurance policy: A legal contract between the policyholder (the insured) and the insurance firm.

Premium: The price or cost of the insurance or what you pay for a policy's protection.

Whether you are buying life insurance, health insurance, car insurance or property insurance, you are buying a program that means savings and protection for you and your family.

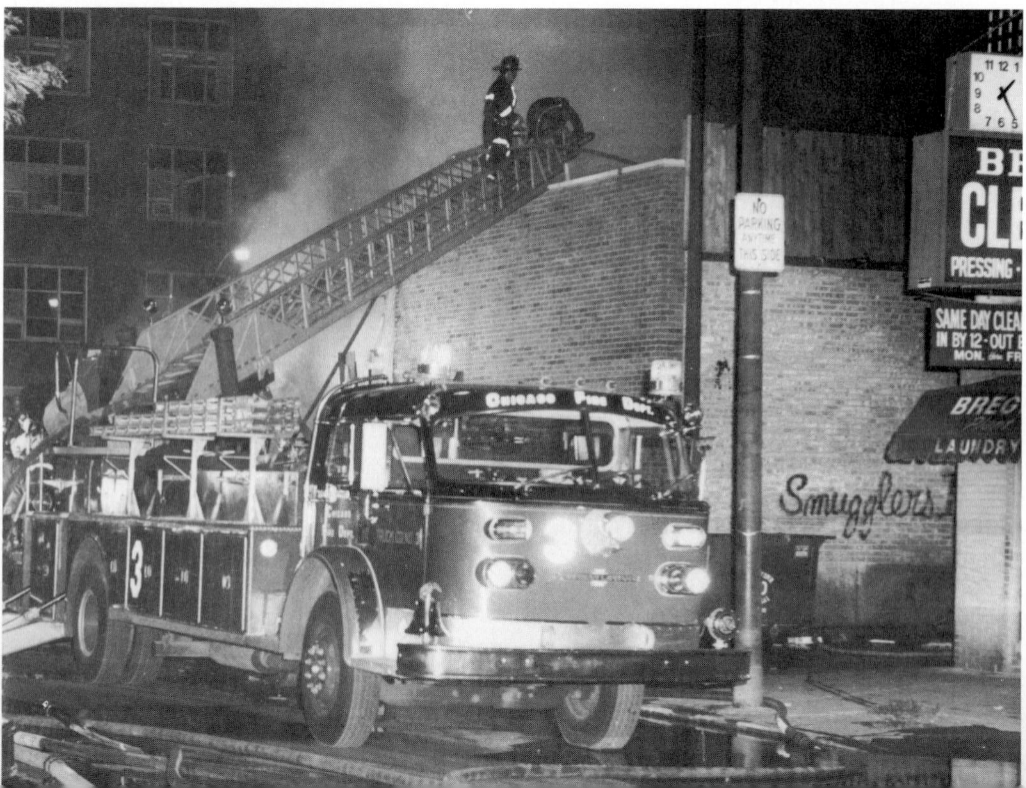

LIFE INSURANCE

Most life insurance policies are bought to replace lost earnings in the event of an early death of a family wage earner or the homemaker. The **insurance policy** pays a certain sum of tax-free cash if the policyholder dies.

All insurance policies do one or two things. The policy gives financial protection only, or it gives financial protection plus a built up cash value (savings).

Three basic types of life insurance—term, whole life, and endowment—have been offered for many years. In addition, variations, or combinations, of these are available. In 1979 universal life insurance was introduced.

The **premium** for, or the cost of, all policies is based on a mortality table. The table lists by age the projected death rate per thousand persons. As required, this table is updated. The current table is the Commissioners 1980 Standard Ordinary Mortality Table.

Regardless of the type of policy you buy, the cost of life insurance goes up each year. On each birthday you are one year older and, thence, have one less year to live.

TERM INSURANCE

Term insurance, as the name implies, is life insurance for one or more years. It gives the most protection for your dollar. The premium buys protection only. At the end of the term, the coverage stops, and, if renewed, the cost goes up since the insured is now older.

Two important options that merit some thought when you buy a term plan are renewability and convertibility. A renewable option lets you renew the policy without a doctor's exam. A convertible option lets you change a term plan to another type of life plan without a doctor's exam. Financial planners say that you should have both options included when you buy a term plan.

Term insurance is a less expensive way for a young family on a small budget and with young children to have financial protection. A large sum of cash for dependent survivors is possible even if a paycheck makes it hard to save. This is called "creating an instant estate."

The variations of basic term life plans are annual renewable term life, decreasing term life, and level term life. Before you buy any insurance plan, check and compare the costs and benefits of each type of plan.

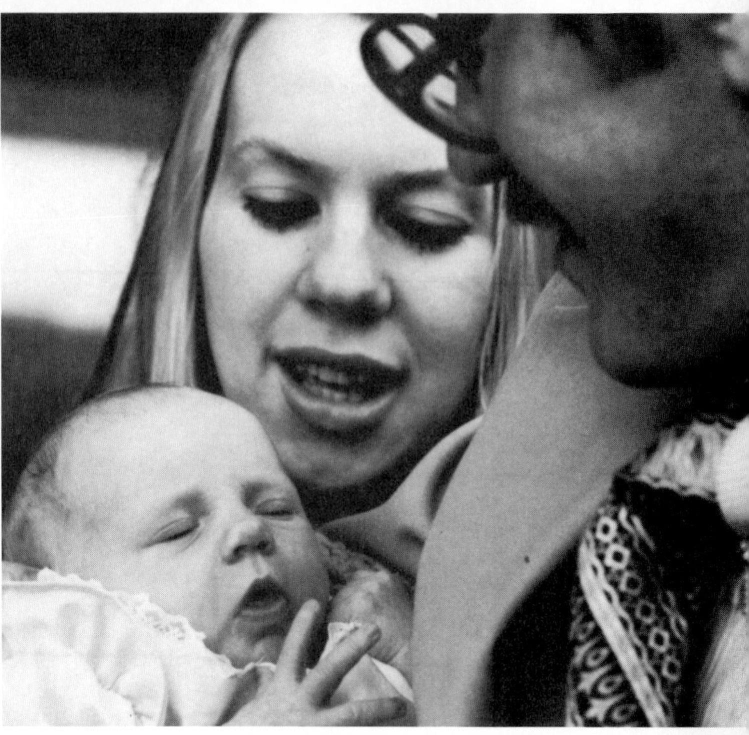

A young family can change their life insurance coverage with a convertible term policy as their family responsibilities change.

WHOLE LIFE INSURANCE

Whole life insurance is also called straight life or ordinary life. The face value and cost remain the same for your lifetime. The cost is based on the policy's face value plus your age and health when you buy the plan. Whole life costs more than term insurance.

Over a period of years a cash value builds up. It builds up slowly and is small in the first several years. Many financial planners say that you should consider a plan with a cash value only if you are going to keep it for fifteen years, twenty years, or longer.

For many years whole life was the type of insurance sold most often. However, due to inflation, sales of this type of plan has declined. Savings and investments may earn more than the cash value of a whole life policy.

A variation of whole life is a limited payment life plan. Limited payment life requires that all the payments be made within a certain time span—twenty or thirty years or until age sixty-five. People who want less financial responsibility during retirement choose this plan rather than whole life.

ENDOWMENT LIFE INSURANCE

An endowment life plan provides payment of its face value to the policyholder. A policy usually matures after fifteen or twenty years or when the policyholder is sixty-five. The cost is very high and the cash value builds up faster than with other types of plans.

When the policy matures, the total cash paid equals the face value. When the policyholder is paid the face value, the insurance protection stops.

UNIVERSAL LIFE INSURANCE

The newest and most innovative type of life insurance is universal life. It combines cash value, or savings, with term coverage. With this plan the cash value earns a higher rate of interest than other cash value plans. You may add to the cash value as desired, as long as you keep the amount of the plan's face value higher than its total savings.

As your needs change, you may, within limits, raise or lower your coverage and cost. Also, your cost for a loan against the cash value is lower than for other types of plans.

Whole life insurance offers a savings and death benefit package. The accumulated premium payments can be returned to you when you cash in the policy or when it matures.

GROUP LIFE INSURANCE

Group life insurance is offered to employees by some companies and unions and by professional, alumni, and fraternal groups to their members. If you are able to take part in a group life plan, it is wise to do so. This applies to both parents in two-income families.

Some firms pay the whole cost while others share the costs of the plan. The cost is small. Employees often can buy additional life insurance and add it to their firm's paid coverage.

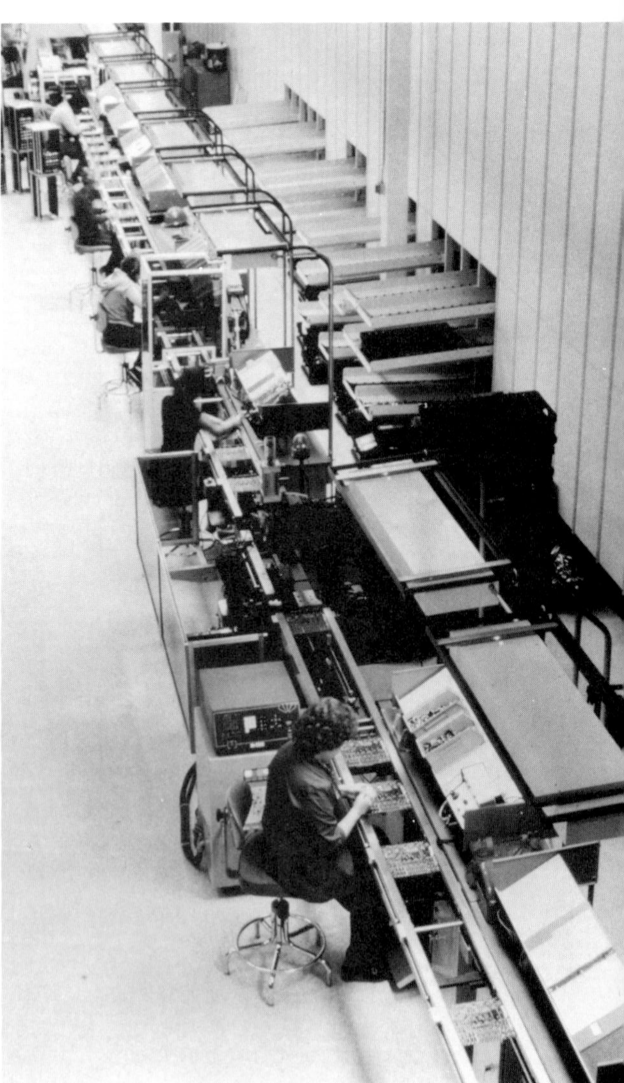

Many employers offer group life insurance to their employees.

SOCIAL SECURITY

Social Security had its start in 1935. Its goal was to give a cash benefit to raise retirement income after age sixty-five. Through the years its benefits were increased. Now they include survivors' benefits, disability income, and health insurance for the elderly.

Both employees and employers pay money to Social Security. Self-employed persons also pay the tax. This money is the source of payments to those who now get benefits. When you retire, workers and employers at that time will fund your benefits.

There is concern about there being enough funds for future Social Security payments. The main concern is the ratio of workers who pay the tax for each person who get benefits. During the early years of the program, this ratio was about sixteen to one. In 1980 the ratio was about three to one. It is thought that it may drop to two to one in the future. This belief is based on the premise that fewer babies are being born, and more people now live longer. This means there may be fewer workers to pay into the fund and a larger group to get payments.

It is doubtful the Social Security program will end. However, over a number of years it may change. Whatever the outcome, it is wise to prepare your own retirement program based on the money you control yourself.

How to Qualify for Social Security

When you are first hired in a job covered by Social Security, you will apply for a Social Security ID card. The number on the card is your Social Security number. It is yours for your lifetime.

Each year your employer reports your pay to the Social Security office in Baltimore, Maryland. Your lifetime earnings record is kept at this office. Job changes and/or changes of address do not affect your record. All Social Security earnings reports go to Baltimore.

It is most important your earnings record is accurate. When you (or your family) ask for benefits, Social Security will check your record to learn whether you worked long enough to get benefits and to determine the amount of the benefit(s) you will get.

Social Security Survivors' Benefits

Social Security survivors' benefits provide payments to qualifying workers and their families. For instance, a parent's employment includes Social Security coverage. If one parent dies, the other parent and children may be able to get survivors' benefits. Qualifying widows, widowers, and parents may also be able to get benefits.

Later in this chapter Social Security benefits that add to retirement income, disability income, and health plans for the elderly will be discussed.

A social security number is needed for everyone who works. The number on the card is yours for your lifetime.

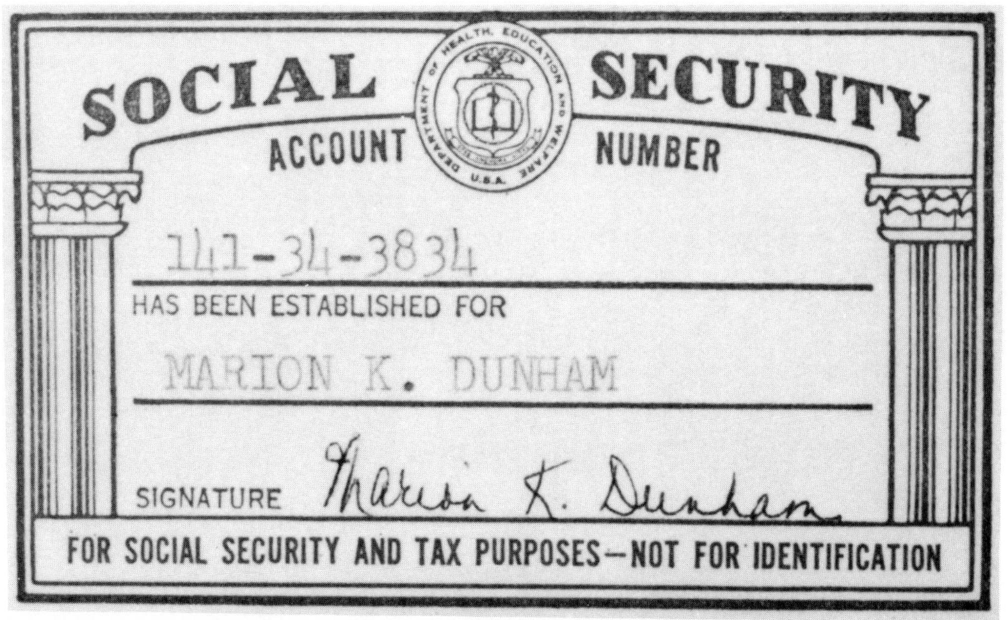

CAR INSURANCE

When you are behind the wheel of a car, there is a lot more involved than getting to your destination. Is the car safe to drive? Are you a safe, thoughtful, and alert driver? And are you prepared for an accident?

If an accident occurs, will you be able to pay for injuries and damages that might happen to you or others, to their cars, and to their property? The answer is probably no, unless you have insurance. Such possibilities are, of course, the main goal of car insurance.

Five basic types of car insurance can be bought: liability (bodily injury and property damage), medical, collision, comprehensive, and protection against uninsured motorists.

LIABILITY COVERAGE

Liability insurance applies to people and property. If an accident is your fault, you are legally bound to pay for bodily injury and property damage.

Bodily injury coverage protects you if you harm or kill a person with your car. It applies to persons in your car, those in another car, and to pedestrians. Financial advisers will tell you to carry a large amount of this insurance. Ask about the cost of different amounts of coverage. More coverage does not always mean a correspondingly higher cost.

Property damage liability applies if your car harms another's property—a car, building, fence, telephone pole, wall, and so forth.

The amount of liability coverage is usually stated in three figures. For instance, 10/20/5 or 100/300/50

If this accident were your fault you would be legally bound to pay for the repair of the mailbox. Liability insurance would help cover the costs.

Insurance "Language"

Liability Insurance
(Bodily Injury and Property Damage)
10/20/5 or 100/300/50

Each number is the coverage limit (maximum amount) in thousands of dollars paid by the insurance firm for one accident. For example:

10 = 10 × $1,000 = $10,000
300 = 300 × $1,000 = $300,000
10/20/5 = $10,000/$20,000/$5,000
100/300/50 = $1000,000/$3000,000/$50,000

The first figure (10 or 100) is the amount the firm will pay for one person's bodily injuries.

The second figure (20 or 300) is the amount the firm will pay for all bodily injuries.

The third figure (5 or 50) is the amount paid for property damage.

Carrying a minimum amount of bodily injury and property damage insurance is required by law in most states.

MEDICAL PAYMENT INSURANCE

Medical payment insurance pays medical costs in spite of who caused the accident. The coverage applies to you and to those in your car. If you are hurt as a pedestrian or as a passenger in someone else's car, you are also covered.

COLLISION INSURANCE

Collision insurance protects you when your car hits another car or object, or when it turns over. Your insurance firm pays for the repairs in spite of who is at fault. Most collision insurance sold has a deductible clause. A **deductible** is a certain sum you pay on each claim. The insurance firm then pays for the rest of the claim. By paying a deductible, you reduce the cost of your car insurance.

COMPREHENSIVE INSURANCE

Comprehensive coverage includes theft and car damage not covered by collision insurance. This coverage includes harm caused by: fire, flood, water, windstorm, hail, earthquake, glass breakage, vandalism, explosion, falling object, riot, and collision with an animal.

You can buy full comprehensive coverage. This means the insurance firm pays 100 percent of a valid claim. However, it is usually bought with a deductible.

UNINSURED MOTORIST INSURANCE

Uninsured motorist insurance applies to bodily injuries received in an accident caused by an uninsured motorist or hit-and-run driver.

In most states an insurance firm pays only the state's minimum liability level. If you can buy more of this type coverage in your state, it is wise to do so.

NO-FAULT INSURANCE

A sixth type of car insurance, no-fault, can now be bought in some states. Its concept arose from criticism of the process used to decide who is at fault when an accident occurs. The process often takes much time, is costly and requires lawyers services. Trials and settlement of claims are often delayed because of the number of cases. The goal of no-fault insurance is to reduce such cost and delay.

In a no-fault state a person's financial losses (medical, hospital, and loss of income) are paid by the insurance firm in spite of who is at fault. Most no-fault states restrict the right to sue. No-fault laws vary from state to state.

A good driving record, driver education certificate and good academic records can help you obtain reduced rates from most auto insurance companies.

HOW CAR INSURANCE RATES ARE SET

The main factor when insurance firms set rates is the dollar amount of claims paid. "Insured" accidents require insurance firms to pay claims. The more dollars used to pay claims, the higher the cost of car insurance.

States are divided into "rate zones." Rates among zones are based on the claims paid in each zone. The more claims paid, the higher the rate.

Within a zone car insurance costs also vary among policyholders. Factors that affect costs include: the number of coverages you buy; the dollar amounts you choose for each coverage; the deductibles; the year, make, and model of your car; your driver class (personal or business); and your driving record. In most states your age, sex, and marital status are also factors. In many states, high grades in school and driver education will lower rates for young drivers.

HEALTH INSURANCE

Working each day to keep yourself fit and healthy is the best and least costly health insurance. But even if you do your part, you cannot be 100 percent sure your "machine" will stay trouble free. An illness or accident can be costly. This is why good health insurance is a key part of an overall protection plan. Its main goal is to help you with the cost if you need costly medical care.

Health insurance plans available are: basic care (hospitalization and surgical), major medical, comprehensive, a Health Maintenance Organization (HMO), group health insurance, and Medicare (Social Security).

BASIC CARE (HOSPITALIZATION AND SURGICAL)

Hospitalization insurance helps to pay for the time you are in the hospital. Benefits help to pay for room, meals, routine nursing care, and minor medical supplies. This type of health plan is offered by commercial and nonprofit companies. Surgical insurance also offered by these firms helps to pay for surgeons' fees and other related expenses.

It is best to buy a plan that pays from 70 percent to 80 percent of "reasonable and customary rates and fees." This is better than fixed amounts. Over a span of time fixed amounts go out-of-date. The rise in hospital room rates is an example. Rates and fees also vary among different parts of the country.

Expenses incurred while you are in the hospital—room, meals, and medical supplies are covered by hospitalization insurance.

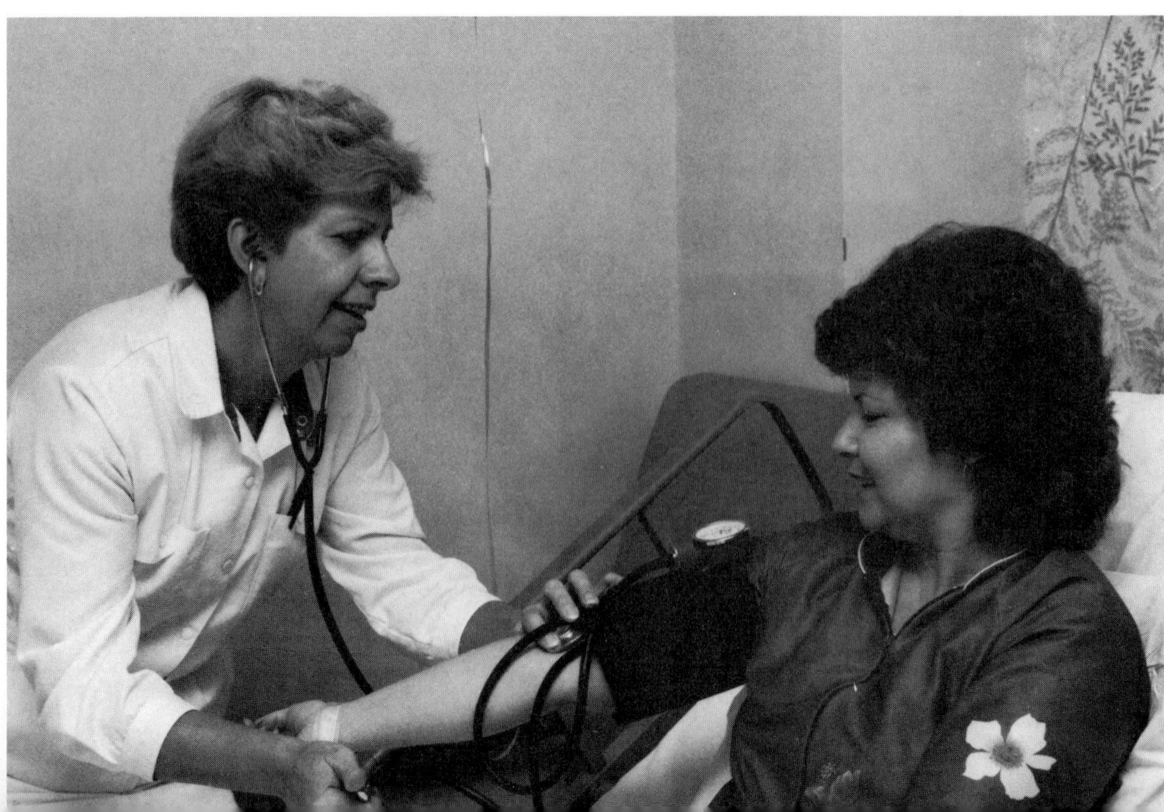

MAJOR MEDICAL INSURANCE

Each of us needs major medical coverage. Otherwise, savings can be wiped out as a result of a high-cost illness or mishap. This plan picks up where a basic care plan stops. Major medical plans include a deductible.

COMPREHENSIVE INSURANCE

Comprehensive insurance include all or most all of the coverage. It combines basic care and major medical plans. It often includes dental, vision, and psychiatric care. Many times it includes a low deductible.

HEALTH MAINTENANCE ORGANIZATION (HMO)

A Health Maintenance Organization is a membership group. You pay a yearly fee and the plan provides for all or most medical needs. Usually you can get most medical services at one place.

To join an HMO, you usually need to pass a doctor's exam. Each year, however, the law requires an "open" period when anyone, in spite of health, can join.

GROUP HEALTH INSURANCE

If you have the chance to take part in a group health insurance plan with your employer, it is wise to do so. Take advantage of all the benefits offered you. It is the least costly plan to buy. Some employers pay the whole cost for their employees. Other plans require employees to pay part of the cost.

If your group health plan provides only basic care, it is best to buy more protection. To do this, buy a major medical policy on your own.

MEDICARE (SOCIAL SECURITY)

Medicare is a federal health insurance program for people sixty-five years old or older. Most people over age sixty-five can have this coverage. The plan includes hospital (Part A) and medical (Part B) insurance. There is no charge for the hospital coverage and the medical part requires a small monthly charge.

COMMUNITY HEALTH SERVICE

Take the time to learn about health resources found in your area. Many hospitals and health agencies offer public health awareness programs. These include talks and demonstrations on heart disease, coronary risk screening, nutrition, exercise, how to quit smoking, stress management, and so on. Many programs are free. For others there is a small charge.

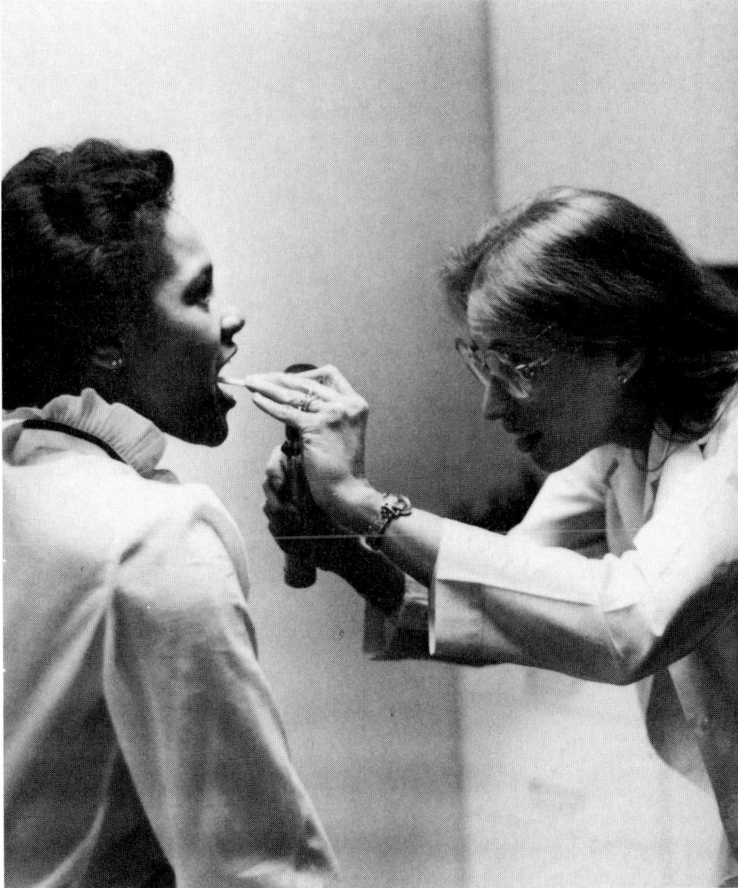

Health insurance, sometimes offered through an employer or school, can help save money on your medical bills.

SHOPPING FOR A CAR

In today's marketplace, the price of a car, whether new or used, is a not cheap. Thus, when shopping for a car, it is wise to make a decision with care and not to buy on impulse.

• Before you shop, take a good look at your financial status. Then decide how much you can pay for a car. Usually, this means how much you can pay each month. This figure should include the finance charge that will be part of your monthly payment.

• To keep a car's cost as low as possible, make as large a down payment as you can. Then pay the balance in as short amount of time as you can. The important thing to remember is that the longer you take to pay back a loan, the higher your interest charge will be.

• Making a choice will be easy if you do your homework first. Visit dealer showrooms and/or used car lots. Study car-buying reference materials at the library, in magazine articles, and in ads. Then decide what make, size, and model you want. When you make these choices, keep in mind gas, upkeep and insurance costs. A high-performance sports car usually costs more to insure.

• Many people who shop for a car do not regard the make or price the most vital factors. It is the car dealer. If you choose a dealer with a good reputation, it may prove well worth it, even if the price is slightly higher than others.

• If the basis of your choice is price only, it may "boomerang" on you. If it is always hard to get warranty work or regular service done well, the value of a lower price is minimal. You must not overlook the value of a fair and highly rated service department.

• If there is an active Better Business Bureau near you, check with them about the dealer(s) with whom you might do business. One phone call may save you much grief. A bureau keeps a file of consumer complaints reported to them. Thus, you can ask about a specific business.

• Before you make a final decision, be sure you understand the car's warranty, or what is and what is not covered and for how long. The dealer should give you a copy when you buy the car. The types of warranties are covered in chapter 14, "Shopping Savvy."

• When you use installment credit to pay for a car, the dealer may ask you to buy credit life insurance. Its purpose is to provide money for payment of your loan in case of your death. When this insurance is part of an installment contract, the cost is high. You will pay a lower cost if you buy a term life plan for the period of your loan from an insurance firm.

• There is an advantage to buying a car from a franchised dealer. If you cannot get a problem settled to your satisfaction, you can contact the manufacturer for help.

DISABILITY OR INCOME PROTECTION INSURANCE

An illness or accident may cause you to be out of work for several weeks or months. Although health insurance would pay for most of the medical bills, what would you and your family live on while you were getting well?

There are several possible sources of income to help a person who has been struck by an illness or accident. An employer's benefits plan may provide for wages during a time of illness. A union contract may provide its members with benefits during sick leave. And if the illness or accident is job related, the person may be able to get benefits from a state workers' compensation fund.

If income sources are limited, a person may want to buy a disability insurance plan. Disability insurance pays a cash benefit to help replace the income lost during sickness. The policies vary greatly, so compare them with care. Check to see how soon after the disability occurs the first payment will be sent. And ask for how long a span of time payment will be sent?

To plan disability income, it is not necessary to replace the amount of your paycheck 100 percent. Most such benefits are tax free. Thus, it is advised to plan an income to replace from 60 percent to 70 percent of your paycheck.

SOCIAL SECURITY DISABILITY BENEFITS

A person can get Social Security disability benefits at any age. However, a person must be disabled for at least a year. Or the condition must be terminal (result in death). The first payment is received five months after the onset of the disability. The benefits are the same as those for a retired person. If a disabled person gets benefits for twenty-four months, he or she qualifies for Medicare.

HOMEOWNER'S AND TENANT'S HOUSEHOLD INSURANCE

Usually, the rent or house payment is your biggest expense. Add to this personal property—household contents and personal belongings. Together the total is a large sum of money.

It is wise to protect your house and property against loss from fire, burglary, and other perils. To do this, buy home-owner's insurance. This covers the house and personal property. A renter's policy is a tenant's plan. Such a plan covers only personal property and not the house.

Homeowner's insurance is designed to help cover the cost of replacing stolen or damaged property.

Different amounts of coverage can be bought. For home owners there is one important point to keep in mind. Keep the house coverage current. It should equal at least 80 percent of what it would take to replace the house. This replacement value is not the same as the market value (selling price). If you keep this coverage level, the insurance firm pays your repair bills for partial loss or damage in full up to your policy's limit.

Both home-owner's and tenant's household plans provide liability coverages, which includes bodily or personal liability, medical payments to others, and damage to another person's property.

Insurance firms say that both home owners and renters should keep an inventory of all personal property. Keep receipts. Take photos to back up your written inventory. It helps greatly when you file a claim to itemize your losses. Do not trust your memory. Keep this record in a safe deposit box or a fireproof box at home.

HOW HOMEOWNER'S AND TENANT'S HOUSEHOLD INSURANCE RATES ARE SET

A number of factors are looked at when the rates are set for home-owner's or renter's insurance plan. The main one is the amount of money insurance firms pay for claims filed by and against policyholders. Others are the local fire department, nearness of a fireplug to the house, building materials used in the house, and your choice of insurance coverage.

INVESTMENTS—MAKING YOUR MONEY WORK FOR YOU

When you invest money, you do it to make a profit. You put your dollars "to work" for you.

What you think of as an investment, someone else might call a savings or retirement plan. This is not important. What counts is that you know what you want your money to do and where to put it to reach your goals. To do this well, you need an investment plan.

It is generally agreed that you invest only money not needed to meet your living expenses. If a family is involved, good life and health plans are top priorities. Enough savings should be on hand to meet emergencies without hardship. Other needs may be to buy a home or to save for a college education.

Many types of investments can be made. The amount of money required to take part or invest varies greatly. The discussion below highlights some of the ways that people choose to put their money "to work"

PAYROLL DEDUCTION PLANS

Employer payroll deduction plans to invest and save were discussed in chapter 11 (page 152). These plans offer good ways to save and/or invest money. Many people use these plans with great success.

It is important for you to know what a vested right is. A **vested right** is your "claim" to the benefits you earned in a firm's pension plan. Usually, your "claim" is based on the number of years of employment. You have a claim even if you leave the firm before you retire, such as when you change jobs, are laid off, or are fired. If you leave a firm before you retire and are partially vested (less than 100 percent), your employer must tell you what benefits are due you.

Sometimes you can get partial vesting after five years in a plan. This is why it is important to learn all you can about pension and other plans at work.

INDIVIDUAL RETIREMENT ACCOUNT (IRA)

The Individual Retirement Account (IRA) has been called "the first tax shelter for the average worker." Effective January 1, 1982, anyone who earned a wage or salary could open an IRA. Prior to this date, only persons who did not take part in an employer's pension plan could buy an IRA.

The purpose of the IRA was to serve as a personal savings plan that allowed individuals to "shelter" some of their current income from Federal Income tax. For example, if an individual put $2,000 of earned income in an account, this amount was deducted from the total earnings reported for income tax purposes. That is, the $2,000 was not taxed. In addition, the compound interest the IRA earned was **tax deferred.** This means that the interest built up tax free until money was taken out of the IRA. For these reasons the IRA has been considered a tax shelter.

However, Congress has been reviewing and proposing new laws that would affect Individual Retirement Accounts. These laws could change the benefits of the IRA as an investment tax shelter. Therefore, before investing in an IRA or any other long term investment program, the consumer should research current information and compare the advantages of the various investment options.

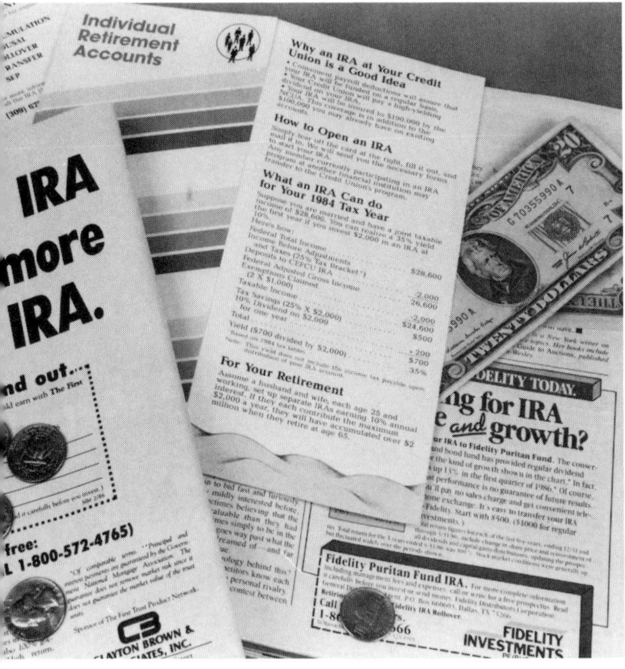

An IRA is a tax shelter that allows individuals to put $2000 of earned income in an account annually. This money can supplement other retirement benefits.

KEOGH PLAN

A Keogh plan is for full or part-time self-employed persons. You may invest 15 percent of your yearly earned income up to a maximum of $15,000.

Both IRAs and Keogh plans can be bought at banks, some credit unions, savings and loans, a brokerage house, and insurance firms.

ANNUITIES

An **annuity** is the opposite of life insurance. An annuity's main goal is to provide income for the person who buys it. Life insurance's main goal is to provide income for a beneficiary.

An annuity is a contract with an insurance firm. The amount you get from an annuity is based on how much money you put into it, the interest it earns, and the number of years you are expected to live. The **annuity rate (yield)** is the amount of income obtainable for each $1,000 of the annuities purchase price. Because payments are made for as long as you live, an annuity has been called protection against living too long.

Annuities are either qualified or nonqualified. You buy a qualified annuity as part of a firm's pension plan, an IRA account or a Keogh plan. You buy a nonqualified annuity with after-tax (income tax paid) dollars. The qualified annuities usually cost less, earn more interest, and make higher payments.

SOCIAL SECURITY RETIREMENT BENEFIT

In order to get the full amount of your Social Security benefit (PIA or primary insurance amount), you must be sixty-five years old. However, you may ask for the benefit any time after age sixty-two. At sixty-two you get 80 percent of your full benefit. At age sixty-three and a half you get 90 percent.

Payment of Social Security benefits does not start automatically. In order to get any benefit, you must ask for it. Make your request at the local Social Security office.

MUTUAL FUNDS

A mutual fund lets a large number of people "pool" their money for investments. A fund gives a person the chance to invest in stocks and bonds with a small sum of money. You buy fund shares. A fund also has the benefits of professional management and diversification. Diversification means you spread the risk of loss among several firms or industries. In other words, you do not put "all your eggs in one basket"—in one firm or industry.

A mutual fund is managed to reach a stated goal. It can be to provide income, growth of capital, or both. Mutual funds provide the chance to invest in stocks, bonds, money markets, and government securities. When putting money in securities, most people have more success if they use a mutual fund rather than doing it on their own.

Before buying shares in a mutual fund, learn as much as you can about funds. Then choose one or two funds with the same goals you have. Compare their performance or "track record" over the years. Doing so lets you know how well the funds are managed. After you make a good comparison, you will be ready to make a final decision—your choice of a fund.

WORDS TO REMEMBER

annuity
annuity rate (yield)
beneficiary
cash value or cash surrender value
deductible
face value
insurance
insurance policy
liability insurance
premium
tax deferred
vested right

CHECKING YOUR UNDERSTANDING

1. What is the main reason for buying insurance? Name five different kinds of insurance available.
2. There is concern about having adequate funds for future Social Security needs. Explain the reasons for this concern.
3. What is the main factor used by an insurance firm to set rates for car insurance?
4. What is the main difference between a life insurance policy and an annuity?
5. Why is it to your advantage to put money in your IRA as early in the year as possible?

APPLYING YOUR UNDERSTANDING

1. Assume you are going to buy your first car. Choose the year, make, and model. Then decide which insurance coverage you will buy. Include deductibles, if any. Do you qualify for any discount.
   Learn what your yearly insurance costs will be from three sources. Report this information in chart form. Itemize coverage. Evaluate the chart content and decide from whom you will buy insurance.
2. Universal is the newest and most innovative type of life insurance. Research this insurance, including its flexibility, the interest your savings earn, and the cost of a loan on the cash value of your policy. Report your findings to the class.
3. Assume you are employed, have enough savings for an emergency fund, and can invest $25 to $30 a month. Consider three investment opportunities. Briefly explain the pros and cons of each. Choose one and explain your choice.

Chapter 14

SHOPPING SAVVY

Has this ever happened to you?

Joyce waited all morning for the mail to be delivered. When it arrived, she saw the small brown package she had been waiting for. Eagerly, she tore open the wrapper and let out a cry of dismay. "These are supposed to be diamond earrings," she wailed, "but where are the diamonds?"

"There, in the middle," pointed her friend Carrie. "My goodness, they're tiny! How big did you think they were going to be?"

"I never thought about it. I just heard the man on TV say, 'genuine diamond earings for $9.99,' so I ordered a pair. I didn't think you'd need a magnifying glass to see them."

"Well, did they say you could send them back if you weren't satisfied?" asked Carrie.

"I can't remember," Joyce moaned. "There's nothing in the box that says anything about it. I guess I wasted my money."

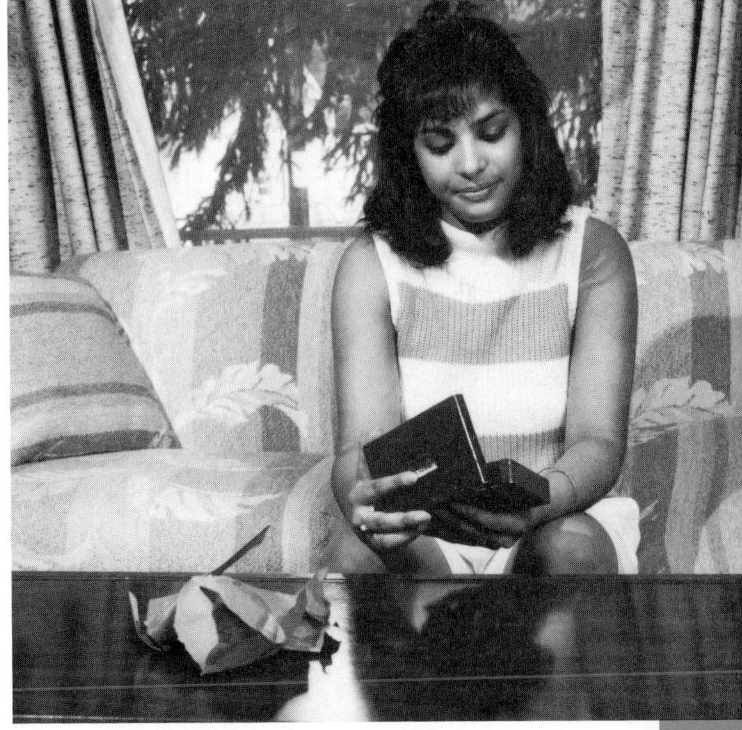

Have you ever wondered why some purchases do not live up to your expectations?

Have you ever thought about how you could learn to be a better shopper?

After reading this chapter, you will be able to

- recognize the factors that affect your decisions to buy;
- know how to use ads and comparison shopping to help you get the best value for your money;
- know your rights as a consumer;
- complain effectively if a product or service does not live up to your expectations.

When Henry Ford made his most famous automobile, it came in one style—the Model T—and it came in one color—black. If he were alive today, he would probably be shocked at all the different makes and models of cars, the range of colors, and the large number of options—from sun roofs to keyless door systems.

When today's consumer is ready to buy, he or she is faced with an array of brands and goods from which to choose. The modern marketplace is highly competitive, with many products fighting for your eye and your money. Price and being in stock are not the only things to think about when you try to decide what to buy. Changing technology, increased communication, more features, and a large number of stores have turned what was once a simple choice into a much more complicated process.

A good shopper is aware of the subtle influences that affect the ways that decisions are made. The wise, or savvy, shopper is one who knows how to evaluate the choices that give him or her the best value for the money and the most satisfaction from the product.

WHAT AFFECTS YOUR BUYING DECISIONS

Suppose you and your best friend each decide to buy a radio. After looking at what is available with care, you choose a small, battery-powered radio with earphones, and your friend chooses a large portable radio with a tape deck. What influenced each of you to make your final choice?

PERSONAL VALUES

Most of us do not have enough money to buy all that we want. We must make choices. These choices are a result of our personal values.

Values are your ideas about what is important and worthwhile. Some people place great value on appearances. They might choose a certain brand of radio because it is "in" or because it is in a style or color that greatly attracts them. Some people value performance. They might choose a radio only for its superior sound quality.

In today's competitive modern marketplace the consumer has an array of goods and services from which to choose.

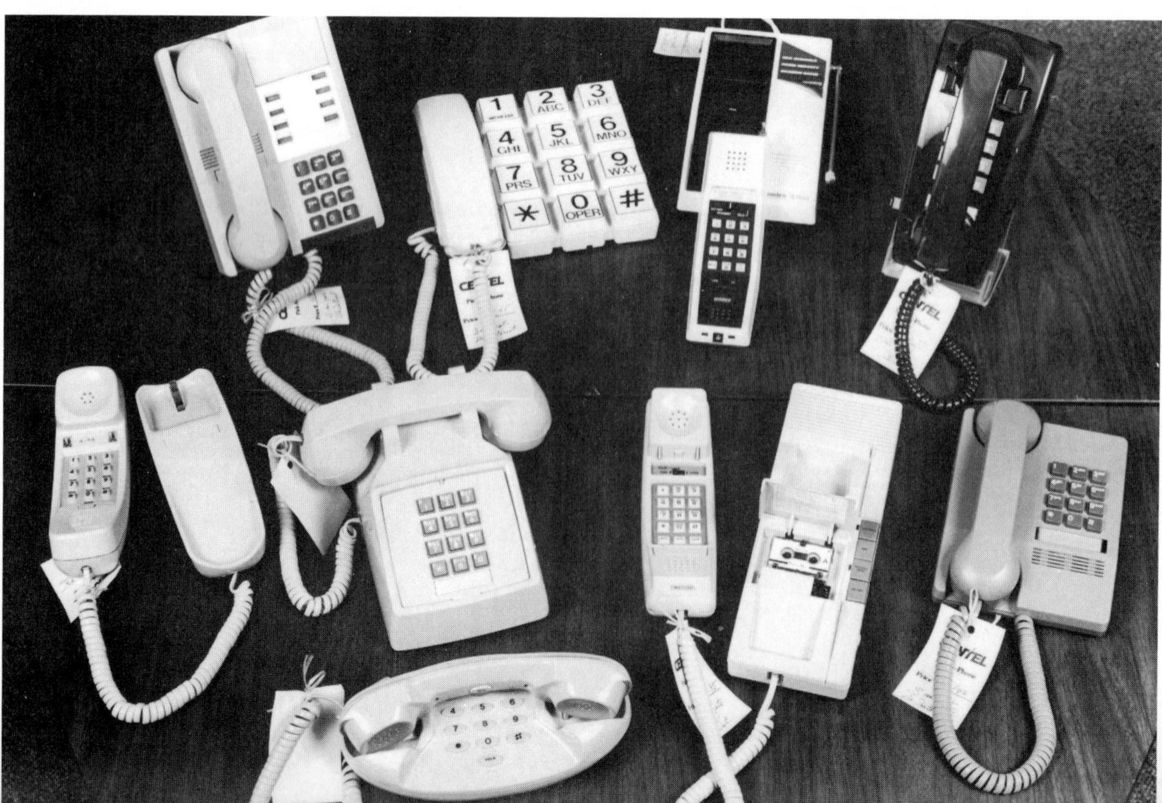

When you select products that are recyclable or biodegradable, you are showing your personal values.

FINANCIAL SITUATION

The money you have to spend can affect your decision to buy in many ways. Very few people have unlimited amounts of money. Most of us must decide how much money we have to spend on a certain item. Then we must choose from among the goods or services that are within our price range.

If the item you want is not in your price range, you have several alternatives. You might wait for the item to go on sale. You might try to find the item in a discount or outlet store. You might delay buying until you save the money needed. You might once again review your budget and eliminate some other expense so that you have more money for this item. As a last resort, you may have to make a different choice or simply do without the item.

NEEDS AND WANTS

Abraham Maslow, a psychologist, studied human behavior and came to the conclusion that all human beings have five basic needs. He listed these needs according to a **hierarchy,** or level of importance.

1. *Survival.* The need for enough food, water, clothes, and shelter to survive.
2. *Safety and security.* The need to be free from physical harm and the security of knowing that one's survival needs will be met.
3. *Belonging.* The need to be part of a family and other groups, such as tribe, clan, or nation, and to love and be loved.
4. *Self-esteem.* The need to have self-respect and a feeling of self-worth.
5. *Fulfillment.* The need to use one's special talents and creativity to reach personal goals and self-satisfaction through one's own efforts.

Before a person can get concerned with one level of needs, the prior level must be met. For example, a person must have enough food, water, clothes, and shelter to survive before he or she will worry about safety and security. In an advanced society like ours, many members have the time and the means to be concerned with all five levels of needs.

A want is a desire for something that we think will give us satisfaction. Our wants are an important part of how we express our need for fulfillment.

It is very easy to confuse needs with wants. For example, what you may need is something to wake you up in the morning. What you may want is a digital clock radio with a snooze alarm. Our wants are often affected by outside factors such as peer pressure, advertising, and features.

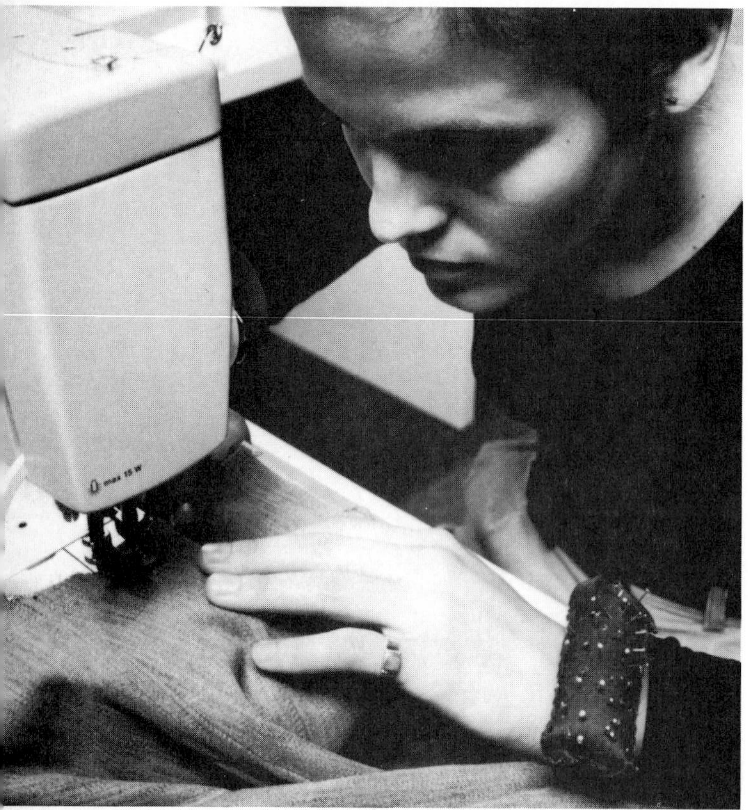

When you use your own special talents and creativity to sew an original design, you are achieving the last stage of Maslow's hierarchy, fulfillment.

How do you think peer pressure has affected the dress of the group above? Explain the positive and negative influence of peer pressure.

PEER PRESSURE

Have you ever gone shopping with a group of friends, and all of you bought the same item? Perhaps, you really did not want it. Or have you ever felt better in a certain outfit just because it was what "everyone else" was wearing? These are two examples of how peer pressure can affect your decision to buy.

A peer group is made up of members who have equal standing in the group. Being a part of a peer group fulfills Maslow's third need—the need to belong. **Peer pressure** is the influence the whole group places on each member to get him or her to conform to the values and standards of the group.

Peer pressure can be good. It may give a person the strength to act in a certain way that is good for his or her development. Peer pressure can also be bad. It may influence you to buy things that you do not need or want or to act in a way that does not reflect your own beliefs and values.

ADVERTISING

In order to buy a product, we must know that it exists. Advertising is one of the ways we find out about it. An ad can tell us about the good points of a product and explain how it will meet a certain need or want. It can also tempt us to buy something that we do not need or that is too costly for our budget.

OTHER INFLUENCES

Other factors can also affect your decisions to buy. These include the good name of the store or the manufacturer, the safety and endurance of the product, the experiences of friends and relatives, and the warranty.

ADVERTISING

If you are like most people, you pay close attention to ads when you are looking for information about products or services. It is important to remember that an ad's main goal is to sell us something. Manufacturers and retailers use ads to try to convince us that their goods or services are what we want to buy.

TYPES OF ADS

There are three basic types of ads—image, factual, and informational ads. An **image ad** appeals to your fantasies, makes a fashion statement, or promotes a store's or manufacturer's name. Most of the space in these ads is given to artwork or a photograph. Most magazine ads, like those for clothes, makeup, and cars, are image ads.

Factual ads can provide many facts about the product or service. Price, features, performance, care needs, and warranties are some of the facts that may be found in such an ad. Factual ads make it possible for you to shop and compare without going from store to store. Newspaper ads and catalogs are usually factual ads.

Informational ads provide you with general information about a type of product, service, or activity, but do not try to sell you a specific one. Many informational ads are paid for by a group of people or manufacturers, such as a professional group, a trade association, or a labor union.

ADVERTISING MEDIA

Media is the means used to convey the advertising message. There are two basic types of media—electronic media, such as radio and TV, and print media, such as newspapers, magazines, billboards, and posters.

Electronic Media

Radio and TV stations sell space, or ad time. Because there are only twenty-four hours in a day, there is only so much space that can be sold. Ad time is more costly at those times when more people watch or listen to a program. In TV, this is **prime time,** the early evening hours when many families turn on their TV sets. In radio, the most costly time to advertise is **drive time,** the morning and late afternoon hours when many people drive to and from work by car.

Radio and TV ads are designed to get your attention and to make you remember the product. Because they are only thirty seconds to sixty seconds long, they usually do not give you many facts. Radio and TV are often used to advertise special sales.

Print Media

Newspapers and magazines also sell space, or a certain size ad. The larger the ad, the more costly it is. Full color ads cost more than black-and-white ones. Certain placements, such as the back or inside front cover of a magazine, costs more than others.

Most magazine ads are used to create an image. They do not usually have a great deal of information. Most newspaper ads are factual or informative. They usually have specific information, such as where to buy the products, what hours the store is open, and how much the product costs.

Billboards and posters are found along the highway, on the sides of a bus, or inside the bus. Because these ads are usually seen for only a short time, the message is brief and bold.

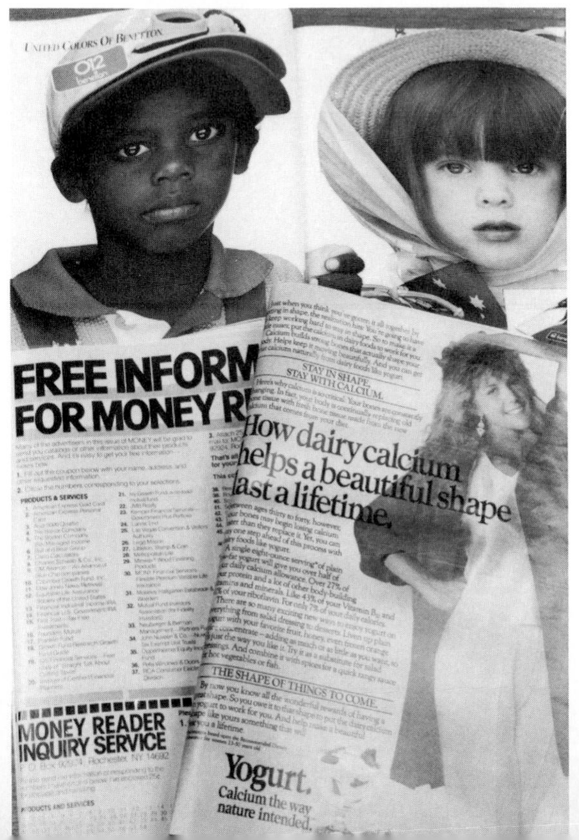

The three types of ads: image, factual and informative are used to sell goods and services. What type of ad do you prefer?

ADVERTISING IN DISGUISE

The familiar media ads are not the only form of advertising. Other kinds may be used to persuade you to buy a product. Some of these are very obvious. Others are so subtle that you may not be aware of how they affect your decisions to buy.

1. *Sales promotion.* Fashion shows, demonstrations, and contests are all ways to make you take note of and buy the product.
2. *Promotional articles.* A magazine or a newspaper will often have an article or an editorial that mentions certain products. If you read these articles with care, you may find that some of them advertise products.
3. *In-store displays.* Window displays, mannequins, and eye-catching arrangements of products are all used to get your attention.
4. *Product placement.* Have you ever wondered why some foods, such as milk or bread, are placed far from the door of your local grocery store? By making you walk through other aisles, store planners hope that you will see and buy other items, too. Items that people buy on impulse or can always use more of, such as batteries, chewing gum, or candy, are placed right next to the cash register. Customers are also encouraged to buy certain products by placing them at eye level, where they can be easily seen.
5. *Package design.* Manufacturers spend a great deal of money to develop and test package designs that will prompt you to buy the product.
6. *Entertainment features.* When a certain product is clearly identifiable in a movie, a TV show, or a music video, it may be part of the story or it may be there to help sell something. Some manufacturers work hard to see to it that their goods are seen in certain forms of entertainment. They hope that if the movie or performer is popu lar, their goods will get some attention and sales.

Subtle advertising techniques are used to persuade you to buy a product. What techniques are used in the pictures to the right?

COMPUTERS IN THE MARKETPLACE

Computers are changing the way we live, work, and shop. Some of these changes have already begun. Others are the wave of the future.

• Imagine that you can see how a style will look on you without having to try it on? A computer-programmed looking glass will let you "try on" clothes programmed into its memory. You will stand in front of the mirror, press a button, and the mirror will reflect your image in each of the outfits.

• Consider a large nationwide chain of stores that does not have a single warehouse. Each store's cash register is hooked up to a computer. When an item is sold, the computer deducts it from that store's inventory. When the stock gets low, the computer orders more so that the store is never out of stock. Buyers can also learn what is selling well to their customers.

• It is 10:00 P.M., and all the banks are closed. You sit down at your home computer, dial up your own access code to connect you with the bank's computer, and take care of all your banking needs.

• Using an 800 phone number, you can use your home computer to make your own flight plans and to print your own airline ticket.

• Computer shopping booths are sprouting up in retail malls, supermarkets, and airports. A color video screen shows pictures and gives facts about more than a thousand products. You make a choice, use your credit card as payment, and the item is delivered to your home.

JUDGING PRICE AND QUALITY

The wise shopper is one who takes the time to evaluate the price and quality of an item. Whether it is a cheap item that you buy often or a costly one that you expect to last a long time, the questions you ask yourself should be the same. The more costly the item, the more time you should spend in getting the answers. After all, if you are not happy with your choice of razor blades or mascara, you can buy a different brand the next time. But if you are not happy with your choice of a winter coat, a bike, or a tape deck, you may have to wait quite some time before you can afford to buy a replacement.

Analyze the following features:

1. *Performance features.* Will the product be able to do what you want it to? For instance, does it run on batteries or electrical current? Is it shockproof, waterproof, or water-repellent? How many miles per gallon does the car get? How many gears does the bicycle have? Shop and compare to find out what types of features are available.

2. *Care and maintenance.* Is the item washable or dry-cleanable? How often will it need to be cleaned or serviced? Do you need special products or tools to maintain it? Consider care and upkeep in terms of both your money and your time.

Judge the quality of products based on performance features, care and maintenance, safety, durability and warranty. Then compare prices of similar items.

3. *Safety.* Does the item need to be flame-resistant? Is it properly wired? Will you need an expert to set it up? Does it have the minimum required safety features? What "extras" does it have?

4. *Durability and usage.* Will the product last as long as you want it to? Examine the workmanship. Are there parts that could break off or come loose? Is the color even? What type of warranty does the store or manufacturer offer?

5. *Price.* Is the price of the item within your budget? How does the price of this item compare with the price of like items? Price is not always a gauge of quality. However, if the price is much higher or much lower than like products, you would be wise to take a closer look at the item. If the price is lower, the item may not have all the features you want. If it is higher, you may be paying for features that you do not want or need.

COMPARISON SHOPPING

In order to judge the price and quality of an item, and then to make a wise buying decision, you will need to gather some information. This research process is called **comparison shopping.**

USE YOUR RESOURCES

Shopping will be easier if you learn as much as you can about a product before you go to the stores. That way you will know what questions to ask.

Word of mouth is a good way to begin. Ask your friends and relatives who own similar products to share their knowledge with you. What do they like or not like about the brand or model they chose?

Make the library your next stop. *The Reader's Guide to Periodical Literature* has lists of names of magazines, as well as the dates and the page numbers, that have published articles on certain topics. Also look at *Consumer Reports,* a magazine that evaluates consumer goods and services.

Study newspaper ads with care. They will give you some facts to use as a basis for comparing price, service, and warranties.

Use the Yellow Pages in your phone book. These lists and ads will give you an idea of who sells what products and brands. If you are looking for a special brand or model, call those stores and ask if they carry it. They may also be willing to give you prices over the phone.

Before you buy a major item, such as a sewing machine, a new or used car, a costly piece of jewelry, or a home computer, you may want to contact the local office of the Better Business Bureau or the Chamber of Commerce. Find out if there are any complaints against the dealer from whom you plan to buy.

Before making a major purchase, visit your local library. It has magazines and articles that can help you evaluate your consumer goods.

STORE POLICIES

There are many different types of stores. Department stores, specialty stores, discount stores, outlet stores, catalog and mail order stores, as well as thrift shops, garage sales, and flea markets, are all sources for many kinds of goods. In unit 4, chapter 17, you will learn about what to expect when you shop in each type of store.

In addition to the type of goods and the price level, there are other customer services that may be important to you.

1. What is the store's policy regarding returns?
2. What kinds of payment can be made?
3. If the item is a major appliance, will the dealer deliver and set it up?
4. Is there a truck service nearby to move large, bulky, or heavy items?
5. Is an alterations or a service and repair department important to you?

SHOPPING SALES

Shopping the sales can be a smart way to get a good price on an item. To be sure you get the quality you expect, it is important to know what the various sale terms mean. Below are some of the common sales terms.

1. Retail price is the price the store usually charges for the item.
2. Markdown is the reduced retail price.
3. Wholesale is the price the store pays the manufacturer for the items.
4. Irregular merchandise has small flaws that will not affect the wear or performance of the product.
5. Seconds are items with visible flaws.
6. Damaged items are torn, soiled, scratched, or dented. Goods marked "as is" are damaged and are sold and bought with that knowledge.

If you can delay your purchase, you may be able to take advantage of some special sales.

1. Clearance sales occur when the store wants to make room for new goods or when a store decides not to carry a certain item in the future.
2. Special buys are items that the store has bought from the manufacturer at a special, low price. There may be two or more reasons for the low price. Perhaps, the store bought a large number of the item. Perhaps, the manufacturer is closing out the style. Or, perhaps, the manufacturer had many items left over that were not sold to other stores.
3. Holiday sales are sales that occur at a certain time of year. These might be national holidays, such as President's Day, or the Fourth of July. They might also be days that the store celebrates, such as a Manager's Sale or a Founder's Day Sale.

Be sure you understand what the various sale terms mean so that you get the quality you expect.

WARRANTIES

A **warranty** is a written guarantee against poor workmanship and materials. It is the store's or manufacturer's pledge that the product will meet certain standards.

If the product comes with a warranty, read it with care before you buy. It is important to know what is covered and what is not covered.

1. Does the warranty cover the whole product or only some parts?
2. How long does the warranty last?
3. Is it the store or the manufacturer who will do the warranty service?
4. Where will the product be serviced? Will it be in your home, at an authorized service center, or must it be shipped back to the manufacturer?
5. Who pays for the labor?

When you buy a product with a warranty, make sure you get a copy of the warranty. If you have trouble with an appliance or a car that is in warranty, have it serviced by an authorized service shop. Your warranty may not be good if you try to fix the item.

CONSUMER PROTECTION

In chapter 12, you learned about certain laws that were designed to help protect the buyer. Several government agencies enforce these laws.

The Food and Drug Administration, or FDA, enforces laws for foods, drugs, and cosmetics.

The Federal Trade Commission, or FTC, has a Bureau of Consumer Protection. It enforces consumer protection laws related to advertising, price fixing, credit, and fraud.

The Office of Consumer Affairs suggests programs for consumer protection and education to the President of the United States.

A warranty may not cover the whole product. Read it carefully.

CONSUMER RESPONSIBILITIES

All of us have had the experience of not being happy with a product. Sometimes the fault has been with the product, and sometimes the fault has been with us.

Before you complain to the store or the manufacturer, make sure that you have read and followed the directions with care. If the label says "dry-clean only," and you washed the garment, you will not get your money back. Use the product only for its intended purpose. If your watch was not labeled waterproof, do not wear it when you go swimming.

HOW TO COMPLAIN EFFECTIVELY

If something goes wrong with a product or a service and it is not your fault, you should make your complaint known to the store or manufacturer. Responsible retailers and manufacturers want to solve the problem and keep you as a happy customer.

Sometimes your complaint will not get the attention it should. If you know how to complain effectively, you will reduce the chances of this happening. Here are some guidelines to follow.

1. Before you approach the store or manufacturer, identify the problem and decide how you would like the matter settled. Do you want the item repaired or replaced, or do you want a credit or a refund? Have your sales receipt and copy of the warranty on hand.
2. Contact the sales or service person involved. Explain your problem well but as briefly as you can. Tell him or her how you would like the problem settled. If this person is vague or evasive, speak with the store or service manager. About 88 percent of all buyer problems are settled at this level.
3. If the store or service center does not help you, contact the manufacturer. Write or phone the person in charge of public relations, product services, or consumer affairs. Many firms have a free 800 phone number for consumer questions and complaints. To find out if a firm has an 800 number, call the information operator at 1-800-555-1212.

If you are not able to get the name of the person in charge of customer relations, write to the firm's president. His or her name and the firm's address can be found in *Standard & Poor's Register of Corporations, Directors and Executives.* Ask your local librarian for help.

ADDITIONAL HELP

If the firm's response does not solve your problem to your satisfaction, you can seek help elsewhere. Contact your city or county consumer protection agency. If need be, contact the state or federal consumer agencies. Look in the phone book under city, county, state, or U.S. government.

Find out if your local newspaper, or radio or TV station has a service to help consumers with their problems. The U.S. Post Office handles complaints about mail order fraud. Private consumer groups include the Better Business Bureau. Such groups help to settle complaints through voluntary arbitration. **Arbitration** is the settlement of a dispute by a person or group chosen to listen to both sides and make a judgement.

THE COMPLAINT LETTER

Complaining by letter is usually more effective than by phone. You can organize your thoughts and explain your problem more clearly. A good letter of complaint should include all of the following:

1. A brief description of the item or service, including any serial or model numbers.
2. The date and the name of the store. If it was a gift and you do not know where it was bought, say so.
3. A statement of the problem, including any attempts you have made to have it repaired at an authorized service center.
4. Copies of all documents, such as sales receipts, warranty, repair bills, and so forth.
5. A request for action on the part of the manufacturer.
6. A reasonable deadline for a response.
7. Your name, address, and work and home phone numbers.

If possible, type the letter. If you write it by hand, make sure it is neat and legible. Keep a copy for your files.

Remember, the person who reads your letter is not the cause of your problem. Do not threaten the firm or be sarcastic or nasty. It may make it harder for you to get your problem solved.

WHEN YOU COMPLAIN . . .

*Identify your purchase, date of purchase, and point of purchase. Include model and serial number, if applicable.

*Be courteous and reasonable.

*Include your phone number(s) in a letter.

*Keep a copy of all correspondence.

WHEN YOU COMPLAIN . . .

*By phone

*State the problem briefly and specifically.

*By letter

5100 North Sherwood
Peoria, IL 61614
August 29, 1986

Mr. Greg Padesky
W.W. GRAINGER, INC.
2305 W. Altorfer Drive
Peoria, IL 61615

Dear Mr. Padesky:

Last week I purchased a boom box, SN-1062, Model LN2. I made this purchase at K's Merchandise, 100 Pioneer Parkway, Peoria, Illinois 61615.

Unfortunately, your boom box has not performed satisfactorily because of the speaker. Therefore, to solve the problem, I would appreciate your repairing the speaker. Enclosed are copies of my receipt, guarantee, and warranty.

I am looking forward to your reply and resolution of my problem, and will wait three weeks before seeking third-party assistance. Contact me at the above address or by phone at home (309-691-3235) or at my office (309-691-4454).

Sincerely,

Dorothy J. Bair

DJB/d

*Request action within a reasonable time period.

*In person

*With a letter, enclose copies of proof-of-purchase and service papers. Always keep the originals of these documents for your records.

*State your settlement preference.

REFERENCES . . .

*Check the use and care instructions, warranty, and hang tags for information about what to do if you have a problem.	*If you do not know the manufacturer of your problem product, check the local library for the THOMAS REGISTRY. This publication lists thousands of products and the manufacturers.	*For the name and address of a company president, check the local library for STANDARD & POOR'S REGISTRY OF CORPORATIONS, DIRECTORS, AND EXECUTIVES.

WORDS TO REMEMBER

arbitration
comparison shopping
drive time
factual ads
informational ads
hierarchy
image ads
peer pressure
prime time
warranty

CHECKING YOUR UNDERSTANDING

1. Make a list of the factors that can affect your decision to buy. Briefly describe how each of them might affect you.
2. Describe the three basic types of ads. Which ones would be more helpful to you when you are ready to comparison shop?
3. Besides advertising, what other resources can you use to comparison shop?
4. What is the purpose of a warranty? Suppose you are trying to compare two warranties. What are some questions you should ask?
5. What steps should you take if you are not happy with a product?

APPLYING YOUR UNDERSTANDING

1. Make a list of five things you have bought in the last month. Can you remember what moved you to buy these items? If you were buying them today, would you make the same choices?
2. Pretend you have to develop an ad for a wrist watch. What would you want to tell the consumer in each of the following: (A) an image ad that will appear in a magazine; (B) a factual ad that will appear in a newspaper; and (C) a radio ad that will promote a special sale?
3. Visit your local supermarket and find some examples of advertising in disguise. Be prepared to discuss them with your classmates.
4. Suppose you are going to take a weekend bike trip and you need to buy a safety helmet. Using the resources at hand, find out as much as you can about bike helmets and report back to the class.
5. Gather and compare copies of warranties for at least five different types of products. If you can, include warranties for a car, a major appliance, a clothes item, and a piece of sports or camping gear.

Unit 4 CLOTHING AND TEXTILES

From the first time humans draped animal skins over their shoulders, clothing has been a part of our lives. As society has developed, the role of clothes has become more complex.

Today clothing is much more than just a way to protect ourselves from the sun, wind, rain, and cold. We use clothes to enhance our personal appearance, to show which group we belong to, to reflect how we feel, to express our values, and to fill our needs to be creative.

In this unit you will learn how to plan and buy your wardrobe with care. You will learn about the principles and elements of design, about fabric characteristics, and about the basics of clothes construction, care, and upkeep. As a result, you will look and feel better in the clothes you now own, you will be more satisfied with the clothes you buy in the future, and your improved shopping and sewing skills will save you time and money.

Chapter 15

DESIGN IN OUR WORLD

Has this ever happened to you?

June was trying to decide what to wear to the party next Friday night. Her best friend, Sara, was helping her choose from a pile of skirts and blouses thrown on the bed. June said, "I really wanted to wear something that would make everyone notice me. That's why I bought this great blouse."

"Isn't it the one that was advertised in the paper last Sunday?" asked Sara.

"Yes," replied June. "It looked so fantastic on the model that I just couldn't resist it. I didn't have time to try it on, so I just ran in and bought it. What do you think?"

"Well," said Sara, "to tell you the truth, it is beautiful, but somehow I just don't think it will look right on you. Why don't you wear the pink one that you got for your birthday?"

"You're right," sighed June. "I don't know why, but everyone always tells me how pretty I look when I wear it."

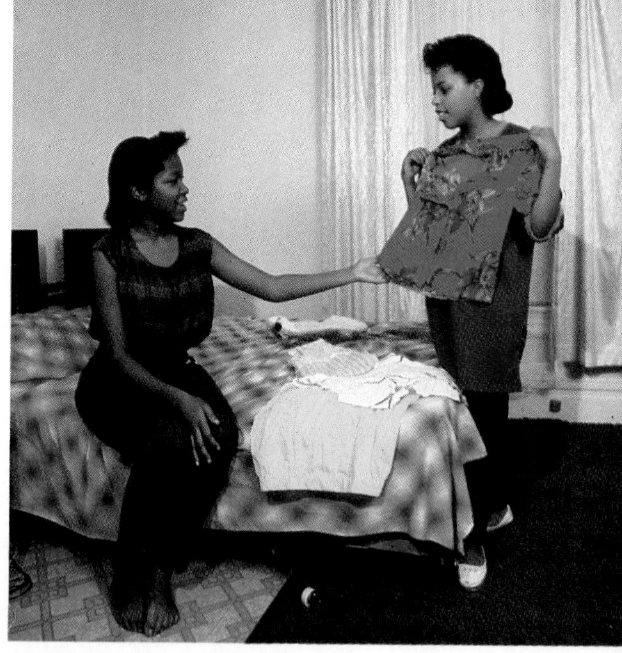

Have you ever wondered why you look and feel better in some clothes than in others?

Have you ever bought something because it looked great in the store without thinking about how it will look on you?

After reading this chapter, you will be able to

- identify the elements of design;
- describe how color influences the way you look and feel;
- understand how the principles of design relate to clothing choices;
- analyze a garment according to the elements and principles of design.

Design is everywhere in our world, from the way a painter fills a canvas with color to the way items of clothing are combined to create an outfit. Have you ever tried to explain why a certain photograph or item of clothing pleases you more than another? Can you visualize how a certain pattern and fabric will look as a garment before you actually sew it? These things are easier to do if you understand the language of design.

THE ELEMENTS OF DESIGN

Line, shape, space, texture, and color are called the elements of design. Think of them as building blocks that can be combined in many different ways to create a design. If you study these elements carefully, you will learn how to create moods, impressions, and illusions.

UNDERSTANDING LINE

Line is the most basic element of design because it creates shape and divides shape into spaces. Line also gives direction, suggests movement, and creates a sense of rhythm. In order to do this, individual lines are either straight or curved, as well as horizontal, vertical, or diagonal.

Straight lines suggest dignity, formality, crispness, and stiffness. Curved lines are soft and graceful, suggesting a relaxed, informal air. They vary from gentle, almost straight, curves to deep, full curves.

Fashion designers, artists, interior designers, and architects combine design elements and principles for a pleasing visual treat.

Compare the lines in these two garments. Notice how the curved lines soften the illusion while the straight lines produce a more harsh or severe look.

Curved and straight lines are often used together to soften the illusion that one type of line may create. For example, if a design has only straight lines, the effect may be harsh and severe or stiff and cold. Adding curved lines softens this effect. If only curved lines are used, the design may appear monotonous or too informal. This effect can be relieved by adding some straight lines.

Creating Illusions

Lines create the illusion of direction and movement. This is because our eyes follow a line. If a line goes up, the eye follows it up. If a line goes across, the eye moves from side to side. An unbroken line carries the eye along smoothly and directly. If the line is broken or changes direction abruptly, as in the case of a zigzag line, the movement is jumpy and erratic.

Vertical lines suggest height, strength, and dignity. In clothing, vertical lines can be used to create the illusion that the wearer is taller and slimmer. Horizontal lines suggest width, quiet, and rest. In clothing, they can be used to create the illusion of a shorter and fuller figure.

If the line is on a slant, the eye follows it in a diagonal direction. The more vertical the diagonal line, the more the eye travels upward. The more horizontal the diagonal line, the more the eye travels sideways. Because they lean, diagonal lines are insecure and need support. Used alone, they give the impression of falling over. When used in combination with straight or horizontal lines, they can make the design more dramatic.

SHAPE

When lines that have different directions are combined, they create the shape, or silhouette, of an object. There are three basic shapes: the square or rectangle, which has four corners; the triangle, which has three corners; and the circle or oval, which has no corners. All other shapes are variations of these three.

SPACE

Line is used to divide shape into various smaller areas, or spaces. For example, if you begin with a rectangular shape, and then draw a diagonal line that extends from one corner of the rectangle to the opposite corner, you create two triangular spaces.

TEXTURE

Texture can be detected by sight and feel. Terms such as rough, smooth, coarse, gritty, slippery, shiny, dull, and plush can be used to describe various textures.

Different textures create different moods or impressions. Think about the texture of fabrics such as silk, velvet, and satin. Their smoothness suggests refinement and luxury. Now think about the texture of denim, corduroy, and suede. Their roughness suggests vigor and ruggedness.

Rough textures and bulky fabrics add to apparent size. Smooth, clingy textures add no bulk but outline the figure. They can be flattering to a well-proportioned figure, but will show every flaw in a less-than-perfect figure. Shiny fabrics tend to reflect light as they follow the curves of the body and call attention to those areas. Smooth, lightweight fabrics that have enough body to hold their shape will lie lightly over the figure, hiding figure irregularities without adding bulk.

Create different moods or impressions by choosing fabrics of varying textures. Compare the mood created by the angora sweater to that of the denim jacket.

COLOR

Can you imagine a world without color, a world where everything looks like a black and white movie? The food you would eat, the clothes you would wear, and the things you would look at would all be black, white, or gray. There would be no blue sky, no green trees, and no red roses.

Color can be used to create a mood, to suggest temperature, and to create optical illusions. Color can add enjoyment, interest, and variety to your life. The key is to learn how to use color effectively.

What Is Color?

As you learned in your art and science classes, when light strikes an object, some light rays are reflected and others are absorbed. Color is the reflected rays of light. Without light, there would be no color. If a vase appears red, it is because the vase has absorbed all the rays that create the other colors, reflecting only the red rays. If all the light rays were reflected, the vase would be white. If all the light rays were absorbed, the vase would be black.

The Color Wheel

The color wheel is an aid in the identification of color. It serves as a guide for putting colors together in pleasing, attractive combinations.

Hue is the name given to a specific color, or pigment, such as red, purple, or turquoise. All color is made up of three colors, or pigments—red, yellow, and blue. These are called the primary colors because they cannot be made from any other colors. The primary colors form a triangle on the color wheel.

If you mix equal amounts of two primary colors, you will get the secondary colors—orange, green, and violet. If you mix red and yellow, the result is orange. If you mix yellow and blue, the result is green. If you mix blue and red, the result is violet or purple. The secondary colors also form a triangle on the color wheel.

If you mix a primary color with the secondary color that is next to it on the color wheel, you will get an in-between, or intermediate, color. The intermediate colors are yellow green, yellow orange, red orange, red violet, blue violet, and blue green.

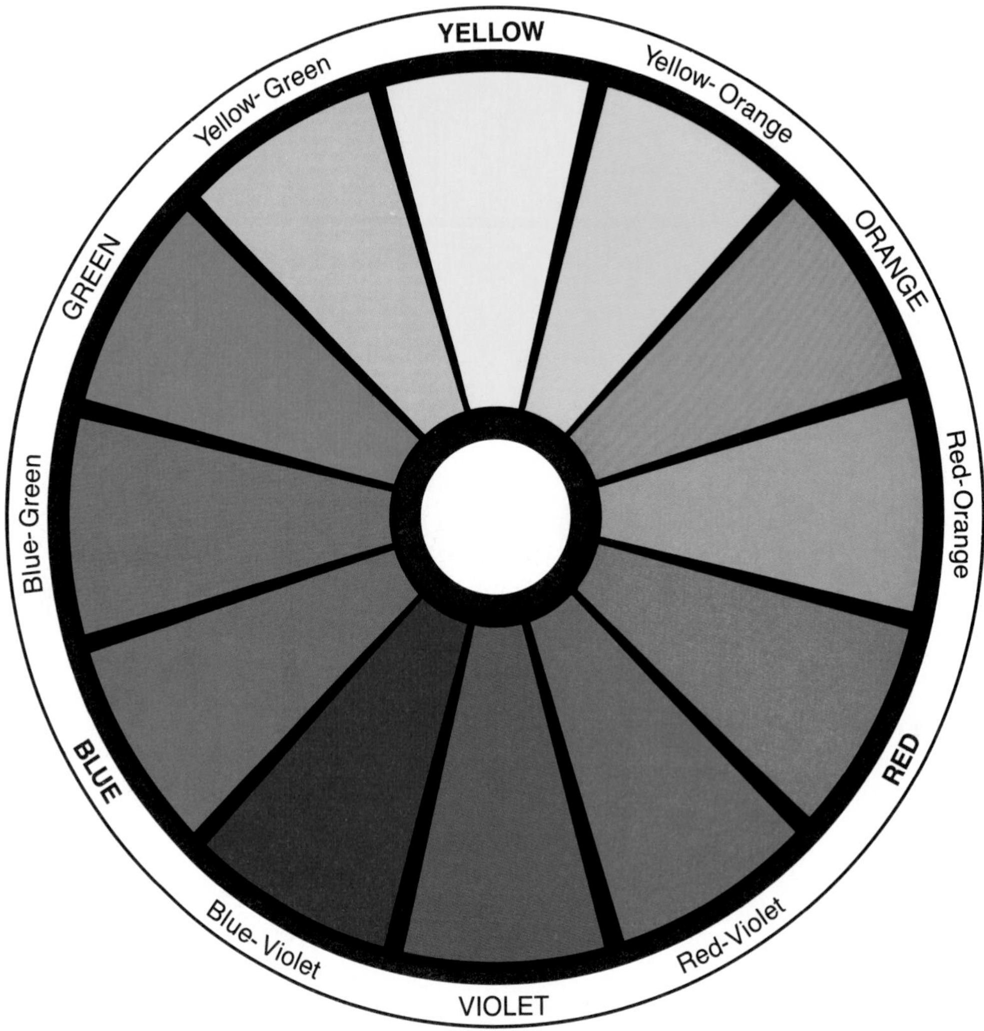

Locate the primary, secondary and intermediate colors. Explain how they are produced.

Color Variations

Colors, as they appear on the color wheel, are known as pure colors. Further variations can be produced by changing the value, or the intensity, of the colors.

The **value** is the lightness or darkness of a color. As you learned earlier in this chapter, black occurs when all the light rays are absorbed. White occurs when all the light rays are reflected. In color language, black, white, and gray are not colors. They are called neutrals, or **achromatics,** meaning without color, and they do not appear on the color wheel. However, black or white can be added to a color to change its value and to create a new hue. Adding black darkens the color and produces a **shade** of the color. Adding white lightens the color and produces a **tint.**

Intensity is the quality of brightness or dullness of a color. Pure colors are the brightest, or most intense, colors. To make a color duller or less intense, you would combine it with some of the color that appears directly opposite it on the color wheel. These two opposite colors are called **complementary** colors. If you combined them in equal parts, the result would be gray.

Complementary colors placed side by side tend to intensify each other. The colors look brighter together than they do when used alone or with another color. For example, putting a red bow on a wreath of Christmas greens makes the red look redder and the green look greener.

Notice how the color intensity is produced by the use of the complementary colors. The red bow on the Christmas wreath and the yellow blouse with the purple skirt enhance the vividness of the colors.

Basic color schemes can be used to decorate a home or plan a wardrobe that creates the desired effects.

Color Schemes

Using the color wheel as a reference, you can make color combinations that are pleasing to the eye. These combinations are called color schemes. The neutral colors—black, white, and gray—may be used as accents for any of these color schemes.

Related color schemes are those that have something in common. They are as follows:

1. **Monochromatic** schemes use only one color. Different shades and tints, as well as textures and intensities, may be used. Light blue with navy blue is an example of a monochromatic color scheme.
2. Adjacent, or **analogous,** color schemes use colors that are next to each other on the color wheel. An example of an analogous color scheme is a combination of blue, blue green, and green.

Contrasting color schemes are those that combine colors that are separated on the color wheel. They are as follows:

1. *Complementary* color schemes use colors that are opposite each other on the color wheel. The colors should be used in unequal amounts. A variety of values and intensities should also be used. This color scheme is particularly effective when it is used with large amounts of black and white.
2. *Double-complementary* color schemes use four colors. This color scheme can be created by using those colors on each side of two, direct complementary colors or by using two adjacent colors and their complements. Double-complementary colors are often used in plaids and prints.
3. *Split-complementary* schemes are three-color schemes. They consist of any one color, plus the two colors on each side of its direct complement.
4. *Adjacent-complementary* schemes use two adjacent colors, plus the complement of the most dominant color.
5. **Triadic-***color* schemes use any three colors that are an equal distance apart on the color wheel.
6. *Accented-neutral* color schemes combine any color or colors with black, white, or gray. The colors must always be used in smaller amounts than the neutrals.

Color and Mood

Split the color wheel down the middle, separating red from red violet and green from yellow green. Notice that the half with the reds and oranges appears warm, while the half with the blues and greens appears cool.

The warm colors of red, yellow, orange, and their variations are brilliant and stimulating. They can actually make you feel warmer and more active. They are aggressive and seem to advance towards you, demanding action. This is the reason they are popular in advertisements.

The cool colors are those that contain some combination of blue. They are restful, creating a serene, relaxed atmosphere. These colors can actually make you feel calm, cool, and rested. That is why these colors are popular for summer clothes and for bedrooms.

Color and Illusion

Color can be used to create illusion, causing an object to appear smaller or larger, taller or shorter, or fatter or slimmer than it actually is. Some colors make the objects they cover look nearer and larger. These are called *advancing colors* because they seem to stand out or come forward. They attract the eye. Warm colors, bright or intense colors, and light colors all tend to be advancing. A brightly colored shirt with dark slacks makes the top of the figure look larger than the bottom part.

Other colors make the objects they cover look smaller and farther away. These are called *receding colors* because they appear to fade or move away from you. The eye passes over them. The cool colors, the dulled or grayed (less intense) colors, and the darker shades of colors tend to be receding colors. If you wish to minimize one area of the body, such as large hips, you will appear slimmer if you wear pants or a skirt in a receding color.

Outfits of all one color make the wearer appear taller and slimmer. Outfits with contrasting colors break the figure into two distinct parts so that the total figure looks shorter.

You can use color to disguise physical flaws. A bright shirt can add the illusion of weight to a thin body while a dark gray or subdued color can minimize large hips or other problem areas.

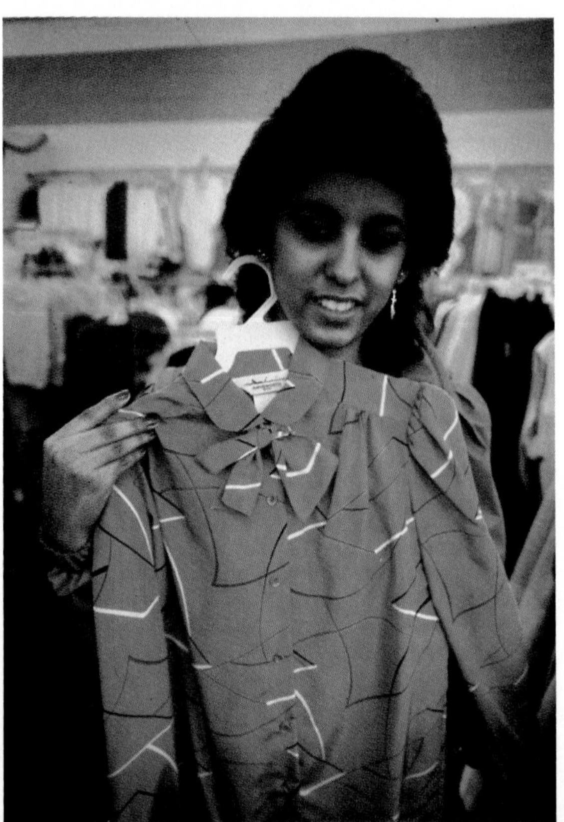

THE PRINCIPLES OF DESIGN

A successful design, one that creates the desired effect, is one that was made by using certain rules, or principles of design. The principles of design are balance, proportion, emphasis, rhythm, and harmony. These rules stay the same whether you want to build a house, design a wardrobe, or landscape a yard. If used in the right way, they will help you achieve beauty and harmony.

BALANCE

Balance is the way the internal spaces of a design work together. These spaces can be defined by line, texture, or color.

Symmetrical, or formal balance, is achieved by breaking up a space into equal parts. Formal balance creates a dignified, proper, sometimes stiff impression. It is a safe and easy-to-use arrangement. Two breast pockets on either side of a shirt and the traditional single-breasted business suit are examples of formal balance.

Asymmetrical, or informal balance, is achieved by breaking up a space into unequal parts. Informal balance creates a subtle, casual impression, which is usually more interesting and dynamic than formal balance. A dress with a diagonal front closing or a shirt with one breast pocket are examples of informal balance.

Which outfits above illustrate symmetrical and assymetrical balance? Which types of balance creates a more dignified, stiff impression?

A lack of balance can make a room or a person seem lopsided. A room may look like it tips in one corner. A person may seem to be all shoulders, or all hips, or larger on one side than the other. If you have a large printed design on one shoulder but none on the other, the body may look unbalanced.

Color can be used to create balance. Warm, bright, or light colors carry more visual weight than cool colors or those of less intensity and value. This means that a subdued, dark, or cool color can be balanced by a smaller amount of a warm, bright, or light color.

PROPORTION

Proportion refers to the relationship of two or more spaces to each other and to the total shape or appearance. If the proportion is good, each part not only has individuality, but the total arrangement is unified. Think about a petite woman wearing a dress with a small print, a narrow belt, and delicate jewelry. The effect is pleasing—everything in scale.

RHYTHM

Rhythm leads the eye smoothly and easily through the parts of a design, relating them to each other. Rhythm creates a mood. Depending on how the combinations of lines, shapes, colors, and spaces carry the eye, the mood can be steady, static, and monotonous, or it can be smooth, slow, and restful. It can be happy, active, and lively or bouncy, jumpy, and erratic. There are several different ways to create these effects in a design.

Repetition is one way. It is achieved by evenly spacing more than one of the same object, such as a row of buttons or bands of braid. Repetition can also be achieved by the clever use of color in several different places, causing the eye to glide around a room or a person. Too much repetition can be spotty or monotonous.

Rhythm can also be achieved by progression, such as different sizes of kitchen canisters. An example of radiation can be seen in pleats flaring from the waistband of a skirt. A sea shell is also a beautiful example of rhythm by transition where curved lines lead the eye in a graceful flow. Plaids, however, are examples of rhythm by opposition. The eye follows a straight line until it intersects another straight line.

The color (red) is repeated in the outfit above creating interest and variety to an otherwise plain outfit.

EMPHASIS

Emphasis helps to give interest to a design. Every design, whether it is a picture, a room, or an article of clothing, should have a center of interest. One part of the design should attract the eye first. Without emphasis, a design is monotonous.

The center of interest can be one large object or a group of small items. Emphasis can be achieved through size or the use of color, pattern, or arrangement. For example, either one bold, oversized piece of jewelry or several small stick pins grouped together can add emphasis to the lapel of a jacket.

One dominant center of emphasis is enough. If there are several equally forceful attention getters, the effect is too busy. Picture in your mind a person dressed in navy-blue jeans, red socks, and brown shoes. Now imagine a yellow shirt and a pink scarf. See how your eye mentally jumps from one area to another without knowing where to stop.

HARMONY

Harmony is the pleasing result of all the other principles of design working together to create the desired effect. In order to be a successful design, it must also be in harmony with its surroundings. The dress or suit that is beautiful on the hanger must also look equally well on you. It should emphasize your best features, creating a flattering and attractive appearance.

A focal point calls attention to the wearer. What clothing items have the teens in the picture below used to achieve a point of emphasis?

HOW TO CREATE THE ROOM SETTING OF YOUR DREAMS

The elements and principles of design that help you create an attractive and harmonious personal appearance are also useful in other areas of your life. These same rules apply whether you paint a picture, take a photograph, or arrange a bouquet of flowers.

Suppose someone gave you the chance to redesign a room in your home. Would you know how to apply the elements and principles of design to create a room setting that was pleasant and attractive? Below are some suggestions to follow:

- *Use color to create mood and illusions.* Do you want the room to be bright and cheerful, warm and cozy, cool and restful, casual or formal, or larger or smaller than it actually is? If your room is dark and gloomy, use warm colors to make it look lighter and more cheerful. Warm colors will also make a cold room appear warmer. Cool colors will make a warm and stuffy room feel cooler and more restful. Dark shades and bright colors will make a large room appear smaller. Light tints will make a small room appear larger. If your room has a high ceiling, you can make it look lower by painting the ceiling a dark color. If your room has a low ceiling, you can create the illusion of height by painting the ceiling the same or a lighter color than the walls. If the room is very small, consider painting the walls, ceiling, and woodwork all the same color. The room will appear larger and more restful, especially if you choose a light or a neutral color.
- *Use line to create the desired effect?* Doorways, windows, draperies, moldings, bookcases, fireplaces, lamps, and pictures carry the eye up and down. They make a room look higher and add dignity. Horizontal lines in chairs and sofa backs, mantels, shelves, counters, table and desk tops, and mirrors create width and restfulness. The curved lines of overstuffed furniture, round tables, lamp shades, and accessories relieve the severity of straight lines by adding softness.
- *Define the space within the room by using small area rugs or groupings of furniture.* Contrasting colors on walls and woodwork tend to make many busy lines that break up the space. If your room is large, this might be a way to divide it into cozy and appealing spaces. However, if your room is small, this might make it appear confused and cluttered.
- *Develop a focal point.* The center of interest could be a specific area, a large object, or a group of small items. A large window, a collection of photographs, an oversized poster, a beautiful rug, a large desk and bookcase, or a canopy bed might be the focal point of your room.
- *Use texture, along with color, to enhance the mood of your room.* Warm, bright or bold patterns, colors, or fabrics add cheer and informality to a room. They also make the areas they cover look larger and nearer. Use rough textures to create a feeling of informality. Use smooth or shiny textures to create a more formal appearance.

YOUR PERSONAL APPEARANCE

The same principles of design that work to develop a flattering wardrobe will also help you select the best accessories, hair style, and makeup for you.

Scarves, ties, collars, necklaces, and earrings are ways to draw attention to your face. The more they contrast with your face, the more your face is emphasized. The day you develop a blemish is the day to avoid contrasting ties, collars, or scarves. Instead, wear a shirt with a matching collar. Consider drawing attention to another part of your body. Wear a contrasting belt, bright shoes, or colorful socks.

Together, the neckline and hair style frame the face. When you choose a hair style, consider the shape of your face, the length of your neck, and the size of your face in relation to your body size. Hair styles and necklines that repeat the face shape emphasize it. A square neckline and a jaw-length hair style with straight bangs will draw attention to a square face.

Local customs and religion dictate the use of makeup. To use it or not to use it is a very personal choice. You do not need makeup to call attention to your best facial features. Do you have lovely skin, lovely eyes, or beautiful hair? Call attention to them by repeating their color or using their complements in your clothes. Have you noticed how a green dress will make red hair—its complement—look redder?

Perhaps you enjoy and want to wear a special color. Yet you realize it dulls your hair or drains the color from your skin or eyes. Try wearing a contrasting collar or scarf to separate the color from your face. Better yet, save such colors for your slacks or skirt.

The idea is for all the elements of your personal appearance to work together to present a picture of harmony. Choose a hair style that is flattering and easy to groom. Choose makeup and clothes in colors that enhance your hair and eyes, as well as flatter your skin tones. Look for clothing styles that complement your figure type. The result will be a pleasing appearance that boosts your self-confidence and creates a good impression on the world around you.

Study and evaluate your hair, skin, eye coloring and features. Plan to use the design elements to create a super personalized look.

WORDS TO REMEMBER

achromatic
analogous
balance
complementary
hue
intensity
monochromatic
proportion
shade
tint
triadic
value

CHECKING YOUR UNDERSTANDING

1. What are the elements of design? Look around the room and explain how they have been used in different combinations to create a design.
2. What is the difference between the value and the intensity of a color?
3. Give examples of four different types of color schemes. Using a color wheel, explain how each color scheme is formed.
4. Define symmetrical and asymmetrical balance and give examples of each.
5. What are the principles of design? Give examples of how someone could use them to enhance their personal appearance.

APPLYING YOUR UNDERSTANDING

1. Go through the pages of a pattern catalog or fashion magazine and pick out several designs that please you. Analyze them in terms of line. Which ones would make a person look taller and thinner, or shorter and wider? What body features do the lines of these designs emphasize?
2. Take a close look at several rooms in your home or school. Can you identify the color schemes? Write a paragraph describing how you feel about one of these rooms. How do the colors and textures used in this room influence these feelings?
3. Examine your wardrobe and pick out the items that always bring you compliments when you wear them. Now analyze them in terms of the principles and elements of design. Why do these items look good on you?
4. Imagine you are four inches shorter than you would like to be. How would you select your clothing to make you seem taller? If you were taller than you would like, how would you make yourself seem shorter?

Chapter 16

THE FABRICS YOU USE AND WEAR

Has this ever happened to you?

Paul and Harry were on their way to the movies, but it was such a beautiful day that they decided to shoot some baskets first. After they were playing for only a few minutes, Paul wanted to stop. "Boy," said Paul, "it's really warm today, isn't it? Aren't you hot in that sweatshirt?"

"No, I'm fine," replied Harry. "Are you sure you're not catching a cold?"

"Maybe I'd better take off this jacket. I'm sweating like crazy in it. And look at my shirt!" exclaimed Paul. "Can you believe how wrinkled it got in just a few minutes? I knew I should have worn my other shirt. I've had it forever but it still looks great."

Have you ever thought about what makes some clothes good for certain activities but not good for others?

Have you ever wondered why some of the items in your wardrobe look great for a long time, while others look faded and worn after only a few months of wear?

After reading this chapter, you will be able to

- understand the difference between a natural and a manufactured fiber;
- explain how fibers are processsed into fabric;
- discuss how finishes can affect the characteristics and performance of fabric;
- utilize the information provided on labels and hangtags.

Have you ever had a garment that faded from dry cleaning? Or a sweater that shrank in the wash? Why are some fabrics commonly used for upholstery while others almost never are?

In Chapter 15 you learned how to use the elements and principles of design to create illusion. In order to translate your ideas into textile products that perform the way you want them to, you need to know something about fibers, fabrics, and finishes.

With so many fabric choices available to the consumer today, it is wise to learn the characteristics that can be expected from different textiles.

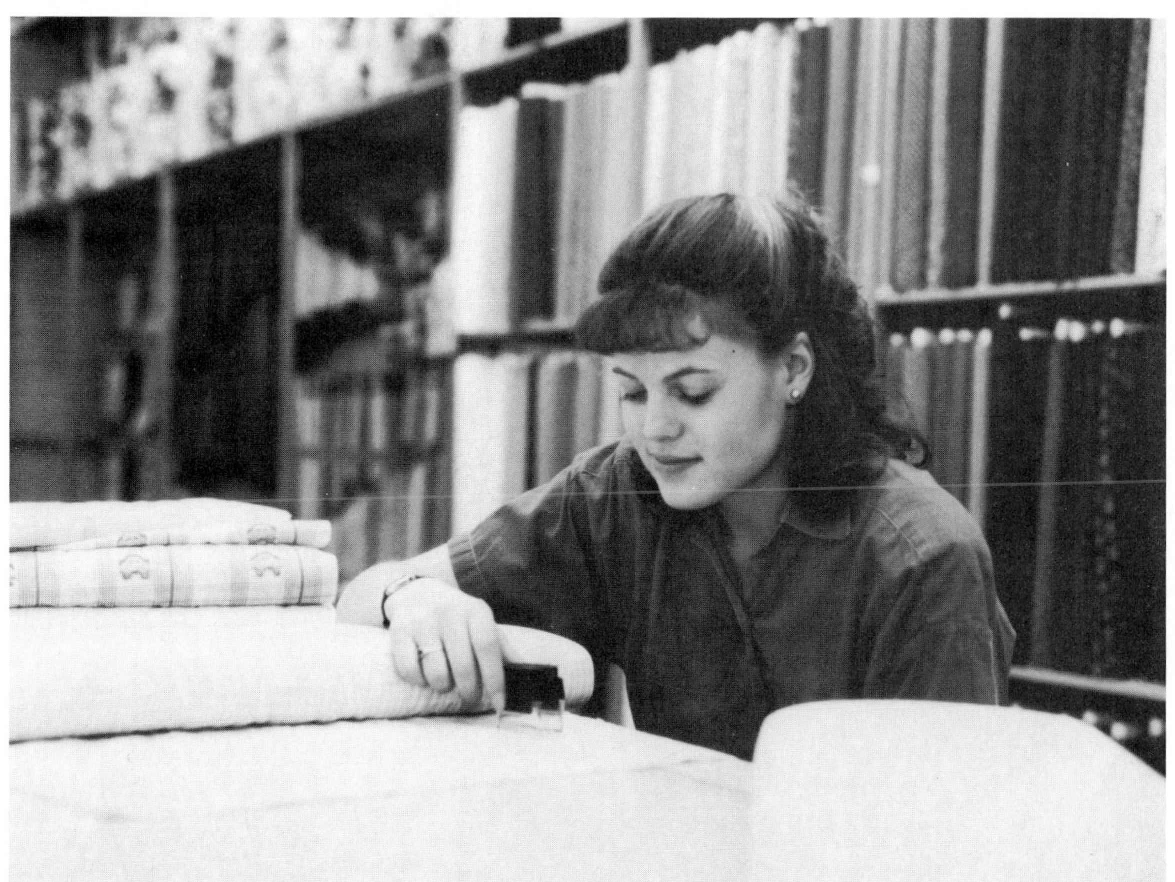

UNDERSTANDING FABRICS

To create a fabric, you must begin with a fiber. Fibers can be natural or manufactured. The fibers are spun into yarns, and then the yarns are formed into woven, knitted, or nonwoven fabrics. Special finishes are put on fabrics so that they will act in a certain way. For example, these finishes can make a fabric extra absorbent, crease resistant, flame retardant, or water repellant. If you have some understanding of how fabrics are made, it will help you choose those that will suit your needs and act the way you want them to.

FIBERS

There was a time when the informed person could tell the content of a fabric by looking at it or by feeling it. Almost all of them were made from natural fibers, such as wool, cotton, linen, or silk. Today, manufactured fibers with names like rayon, polyester, triacetate, and acrylic can be used alone or blended with other fibers so that they imitate natural fibers.

NATURAL FIBERS

Natural fibers are those that come from plants and animals. They exist in nature in a fibrous form. Cotton and linen are the main plant fibers. Silk and wool are the main animal fibers. Each natural fiber has its own set of pros and cons. As you will learn later in this chapter, many of the cons can be overcome by blending them with other fibers or by treating them with special finishes.

Cotton

Cotton comes from the boll, or seed pod, of the cotton plant. Under a microscope, a cotton fiber looks like a twisted ribbon. Cotton has several advantages. It is strong, absorbent, and comfortable to wear. It can be washed at high temperatures and with strong soaps or detergents. It dyes readily. Mercerized cotton has been washed with a special solution and then dried under conditions to add strength and luster to the fiber.

The main disadvantages to anything made from 100 percent cotton are that it will wrinkle easily and can shrink. It may also mildew, and it is flammable.

Cotton, the most widely used natural fiber, is strong, absorbent and comfortable to wear.

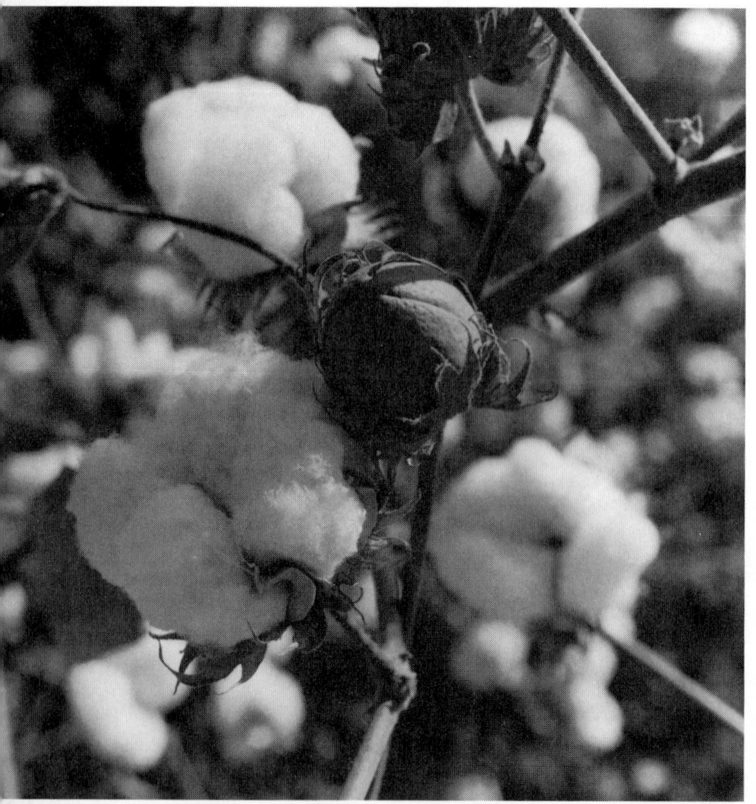

Linen

Linen comes from the inside of the stem of the flax plant. Under a microscope, a flax fiber looks like a bamboo pole. Linen is stronger than cotton. It is very absorbent and it dries quickly. Linen can be washed, bleached, and ironed at high temperatures. Because linen has a natural luster, it is seldom mercerized.

One disadvantage to anything made from 100 percent linen is that it is not very resilient. This means that it will not spring back into shape after it has been crushed or stretched. As a result, it wrinkles easily. In addition, linen can shrink and may be damaged by mildew.

Wool

Wool comes from the furlike covering, or fleece, of a sheep. Under a microscope, a wool fiber is crimped, wavy, and covered with overlapping scales. Wool is one of the most resilient fibers. It springs back into shape when crushed, wrinkled, or stretched. It is warm and durable. It is naturally flame resistant. This is why a wool blanket can be used to smother a fire.

The disadvantages of 100 percent wool include the fact that it shrinks and is weaker wet than dry. That is why most wool fabrics should be dry-cleaned or washed carefully by hand in cold water. Wool sweaters should be dried on a flat surface. Wool can also be damaged by moths, carpet beetles, and other insects.

Linen, a natural fiber that comes from the flax plant, wrinkles easily.

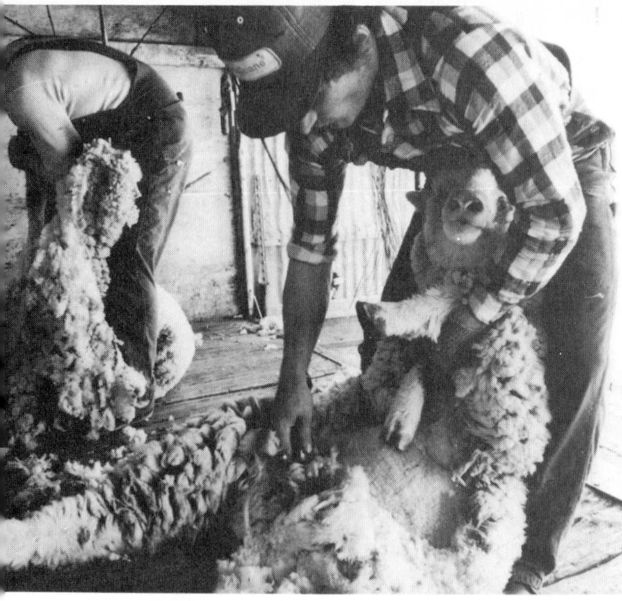

Wool, which comes from sheep, is good to wear in cold weather. It keeps the body warm and is flame and wrinkle resistant.

Silk

Silk comes from the glands of the silkworm larva as it spins its cocoon. Under a microscope, silk looks like a glass rod with an irregular surface. Silk is lightweight, strong, and comfortable to wear. It has elasticity and resists wrinkling. It can be dyed in bright colors and prints.

While some silks can be washed, most must be dry-cleaned. Strong soaps, bleaches, high water temperatures, hot irons, and abrasion can all harm silk fibers. In addition, body perspiration may harm the fibers and fade the dyes.

Silk, which comes from the glands of the silkworm larva, is strong, lightweight and comfortable to wear.

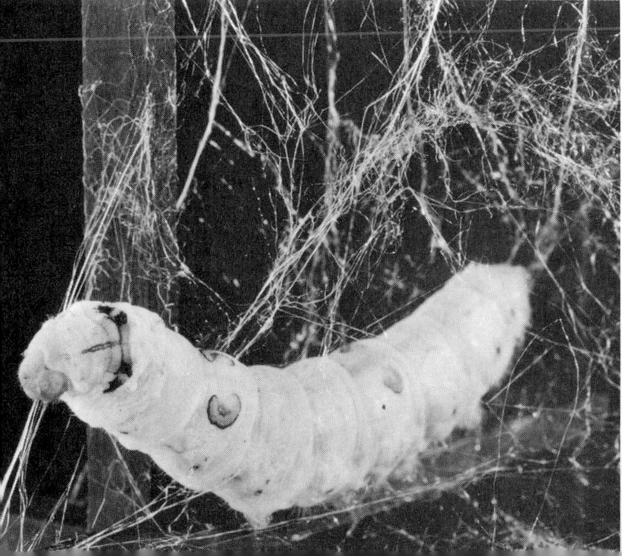

MANUFACTURED FIBERS

Manufactured fibers can be made in one of two ways. Some of them are made by taking natural materials and changing their form. Acetate and triacetate are two examples of fibers made from cellulose. Rayon is made from the cellulose found in wood pulp and cotton linters, the tiny cotton fibers too small to be twisted into yarns.

Other manufactured fibers, sometimes called **synthetic** fibers, are made from chemicals. No natural materials are used. Instead, various chemical elements are combined. Acrylic is a synthetic fiber made from elements taken from coal, air, water, petroleum, and limestone. A common way to make nylon is to combine carbon (from petroleum or natural gas) with nitrogen and oxygen (from the air) and hydrogen (from water).

Manufactured fibers are formed by combining the natural materials or the chemicals into a liquid called **dope.** The dope is forced through tiny holes in a spinneret. This forms the fibers.

The dope of polyester is forced through the tiny holes of a spinneret to make brightly colored yarns.

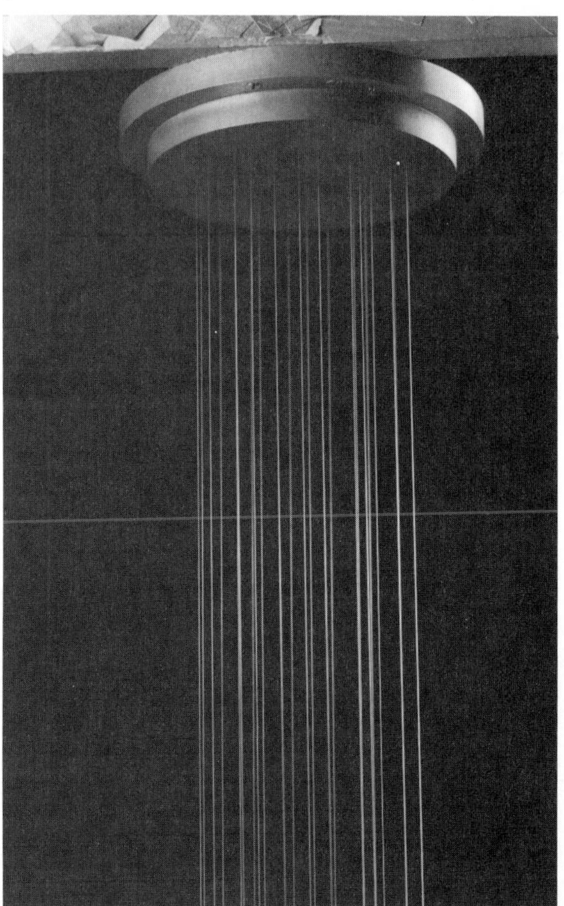

COMMON CLOTHING AND HOUSEHOLD FIBERS

Generic Name	Advantages	Disadvantages	Major Uses
Rayon	• Highly absorbent, making it cool and comfortable to wear • Blends well with other fibers • Dyes easily • Relatively inexpensive • Good drapability	• Susceptible to mildew • Weakened when wet • Has low resiliency • Damaged by acids • Requires low ironing temperatures	• Blouses, dresses, coats, jackets, lingerie, linings, rainwear, sportswear, suits, ties, and work clothes • Bedspreads, tableclothes, blankets, carpets, curtains, draperies, sheets, slipcovers, and upholstery
Spandex	• Great stretchability—up to 500 percent with great recovery to normal size • Lightweight • Resists body oils better than rubber and is stronger	• May be damaged by chlorine bleaches • May yellow on exposure to light	• Athletic apparel, bathing suits, laces, foundation garments, and support and surgical hose
Triacetate	• Good pleat retention • Shrink and wrinkle resistant • Washes easily • Stays white if not dyed	• Poor abrasion resistance • Damaged by light • Soluable in acetone and acetic acid • Moderately flammable • Low wet strength	• Dresses, pleated garments, and blouses
Cotton	• Very absorbent, making it cool to wear • Adds absorbency to blends of cotton and synthetics • Launders well and can be bleached or boiled to sterilize • Takes dyes and other finishes well • Can be ironed at high temperatures without scorching or melting • Durable with excellent wear life • Has no pilling • Resistant to moths	• Wrinkles and creases easily unless treated with special finish • Shrinks in hot water unless pretreated • Susceptible to mildew growth if left in warm, damp place • Rots if exposed to bright sunlight for long periods • Burns readily	• Underwear, nightwear, T-shirts, shirts, jeans, sportswear, blouses, socks, and jackets • Curtains, towels, bed linens and spreads, tablecloths, rugs, and slipcovers
Linen	• Very absorbent and cool to wear • Durable and long lasting • Can be ironed at high temperatures without scorching • Makes a smooth, lustrous fabric • Does not lint • Resistant to moths	• Wrinkles very easily unless treated with special finish • Expensive and must often be dry-cleaned to prevent shrinkage and color loss • Susceptible to mildew, rotting, and color fading • Burns readily • Has poor crease retention	• Skirts, slacks, dresses, suits, and handkerchiefs • Draperies, slipcovers, upholstery, and kitchen or hand towels

COMMON CLOTHING AND HOUSEHOLD FIBERS (Continued)

Generic Name	Advantages	Disadvantages	Major Uses
Wool	• Lightweight • Absorbent of moisture in vapor form • Naturally water-repellent to liquids • Resiliency of fibers gives crease resistance and recovery • Can be shaped and tailored easily • Durable and long wearing • Flame resistant and burns slowly • Insulating capacity makes it warm in winter and cool in summer	• Shrinks easily unless blended with synthetics or pretreated for shrinkage control • Susceptible to damage from moths and carpet beetles • Must usually be dry-cleaned unless blended with more stable fiber	• Suits, sweaters, skirts, slacks, and dresses • Carpets, upholstery, and blankets • Fire blankets • Felts
Silk	• Very absorbent and cool to wear • Luxurious look and feel • Lightweight but strong • Resists wrinkles and soil	• Expensive • Tends to yellow with age • Susceptible to damage from silverfish, exposure to sunlight, perspiration, and detergents • Must usually be dry-cleaned • Water-spots	• Blouses, dresses, suits, shirts, scarves, neckties, and lingerie • Draperies, lamp shades, upholstery, and pillows
Acetate	• Luxurious appearance and feel • Drapes well and dyes beautiful colors • Relatively inexpensive • Resists moths, shrinking, and mildew • Cool	• Is a weak fiber and must be washed or dry-cleaned with care • Glazes and melts easily unless ironed at low temperatures • Must have a special finish to be crease resistant • Dissolves in nail polish remover (acetone)	• Blouses, dresses, lingerie, linings, shirts, slacks, and sportswear • Draperies, upholstery, and pillow covers
Acrylic	• Resilient and lightweight • Quick drying • Warm like wool when textured • Resists moths, oil, sunlight, and chemicals • Very stable to laundry • Can be heat-set • Good pleat retention and wrinkle resistance	• Pills easily and tends to roughen in texture • Heat sensitive	• Sweaters, dresses, slacks, children's wear, sportswear, socks, and work clothes • Blankets, carpets, draperies, and upholstery
Modacrylic	• Soft and resilient • Abrasion and flame resistant • Dries quickly • Retains shape • Resists moths, mildew, acids, and alkalies • Warm, pleasing feel • Wrinkle resistant	• Heat sensitive and may shrink drastically when exposed to heat • Accumulates static electricity	• Pile fabrics, trims, linings, and children's sleepwear • Awnings, carpets, draperies, curtains, scatter rugs, and stuffed toys

COMMON CLOTHING AND HOUSEHOLD FIBERS (Continued)

Generic Name	Advantages	Disadvantages	Major Uses
Nylon	• Exceptionally strong and abrasion resistant • Easy to wash and dries easily • Lustrous and supple • Dyes a wide range of colors • Resilient • Resists mildew, insects, and alkaline substances • Can be heat-set in pleats (thermoplastic) • Resists nonoily stains	• Hydrophobic—nonabsorbent • Damaged by sunlight, especially dull types of nylon • Accumulates static electricity • If white, readily picks up dyes and soil from other garments in laundering, causing graying • Susceptible to pilling	• Blouses, dresses, foundation garments, hoisery, lingerie, raincoats, and ski and snow apparel • Carpets, bedspreads, draperies, curtains, and upholstery
Olefin	• Nonabsorbent but has wicking properties that carry moisture to the surface where it can evaporate • Abrasion resistant • Quick drying • Very lightweight and strong • Resists soil, mildew, perspiration, rot, and weather	• Sensitive to heat with low melting temperature • Shrinks when exposed to heat • Absorbs mineral and vegetable oils, causing swelling	• Panty hose, underwear, men's hose, and sweaters • Indoor and outdoor carpets, slipcovers, upholstery, carpet backing, marine cordage, seat covers for automobiles, and outdoor furniture
Polyester	• Strong and shape retentive (dimensional stability) • Resists stretching and shrinking • Resists most chemicals • Easy to wash and dries quickly • Wrinkle and abrasion resistant • Excellent wash-and-wear traits • May be heat-set	• Easily soiled and stained by oily soil and oil-borne stains • Some fabrics may pill if made from staple yarns • Low-moisture absorption • Heat sensitive	• Blouses, shirts, children's wear, underwear, lingerie, sportswear, slacks, skirts, dresses, ties, suits, blended fabrics, and fiberfill • Carpets, curtains, draperies, sheets, pillowcases, table linens, and kitchen linens

Generic Groups

Manufactured fibers are grouped according to their chemical makeup. These are called **generic** groups. The best-known generic groups are acetate, acrylic, modacrylic, nylon, olefin, rayon, polyester, and spandex. Several manufacturers may make the same generic fiber. To distinguish their products, they use their own **trade names.** For example, Acrilan, Creslan, and Orlon are all acrylic fibers made by different manufacturers. Dacron, Fortrel, Trevira and Kodel are all trade names for polyester.

YARNS

Fibers in their natural forms are too delicate and too tiny to weave or knit into fabric. They must first be twisted together or laid side by side to form a continuous strand. These strands are called yarns.

Each yarn has different traits. These traits are affected by the length of the fibers, the number of strands, the way the strands are twisted together, the amount of texture the yarn has, and the types of fibers used.

LENGTH OF FIBERS

There are two different terms used to describe the length of fibers. A **staple** fiber is one that is short enough to have its length measured in inches or centimeters. A **filament** fiber is one that is measured in yards or meters.

Silk is a filament fiber. All other natural fibers are staple fibers. All synthetic fibers are first made as long, filament fibers. However, these fibers can be cut into shorter, staple lengths than can be used to make fabrics that look like cotton, linen, or wool. Yarns made from staple fibers are rougher and fuzzier than those made from filament fibers.

PLY AND TWIST

Ply refers to the number of individual strands of fiber that make up a yarn. **Twist** refers to the way the plies are put together to form the yarn.

Single, or one ply, yarn consists of one strand of fiber. Ply yarn is made by twisting two or more single strands together. Cable yarn is made by twisting two or more plies together. If the two plies are not the same, the yarn is called a novelty yarn.

As an experiment, examine a length of sewing thread. It is a single yarn. Take two strands of the thread and twist them together. You have just made a ply yarn. Now make a second ply yarn and twist the two plies together. You now have made a cable yarn. Can you see how the yarn gets stronger as you increase the number of plies?

Twist refers to the way the plies are put together to form the yarn. Yarns with a low twist are loosely constructed. As a result, they are softer, weaker, and more lustrous than those with a high twist. In addition, they may pill and snag more easily. Yarns with a high twist are tightly constructed. They are used to make fabrics that are firm, strong, and dull in finish. Fabrics made from highly twisted yarns, such as crepe, may shrink.

BLENDED YARNS

Yarns can be created by combining more than one fiber. These yarns are called blended yarns. This is done to improve the performance or to change the way the basic fiber looks. In order to benefit from that fiber's traits the yarn should contain at least 15 percent of the fiber. Cotton is often combined with polyester to make a fabric that looks and feels like cotton but that does not wrinkle. Silk can be blended with wool to make the wool shiny and more lustrous.

TEXTURED YARNS

Yarns can be permanently shaped into curls, loops, zigzags, or waves. This process, called texturizing, makes the yarn bulkier and softer. Depending on the type of texture, traits such as stretch and recovery, wrinkle resistance, and breathability can be added to the yarn. You will learn about these traits later in this chapter.

The strength of simple yarns is determined by the ply and the twisting of the yarn. The variety of novelty yarns depends upon the different single yarns twisted together.

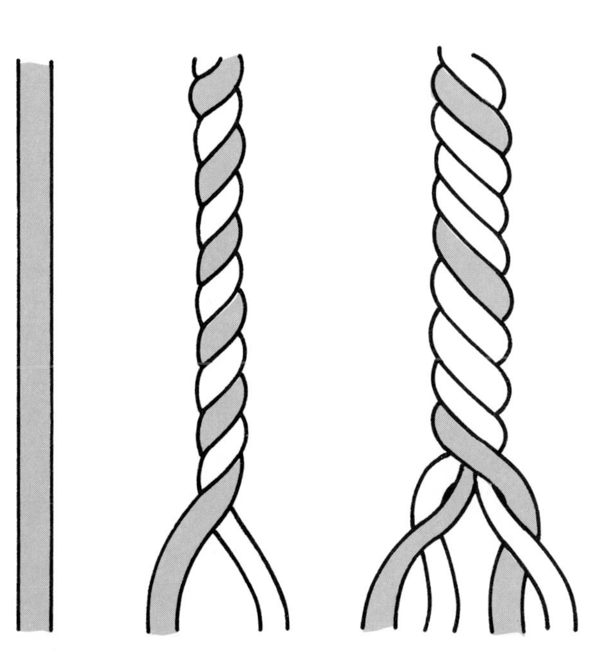

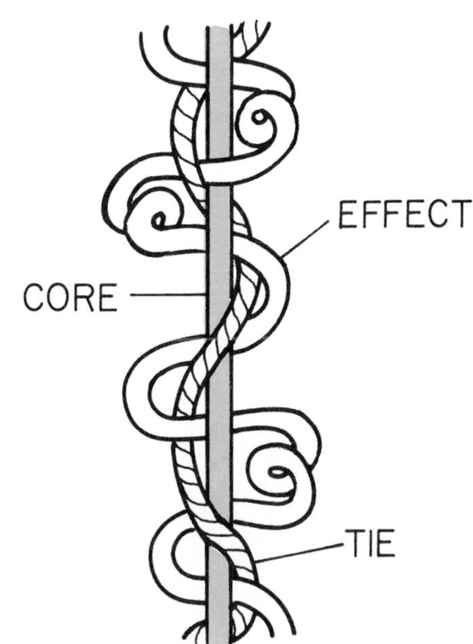

DOES THE FABRIC SUIT YOUR NEEDS?

How do you know what to look for in a certain fabric? How do you know if you will get the best fabric value for your money? Read the labels and hangtags carefully. They give the clues that will help answer these questions. Because no one fabric can do everything, you will have to decide which performance traits are most important to you.

• Is the fabric strong enough for the way you plan to use it? Some fibers are naturally stronger than others. Tightly woven or knitted fabrics are usually stronger than loosely woven or knitted fabrics.

• Will the fabric keep its shape after wearing or cleaning?

• Will the fabric be able to regain its shape after crushing or wrinkling? Crush a corner of it in your hand to see how it reacts.

• Will the fabric wear out easily? Have you ever seen the tiny balls of fiber that sometimes build up where the fabric rubs against something? This pilling can take place on the inside neck of a collar, at your side where you carry your books, or on the inner-thigh area of pants.

• Will the colors fade or run when the garment is washed? If the label says to "machine wash separately," that is a clue which tells you that they might run. If the label says "colorfast," it means that the color is in the fabric permanently.

• Will the fabric absorb, or take in, moisture? Some fibers, such as cotton and wool, are very absorbent. Others, such as polyester and nylon, are not. If you perspire a great deal or plan to wear the garment for active sportswear, absorbency is important.

• Will you have to dry-clean the fabric or can it be washed?

• Will it shrink? How much?

• Has it been treated with any special finishes to make it stain and spot resistant?

• Does the fabric stretch? This trait can be important when you choose items such as swimsuits, exercise wear, and ski pants.

FABRIC CONSTRUCTION

Yarns are joined together to create fabric. The most common methods of doing this are weaving and knitting. Other methods include crocheting, felting, looping, and interlocking with an adhesive substance.

WEAVING FABRIC

Weaving involves interlacing two or more sets of yarns at right angles. Weaving is done on a machine called a loom. The **warp** yarns are the ones that are strung lengthwise on the loom. They determine how long the finished piece of fabric will be. The other set of yarns, called **woof, weft,** or filling yarns, are woven or interlaced in a crosswise fashion on the loom. This interlacing forms a smooth woven edge along the length of the fabric called a **selvage.**

There are three basic weaving patterns—plain, twill, and satin. Variations of these three weaves are used to make different and complicated effects.

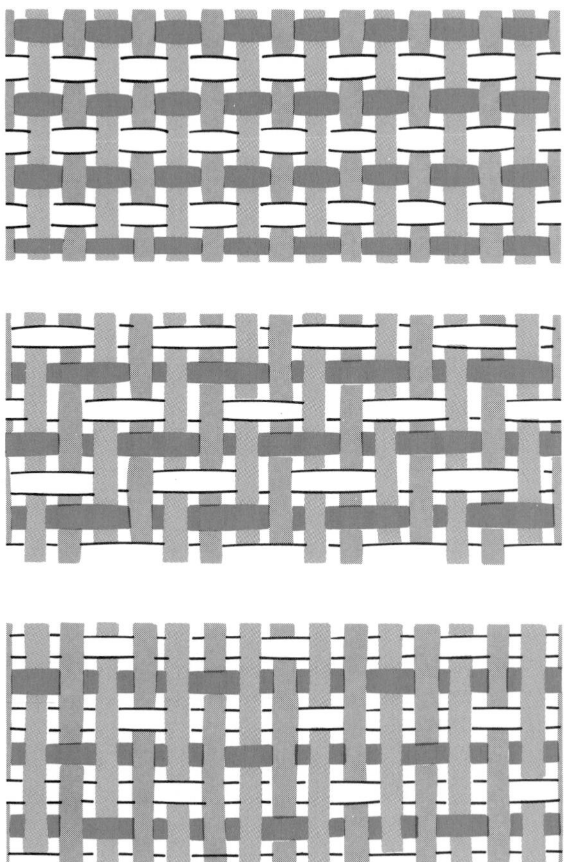

The three basic weaving patterns are plain, twill and satin weaves.

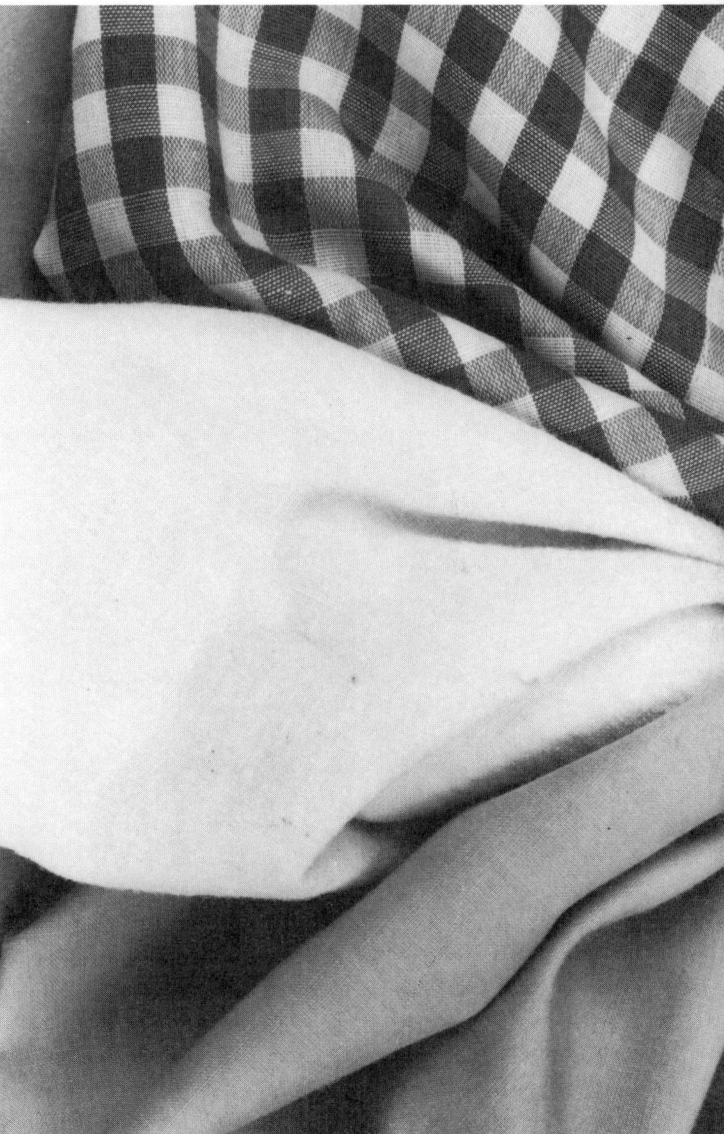

Plain weave is a simple weave. Plain weave fabrics include gingham, muslin, percale, madras and crepe.

Plain Weave

The plain weave is a simple weaving process. The filling yarn passes under one warp yarn and then over one warp yarn. This pattern is repeated across the width of the fabric. Because this is the easiest weave to do, it is also the least costly to do. Some examples of plain-weave fabrics are gingham, muslin, percale, madras, and crepe.

There are several common variations of the plain weave. In the basket weave, two or more filling yarns pass under and then over the same number of warp yarns. Monk's cloth and oxford cloth are two kinds of basket-weave fabrics. The rib weave has a ribbed effect that is made by using heavier yarns in one direction than in the other. Poplin and broadcloth are two kinds of rib-weave fabrics. The leno, or gauze, weave is made by twisting or crossing two warp threads after each filling thread has been added. The result is a strong, open, lacelike fabric such as marquisette, a sheer, gauzy fabric used for curtains and evening wear.

Twill Weave

The twill weave can be recognized by the parallel diagonal lines or ridges that run through the fabric. The filling yarn passes under and over one or more warp yarns. For example, the weaving pattern could be over one, then under three yarns or over two, and then under two yarns. In each successive row, the filling yarn moves one step to the right or left to form the diagonal line.

Twill-weave fabrics are usually tightly woven from strong yarns. They are firm and durable, keep their shape, and hold creases well. Gabardine and denim are examples of twill-weave fabrics.

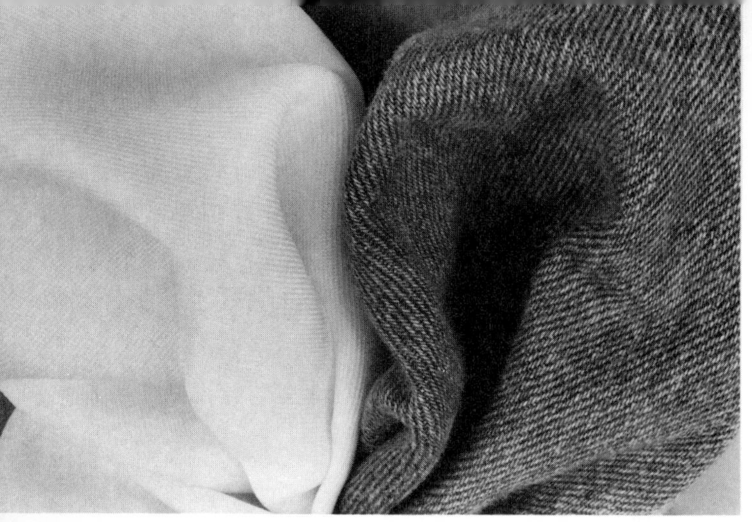

Twill weave fabrics, noted for their strength, include gabardine and denim.

Satin Weave

A satin weave has yarns that "float" on the surface of the fabric to give it luster and shine. In order to create the shiny quality, yarns made from silk or other smooth, lustrous fibers, such as nylon, rayon, or polyester, are used. Closely woven satin is firm and durable. However, because of the long floats, the fabric may snag easily.

Other Weaves

Other variations of these basic weaves are the pile weave and the figure weaves. The pile weave has an extra set of yarns that forms loops which extend above the surface of the fabric. The loops can be cut or left alone. Terry cloth is one kind of a loop-surface pile weave. Corduroy, plush, velvet, velveteen, and fake fur are all fabrics with cut loops.

Figure weaving includes two types of construction. In one, a third set of yarns is used to make the design. In the other, only two sets of yarns are used. The design is made by changing the weaving pattern. The jacquard weave is an example of this type of figure weaving.

KNITTING FABRIC

Have you ever done some hand knitting or watched a friend knit? Perhaps you know the process of using needles to form interlocking loops from a single yarn. Commercial knitting done by machines was based on this process.

Weft Knits

Weft knitting is similar to hand knitting and has the same general traits. It is done with only one yarn. On the right side of the fabric, the loops form clearly seen vertical rows called wales or ribs. On the wrong side, the loops form clearly seen horizontal rows called courses. Most weft knits stretch in both the lengthwise and the crosswise direction. Because they are made from one yarn, they tend to "run" if a thread is broken. Women's hosiery and jersey fabrics are examples of weft knits.

A weft knit that is made with only one set of needles is called a single knit. A double knit is a variation of a weft knit. Two sets of needles knit two pieces of fabric and interlock them in one process. One side of the fabric has fine ribs. The other side has a diamond-like pattern. Double knits are heavier and hold their shape better than single knits.

Satin fabric uses the satin weave to produce a fabric with a shine.

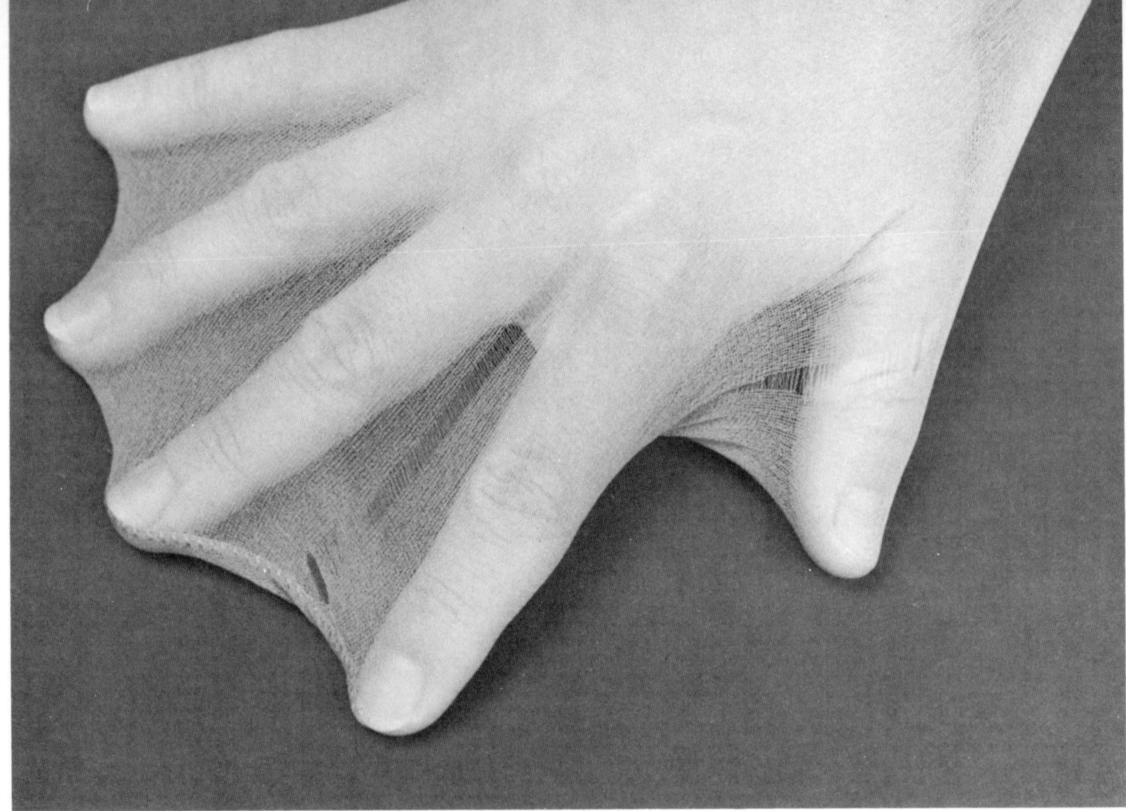

Leotards, women's hosiery and knit shirts are examples of weft knits. They tend to "run" if a thread is broken.

Warp Knits

Warp knitting uses several yarns at one time. The resulting fabric has lengthwise wales on both sides. Warp knits are usually stronger and firmer than weft knits, and they do not stretch as easily. Because the loops are interlaced so that each stitch is locked, they do not run if one of the loops is broken. Tricot, often used for lingerie, is one kind of warp knit. Another type of warp knit is a raschel knit. This knit has an extra yarn stitched in to make a textured or patterned design.

NONWOVENS

Nonwoven fabrics are made by applying heat, pressure, and sometimes an adhesive substance to make the fibers cling together. Felt fabrics, many filters, and nonwoven interfacings are made this way.

STRETCH FABRICS

Stretch fabrics, both woven and knitted, are becoming more common as manufacturers find out how to build stretch traits into the yarns themselves. Many of the texturing processes that build crimp into the yarns add stretch to fabrics. Stretch can also be achieved by adding a core of stretchable fibers, such as spandex, to the yarns.

FABRIC FINISHES

Fabric finishes can be divided into two groups—those that change the look and feel of the fabric and those that change the way the fabric acts.

ADDING COLOR

Color can be added before or after the yarn is formed into cloth. It can be introduced as a dye or printed on the fabric.

Dyeing

Man-made fibers can be colored by adding dye to the dope while it is in liquid form. Fibers spun from colored dope are very colorfast because the color is part of the fiber itself.

Both natural and man-made fibers can be dyed after they have been spun but before they are made into yarns. Yarns can be dyed before they are woven or knitted into cloth. Plaids and check fabrics that have no right or wrong side are made this way.

Once the yarn is formed into cloth, it can be colored in several ways. It can be dyed all at once by a process called piece dyeing. Piece-dyed fabrics look the same on both sides. Some fibers accept the same dye better than other fibers. The result is a piece-dyed fabric with a two-tone effect.

Printing

Fabrics can also be colored by printing them. The best-known way is roller, or direct, printing. The fabric passes through a press that has one roller for each color of the design. Each roller has raised areas that match the places where that color is seen in the design.

Other kinds of roller printing are discharge and resist printing. In discharge printing, the fabric is dyed first. Then, a white design is made with bleach, which chemically removes some of the dye. In resist printing, the fabric is first printed with a dye-resistant chemical. When the fabric is dyed, the printed area stays uncolored.

This fabric has been piece-dyed or dyed all at once.

ADDING TEXTURE

Most fabrics have some type of finish applied to improve the surface texture and the feel of the fabric.

Below is a list of a few of the more common texturizing finishes.

1. **Calendering** smooths the fabric and gives it more luster by passing it between two hot rollers. Embossed fabrics are made when the fabric is calendered with engraved rollers. The result is a raised design. Glazed fabrics have a resin that is put on as they pass through the calender. The result is a fabric with a highly polished surface, such as chintz.
2. **Delustering** is a process that treats fibers or fabrics with chemicals to reduce their gloss.
3. **Napping** creates a soft, fuzzy surface by using wire brushes to raise the short fiber ends of staple yarns. Flannel is one kind of a napped fabric.
4. **Sizing** refers to the process of adding starches or resins to the fabric for extra body. Sizing is usually only a temporary finish.

IMPROVING FABRIC PERFORMANCE

Many finishes do not add anything to the eye appeal of the fabric. However, they do make a great deal of difference in how the fabric acts.

Crease- and wrinkle-resistant finishes help stop the fabric from wrinkling or help it to recover more quickly when it does wrinkle.

Durable press and wash-and-wear finishes also help the fabric to wrinkle less during wear. The fabric can be washed and dried by machine. It will need little or no ironing as long as the care instructions are followed closely.

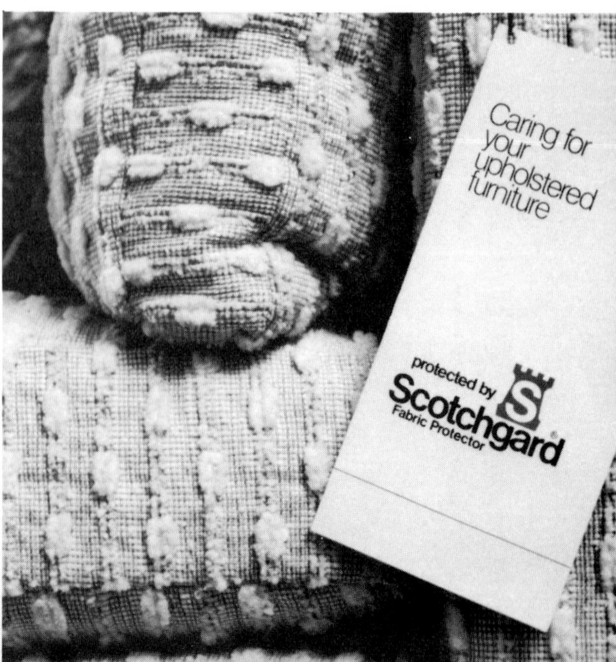

Caring for your upholstered furniture
protected by
Scotchgard
Fabric Protector

Today finishes are added to fabrics to protect them against soils and stains, moths, water, shrinking and flames.

Shrink-resistant finishes ensure that the fabric will not shrink or will shrink only a little bit. Sanforizing is a patented process that guarantees the fabric will shrink no more than 2 percent during future launderings.

Soil-release finishes make it easier to remove soil and oily stains from durable press fabrics and fabrics made from man-made fibers.

Stain- and spot-resistant finishes help fabrics to repel water-based and oil-based stains. These finishes are often used on fabrics from which table linens, upholstery, and clothes are made.

Antistatic finishes stop fabrics from clinging. These finishes are used often on lingerie fabrics.

Absorbent finishes help the fabric to absorb moisture more easily so that it is more comfortable to wear. Many fabrics that are used for active sportswear are treated with such finishes.

Waterproof finishes coat or treat the fabric so that it will not absorb water. Because some of these finishes stop body moisture from evaporating, the fabric may not be comfortable to wear. New microporous waterproof finishes have been found to stop this problem.

Water-repellent finishes help a fabric resist water. Because the fabric stays porous, it is still comfortable to wear. However, it will eventually become wet. The finish may need to be renewed when the garment is dry-cleaned. Raincoats are often treated with this finish.

Flame-retardant finishes help reduce flaming or burning in fabrics that have been exposed to flame or high heat. These finishes are used on some camping gear, children's sleepwear, and other clothing. Special care may be required to keep up the finish.

Other performance finishes stop mildew, repel moths and other fiber-eating insects, and check the growth of bacteria and perspiration odors.

LABELS AND HANGTAGS

When you consider buying a garment or a piece of fabric, how do you know what the fiber content is? How do you know how much it will shrink? How do you know what type of care the fabric will need? These questions and more can be answered by carefully reading and understanding the information on the labels and hangtags.

Upholstered furniture, carpeting and table linens are often treated with a stain and spot repellent. How does this increase the life span of the furnishings?

MANDATORY INFORMATION

In 1958, Congress passed the Textile Fibers Products Information Act. This law states that there are five kinds of information that must appear on labels, which must be attached to the garment. If you are buying fabric by the yard, this information must be attached to the fabric bolt.

1. *Fiber content.* Any fiber that makes up 5 percent or more of the garment by weight must be listed. The generic name of the fiber must be given.
2. *Percentage of fiber.* Fibers must be listed in the order of their weight. The fiber in the greatest amount is listed first. The fiber in the least amount is listed last.
3. *Brand label.* The label must tell you who is responsible for the product.
4. *Country of origin.* The label must tell you where the garment was made, such as "Made in the Philippines" or "Made in Hong Kong." All textile products made in the United States must have a label that says "Made in U.S.A."
5. *Care requirements.* The label must tell you how to wash or dry-clean the garment. It must also tell you if ironing is required and give the proper iron temperature. It must tell you if the fabric can be bleached and state what type of bleach is safe.

VOLUNTARY INFORMATION

Hangtags give voluntary information. They may tell you about how the fabric was made, describing it as a knit, a woven, a nonwoven, or a stretch fabric. Special finishes may be listed and described. Sometimes the hangtag will tell you how much the fabric may shrink. Hangtags can also act as advertisements and include such things as the logo, or symbol, for the product or maker, and words like "easy care," "elegant," "rugged," and "As seen in *Seventeen Magazine.*"

LOOK BEFORE YOU BUY

Fabric performance depends on the fibers used, the types of the yarns used, and the method used to make the cloth. Chemical and mechanical finishes put on the fabric can add desirable traits. As a consumer, you have two duties. The first is to know what you can expect from fabrics. The second is to examine carefully the item you wish to buy. Study the fabric and read the information found on the labels and hangtags. If you fulfill these duties, you will be able to make an informed buying decision.

Read clothing labels carefully. They are your clue to understanding the performance characteristics and care requirements of the fabrics in your life.

WORDS TO REMEMBER

calendering	generic	sizing	twist
delustering	napping	staple	warp
dope	ply	synthetic	woof (weft)
filament	selvage	trade name	

CHECKING YOUR UNDERSTANDING

1. What is the difference between a natural and a manufactured fiber? Give some examples of each. What is the difference between a generic name and a trade name? Give an example.
2. List the four best-known natural fibers. What are the advantages and disadvantages of each?
3. Explain what is meant by the terms *twist* and *ply*. How do they affect the looks and performance of a fabric?
4. Name and describe three finishes that can change the texture of a fabric and three finishes that will change its performance.
5. Describe the information that you might find on a label and a hangtag. By law, what information must appear there?

APPLYING YOUR UNDERSTANDING

1. Examine your wardrobe to identify the clothes that you wear only for active sports and the ones you wear only when you dress up. What is there about the fabrics that make these clothes good for one activity but not good for another?
2. As an experiment, go "window shopping" at your local fabric store. By feeling and looking at the fabric, can you guess the fiber content of a few of them? Can you guess how you would take care of them? Now take a look at the labels to see if you are right.
3. Pretend you are shopping for a raincoat and a jogging suit. What kind of fabric would you want for each of these items?
4. Pick out a room in your home or school. Take a close look at the fabrics that are used. Why are these fabrics good choices for the room setting? Would you want to wear a garment made from any of these fabrics? Explain why or why not.
5. Collect swatches of several fabrics. Can you tell which ones are knits and which ones are wovens? Can you identify the various types of weaves? Are any of them nonwovens? If necessary, use a magnifying glass so that you can see the details clearly.

Chapter 17 SMART SHOPPING

Has this ever happened to you?

Mark's brother was sitting in the living room watching TV when Mark came in. "Hey, Craig," said Mark, "I've got a big date tonight. Can I wear your new blue sweater?"

"No way," replied Craig. "I have plans to wear it . . . and besides, didn't you just buy a new red one yesterday?"

"Yeah," Mark grumbled, "but I don't have a shirt to wear with it. Besides, blue is Carrie's favorite color and I really want to impress her."

Craig looked at his watch. "It's only 4:00 p.m. You haven't worn that sweater yet so why don't you take it back to the store and get another one?"

"I can't," wailed Mark. "The salesperson told me it was a final sale and that I couldn't bring it back or exchange it. And if I go and buy another one, I won't have enough money left for my date tonight. C'mon, Craig, be a sport, huh?"

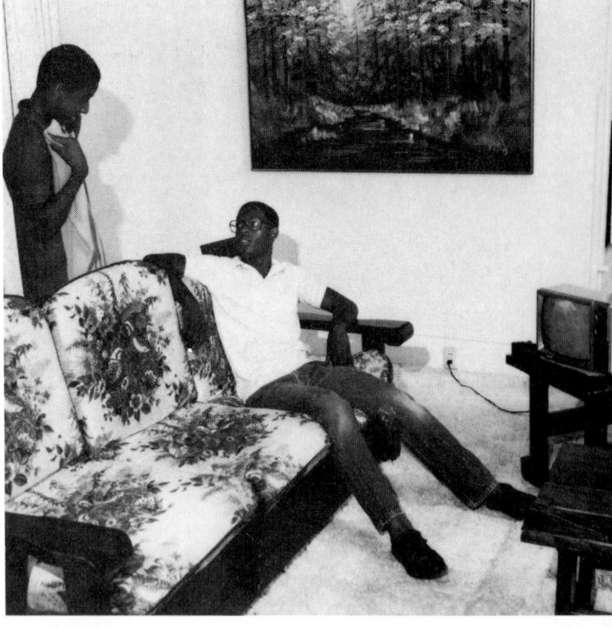

Have you ever bought something new only to find out when you got it home that it did not go with anything else in your wardrobe?

Have you ever wished you knew how to be a smarter shopper so that the clothes you bought were not only clothes you liked, but clothes you could use and afford?

After reading this chapter, you will be able to

- analyze and revise your wardrobe so that it is suitable for your tastes and activities;
- know what to expect when you shop in various kinds of stores;
- talk about the different ways used to pay for a purchase and give the pros and cons of each.

When a special occasion arises, are you one of those people who always feels you have "nothing to wear?" If so, you are not alone. Did you know that most people wear 10 percent of their wardrobe 90 percent of the time? That means they wear the same things over and over, while they let other garments lie or hang unworn in drawers and closets. Often, this has nothing to do with how much clothing they own or how much money they spend. People with small clothing budgets may have as many unworn clothes or may feel they have nothing suitable to wear as often as those with larger clothing budgets.

Have you ever wondered why some people seem to have better luck with their clothing purchases, regardless of how much money they spend? Fortunately, luck has very little to do with it. They are the people who have learned the rules of being smart shoppers. They know how to examine their wardrobe so that they can judge their needs and learn from their mistakes. They know where to shop. They know how to make their choices so that the items that are not suitable stay in the store. They also make sure that they know about the various ways to pay for their purchases.

ANALYZING YOUR WARDROBE

The first step in becoming a smart shopper is to analyze the clothes you own. Once you have done this, you will be able to see why some of your clothes have stayed in style longer than others. You will be able to decide which clothes are still tasteful and which ones should be thrown out. And you will know what items you need to fill in the gaps in your wardrobe.

You can solve your wardrobe problems. Begin by analyzing each garment in terms of your tastes, lifestyle and activities.

FASHION TERMS

Before you begin to analyze your wardrobe, it will be helpful if you could label the clothes in your closet in certain fashion terms. If you learn to know the differences among fads, classics, and trends, you will be able to see why some clothes stay in fashion for a very long time, while others pass out of date very quickly.

A Fad

A **fad** is a fashion that is popular for a very short time. A fad can be a style, such as army fatigues or miniskirts. A fad can be a color, such as fuchsia or parrot green. A fad can be an accessory, such as leg warmers or a lace scarf. A fad can also be a certain look, such as "punk rock." Fads are often inspired by popular movies, television shows, rock stars, and sports figures.

A fad is a fashion that is popular for a very short time. What fads are popular now?

A Classic

A **classic** is a traditional style that stays in fashion for a long time. Button-down shirts, loafers, pleated skirts, blazers, blue jeans, and turtleneck sweaters are all classic styles.

This classic look of a button-down shirt, sweater and loafers is a traditional style that has stayed in fashion for a long time.

A Trend

A **trend** is a slow change in a certain style or way of wearing clothes. For example, in the late 1960s and early 1970s skirts were very short. Slowly, skirt lengths became longer. In the late 1970s and early 1980s, it was high fashion to wear mid-calf-length skirts with boots or dark stockings. By the mid-1980s, the popular skirt length was just below the knee. Men's ties have gone through similar changes. In the 1940s they were very wide, but by 1960 they were very narrow. Then, in the 1970s, when suits with wide lapels were popular, ties became wider. By the 1980s, when styles became more conservative, ties narrowed to a medium width. These slow, recurring changes in styles are called **fashion cycles.**

It can be difficult to tell the difference between a fad and a trend. Sometimes, you have to wait to see if a style is still around for a second season. When shoulder pads reappeared in women's clothes in the early 1980s, many people at first thought it was a fad. However, it turned out to be a trend. Shoulder pads continued to be popular for several years.

TAKING INVENTORY

An **inventory** is a detailed list of goods or property. Taking inventory is an essential first step in analyzing your wardrobe.

Begin by preparing a form for a personal inventory record. This will enable you to write down everything in a way that will be helpful to you. Once your form is filled in, it will be easy to see if you have too many of one type of garment or not enough of another.

To prepare the form for your personal inventory record, make a list of all your activities, such as school, job, sports, social events, hobbies, and even sleeping. Write down each of these activities as a heading across the top of a sheet of paper. Then, as you look through your drawers and closets, list under each heading those clothes that are suitable for that activity. Because many clothes and accessories are suitable for more than one type of activity, a garment may be listed in more than one column.

The second step is to remove everything from your closets and drawers. Sort them into three piles: the things you wear 90 percent of the time, the things that you wear now and then, and the things that you never wear.

Begin with the clothes in the 90 percent pile. Decide for which activities each garment is worn and enter it in the appropriate columns. When you list a garment, write down the type, such "dress" or "coat," the color, and a short description, such as "dressy," "casual," or "classic." Once you have listed the garment in the proper columns on your inventory form, return the item to your closet or drawers.

Now look at the pile of clothes that you seldom wear. Before listing each of these garments, try to figure out why you do not wear it more often. Perhaps the garment is good only for special events. If that is the case, enter the item on your inventory form and return it to your closet. Perhaps you bought the garment because it was a fad and now it looks out-of-date. If you have a great many fads in this pile, you may need to rethink your buying habits. Perhaps the garment is not comfortable or does not go with the other clothes in your wardrobe. In that case, add the garment to the third pile of clothes.

PERSONAL INVENTORY RECORD

	School	Job	Sports	Special Events	Hobbies
Slacks					
Shirts					
Jackets					
Skirts					
Sweaters					
Accessories					

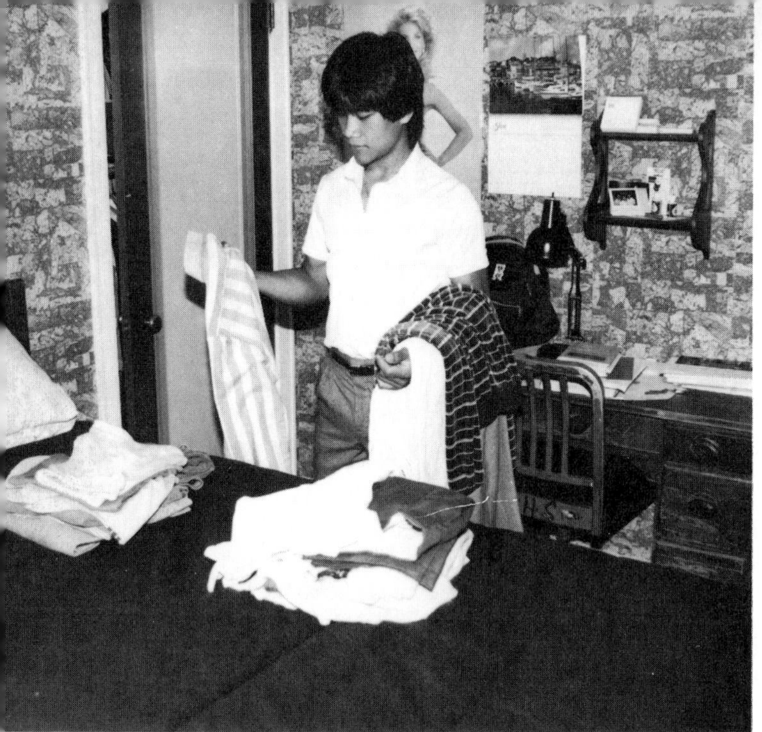

Some clothes have built-in versatility, they can be worn for more than one activity. What clothes in your closet are versatile?

Dyeing is an inexpensive way to redesign clothes and to create a new garment for your wardrobe.

ANALYZING THE ALTERNATIVES

The third step is to examine the pile of clothes that you never wear and decide what to do with each garment. These clothes are candidates for the four "Rs"—repair, redesign, recycle, or reject.

Repairs

Many times, all a garment needs to make it useful is some small repair or alteration. Perhaps it needs some buttons. Perhaps the hem is the wrong length or has been torn out and needs to be resewn. In chapter 18, you will learn how to make some of these small repairs.

Redesigning

Some garments can be redesigned to make them look new again. A full garment might be altered to make it look more fitted. A pair of pants might be made into shorts. A shirtdress might look very different if it were cut off to tunic length and worn over pants. Some coats can be made into jackets. Some jackets can be made into vests. If the color has faded, or if a white garment has turned permanently gray, perhaps dyeing it a new color is the answer. Look at current fashion magazines for ideas. If your ideas are more advanced than your sewing skills, get help from a friend or family member who sews.

Recycling

What can you do with clothes that are still in good condition but cannot be repaired or redesigned into a garment that you want in your wardrobe? What do you do with a wearable garment that you no longer like or that does not go with anything else in your wardrobe? A third choice is to recycle it so that it becomes part of another person's wardrobe. Perhaps you could pass the garment along to a younger family member. Or you and your friends could hold a clothes meet and trade garments. The shirt or blouse that is not flattering to one person might look great on another.

Perhaps there is a charity or a **thrift shop** that you could give these garments to. Perhaps there is a **consignment shop** near your home that will sell your used clothes for you. This type of store puts your clothes up for sale, but you do not get any money until the store sells the items. The store takes a percentage of the selling price and then gives you the balance. If the store cannot sell them within a certain length of time, you must come and pick up the items. If you do not want them or forget to pick them up, the store may give your clothes to a charity.

Consider taking clothes that you no longer wear to a thrift shop or a consignment store, so that other people can benefit from the garment.

Rejects

These are clothes that are too worn or too stained to be of use to anyone. If this is the case, throw them away. If the fabric is very absorbent, such as 100 percent cotton or a cotton blend, you might wish to put it in the family rag bag. You can use these cloths to dust, wipe, and polish furniture and floors. Be sure to remove any trims, hooks, and snaps that might scratch the surfaces that you clean.

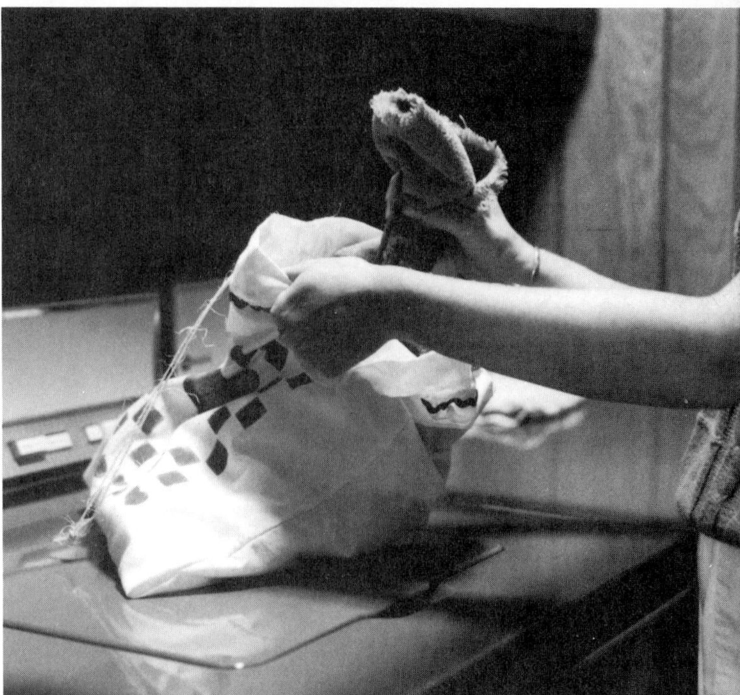

Add retired garments made from 100% cotton or cotton blends to the family rag bag. They come in handy for cleaning furniture and floors.

FILLING IN THE GAPS

Once you have decided which clothes are usable, you will be ready to make a final analysis of your wardrobe. To do this, you will need to look at your inventory form.

At this point, your inventory form should list all the clothes that you can currently wear, plus those that you plan to repair or redesign. Compare your list of activities with your list of clothes. Do you see any problems? Are some areas blank? Do you have several garments for rare events and only a few for common activities? How many garments do you feel you need for each kind of activity?

Make a list of the clothes you think you need to make your wardrobe more suitable to your lifestyle. Include the color and the type of fabric. Now look at this list in terms of your clothing budget. Do you really need everything on your list? Could some of your "wants" be set aside until they go on sale? Evaluate your sewing skills. You might save money if you sew some of your own clothes. Decide which clothes you want to sew and which you want to buy.

Use this list as your shopping plan. That way, the clothes you buy or sew will be well planned and usable.

EVALUATING YOUR SELECTION

Once you find a garment that you think you like, how do you decide if it really belongs in your wardrobe? Your answers to the questions below will tell you what you need to know.

Ask yourself these questions before you try on the garment:

• *Will it go with the rest of my wardrobe?* Do not be tempted to buy a red shirt if a blue one is what you really need.

• *Does it suit my life-style?* If most of your activities require very casual clothes in washable fabrics, a dry-clean-only silk dress is probably not the best choice unless it is for a very special occasion.

• *What are the care requirements?* Will you really take the time and trouble to hand wash that sweater? If the shirt has to be ironed every time you wear it, will it end up in an ironing basket?

• *How long can I expect this garment to stay in fashion?* The smart shopper sticks to classic styles when choosing garments that must last for several seasons. The smart shopper may occasionally purchase a fad item, but it generally will be an inexpensive item.

• *How much will it cost me to take care of this garment?* It costs more to dry-clean a garment than to wash it. A pale garment will need to be washed or cleaned more often than a dark one.

• *Is the quality worth the price?* Think about all the things you learned about fabric performance in chapter 16. Do you think you are paying for a fabric that will perform the way you expect it to? Now look at the quality of the workmanship. Look at the seams, the closures, the hemline. Is everything stitched neatly and securely? Are all the curves smooth and the corners sharp? As you learn more about sewing your own clothes in chapters 19 and 20, you will become a better judge of workmanship.

If you are satisfied with your answers to those questions, it is time to take the garment to the fitting room to try it on. Once you do, there are two more questions to consider:

• *How does the garment look on you?* Does it fit properly? Is it a flattering style and color? Does it stress your good points while it plays down others? Think about all the things you learned in chapter 15 about the elements and rules of design.

• *Is it comfortable?* Stand up and raise your arms over your head. Then, bend over and try to touch your toes. Now sit down. How did the garment feel when you did each of these things?

WHERE TO SHOP

Once you have analyzed your wardrobe and drawn up a shopping plan, you must put that plan into action.

Newspapers, radio, and TV are full of ads from all kinds of stores. Catalogs and brochures urge you daily to buy things through the mail. How are you going to decide where to buy the things you need? Before you begin, it will help to know something about all the different kinds of stores.

The kind of store you choose will rest on the type and choice of merchandise, the price, the locale, the special services, the sales staff, and the reputation. Some of these things may be important to you; others may not.

DEPARTMENT STORES

Department stores are stores that carry a wide range of many types of goods. They usually have clothes for all family members, from infants to adults. These stores also may carry other items, such as makeup, appliances, furniture, and sporting goods.

Department stores usually have a head office or main store, as well as other stores called branches. The items in each store are organized into areas called departments. These departments may be arranged by the types of items sold there, such as shoes, skirts, coats, and so forth. They also might be arranged according to fashion and price, such as designer clothes and budget.

Department stores also offer services that most other kinds of stores do not. These services include gift wrapping, alterations, repairs, hair styling, and many others.

Department stores carry goods from many manufacturers. Sometimes, they ask a manufacturer to make items for their stores only. The store then puts its own name, rather than the manufacturer's name, on the item. This is known as a **private label.**

Department stores offer a range of sizes, styles and goods to choose from, as well as gift wrapping, alterations and hair styling.

SPECIALTY STORES

A specialty store is a store that has a small range of items. The store may carry clothing for one group of people, such as children, working women, teenagers, or expectant mothers. It may also carry one type of goods, such as camping gear, costumes, shoes, swim suits, toys and games, or gifts and flowers. Specialty stores that carry high-fashion clothes or unique items are called **boutiques.**

Most specialty stores are owned by one or more persons. Salespeople will usually give you special care. Many of these stores will special order an item for you if they do not have the size or color you want. If you return an item, some stores will not give you back your money. Instead, they will give you credit toward another item in the store.

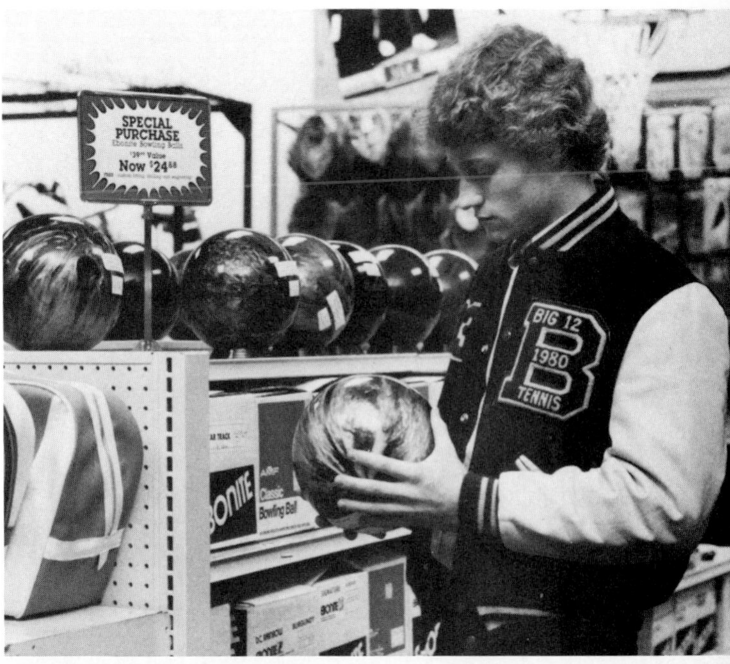

This speciality store specializes in sporting goods. Only merchandise related to sports is carried here.

DISCOUNT STORES

Discount stores are stores that usually charge lower prices for their goods than other stores. To be sure you get a good price, you must learn to compare prices and quality. Other kinds of stores may have special sales with lower prices than the discount stores.

When discount stores first opened, you had to pay cash for the items you bought. Today, most discount stores will let you pay by check. Some of them will also let you pay by credit card.

OUTLET STORES

An **outlet store** sells only the items made by the manufacturer that owns it. Sometimes more than one manufacturer will own an outlet store together.

Some outlets have dressing rooms where you can try on clothes. Others do not. This means that you should be familiar with the brand of clothes and the size you wear in that brand before you go to the outlet. If you do not, you may waste your money and end up with a garment that you will have to give to someone else.

Most outlet stores require cash, though some will take checks. They seldom take credit cards.

VARIETY STORES

Variety stores are stores that sell many kinds of merchandise. Drugstores, supermarkets, and five-and-dime stores are all variety stores. Clothes are usually only a small part of what they sell. Although the clothes section is small, this type of store may be a handy source for items such as underwear, hosiery, and some accessories.

CATALOG AND MAIL ORDER STORES

In the 1970s, when gasoline prices soared, people began to look for ways to use their car less often. Catalog and mail order shopping began to grow more popular. For many people, it is an easy way to shop because it saves time and effort. Many mail order houses specialize in goods that are not easy to find in most stores.

The mail order house sends you a catalog or a brochure. You order what you want with a mail order form or with a phone call. Some mail houses have an 800 number, which means that they pay for the phone call. Otherwise, you must pay for the call.

There are some draw backs to mail order shopping. You do not always know exactly what an item looks like. You cannot be sure that it will fit or that the color will match. Most mail order houses will return your money if you are not happy with your purchase. As a safeguard, however, always read the fine print in the catalog about return policies and guarantees.

Don't rely on discount stores to be less expensive. Compare quality and price of similar merchandise before making your purchase.

Catalog shopping dates back to the turn of the century. It is a convenient way to shop especially if you know exactly what you want.

OTHER PLACES TO SHOP

In the past several years, bazaars, flea markets, fairs, and garage sales have become popular events. Going to them has become a social event as well as a shopping activity.

Thrift shops also have become popular places to shop. This is especially true for young persons who want to find and wear clothes from 1950s and 1960s, which has become a popular fad. **Thrift shops** are stores that carry used clothes and household items. Many of these stores are run by church groups.

Bazaars, flea markets, and fairs rent booths or tables to people at convenient locations, such as churches, schools, shopping malls, parking lots, or fields. These people sell new items, bought directly from a factory, or used items. A flea market, bazaar, or fair may be held only at certain times of the year or on certain days of the week. If it is a regular event, the same vendors, or people who sell the goods, may not be there every time you go.

Garage sales and tag sales are usually held by one or more families. They can be an enjoyable way to get rid of clothes and other items that the family no longer wants or uses.

You must take care when you shop in any of these places. If you do, you may be able to find something new at a very good price, something used that is in good shape, or a rare item. You will probably have to pay in cash, and you will not be able to get your money back if you change your mind.

PAYING FOR YOUR PURCHASES

There are many ways to pay for your purchases. Your options include cash, a check, credit card, layaway, money order, or C.O.D. As you have just learned, different kinds of stores permit various types of payment. Even if a store lets you choose the way you pay; you must look at the pros and cons of each and choose the way that is best for you.

CASH

All stores take cash. It is the simplest form of payment. Paying cash is an easy way to stay within your budget. If you always pay in cash, you will not spend more money than you have. However, if you order something by mail, you should not send cash because it can easily be stolen and you will not be able to prove that you sent it.

CHECKS

Paying by check is almost as easy as paying by cash. You put your money in the bank and the bank provides you with a series of checks. Each time you use a check, you write down the name of the payee and the amount paid in the check register. After subtracting the amount paid from the previous balance, you find your new balance, or the money you have in the bank.

It is important to balance your checkbook after each transaction so that you know how much money you have in the bank.

CREDIT CARDS

When you buy on credit, you are buying something based on your promise and ability to pay in the future. Credit cards are handy because you do not have to keep large sums of cash on you. It is also easier to return or exchange an item. A credit is simply made to your account.

When paying with credit be sure to budget the payment that will be billed within the month.

LAYAWAY

When you buy an item on layaway, you give the store a **down payment,** or part of the cost, and agree to pay the balance by a certain date. In return, the store holds the item for you. Once the balance is paid, the item is yours.

An advantage to this way of paying is that you can buy something on credit even if you do not own a credit card. Although there may be a service charge, you will not have to pay any interest. A disadvantage is that you do not have the item until the store gets its money. In the meantime, the store can use some of your money interest free.

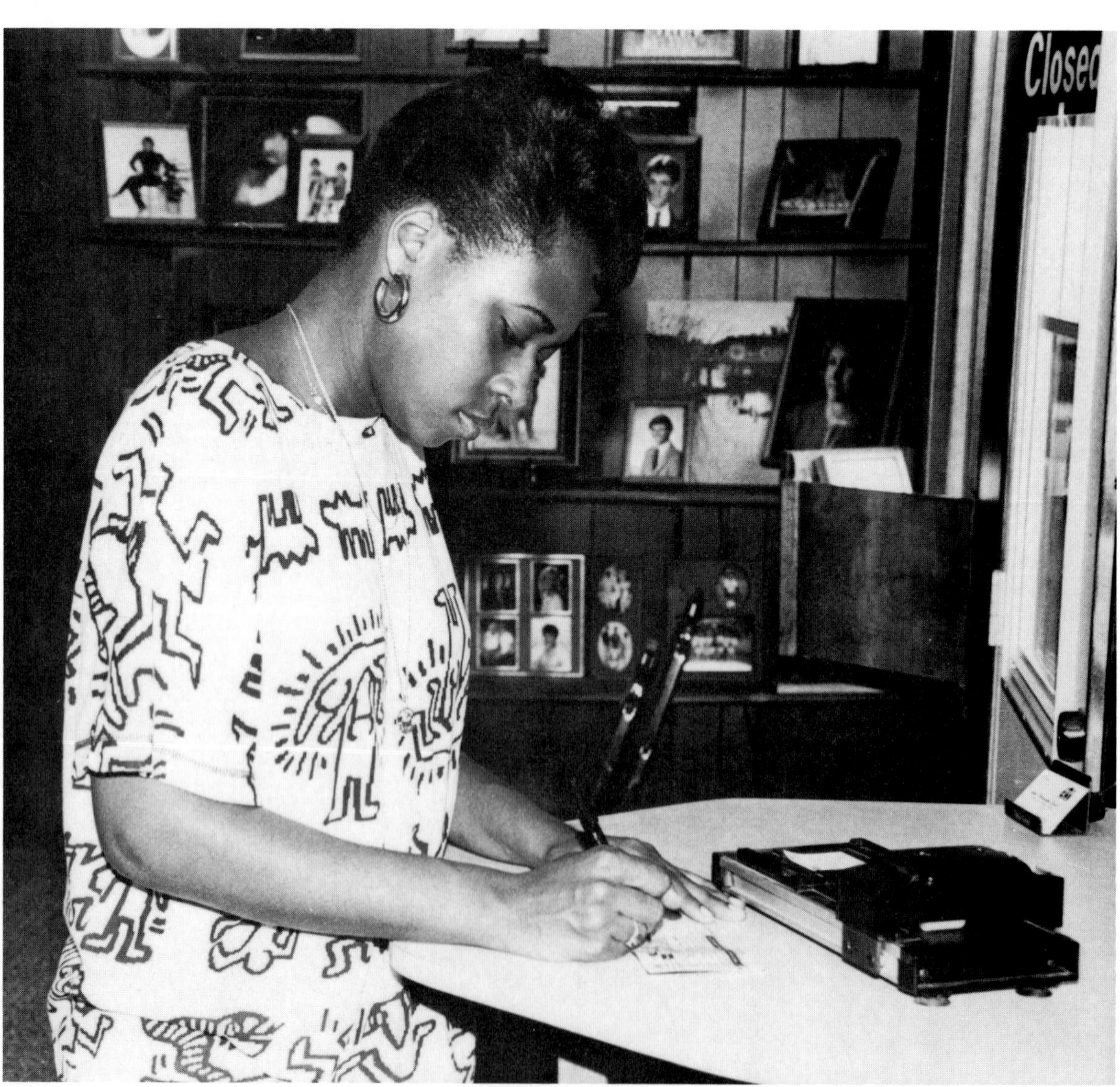

MONEY ORDERS

A money order is similar to a check, but you do not have to open a checking account. Instead, you take your money to a bank or post office and exchange it for a check made out for a certain amount to whomever you wish. When that person or company receives the money order, they can exchange it for cash at the bank.

If you do not have a checking account or a credit card, a money order is a way to pay for an item that you order from a catalog or a mail order company.

C.O.D. PURCHASES

C.O.D., or cash on delivery, is another way to pay for items that are mailed to you. When the package arrives, you must pay the money to the delivery person. Many stores will not ship C.O.D. Those that do may ask for a small down payment and charge a delivery fee.

KNOW BEFORE YOU GO

To be a smart shopper you must do some preplanning. Know your needs before you go to the store. That way you will not come home with a "great" bargain that does not go with anything else in your wardrobe. Know what to expect from the type of store where you are shopping. Do not expect the salespersons in a discount or outlet store to be as helpful as those in a department store or specialty shop. Decide in advance how much you have to spend and how you are going to pay for your purchases. That way you will not get your heart set on something you cannot afford.

Get the most from your clothing dollars by identifying your needs, planning your shopping strategies and knowing where to shop.

Review CHAPTER 17

WORDS TO REMEMBER

boutique
classic
C.O.D.
consignment shop
down payment
fad
fashion cycle
inventory
outlet store
private label
thrift shop
trend

CHECKING YOUR UNDERSTANDING

1. What are the differences among fads, classics, and trends? Give at least two examples of each.
2. What are the benefits of taking an inventory of your wardrobe? What can you do with the clothes that you seldom or never wear?
3. Describe the various kinds of stores where you can buy clothes.
4. If you needed an item of clothing but did not have the cash handy to pay for it, what ways of payment could you use? Which ones would you use if you needed the garment right away?
5. If you want to order something from a catalog or by mail, how would you pay for it? What are the pros and cons of each method?

APPLYING YOUR UNDERSTANDING

1. Pick out one garment from your wardrobe that you seldom wear. Make sure it is one that is in good shape. How many ways can you think of to redesign this garment? Be as creative as possible, then decide which ways are best in terms of your budget and sewing skills.
2. Visit several banks and stores that offer credit cards and ask them for a copy of their credit card agreement. Read the agreements carefully and be ready to discuss how they differ.
3. Go through the newspaper to see if you can find ads from several kinds of stores, such as a department store, a specialty store, a discount store, and an outlet. What do their ads tell you about the differences among these stores?
4. Get together with your classmates and bring in several different mail order catalogs. Examine them carefully. Which ones seem to give you a better idea of what the merchandise is really like? Is it because of the picture or the description or both? Compare the various refund and return policies.
5. Make a list of the five stores you shop in most often. Now analyze why you are a frequent customer. Is it the price, the service, the type of goods, the locale? Does this tell you anything about yourself as a shopper?

Chapter 18

CLOTHING CARE AND MAINTENANCE

Has this ever happened to you?

Marcie was upstairs getting ready to go out when she heard a car pull into the driveway. "Mom," she called downstairs frantically, "please tell them to wait. I'm not ready yet."

Marcie heard her mother go to the front door. A few minutes later, her mother came to her bedroom door. "Bobbie says if you're not downstairs in five minutes, they're all leaving without you."

"But they can't!" wailed Marcie. "I've been waiting all month to see that movie."

"Then why aren't you ready?" asked her mother.

"Well," Marcie began, "first my skirt needed ironing, then my blouse was missing a button. I hate the way I look in this sweater but the other one was dirty . . . and now one of my shoes is missing. *Please* ask them to wait."

Her mother nodded and headed back downstairs. Marcie was on the verge of tears. "Why does everything happen to me? I must be jinxed or something!"

Have you ever wondered how some people always manage to look neat and well-groomed?

Have you ever thought about how you could plan an easy-to-follow system for taking care of your wardrobe?

After reading this chapter, you will be able to

- understand that responsible clothing care will save you time and money, and make good first impressions;
- describe daily, weekly, and seasonal wardrobe maintenance;
- develop a system for organizing your storage space;
- recognize the benefits of making minor repairs on your garments.

In the earlier chapters of this unit, you learned how to use the elements and principles of design to create a pleasing appearance. You learned what performance traits to look for in the fabrics you choose. You also learned how to analyze your wardrobe and how to shop wisely for your clothes. However, all of this knowledge will be wasted unless you learn how to take care of your wardrobe.

TAKING RESPONSIBILITY

If you learn and follow the rules of wardrobe care, you will be able to make a better impression on other people. You will be able to keep your favorite clothes looking like new for a longer time. And, once you make up and follow a routine, you will find that it actually saves you time.

FIRST IMPRESSIONS

When you are meeting a group of people for the first time, why do you quickly like some people more than others? What is it about one person that makes you want to talk to him or her, while another person seems less interesting?

A **first impression** is an image someone forms about you when they meet you for the first time. Whether you know it or not, your clothes, your grooming, your mannerisms, the tone of your voice, and the expression on your face send out messages to the world around you. People respond to those messages in a positive or a negative way.

Most people respond in a positive way to a person who is well-groomed and dressed in clothes that are right for the occasion. They tend to think that the person with a neat appearance is more responsible, more mature, smarter, and more pleasant to be with than the person who is sloppy and not groomed well.

What first impressions do each of these images create? How does the posture affect the impression?

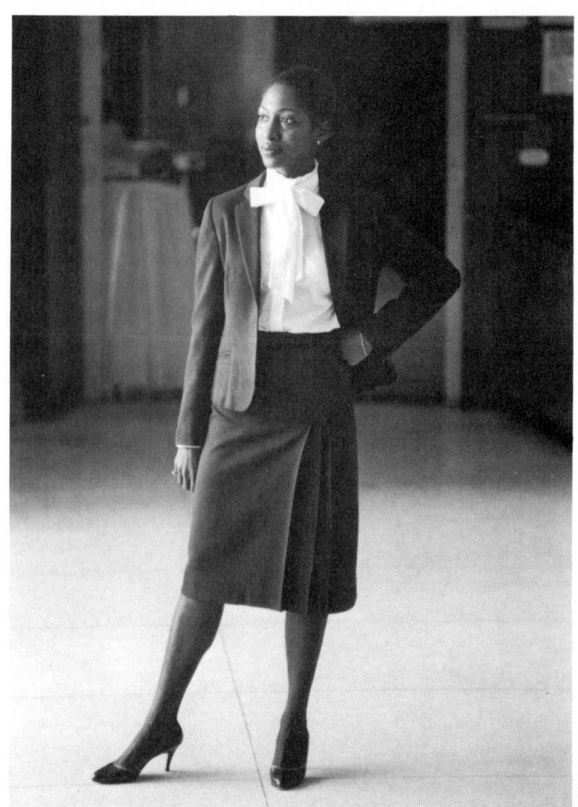

SAVING TIME

Once you make up a plan to care for and maintain your wardrobe, you will find that you actually have more time for the things you want to do. Clothes that are hung up after each wearing will not need to be cleaned and pressed as often as clothes that are left in a pile on the floor. Clothes that are stored in an organized manner are easier to find than those that are left lying around or put away carelessly. Rips, holes, and tears are easier and quicker to fix when they are small.

SAVING MONEY

Routine maintenance can save you money. For example, clothes that are aired out and brushed between wearings will not need to be sent to the cleaners as often. Clothes that are well cared for last longer. And when your clothes last longer, that saves you money. Learning how to sew on a button, fix a hem, or mend a seam will save you the cost of paying someone else to do it for you. It will also stop your garment from becoming damaged beyond repair. It makes more sense to mend a garment that is in otherwise good shape than to buy a new one.

A little bit of routine care, such as brushing a jacket, will make your clothes last longer and save you money.

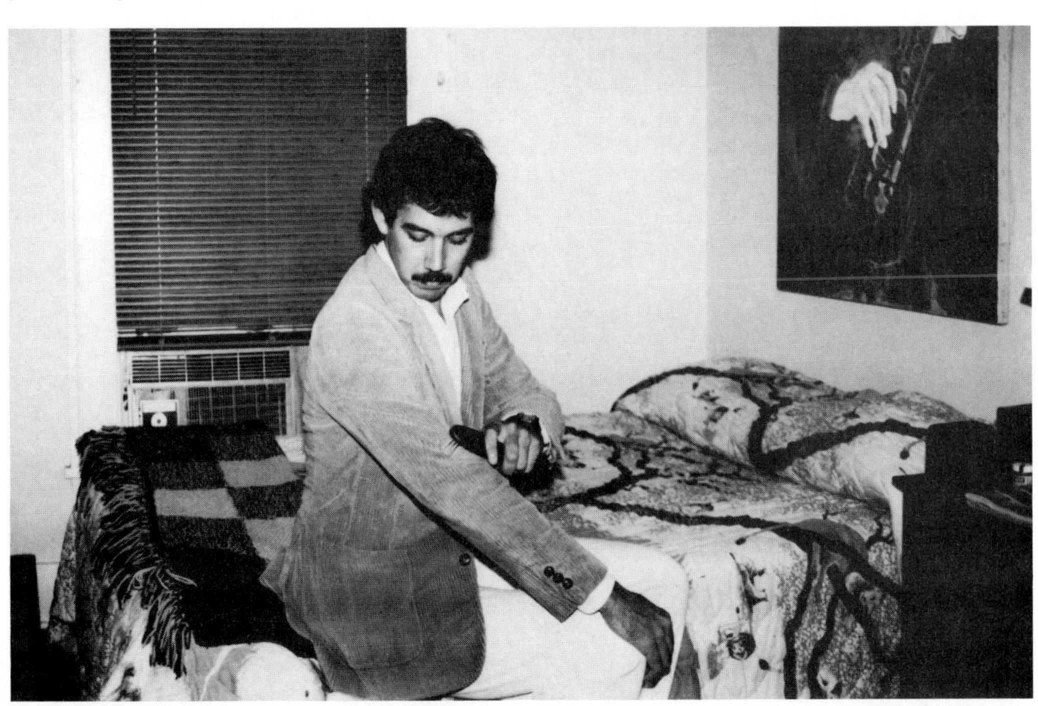

DEVELOPING A SYSTEM

A **system** is a logical, orderly way to do something. It is a plan of action. Taking care of your wardrobe is a two-step system. The first step is to organize your storage space. The second step is to make up a daily, weekly, and seasonal routine to care for your clothes.

ORGANIZING YOUR STORAGE SPACE

Have you ever heard the saying "a place for everything and everything in its place"? It is good advice to follow when you are organizing your storage space. Some clothes will last longer if you hang them up carefully in a closet. Other clothes should be folded and stored in boxes or drawers. If everything has its own space, and you always put it back in that place, it will be easier to find when you need it.

A Personal Matter

An efficient closet space is a very personal matter. No two persons, no two wardrobes, and no two living spaces are alike. You might have a small or a large closet. You might have your own or you might share one with another family member. You might be able to increase your storage space with a large dresser or a few drawers. You might be able to store out-of-season clothes in an attic, a storage room, or in boxes under your bed. No matter what your personal situation, there are things you can do to get more use out of the space available to you.

EXPANDING YOUR CLOSET

There are many simple, but cheap, ways to arrange your closet space so that clothes and belongings are organized and easy to find.

- Use the closet frame and the back of the closet door for more storage space. Plastic, ceramic, or wire hooks make good places to hang nightwear and jeans. For a cheap substitute, use nails.
- Hang pegboard on the inside of the closet door or to the back wall of the closet. It will give you plenty of space to hang belts, scarves, bags, or clothes brushes.
- Scarves can be hung in a variety of ways. One way is to attach them to a skirt hanger or a man's pants hanger so they hang flat. Another way is to put spring-action clothes pins on the crossbar of a wire coat hanger and then hang the scarves by one corner from each of the clothes pins. This also makes a good belt rack.
- Screw cup hooks into the bottom of the crossbar on a large wooden hanger. This is a good place to hang belts or necklaces.
- A man's tie rack mounted on the wall or on the back of a closet door can be used to store ties or belts.
- Use see-through wire baskets on shelves or on the floor to hold items that must be folded.
- A plastic tableware organizer is a cheap, but effective, way to keep your jewelry sorted out. Put it on a shelf in your closet or in a drawer.
- Hang your shoes in shoe bags or leave them in their boxes and stack them on a shelf or on the floor. Label the end of each box with a description of the shoes inside. That way you will not need to open all the boxes to find the right pair of shoes.
- Flea markets, yard sales, and thrift shops are all good sources for items such as towel racks and kitchen mug racks that can be used for hanging belts, ties, or jewelry. You might also get a good buy on sturdy wooden hangers and garment bags.

Arranging Your Closet

Hang the long garments in one part of the closet. Then, hang all the short garments, such as skirts, shirts, blouses, slacks, and jackets, in another part of the closet. You may be able to make more storage space by adding a second row below the short garments. You can buy special rods for this purpose or you can hang an old broom handle to the top rod with pieces of rope.

Do not hang sweaters, knits, or bias-cut clothes. They will stretch out of shape on a hanger. Instead, fold them and store them on a shelf in the closet, in a drawer, or in a box under your bed. If you use a box, make a list of what is in it and tape the list to the top of the box. That way, if you need something, you will know just where to find it.

By organizing your storage space and carefully putting your clothes where they belong, you will spend less time looking for them.

Shelves above the rod can be used to store handbags, extra shoes, and boxes for sweaters. Use clear, plastic boxes so you can see what is in them or clearly label the ends of the cardboard boxes.

Fabrics that shed, such as mohair or angora, should not be stored next to fabrics like velvet and corduroy that attract hairs and fibers. That way, you will not have to spend time brushing off a garment before you wear it.

All clothing experts suggest using padded, wooden, or plastic hangers rather than wire hangers. Wire hangers are used by dry cleaners as an inexpensive means of holding clothes. They were not meant to be permanent storage items. They tend to crease clothes along the shoulders and may even poke holes in some fabrics. If they are the only type of hangers that you have, pad them in some way. You might wrap the wire with scraps of fabric or old ties or scarves. You might crochet binding around the wire, using odd scraps of yarn, strips of cloth, or old nylon hosiery. You can even make fitted covers out of quilted or felt fabric scraps.

Garment bags help to protect your better clothes. Fabric bags are best. They keep the garments clean while letting them breathe. Leather, silk, fur, and down-filled clothes should never be stored in plastic cleaner's bags. They need air circulation to prevent mildew. An old, clean sheet draped around the garment is an easy, cheap way to make a garment bag.

Fold or hang and store out-of-season clothes in a special place so that only the clothes you are currently wearing are in your closet.

DAILY CARE

One of the worst things you can do to your clothes is to leave them in a pile on the floor or on a chair. You only make more work for yourself. Odors, wrinkles, and soil spots will increase. Stains can become permanently set. Clothes may need double or triple the amount of work to get them ready to wear again.

When you take off a piece of clothing, take a good look at it. Is it clean enough to be worn again? If the answer is yes, brush off any dust, dirt, or lint and put it on a hanger. Fasten any zippers, buttons, or other closures so that the garment hangs straight. Then, before putting it in the closet, let it hang for a few hours in a place where air can circulate around it. This will give the garment a chance to air out, let body moisture dry up, and allow wrinkles to hang out.

It is a good idea to get into the habit of pressing a garment before you put it back in the closet. That way, it will be ready the next time you want to wear it. Some clothes, such as those that have a large amount of linen or wool, need no more than a steam pressing. An easy way to do this is to let the garment hang in the bathroom while you take a shower. The steam and heat may be enough to remove the wrinkles. Be sure the garment is thoroughly dry before you hang it back in the closet.

If the garment is soiled, put it in the laundry basket or in a special place to remind you to take it to the dry cleaner. If it is stained, try to remove the stain as soon as possible. The longer a stain stays in a fabric, the harder it is to remove.

At the same time you are looking for soil or stains, also look to see if repairs need to be made. If you mend a garment before you put it back in your closet, it will be ready to wear the next time you need it. Because cleaning can put strain on the damaged area, garments should be repaired before being laundered or dry-cleaned. It may help you to be more organized if you have a hook or part of your closet where you can hang clothes that need cleaning or mending. When you have a few minutes free, the clothes that need care will be in one spot.

Properly remove stains as soon as possible to prevent them from permanently setting into the fabric.

STAIN REMOVAL

General points to remember:
- Identify the stain.
- Identify the fiber content of garment.
- Treat immediately: fresh stains are easier to remove than old ones.
- Test a stain remover on a seam, facing, or hem to check for color change or damage.
- Blot or scrape off excess stain.
- Work on wrong side—push stain out, not in.
- Work patiently and carefully.
- Do not use hot water on an unknown stain.
- Follow directions and safety suggestions when working with spot removers.
- If stain is large or stubborn, take garment to your dry cleaner and tell him what the stain is.
- Many stains can be removed through regular washing.

Almost 75 percent of all stains can be removed from washable garments by using cool water to dilute the stain or by soaking it in cool water, rubbing with detergent, and then laundering. Use liquid detergent or make a paste of powdered detergent and water. Use the hottest water possible for the fabric. Use a chlorine bleach if the fabric will stand it.

Specific stains can be removed from washable fabrics by using the following methods:
- *Adhesive tape.* Rub with ice to harden. Scrape. Rub in heavy duty detergent and grease solvent. Soak overnight. Lift off stain. Launder.
- *Alcoholic beverages.* Sponge with cool water. Rub with detergent. Launder.
- *Ballpoint pen.* Sponge with rubbing alcohol *or* spray with hair spray. Rub with detergent. Launder garment.
- *Blood.* Soak in cool water. Rub with detergent. Rinse. If stain remains, add ammonia and repeat detergent treatment. Launder.
- *Candle wax.* Rub with ice to harden. Scrape. Place stain between paper towels. Press with warm iron. Place face down on paper towel. Sponge with cleaning solvent. Let dry. Launder.
- *Carbon paper.* Rub detergent into stain. Rinse. Add a few drops of ammonia if stain remains. Repeat detergent treatment. Launder.

STAIN REMOVAL (Continued)

- *Carbon paper—duplicating.* Sponge with rubbing alcohol. (Dilute two parts water with one part alcohol when using on acetate.) Let dry. Rub with detergent. Launder.
- *Catsup.* Scrape. Sponge and/or soak in cool water. Rub with detergent. Launder.
- *Chewing gum.* Rub with ice to harden. Scrape. Let soak in heavy duty detergent and grease solvent overnight. Lift off. Launder.
- *Chocolate.* Sponge and/or soak in cool water. Rub with liquid detergent. Rinse. Let dry. Use spot remover to remove greasy stain. Launder.
- *Coffee, tea.* Sponge and/or soak in cool water. Rub with detergent. Launder.
- *Cosmetics.* Dampen stain. Rub with detergent until suds are thick and outline of stain is removed. Use spot remover to remove greasy stain. Launder.
- *Crayon (few spots).* Scrape, then do the same as for cosmetics.
- *Crayon (load of cloths).* Wash with hot water (if possible for fabrics) using detergent and one cup baking soda *or* dry-clean.
- *Cream, ice cream, milk.* Sponge and/or soak in cool water. Rub in detergent. Rinse, let dry. Use spot remover to remove greasy stains. Launder.
- *Deodorants, antiperspirants.* Rub with detergent. Launder garment. Restore color with ammonia (new stains) or vinegar (old stains). Rinse.
- *Dye transfer.* May be impossible to remove. Use a color remover on white fabrics. Soak colored fabrics in a presoak. Launder.
- *Fingernail polish.* May be impossible to remove. Sponge with nail polish remover, except on acetate. Let dry. Rub in detergent. Launder.
- *Fruits, berries.* Sponge and/or soak in cool water. Rub with detergent. Launder. (If safe for fabric, pour boiling water through spot.)
- *Grass.* Sponge and/or soak in cool water. Rub with detergent. Launder. If stain remains, sponge with rubbing alcohol if it is safe for the fabric.
- *Gravy.* Sponge and/or soak in cool water. Rub with detergent. Rinse. Let dry. Use spot remover if greasy stain remains.
- *Grease, oils.* Soak in cool water. Rub in detergent. Rinse. Dry. Use grease solvent if stain remains. Launder garment.
- *Ink, regular.* Rub with detergent. Rinse. Soak in presoak or oxygen bleach using hottest water safe for fabrics. Launder.
- *Liquid paper.* Scrape. Use a prewash spot and stain remover. Repeat if needed. Rub in detergent. Launder garment.
- *Mayonnaise.* Soak in cool water. Rub in detergent. Rinse. Dry. Use grease or cleaning solvent to remove greasy stain if needed. Let dry. Launder.
- *Mildew.* Launder fabric. Dry in sun. If stain remains, soak in chlorine bleach, if it is safe for the fabric, diluted with water for ten to fifteen minutes. Rinse. Launder again.
- *Mud.* Brush off after drying. Sponge and/or soak in cool water. Rub with detergent. Launder.
- *Mustard.* Rub in detergent. Rinse. If stain remains, soak in presoak. Launder.
- *Paint, oil base.* If dry, nothing will remove it. Use turpentine or paint thinner. Sponge with solvent. Let dry. Rub in detergent. Launder.
- *Paint, water base.* If dry, nothing will remove it. If wet, sponge with water, and do not let the stain spread. Rub in detergent. Launder.
- *Perfume.* Sponge and/or soak in cool water. Rub with detergent. Launder.
- *Perspiration.* Rub in detergent. Launder. If odor remains, rub in deodorant soap and launder again. If color changed, try to restore with ammonia (new stains) or vinegar (old stains). Rinse. Use grease solvent to remove grease stain.
- *Ring-around-the-collar stain.* Rub in detergent. Let stand for thirty minutes. Launder.
- *Rust.* Spread stained area over a pan of boiling water. Squeeze on lemon juice. Sprinkle on salt. Let dry in sun. Rinse. Launder.
- *Salad dressing.* Sponge or soak in cool water. Rub in detergent. Rinse. Let dry. Apply grease solvent. Launder. Use bleach if it is safe for the fabric.
- *Shoe polish.* Rub in detergent. Rinse. Let dry. Sponge with rubbing alcohol. Let dry. Apply grease solvent. Launder. Use bleach if it is safe for the fabric.
- *Soft drinks.* Some of these cannot be seen after they dry, but they turn yellow with age or heat. The yellow stain may be impossible to remove. Sponge and/or soak in cool water. Rub with detergent. Launder. If stain remains, soak in oxygen bleach and hottest water safe for the fabric. Launder.
- *Tar, asphalt.* Scrape. Sponge with grease solvent. Repeat if needed. Or let soak in heavy duty detergent with grease solvent overnight. Lift it off. Launder.

REGULAR CARE

Some clothes maintenance tasks will need to be done on a regular basis. Most people like to do their laundry and to go the dry cleaners once a week.

Prompt laundering or dry-cleaning helps to remove stains before they have a chance to set and become impossible to remove. Some stains caused by sugar cannot be seen for weeks but then slowly grow visible when it is too late to remove them. Different stains need different treatments. If you know what the stain is, be sure to tell the dry cleaners when you drop off your garment. If the dry cleaners know what it is, they have a better chance to remove the stain.

Care Labels

How do you know if a garment should be washed or dry-cleaned? As you learned in chapter 16, by law every garment must have a label that tells you how to clean the garment. For the best results, it is vital that you understand the care label terms.

1. Only the washing or dry-cleaning process on the care label has been checked as safe for use. The manufacturer has to give you only *one* method of safe care, even though others may be used. If the label says "machine wash and dry," you can wash and dry the garment by any method at any temperature. If it says "dry-clean only," any dry-cleaning method may be used.

2. If no temperature setting is mentioned for the washing machine, the dryer, or the iron, it is safe to use any temperature or setting you wish—hot, warm, or cold.

3. If you are given no ironing instructions, it should not be necessary to iron the garment. If ironing is needed, even for a "touch-up," the label must say so.

4. If bleach is not mentioned, any type of bleach may be used when needed. Chlorine bleach is one type of bleach that is harmful to some fabrics. If this is the case, the label will say "use only nonchlorine bleach when needed." If all types of bleach are harmful, the label must warn "no bleach."

Wash or dry clean? Cold or hot water? Read the care labels and your questions will be answered.

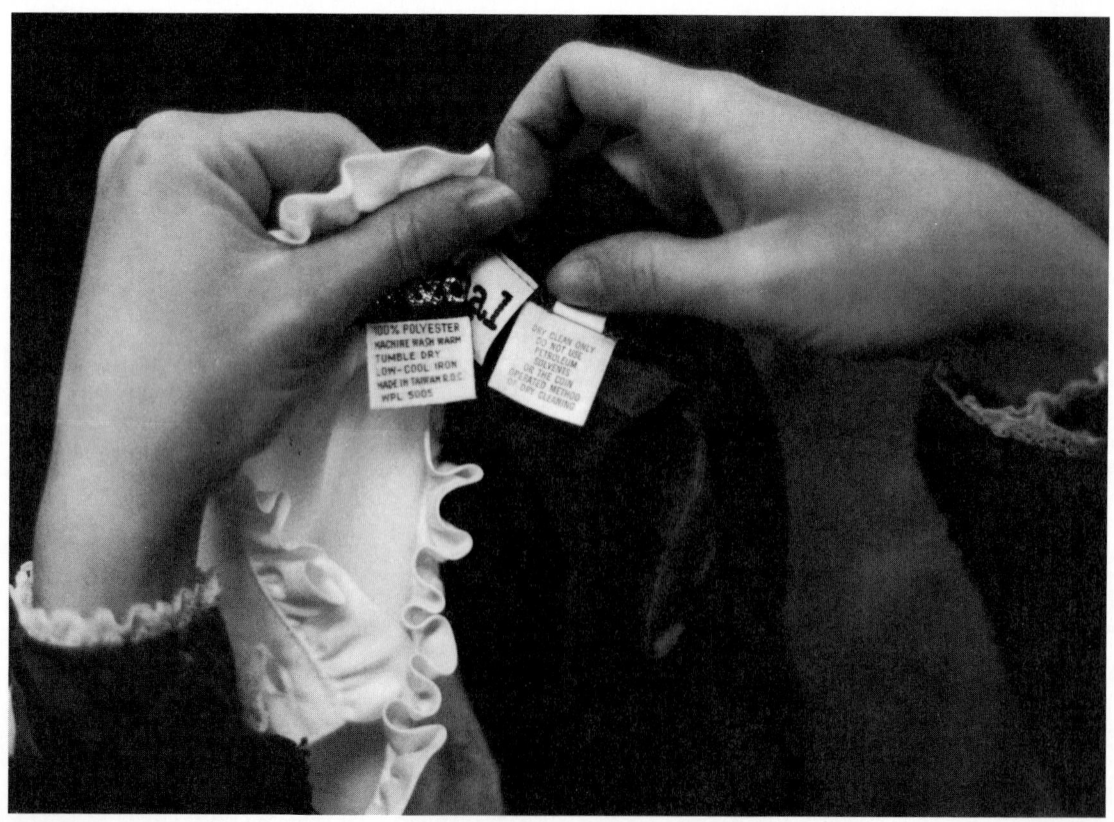

Laundry Procedures

Before you put your clothes in the washer, take a few minutes to get them ready. Shake off loose dirt. Take all items from the pockets and turn the pockets wrong side out. Brush off the dirt and lint that gets caught in pockets and cuffs. Zippers, velcro closures, and hooks and eyes should be fastened to protect them during washing. Loose tie strings, such as those on aprons and pajamas, should be tied together so they do not get caught in the washer. Pretreat spots and stains before the clothes are put into the wash. If you do not, the wash and dry process might set them permanently. For heavily soiled spots, use full strength, liquid detergent and rub it in thoroughly.

Divide the clothes into compatible loads for washing. White clothes should be washed separately. This stops them from picking up colors from other clothes. They can be washed in hot water. Brightly colored clothes should be washed together because they need cool water. Dark clothes can be washed together in one load or separately, depending on what the care label says. If the label says "Machine Wash Separately," the color will probably run. Brightly colored clothes should be washed in cold water so that the colors will not fade. Clothes labeled "Machine Wash—Delicate" should be washed together.

Before you add the detergent to your wash, read the directions and follow them exactly. For example, some detergents must be dissolved in the wash water before the clothes are added, while others can be added full strength after the clothes are put in. Most manufacturers suggest that you wash an "average" load with "average" soil in sixteen gallons of water. If your clothes are dirtier than average, you will probably need to add a little bit more detergent.

Do not pack the clothes too tightly in the washer. You want to leave enough room for them to move around freely in the water so that they will be well washed and thoroughly rinsed.

Drying Procedures

The care labels on your clothes will say if they can be dried by machine and what temperature setting to use. If the label says "Durable Press" or "Permanent Press," remove the garment as soon as the drying cycle is finished. If you do not, wrinkles may develop.

Pressing and Ironing

Thanks to crease-resistant fibers and fabric finishes, many clothes need little or no ironing. They may, however, need a light touch-up with a warm iron. Most irons are clearly marked with the temperature ranges for the various types of fabrics. It is vital to set the iron at the right heat setting for the fabric you want to iron. Most synthetic and man-made fibers will not endure the heat needed to iron cotton and linen.

When you can, turn the garment wrong side out and iron on the wrong side. Many fabrics, such as dark colored ones, develop a shine or show the impression of the iron when they are ironed on the right side. If you must iron on the right side, use a lightweight **press cloth** between the fabric and the iron. If you do not own a press cloth, a piece of cheese cloth or a man's cotton handkerchief can be used.

Steam, a damp press cloth, or a light spray of water helps the iron to do its job faster and better. An old plastic spray bottle, such as the ones cleaning liquids come in, can help. Rinse it out, fill it with fresh water, and lightly spray the area to be ironed.

Many people think that "to iron" and "to press" mean the same thing, but they are really two different processes. To **iron,** you move the iron in a back-and-forth motion over the surface of the fabric until the wrinkles vanish. To **press,** you move the iron from place to place by picking it up and putting it back down in an overlapping pattern. There is no back-and-forth motion.

Pressing helps to avoid forcing new, unwanted wrinkles into the fabric. It is a good technique to use when the press cloth makes it hard to see what you are doing. Pressing also prevents stretching the fabric out of shape. Sewing instructions always tell you to press, not iron, as you sew so that you do not distort the smaller shapes that make up a garment.

SEASONAL CARE

Your closet will be less crowded and your clothes will have more room to breathe if you store out-of-season clothes in some other place. Drawers, extra closets, or boxes under the bed or on shelves make good storage places.

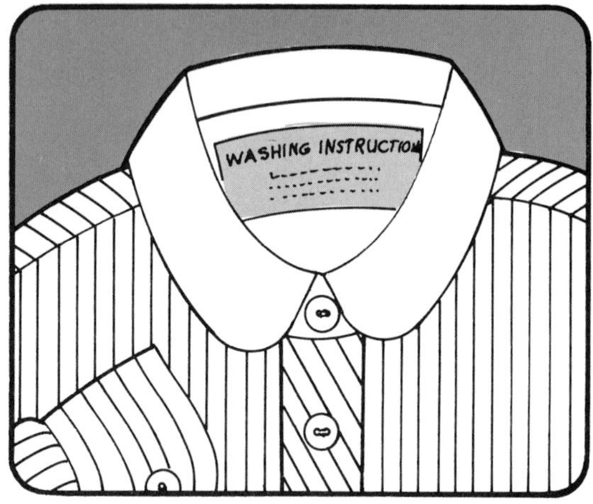

1. READ CARE LABELS.

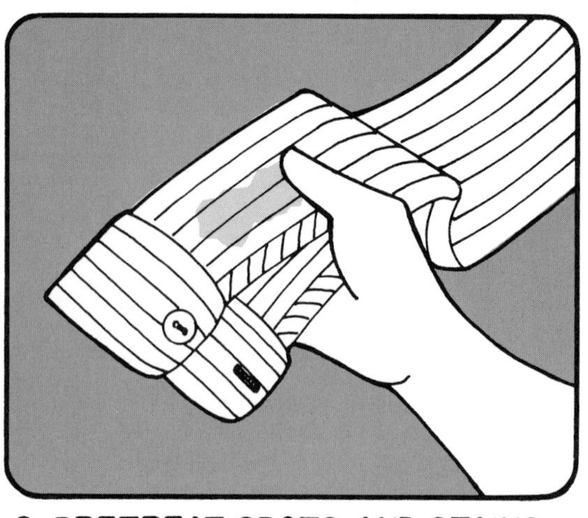
2. PRETREAT SPOTS AND STAINS.

3. DIVIDE CLOTHES INTO COMPATIBLE LOADS FOR WASHING.

4. READ AND FOLLOW DETERGENT DIRECTIONS.

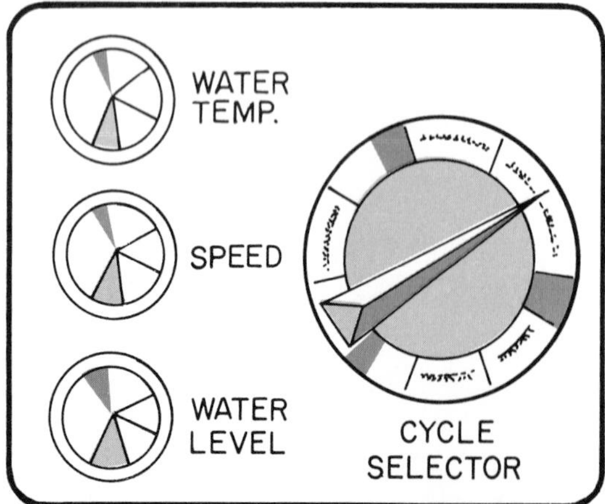

5. SELECT THE RIGHT WATER TEMPERATURE AND WASHING ACTION.

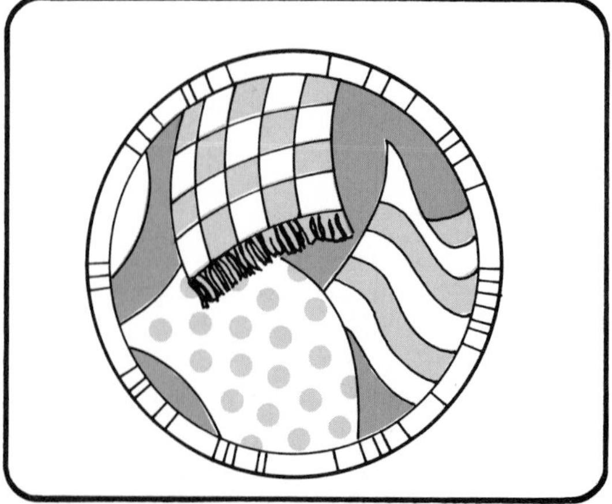
6. DRY CLOTHES PROPERLY.

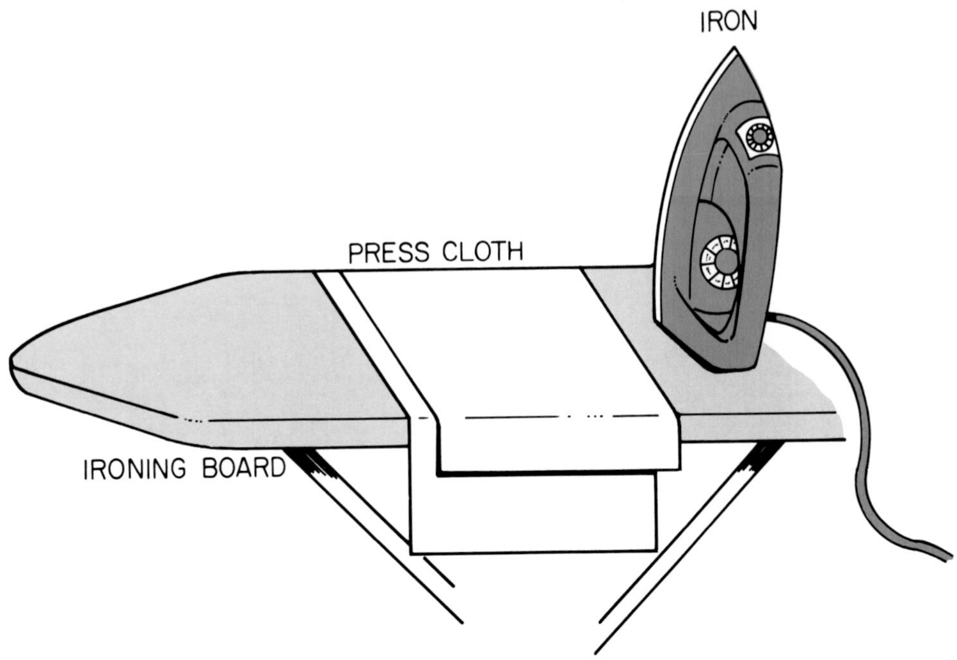

Achieve professional results in ready-made and home-sewn clothes by using good quality pressing equipment.

Before you pack away your clothes, be sure they are clean and mended. Any fiber that can be damaged by insects, such as wool, should be packed away with moth balls. Knitted and woolen clothes should be folded for storage. Place white tissue paper in the folds to help prevent wrinkles. Never use newspapers or printed papers. The inks may stain the fabrics. Many items, such as sweaters, take less storage space and get fewer wrinkles if they are rolled rather than folded. Cotton and linen clothes should be packed away unironed. If ironed, they may yellow while in storage. Besides, they usually need to be ironed or pressed when they are unpacked.

If you live in a climate where drawers, boxes, and suitcases quickly develop a musty odor, pack a small bar of soap with the clothes. It will prevent the musty odors from forming.

MAKING SMALL REPAIRS

If you get into the habit of mending your clothes while the damage is still small, you will benefit in two ways. First, you will save time. It is quicker to do mending jobs while they are still small and simple. Second, you will save money. If you ignore the damage when it first appears, you may find that it increases to the point where the garment cannot be saved.

REPLACING BUTTONS, SNAPS, AND HOOKS

Fasteners such as buttons, snaps, and hooks are easy to replace. To make your sewing go fast, cut a piece of thread about forty-eight inches long. Use a color that matches your garment. Fold the thread in half and push it through the eye of the needle so you will be sewing with four strands of thread at once. That way you will need to take only two or three stitches to secure the fastener.

Your sewing will be neater if you do not knot your thread. Instead, take a few small backstitches on the underside of your fabric to lock the thread at the beginning and end of your stitching. Cut off the thread tails close to the fabric.

Buttons

Buttons need to be sewn on so that there is some "give" to leave room for the layers of fabric that surround the buttonhole. Some buttons have a built-in stem, or **shank**, at their base that automatically creates the needed space. If your button does not have a shank, you can make the extra space by putting an object, such as a toothpick or a match stick, on top of the button and sewing over it. When your stitches are made, pull out the toothpick, hold the button so it is away from the fabric, and wrap the thread around the stitches a few times to form a thread shank.

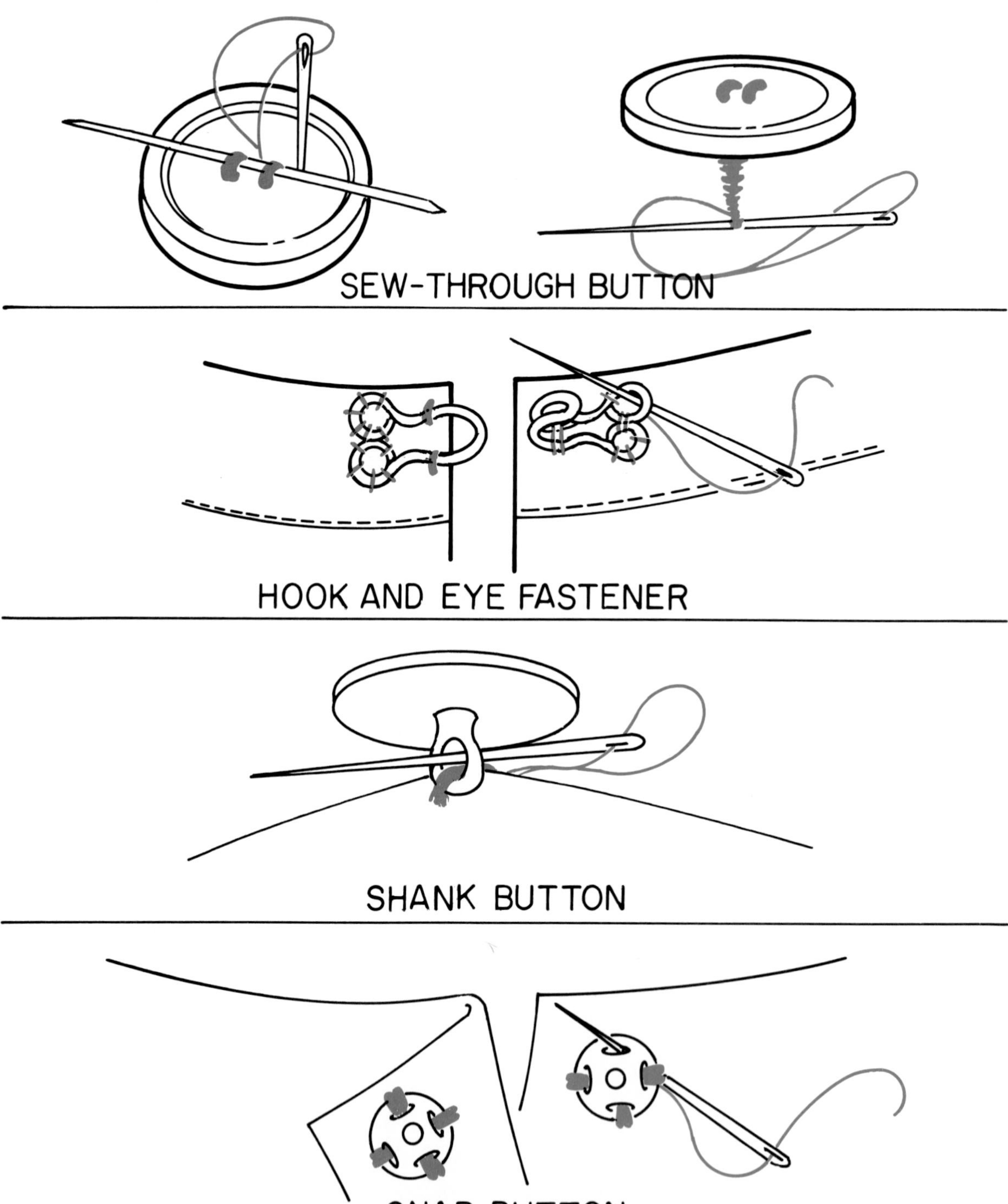

Fasteners can be decorative as well as functional. Select the fastener suitable for the weight of the fabric and style of the garment.

Snaps

Snaps are a two-part fastener. The top half is called the **ball** and the bottom half is called the **socket**. If the edges of the garment overlap, the ball part of the snap is always sewn on the underside of the top layers.

Sew the ball part in place first by taking two stitches through each hole. Be sure to pick up only a few threads of the fabric with each stitch. This will keep your stitches from showing on the outside of the garment. As you go from hole to hole, tunnel the needle through the layers of fabric. To mark the spot for the socket, rub the ball with chalk and press it in place. Sew the socket on this mark.

Hooks and Eyes

Hook fasteners come with a hook and two styles of eyes. The bar, or straight eye, is used on garment edges that overlap. The curved eye is used on garment edges that meet.

Place the hook so that it is slightly inside the edge of the garment. If the garment edges overlap, the hook is sewn to the underside of the top lays. Sew two short stitches through each circle. Be sure to pick up only a few threads of the fabric with each stitch. After the circles are sewn, tunnel the needle through the layers of fabric to the head of the hook. Take two stitches across the hook at the curve.

To apply the bar eye, rub the hook with chalk and press it in place. This will mark the spot for the eye. Sew the eye over this mark.

To apply the loop eye, place the loop so it extends slightly beyond the garment edge, opposite the hook. Sew it in place.

BACKSTITCH

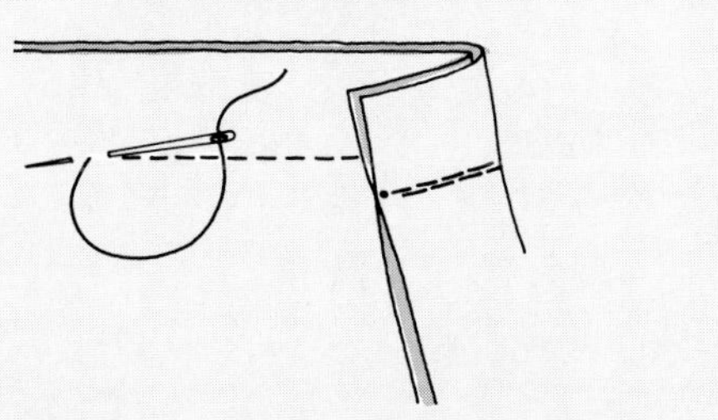

The backstitch is one of the strongest handstitches. It is used to mend machine-stitched seams and to fasten thread ends securely.

Begin with a small running stitch. Then insert the needle back at the beginning of the first stitch, and bring it out again one stitch length in front of the thread. Keep inserting the needle in the end of the last stitch and bringing it out one stitch ahead. The stitches on the underside will be twice as long as those on the upper side.

MENDING SEAMS

You can mend a ripped seam by hand with a backstitch or on the sewing machine. Begin and end your stitching about one inch (2.5 cm) from the beginning and end of the break. If the seam is in a spot that takes extra stress, such as the underarm or crotch seam, use a double row of stitching one-eighth inch (3 mm) apart.

REPAIRING HEMS

Many clothes have hems that are sewn by machine with a straight stitch. These hems are very secure and rarely rip out. You might, however, want to change the length of a garment with this type of hem. To do so, choose a stitch length and thread color that match the factory stitching closely.

Some clothes have been machine stitched with a chain stitch. You can mend this type of hem with hand-sewn hem stitches that are almost invisible on the outside of the garment. The section on hems in chapter 20 will give some suggestions for various hem stitches. Begin and end your stitches about one inch (2.5 cm) from the beginning and end of the break.

MENDING HOLES AND TEARS

Holes in clothes can be mended by darning, patching, or reweaving. You might also think about covering the hole with a band of ribbon, lace, or bias tape, a purchased applique, or an applique you have made from scraps and bits of trim.

If the garment is a casual one, such as a well-worn pair of jeans, you might want to cover the hole with an iron-on patch. You might also darn it on your sewing machine. **Darning** is a network of stitches used to fill in a hole. Your sewing machine manual will probably give you directions on how to darn on your machine.

If the garment is part of your "good" wardrobe, you will want to make the mend as invisible as possible to the naked eye. If you cover the hole with some type of trim, you may also have to add that trim to some other part of the garment. That way, the repaired garment will have a balanced appearance. If you do not want to mend the hole yourself, you can take the garment to a person who does **reweaving**. This specialist uses yarns from the inside parts of the garment to repair small holes and tears so they are barely visible. Their work is costly but worth it if you can salvage an expensive garment.

Review CHAPTER 18

WORDS TO REMEMBER

backstitch
ball and socket
darning
first impression
iron
press
press cloth
reweaving
shank
system

CHECKING YOUR UNDERSTANDING

1. What are the advantages of making a personal plan for clothes care and maintenance?
2. List some ways a person could make his or her storage space more efficient. How could one do this without spending a great deal of money?
3. Describe those wardrobe maintenance tasks that should be done on a daily, weekly, and seasonal basis.
4. Describe the basic procedures for doing laundry. Why are care labels so important? Give some examples of the information they provide.
5. Why is it important to do small repairs on a regular basis? Give some examples of small repairs that you might make on your wardrobe.

APPLYING YOUR UNDERSTANDING

1. Go through several newspapers or magazines and pick out pictures of five people. Make sure the pictures clearly show the person's clothes. Based on what they are wearing and how they are groomed, what would be your first impression of each of these people?
2. Pretend that your favorite shirt has a hole in the front, just below one shoulder. How many ways can you think of to mend it?
3. Take two scraps of the same fabric and stain each of them with common substances such as mustard, catsup, lipstick, ballpoint pen ink, grass, tea, chocolate, and grape juice. Using the information on the stain removal chart, remove the fresh stains from one set of scraps. Allow the other set to dry for a least a week and then try to remove the stains.
4. Analyze your personal storage space and make a list of five ways you can make it more efficient. Set yourself a deadline to do this.
5. Visit your local dry cleaner and find out how much it costs to clean a pair of wool slacks and a wool blazer. Pretend you wear these garments at least once a week. Figure out how much it would cost you if you had to have each of these items cleaned twice a month for the next six months. If you took very good care of them so that they only had to be cleaned twice in six months, how much money would you save?

Chapter 19

PREPARING TO SEW

Has this ever happened to you?

Andy, Stephanie, and Patti were eating lunch together in the school cafeteria. Patti was admiring Stephanie's blouse. "I really like that color and fabric," she said. "That's a super bracelet, too."

"Thanks," replied Stephanie. "I couldn't find the kind of blouse I wanted anywhere, so I decided to sew one. I even saved enough money by sewing it to buy a bracelet to go with it."

"I wish I could sew," sighed Patti, "but I'd probably be all thumbs."

"No, you wouldn't," volunteered Andy. "I can sew."

"You!" exclaimed Patti. "Where did you learn to sew?"

"Last year in home economics class," replied Andy. "I made a vest for myself that turned out great, so this year I made pillows for my brother and sister for Christmas. I put their initials on them and picked out colors that matched their bedrooms. Everyone thought they were super."

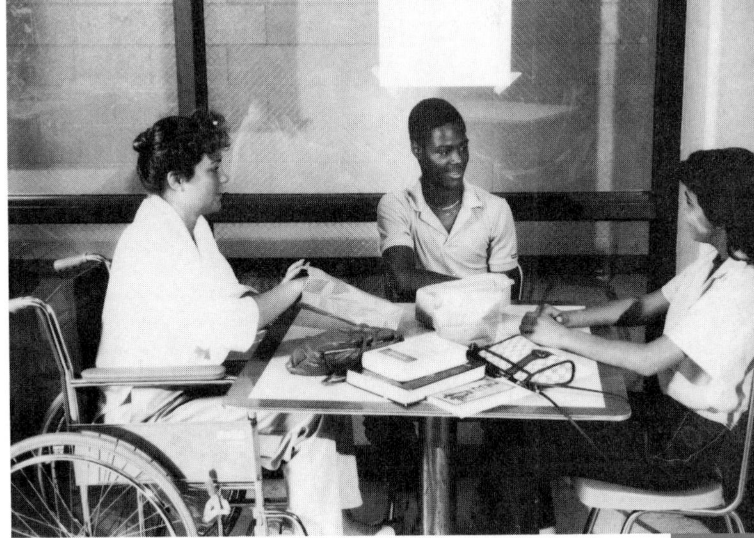

Have you ever been surprised to find that something you admired was made by the person who was wearing it?

Have your ever thought about the benefits of being able to sew and wondered if you could learn how?

After reading this chapter, you will be able to

- understand how to choose a pattern in the proper size and figure type and a fabric that is suitable for the pattern;
- know the importance of preshrinking and straightening your fabric;
- make simple length and width adjustments on your pattern;
- show the procedures to follow as you lay out, pin, cut, and mark your garment.

Some people would call sewing a leisure activity, much like playing sports or taking part in an after-school club. Others would say that it is something done by those who have a special talent.

But sewing is more than a hobby. It is a skill that anyone can learn. Whether you learn how to sew well enough to make many of your own clothes or just to do simple repairs, you will gain many benefits from learning about how clothes are made.

Sewing saves money. It is possible to save up to 50 percent on the cost of clothes you make yourself. It is also less costly to repair your own hems, replace your own buttons, and mend your own clothes than to pay someone else to do it for you.

Sewing saves time. When you need a garment repaired immediately, is it not faster to do it yourself than to take it to a professional sewing shop or to plead with a family member to do it for you?

Sewing makes you a better consumer. You begin to look at ready-to-wear clothes in a new light. You become aware of details that reveal the quality of a garment. You look at the spacing of the stitches, the width of the seams, how well trims and fasteners are attached, and the quality of the fabric.

SELECTING A PROJECT

The key to learning to sew is to choose a project you like, one that is equal to your sewing skills and that will help you to create a flattering personal image. How are you going to know by looking at a picture in a pattern catalog and at the fabric in the store if you are going to like the final result? The answer rests on your experience and knowledge.

You probably already have more experience and knowledge than you think you do. After all, you have worn clothes all your life. Some of them looked and felt better than others. In chaper 17 you learned how to analyze your wardrobe. Think about the style and fabric of the clothes that were in your 10 percent pile. Compare those with the items that you gave away. Now think about what you learned in chapter 15 regarding the elements and principles of design. All of this knowledge will help you to select a flattering mix of pattern and fabric.

The ability to make your own clothes can be an outlet for creative expression as well as a self-satisfying, rewarding accomplishment.

SELECTING THE PATTERN

If you have done little or no prior sewing, choose a very simple design. Many patterns have labels, such as "Easy," "Very Easy," "Fast and Easy," or "Easy to Sew." These patterns would be a good choice for a beginner. They usually have fewer pattern pieces, simple-to-follow layouts, and easier construction techniques.

If you have done some sewing, choose a project that will teach you one new technique, such as making pleats or cuffs. Or choose an easy pattern, then pick out a fabric that needs some special handling, such as a plaid or stripe that must be matched.

DETERMINING YOUR PATTERN SIZE

The garment you make should fit as well or better than the clothes you buy ready-made. To make sure that this happens, it is important that you buy a pattern that is the right size for you.

When selecting a pattern, determine the amount of time you have to complete the project. Then choose a pattern appropriate for your time constraints and skill level.

Patterns are made in several different **figure types,** or size ranges. These figure types are based on body contours and proportions, not on age groups. An older woman might wear a junior petite size; a teenage girl might wear a Misses' size.

Have you ever noticed that you sometimes wear a different size garment depending on who the manufacturer is? That is why you cannot assume that you wear the same size in a pattern as you do in ready-to-wear clothes. Pattern makers have tried to make patterns so they are like ready-to-wear sizes. However, they also give you a measurement chart at the back of the pattern catalog so that you can choose the size that matches your measurements most closely.

Ideally, measurements should be taken over undergarments, not over clothes. If need be, take them over snug-fitting clothes, but take off sweaters, belts, jackets, and other bulky items. For accuracy, have someone else help you measure.

To take your measurements, use a firm tape measure, or one that will not stretch with use. Tie a string around your waist to mark its location. You will want to record your height and your circumference measurements. Females will also need to take their back waist measurement. Males should note their neck size and their shirt sleeve length. Record your measurements as shown in the chart below.

Refer to the chart below or to one in the back of the pattern catalogs to determine your figure type and your pattern size. Females should choose dress and blouse patterns based on their bust measurements. Males should choose jacket patterns based on their chest measurements. They should choose shirt patterns based on their neck measurements.

If you are picking out a pattern for pants or a skirt, choose your pattern size by your waist measurement. However, if your hips are more than two inches larger than the hip measurement that corresponds to your waist size, buy the pattern by hip measurement.

PATTERN SIZE MEASUREMENTS

Height	
Bust/Chest	
Waist	
Back Waist (female)	
Hip or Seat	
Neckband (male)	
Shirt Sleeve Length (male)	

Female

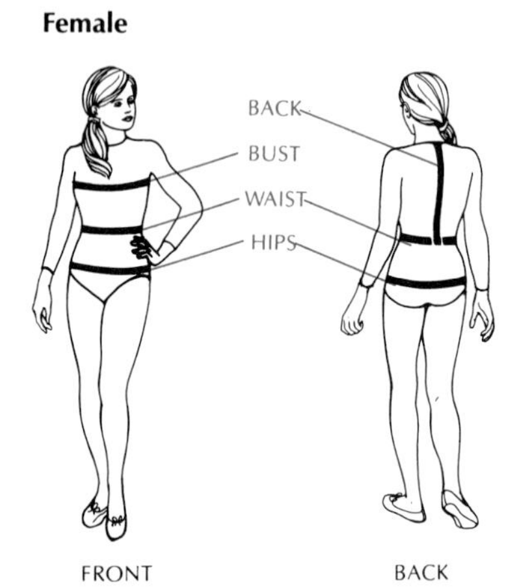

Male

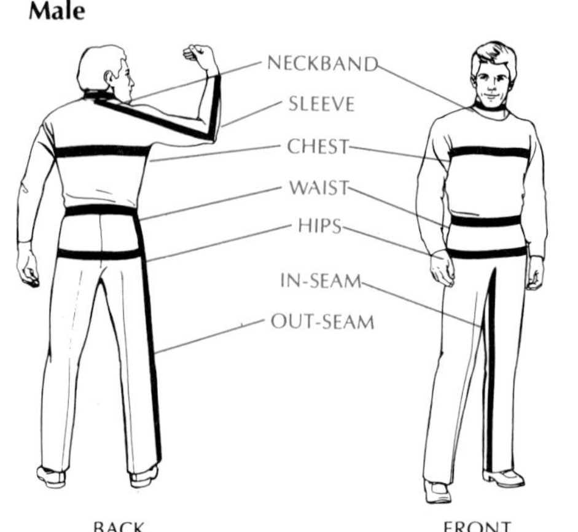

Taking Your Measurements

Depending on the garment you're buying, you will need to take different measurements to determine your size.

In a man's shirt, for example, neck and sleeve measurements are most important. For a woman's dress, the measurements needed to find the right size are bust, waist, and hips.

To find out what size you wear, take your measurements according to the following instructions. Then compare your measurements to those on a size chart. Most clothing stores have size charts available.

How To Measure

Measuring to check your size is not difficult. Remember to stand naturally, and to hold the tape taut, but not tight.

Height Stand against the wall (barefooted). Have another person make a mark level with the top of your head. Measure from this point to the floor. For pants and skirt measurements, it is best to wear shoes.

Bust or Chest Measure over the fullest part of the bust or chest, with the tape straight across the back.

Waist Measure the smallest part of the natural waistline.

Hips Measure at the fullest part of the hips in a straight line around the body.

Back Measure from waist to neck.

In-Seam Place pants that are the correct length on a flat surface. Measure along inner seam from the bottom of one leg to where the two legs meet.

Out-seam Measure from waist to point where pants bottom breaks slightly on shoe.

Neckband Measure around the fullest part of the neck for neckband size, adding ½ in or 1 cm for wearing ease.

Sleeve Bend arm up. Measure from base of neck across center back to elbow, across elbow crook, and up over wrist bone.

SELECTING FABRIC

Once you have chosen your pattern, you will want to make sure you pick out a suitable fabric. Every pattern has a list of suggested fabrics that is printed on the back of the pattern envelope. These are the fabrics that are suitable for that design.

In order to be happy with the results, you must choose one of these fabrics or a fabric that has a similar hand. **Hand** refers to the way a fabric feels and how well it drapes. Draping is a fabric's ability to hang in loose folds. Terms such as *soft, crisp, firm,* or *stiff* are used to describe hand.

The back of the pattern envelope will also tell you if the design is not suitable for some fabrics, such as plaids, stripes, diagonals, and checks. Sometimes, the design lines of the garment would make it impossible to match the design lines on the fabric.

As you pick out your fabric, keep in mind what you learned in the other chapters of this unit about the traits of some fibers and fabrics. Read the labels for fiber content and care needs. Get the best value you can for the money you spend and the time you take to sew.

INTERFACING

Interfacing is an extra layer of cloth that adds shape and strength to parts of the garment that are subject to more stress. It adds firmness and body to parts such as collars, cuffs, lapels, waistbands, neckline facings, buttonholes, and patch pockets.

Special woven, nonwoven and knit interfacing fabrics are made in many types and weights. Some of these are sew-in interfacings, and others are fusibles. A **fusible** interfacing is one that is put on the garment with your iron, using a combination of heat, steam, and pressure to make it bond to the fabric.

Your choice of interfacing should be based on your garment fabric. The interfacing should not be heavier than the outer fabric. Color also needs to be considered. Most interfacings come in basic colors, such as black, white, beige, and gray. An interfacing that is too dark or too light might make shadows on the outside of your garment. The interfacing should also have the same care needs as the fabric. If one is washable, the other must also be washable.

Interfacings are added to the areas of the garment that need reinforcement, such as collars, cuffs and waistlines. Use an interfacing that is suitable for the weight of the fabric.

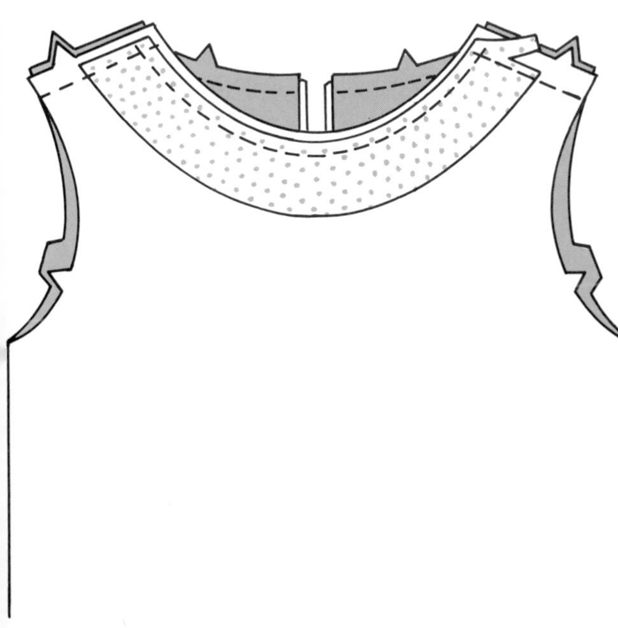

LINING

Lining gives a garment a finished look by covering all the raw edges and construction details. Coats and jackets often have linings. They can also be found in other clothes, such as skirts, slacks, and vests.

A lining is made separately and sewn into the garment. A lining fabric should be closely woven to wear well. If it is firm or slightly stiff, a lining will add more body to the garment, and it will also help stop wrinkles.

SELECTING NOTIONS

The back of the pattern envelope will also list the notions that you will need to buy to complete your garment. **Notions** are things such as buttons, zippers, snaps, seam tapes, hooks and eyes, shoulder pads, and elastic. As you choose these items, keep in mind the care needs of the fabric. You would not want to put dry-clean-only buttons or trim on a garment you intend to wash.

A. Thread (polyester thread, mercerized thread, elastic thread), B. Buttons, C. Zippers, D. Seam tapes, E. Hooks & eyes, F. Elastic, G. Velcro, H. Trims, braids, appliques.

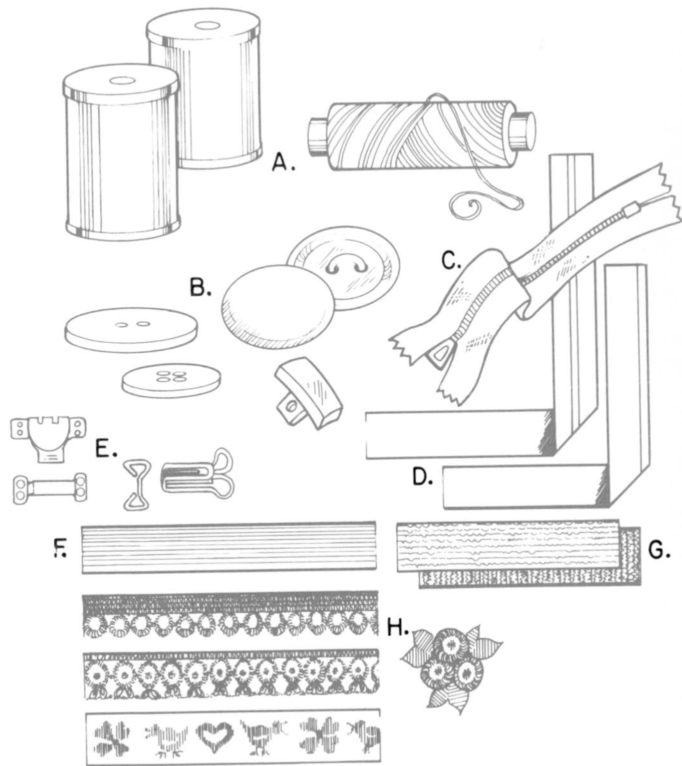

Thread

The most common sewing threads are made of 100 percent polyester, cotton wrapped around a core of polyester, mercerized cotton, and silk. **Mercerization** is a process that adds luster to a fiber and improves its ability to absorb dyes.

Mercerized cotton thread is good to use with all natural fiber fabrics. Silk thread can be used on silk or wool cloth. Polyester thread and cotton-wrapped polyester thread are good to use with almost all natural and synthetic fabrics. Because they are stretchier and stronger than any cotton thread, they are good to use with knits and stretch woven fabrics.

Buy a good quality thread in a color that matches your fabric. If you cannot decide between two shades, choose the darker shade. Thread looks darker when it is wound on a spool than when it is stitched on fabric. As a general rule, it is not a good idea to use a "bargain" thread for machine stitching.

FABRIC TRAITS CAN AFFECT PATTERN LAYOUT

Some fabrics have traits that must be carefully considered both before you buy them and when you lay out your pattern pieces. You may have to buy more fabric, follow a special layout, or vary the layout given in the pattern guide.

• Does the fabric have an all-over print or pattern, with no clear design or direction? If it does, it can be cut the same as any plain fabric.

• Does the fabric have a nap, such as corduroy, velvet, or velveteen? If so, you will have to use the "with nap" layout on your guide sheet. This layout is set up so that the top of each pattern piece is heading in the same direction. Because of the way napped surfaces reflect the light, these fabrics appear to change color depending on whether the nap runs up or down.

• Does the fabric have a one-way design? If so, you will also need to use the "with nap" layout.

• Is the design printed off-grain? If it forms a pattern that needs to be matched, you will never be able to straighten it so that both the grain and the print motifs are aligned. You will probably be better off if you leave this fabric in the store.

• Does the fabric have a diagonal design? Diagonal fabrics should also be cut following the "with nap" layout. If you do this, you will be sure that the diagonal slants around the garment in the same direction.

• If your fabric is a knit, does it have a lengthwise crease where it was folded on the bolt? This center fold line is hard to remove in some knits. Press it carefully before you lay out the pattern. If the crease does not disappear, refold the fabric so that the crease line can be avoided or placed in an inconspicuous spot.

PREPARING THE FABRIC

If your fabric is washable, preshrink it. This can be done by following the care instructions for washing and drying the fabric. Even if the fabric is labeled "preshrunk," it may shrink more. Besides, washing will remove any sizings that may have been added to give the fabric a temporary, crisper finish. You will want to wash out this finish so that there will be no surprises later on about what this fabric is really like. You can preshrink wool fabrics by pressing them carefully with a steam iron or by taking them to a dry cleaner for steaming.

STRAIGHTENING

If possible, woven fabric should be grain perfect before the garment is cut out. **Grain perfect** means that all the crosswise and lengthwise yarns lie at right angles to each other, just the way they were first set up on the loom.

Sometimes, a fabric is pulled "off grain" during the weaving process. If you do not straighten the fabric, you may have problems after the garment is made. As a garment hangs, whether it is on your body or in your closet, the yarns will begin to go back to their original, perpendicular position. This can result in a misshapen garment. Permanent press fabrics cannot be straightened because the finish that creates the permanent press traits also sets the yarns permanently in place.

How will you know if your fabric is grain perfect? Begin by gently pulling out a crosswise thread all the way across the fabric at both ends, between the two selvages. Working on a large flat surface, such as a table or the floor, fold the fabric in half lengthwise. Then, pin the fabric together around the edges, carefully matching the selvages and the pulled threads at either end. Do all three edges align? Does the fabric lie flat without puckering? If it does not, the fabric is off grain and must be straightened.

To straighten, steam press the fabric until the puckers disappear and the threads are aligned. If the fabric is very off grain, unpin it and find out which way the crosswise threads slant. Gently pull the fabric on the bias in the direction opposite to the way the threads slant.

You cannot pull a thread in a knit fabric. To keep a knit on grain as you cut, you must lay it out on a flat surface and smooth it out so that the lengthwise ribs are all straight and parallel to each other. Do not let any of the knit fabric hang over the edge of your cutting surface. The weight of the fabric will distort the knit.

PREPARING THE PATTERN

Open up the pattern envelope and take out the pattern pieces for the version you want to make. Spread them out flat and press with a cool, dry iron to remove creases or wrinkles.

PATTERN SYMBOLS

Patterns have special marks, such as notches, circles, arrows, and broken lines. These symbols tell you where to make adjustments, where to join the garment parts, where to fold, where to cut, and where to sew.

If you learn the common symbols and marks in the chart "Common Pattern Symbols and Markings," you can make almost any garment. Unusual marks will be explained in your pattern instruction sheet.

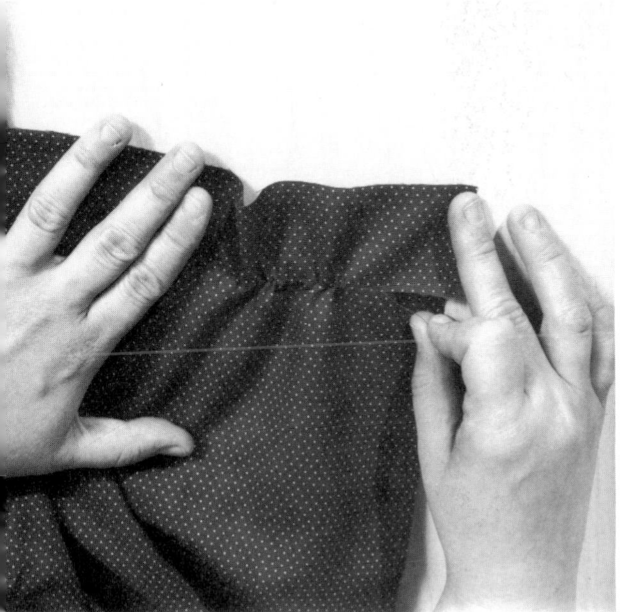

Handle your fabric properly from the start by checking and making the fabric grain perfect.

Symbol	Description
	**Grainline.** Heavy solid line with arrows at each end.
	**Fold Bracket.** Long bracket with arrows at each end or "place on fold" instruction.
	**Cutting line.** Heavy solid line along outer edge of pattern. May also designate a "cut-off" line for a certain view.
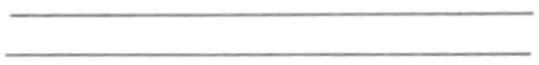	**Adjustment line.** Double line indicating where pattern can be lengthened or shortened before cutting.
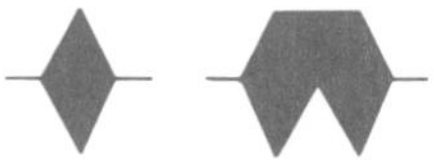	**Notches.** Diamond shapes along cutting line, used for matching seams. Numbered in order in which seams are joined.
	**Seamline.** Long, broken line, usually five-eighths inch (1.5 cm) inside cutting line. Multi-sized patterns do not have printed seamlines.
	**Foldline.** Solid line marking where garment is to be folded during construction.
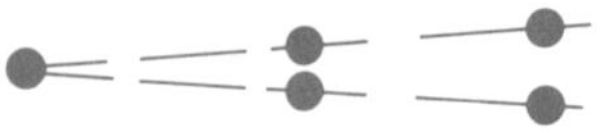	**Dart.** Broken line and dots forming a V-shape, usually at hipline, bustline, or elbow.
	**Dots (large and small), squares or triangles.** Usually found along seamlines or darts.
 EASE	**Easing line.** Short, boken line with small dot at each end, marking area to be eased.
 GATHER	**Gathering lines.** Two solid or broken lines, or small dots at each end, marking an area to be gathered.
 3" (7.5 cm) HEM	**Hemline.** Hem allowance is printed on the cutting line.
	**Zipper placement.** Parallel rows of triangles along seamline where zipper is to be inserted.
	**Detail positions.** Broken lines indicating placement of pockets, tucks, or other details.
	**Button and buttonhole placements.** Solid lines indicate length of buttonhole; "X" or illustration shows button size and placement

FITTING THE PATTERN

Proper fit begins with the selection of the right size pattern in the right figure type category. The next step is to compare your measurements with those of the pattern itself. Then, analyze your figure to make the needed changes. Changes in length or width that can be made on the pattern tissue before the garment is cut out are called pattern **adjustments.** Most people find that these simple length and width adjustments are enough to get a good fit.

Pattern **alterations** are more difficult changes that affect the contours of the garment. Pattern alterations may be needed if you have figure variations, such as a sway back, a large bust, very broad shoulders, or a thick neck. If you need a pattern alteration, there are sewing books and special patterns that will tell you how to do it. People with figure variations can sometimes avoid the need to make alterations by choosing styles that fit loosely through their "problem" area.

EASE

All patterns are made up with a certain amount of ease or extra room. There are two types of ease.

Minimum ease is the amount needed to let the body move. The amount of minimum ease is determined by the fabric recommendations. A pattern that is made for stretch wovens or knits will need less ease than one made up for stable knits or wovens.

Designer ease is the amount of extra room that makes the garment look the way the designer wanted it to look. Designer ease is the difference between a garment that is "loosely fitted" and one that is "closely fitted."

Because the amount of ease varies from one pattern to the next, it is not a good idea to compare your measurements with those of the pattern tissue. Instead, compare your measurements with the ones on the pattern envelope for your size. Differences between these two sets of measurements will tell you where and how much adjustment needs to be made.

The minimum ease of the garments below is the same but the designer ease differs. This creates the special look the designer is attempting to achieve.

LENGTH ADJUSTMENTS

Length adjustment lines are usually found several inches above the waistline on bodices and shirts, in the hipline area on pants and skirts, and above or below the elbow on sleeves.

If the pattern does not have a "lengthen or shorten" line it means that you will distort the design if you change the length within the body of the pattern. These styles can be adjusted only on the hemline edge.

To shorten, fold a tuck in the pattern along the line shown. Remember that a fold is a double thickness, so the fold should be half the amount you need to shorten. For example, to shorten the pattern one inch (2.5 cm), make a one-half-inch (13-mm) tuck. Pin or tape the tuck in place.

To lengthen, cut the pattern along the adjustment line. Pin or tape one part of the pattern piece to a strip of tissue paper. Measure and draw a line to show the amount to be added on the tissue paper. Pin or tape the other part of the pattern in place on this line. Be sure to keep grainline markings aligned. Redraw any cutting lines, fold lines, or seam lines that are affected by the adjustment.

Remember to make your adjustments on all related pattern pieces. If you have adjusted the front piece, you must also adjust the back piece. You may also need to adjust the pieces for facings, interfacings, and **plackets** (slits that form closures).

Many patterns have adjustment lines printed on the pattern pieces. Other patterns are lengthened or shortened at the lower edge.

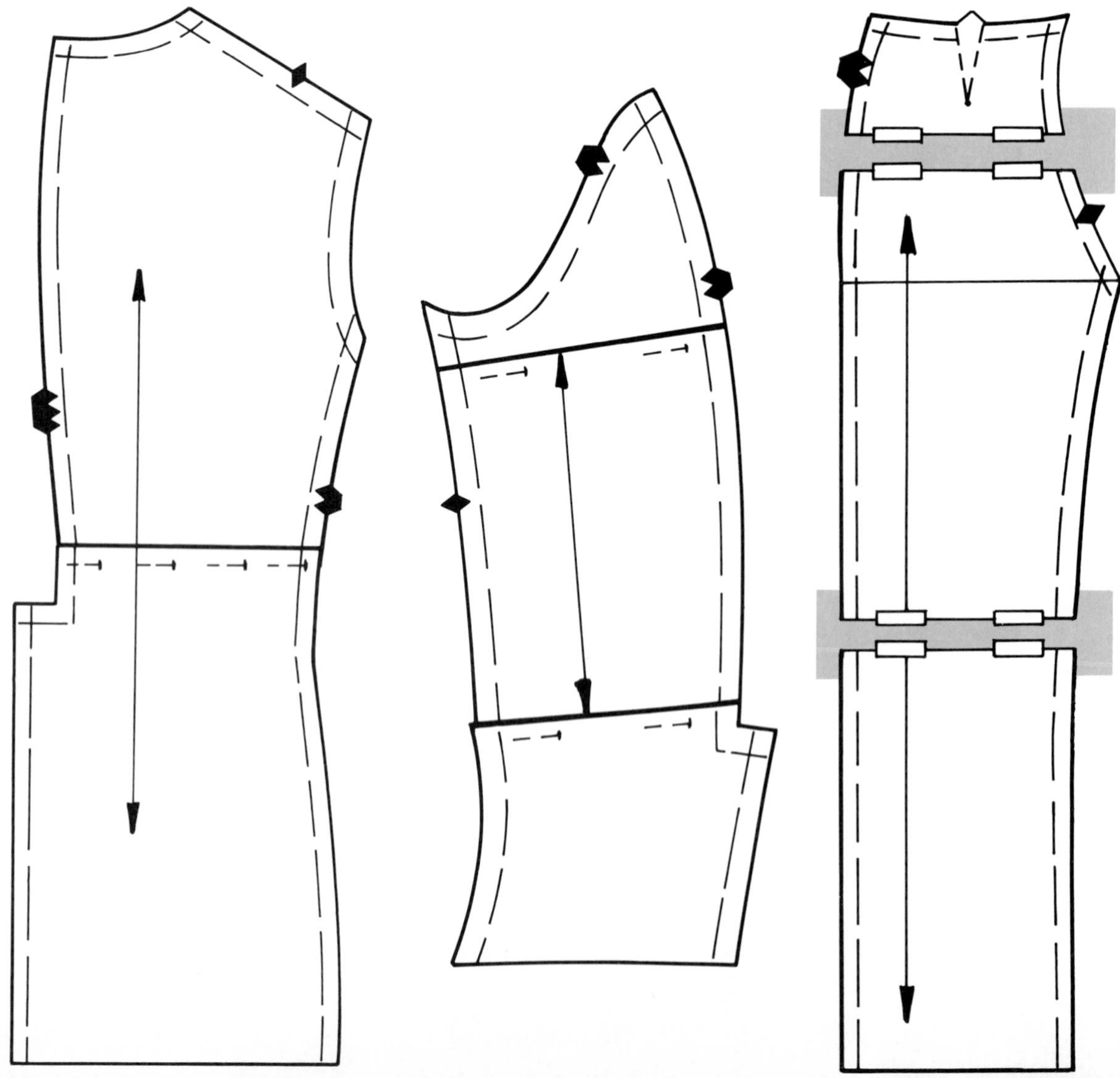

CIRCUMFERENCE ADJUSTMENTS

Circumference adjustments are changes in the width of the pattern, usually at the waist or hip areas. These adjustments are made at the side seams only. Making changes at the center foldline or seamline would change the lines of the garment.

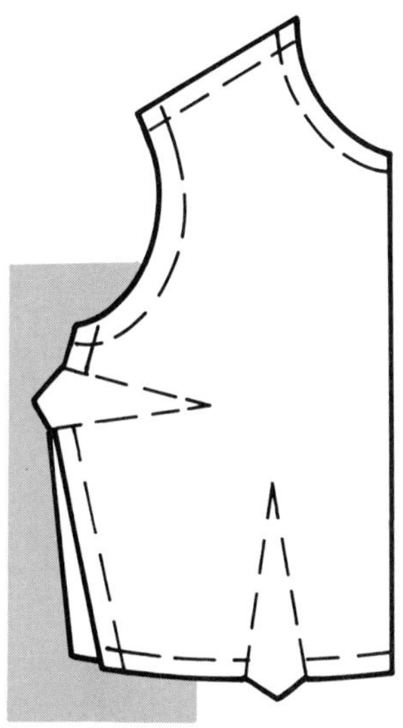

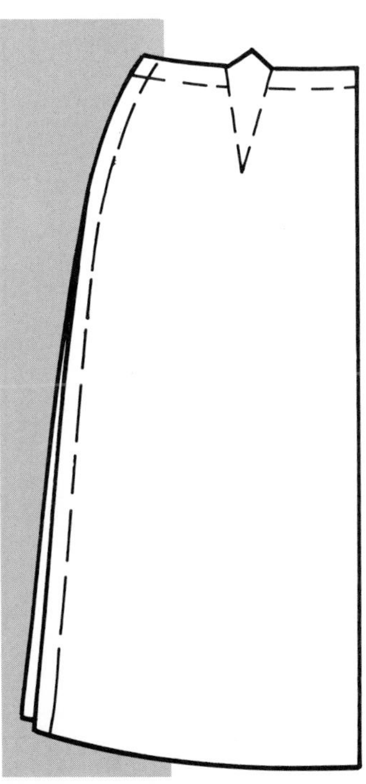

To increase the width, divide the total amount of the change by four. Add this amount at each side seam. The adjustment may not be needed for the whole length of the seam. For example, the waist may need to be enlarged but the hips may not. If this is the case, taper back the new cutting line to the original one.

A pattern can usually be made smaller by taking a wider seam allowance when the pieces are sewn together. To figure how much you must take in at each seam, divide the total amount of the change by four. Make a note at the right places on your guide sheet so that you will remember to make the adjustment when you sew these seams.

LAYOUT

Your guide sheet will give several layouts for various sizes and fabric widths. Locate the layout that is right for your size, the one you have chosen, and your width of fabric. Draw a circle around this layout. Then, each time you glance at the sheet, your eye will be drawn to the right layout.

Circle and follow the layout that is right for your size, the view you have chosen, and your width of fabric.

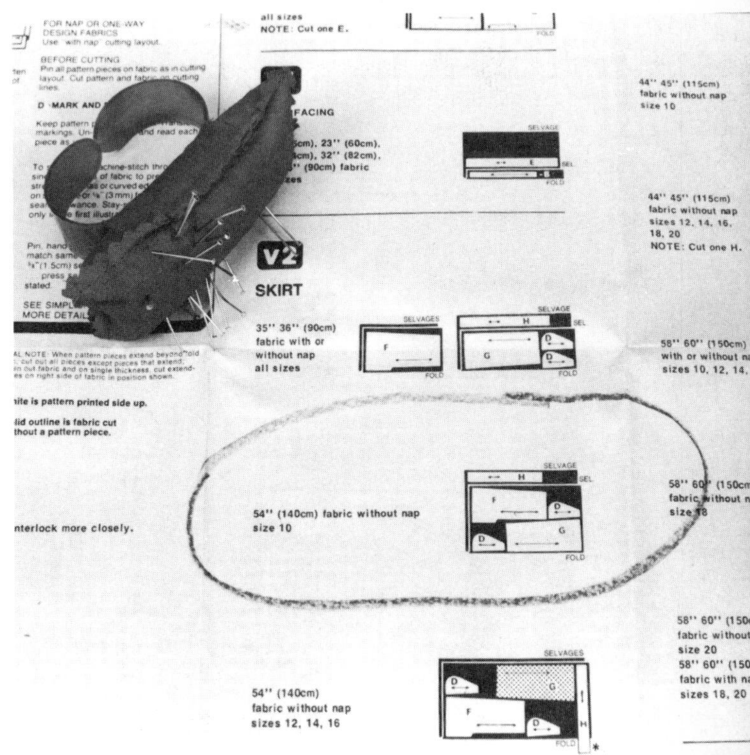

PINNING

Place all the pieces of the pattern on the fabric as shown on your pattern's guide sheet. Do this before you pin any of the pieces in place. The "place on fold" lines should be placed along the straight fold of the fabric, and the grainlines should be placed so that they are parallel to the selvage edge.

When you have laid out all the needed pattern pieces, pin them in place, beginning with the large pieces. Pin the pieces with foldlines first and then move on to the other large pieces. Place the pieces as close together as possible without overlapping the cutting lines.

If the pattern piece has a grainline instead of a "place on fold" line, it should be placed so that the grainline is parallel to the selvage edge. Pin one point of the grainline arrow in place. With a tape measure or a yardstick, measure from this point to the closest edge of the fabric. Then, shift the pattern piece until the point of the other arrow is the same distance from the edge. Pin the second point in place.

Smooth out the pattern and place a pin diagonally in each corner. Then, place a pin at each of the pattern notches. To finish pinning, place pins every three inches to six inches (7.5 cm to 15 cm) along each edge of the pattern. Pins should be placed at a right angle to the cutting line, with the head toward the center and the point facing, but inside of, the cutting line.

Measure the grainline of the pattern pieces to be sure that they are parallel to the selvage area.

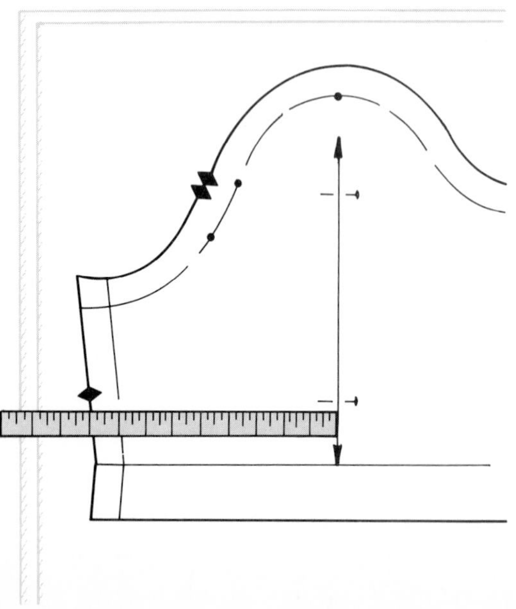

CUTTING

Use sharp dressmaker's shears, preferably ones with bent handles. It is important to keep the fabric as flat as possible while you cut it. Bent-handle shears make this much easier. Pinking or scalloping shears should not be used to cut out a garment. They are designed to make a seam finish after the seam has been sewn.

Hold the shears in your cutting hand. Hold the fabric flat with your other hand. Cut in long, even strokes, and do not close the blades completely. This will give you a smooth, even edge. Use the tip of the shears only when you need to cut around small areas, such as the notches.

This person is cutting exactly on the cutting line using long sharp shears to make steady even slashes.

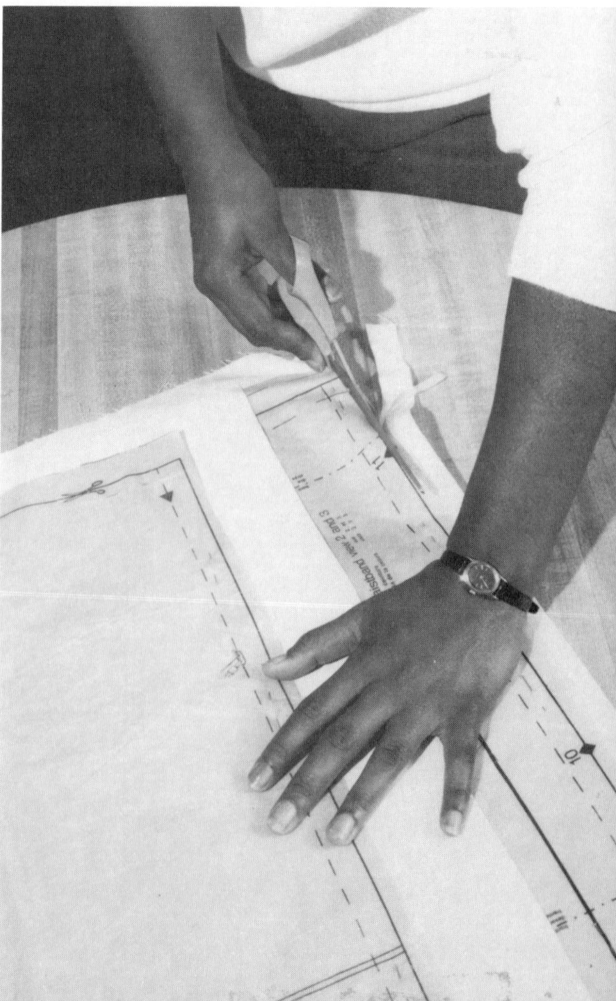

MARKING

The symbols on the pattern are important. They tell you exactly where a dart is, where a seam starts or stops, and how two parts fit together. All dots, squares, and triangles printed on the pattern tissue should be transferred to the fabric. Each has a purpose and will be referred to in the pattern's instructions. It is not necessary to mark seamlines and hemlines.

The two most common ways to mark symbols on fabric are a tracing wheel and tailor's chalk. They are useful to make marks on the wrong side of most fabrics. However, these two methods are not used on some fabrics. They will show through on the right side of sheer and white fabrics. On fabrics with textured surfaces, the marks may not show up clearly. In these cases, a tailor's tack, or thread markings, should be used.

TRACING WHEEL

A tracing wheel is a sewing aid that looks like a small pizza cutter. It is used with special carbon paper, called dressmaker's carbon. Use a saw-toothed wheel for most fabrics and a smooth-edged wheel for delicate fabrics.

To use a tracing wheel, place the colored sides of the carbon paper on the wrong sides of the fabric. Place the edge of a ruler along the line you wish to trace. Lightly pass the edge of the tracing wheel over the pattern lines.

TAILOR'S CHALK

To use tailor's chalk, push a pin through both layers of the fabric at each mark, forcing the head through the tissue. Remove the pattern. Make a small chalk dot at each pin on the wrong side of both layers of fabric.

TAILOR'S TACKS

To make tailor's tacks, use a double thread without a knot. Take a small stitch through the pattern and both layers of fabric at the symbol. Pull the thread through, but leave at least a one-inch (2.5-cm) tail. Take a second stitch that intersects the first stitch at a right angle, leaving a loop of one inch (2.5 cm). When you are ready to sew, unpin the pattern tissue and gently pull the thread loops and ends through the paper pattern. Pull the two fabric layers apart as far as the loops will allow. Cut the threads between the fabric layers.

READY TO SEW

Once you have made all the markings on your garment parts, the preliminary work is done. Now you are ready to sew.

Transfer the construction symbols and lines from your pattern to the wrong side of each garment section using carbon paper, tailor's chalk or "tailor's tacks".

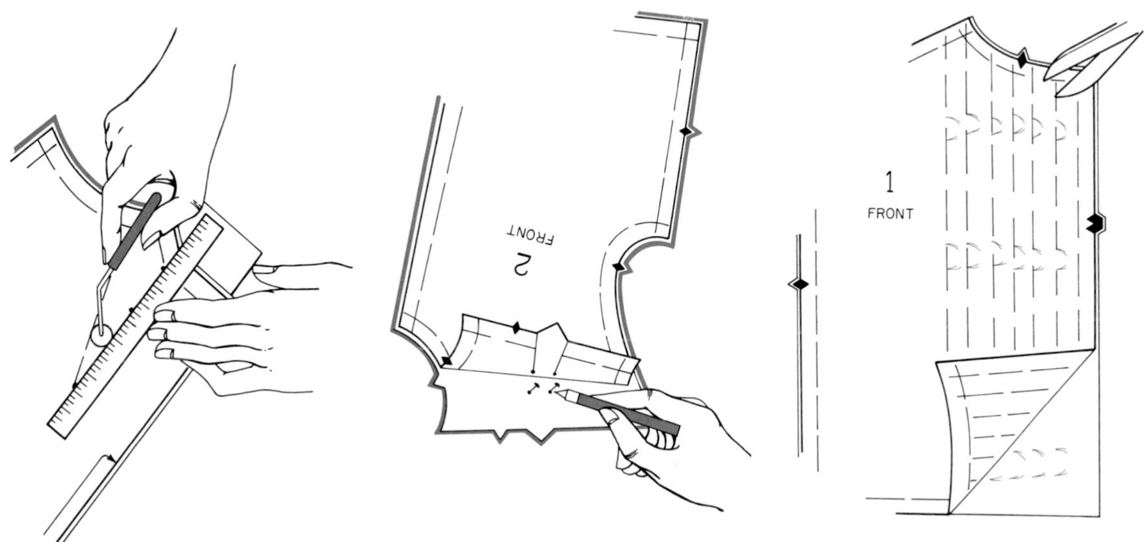

WORDS TO REMEMBER

adjustments	hand
alterations	interfacing
designer ease	mercerization
figure type	minimum ease
fusible	notions
grain perfect	placket

CHECKING YOUR UNDERSTANDING

1. How can you determine your correct figure type and pattern size? List all the measurements you would need to take.
2. How do you go about choosing a fabric, an interfacing, and a lining that are suitable for your pattern?
3. Explain why it is important to use a fabric that is grain perfect. Describe how you would straighten the grain on a fabric that needed it.
4. Define what is meant by ease. Explain the difference between minimum ease and designer ease.
5. Describe the proper ways to lay out your pattern.

APPLYING YOUR UNDERSTANDING

1. Pick out several garments in your wardrobe and compare the hand of the fabric to the silhouette of the garment. Can you see why some of these styles are suitable for soft, fluid fabrics, while others look better in firm, crisp fabrics?
2. Go through the pattern catalogs and pick out one pattern that is right for your current level of sewing expertise. Now pick out three patterns that will each teach you a new sewing technique.
3. Look at the back of a pattern envelope and identify all the information that is given. Make a list of all the things you would need to buy if you were going to follow that pattern.
4. Once you and your classmates have cut out your garments, trade samples of leftover fabric. Experiment with different marking methods. Which methods work best on which fabrics? Can you explain why?
5. Pretend that you have a piece of stretch velour, a piece of denim, and a piece of lightweight silk. Go through the pattern catalog and pick out two or three designs that are suitable for each fabric. Why did you choose these designs?

Chapter 20
Constructing a Garment

Has this ever happened to you?

Classes were over for the day, and Michele was in the home economics room working on her sewing project when her best friend Louise burst into the room.

Louise blurted, "Dick and Kathy and I were just talking about our act in next month's talent contest, and we have a super idea for costumes. See, we even made a sketch. What do you think?"

"They're great," replied Michele, "but where are you going to get them?"

"We thought maybe you'd help us make them. You sew better than any of us," answered Louise.

"You know, I just took a new job after school. I'd never get them done by next month," said Michele.

"We've got that all figured out," Louise declared. "Kathy and I will go shopping for everything. Then, you can show Dick how to cut out the pattern. You can teach Dick and I how to press the seams the way you said Miss Wilcox taught you. We'll do that while you and Kathy sew. That way, we'll be able to get them all done and they'll look like they were made by experts."

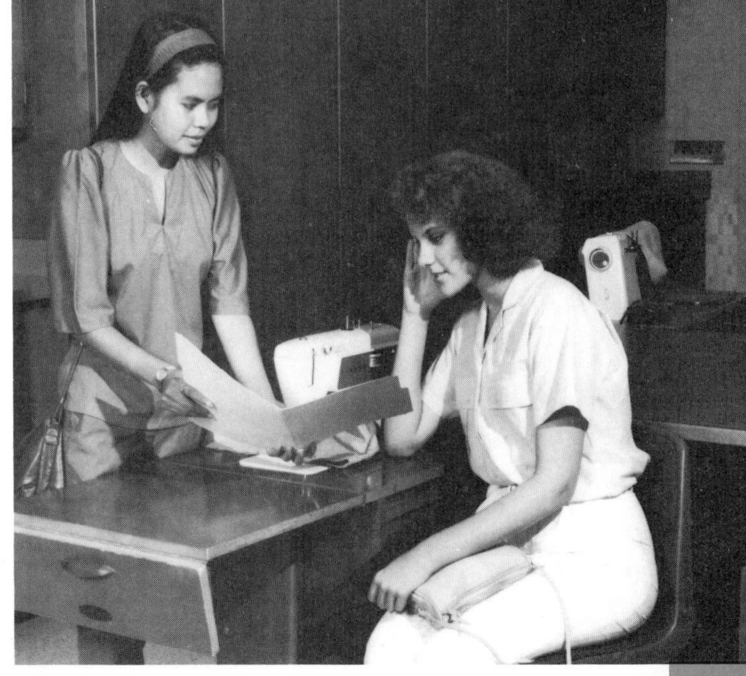

Have you ever wondered why some people seem to spend less time on their sewing projects, but get better results than you do?

Have you ever thought about how you could improve your sewing skills?

After reading this chapter, you will be able to

- describe the three methods of organizing your sewing projects;
- know the sewing procedures that will result in a garment which looks professional;
- choose a seam finish that is right for your fabric;
- know the steps to achieve a good fit.

Before you start to sew, take a few minutes to read through the sewing directions on the instruction sheet or guide sheet, in your pattern envelope. These step-by-step directions will show you with words and drawings how to sew your garment. Use a yellow marking pen to highlight any sewing terms or methods that are new to you. Some of these terms may be defined in a special glossary on the guide sheet. For other terms or for more information about methods that are new to you, you may wish to get a book on basic sewing. This chapter has some general sewing information, as well as fitting techniques, that will supplement the guide sheet.

The instruction sheet, or guide sheet, in the pattern envelope is a set of step-by-step directions that explain how to sew the garment.

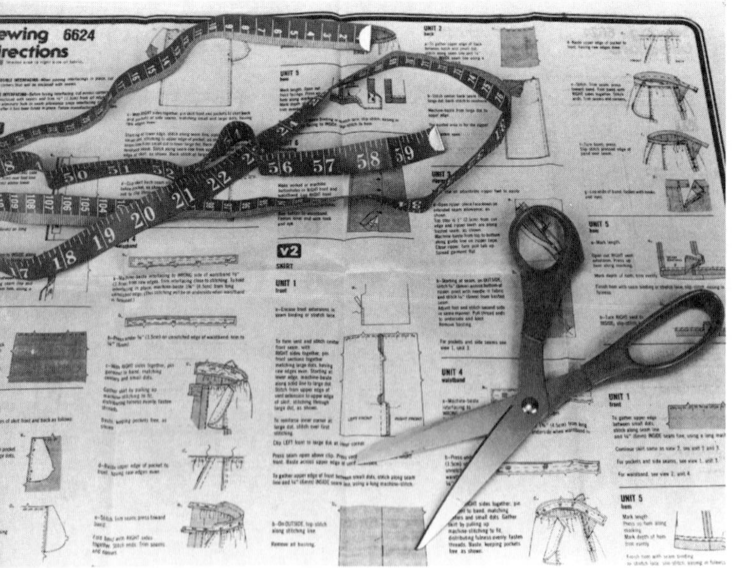

CONSTRUCTION METHODS

When you sit down to sew a garment, there are several ways to set up your sewing procedures. Which one you choose rests on your personal preference and your level of sewing skill.

UNIT CONSTRUCTION

Unit construction means that every unit is done, no matter how small, before you begin to sew the units together. For example, if you were making a dress with a waistline seam, you would be apt to sew it together in the following way:

Step 1. Make the bodice, along with details such as darts, collars, and pockets, as one unit.

Step 2. Make the sleeves as another unit, and then join them to the bodice at the underarm seam.

Step 3. Make the skirt as another unit.

Step 4. Stitch the bodice and skirt together at the waistline seam, complete the hem, and attach any fasteners.

The unit construction method is very useful when a garment has a lot of details, such as pleats, welt pockets, tailored collars, and lapels.

FLAT CONSTRUCTION

Another method of sewing is **flat construction.** With this system, you do as many details as you can on each part of the garment while it is still flat. If you were making a dress with this method, these are the steps you would follow:

Step 1. Complete all the details on the bodice front and skirt front and stitch them together at the waistline seam.

Step 2. Complete the bodice back and skirt back and stitch them together at the waistline seam.

Step 3. Sew the garment together at the shoulder seams, finish the neckline area, and join the sleeves to the garment at the armhole seam.

Step 4. Sew the garment together at the sides and underarms in one long seam, complete the hem, and then attach the fasteners.

Many easy patterns that do not have many curves, such as men's shirts and children's clothing, are put together using the flat construction method.

ASSEMBLY LINE METHOD

The **assembly line method** requires you to arrange the sewing steps in the guide sheet in a new way. This way must let you work on different parts of the garment at the same time.

Step 1. Sit down at the sewing machine and sew as many seams as you can. Do not, however, stitch any intersecting seams.

Step 2. Pick up your scissors and notch, clip, trim, and grade whatever is necessary.

Step 3. Go to your ironing board and press all these seams.

Repeat steps 1—3 until the garment is completed.

Anyone who uses this method must thoroughly understand how a garment is put together. It is often used by sewers who have a great deal of expertise and who want to sew very quickly. However, there are times when even a new sewer might use this method. Suppose you are making duplicates of the same item, such as Christmas stockings or gift pillows. If you followed this method, you could sew faster by working on all the pillows at the same time, rather than doing them one at a time.

The assembly line method is used when you are making duplicates of the same item, such as craft projects, pillows, or Christmas stockings.

Managing Your Life

A PROFITABLE HOBBY

Have you ever thought about how you could use your sewing skills to earn some extra money? You do not have to be an expert to turn your hobby into a profitable venture.

- *Consider starting a small repair business.* Start by doing small repairs, such as mending hems, restitching seams, replacing buttons. As you get more skilled, you may want to do some simple alterations. Many dry cleaners offer these services. Visit some of them to find out what they charge so you can match or beat their prices.
- *Work up a line of unique clothes, such as sweatshirts.* You might buy the sweatshirts and then add the trim yourself. Talk to some local boutiques to see if any of them would be willing to sell your sweatshirts on consignment. This means that the store agrees to show your sweatshirts and, if they sell, take a percentage of your profit. If your sweatshirts do not sell, you must take them back after a month or so.
- *Design a gift that can be personalized for a holiday.* For example, you could make red valentine pillows in the shape of a heart. Then you could use liquid rhinestones to write personal messages. If you are going to make customized items, ask for part of the cost as a down payment. That way you will not be stuck with a pillow you cannot use that says, "I love you Jack."
- *Get a part-time job in a fabric store.* Such stores are always looking for good help that enjoys and knows something about sewing.

Whatever you decide to do, start your business slowly so that you do not end up with more work than you can do. Keep records of how much you spend on supplies and how much time it takes you to make or repair an item. If necessary, ask yourself how you can cut your costs and/or raise your sewing efficiency. Review these records regularly to make sure you are getting a fair price for your time and your skills.

THE BASICS OF CONSTRUCTING A SEAM

No matter what type of project you are making, you should know the basic techniques for stitching a seam. If you know and use these techniques, your finished garment will look like it was sewn by an expert.

PINNING

Unless the pattern guide tells you otherwise, most seams are pinned and stitched right sides together.

To begin, match the two pieces of fabric together at either end of the seamline. Place a pin at a right angle to the cut edge at each end. Then match and pin the garment parts together at notches or other matching points. If necessary, place more pins between these pins. Use just enough pins to hold the garment parts together for stitching. You will pull out the pins as you stitch, so too many pins will slow you down.

STITCHING

The standard seam allowance is five-eighths inch (15 mm) on all seams. If the seam allowance is a different width, there will be a note on your pattern tissue. It is vital to cut out your garment exactly on the cut lines shown on the pattern tissue. It is also vital to stitch all seams accurately. If you do not, the garment parts will not fit together the way they should, and the finished garment will not be the right size. For example, if you sewed each shoulder seam one-eighth inch (3 mm) narrower than it should be, you would be making the seam allowances smaller and the garment larger. You would be adding one-fourth inch (6 mm) at each shoulder, or one-half inch (13 mm) to the total neck edge. The collar or the neckline facing would be too small for the neck edge of the garment.

Sew straight even seems by lining up the cut edge of the fabric with the right markings on the throat plate.

Most sewing machines have stitch guides cut into the throat plate under the needle. To sew straight, even seams, you line up the cut edge of your fabric with the right marking as you stitch. If your machine does not have stitch guides, you can make your own stitch guides with masking tape. Use a wide strip of tape and, measuring from and to the right of the needle, mark various widths on the tape.

As you stitch, gently guide the fabric with one hand in front and the other hand behind the presser foot. As you do this, keep your eye on the cut edge of the fabric, rather than on the needle. Your stitching will be straighter.

As you come to each pin, stop and pull it out rather than stitching over it. If a needle hits a pin while stitching, it can dull or break the needle, bend the pin, or make a weak spot in the seam. Be sure, too, to keep your fingers out of the way of the moving needle.

When stitching a corner, stop just one stitch short of the corner point. Then, take one stitch diagonally across the point and continue stitching down the other side. This technique will result in a sharper point once the seam is trimmed and pressed.

TRIMMING

Your goal is to make a garment with seams that lie flat and smooth. To do this, you will need to know some trimming and grading techniques.

As a rule of thumb, any seam that you can see when the garment is wrong side out will not need special treatment with your scissors. **Enclosed seams,** or seams that are hidden between layers of fabric, should be trimmed to reduce bulk. Some enclosed seams include those inside a pocket, a collar or a cuff, or under a facing.

To **trim** means to cut off part of the seam allowance so that it is a narrower width. As a rule of thumb, if the seam allowance is five-eighths inch (15 mm), it is usually trimmed to one-fourth inch (6 mm).

Once the seam is trimmed, it will need to be graded. **Grading** is the process of trimming each seam allowance to a different width. Its goal is to stop a ridge from forming on the outside of the garment when both seam allowances are pressed in the same direction. As a rule of thumb, the seam allowance that will be closest to the garment is left the widest.

Trimming, grading, clipping, and notching are four frequent steps to take in sewing necklines, armholes, and waistlines.

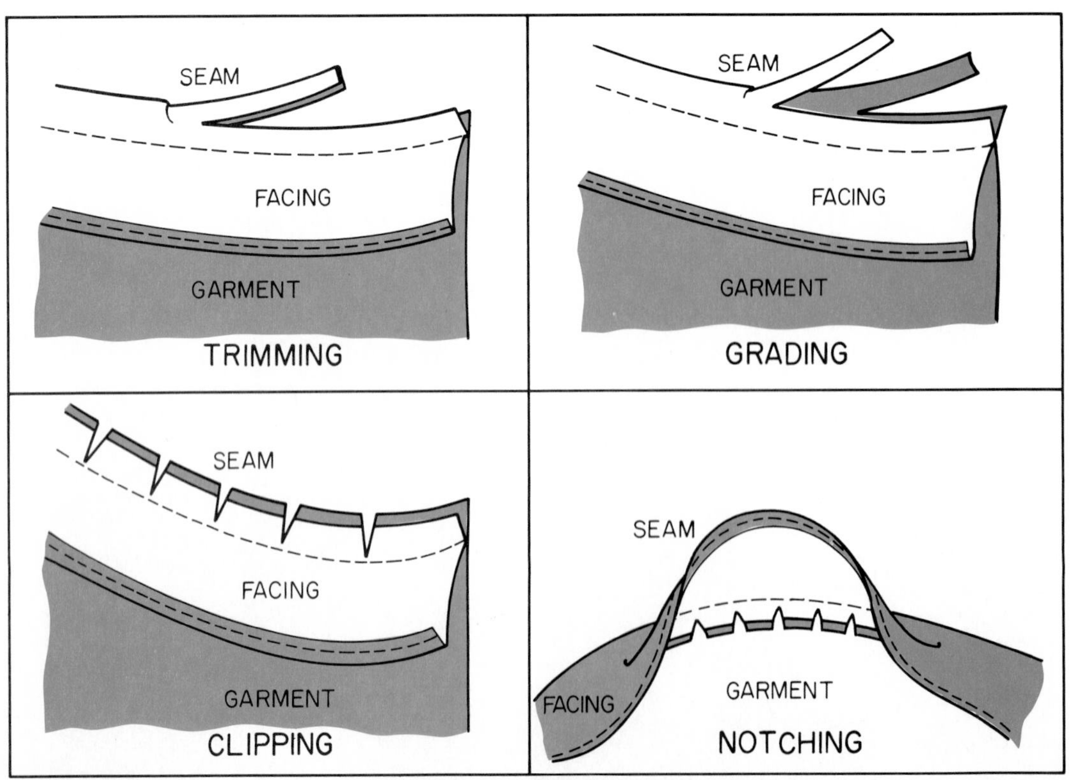

Curved Seams

Curved seams need more handling to make them lie flat when pressed and hidden.

Clips are small cuts in the seam allowance. They let the outer edge of the seam allowance spread out and lie flat when the seam is pressed. Inside, or concave, curves should be clipped.

Notches are small wedges of fabric that are cut from the seam allowance. If a convex curve is not notched, there will be too much fabric in the seam allowances. This excess will form small bumps and ridges on the completed garment. Outside, or convex, curves should be notched.

Clips or notches should be spaced from one-half inch to one inch (13 mm to 25 mm) apart along the curve. The deeper the curve, the more closely spaced the clips or notches should be. Clip or notch just to, but not through, the stitching line.

Corners

To get rid of the bulk of extra fabric, you should trim corners diagonally and close to the stitching line. Do not trim too close or the fabric will fray at the point when the corner is turned and pressed. Trim the corner after you trim and grade the seam allowances.

SPECIAL SEAM TECHNIQUES

Sometimes, the pattern guide calls for more special techniques to get the desired look.

Staystitching

Staystitching is a line of stitching that stops curved or bias edges from stretching out of shape as they are handled. These machine stitches are placed just inside the seamline while the garment part is still flat. As you study your pattern guide, you will note that it sometimes tells you to staystitch some garment edges. This is done before any seams are sewn.

Staystitching should be done with, or in the same direction as, the fabric grain. This is called **directional stitching.** To find grain direction, run your finger along the edge of the fabric. If the yarns curl smoothly against the fabric edge, you are going with the grain. If the yarns push apart, you are going against the grain. Directional stitching helps to stop the garment from stretching or changing shape as you stitch. Whenever you can, use this technique to stitch seams as well as to staystitch edges. If a seam that is staystitched needs to be clipped or notched, cut just to, but not through, the lines of staystitching.

Easestitching

Easestitching is a technique that is used to join a larger garment part to a slightly smaller one. To easestitch, stitch close to the seamline with a long machine stitch. The stitching should lie slightly beyond the marks shown on the pattern tissue. When you are ready to sew the two parts together, match the marks and pin. Work with the easestitching facing you and pull up the thread to spread out the fullness evenly. Stitch along the seamline. Be sure not to stitch in any folds or gathers.

***Direction stitching* is the technique of stitching with the grain of the fabric to prevent stretching. *Easestitching* is the technique to join a larger garment part to a slightly smaller one.**

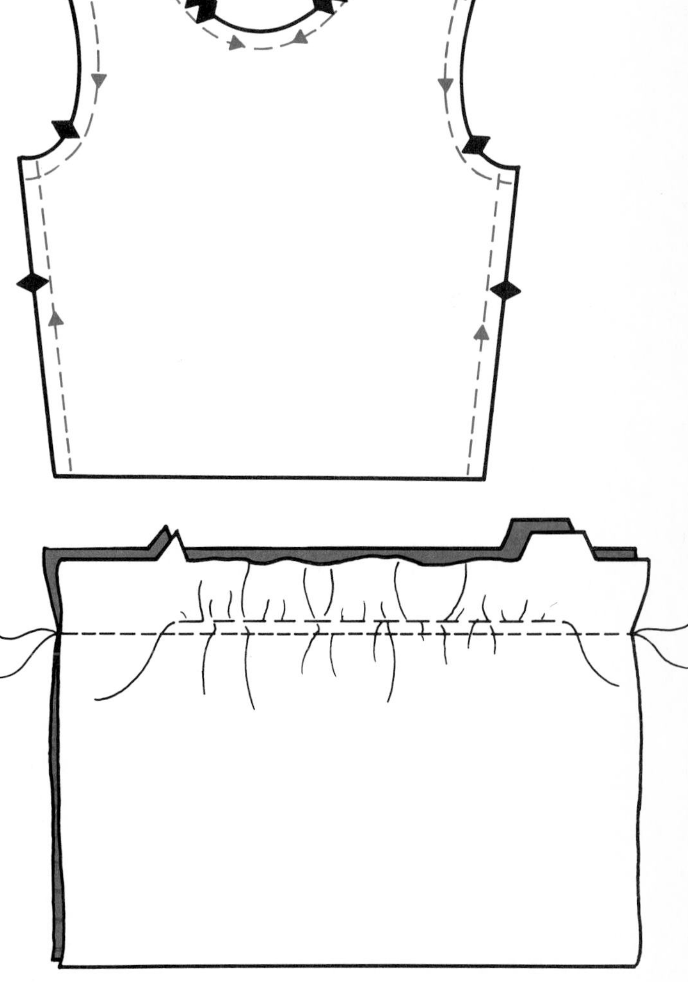

Careers A BRIEF LOOK

CLOTHING AND TEXTILES

If you like to work with fabrics, possess an artistic flair, have a keen eye for fashion, and can communicate your ideas to other people, then you may want to pursue a career in the clothing and textiles field.

If you are interested in this field, you can start learning now. Here are just a few things you can do. You can take a part-time job in a clothing store, improve your sewing skills, visit the costume collection at your local museum, and read the fashion magazines. You can also learn to communicate well, whether your talent is writing, sketching, public speaking, or photography.

Entry Level Jobs
Assistant buyer
Copywriting assistant
Display assistant
Fashion model
Retail salesperson
Shipping clerk
Stock clerk

Jobs That Require More Training
Alterations expert
Boutique/specialty store owner
Buyer
Clothing instructor
Commercial artist
Computer operator
Customer service representative
Cutter
Display artist
Dressmaker/tailor
Dry-cleaning specialist
Fashion coordinator
Fabric designer
Fashion designer
Fashion director
Fashion editor
Fashion illustrator
Fashion photographer
Fashion stylist
Pattern maker
Sales representative

Jobs That Require an Advanced Degree
Consumer education specialist
Costume historian
Extension home economist
Market researcher
Textile chemist

For more information, write to:

American Apparel Manufacturer Association
1611 N. Kent St.
Arlington, Virginia 22209

American Textile Manufacturer Institute
1101 Connecticut Ave., N.W., Suite 300
Washington, D.C. 20036

National Cotton Council of America
1918 North Parkway
Memphis, Tennessee 38112

Understitching

Understitching is an extra row of stitching that stops a facing or a layer of fabric from rolling to the outside of the garment. Do this stitching after you trim, grade, and clip or notch the seam allowances. Press the seam allowances toward the facing. Work from the right side of the garment and stitch one-eighth inch (3 mm) from the seamline through the facing and seam allowances only.

Topstitching

Topstitching is a row of stitching that can be seen on the outside of the garment. It can be both decorative and functional. Topstitching can be used to stress design lines, such as seamlines. It can be used to secure and decorate details such as patch pockets and pleats. It can also be used to keep garment edges, such as necklines, collars, and hemlines, crisp and flat.

To topstitch, stitch with a slightly longer stitch length, eight to ten stitches per inch (per 2.5 cm). Stitch an even distance from the seamline or garment edge and through all the garment layers. Use thread that matches or contrasts. Use regular thread or, for a more decorative look, use one of the special topstitching threads.

Edgestitching

Edgestitching is topstitching done close to the seamline or garment edge. It is almost always done in regular thread. When used, edgestitching is less visible and less decorative than topstitching.

DARTS

Darts are often used to build shape into a garment. They are used to shift fullness from one part of the garment to another. The most common darts are bust darts, waistline darts, and elbow darts.

Darts are made after the staystitching is done, but before the garment seams are stitched. Fold the fabric so that the dart marks match and pin it. Begin at the wide end of the dart, and sew toward the point. The last two or three stitches should be right on the fold. To secure the stitching, tie the ends of the thread in a knot, and then cut off the thread tails.

Darts are used at the waistline and bustline to control fullness and to build shape into a garment.

GATHERS

Gathers are a way to control and spread out the fullness in a garment. You start your gathers with two rows of machine baste stitches. To **machine baste,** use long machine stitches to hold the fabric in place only until the permanent seam is stitched.

Why should you use two rows of machine basting for gathers? There are two reasons. First, they make it easier to spread out the gathers evenly. Second, if one of your threads should break, you will not have to start all over again.

Begin by adjusting the stitch length on your machine to six to eight stitches per inch (3 to 4 mm in length). Working on the part to be gathered, stitch one row of basting along the seamline. Stitch a second row one-eighth inch (3 mm) away, but within the seam allowance. Pin the two garment parts together. Be sure to match the markings. Adjust the part with the basting stitches to fit by pulling up on both bobbin threads at the same time. As you pull the threads, gently slide the fabric along to make the gathers. To secure the thread ends, wrap them around a pin in a figure eight (8). Spread out the gathers evenly. Then, pin them in place about every one-half inch (13 mm). Work with the gathered side facing up, and stitch along the seamline.

There is a second way to gather that works very well on heavy fabrics. It also is less apt to break the threads as the gathers are formed. To use this method, adjust your machine to stitch a long, wide zigzag stitch. Place a piece of light cord or heavy thread just next to the seamline, within the seam allowance. Zigzag over it. Be sure that your zigzag stitches do not go over the seamline into the garment area. Also make sure the cord is not caught in the stitching. To form the gathers, pull up along one end of the cord and slide the fabric along its length. Once the seam is permanently stitched, the cord is pulled out.

PRESSING

One of the basic rules of sewing is "press as you go." Every person who sews should memorize the following: *Never cross one line of stitching with another until the first one has been pressed.*

As you complete each step of stitching, press it before you go on to the next step. You should use the same method to press each garment part. The stitches should always be pressed flat, first on one side of the garment part, then on the other. This blends the stitches. Then the seam, dart, and so forth should be pressed open or to one side as shown in your pattern guide.

In chapter 18 you learned the difference between "pressing" and "ironing," as well as the importance of using a press cloth. As your sewing skills grow, you may want to learn to use some of the more advanced pressing aids. Pressing hams, pressing mitts, sleeve boards, and point pressers all have specially shaped surfaces that make it easier to press curves and small-detail areas.

SEAM FINISHES

A **seam finish** is any treatment that stops the fabric from fraying on the inside of a garment. It makes the seams stronger and helps to protect them during washing or dry-cleaning. This means the garment will last and look new longer.

If the seam is not an enclosed seam, it should be finished. Seams should be finished after they are sewn, but before they are joined to a second seam.

Below are three basic seam finishes. One of them can be used for almost any fabric you choose. You can also use these treatments to finish the edge of hems and facings.

Finish seams with a zigzag, hemmed, or pinked seam finish to prevent raveling and to create a more professional look.

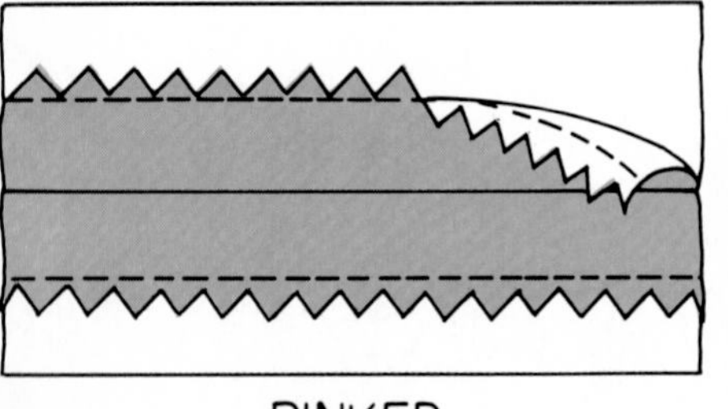
PINKED

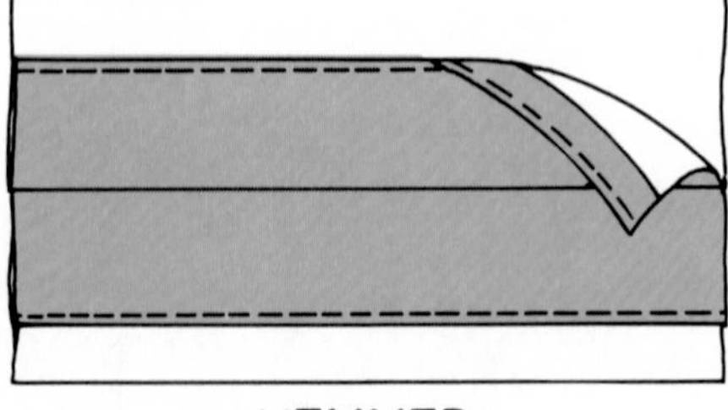
HEMMED

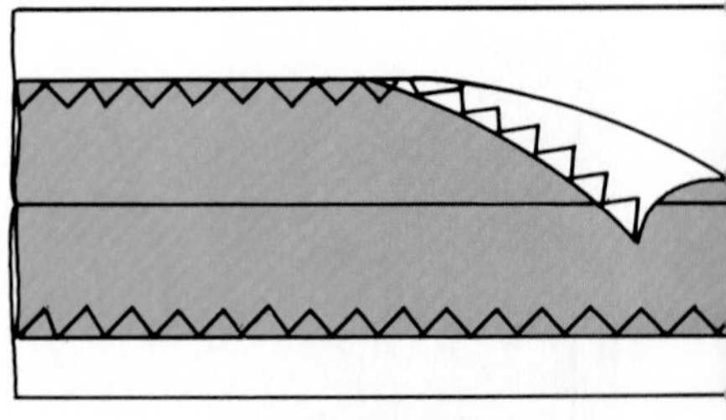
ZIGZAG

1. The stitched and pinked finish is good to use on firmly woven fabrics. Stitch one-fourth inch (6 mm) from the raw edge of the seam allowance. Press the seam open. Using pinking or scalloping shears, trim the edge close to the stitching line.

2. The turned and stitched finish is good to use on light and medium weight woven fabrics. Press the seam open before you start. Fold the raw edge under one-eighth inch to one-fourth inch (3 mm to 6 mm). Press as needed. Edgestitch close to the folded edge.

3. The zigzag finish is good to use on almost all fabrics. It is very good for knits because it has built-in stretch. Press the seam open before you start. Adjust your machine for zigzag stitch. Stitch near, but not over, the edge of the seam allowance. Trim the excess seam allowance close to the stitching. Some machines have finishing stitches, such as the overcast, the overedge, and the three-step zigzag stitch. These are all similar to the basic zigzag seam finish.

FITTING

A garment should be tried on several times during the sewing process to check the fit. In chapter 19 you learned how to measure yourself carefully. You also learned how to make the right adjustments on your pattern tissue before you cut out your garment. If you follow these methods, your fitting changes, if any, should be minor ones.

THE FIRST FITTING

Your first fitting should take place as soon as the major seams are joined. If you are concerned about how the garment will fit, machine baste these seams together for the fitting. If you are using the flat construction method, machine baste the side seams. At this point, details such as collars, sleeves, facings, and waistbands should not be sewed to the garment. If you are trying on pants or a skirt, baste a strip of grosgrain ribbon in place where the waistband will be.

Wear the underwear you plan to wear with the finished product. Put on the garment, right side out, and pin any openings closed the way they will be on the finished garment. Stand in front of a full-length mirror and analyze the fit. Begin at the top of the garment and work your way down. Check the following:

1. Does the neckline lie smooth with no pulling or gapping?

2. Do the shoulder seams rest smoothly on the shoulders?

3. Do the darts taper toward the fullest part of the body?

4. Are the seams at center front and center back in the center of the body, and do they hang at right angles to the floor?

5. Are the side seams straight and at right angles to the floor?

6. Is the garment too tight or too loose in the chest, waist, or hip area?

7. Is the waistline seam in its proper place on the body?

8. Can you sit, stand, stretch, and bend with ease?

Indicate the changes that need to be made, and then remove the garment with great care. Restitch any new lines before you take out the basting or stitching lines you made before the fitting. Remove these old stitches before you press the new seams.

As you go along, try your garment on for fit. It is much easier to make minor adjustment during construction, rather than making a major alteration at the end.

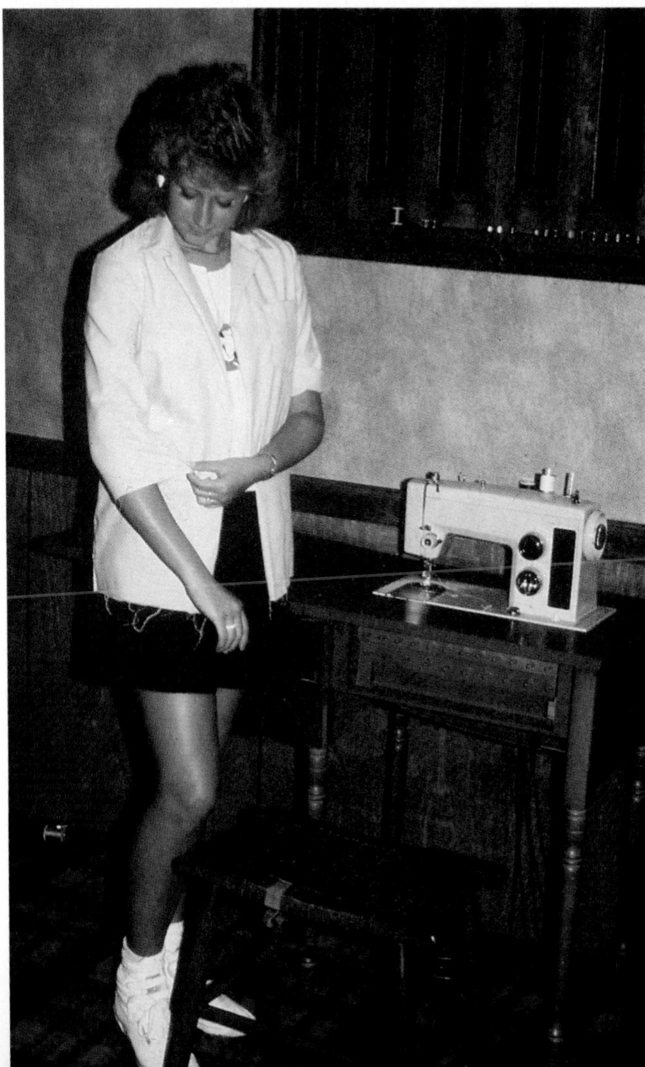

THE SECOND FITTING

To prepare for the second fitting, sew on facings and collars, and baste sleeves and waistbands in place. Pin up the lower edge of the garment along the suggested hemline. Place these pins at right angles to the floor so that the hemline hangs smoothly and evenly. Review everything you checked in the first fitting, and then check the following:

1. Does the collar sit smoothly on the body in an even roll?
2. Does the seamline of a set-in sleeve lie at the tip of the shoulder bone?
3. Do the sleeves hang straight from the shoulder to the elbow?
4. Is the sleeve the right length? If it is a full-length sleeve, the hemline or cuff edge should be at the wrist bone.
5. Are the markings for buttons and buttonholes, snaps, or hook and eyes at the right places on the garment?
6. Is the marked hem length a flattering one for you? For pants, the front should just brush the top of the shoe and the back should hang about one-half inch (13 mm) below the top of the shoe. For a dress or skirt, mark and pin the exact and even hemline with the method described below.

Marking the Hem

Once you have chosen a flattering length for the hemline, you should pull out the pins and mark the hem length so that it is straight and parallel to the floor. For more accuracy, measure the hemline up from the floor, rather than down from the waist. Thus, it is better to have someone else mark the hem length for you.

Use a hem marker adjusted to the right length or a yardstick held at a right angle to the floor. Stand up straight and do not try to watch the person who is marking your hem length. When you look down, you unconsciously lean forward. When you do this, the garment dips in the front and changes the length of the hemline. You should stand still while the person doing the marking moves around you.

Pins should be placed parallel to the floor every three inches to four inches (7.5 cm to 10 cm) around the hemline. Once the hemline is marked, take off the garment and turn it wrong side out. Measure the distance from the pin line to the edge of the garment and trim away excess fabric so that the hem allowance is even.

Hem Finishes

Almost every hem needs some type of hem finish before it is sewn to the garment. The type of hem finish to use depends on the fabric and the type of garment. The stitched and pinked finish or the zigzag finish described on pages 274–275 would both make good hem finishes. Other common hem finishes are the turned-under finish and seam tape or lace. For the turned-under finish, fold the raw edge of the fabric under one-fourth inch (6 mm) and press. With seam tape or lace, hide the raw edge of the fabric under the tape. Place the tape one-fourth inch (6 mm) over the edge, and then edgestitch it in place.

Attaching The Hem

The hem can be sewn to the garment by hand or by machine.

By Machine

Topstitch the hem in place with one or more parallel rows of stitching.

By Hand

There are four hand stitches that are often used for hems.

1. The blindstitch can be used with all types of fabrics and hem finishes. It allows for movement without pulling and is hard to see on the outside of the garment.
2. The catchstitch is a good choice for hemming knits and stretch fabrics.
3. The slipstitch is used to join the turned-under finish to the garment.
4. The hemming stitch is used to join a hem to a seam tape or lace finish.

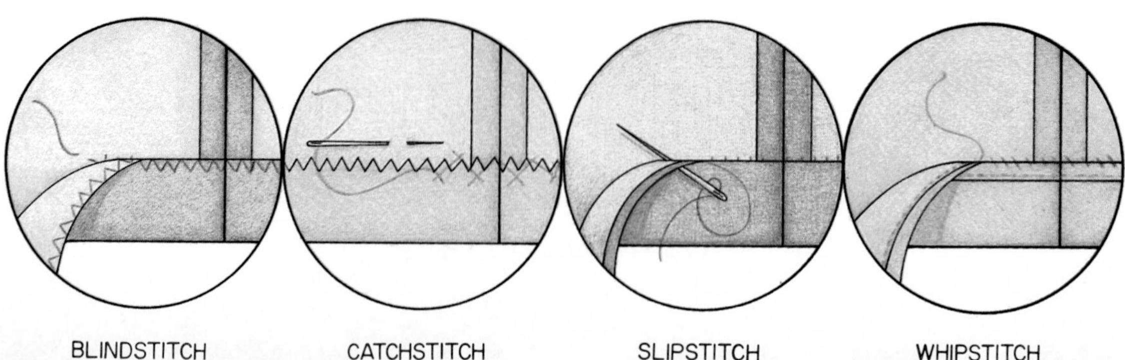

WORDS TO REMEMBER

assembly line method
clip
directional stitching
easestitching
edgestitching
enclosed seam
flat construction
grading
machine baste
notch
seam finish
staystitching
topstitching
trimming
understitching
unit construction

CHECKING YOUR UNDERSTANDING

1. What is the difference between the unit construction and the flat construction methods?
2. What special sewing and trimming techniques would you use to stitch an outside curve, an inside curve, and a seam with a corner?
3. Describe two ways to make smooth, even gathers.
4. Explain how to press a seam the right way.
5. How would you prepare a garment for your first fitting? What are some of the things to look for as you examine the fit?

APPLYING YOUR UNDERSTANDING

1. Collect a man's shirt, a woman's blouse, and a child's garment. See if you can decide which construction method was used.
2. Make two sample curved seams. On the first sample, stitch the seam, and then turn it and press it. On the second sample, stitch and then trim, grade, and clip or notch it. Press this seam using the right pressing methods. Compare the two samples.
3. Examine the fabrics that you and your classmates are using for your current sewing projects. What seam finishes would be suitable for each of these fabrics?
4. Take a close look at several ready-to-wear garments. Note which ones were made with sewing techniques such as staystitching, understitching, topstitching, edgestitching, seam finishes, and hem finishes. Comment on how these techniques affect the overall appearance and quality of the garments.
5. Try on a garment that you know fits you poorly. Look at it in the mirror and decide what changes you would make if you were sewing the garment.

Unit 5

FOODS AND NUTRITION

Good nutrition and good food preparation go hand in hand. A daily diet of healthful food, along with exercise and rest, will help you to look and feel better and to have vitality and energy for your active life-style. But nutritious food must also be properly prepared and served to keep as many of the nutrients as possible. It should taste good and look attractive.

In this unit, you will learn why a good diet is vital to your well-being, and you will see how to make a daily choice of foods that supply good nutrition. You will find information about how to buy and store foods. You also will learn about food package nutrition labeling, unit pricing, and open dating. Given also are techniques for food preparation and suggestions for meals that can be made up in minutes.

With good food management skills you will be able to plan, prepare, and serve meals that are healthful, attractive, and not costly. In addition, you will learn to use your food preparation skills as a form of creative expression.

Chapter 21
NUTRITION AND YOU

Has this ever happened to you?

As Lynn and Terry were talking about the pros and cons of the grapefruit, low protein, and low carbohydrate diets, their friend Jean walked up.

"Jean, you really look terrific. How much weight have you lost?" asked Terry.

"And how long did it take you?" added Lynn.

"Oh let's see," paused Jean, "I have been on the diet for four weeks, and I have lost about ten pounds. It's great. I feel so much better, and now I can wear clothes that haven't fit for over a year!"

"That's super!" exclaimed Lynn. "How did you do it?"

"First of all, I talked to the school nurse and my home economics teacher, Mrs. Snyder. Both of them gave me similar advice," stated Jean. They said, "Eat a well balanced diet and exercise. Mrs. Snyder said that I should start by eating smaller portions of food and to cut out foods rich in fat and sugar. So that, in addition to taking my daily aerobic class, has made the weight loss quite simple."

"You make it sound so easy," stated Terry.

"Well, all I know is that it is the first diet plan that has worked for me, and I feel full of energy," said Jean.

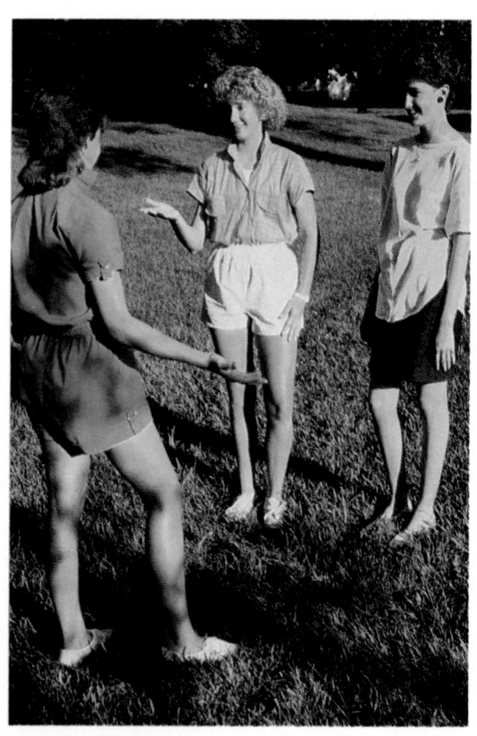

"I have heard enough," responded Terry. "It's time that I did something to get rid of my extra seven pounds. Is there any room left in your aerobic class and where do I sign up?"

Have you ever wondered how diet and exercise affect your overall health?

Have you ever thought about what it means to eat a well-balanced diet?

After reading this chapter, you will be able to

- evaluate the reasons why you eat;
- identify factors that influence your food choices;
- trace the path of food as it is digested in the body;
- describe the kinds of nutrients and identify the best food sources of each nutrient;
- explain how nutrients work in the body.

PLANNING GOOD NUTRITION

Good nutrition is a lifetime investment. What you eat now will affect how you look and feel throughout your life. Have you ever thought about your different food choices? Do you know what types of foods contribute to your energy level, vitality, and appearance? If you are going to manage all the areas of your life, you need to have a knowledge of your diet and know how to control it.

In order for your body to perform in its peak condition, you need to give it fuel. Make healthy food choices everyday to ensure energy and vitality throughout the day.

EVALUATING WHY YOU EAT

The main reasons why you eat are to satisfy your physical, psychological, and social needs. Sometimes you may find it hard to separate each need. Your food decisions might be based on a combination of all these factors. For example, if you have not eaten for a long time, you might feel cross or grumpy. Or even if you are extremely hungry, you may want to wait and eat with your family or friends.

Physical Needs

Food is a basic need. It is the fuel you use to think, work, and play. It is the source of energy that is needed for circulating blood, digesting food, and other vital processes.

Your physical appearance and health are directly related to the food you eat. The condition of your eyes, hair, skin, teeth, and your overall well-being depend on your diet. Your diet will determine whether you will grow to the height set by heredity, and if your body, during times of rapid growth, will have the nutrients it needs to build new tissues. By eating a variety of foods, you can help to ensure that you will get all the nutrients your body needs for maximum growth and health.

Psychological Needs

Foods also help you meet some of your psychological needs. Have you ever found yourself reaching for a cookie or candy bar as a means of a reward? Or have you felt stress before a big exam and found that you were unable to eat? Your feelings and emotions are closely linked to what you eat. You may eat because you are bored, excited, lonely, or upset. Being aware of how your emotions affect your eating habits can help you control your diet.

Social Needs

Food also fills a social need. It is used as part of hospitality, and it is a focus for religious and family traditions. When you visit a friend, he or she usually offers you food and a drink as an expression of welcome. Parties are planned around food. Food and friendship, fun, and caring are all things that often go together.

Whether you eat to meet a physical, psychological, or social need, it is important for you to know the reasons why you eat. You may find that you are developing poor eating habits that could cause you to gain weight in the future. Or you may find that you have not been eating the types of foods that nourish and build strong, healthy bodies.

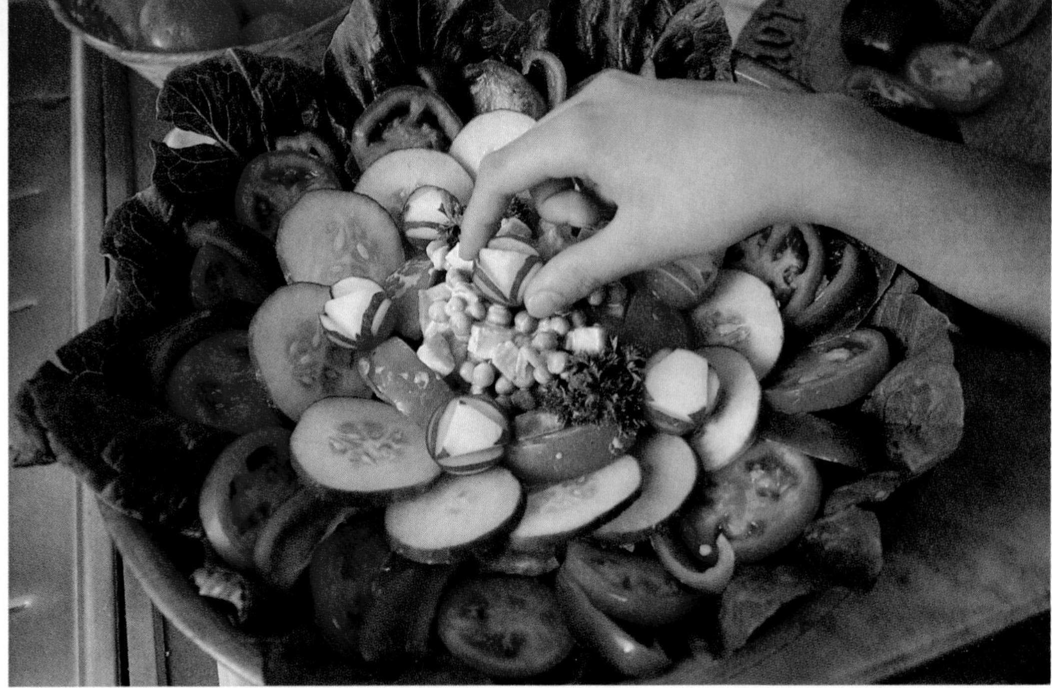

Serving foods in attractive ways, sampling foods from other cultures, and experimenting with seasonings are just a few ways that food can be used as a form of creative expression.

FACTORS AFFECTING FOOD CHOICES

If food helps to meet some of your basic needs and desires, why do not all people cook and eat the same foods? What affects food choices? Resources, social and ethnic influences, customs and traditions, and current trends in foods all affect the choices that you make.

Availability of Resources

Resources. Your resources will affect your food choices. The amount of money that you have to spend on food, your available time, skills and equipment, and your knowledge will affect your food decisions.

Each time that you make a food decision, you weigh each of your resources and decide how to use it. Sometimes you may choose to use your skills and equipment to prepare a recipe from scratch. Other times you may choose to save time and spend more money to prepare a meal with a packaged food product.

Geographic location. Where you live affects the types and availability of foods that you can choose from. A large variety of saltwater fish can be found in regions that are close to the seashore. In states like California and Florida, citrus fruits are plentiful. And in regions such as the Midwest, pork may be more available. Even if foods are available from other regions, the foods grown nearby are usually cheaper.

However, where you live does not affect your food choices as much as it did your grandparents'. Modern transportation has made it easy to ship foods long distances, and food processing and storage have made it easy to keep foods longer.

Social and Cultural Influences

Family. Your food tastes and preferences probably can be traced to your family. The family guides a child's food choices, and from these choices adult eating habits take shape. Family recipes, the kinds of spices and flavors, and eating patterns are passed along within the family unit.

Friends. Many times friends affect your food choices. They may convince you to eat when you are not hungry or they may suggest that you eat foods that are not nutritious. This kind of influence can have a negative impact on your health. In contrast, peer pressure can be good when friends encourage each other to eat healthful foods.

Religious and holiday customs. Holidays are often observed with special meals. Stores are stocked with foods that are more plentiful during these times. Turkey for Thanksgiving and ham for Christmas are two kinds of food that are eaten on holidays.

Ethnic and cultural. Ethnic background and culture also teach individuals to prefer certain foods. The area in which you live, your religion, and ethnic group are parts of your culture. Spareribs and sauerkraut, corn beef and cabbage, black-eyed peas, and pinto beans are some of the foods that appeal to people who share common cultures.

Ethnic and religious customs influence your food choices. What customs and traditions are observed by your family?

Read the labels and compare food products. Foods that claim to be healthful may actually be high in fat, sugar, or salt.

Current Trends

Advertising. Ads for food products have increased greatly in recent years. Each year food processors spend billions of dollars trying to sell their products. These ads, which are usually done with an emotional appeal, help the consumer to stay up to date on new food products.

Some ads give you data about the benefits of the product. For instance, an ad might tell you that the product is low in sugar, low in salt, caffeine free, or has fewer calories.

However, many times foods are advertised in a way that makes one believe that the food is healthful when actually it is high in fat, sugar, or salt. This means that you, the consumer, must be able to read and check food labels for accuracy of fact and not be misled by "slick" ads.

Technology. Advances in transportation, storage, and technology have made it possible for you to enjoy a variety of foods year round. These changes have brought more foods to the grocery shelves and have given the consumer more convenience and storage capabilities. For instance, health foods with no additives, convenience, ready to heat and eat, freeze dried, and irradiated foods are just a few foods available due to the changes in technology.

Changing life-styles. More opportunities to travel and more mobility have given Americans the chance to experience many regional and ethnic customs and foods. These factors, as well as the influx of many cultural groups to our country, have changed food habits.

The change in family life-style has also affected food choices. With more women employed outside the home, more one-parent families, and smaller households, a trend has developed toward more convenience foods and smaller, one-serving packages of foods that can be cooked quickly and easily by any family member.

Another growing trend has been due to studies that indicate a strong link between diet and health. More food products are free of additives, supplemented with vital nutrients, and/or are lower in calories. Such foods appeal to those who are health conscious.

Grocery stores and ethnic restaurants offer a variety of foods that meet the increasing demand for ethnic foods. What ethnic varieties have you tried lately?

HUMAN ENERGY NEEDS

You have probably heard of calories. Perhaps, you have even counted them. But do you know what calories are? A **calorie** is a term used to measure energy or heat. One calorie is the amount of heat required to raise the temperature of 1 kilogram of water 1° C. Calories are used to measure the amount of energy or heat that is released from the food you eat. They are also used to measure the amount of energy used by the body.

The number of calories you need depends on your age, sex, height, weight, body frame, and activity level. Calorie needs may be different for active teenagers who are the same age but a different sex. A female between fourteen and eighteen years of age, and between 114 and 119 pounds, needs about 2,300 calories per day. A male the same age, but 130 pounds needs about 3,000 calories per day.

Exercise and the physical upkeep of your body burn calories. The calories you eat but do not burn are stored as fat. If you want to lose weight, you should eat less and exercise more. To gain weight, you need to eat more calories than your body burns.

CALORIES USED FOR ACTIVITIES

Type of Activity	Calories per hour
Sedentary	80 to 100
Activities done while sitting, with little or no arm movement. Reading; writing; eating; watching television or movies; sewing; playing cards.	
Light	110 to 160
Activities done while standing that require some arm movement, and strenuous activities done while sitting. Preparing food; doing dishes; dusting; handwashing small articles of clothing; ironing; walking slowly; personal care; rapid typing; filing in an office.	
Moderate	170 to 240
Activities done while standing that require moderate arm movement and activities done while sitting that require vigorous arm movement. Making beds, mopping, and scrubbing; sweeping; light polishing and waxing; laundering by machine; light gardening and carpentry work; walking moderately fast.	
Vigorous	250 to 350
Heavy scrubbing and waxing; handwashing large articles of clothing; hanging out clothes; walking fast; bowling; golfing; gardening.	
Strenuous	350 or more
Swimming; tennis; running; bicycling; dancing; skiing; football.	

COUNTING CALORIES

Whether you are fat, thin, or just right, the calories in the food you eat do count. Follow the steps below to see how your calories add up.

1. Every day the average fifteen-to-eighteen-year-old male uses about 19 calories per pound of body weight. The average female uses 18 calories per pound of body weight. If you spend more than an hour each day doing heavy or moderate exercise (anything besides walking), add two to this figure. If you are less active, subtract two.
2. Now calculate the calories you use:

______ your weight in pounds

× ______ calories per pound

= ______ daily calorie use

To gain a pound, you will need to eat 3,500 calories more than your body will use. To lose a pound, you will need to eat 3,500 fewer calories than your body needs. (Or you can eat 2,500 fewer calories and burn 1,000 extra calories through exercise.)

Since calories are the key to weight control, it is important to learn the approximate calorie count of the foods you eat often. Remember that carbohydrates, fats, and proteins each supply calories. Buy an inexpensive calorie guide and check to see which foods have fewer calories and which have more.

You can recognize foods high in calories by their taste and texture. Foods that are generally higher in calories will have these characteristics. They may be:

- Greasy—crisp or contain a lot of oil or fat (potato chips, french fries, fried chicken, and butter)
- Smooth and thick (milkshake, sauces, gravies, salad dressings, mayonnaise, and peanut butter)
- Sweet and gooey (candy, soft drinks, sweet baked goods, and desserts)
- Compact or concentrated (jams and stuffings for poultry)

Foods that are lower in calories will have these characteristics:

- Juicy or watery (oranges, pears, grapefruit, or other fruit)
- Bulky but not fat (lean fish, poultry, and meat)
- Coarse with fiber but little fat (celery and other greens, and whole grain breads and cereals)
- Watery-crisp (apples, carrots, and other fruits and vegetables)
- Puffed or airy (unsugared, enriched cereals)

Whether you count calories by number or identify them by tastes and texture, counting your calories pays big dividends!

THE NUTRIENTS

Nutrients are substances found in foods that supply the body with nourishment and energy. The basic nutrients—carbohydrates, fats, protein, vitamins, minerals, and water—are vital for good health.

CARBOHYDRATES

Carbohydrates are the most important source of food energy. They are made up of the elements carbon, hydrogen, and oxygen. The two basic carbohydrates are simple (sugar) and complex (starches) carbohydrates. Grains, beans, fruits, and vegetables are the most common sources of carbohydrates.

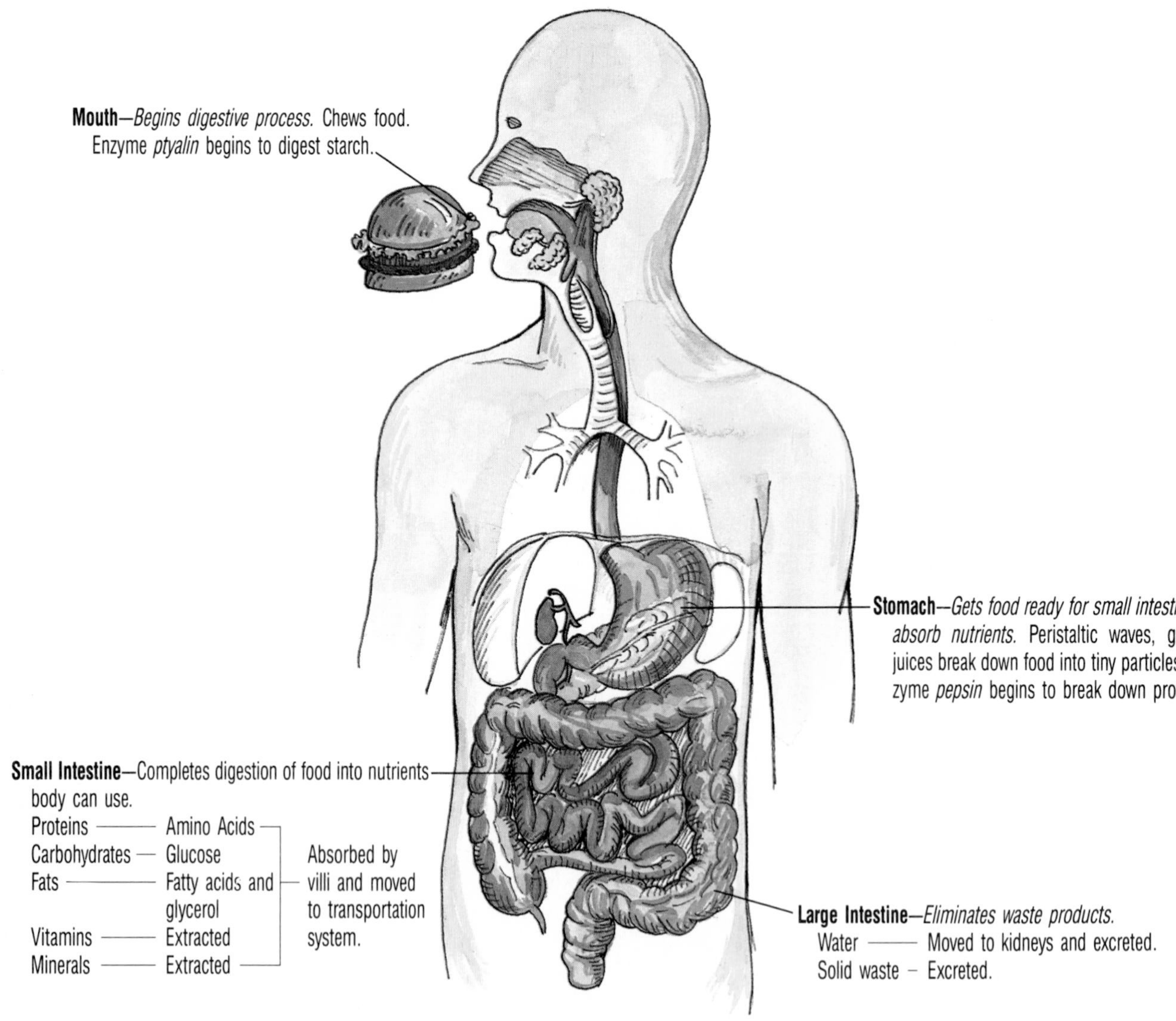
HOW FOOD IS DIGESTED
Mouth—Begins digestive process. Chews food. Enzyme ptyalin begins to digest starch.
Stomach—Gets food ready for small intestine absorb nutrients. Peristaltic waves, gastr juices break down food into tiny particles. E zyme pepsin begins to break down protein
Small Intestine—Completes digestion of food into nutrients body can use.
Proteins — Amino Acids
Carbohydrates — Glucose
Fats — Fatty acids and glycerol
Vitamins — Extracted
Minerals — Extracted
Absorbed by villi and moved to transportation system.
Large Intestine—Eliminates waste products.
Water — Moved to kidneys and excreted.
Solid waste – Excreted.

When carbohydrates are taken from the natural sources, they are referred to as "refined" or "processed." Refined carbohydrates are added to other foods (often in concentrated amounts) that do not naturally contain them. For instance, sugar taken from sugar cane is added to cookies, candy, cakes, and pies. These foods have far fewer nutrients than calories. And that is why some people refer to the carbohydrates in these foods, the refined sugar and starches, as empty calories. The two kinds of carbohydrates are sugars and starches.

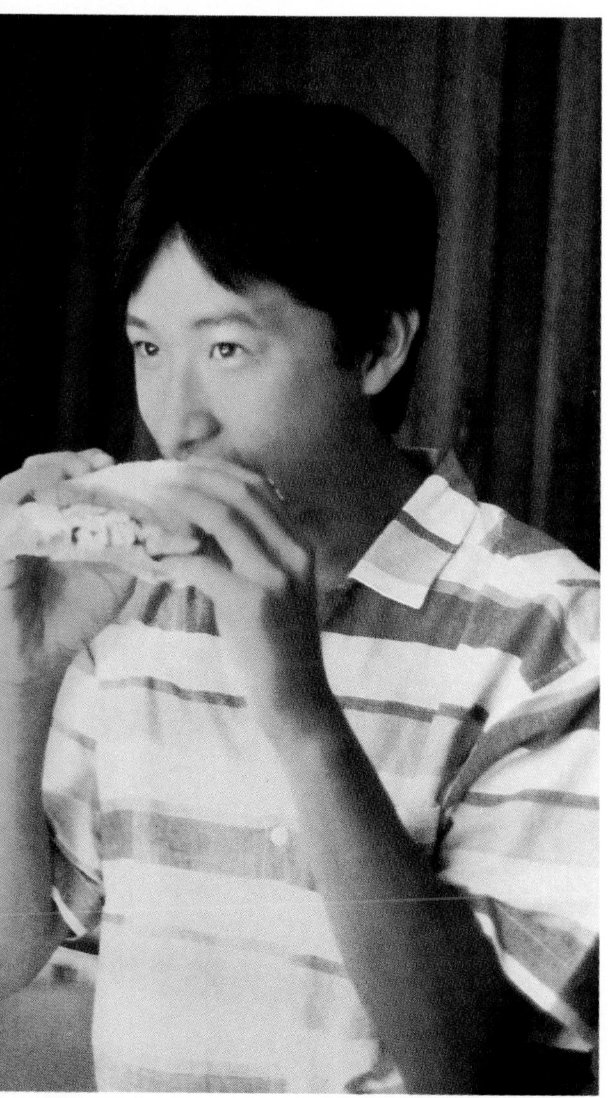

Complex carbohydrates, such as whole grain breads and cereals, are good energy sources and supply the body with the best type of carbohydrates, as well as fiber.

Sugars. There are several types of sugars—glucose, fructose, sucrose, maltose, and lactose. Simple sugar, known as glucose, is found in foods such as grapes and sweet corn. Fructose, the sweetest of all sugars, is found in foods like honey and ripe fruits. The sweetner sucrose is found in cane sugar and table sugar. Maltose is found in breads and cereals, and lactose, the only animal source, is found in milk and milk products.

Starches. All starches and sugars are broken down into glucose and fructose when digestion is completed. Their chief function is to provide energy. This enables the body to work and release the heat needed to maintain body temperature. Foods such as corn, breads, cereals, pasta, and rice supply the body with starches.

Some people think that foods high in carbohydrates are naturally fattening. Ounce for ounce, they have the same number of calories as protein (4 per gram) and less than half those of fat (9 per gram). Natural carbohydrates can be a rich source of the vital nutrients your body needs. For instance, apples and oranges do not have many calories, but they do have vital nutrients.

Health experts suggest that you eat more complex, natural carbohydrates. About 55 percent of a person's daily calorie intake should be carbohydrates. Forty-five percent should be starches and sugars that occur naturally in foods. Only 10 percent should be from refined carbohydrates.

ARE YOU GETTING ENOUGH FIBER DAILY?

You have seen ads that say your favorite cereal or bread product contains fiber. Possibly you have read bits and pieces of information about fiber, but do you still wonder what it is?

Dietary fiber, also known as roughage, comes from the undigestible part of the plant cell wall. It provides no calories, vitamins, or minerals. Instead, fiber moves food through the digestive tract from the mouth to the large intestine acting like a natural laxative. Fiber helps to get rid of waste products from the body.

Because fiber provides bulk, it makes you feel full after eating. In that way you can eat more food for fewer calories.

Some experts claim that fiber plays a role in lowering blood cholesterol and sugar levels. This can be important to people at risk for heart disease and those who have diabetes.

There are several types of fibers that work differently in your body. Therefore, you need to eat a variety of foods with natural fibers in order to get the type you need. The best food sources of fiber are whole grains, beans, fruits, vegetables, nuts, and seeds.

FAT

Fat is found in animal products, grains, nuts, seeds, and some plants and vegetables. It can easily be recognized in butter, margarine, oils, and the fat in meat and poultry. However, fats are not visible in many fatty foods such as whole milk, egg yolks, nuts, and chocolate.

Fat in the diet helps to satisfy the appetite. It also slows the return of hunger because it takes longer to digest. The body uses fat:

1. as a source of essential fatty acids;
2. to transport fat-soluble vitamins (A, D, E, and K);
3. as a source of heat and energy;
4. to cushion vital organs and to help prevent injury.

Fats are classified by the amount of hydrogen found in their fatty acids. **Saturated fats** have more hydrogen and are solid at room temperature. They are found in foods of animal origin such as meat, dairy products, and egg yolks. **Unsaturated fats** have less hydrogen and are liquid at room temperature. They are found only in fish and plants, like corn and peanuts. Polyunsaturated fats have the least amount of hydrogen.

There is much debate about the role of cholesterol and saturated fats in the diet. **Cholesterol** is a fatlike substance. It is a normal part of blood, tissues, and digestive juices, and it covers nerve fibers. Body cells use it to produce vitamin D and certain hormones, including sex hormones. However, when too much cholesterol is in the diet, the blood vessels become lined with it. This makes the blood vessels rigid and interferes with the flow of blood.

Research shows that saturated fat may cause the body to make more cholesterol. There is some evidence that a high level of cholesterol in the blood may lead to a greater risk of heart disease. However, there is no agreement over whether the amount of cholesterol in the blood is affected by the amount eaten. Much scientific data does suggest that there is a relationship between a diet rich in saturated or animal fats and cholesterol and heart disease.

Fats are not visible in many fatty foods, such as whole milk, egg yolks, nuts, chocolate, and peanut butter.

PROTEIN

Proteins are vital to life. They promote growth and maintain and repair body tissues. Proteins are made up of amino acids. The human body needs twenty-two amino acids. Eight of these must come directly from the food you eat, while the other fourteen are made by the body.

Amino acids are the building blocks of protein. They are chemical compounds that are made up mainly of carbon, hydrogen, oxygen, and nitrogen. The amino acids link together in various ways and amounts to form the many different kinds of proteins.

Proteins are classified by their amino acid content. Those that have eight basic amino acids are called **complete proteins,** or high quality proteins. Those that lack one or more basic amino acids are called **incomplete proteins.**

Complete, high quality proteins are found in milk, cheese, fish, poultry, and eggs. Sources of incomplete proteins are dried peas and beans (legumes), peanut butter, and whole grain breads and cereals.

A person can combine some incomplete proteins at the same meal to help the body build a complete protein. This is done by combining foods such as corn and lima beans, black beans and rice, baked beans and brown breads, macaroni and cheese, or peanut butter and whole grain bread. These combinations provide all the amino acids needed to form a complete protein.

Incomplete protein foods, such as beans, can be combined with other foods at the same meal to build a complete, low-cost protein source. What foods could you use with these beans to make complete protein meals?

VITAMIN CHART

Vitamin	Some Food Sources	Major Functions	Deficiency Symptoms
Fat-Soluble A	liver, carrots, sweet potato, dark-green leafy vegetables, broccoli, winter squash, apricots, cantaloupe, peaches, milk, eggs, cheese	important for good vision, especially in the dark; helps keep skin, mucous membranes, bones, teeth healthy	night blindness, permanent blindness, poor growth
D	saltwater fish and their oils, fortified milk and margarine, eggs, liver, butter; body also can make in sunlight	helps form bones and teeth; needed to help body use calcium and phosphorus	rickets (bone deformation), softening of bones
E	seeds, fats, polyunsaturated oils of vegetable products, whole grains, wheat germ	helps vitamin A and some fatty acids work; helps form and keep healthy red blood cells	none known, except anemia in premature infants
Water-Soluble B_1 (Thiamine)	pork, liver, cashews, whole-grain or fortified cereal products, dried peas and beans	promotes growth, muscle tone, good appetite	loss of appetite, depression, muscle tenderness, low blood pressure, tiredness; extreme deficiency causes beriberi
B_2 (Riboflavin)	milk, milk products, liver, dark-green leafy vegetables	helps body release energy from proteins, carbohydrates, fats	cracks at corners of mouth, sore lips, red tongue, poor growth, sensitivity to light, watering eyes
Niacin	meat, poultry, fish, liver, whole-grain or fortified cereal products, cereal brans	helps body release food energy, aids digestion, promotes normal appetite	tiredness, skin and digestive problems, depression, anxiety; extreme deficiency causes the disease pellagra
Folacin	dark-green leafy vegetables, liver, dried beans and peas, nuts, whole-grain or fortified cereals, seeds	helps form red blood cells; helps enzymes and other biochemical systems work	anemia, digestion problems
B_6 (Pyridoxine)	liver, poultry, meat, vegetables, whole-grain or fortified cereals, seeds, bananas, avocados	helps body use protein and amino acids	anemia, irritability, convulsions, skin and nerve problems, cracks at corners of mouth
C (Ascorbic Acid)	citrus fruits, strawberries, cantaloupe, cabbage, broccoli, dark-green leafy vegetables, green peppers, tomatoes	helps form cells; helps body use iron; aids in healing wounds	scurvy; easy bruising; slow wound healing; fatigue; muscle ache; swollen joints; problems with skin, teeth, gums, blood vessels

VITAMINS

Vitamins are the regulators of vital body processes, such as bone and blood formation. They are absorbed by the body and used in their original form. They regulate the growth of tissues and help body cells to release energy from carbohydrates, fats, and proteins. Vitamins are classified as fat-soluble or water-soluble. The functions, sources, and deficiencies of each vitamin are described in the chart on page 290.

The Fat-Soluble Vitamins

The **fat-soluble vitamins,** vitamins A, D, E, and K dissolve in fat. They are stored in the body. They do not dissolve as easily as the water-soluble vitamins. However, they can be destroyed when exposed to air for a long time or if the food becomes rancid, wilted, or dried out. Proper preparation and storage are essential if the vitamin content of the food is to be preserved.

Vitamin A (Retinol). Food sources of vitamin A are liver, eggs, cheese, butter, fortified milk and margarine. It is also found in yellow-orange and dark-green vegetables and fruits. Colors are a good clue to the presence of vitamin A in food. Carotene is yellow or orange-yellow, giving foods such as carrots their color. In some vegetables, carotene is camouflaged by the chlorophyll and becomes a deep green color. Since vitamin A is stored in the liver, people who take large doses of vitamin A supplement run the risk of building up harmful levels of it in their bodies. Unless prescribed by a doctor, vitamin A is best obtained from the food you eat.

Vitamin D (Calcieferol). The best sources of vitamin D are saltwater fish and their oils, and fortified milk and margarine. It is also found in eggs, liver, and butter in small amounts. The body can make vitamin D from sunlight. Vitamin D is stored in the liver.

Vitamin D is needed for the absorption of calcium. Both play a role in helping bones to form. Larger amounts of vitamin D are therefore required during the periods of rapid growth—infancy, childhood, and adolescence.

Vitamin E (Tocopherols). Good food sources of vitamin E are wheat germ, milk, egg yolks, liver, vegetable oils, green leafy vegetables, and whole grain cereals.

Vitamin E in the body helps vitamin A and some fatty acids to work by keeping them from being burned for energy. It helps to form red blood cells, muscles, and other tissues. Deficiency of vitamin E has not been known except in cases of anemia in premature infants.

Vitamin K. Another fat-soluble vitamin, vitamin K, is made in the body by bacteria in the intestines. Good food sources are dark-green leafy vegetables, cabbage, cauliflower, peas, potatoes, liver, and cereals. This vitamin helps blood to clot and maintains normal bone growth and maintenance.

Dark green leafy vegetables, carrots, cheese and butter are good sources of the fat-soluble vitamin, vitamin A.

The Water-Soluble Vitamins

The *water-soluble vitamins,* vitamins B and C, dissolve in water. They can be dissolved in cooking water and are easily destroyed by light, heat, or oxidation. Since these vitamins are not stored in the body, they need to be replaced daily.

The B vitamins. All eight of the B vitamins are very similar, though they have different functions. The B vitamins are: Thiamine (B_1), Riboflavin (B_2), Niacin, Vitamin B_6 (pyridoxine), Vitamin B_{12} (cobalamins), panothenic acid, biotin, and folic acid.

The water-soluble B vitamins can be found in meat, poultry, fish, eggs, and whole grain cereals. They work together to affect the skin, nervous and digestive systems.

Liver is a rich source of the B vitamins. Other good sources are meat, poultry, fish, eggs, whole grain cereals, nuts, dried peas, beans, peanut butter, and dark leafy vegetables.

These vitamins need to be replaced daily since they are not stored in the body. Deficiencies can cause a number of symptoms that depend on the B vitamins that are missing or in short supply. The areas most affected may be the skin and the nervous and digestive systems. Other symptoms are dizziness, moodiness, vision problems, and anemia.

Vitamin C. Vitamin C is a water-soluble vitamin. Citrus fruits such as oranges, grapefruit, and lemons, strawberries, papayas and cantaloupes are fruits that are good sources of vitamin C. Vegetables high in vitamin C are broccoli, raw cabbage, potatoes, dark-green leafy vegetables, peppers, and tomatoes.

Vitamin C and calcium help to build and maintain healthy bones and teeth. Vitamin C plays a key role in blood formation and keeps blood vessels strong. It helps the body fight disease, keeps other vitamins from being burned for energy, and helps to form and to maintain collagen, the substance that binds cells together.

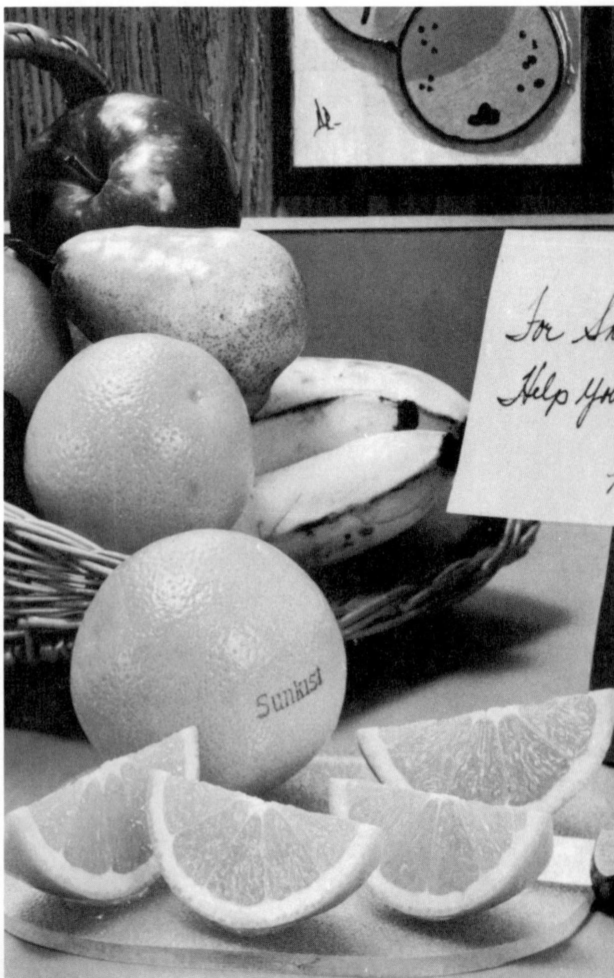

Good sources of vitamin C include fruits, such as citrus fruits and strawberries. What vegetables are good sources of vitamin C?

MINERAL CHART

Mineral	Some Food Sources	Major Functions	Deficiency Symptoms
Calcium	milk, milk products, dark-green leafy vegetables, fish with small edible bones	necessary for bone and teeth formation, blood clotting, nerve transmission	teeth and bone problems, stunted growth, osteoporosis
Iodine	saltwater fish, shellfish, iodized salt	necessary part of thyroid hormone (thyroxin), which regulates metabolic rate	goiter (enlargement of thyroid gland)
Iron	liver, beef, pork, nuts, dried beans and peas, enriched breads, dark-green leafy vegetables	helps make hemoglobin (part of red blood cells) and enzymes that help body use energy	tiredness, paleness, brittleness of fingernails
Magnesium	whole grains, dark-green leafy vegetables, legumes, nuts, organ meats, bananas	helps body make protein from amino acids; helps nerves and muscles work	growth failure, behavioral problems, shaking, spasms
Phosphorous	milk, milk products, meat, fish, poultry, eggs, legumes, nuts	necessary for bones and teeth, acid-base balance; helps cells use energy	abnormal sensations in hands and feet, weakness, seizures
Zinc	oysters, beef, pork, liver, dried peas and beans, whole-grain or fortified cereals, nuts	helps make several enzymes and insulin	delayed healing, retarded physical development, hair loss

MINERALS

Minerals become part of body structures, such as bones, teeth, and blood cells. They help to regulate the body, are absorbed in their original form, and work together to help form bones and teeth.

The minerals calcium, potassium, magnesium, phosphorous, sodium, chlorine, and sulfur are found in your body in large amounts. Your body needs smaller amounts of iron, copper, iodine, flourine, cobalt, manganese, chromium, selenium, and zinc.

Plan your diet to include enough good mineral sources. The chart above shows the best sources of minerals. By including milk, fruit, vegetables, whole grain cereals and breads, eggs, and meat in your diet each day, you should get the minerals your body needs. Please note that large daily doses of mineral supplements can cause health problems and even death.

Calcium and Phosphorus. Both calcium and phosphorus are found in milk and milk products such as cheese and yogurt. They play an important role in building strong bones and teeth. However, calcium is first used for nerve impulses, heart function, muscle contraction, blood clotting, and the activation of some enzymes. Only after these needs are met does the body put the unused calcium in the bones and teeth. If there is not enough calcium for these functions, it is taken from the bones. Bones constantly gain and lose calcium as needed.

Magnesium. Magnesium is found in organ meats, whole grain cereals and breads, nuts, dried beans and peas, green leafy vegetables, bananas, egg yolks, and milk. Magnesium plays a role in the

STRENGTHEN YOUR BONES

If you like to drink milk, eat yogurt, and snack on oranges and broccoli, you may not have to worry about the possibility of getting osteoporosis later in life. But for many adults this is a real problem.

Osteoporosis, a thinning of the bones, results when there is prolonged lack of calcium in the diet. Since the calcium is constantly taken from the bones, the bones become weak, thin, and brittle over a period of time.

Older people, especially inactive women, are prone to develop this condition. And once this condition occurs, it is too late to reverse it.

Health experts now urge people to eat more calcium-rich foods early in life to stop the loss of bone mass. It is important to include dairy products and other good sources of calcium—such as dairy products, oranges, sardines, broccoli, and collard and mustard greens—in your diet every day.

Progressive Spinal Deformity in Osteoporosis

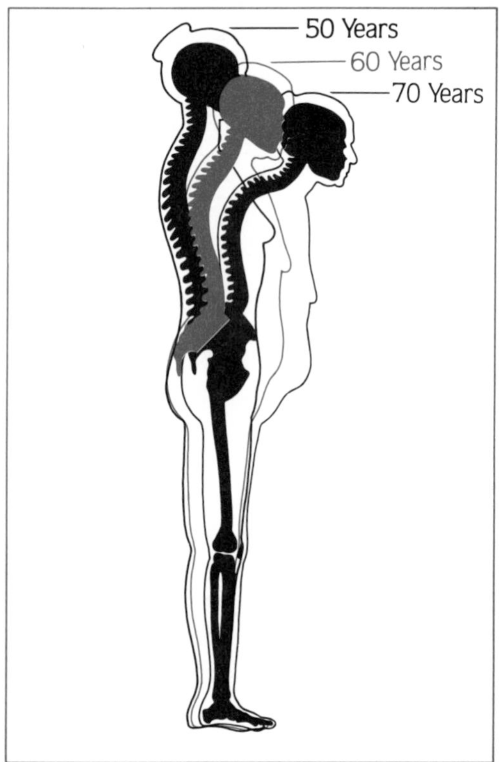

Osteoporosis, a loss of bone mass, has been linked to a deficiency of calcium. What foods can you eat to replenish your supply of calcium daily?

health of nerves and muscles, building bones, and in using carbohydrates and proteins. A sign of magnesium shortage is shaking or muscle tremor. Shortages are found in people, such as alcoholics and drug addicts, who do not eat enough foods. A balanced diet will supply ample magnesium for health.

Chlorine, Potassium, and Sodium. Three minerals, chlorine, potassium, and sodium, are found in most foods. Foods especially high in potassium are fish, meat, bananas, citrus fruit, and milk. Sodium is found in table salt, other flavoring agents, and condiments such as soy sauce, relish, and preservatives, such as sodium nitrate. Health experts say that salt intake should be reduced by everyone, especially those at risk for high blood pressure.

Iron. Iron is a vital mineral that teams up with protein to make the red substance of blood, hemoglobin. This is the oxygen-carrying part of the red blood cells. Iron is found in all cells and helps them to use oxygen.

Liver is the best source of iron. Other good sources are kidney, heart, lean meats, egg yolks, dried beans and peas, spinach, nuts, dried fruits, and whole grain enriched cereals. The body uses iron from vegetable sources better if some vitamin C or a small amount of meat is eaten at the same time.

Iodine. Iodine occurs in saltwater fish and shellfish. People who lived far from the oceans often suffered from a condition called goiter, a swelling of the thyroid gland. This was caused by a lack of iodine in the diet. Today this condition is less common because people use iodized salt to which iodine has been added.

Zinc. Zinc is essential for growth, reproduction, and in helping wounds to heal. Too little zinc can result in slow healing, poor appetite, loss of the sense of taste, and retarded growth. People who do not eat meat have a hard time getting enough zinc.

WATER

Water is the basis of all body fluids. It helps to maintain normal body temperature and lubricates the body's joints. It helps with digestion, getting rid of body waste, and other bodily functions. Because of its importance to the diet, it is considered a nutrient.

Water may also be part of a beverage, soup, or part of the foods you eat. Six to eight glasses of water each day is enough for normal body activity. When there is excessive perspiration or illness, more water may be needed.

THE RDA CHART

The RDA chart gives the amounts of nutrients and calories needed by healthy people throughout life. It lists age groups, weights, and heights. The amounts given are a little higher than those needed with the exception of calories. This slight excess provides a margin of safety for those who may need a little more of the nutrients.

A simple version of the RDA has been prepared by the Food and Drug Administration for easier use. It is known as the U.S. RDA (United States Recommended Daily Allowances). Listed are the percentages of nutrients that will generally meet the average needs of all persons one age group. (See appendix page 442).

People often need more or fewer nutrients than are shown in the chart. For example, growth spurts in adolescence create the need for more nutrients. Activity levels and special conditions, such as pregnancy, also affect nutrient needs.

Nutrition research continues. A great deal must be learned about the role of nutrition in the body. Only twenty-four of the fifty known nutrients have been sufficiently researched. Much still must be studied about the interrelationship of nutrients to health, fitness, and overall well-being.

WORDS TO REMEMBER

calorie
carbohydrate
cholesterol
complete proteins
fat-soluble vitamins
incomplete proteins
nutrients
osteoporosis
saturated fats
unsaturated fats
water-soluble vitamins

CHECKING YOUR UNDERSTANDING

1. Consider your activity level, sex, age, and height. Calculate the number of calories you need daily in order to maintain your ideal body weight.
2. List and define each of the five basic nutrients. Describe the main function of each nutrient in your body.
3. What is the difference between saturated and unsaturated fat? What do scientists think the relationship is between saturated fat and cholesterol?
4. State the difference between complete and incomplete protein. What incomplete protein foods can be combined at the same meal to form a complete protein.
5. Discuss the difference between fat-soluble and water-soluble vitamins. Identify the specific vitamins that are classified in each group.

APPLYING YOUR UNDERSTANDING

1. Discuss and give an example of how food fulfills physical, psychological, and social needs.
2. Analyze the food choices that you make. Name a food resource, social and cultural custom, and the influence of family and friends that affect your food decisions.
3. What foods should be included in the diet to prevent the likelihood of developing osteoporosis later in life? What other measures should be taken?
4. Many diets are deficient in iron. Assume that you have been told that you should include more iron-rich foods in your diet. What foods would you add, and which ones would you eat more of?
5. Discuss the risks of self-prescription dietary supplements. Who should take supplements? Why is taking fat-soluble vitamins and minerals a greater risk than taking water soluble vitamins? What is the best way to get the nutrients you need?

Chapter 22
MANAGING YOUR MEALS

Has this ever happened to you?

Mary was having some friends over for dinner. As she was talking to Tad, she learned he was on a salt-free diet. She wondered what to plan.

"What foods can you eat, Tad?" she asked. "I can eat most food," Tad replied. "I avoid most main dishes that come frozen or canned. Usually canned or dried soups contain too much salt for me. I also watch what I add to food, such as catsup and soy sauce. But don't be too concerned. Just serve my food without sauces. I'll bring my own salad dressing if you plan to have a salad."

Mary was interested in serving a tasty meal without too much salt to everyone. She read all the labels as she shopped. She chose recipes that called for lemon juice and herbs for seasonings. Everyone agreed the meal tasted delicious. And Tad was really pleased not to have to feel different.

Have you ever worried about preparing a meal for a friend who was on a special diet?

Have you ever tried recipes for special diets and found them to be very tasty?

After reading this chapter, you will be able to

- develop a menu that is based on the *Daily Food Guide;*
- explain the relationship among diet, exercise, and health;
- identify and evaluate the resources that affect menu planning and recipe choices;
- list the factors that affect the appeal of a meal.

Whether you make your school lunch, prepare dinner for six people, or plan a weekly menu for your active life-style, good meal management can help you reach your goal. **Meal management** means to plan, choose, and serve meals that make up a healthful, balanced diet.

To help you successfully manage your meals, there are guidelines or tools to use. The use of these tools can help you be sure that you are getting enough nutrients and that you are using your resources wisely to plan and serve appetizing meals.

THE FOOD GROUPS

One tool to help simplify the task of meal management is the **Daily Food Guide.** This guide divides foods into five groups according to the nutrients they contain. They are: the fruit and vegetable group; the bread and cereal group; the meat, poultry, fish, and dried beans group; and the milk and cheese group. These four main groups have nutrients essential for good health. The fifth group, the fats, sweets, and alcohol group, are foods that are not vital for good health.

Recommendations have been made for the number and size of servings to be eaten for each of the main food groups. No serving recommendations are made for the fats, sweets, and alcohol group. If you plan meals around the Daily Food Guide, follow the serving recommendations of each group, and eat a variety of foods, you will get all the nutrients you need.

THE FRUIT AND VEGETABLE GROUP

Foods in the fruit and vegetable group are broccoli, cauliflower, cabbage, carrots, potatoes, squash, cucumbers, tomatoes, peppers, apples, oranges, grapes, and watermelon. It is recommended that four servings from the fruit and vegetable group be part of the diet each day. In addition, one serving from a good source of vitamin C, such as citrus fruit, should be eaten each day. Good vitamin C sources are oranges and other citrus fruits, strawberries, and tomatoes. Fruits and vegetables that contain vitamin A should be eaten three to four times a week. Good sources of vitamin A are green leafy vegetables, such as kale and spinach, and orange vegetables, such as squash and carrots. Peeled fruits and vegetables and those with seeds are a good source of fiber and should also be eaten daily. Sample serving sizes from this group are one orange, a half cup of cooked vegetables, one cup of fresh berries, or one cup of leafy vegetables.

The fruit and vegetable group is made up of foods that are rich in vitamins A, C, and fiber. They provide calcium, phosphorous, iron, and B vitamins.

THE BREADS AND CEREAL GROUP

The bread and cereal group are foods such as whole grain or enriched breads, cereals, rice, grits, cornmeal, noodles, and other pasta. The recommendations are to eat four servings from this group each day. Sample servings from this group are one cup of ready-to-eat cereal, one-half to three-fourths cup of cooked cereal, rice, or pasta, one slice of whole grain or enriched bread, two tortillas, one bagel, or one four-inch pancake. This group supplies the diet with carbohydrates, iron, and B vitamins.

THE MEAT, POULTRY, FISH, AND BEANS GROUP

Foods in the meat, poultry, fish, and beans group include all cuts of beef, pork, veal, lamb, eggs, poultry, fish and shellfish, as well as dried beans and peas, nuts, peanuts, and peanut butter. The recommendations for this group are to eat two servings daily. A serving from this group is two to three ounces of lean cooked meat, two medium eggs, one-third cup of canned tuna or salmon, four tablespoons of peanut butter, or one small chicken leg. The meat, poultry, fish, and beans group supplies protein, iron, and B vitamins.

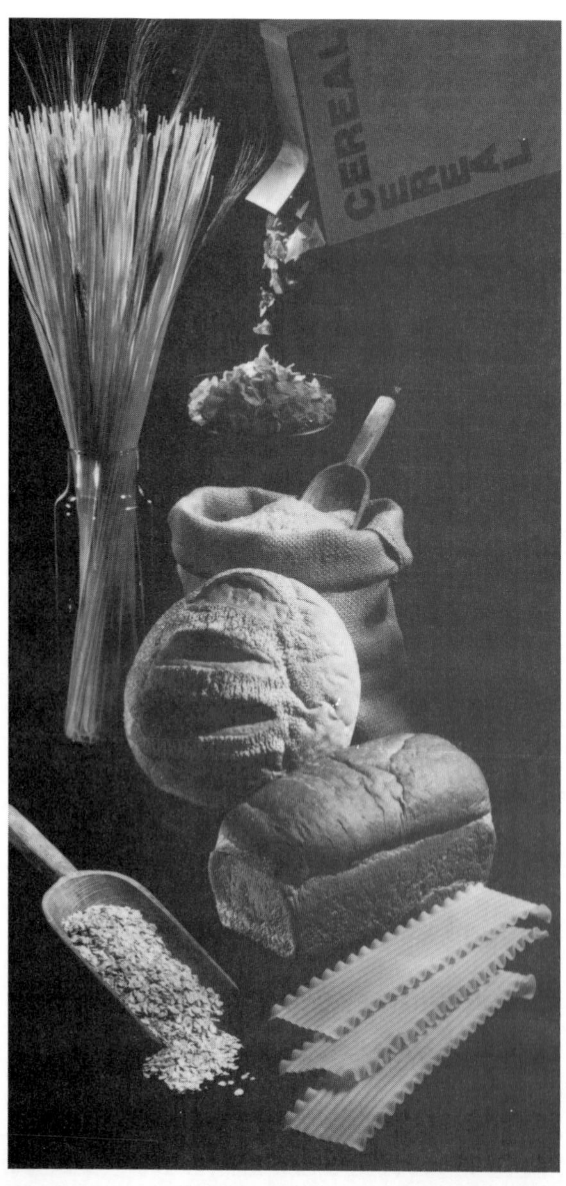

THE MILK AND CHEESE GROUP

Foods in the milk and cheese group are milk, buttermilk, and other dairy products such as cheese, yogurt, and cottage cheese. Teenagers need four servings from the milk and cheese group daily. One cup of milk or yogurt, two slices of American or Swiss cheese, or one-half cup of cottage cheese each equals one serving from this group.

Foods in the milk and cheese group are rich in calcium and riboflavin. They also provide protein and vitamins A, B_2 and B_{12}. In addition, vitamin D is usually added to milk.

FATS, SWEETS, AND ALCOHOL GROUP

The fats, sweets, and alcohol group contains foods such as candy, butter, margarine, syrups, soft drinks, honey, jelly and jams, and alcoholic drinks. These foods are high in calories and low in nutrients. Foods in this group supply so few nutrients that no serving recommendations are given.

NUTRIENT DENSITY

Another tool to help you make wise food decisions is to choose foods based on their nutrient density. **Nutrient density** is the ratio of nutrients in a food to the number of calories. Foods that are nutrient dense offer more nutrients percentagewise with fewer calories than do other foods. For example, one cup of orange juice has a high nutrient density of 96 percent, while a Danish pastry has a low nutrient density of 14 percent.

If you look at the main four food groups, you can see how each relates to nutrient density. The fruit and vegetable group is nutrient dense in vitamins A and C. The bread and cereal group is nutrient dense in carbohydrates, thiamine, iron, and niacin. The meat, poultry, fish, and beans group is nutrient dense in protein, niacin, iron, and thiamine. The milk and cheese group is nutrient dense in calcium, riboflavin, and protein. And the fats, sweets and alcohol group is a low nutrient density group.

As you plan, try to choose a lot of nutrient dense foods from each food group. Look at a nutrient chart if you are not sure of the nutrient density of a food. This process can be one way to help you reach your goal of a healthful diet.

DEVELOPING HEALTHFUL EATING HABITS

Throughout your life you have been encouraged to eat certain foods and to limit or avoid eating other foods. What foods do you really need to stay fit and healthy?

This is a hard question to answer because experts do not always agree. However, it is generally agreed that the average American eats too much fat, sugar, and sodium and too little fiber. It is estimated that 40 percent of all Americans weigh too much. And diet and life-style choices have been linked to health problems such as high blood pressure, heart disease, obesity, and cancer.

These are life-threatening conditions and diseases that can be prevented or controlled through good nutrition. The **Dietary Guidelines** are recommendations that were prepared by the U.S. government to encourage people to improve their health by changing their eating habits.

DIETARY GUIDELINES

- Eat a variety of foods
- Maintain desirable weight
- Avoid too much fat, saturated fat, and cholesterol
- Eat foods with adequate starch and fiber
- Avoid too much sugar
- Avoid too much sodium
- If you drink alcoholic beverages, do so in moderation

MANAGING MEAL PATTERNS

Your **meal patterns** or eating habits affect your health too. What type of meal patterns do you have? Do you eat breakfast every day? Do you find yourself eating food throughout the day?

If you do not eat breakfast, you are failing to give your body the energy it needs, as well as the amino acids it needs, to keep building new cells.

Ideally, breakfast should provide about one-fourth to one-third of the calories and nutrients that you need. If you are a person who does not like eggs, toast, and juice in the morning, try a breakfast alternative. A protein blender drink, a bran muffin, or an orange and a slice of cheese might appeal to you.

If you pack your lunch, it is fairly easy to include foods from each of the main foods groups. A meat or peanut butter sandwich, a piece of fruit, and milk is a fairly common lunch. If you eat in the school cafeteria, choose nutritious foods from a variety of sources. Ideally, lunch should be the largest meal of the day so that you will have time to work off the calories during the balance of the day.

The evening meal is the time when the most variety can be included. During this meal, plan to eat the foods that will combine with foods eaten earlier to equal the total number of servings from the food groups that you need each day.

If snacks are part of your meal pattern, be sure that you choose snacks from the basic four food groups. Some popular snack items such as candy, potato chips, and corn chips are high in calories and low in nutrients. Instead, choose unbuttered popcorn, nuts, fruit, or raw vegetables.

Another common meal pattern is eating out. At a family-style restaurant, you can select from salads, vegetables, and foods that are baked or broiled.

However, if you eat at a fast-food restaurant, it will be harder to control what you eat. Fried foods are high in saturated fats, and typically fast foods are high in fat, sugar, and salt. To improve your choices, choose milk instead of a soft drink, add a salad, ask for foods that are not fried or salted, and take advantage of new low calorie menu items.

DIET, EXERCISE, AND HEALTH

Nutritionists and health experts agree that there is a relationship among diet, exercise, and health. A person cannot rely solely on nutrition to assure good health. Exercise is also needed.

Your body needs a minimum level of physical activity. Below this level, your body begins to deteriorate. Thus, you should plan an exercise program—one that you will enjoy—and take part in it at least one hour, three times a week. This amount of exercise will give you good muscle tone, improved blood circulation, and a stronger heart and lungs. Exercise also helps to get rid of anxiety and tension, and it helps to fight depression.

Exercise raises metabolism. **Metabolism** is your body's ability to burn calories. When you are active, you can eat more calories and still maintain your weight. If the calories you eat are in carefully chosen foods, you will have more of the nutrients you need.

Exercise can help keep the body active. How do the following activities increase muscle tone, improve circulation, and build a stronger heart and lungs?

Managing Your Life

USING THE DAILY FOOD GUIDE

Does 4-4-2-4 mean anything to you? It is called the Daily Food Guide, and it is the secret to a nutritionally balanced diet. Using this plan every day, you should eat:

- 4 servings of fruits and vegetables
- 4 servings of breads and cereals
- 2 servings of meat, poultry, fish, or dried beans
- 4 servings of dairy products

By using this plan, you can see that you get all the nutrients you need. Just follow these easy steps.

1. Keep a record of what you have eaten for three or more consecutive days. Be sure to include snacks and the serving sizes of the foods you have eaten.
2. Identify the food group each food belongs to.
3. Total the daily number of servings from each group.
4. Compare your list with the number of servings suggested for each group in the Daily Food Guide.
5. Now answer the following questions:
   - Have you eaten at least the number of servings suggested from each group?
   - Is there a good source of vitamin C listed each day?
   - Have you eaten a dark-green or deep-yellow fruit or vegetable every other day?

Now you are able to identify the nutrients that you are missing. If you find you do not eat enough servings from a food group, think of ways to change your eating habits. For instance, if milk is missing from your diet, you could choose milk instead of a soft drink for lunch. Or you could add two slices of cheese to your hamburger. By using the Daily Food Guide, it will be easier for you to analyze your diet and add the nutrients that you lack.

Once you have become familiar with how the Daily Food Guide works, you can use it as a tool to plan your meals. The Guide will help you to include all the nutrients you need. These same food groups can be used to plan meals throughout your life cycle. Although the number and size of servings may change during the life cycle, this approach will always result in a balanced diet.

PLANNING YOUR NUTRITIONAL NEEDS

Your nutritional needs will change as you pass through the life cycle—the various stages of life from birth to old age. Age, activity level, and health all affect the calories and nutrients you need.

PREGNANCY

During pregnancy the eating habits of your mother affected you. A growing baby depends on the mother for nourishment. Thus, the mother is the source of nutrients needed for the baby's rapid growth and development.

A pregnant woman needs to eat a wide variety of foods, carefully chosen from the main food groups in the Daily Food Guide. It is advised that the woman increase her intake to three or more servings from the meat, poultry, fish, and beans group and to four or five servings from the milk and cheese group. Refer to "Managing a Safe and Healthy Pregnancy," chapter 8.

INFANCY

After birth and for the first several months, babies are fed liquids. They either are breast fed or drink a prepared formula. The breast-feeding mother must keep eating nutritious foods since her baby will continue to depend on her for the nutrients required.

The doctor's recommendations for formula should be followed with care. Cow's milk alone cannot be used. It is hard for babies to digest, and it lacks iron. Later, solids are added to the diet, and commercial baby food or foods prepared at home may be fed to the infant.

SCHOOL-AGE CHILD

Early eating habits shape adult eating habits and patterns. Thus, children should be offered a variety of foods from each of the main food groups. Since children's stomachs are small, they need smaller portions of foods at meals and healthful snacks between meals.

ADOLESCENCE

During the adolescent years the body changes quickly, and growth occurs at a tremendous rate. This and increased levels of activity make it necessary for teens to eat healthful foods at meals and as snacks.

Problems can arise when the foods are chosen from high fat or sugar foods and soft drinks. These foods do not provide the nutrients that active teens need at a time of rapid growth.

All teenagers should eat the same basic types of foods in a balanced diet. The more active you are, the more food you will need. To maintain the same weight means that you must use all the calories you take in for your energy needs.

If you want to lose weight, be careful that the diet you choose does not rob your body of needed nutrients. Avoid crash diets, weight loss pills, and other fads reported to help you lose weight. Just choose foods with fewer calories and maximum nutrient density. Eat smaller portions from all the food groups and exercise more.

If you want to gain weight, add more or larger servings from the main food groups to your diet. Choose foods that are higher in calories, such as beans, peas, peanut butter, or avocados. You may find that you will gain weight more readily if you eat five to six small meals a day rather than three large meals.

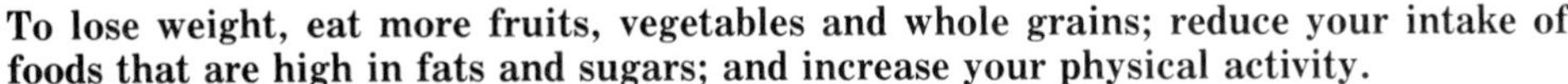

To lose weight, eat more fruits, vegetables and whole grains; reduce your intake of foods that are high in fats and sugars; and increase your physical activity.

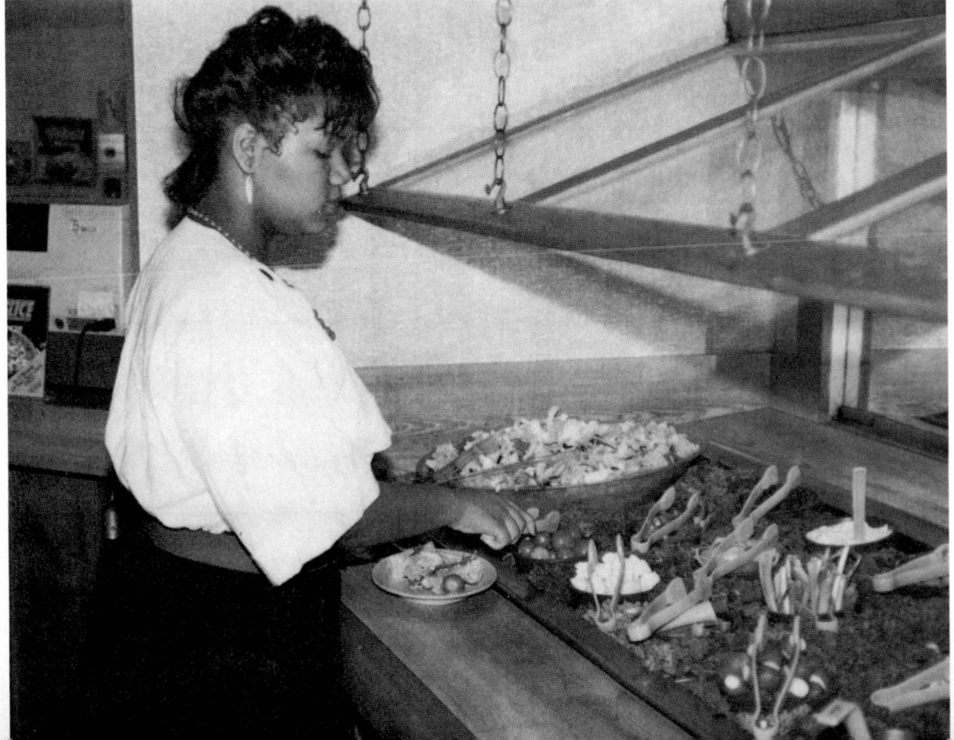

NUTRITION AND THE ATHLETE

Teenagers who take part in sports need to eat more food for energy. Energy is made from stored nutrients. Carbohydrates, fats, and protein work together to provide the energy needed for sports. It is not the food you eat just before an activity that provides energy.

Vitamins are needed to help with the conversion of fats, protein, and carbohydrates into energy. Vitamins do not supply energy, as is commonly thought.

Too many minerals and vitamins taken in the form of supplements are wasteful. In some cases they can be harmful. Salt tablets, for example, can irritate the stomach lining and cause dehydration by drawing fluids from the body. A balanced diet supplies all the vitamins and minerals you need.

Water intake should never be limited. Water is needed to prevent dehydration, heat stroke, organ damage, and even death. It cools your body more efficiently than juices or sports drinks because it leaves the stomach more quickly.

Protein does not increase muscle mass. Carbohydrate is the nutrient source for muscles, not protein. If an athlete does need slightly more protein, it is probably already in his or her diet. The average American eats one to two times as much protein as needed. Thus, most Americans have more than enough protein, even the athlete.

ADULTS

As people grow older and complete their growth, they tend to be less active. As a result, their food needs change, and they need to eat fewer calories to avoid weight gain.

THE RETIREMENT YEARS

Older people need the same nutrients as they did when they were younger. However, they need fewer calories. This is a result of the body's basic processes slowing down and reduced physical activity. The elderly should choose nutrient dense foods from the Daily Food Guide for their diets.

Special programs have been set up to help people over sixty improve their diets. As part of Title VII, the Older Americans Act, help is offered through programs such as Supplemental Social Security, Food Stamps, Food Pantries, and Surplus Commodity Distribution. The need for social contacts and people to eat with is met through group meals at senior centers. Home-delivered meals are brought by volunteers who are part of programs such as Meals on Wheels.

SPECIAL DIETS

The need for a special diet can arise at any age. For instance, a person getting over a stomach disorder may need a light diet, made up of clear soups, toast, and jello. A person with a chronic disease may be given a prescribed diet. For instance, a diabetic diet controls sugar and caloric intake.

When a doctor or a dietician prescribes a special diet, it should be followed closely. If the patient becomes discouraged, you can offer encouragement. You can also help keep a person interested in the diet by serving food attractively when you are in charge.

A prescription for a special diet need not be a cause for alarm. While certain foods may be forbidden or restricted, there are many others in the main food groups that can supply the nutrients needed.

Learn to budget your time and money by taking advantage of seasonal foods, planning menus ahead, and using leftovers for meals the following day. How does this pita pocket sandwich use leftovers?

EVALUATING RESOURCES

Each step in the meal management process takes planning. As the meal manager you will need to answer several questions before you begin. Ask yourself these questions.

1. How many people will you be serving?
2. Do any of the people have special dietary concerns?
3. What food is available?
4. Will the foods taste right together?
5. Does the meal provide balanced nutrition?
6. How does the meal fit into the budget?
7. Do I have the skills needed?
8. Is the equipment needed available?

You can easily achieve the end product you want if you use good management strategies. A planned approach will help you to use your resources—time, money, skills, and kitchen equipment—wisely.

TIME

The time available to plan menus and prepare food often determines what can be chosen. The time you spend in planning a meal often saves time in the overall process.

Choose recipes that can be prepared in the time available. A simple meal may be a better choice when time is limited. You can also shorten preparation time by using packaged foods and by storing supplies and cookware so that you can reach them easily. Using a microwave oven, blender, or food processor may also shorten the preparation time.

Preparing foods ahead and reheating them just before serving them is another time saver. Or by using a crock pot, you can prepare foods that will be ready to serve at a later meal.

SKILLS

It is best for the unskilled cook to use only simple recipes. Practice will lead to mastering cooking skills. Besides, learning how to use small appliances safely and well will improve your skills in the kitchen.

BUDGET

There is usually a limited sum of money that can be spent on food. However, this will not stop you from getting all the nutrients that you need. For instance, you can choose a cheaper source of protein, such as a hamburger patty or eggs, rather than a more costly protein source, such as a sirloin steak. Or you can plan your meal around the fruits and vegetables that are in season. You will learn more ways to save money in the next chapter.

EQUIPMENT

Look at your meal plan. Will you have all the appliances needed? Can others be substituted? Are there any conflicts? Is the oven temperature the same for all the foods to be cooked at the same time? And are you using the appliances available to help save work and time in the preparation of your meal?

PERSONAL PREFERENCES

Your values and food preferences will affect your satisfaction with the meal you cook. If you are vegetarian, prefer low-fat foods, or are trying to avoid sugar and salt, the meal you cook will reflect these values.

SEASONAL CONSIDERATION

Choosing foods that are in season will reduce your food costs. Their fresh taste will be pleasing to you. Seasonal foods are usually plentiful and reasonably priced in your local food store. Those out of season are more costly and may be of poor quality.

MEAL APPEAL

Aside from offering good nutrition, the meals you prepare will be more appealing if they look, taste, and smell good. A meal manager can vary the tastes, temperatures, textures, colors, and shapes of the foods served to improve their appeal at a meal.

Flavor. There are four basic flavors: sweet, sour, salty, and bitter. These basic flavors mix together in different combinations to form the hundreds of subtle flavors that we all enjoy.

When serving a dish with a strong flavor, such as a spicy food, be sure that the other dishes are mild in flavor. Also avoid serving two distinct flavors, such as curry and spicy foods, at the same meal.

Texture. The crunch of celery sticks, a crisp, cool salad, or a juicy orange are just a few kinds of textures that you can feel in your mouth. When planning a meal, combine and contrast different kinds of food textures.

Temperature. Vary the temperature of the food that you serve. If you serve a warm stew, contrast it with crispy bread and a cool salad.

Meal appeal is also affected by the climate or temperature of the outdoor weather. A cool salad is more appealing on a hot day, and a hot drink is more inviting on a cold day.

Color. The eye appeal of food helps to stimulate your appetite too. Foods look more appealing when there is variety of colors.

Describe how this Mexican fiesta dinner makes appetizing use of flavor, texture, shape and size, and temperature.

Home computers can be used to plan menus, file recipes, analyze diets, and control food expenses.

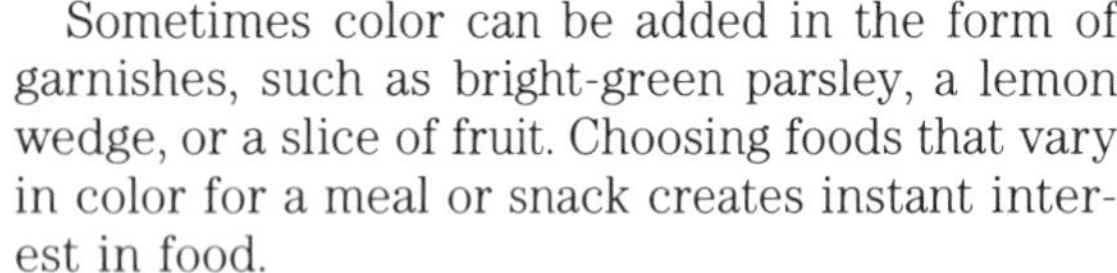

Sometimes color can be added in the form of garnishes, such as bright-green parsley, a lemon wedge, or a slice of fruit. Choosing foods that vary in color for a meal or snack creates instant interest in food.

Shapes. Shapes and sizes of foods can be changed to add interest and variety in the menu. Meat can be sliced, diced, ground, cubed, or served whole. Cheeses, fruits, and vegetables can also be cut into many shapes.

PLANNING A MENU

A **menu** is a list of dishes to be served at a meal. Writing a menu helps you to identify the foods and other things you will need to prepare the meal.

Some foods on a menu can simply be served in the form in which they are bought. Other foods must be cooked. A recipe gives you the directions you will need to prepare the food, as well as the ingredients needed and their amounts.

There are many sources of recipes. Personal collections, cookbooks, newspapers, and magazines are just a few. Some creative people who are experienced cooks like to develop their own recipes.

Whether you are preparing a simple or an elaborate meal, you can manage it better if you follow these steps:

1. Read the recipe beforehand.
2. Figure out the time and sequence for preparing a meal.
3. Assemble equipment and ingredients.
4. Do pre-preparation work.
5. Simplify your work techniques.
6. Clean up as you work.

If you review the section on managing your resources in this chapter, you will find some tips on menu planning. Probably the most important part of success is planning ahead. Follow a time schedule to help you prepare and serve all the foods on a menu at the same time.

WORDS TO REMEMBER

Daily Food Guide
Dietary Guidelines
meal management
meal patterns
menu
metabolism
nutrient density

CHECKING YOUR UNDERSTANDING

1. Define meal management. Discuss the role of the *Daily Food Guide* in managing the meals you eat.
2. Define nutrient density. Give examples of three foods that are nutrient dense. Discuss the reasons why there is a greater need for foods that are nutrient dense during pregnancy.
3. What is the effect on your ability to have a balanced diet if you have poor meal patterns? If you skip breakfast, what is likely to be the effect on your nutritional health?
4. Describe the relationship among exercise, metabolism, and the food you eat.
5. Discuss the reasons for the changes in the serving recommendations in the Daily Food Guide during the life cycle.

APPLYING YOUR UNDERSTANDING

1. Organize a brown-bag lunch club. Plan menus for meals that are balanced for at least three days. Try a brown-bagger lunch special using a long loaf of French bread, and meat and cheese, and a salad bar swap for starters. Be sure to include foods from each of the main food groups.
2. Write an article for your school newspaper that makes diet recommendations for athletes.
3. Collect pictures of meals from magazines. Predict their appeal. Prepare and evaluate at least two meals and compare the results with your expectations.
4. List the factors that affect your ability to plan and prepare meals. Plan a week's menu that considers your resources and the *Daily Food Guide.*

Chapter 23

SHOPPING FOR FOOD

Has this ever happened to you?

Alan and Kevin were having a video night at Kevin's house. They wanted to serve the gang pizza and were trying to decide what kind to get.

Alan suggested, "Let's have a make-your-own pizza party! We can get several of those frozen pizzas with the little packs of toppings."

Kevin looked at the price of one box and whistled. "There must be a cheaper way. Alan, just look at that price. We couldn't afford more than three, and I could eat one all by myself."

They looked around the store and asked a clerk to help them. They found frozen pizza, fresh pizza, ready-to-bake pizza, pizza mixes, pizza sauce, and pizza toppings. They wondered which to choose.

They were thinking about using English muffins and canned pizza sauce when Kevin noticed a special on French bread. He quickly figured the cost of the sauce and the bread and discovered they'd have enough money for the toppings they wanted. He called to Alan, "I've found a solution. Come and see."

Have you ever compared the costs of various forms of the same dish?

Have you ever looked around a supermarket to see the different forms of a food you could find?

After reading this chapter, you will be able to

- describe food shopping skills that can save time, energy, and money;
- choose the most appropriate store for your food needs;
- explain how the information on a food label can be used in comparison shopping;
- identify the role of the government in regulating food processing and packaging.

The last time you shopped for food did you stay within your budget and choose healthful foods? Or did you choose processed, convenience foods that were low in nutrients and more costly? Getting good nutrition for each dollar you spend does not happen by chance. It takes a planned, businesslike approach to make wise food purchases.

SHOPPING FOR FOOD

Before you step into a store, you will need to have made most of your food shopping plans. Start by deciding what your menus will be for one week or more. This will help you to include all the foods needed for balanced, nutritious meals and save you time. First, you can plan creative ways to serve foods that you have already prepared. For instance, the leftover pot roast can be used for another meal or the casserole served at dinner can be used for lunch the next day. Second, you will only have to shop once, thus saving many trips to the store.

Before you shop, you will also need to see how much room you have for food storage. Food spoils and is wasted if it is not stored properly. **Perishable foods,** such as meat, poultry, fish, dairy products, and ripe fruits and vegetables, spoil easily unless they are kept at the right temperature.

FOOD BUDGET

In an age when lots of food choices exist, it is important to watch your food dollars closely. Making sure you are informed and buying food with care can make a big difference in the dollar amount of your food bill.

In order for a food budget to work, the family must make certain decisions about resources, priorities, and management. And since each family is unique, these decisions and the food budget will vary greatly from one family to another.

DETERMINING YOUR FOOD BUDGET

The family budget is spent on the following: housing, transportation, food, clothes, health care, and entertainment. Some of these costs are fixed and cannot be altered. However, the food budget varies in cost, usually from 20 percent to 25 percent of the total budget. Families can adjust their food costs by spending more of their income on food or by choosing to buy fewer high-cost food items.

FACTORS THAT INFLUENCE FOOD BUDGETS

The food budget is influenced by the family income, the use of good consumer skills, and the management of time, money, and skills. In families where some of the food is grown at home, less money is required for food purchases.

The ages and stages, activity levels, special dietary concerns, and values of the family members also affect the food budget. A family that has three growing, active teens will have higher food bills than a family that has three younger children. And if one family member is on a diet because of illness, allergies, or weight concerns, special food products may increase the need for money in the food budget.

Family values play an important role in the food budget too. A family that likes to serve lavish foods to family and guests, to entertain on a large scale, or to experiment with gourmet foods will see this as a priority and budget more money for food.

Take advantage of seasonal foods and grocery store specials by planning weekly menus before you step into a store.

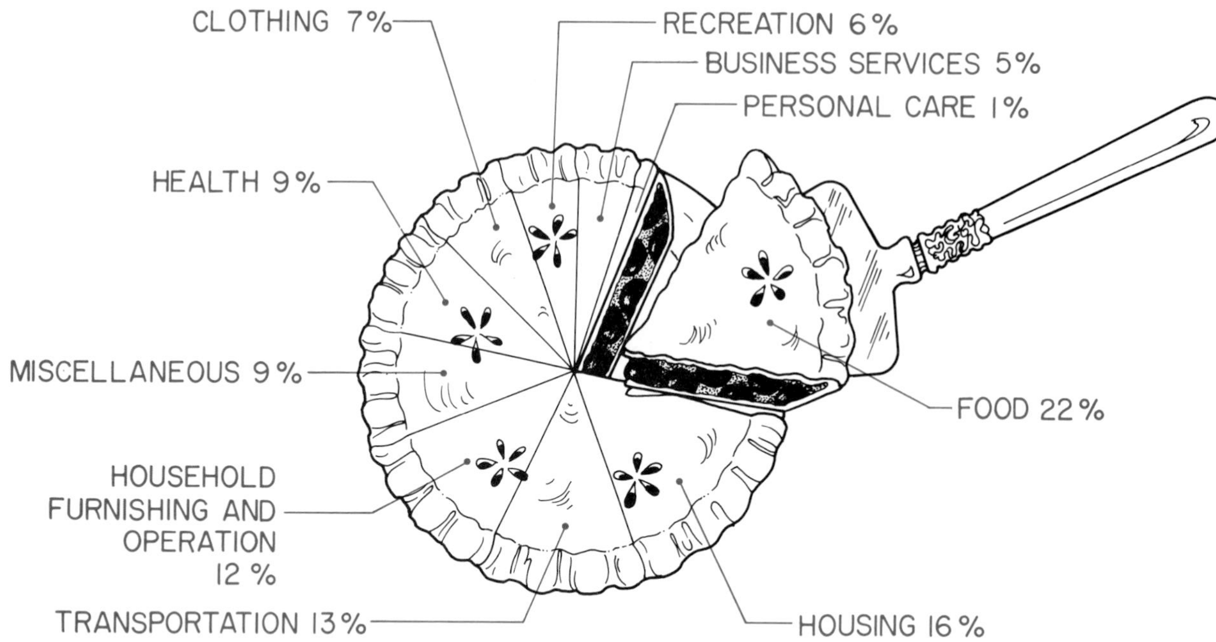

The food budget is a flexible expense, accounting for 20%–25% of the family's budget. By carefully planning and making wise purchases you can make a big difference in the amount you spend for food.

Finally, the management of time, energy, and resources will affect the food budget. People who have little time may buy prepackaged, premixed convenience foods or foods that are delivered to the home. Because service adds to the cost of food, food costs can be reduced if you shop for and cook your own food, thus trading time for money. Other people will reduce food costs by not wasting food or by improving their cooking or buying skills.

COMPUTING COST PER SERVING

Once you know how much money you have to spend for food and the priorities and needs of the family, you can begin to plan how to spend your food dollars. To control spending, you must know how much can be spent for each meal for each person.

After figuring how much you can spend for each day, you can look to see how much each food will cost per serving. This will help you to decide whether to choose a different food in the same food group. For instance, if a pound of hamburger costs $1.60 and will serve four people, it will cost $.40 per person. You might compare this with prices per serving of fish or poultry to see which food fits your daily food budget.

UNIT PRICING

Another important skill in keeping within your food budget is to choose the food you need at the lowest price. You can do this by comparing the unit price of each food item. **Unit pricing** is the cost per unit of measure. These units may be kilograms or pounds, grams (ounces), or liters (quarts or pints). The unit price is usually on the package label or on the edge of the shelf near the food.

To figure the unit price, divide the price of the unit of measure to get the price per unit. Compare this cost with other food brands and different sizes of cans. This will help you to decide whether three small cans or one large can would be a better choice. Plus you can compare brands and forms of food to see which is the better buy.

PLANNING A MENU

Once you have thought about food in relation to time and money, you are ready to write down your menus. A good menu plan will consider good nutrition, family needs, life-styles, food preferences, and costs.

Unit pricing can help you compare the cost of different forms of food. For example, the cost of peaches in each form: fresh, frozen, canned and dried can easily be compared.

USING NEWSPAPERS AND OTHER RESOURCES

Newspaper food sections and ads, store brochures, and family magazines are good resources to use as you plan. They provide information about menu ideas and food costs, and some offer coupon savings.

MAKING A LIST

Once you have planned the menus, you are ready to make a shopping list. Check recipes for ingredients. Be thorough as you make your list. Write down the exact amounts for the items that you will need.

To save time and for shopping ease, arrange the shopping list in order. Group similar foods together, such as meats or dairy products. If shopping at more than one store, make a list for each store. When you have completed the list, check the freezer, refrigerator, and storage shelves to see what foods are on hand.

SHOPPING STRATEGIES

Specials, promotions, two-for-one sales, and coupons offer ways to save money. You can save money by buying staples only when they are "on sale." Specials are announced in the newspaper, and unadvertised store sales occur as well. Take advantage of good sales by keeping your shopping lists and menu plans flexible.

Using Coupons

Using "cents off" and refund coupons also offer savings. Coupons offer you cash discounts at the checkout stand or money back if you send in proofs of purchase. But be sure you would buy the item under normal circumstances. Before you use coupons, compare the price with other similar foods packaged under store brand or generic labels.

The newspaper food section is a helpful resource when planning menus. It features recipes using seasonal foods that are lower in cost and at their peak in flavor.

Take advantage of coupons for food products that you normally would purchase. Some supermarkets even offer double and triple value for coupons.

Using Food Stamps and Commodities

Families who meet income guidelines can get surplus foods or commodities. Some of the foods offered are cheese, dried milk, butter, rice, honey, corn meal, and flour. These foods are bought and passed out by the U.S. Department of Agriculture. These foods can play an important part in stretching the food dollars of the people who receive them.

Food stamps are bought by low-income families from the federal government at a discounted rate. The food stamps are then used to purchase food in local stores. While stamps do increase buying power, people on food stamps must budget both money and stamps with care to meet monthly food needs.

THE STORE

If you are like most consumers, you shop in a store that gives you the best quality and most food for your money. You also expect prompt, friendly service.

When surveyed, consumers ranked the following factors from most to least important:

1. speed at the checkout counter
2. low food prices
3. quality and freshness of meats
4. convenience of location
5. appeal and cleanliness of the store
6. variety of groceries
7. quality and freshness of produce

Price, quality, and selection of food differ among stores. Choosing the best place to shop is important. The information in the box, "Types of Stores," is an overview of the pros and cons of the different types of stores.

To select the store that you will use regularly, visit each store in your area. Look for features such as

1. stable, low prices on frequently purchased items;
2. good quality store brands and selection of generic foods;
3. fresh, good quality meats, produce, and dairy products;
4. honesty in pricing, weights, packaging, and advertising;
5. a clean, convenient location with a helpful, friendly staff.

TYPES OF STORES

- *Supermarket.* Supermarkets or chain stores usually have seven departments: meat, produce, dairy, frozen foods, bakery, grocery, and nonfoods. Many have onsite bakeries and delicatessens, catering services, and salad bars. They usually sell nonfood items too, such as drug and beauty items and other household supplies. Because of their large volume buying power, supermarkets can usually offer cheaper prices.
- *Discount or warehouse stores.* Discount stores offer fewer departments and reduced services. Many stock foods on shelves in open boxes. Discounts are given for food bought in large amounts, such as by the case. Discount stores feature "everyday" low prices instead of special sales.
- *Food cooperatives.* Co-ops are groups that have organized to buy food in bulk at wholesale prices, thus avoiding the middleman. The advantages of cooperative buying may be reduced costs and fresher foods. The disadvantages may be fewer food choices and a lack of convenience.
- *Convenience stores.* Often called minimarkets, these stores meet the need for quick and convenient supplies or for people who do not have the transportation or time to go to a supermarket. Choices are limited and prices are higher. They usually offer twenty-four-hour service.
- *Speciality food stores.* These stores usually offer only one type of food. Bakeries, cheese stores, meat shops, and ethnic shops are all speciality shops. Prices are higher at these shops because the food is of higher quality.
- *Neighborhood grocery stores.* These may be independent supermarkets or small grocery stores. Delivery, charge accounts, and special order services are often offered. Choices are limited and prices are higher.
- *Farmer's market and roadside stands.* These are open on a seasonal basis. Fresh produce is offered for direct sale from the local farms. If prices are good, these places may be the best sources of fruits and vegetables.

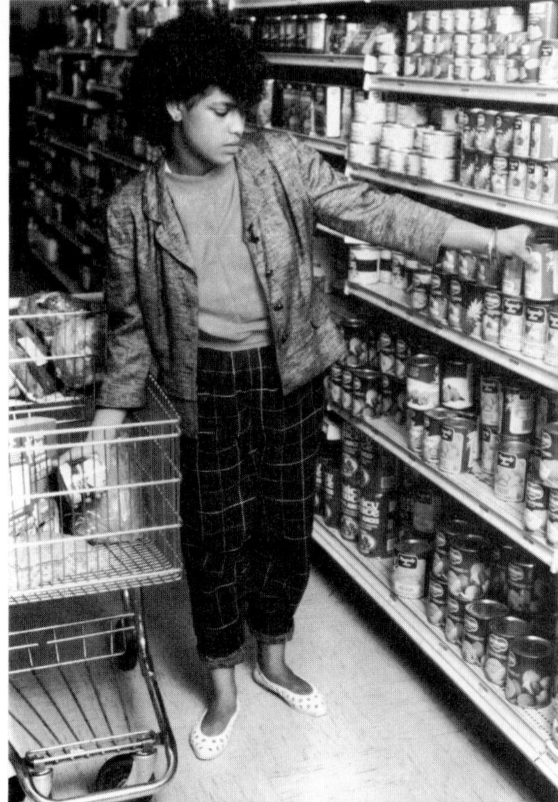

If you limit the number of stores in which you shop, know the layout of the store, and are familiar with the products offered by a store, you can save time.

What information is required by law to be on a food label?

LABELING—WHAT'S IN A NAME?

Are you a label reader? Reading labels is important if you want to improve your diet and get good value for your money. Since more than half of the food you eat comes in packages, you need to know how to read labels to get the information you need to make better choices.

LABEL INFORMATION

The name on a label can tell you what is in the package. For example, fruit juice must contain 100 percent real juice, while a juice drink can have from 35 percent to 69 percent fruit juice. And if you buy a fruit drink, it is only required to contain 10 percent to 34 percent fruit juice. Did you know that the first food listed in the name is the main ingredient? For example, chicken and rice must have more chicken than rice.

As required by law, every label must contain the following information:

1. the name of the food
2. the net weight of the contents, including liquids
3. the name and address of the manufacturer, packer, or distributor
4. the ingredients listed in order from the largest amount to the smallest by weight

The label identifies the food or food product, tells the form of the food—such as sliced, whole, or chunk—and what the food is packed in—such as water, syrup, or its own juices.

Spices, flavorings, and coloring do not have to be listed individually. However, the label must state that they have been used, and it must list the preservatives used.

Foods such as eggs and fresh meat are graded or inspected. The grade shield or inspection mark is stamped on the package or product. Foods are also graded for quality.

Some foods are called **imitation foods.** These foods are made to look and taste like natural foods. Some imitations offer a low cost alternative, such as margarine for butter. Others, such as egg substitutes, were developed for special diets prescribed by doctors.

If the imitation food is not as nutritious as the food replaced, it must be labeled imitation. If the product is similar to the real food and just as nutritious, it must be given a new name, such as margarine, which is a butter substitute.

Nutritional Labeling

Nutritional labels can be useful when shopping. Any food package that says the food in it is healthful must contain a nutritional label. Other food items contain nutritional labeling as a service to the consumer. You can use the list of nutrients on each container to compare and choose the brands that give you the most for your money.

Nutritional labels must give the following information:

1. serving size and the number of servings in a container
2. calories in a serving listed in grams
3. grams of protein, carbohydrates, and fats in each serving
4. percentages of the U.S. RDA for protein and for at least five vitamins (vitamins A and C, thiamine, riboflavin, and niacin) and two minerals (calcium and iron)

In addition, the labels may contain facts about the amounts of sodium, fat, cholesterol, and the percent of the U.S. RDA for twelve other vitamins and minerals. If the food is usually combined with another food, such as cereal and milk, there may be two lists—one for each nutrient in the food when eaten alone and one for the nutrients when eaten in their combined form.

UNIVERSAL PRODUCT CODE

As you look at labels, you may see a small block of ten bars with some numbers to one side. This is the **Universal Product Code,** or the UPC. This code is used by stores to save labor costs. Instead of pricing individual items, the clerk uses a laser beam to scan the bars at the checkout counter. The scanner electronically transmits the code to the computer. The computer identifies the items, locates and rings up the prices, and keeps an inventory of the items purchased.

The customer benefits, too. The computer transmits the price and name of each item to the computerized cash register. The information is flashed on a small screen for the customer to see. Some stores even use a voice synthesizer that announces the information. The name and price of each item is printed on the cash register tape. This makes it possible to check the price you paid for the item either at the point of purchase or when you arrive home.

When a food product claims that it is nutritious, it must include a nutritional label. Other food products add nutritional labelings as a service to the consumer. This helps you to compare calories and nutrients.

The universal product code (UPC) enables a scanner to electronically transmit the code to a computer. The computer transmits the price and name of each item to the computerized cash register receipt.

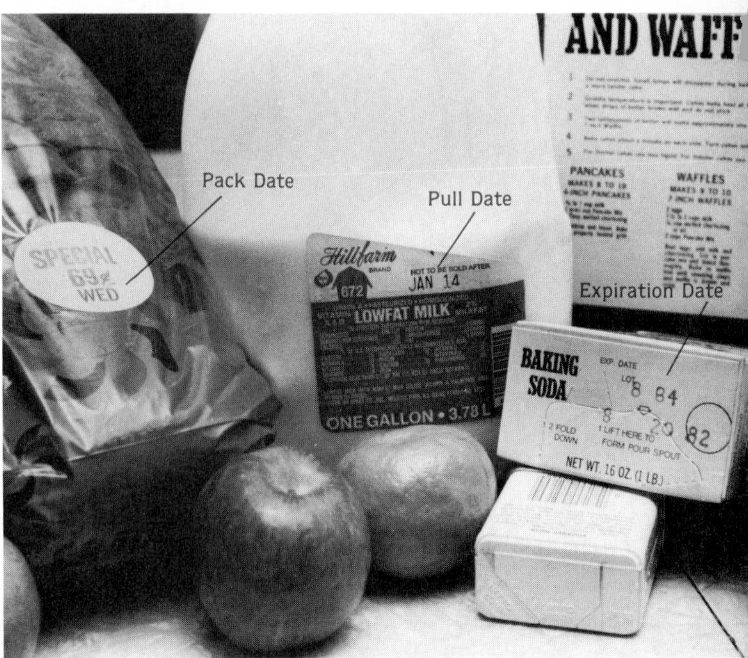

Read the dates on packages to help you determine the freshness of the product.

GENERIC AND STORE LABELS

Foods packaged under **generic** or store labels are usually cheaper than nationally advertised brands. Generic products are those packaged with plain labels and no brand names. The lack of advertising costs and plain packaging reduce the price of the item.

Generally, store brands or private labels are similar to or slightly lower in quality than nationally advertised brands. Generic products may contain varying grades of foods. Sizes, colors, and textures of the food may be different within a container. However, this does not affect the nutritional value nor the taste.

OPEN DATING

Open dating is a system of date coding food products. The date may appear as January 23, 1987, or as 1-23, 123, or 1237, each meaning the same as the first date. You can find dates on the tops or bottoms of food containers. The date may be the pull date, the quality assurance or freshness date, an expiration date, or the pack date. It is often hard to use the dates because they do not always mean the same thing, and the code is often difficult to understand.

The pull date is the last day the product should be sold. It allows time for home storage and use before spoiling. Milk and dairy products, meat, poultry, and fish products are likely to have pull dates. These products are not safe to eat after this date and can not be sold.

The quality assurance or freshness date usually appears on foods such as peanut butter, cheeses, breakfast cereals, ready-to-bake biscuits, and mayonnaise. Statements such as "better if used before" or "best when purchased by" appear on the labels. The flavor and quality is better when the product is used by the date stamped on the label.

The expiration date generally means do not use after the date shown. This date seldom appears except on yeast packages.

Canned food products and packages of frozen foods have pack dates. The pack date does not tell you how long you can expect a product to be good.

STRETCH YOUR FOOD DOLLARS

The following guidelines will help you stretch your food dollars. Keep the following ideas in mind as you plan your meals.

• Meats are usually the most costly food items on a shopping list. If you are on a low budget, serve meat no more than once a day. Instead of making a lunch meat sandwich, make one of peanut butter. For main dishes you can choose meats that are cheaper but take a longer time to cook, such as a chuck pot roast. Or you can eat hamburger or ground turkey in place of more costly cuts of meat.

• Meat will go further if you mix it with other foods. A meatloaf, for instance, uses bread crumbs to extend ground beef. Some other ideas are stews and casseroles that extend meat with rice, spaghetti, noodles, or potatoes. You might also use canned meats, canned fish, and poultry, all of which are cheaper.

• Another strategy is to use dried beans or peas, eggs, and cheese for meat. Also, if you spend too much on one meal's portions, you can use these cheaper items to balance your budget again.

• Canned vegetables and fruits, especially store and generic brands, are cheaper. Buy seasonal fresh fruits and vegetables. Stock up on frozen vegetables when they are on sale.

• Use dried milk in cooking. Or use it to extend whole milk by mixing equal parts of each together. Evaporated milk is a good stand in for cream.

• Use cooked cereals in place of the more costly ready-to-eat cereals. Or buy generic brands or bigger sizes of ready-to-eat cereals. Day-old bread and rolls save money, too.

• To further save money, cut down on snack foods that are costly and poor in nutrients. Instead, use fruit juices, popcorn, and nuts in place of candy, soft drinks, and chips.

BUYING CONVENIENCE

When you buy convenience foods, you are, in a sense buying time. Much of the time you would spend preparing the food is saved since the convenience food shortens the number of steps needed to prepare the food and to cleanup.

CONVENIENCE FOODS

Convenience foods come in many forms: canned, frozen, freeze dried, dehydrated, premixed, and ready to serve. Demand for these foods has risen along with the demands on people's time.

Each person who plans meals must evaluate convenience foods with the following points in mind: the cost of the ingredients, taste, nutritional value, cost in relation to the food budget, time of preparation, and costs in time and money if a similar food was prepared at home.

If you look at the costs of convenience foods, you will find great variations. Products also vary in quality and nutritional content. Evaluate each purchase with care.

NATURAL AND ORGANIC FOODS

You have probably heard claims of superiority for foods that are "natural." Natural foods are generally those foods that have no artificial ingredients. They also are not processed beyond what would normally be done in a home kitchen.

Despite claims to the contrary, natural foods have no more nutrients than regular foods. Further, some of those that claim to be "natural" are really highly processed and have artificial ingredients. Paying more for "natural" foods does not always buy better nutrition.

If you choose a "natural" food, read the label with care. Find out what you are or are not getting for the extra money you are paying.

Organic foods are grown without the use of chemical fertilizers or pesticides. Manure and decayed plant matter are used in place of chemicals. Careful studies of organic foods have found no difference in the nutrient content of organic food.

Convenience foods vary in quality and nutritional content. Compare ingredients, taste, cost, and time savings when using convenience foods.

WHAT ABOUT ADDITIVES?

If natural foods are not always superior in nutrition, what about foods with additives? Are they harmful to your health? You have probably heard a lot of talk about additives. The information that follows will help you understand why additives are added to food.

Food additives include many thousands of substances that are added to foods during processing. Most are added on purpose, while others are added by chance from processing, packaging, handling, and storage. Food additives are used for many reasons, such as

1. to improve nutritional value;
2. to maintain texture;
3. to prevent spoilage;
4. to enhance flavor and color;
5. to speed the aging process;
6. to sweeten;
7. to improve the keeping qualities by controlling acidity;
8. to stabilize ingredients.

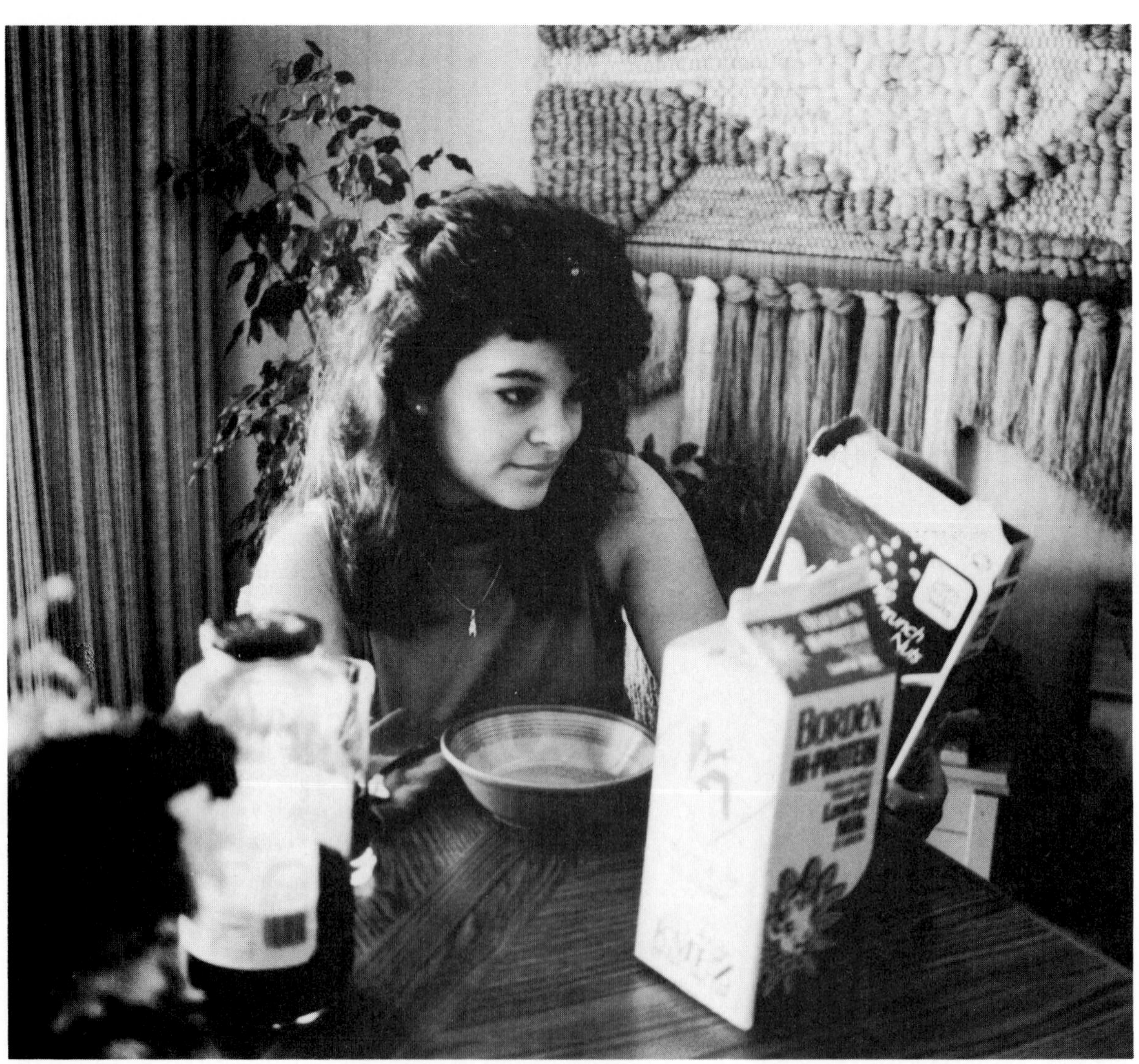

Read food labels to determine what additives have been added. Can you explain the purpose of the food additives used in the box of cereal?

When foods have nutrients added, they are said to be enriched or fortified. Both terms mean the same thing. In general, foods that are labeled **enriched** have had the nutrients lost in processing replaced. The term fortified usually is found on the label of foods that do not normally contain the nutrient.

There is a reason for adding nutrients to food. Vitamin D is added to milk to help the body absorb the calcium in milk. The label on a package of instant rice lists niacin, iron, and thiamine as being added to give the rice more nutritional value. Flour and grain products are often enriched to replace nutrients lost in refining and processing. Some breakfast cereals are fortified with a long list of nutrients. This is done so that they can provide a balanced meal when eaten with other breakfast foods such as juice and milk.

If you use sugar, salt, pepper, spices, baking soda, lemon juice, vinegar, or cornstarch, you are using food additives. There are at least 2,600 additives. Of the 1,500 pounds of food consumed by the average American adult, 150 pounds are additives. About 93 percent of this is made up of sweetners and salt. Chemicals make up about 1 percent.

ROLES OF GOVERNMENT AND INDUSTRY

Federal laws direct that all food sold across state lines must be safe, clean and honestly prepared, packaged, and labeled. Plants where foods are processed are inspected by government agents periodically. If evidence is found of violation, the producer may be taken to court.

In the United States, the Federal Food, Drug, and Cosmetic Act of 1930 sets the standards for the food industry and requires truthful labeling. This act has been amended several times to keep up with changes in the food industry. This law requires that a manufacturer must prove a new additive is safe before using it. The Food and Drug Administration (FDA) is responsible for enforcing the law and testing additives before approving their use.

In 1980, the FDA began a review of the additives that had been placed on the Generally Recognized as Safe (GRAS) list. The purpose was to check their safety against newer standards. The GRAS list includes commonly used substances that are added to food, such as salt, sugar, and various spices, as well as vitamins and minerals, to name a few. Any additives on the GRAS list may be used by a food processor without getting further permission. Some additives have been removed from the GRAS list. One was saccharin, which was found to cause cancer when given to animals in large doses. Thus, a warning label is put on all foods that contain saccharin.

Permission must be obtained if the food processor wants to use an additive not on the GRAS list. The firm is responsible for testing the product and showing proof of its results. Then approval can be obtained from the FDA. The law requires that the additive must be safe in the amount used, will help to improve the product, and will not be in violation of the 1958 Food Additive Amendment to the Food, Drug, and Cosmetic Act. Both business and government share the responsibility to supply wholesome, safe food.

LABELING LEGISLATION

You have already read about what is required to be on a label. But did you know that some products have names that are covered by a standard of identity? This determines what name may be listed on the label.

A **standard of identity** lists the key ingredients and the minimum amount of each that must be found in a product. Over 250 foods have standards of identity. Bread, jam, peanut butter, and margarine are among the foods covered. Foods that have a standard of identity do not need to list these ingredients on the label, however, any added nutrients must be listed.

Review CHAPTER 23

WORDS TO REMEMBER

enriched
food additives
generic foods
imitation foods
open dating
perishables
standard of identity
unit pricing
Universal Product Code

CHECKING YOUR UNDERSTANDING

1. What is unit pricing? Discuss how it can be used to save you time and money.
2. What is meant by an imitation food? When must a product be labeled as an imitation and when must it be given a new name?
3. Describe the Universal Product Code. How is the Universal Product Code used in the store?
4. What are generic and private labels? What are the pros and cons of buying generic and private label products?
5. What are the four common types of open dating?

APPLYING YOUR UNDERSTANDING

1. List the factors you should consider when you plan a menu. What are the advantages of making up a shopping list from your menu plan?
2. Collect samples of coupons and ads for store specials. Discuss how you can use coupons and store specials to save money.
3. Make a list of factors you would look for when choosing the best store for your food needs.
4. Collect food labels. Explain how to use the information given on a food label to help you compare prices and nutritional value.
5. Describe the role of government in the regulation of food production and packaging.

Chapter 24
SELECTING AND STORING FOOD

Has this ever happened to you?

"I'll help you fix dinner tonight," remarked Bill, Ron's best friend. "I like to cook."

"That would be great," replied Ron. "Then we can play some basketball after dinner. For dinner we can have fish, salad, garlic bread, and fruit. Why don't you begin by fixing the fish."

Bill went to the refrigerator and searched for the fish. He found it in the same package that it had been wrapped in by the store. As he tore open the plastic, he was struck by the bad odor. "Hey, we're not having this for dinner!" exclaimed Bill. "It should have been eaten days ago."

"Oh, you're right," stated Ron as he spied the lettuce on the open shelf in the refrigerator. "I guess we will have to settle for a salad and garlic bread. But look at this lettuce! It's all dried out and brown. I don't think it will taste very good."

"Nor will this garlic bread," said Bill as he reached for the bread loaf. "Unless, of course, you like mold!"

"Gosh, Bill," stammered Ron. "I feel embarrassed for inviting you to my house for dinner. This food looked fine three days ago. I don't know what happened."

"Knowing how to cook is only half the battle. Knowing how to choose and store food is the other half. You could use some help in both areas," advised Bill. "But don't worry. We won't starve this time. Let's go over to my house. There are hamburgers and vegetables that we can fix."

Have you ever planned to prepare a dish only to find the food was spoiled?

Have you ever wondered how long food would stay fresh in the refrigerator?

After reading this chapter, you will be able to

- recognize the importance of comparing the costs of different forms of food;
- select the food that is the best quality for the lowest cost for the intended use;
- discuss the importance of correct food storage;
- distinguish between the functions of inspection and grading of certain foods;

Step into any food store and you will soon see that you have many, many choices of food. Choosing a food product that gives you the best value, taste, quality, and satisfaction for your money takes practice.

But there is more to choosing food. Once you get home, you must know how to store food so that quality and nutritional value are protected. Using the best storage method for the food you have chosen is essential to maintain its quality taste, texture, freshness, and appearance. And proper storage will help to reduce food spoilage, which wastes dollars and can cause serious illness.

FRUITS AND VEGETABLES

Fruits and vegetables play an important role in menu planning. They are versatile foods that add color, flavor, texture, and nutrition to the menu. You can serve them raw as snack food, steamed as a healthful side dish, or mixed with other foods to make interesting salads, casseroles, or desserts.

FORMS

Fruits and vegetables come in many forms: fresh, frozen, canned, dried, or as juices. The best form depends on what you plan to do with it. For instance, frozen strawberries would not be the best choice for a school sack lunch. To decide what form to buy, consider how you will store and use the items, as well as the cost and nutritional value.

Whether to buy fresh or frozen, dried or canned, precooked or enriched products, are just a few of the choices you have when selecting and purchasing food.

Make a list of the fresh fruits and vegetables that you have tasted. How many of the over 70 varieties of fresh fruits and 200 varieties of vegetables have you tried?

BUYING AND STORING FRESH FRUITS AND VEGETABLES

When choosing fresh fruits and vegetables, also called **produce,** choose those that are seasonal. **Seasonal** fruits and vegetables are plentiful during certain times of the year. At these times their quality will be at a peak and prices will be lower. Choose fresh fruits and vegetables that have the richest colors. A rich, deep color indicates a more nutritious food product.

Buy only as much produce as you can store correctly and use within the storage life of the fruit or vegetable. On the average, most fruits and vegetables can be stored from two to five days. Root vegetables will last from one to several weeks. Apples and citrus fruits will last as long as two weeks if they are stored in the refrigerator.

The best storage place for most produce is in the cool, moist air of the refrigerator. Plastic containers, plastic bags, or the refrigerator's crisper compartment help to maintain crispness and freshness. Wash vegetables before you store them only if absolutely necessary and then dry them thoroughly. Wash fruit with care to remove dirt and pesticide and dry before you store or serve them. Store potatoes, onions, and late fall vegetables in a cool, dry, dark place.

BUYING AND STORING FROZEN FRUITS, VEGETABLES, AND JUICES

Of the processed fruits and vegetables, frozen fruits and vegetables are the closest in flavor and nutrition to fresh produce. Keep frozen fruits and vegetables at a temperature of 0° (18°C). Thawing and refreezing affects the color, texture, taste, and the nutritional value of the product.

Frozen vegetables are available year-round, offer high nutritional value, and have a well preserved natural color and flavor. However, gourmet vegetables, with specialty sauces, tend to be more expensive.

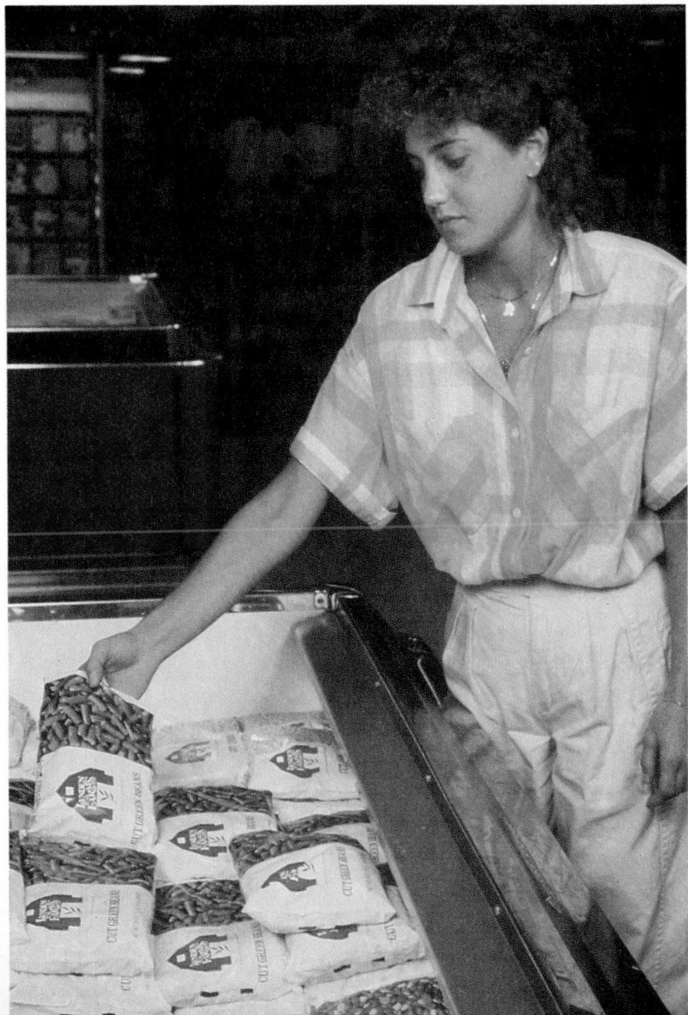

The prices of frozen fruits and vegetables vary depending on the size of the package and whether the products are whole, sliced, or cut in pieces. Compare the unit price per package and judge the best choice in terms of how the food will be used.

When buying frozen produce, choose only those that are solidly frozen. Avoid packages that are stained or broken. Purchase frozen products last. Then put them in the freezer as soon as you get home. Under the best conditions, storage life may be eight to twelve months from the time of purchase.

When the product has been defrosted, use the food promptly or it may spoil. Juices made from frozen concentrates should be used within two to three days after you mix them.

BUYING AND STORING CANNED FRUITS, VEGETABLES, AND JUICES

Canned fruits and vegetables can come whole, sliced, diced, chunked, or crushed. Choose the style that is best for the recipe you are using.

The cost of canned fruits and vegetables fluctuates with the season. Take advantage and stock up on canned goods during harvest time when the prices are at their lowest.

When shopping for canned goods, be sure to check that the cans and jars of food have been tightly sealed. Small dents usually do not affect the seal, but avoid buying cans that are badly dented, rusted, leaking, or bulging. If there is a sudden release of pressure, a bad odor, or poor color when you open the can, destroy the food rather than run the risk of getting food poisoning.

It is best to use canned nonacid vegetables, such as peas, corn, and potatoes within four to six months after you have bought them.

Unopened canned fruit, juices, and vegetables will keep for eight to twelve months if they are stored in a cool, dry place. After that, they lose their quality.

Once opened, canned fruits, juices, and vegetables start to perish. Store any unused portions in airtight containers in the refrigerator, and use within two or three days.

Carefully read the label to determine if the fruit is packed in syrup, juice, or water. Syrups are usually concentrations of sugar and add calories to the product.

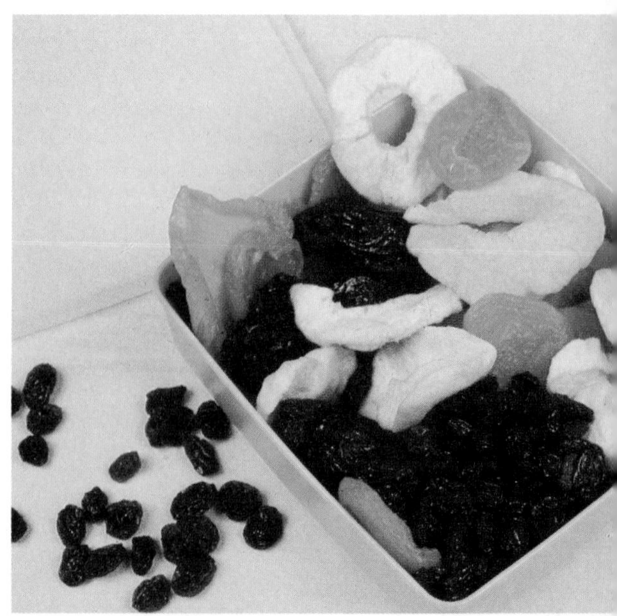

Dried fruits, such as raisins, apples, apricots, and bananas are excellent sources of concentrated energy and good snack foods.

BUYING AND STORING SALAD GREENS

When you think of salad greens, do you automatically picture iceberg lettuce? Iceberg is the most popular lettuce because of its crisp, mild tasting, pale green leaves. It stays crisp longer than other lettuces. But there are many kinds of lettuces that range in flavor from mild to sharp to bitter.

To choose high quality salad greens, look for fresh, bright products. Avoid those that look wilted or have browned edges, rust spots, bruises, or signs of insects. Be careful also of those that are too wet or too exposed to the sun in the stores. This produce will spoil more rapidly.

Salad greens perish quickly if they are not stored correctly. Special care must be taken if they are to keep their original food value and appearance. All greens must be washed thoroughly to remove all traces of dirt, grit, and pesticide. Dry greens with care by spin drying or blotting them gently with paper towels after washing to maintain fresh quality.

Experiment with different types of salad greens. Combine a stronger flavored lettuce, such as Belgian endive, with milder greens.

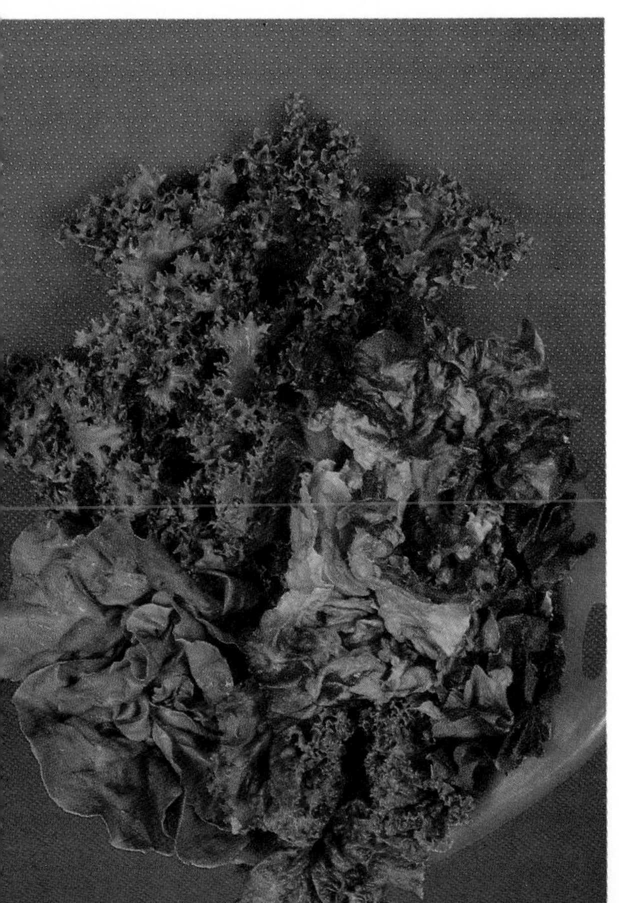

BREADS AND CEREALS

Grain products include bread, pasta, rice, breakfast cereals, flours, and other foods made from grains. They are made from the kernels or seeds of cereal grasses. The most widely used grains are wheat, rice, corn, sorghum, oats, rye, barley, and buckwheat.

PROCESSING

Whole grain breads and cereals are more nutritious and have a fuller flavor than processed grain products because they contain all the parts of the kernel. In **refined,** or processed, grain products part of the kernel is removed, thus destroying many nutrients.

About 80 percent of the essential nutrients are removed when whole grain products are processed. Processing leaves only one-fourth of the vitamin E and 7 percent of the fiber from the original grain. Vitamin E is further destroyed when the flour is bleached. Therefore, grain products such as rice, all-purpose flours, white bread, pasta products, breakfast cereals, and baked goods are enriched or fortified to replace the nutrients lost in processing.

The three main parts of the grain kernel are the bran, endosperm and germ.

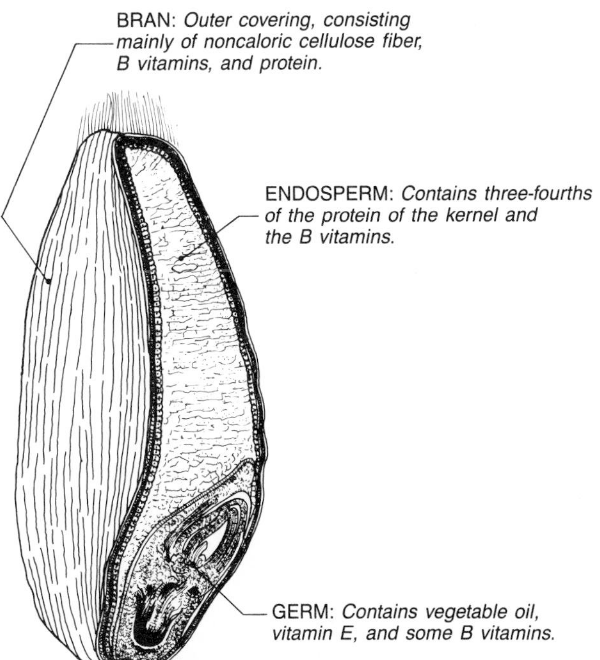
BRAN: *Outer covering, consisting mainly of noncaloric cellulose fiber, B vitamins, and protein.*
ENDOSPERM: *Contains three-fourths of the protein of the kernel and the B vitamins.*
GERM: *Contains vegetable oil, vitamin E, and some B vitamins.*

BUYING AND STORING GRAIN PRODUCTS

Flour refers to all-purpose or general purpose wheat flour. All-purpose flour is milled from a blend of hard and soft wheats. It is mixed so that it can be used to bake yeast breads that require gluten development, as well as to bake cakes and pastries.

Other flours are cake flour, bread flour, self-rising flour, instant flour, and whole wheat or graham flour. All-purpose flour is usually the best type of flour for home use. Whole grain flours keep best when cooled to retard spoilage.

Pasta

All macaroni and noodle products are called pasta. They are made from durum wheat or semolina flour and water. This flour has a high-protein quality, yellow color, and a nutlike taste. Federal law requires that noodles contain 5.5 percent egg solids. Green noodles have about 3 percent spinach solids.

Pasta dough comes in about two hundred different shapes and sizes. The three main forms of pasta, which are dried and sold in boxes or plastic bags, include spaghetti, macaroni, and lasagna noodles. Dried pasta should be stored in a clean, dry shelf and protected from dust and insects.

Rice

Rice is sold in three sizes—short, medium, and long. Long rice is the type most often served alone or along with a main dish because it stays dry and fluffy when cooked. Short and medium grains have small round kernels that are sticky when cooled. They are used in rice puddings and rice molds and croquettes.

There are several kinds of rice sold: white or polished rice, brown rice, parboiled or converted rice, instant or precooked rice, and wild rice.

Store uncooked rice at room temperature in a tightly sealed container to keep out moisture and insects. White rice will keep for many months, while brown rice is somewhat more perishable.

Breakfast Cereals

Breakfast cereals come in four forms—ready-to-eat, instant, quick cooking, and regular. The least costly per serving are regular cereals that need to be cooked. Cereals that are ready-to-eat, especially those that have sugar and/or fruit added are the most costly. Instant cereals that only need to have hot water added are almost as costly as cold cereals.

Cereals should be stored on a clean, dry shelf. Ready-to-eat cereals can be stored in the box in which they were bought. Uncooked and instant cereals can be stored in their original boxes. Keep them tightly closed when not in use, or transfer them to plastic or glass containers with lids.

Wrap breads tightly and store in a breadbox. In warm weather, store them in the refrigerator to slow down the growth of mold.

BUYING AND STORING OTHER GRAIN PRODUCTS

Oats are sold as flakes or oatmeal after the hulls are removed. Quick-cooking oats are thinner flakes than the regular or "old fashioned" oats. Oatmeal can be used in main dishes, breads, cakes, cookies, and other desserts, as well as oatmeal cereal.

Rye, barley, and buckwheat flours are usually mixed with wheat flour in baking. Buckwheat flour is often used in pancakes and crepes. Kasha, which is used in place of rice or potatoes, is buckwheat that is made into hulled, toasted oats. Pearl barley is hulled, polished barley. Both the regular and quick-cooking forms can be used in stews or soups to flavor and thicken them as well as for more nutritional value.

Whole grain products should be stored in a tightly wrapped plastic bag, foil, or covered container and refrigerated for longer storage. This will stop their drying out and losing their flavor and nutrients. If they are stored at room temperature, they will become rancid or smell and taste bad. **Rancidity** is caused by the breakdown of fats in food. Refrigeration retards rancidity.

Add wheat bran to cereals to replace the fiber lost during processing. Sprinkle wheat germ on a variety of foods to improve the nutritional value and flavor.

PROTEIN FOODS

Many cooks plan their menus around a main dish of meat, poultry, or fish. Americans spend about one-third of the family's food budget on these high-quality protein foods.

MEAT

Beef, veal, pork, and lamb are the types of meat that you will use most often. Beef and veal come from cattle, pork comes from hogs, and lamb comes from sheep.

Inspection and Grading

All meats shipped across the state lines are federally inspected and stamped to show that the meat meets the standards of the Wholesome Meat Act of 1967. An inspection stamp tells you that the meat is wholesome or safe to eat.

Meats are also inspected and graded according to quality. While grades do not always indicate the flavor and tenderness of meat, they are one of the few guidelines that you have as a consumer. Shield-shaped stamps show which meats have been graded by the USDA for quality. Quality grading is based on texture, firmness, and color of lean meat, the age and maturity of the animal, and the degree of marbling. **Marbling** is the amount of fat seen in lean meat.

Pork is seldom graded since it usually comes from young hogs and is all of one quality.

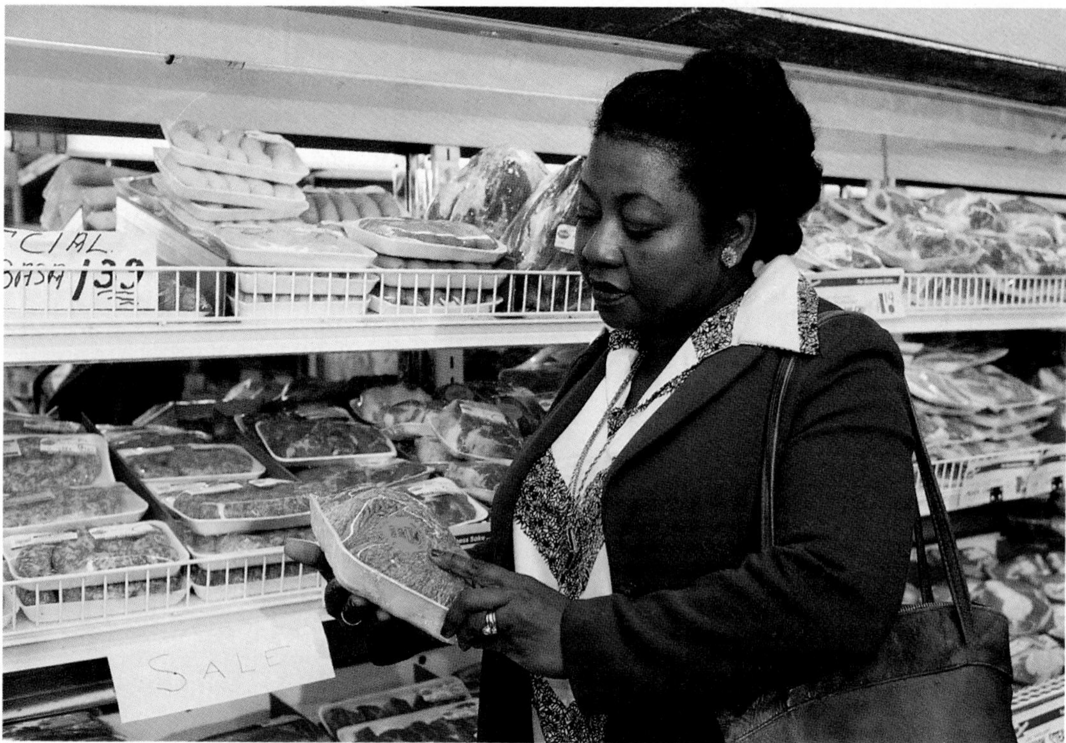

The three top USDA grades for beef, veal, and lamb are prime, choice, and good.

- **Prime—Well marbled with fat flecks; sold primarily to restaurants and speciality meat markets.**
- **Choice—Grade sold in most meat markets.**
- **Good—Ungraded, marked "generic" or sold under a store's or meat packer's own brand label.**

Cuts of Meat

A **cut of meat** is a portion of meat cut away from the animal carcass. Meat cuts are based on two factors, the muscle and bone structure of the meat, and the uses of the meat and the cooking methods usually used to cook the different parts of the animal.

Knowing where the cut of meat comes from can help you judge tenderness. The cut also determines the price you pay, as well as how you cook the piece of meat.

Cuts of meat and certain internal organs are grouped by tenderness. The three categories are:

1. Tender cuts: the loin and ribs of beef, veal, lamb, and pork; the leg of veal, lamb, and pork.
2. Less tender cuts: the round, rump, flank, and chuck of beef; the shoulder and breast of veal and lamb; the shoulder of pork.
3. Variety meats or organ meats: the liver, kidney, heart, tongue, brains, and sweetbreads of beef, veal, and lamb.

Processed Meats

Some meats are processed by canning, freezing, freeze-drying, drying, and pickling. The most costly processed meats are cold cuts. They are high in fat and are made from the lowest, toughest grades of meat. Many processed meats are **cured** by treating them with curing ingredients such as salt, spices, nitrates or nitrites, and sugar. Curing slows spoilage and gives cured meat its particular taste and color. Both fresh and cured meats may be smoked to help preserve the meat further.

POULTRY

Poultry refers to chickens, turkeys, ducks, and geese. The forms poultry comes in are fresh, frozen, canned, live, freeze-dried, smoked, and specialities such as preserved duck.

Sources of Poultry

Chickens are sold whole, cut up, packaged by the individual parts, and fresh, chilled, or frozen. Poultry can come in many forms, such as canned boneless chicken, frozen precooked chicken, sandwich spreads, and chopped, pressed lunch meats.

Turkeys are packaged whole, prestuffed as boneless rolls, ground, or in parts. They may be bought fresh, chilled, or frozen. Turkey is also sold smoked or cured and in a variety of turkey products, such as turkey ham or lunch meats.

Processed turkey products and textured vegetable protein foods offer consumers a product that tastes similar to beef, but is lower in cholesterol and fat.

Inspection and Grading

Quality grading for poultry is voluntary. Grade A poultry is the highest grade given to poultry that is fully fleshed and meaty. Grade B is slightly less meaty and less attractive in appearance. Poultry below Grade A is seldom graded. They may be sold as generic or store brands, or simply ungraded.

FISH

Since grading for fish is also voluntary, it is best to buy fish from reliable sources. Grades when used are U.S. Grade A, U.S. Grade B, and Substandard. Grading can help you choose fish that is wholesome, good quality, and fresh. If the fish is not graded, look more carefully at each form of fish sold. Fresh fish should be bright, clear, with bulging eyes, bright red gills, and skin that is smooth but not slimy. It should have a mild, agreeable smell.

All fish products are high in nutrients and are a good protein source. Finfish, such as trout and halibut, have a center spine and bones. Shellfish, such as shrimp and lobster, have a shell and no spine or bones.

FOOD FOR A HEALTHY BODY

You know what foods your body needs each day to keep up with your active life-style. But how can you apply your knowledge of nutrition when you are faced with the many choices in each department of the store? Here are some tips for each of the main food groups:

- *Fruits and vegetables.* Get in the habit of having fruits and/or vegetables with each meal. Take time to compare the costs of your choices in fresh, canned, and frozen forms. According to the USDA, fresh carrots, frozen lima beans, and canned peas are always best buys. Check this out!
- *Breads and cereals.* Look for ready-to-eat cereals with grains listed as the first ingredient, not flour or sugar. Choose whole grain products for fiber and nutrients.
- *Meat, poultry, fish, and beans.* Remember a serving of meat only needs to be two to three ounces. Buy large cuts of meat and cut them into portions for just one meal. Wrap individually and freeze. Compare the costs per serving rather than per pound. Use this formula to compare the costs of the actual lean meat in different types of ground beef:

$$\text{cost per pound of lean portion} = \frac{\text{price per pound} \times 100}{\text{\% lean (80, 70 etc.)}}$$

Buy whole poultry. Use all the parts. Choose tuna and other fish packed in water. Remember size and color of eggs are not related to quality. Try beans and other legumes in salads.
- *Milk and cheese.* Milk and cream product costs are affected more by butterfat content than nutritional value. Cheese is a good source of protein but a poor source of iron. Include iron-rich foods such as enriched cereals, bread, or green leafy vegetables when cheese is the main source of protein. Use reduced fat cheese.

No matter what you buy, read the labels. They are your only clues to what is inside. Compare weights, contents, and unit prices before deciding which product suits your needs. This is the secret to successful shopping!

Forms of Fish

Fresh fish can be bought in the following forms:

1. whole
2. drawn (entrails removed)
3. dressed (cleaned and scaled and with the head, tail, and fins cut off)
4. steak (cross section of dressed fish)
5. fillets (sides of fish cut away from backbone, usually boneless)

Frozen fish may be sold whole, as fillets, or as steaks. Fish sticks, cut from fillets, may be breaded and then frozen. Lobster tails, frozen crab meat, scallops, and shrimp are also sold frozen. Choose only fish that is solidly frozen.

Canned fish includes finfish and shellfish. Salmon, tuna, and sardines are some popular canned finfish items. Oysters, lobsters, crab, and shrimp are sold ready to use. Since canned fish is already cooked, it is a useful convenience item to have on hand.

Cured fish may be smoked, dried, salted, or pickled. It is sold in delicatessens and in cans. Some examples are smoked mackerel, salted cod, dried tuna, and pickled herring.

STORING MEAT, POULTRY, AND FISH

Store fresh meat, poultry, and fish in the coldest part of the refrigerator and use within two days. Wrap fresh, unfrozen meats and fish loosely in foil or plastic wrap. When storing poultry, remove the wrapping, wash, and loosely rewrap the bird. Wrap the giblets in a separate package.

Frozen meat, poultry, and fish will keep its quality if the freezer temperature remains at 0° F. (− 18°C) for up to six months. Wrap meats, fish, and poultry in a thick-gauge plastic wrap, freezer wrap, or heavy duty aluminum foil. Seal the package tightly and label and date the contents.

In general, cured meats need refrigeration. They can be kept in the wrappers they came in. Canned meat, poultry, or fish should be kept in a cool, dry storage shelf.

NUTS AND LEGUMES

Nuts are the dried fruits or seeds of plants that consist of a kernel usually enclosed in a shell. They are more than a snack food, and they can be used in main dishes as the protein source. They are rich in nutrients but, because they contain a high amount of vegetable fat, they should be limited in the diet.

Nuts can be purchased in the shell, shelled, and in packages or in cans, and jars. They come whole and in halves, sliced, slivered, or broken pieces. Choose the form based on how you will use the nuts. Nuts that are advertised as "fresh crop" usually are higher in quality.

Use shelled or unshelled nuts as soon as possible. Store those that will not be used in a short time in the refrigerator or freezer. Freezing nuts can stop the oil from becoming rancid. Packaged nuts will keep for a month in the refrigerator. Nuts in cans or jars will keep for up to a year from the packaging date.

Legumes are seeds that grow in a pod such as beans or peas. These incomplete proteins are high in essential amino acids. When legumes are eaten with grain products, nuts, or small amounts of animal protein, they form complete proteins and become low-cost substitutes for meat. The legumes that are the best sources of protein are soybeans, peanuts, and chick peas.

Beans and other legumes are also sold in cans, both dried and ready to eat. Pork and beans and chili are long standing convenience foods.

If stored properly in a cool, dry place, dried legumes will keep for months. Once opened, they should be put in containers with tight-fitting lids.

EGGS

Eggs are sold by grade and size, and in some areas by whether the shell is brown or white. The color of the egg shell does not affect either nutrition or taste. Eggs may be bought fresh, liquid, frozen, dried, and ready to heat and eat as part of frozen meals. Compared to other high-protein foods, eggs are a good buy.

Grades

Eggs are graded by sorting them by their quality and weight. Egg quality is judged by four factors: the clarity and thickness of the white, the condition of the yolk, the condition and size of the air cell, and the texture and condition of the shell. Grade and size are two separate factors.

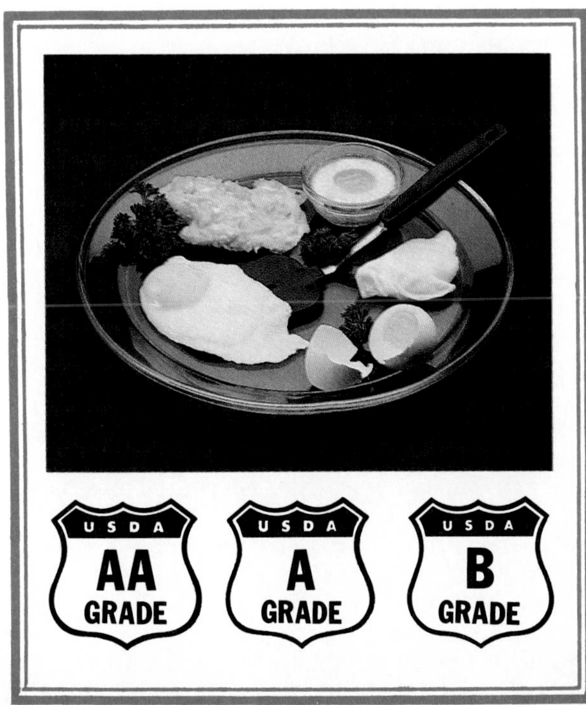

These shields indicate the quality of eggs you are buying. U.S. Grade AA, makes more attractive fried or poached eggs. U.S. Grade A, are good all purpose eggs, and U.S. Grade B, are best used for cooking and baking.

Sizes

The size of an egg refers to the minimum weight of a dozen eggs. The sizes generally available are jumbo, extra large, large, and medium. The size of an egg is not a factor of its quality.

Storage of Eggs

Fresh eggs should be stored unwashed in their store container instead of in the egg rack in the refrigerator. Leftover whites may be stored in a covered container or frozen. Yolks should be covered with a thin layer of milk or water and tightly covered. Dried whole egg or egg yolk powders, because of the high fat content of the yolk, cannot be stored for long periods of time.

DAIRY PRODUCTS

From soups to desserts and from beverages to snacks, dairy products are used the world over as a wholesome, nutritious food. Milk, cheese, yogurt, milk drinks, buttermilk, and frozen desserts are some examples of dairy products.

MILK

Most milk and milk products are **pasteurized,** which means that harmful bacteria have been heated and killed. The pasteurizing of milk involves quickly heating the milk, holding it at that temperature, and then letting it cool. You will also note that some milk products are **homogenized.** During this process fat globules are broken up and suspended throughout the milk so that they will not separate out as cream.

Forms of Milk

The most common type of milk product is fresh milk that is sold as whole milk, low-fat, or skim milk. Whole milk has at least 3.25 percent milk fat. Low-fat has 2 percent milk fat, and skim or nonfat milk has had all the fat removed. Both whole and low-fat milk may be homogenized.

Nonfat dried milk, an economical form of milk, is made by removing the water and most of the fat from pasteurized fluid milk. Since nutrients are lost when fat is removed, nonfat dried milk is fortified with vitamins A and D, as are low-fat and skim milk.

Both evaporated milk and condensed milk have about half of the water removed before they are sterilized and canned. Condensed milk is sweetened by adding about 44 percent sugar. Evaporated milk can be used full strength in place of cream or mixed with water and used as milk. Sweetened condensed milk is used in candy and dessert recipes.

Cultured buttermilk is pasteurized skim or low-fat milk that has been soured by lactic acid-producing bacteria or similar culture. Yogurt, a custardlike milk product made from whole or skim milk, is also cultured.

Buying and Storing Milk

Before you choose the form of milk to buy, think about how you will use it. Fresh milk is the most costly, but it is preferred for drinking.

Dried, nonfat milk costs about one-third as much as fresh milk. It is ideal to cook with or to blend with whole milk for drinking. Canned milk is also less costly than fresh milk and it has a long shelf life.

Do you know the difference between ice cream, ice milk, and fruit sherbert? Ice cream contains at least 10 percent milkfat; ice milk is made with 2–7 percent milkfat but more sugar; and fruit sherbet has only 1–2 percent milkfat but more sugar.

Fresh milk and dried milk, as well as canned milk that has been opened, should be placed in a closed or covered container and refrigerated right away. Storage temperatures should be 40°F. (4.4°C). Fresh and canned milk that has been opened will keep about three to five days or longer if it is kept cold. Thaw frozen milk in the refrigerator to prevent spoilage. Store unopened cans of milk in a cool, dry place. Containers of dried milk should be tightly closed after each use, or the milk will pick up moisture and spoil. Nonfat dried milk can be stored at room temperature for a few months if kept dry; however, whole dried milk should be stored in the refrigerator and used within a few weeks.

TYPES OF CHEESE

Most cheeses in the United States are made from cow's milk. However, cheese can also be made from the milk of goats or sheep. There are three types of cheeses. The first is called fresh or unripened cheese. Such cheeses are cottage cheese, cream cheese, and ricotta cheese, all of which have a mild, delicate flavor and aroma. The second type is often called the natural cheeses. These cheeses are cured or ripened, or allowed to mature. Natural cheeses include most kinds of cheese in the market. These cheeses have a sharper, richer, or fuller flavor. The third kind of cheese is made up of one or more kinds of natural cheese plus an emulsifying agent and is called processed cheese. To enhance nutritional value, milk solids are often added. After the pasteurization process, cheese is molded and sealed in packages that need no refrigeration until they are opened.

Buying and Storing Cheese

To determine the best buys in cheese, compare cost. Mild, soft cheeses and pasteurized-processed cheese usually cost less than aged or sharp cheese. However, pasteurized processed cheese is more costly when it is packaged in cans. Consider the packaging and the form of the cheese, too. For example, shredded or cubed cheese, or cheese in small packages costs more than cheese bought in a large round, wedge, block, roll, or stick. Buy only what you can use in a reasonable time, because cheese will mold or spoil. Plan to use soft cheeses before the freshness date on the package.

Cheese keeps best in the refrigerator, with the exception of unopened processed cheese. Read the labels on cheese products for instructions for storage after opening. All cheese should be stored in an airtight container or wrapped to keep air out and the cheese moist.

Cheese, an excellent snack when combined with fruit, is available in many varieties. Some are rather mild in taste; others are very sharp.

WORDS TO REMEMBER

cured meat	legumes	produce	seasonal
cut of meat	marbling	rancidity	
homogenized	pasteurized	refined	

CHECKING YOUR UNDERSTANDING

1. Why should you buy produce when it is in season? How are prices for other than fresh produce affected by the harvest of a product?
2. Discuss why it is necessary to enrich or fortify grain products after they have been refined.
3. How can you tell if a food has become rancid? What foods are apt to become rancid and how can you slow down the process?
4. Make a list of the tender cuts of meat. What is meant by marbling?
5. Describe the process of pasteurization and homogenization of milk. How does the consumer benefit from these processes?

APPLYING YOUR UNDERSTANDING

1. Make a list of the fruits and vegetables you and your family like. Visit a supermarket to find out how each form is sold. Figure out the cost per serving for each form. Report the best forms to buy to the class.
2. Find out the price per serving of ready-to-eat cereal, which is plain, sugared, and with fruit added. Compare these to the costs of cooked and instant cereal. Which is the least costly? Which is the most refined or processed?
3. Interview a butcher. Ask to be shown the grading and inspection stamps on meat, poultry, and fish sold in the store. Ask the butcher to tell you other things to look for when you buy each of these meat products. Report to the class.
4. Plan two menus, one using a legume as the protein source and a second one using meat as the protein source. Find out the cost of each meal per person. Research and discuss the nutritional benefits of legumes. How can they be used to stretch a limited budget?
5. You have just returned from the supermarket and are putting the food away. Make a list of each of the food groups and tell how you would prepare the food for storage and where you would store it. Also tell how long you would expect the food to stay fresh or edible.

Chapter 25

KITCHEN KNOW-HOW

Has this ever happened to you?

Spring break had come, and Jan was helping her older sister unpack and move into a tiny studio apartment.

"Sara, I really like your new apartment. The location is convenient for your job and school, and the pool will be great during the summer. But where are you going to put all of your things?" asked Jan.

"Good question," replied Sara. "I guess it's going to be a true test of creativity to get all my belongings in here, especially in the kitchen!"

Looking around, Jan agreed. "Yes, you don't have many cupboards in the kitchen, and the ones you have are deep and an awkward shape. Once you put pans or dishes away, you are going to have a hard time finding them again!" said Jan.

"Oh, I know," replied Sara. "That's why yesterday I bought some pull-out trays and a revolving shelf for the deep cupboards. I am also going to put cork on one of the walls so that I can display and store some kitchen tools on it."

"Good idea," said Jan. "Tomorrow I'll bring you mom's book on spacing saving. It has hundreds of do-it-yourself ways to

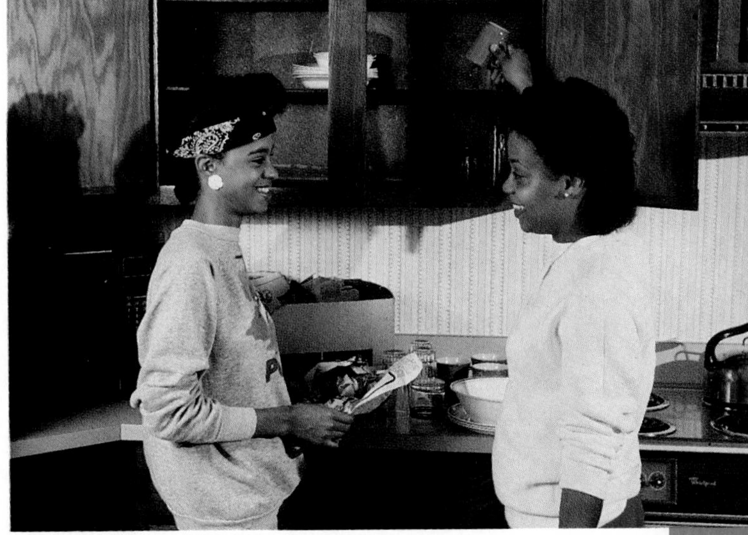

organize space and work areas. With a little help from the book, we'll get this kitchen organized and working efficiently in no time!"

Have you ever tried to improve a poor storage situation by creatively exploring other options?

How can organization of equipment in a kitchen improve efficiency?

After reading this chapter, you will be able to

- analyze kitchens for efficiency and plan the best use of your kitchen to meet your needs;
- evaluate types and uses of kitchen appliances and other food preparation equipment;
- explain the parts of a recipe and describe proper measurement procedures;
- describe food safety hazards and how to prevent accidents in the kitchen.

A well-organized kitchen can save a cook time and energy. Though you probably can do little to change the shape of your kitchen, you can organize the space you have for a more efficient use of space.

PLANNING WORK AREAS

Kitchens are usually broken up into **work centers.** Each center has appliances, equipment, and enough work space and storage area for the work done there. By arranging equipment and work areas, your work can flow smoothly and efficiently.

When you cook, you move back and forth among the three areas—refrigerator-freezer, sink, and range. These three units form the major work centers. A mixing center should also be part of the kitchen plan. Other centers such as the eating center, planning center, and laundry center may be included if space permits.

The refrigerator-freezer, sink, and range are the main work centers in the kitchen. What other centers are included in the kitchen above?

THE WORK CENTERS

The refrigerator center should have at least 75 cm (30 in.) of counter space next to it for loading and unloading food from the refrigerator. It is ideal if items such as waxed paper, foil, plastic bags, and other containers can be stored nearby.

The range center should have at least 60 cm (24 in.) of counter space on at least one side of the range. Cabinet storage is needed for foods such as canned vegetables, frying fats and oils, seasonings, rice and pasta. Equipment stored at this center includes a can opener, ladles, stirring spoons, turners, serving bowls, saucepans and pots, frypans, and pot holders.

The sink or cleanup center may have appliances such as a dishwasher, food waste disposer, and trash compactor. Cleanup activities include not only washing dishes but also cleaning fruits, vegetables, and other foods. Here, there should be enough storage space for items such as measuring cups, paring knives, cleaning brushes, wastebasket, detergent, dishcloths and towels, and scouring powder.

A mixing center can be the counter space between two centers. For instance, it may be the area between the range and refrigerator or any other area that has enough counter space for you to work. The mixing area should be at least 90 cm (36 in.) wide. Store mixing and measuring equipment, knives, and baking pans in this area.

THE WORK TRIANGLE

If possible, the three major work centers—refrigerator-freezer, range, and sink—should be located so that each is at the point of an imaginary triangle. This area is called a **work triangle.** You move back and forth among the three points of the work triangle many times. The general procedure is to take food out of the refrigerator, freezer, or cabinet, clean it if necessary, prepare it, and then cook and serve it. This is known as the **work flow.** Ideally, the three major appliances should reflect the work flow and the total distance among the three points should not be more than 6 m (21 ft.) long.

The work triangle is usually an integrated part of basic kitchen plans. The five most commonly used plans are (1) wall, (2) corridor, (3) L-shape, (4) U-shape, and (5) island or peninsula kitchens.

A one-wall kitchen plan will have appliances lined up against one wall with storage cabinets and counter space between them. This arrangement is used where space is limited, as in apartments. For most people this type of kitchen does not provide enough counter or storage space.

Notice how the work triangle is an integrated part of each of the basic kitchen plans. How does the work triangle help the cook work more efficiently?

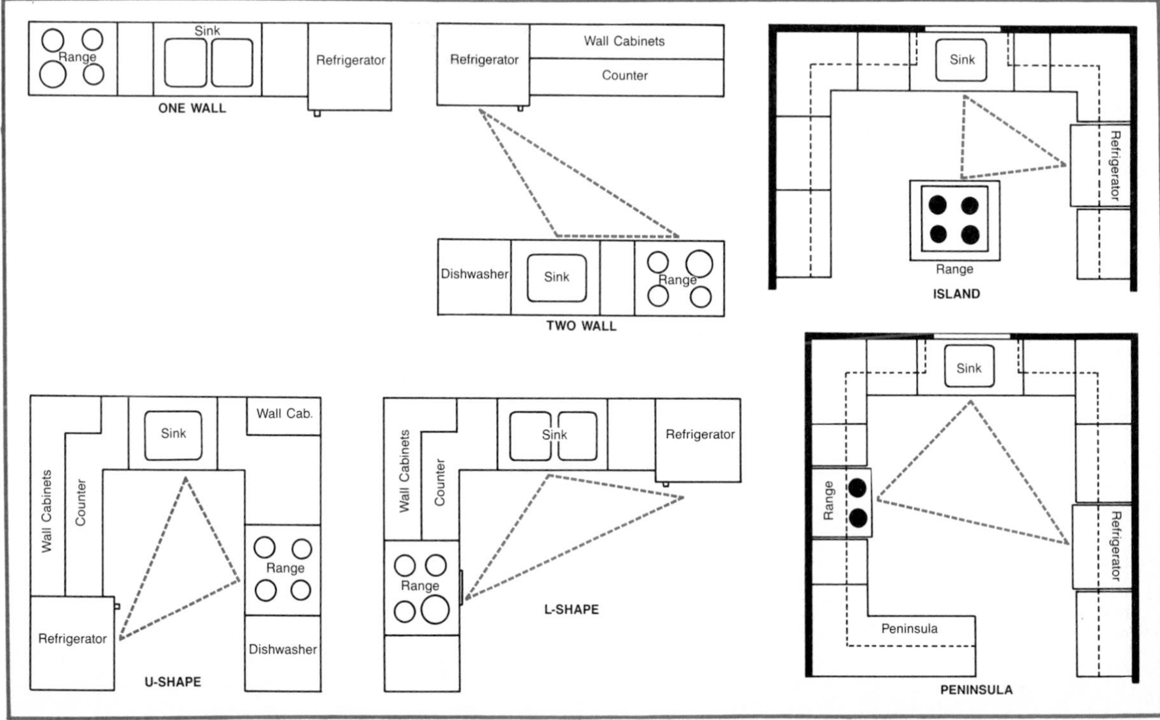

A corridor kitchen plan will have appliances, cabinets, and counter space arranged on two facing walls. Usually the room is long and narrow. If the room is not too long, this can be an efficient kitchen.

The L-shape kitchen plan has a continuous line of appliances and cabinets on two adjoining walls. It can be efficient, especially in a large room.

A U-shaped kitchen is a continuous row of appliances and cabinets on three adjoining walls. It usually has the least walking distance between appliances, and it is a very desirable plan because it is more compact.

An island or peninsula kitchen plan is used in a large kitchen. It calls for a counter or island in what might otherwise be unused space. A peninsula or extension of one of the counters is a similar plan.

KITCHEN STORAGE

Storage is very important in kitchen plans. You may not be able to add storage space in a small kitchen, but you can make better use of the space you have by organizing it well. Storage aids, which can help solve some of your space problems, are available in most housewares departments. Storage tips on page 339 list other space-saving techniques.

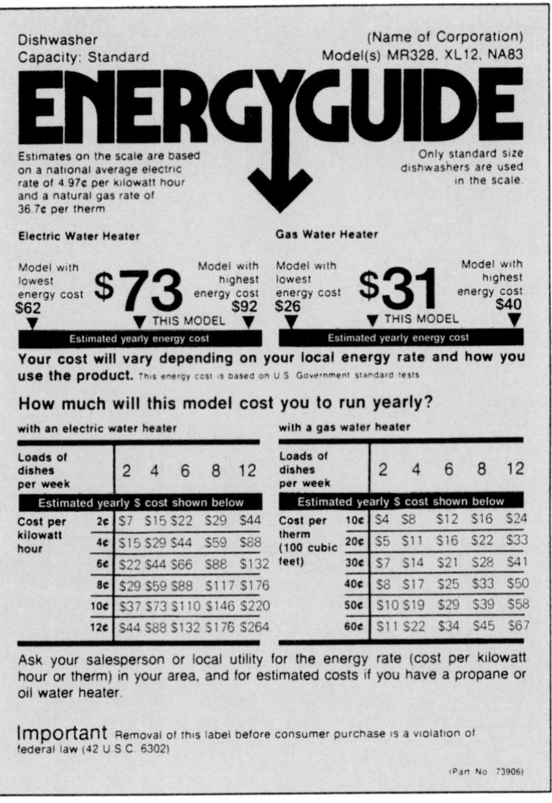

Dishwasher (Name of Corporation)
Capacity: Standard Model(s) MR328, XL12, NA83

ENERGYGUIDE

Estimates on the scale are based on a national average electric rate of 4.97¢ per kilowatt hour and a natural gas rate of 36.7¢ per therm.

Only standard size dishwashers are used in the scale.

Electric Water Heater

Model with lowest energy cost $62 — $73 THIS MODEL — Model with highest energy cost $92

Estimated yearly energy cost

Gas Water Heater

Model with lowest energy cost $26 — $31 THIS MODEL — Model with highest energy cost $40

Estimated yearly energy cost

Your cost will vary depending on your local energy rate and how you use the product. This energy cost is based on U.S. Government standard tests

How much will this model cost you to run yearly?

with an electric water heater

Loads of dishes per week		2	4	6	8	12
Estimated yearly $ cost shown below						
Cost per kilowatt hour	2¢	$7	$15	$22	$29	$44
	4¢	$15	$29	$44	$59	$88
	6¢	$22	$44	$66	$88	$132
	8¢	$29	$59	$88	$117	$176
	10¢	$37	$73	$110	$146	$220
	12¢	$44	$88	$132	$176	$264

with a gas water heater

Loads of dishes per week		2	4	6	8	12
Estimated yearly $ cost shown below						
Cost per therm (100 cubic feet)	10¢	$4	$8	$12	$16	$24
	20¢	$5	$11	$16	$22	$33
	30¢	$7	$14	$21	$28	$41
	40¢	$8	$17	$25	$33	$50
	50¢	$10	$19	$29	$39	$58
	60¢	$11	$22	$34	$45	$67

Ask your salesperson or local utility for the energy rate (cost per kilowatt hour or therm) in your area, and for estimated costs if you have a propane or oil water heater.

Important Removal of this label before consumer purchase is a violation of federal law (42 U.S.C. 6302)

(Part No. 73906)

Use the information on energy guide labels to compare the annual operating costs between similar appliances.

SELECTING KITCHEN APPLIANCES

As you learn to cook, you will need to learn how to choose and use kitchen appliances. Appliances are grouped basically into two groups—major appliances and *portable* or small appliances.

MAJOR APPLIANCES

Major appliances include the refrigerator, range, dishwasher, food waste disposer, and trash compactor. They are usually your most costly items when furnishing a kitchen. Chapter 31 lists steps to take before buying appliances. Other things to consider are the energy and safety requirements of the appliances.

Energy Requirements

Energy guide labels that appear on most large appliances, such as refrigerators, freezers, and dishwashers, can give you an idea of how much it will cost to run the appliance for one year. The large figure in the center of the label is the energy-cost number. If you use this information, you can compare the operating costs of similar appliances. The appliance with the higher number will cost more to run.

The American Gas Association (AGA) seal is placed on tested gas appliances. The Underwriter's Laboratories (UL) seal certifies that an electrical appliance is safe to use.

GETTING RID OF KITCHEN CLUTTER

When you work in the kitchen, do you always have to search for the right knife, bowl, or measuring cup? Is your kitchen disorganized and full of clutter? If it is, perhaps now is the time to get your kitchen organized. Use some of the space-saving suggestions below to solve your kitchen storage blues. Not only will you get rid of kitchen clutter, but it will also help you work more efficiently.

Drawers and Cupboards

- Use dividers in drawers to create distinct spaces for items. For instance, store all spatulas in one compartment, and cooking spoons in yet another compartment.
- Divide a deep drawer using vertical, or upright, dividers. This can provide practical storage for shallow items—cookie sheets, baking pans, muffin tins, pot tops, and trays.
- Use trays or baskets, and locking plastic organizers to make drawers turn into the shape you need.
- Add a portable sliding shelf to cabinets so that you can pull out the entire shelf and easily reach the items in the back.
- Install lazy susans or revolving shelves for corner cabinets or deep cupboards where items are hard to reach.

Undersink and Undercounter Storage Accessories

- Plastic dishpans and stacking bins can help you organize undersink clutter.
- Mount a paper towel dispenser to the inside of the cabinet door or mount a towel rack and hang towels and dishcloths.
- Attach storage bins under counters and use to store flour, sugar, and other staples.
- Attach door shelves to maximize your storage space. Use these shelves for lightweight, narrow items or for paper goods.

Walls

- Install pegboard or bulletin board on walls to expand storage space. Pegboard is both decorative and useful. It is a thin woodlike board with holes and special hooks inserted into the holes and it is used to hang utensils and tools.
- Hang a metal frame from the ceiling to display and/or hang, skillets, pots, and pans.
- Accessorize the kitchen with an attractive, matching spice rack. It not only serves as decoration but is also convenient.

Counter

- Knife storage requires some special thought. First, consider safety. Knives should not just be tossed into drawers with other utensils. A simple knife rack is the answer. There are knife holder blocks, hanging racks, or magnetic-strip racks available at department, cookware, or cutlery stores.
- In small kitchens with very limited storage space, equipment can be left on the counter covered or in containers within easy reach. Equipment that is used less often and some canned goods may have to be stored elsewhere in the home.

Safety

When buying gas and electric appliances, look for seals showing that the products meet required standards.

The **American Gas Association (AGA) seal** found on all gas appliances shows that the unit has been tested by the AGA laboratories. These products meet the safety and performance standards set up by the National Standards Institute.

The **Underwriters' Laboratories, Inc. (UL) seal** found on all electrical equipment and appliances shows that the unit has been tested and approved as being safe to use. These products have passed tests and are periodically looked at again for safety.

Refrigerator-Freezer

When you buy a refrigerator ask yourself these questions:

1. Does it provide the space you need for the kind and amount of food you buy?
2. Will it fit the space in your kitchen?
3. Is it easy to clean and are the shelves adjustable?
4. Does it have separate temperature controls for the refrigerator and freezer?

There are two types of regrigerator-freezers: a conventional model that has one outer door and a combination model that has two outer doors.

The conventional model has storage for fresh and frozen food. The frozen food compartment is found at the top and enclosed with a lightweight inner door. The freezer maintains a temperature around 12° C to −10° C (10° F. to 15° F.) and can be used to store already frozen foods up to two weeks. It is not cold enough to freeze fresh foods.

The combination model will have the freezer separated by a second door at the top, bottom, or on the side of the appliance. The freezer maintains a temperature of −18° C (0° F.) and can be used to store fresh or already frozen foods.

Refrigerators can be bought as manual defrost, automatic defrost, or frostless. Manual defrost models, the least costly, must be manually defrosted on a regular basis. The refrigerator part of the automatic defrost appliance will defrost itself. But the freezer will have to be manually defrosted.

The frostless refrigerator, the most costly type of refrigerator, has no visible frost in either the refrigerator or freezer. Defrost water is drained automatically.

Range

A range usually has four surface cooking units that vary in size, an oven, and a broiler. The three types of ranges are the free-standing, built-in, and counter models.

The free-standing range varies in size from 60 to 100 cm (24 to 40 in.). Some have one oven and a broiler along with extra storage space, while others may have two ovens.

The built-in range has two separate units—oven and surface cooking units—built into kitchen cabinets.

Counter model ovens are small appliances that can be kept on a counter. They can be a conventional oven or a microwave oven.

Some ranges have self-cleaning ovens. There are two types—self-cleaning and continuous-cleaning.

What ways can you conserve energy when using the major appliances, such as the refrigerator, range, and dishwasher?

The self-cleaning oven has a control and lock to start the cleaning process. The oven reaches a very high temperature, over 380° C (750° F.), to clean. This feature adds to the cost of the range.

The continuous-cleaning oven has a special coating on the oven walls, usually dark, dull, and lightly rough. Food spatters will spread on the coating and oxidize over a period of time. This feature adds to the cost, but not as much as self-cleaning ovens.

Other features found on ranges are clocks, timers, automatically controlled ovens, electric outlets, thermostatically controlled surface units, and oven/broiler rotisseries.

Ranges are either gas or electric. Both types perform well. You may have your choice of either, but in some areas or homes, you may be limited to only one fuel source.

Microwave Oven

A microwave oven can reduce cooking time. The oven cooks food with waves of energy called microwaves. A magnetron, which produces these waves, is found in the oven.

When foods are cooked in a microwave oven, they do not brown. Thus, some ovens are available that include a browning unit.

Other features available on microwave ovens are temperature probes, variable powers, rotating lower shelves, oven racks, and steam-sensing controls. Ask a salesperson to show you the various features, and then you can decide what features you would use most often.

Dishwasher

The automatic dishwasher not only helps with postmeal cleanup, but it also improves sanitation in the kitchen. There are two types of dishwashers—built-in and portable.

The built-in dishwasher is installed under the kitchen counter. The portable model has casters so it can be rolled to the sink for use and stored wherever convenient. Dishwashers are available as top-loading or front-loading. The front-loading ones can be built into cabinets or closets.

Dishwashers have a number of cycles and features, depending on the model and manufacturer. Washer cycles include the following: normal, short, or single-wash cycles for average soiled loads; power scrub for heavily soiled pots, pans, or casseroles; gentle for fine china and crystal; and plate warmer to warm plates just before serving a hot meal.

BENEFITS OF SMALL EQUIPMENT

Portable appliances, which can be moved from one place to another, include toasters, coffee makers, blenders, food processors, and electric skillets.

Portable appliances can make cooking easier. For instance, it is easier to grate large amounts of cheese in a food processor than with a hand grater. Other portable appliances save energy. Baking two potatoes in a toaster oven uses less energy than baking two potatoes in a conventional oven. Some portable appliances increase cooking capacity. For example, if all the surface units on a range are in use, a coffee maker lets the cook brew coffee at the same time.

Before you buy a portable appliance, be sure that you do not have one that does a similar job. For instance, you can crush crackers into fine crumbs using a blender or a food processer. An electric skillet can fry, roast, or simmer foods. If the skillet has a broiling element, it will also broil. Some mixers have blender and meat grinding attachments that increase their versatility .

Portable appliances can reduce the amount of time it takes to prepare a meal, as well as save energy.

CARING FOR KITCHEN EQUIPMENT

Before you use a new appliance, read the owner's manual that comes with it. It will give you the use and care instructions and tell you always to use the piece of equipment only for its intended use.

If you are replacing an appliance, do not assume that the new one works the same way. And when using any electrical appliance, follow the safety procedures listed on page 347.

FOOD PREPARATION TOOLS

Kitchen equipment includes cooking and baking utensils as well as hand tools used to measure, mix, and prepare food. When you start to equip your first kitchen, choose utensils that will serve many purposes. For instance, an ovenproof bowl can be used to mix food, bake a casserole, and as a serving dish.

When you buy a kitchen tool, be sure it meets your needs. Consider storage space and the cost of an item in relation to its use. Look for well-constructed tools that will stand up under use. Good tools seldom have to be replaced.

Kitchen tools can be grouped by how and when you use them. You will need some tools to help you prepare food before it is cooked. For instance, you will need tools to cut, peel, and grate foods. You will need other tools with which to measure, cook, and bake. You may also want some special tools for special jobs. For instance, you can crush garlic with a knife, but a garlic press makes the job easier. The chart on pages 342-344 lists the types and uses of the various kitchen tools.

PREPARATION TOOLS	
Liquid measuring cups have handles and pouring lips, and are used to measure liquid ingredients. They have a pouring spout and a small headspace at the top to prevent spills. They show measures on the sides—ounces and cups on one side and liters on the other. They come in 240-ml and 480-ml (1- and 2-cup) sizes.	
Dry measures are used to measure dry ingredients such as flour and sugar. Dry measures are available in a set of four cups—¼ cup, ⅓ cup, ½ cup, and 1 cup. A set of metric measures includes 50 ml, 125 ml, and 250 ml.	
Measuring spoons are used to measure small amounts of liquid and dry ingredients. They come in a set of four spoons—¼ teaspoon, ½ teaspoon, 1 teaspoon, and 1 tablespoon. A set of small metric measures includes 1 ml, 2 ml, 5 ml, 15 ml, and 25 ml sizes.	
Hand egg beaters or **wire whisks** are handy to have for ease of mixing batters. Egg beaters should be comfortable to hold and should turn easily. Whisks usually are made of metal and are used for medium and lightweight beating jobs.	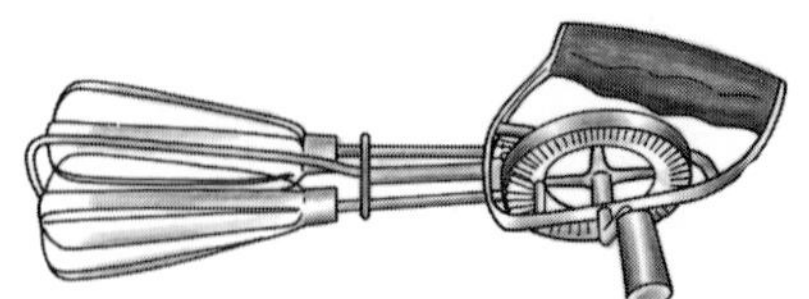
Cooking spoons and **forks** should have extra long, heat-resistant handles. Extra long handles help keep hands away from hot food, steam, and spattering fat. Spoons may be solid or perforated.	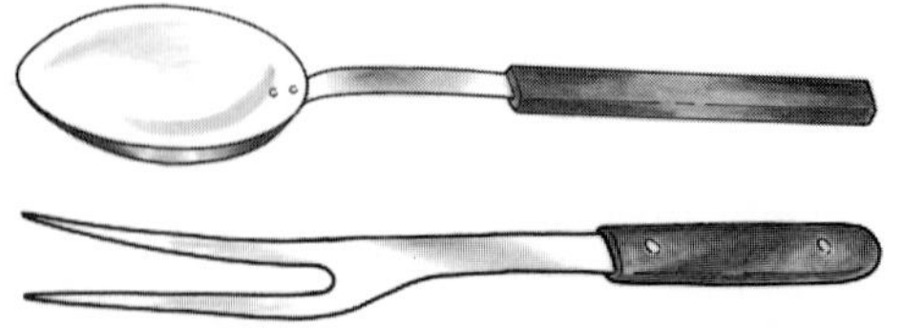

Metal tongs make it easy to turn hot food in a pan or to remove it from hot fat.

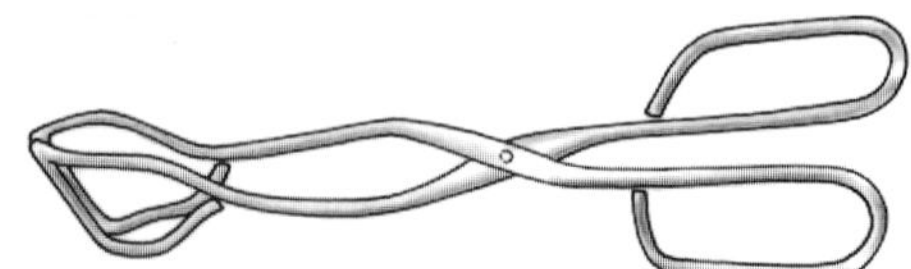

A set of **mixing bowls,** made of glass, earthenware, stainless steel, or aluminum should be part of a well-equipped kitchen. Glass and earthenware bowls chip and break easily, so they must be handled with care. Aluminum will darken egg white mixtures.

A selection of **knives** will make kitchen work much easier. Knife handles can be wood, plastic, or a combination of wood and plastic. The handle portion of the blade should extend into the handle at least one-third of the way and be attached with at least two rivets.

COOKING AND BAKING TOOLS

Saucepans usually have one handle while pots have two. They come in assorted sizes and may have lids to match. Pans can be made of metal, glass, or metal covered with enamel. Pots are usually made of metal.

Fry pans can be made of metal or glass ceramic. They also come in assorted sizes, usually given in inch diameter, such as ten inches. Some will have matching lids.

Casseroles can be made of many different materials, usually measured by quart sizes. Most come with matching lids.

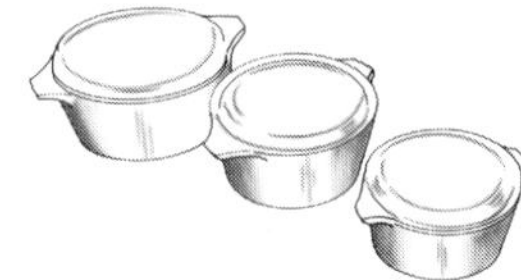

Baking pans are usually made of metal but some are made of ovenproof glass. There are different types of specialized pans for baking, such as bread pans, cake pans, cookie sheets, pie pans, or angel food cake pans.

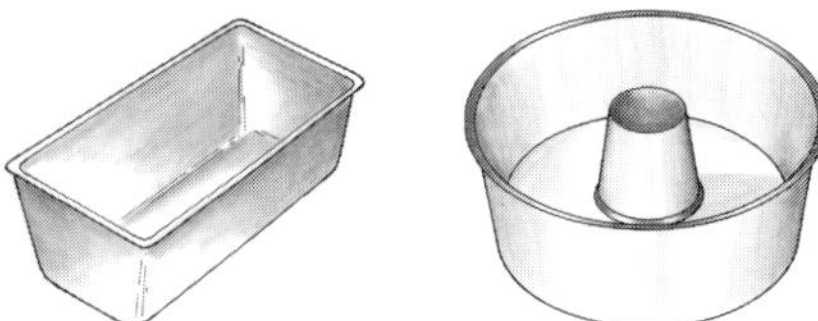

Roasting pans are large, heavy pans either rectangular or oval. Usually they will have a trivet or metal rack.

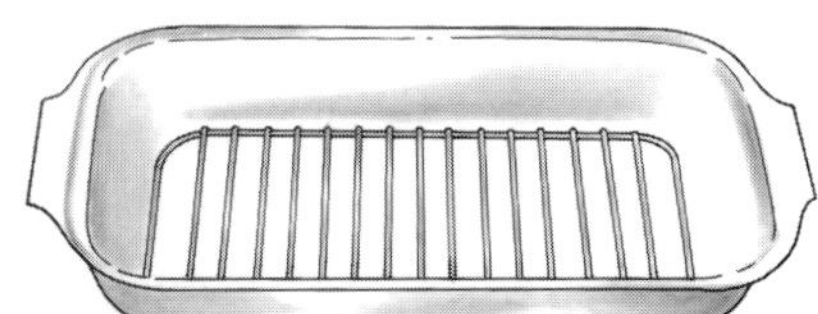

SPECIALTY TOOLS	
A **colander** is a large perforated bowl for draining liquid from food such as cooked spaghetti.	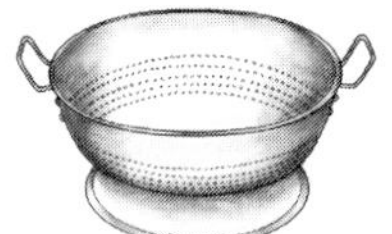
Thermometers—Meat thermometers measure the internal temperature of roasts and poultry to show when food is cooked. Candy thermometers measure the temperature of sugar syrup in a pan, and fit inside pan. Deep-fat thermometers measure the temperature of oil for deep-fat frying. Oven thermometers measure the temperature inside the oven.	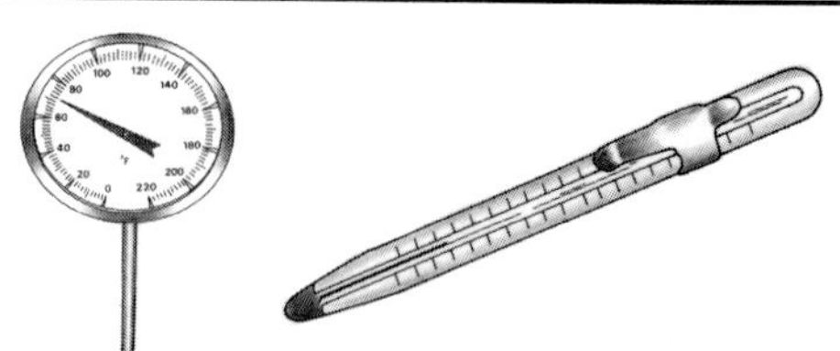
Wire cooling racks are used for cooling cookies, cakes, and breads.	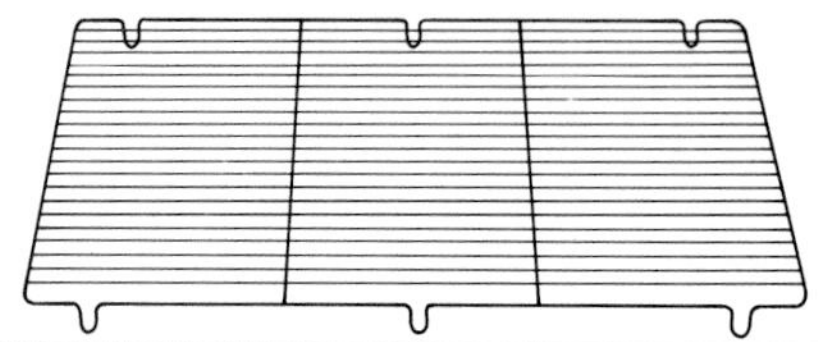
Steamers are used for steaming food, such as vegetables.	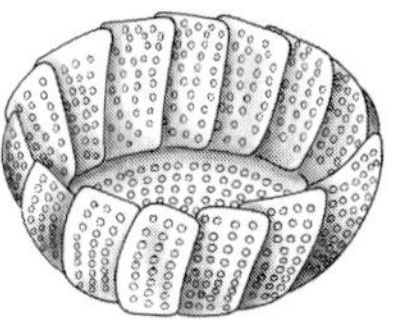
Graters are used to grate, shred, or slice vegetables and cheese.	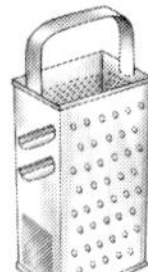
Flour sifters are used for sifting and adding air to flour and other dry ingredients. Mixes dry ingredients.	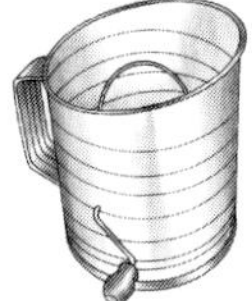
Kitchen shears are used for cutting dried fruits and vegetables, trimming fresh herbs, and cutting pastry.	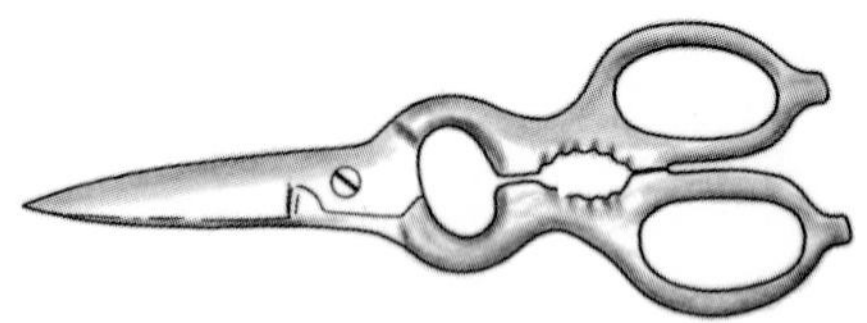

SYMBOLS AND ABBREVIATIONS

Metric Symbols	Customary Abbreviations	
milliliter . . . . mL	teaspoon . . . . tsp.	quart . . . . qt.
liter L	tablespoon . . . . Tbsp.	gallon . . . . gal.
gram . . . . g	cup . . . . c.	ounce . . . . oz.
degrees Celsius . . . . . . °C	pint . . . . pt.	pound . . . . lb.
	degrees Fahrenheit . . °F	

READING A RECIPE

A **recipe** is one of the most important tools in food preparation. It is like a road map that gives you directions. If followed properly, you will end up with an attractive and good-tasting food dish. A recipe should give you the following information:

1. A list of ingredients and amounts of each. Ingredients should be listed in the order in which you will use them. Amounts may be given in volume measures, such as milliliters (cups or spoons), or as a certain number of pieces, such as two eggs.
2. Specific instructions for combining ingredients. The instructions should be given step by step and clearly stated so you know what you are to do.
3. How long and at what temperature to cook the food.
4. What size of pan to use and how many servings you can expect to get.

Before you start to cook, always read through the entire recipe. Check to see that you have all the ingredients, tools, and skills needed for the recipe. Be sure you know exactly what you will need to do. If you are not sure what a term means, look it up in a cookbook or a dictionary.

Some recipes are written with standard symbols and abbreviations. You will save time if you memorize the meaning of these abbreviations.

BASIC EQUIVALENTS

3 teaspoons	= 1 tablespoon
1½ teaspoons	= ½ tablespoon
2 tablespoons	= 1 (fluid) ounce
4 tablespoons	= ¼ cup = 2 ounces
5 tablespoons + 1 teaspoon	= ⅓ cup = 2⅔ ounces
8 tablespoons	= ½ cup = 4 ounces
10 tablespoons + 2 teaspoons	= ⅔ cup = 5⅓ ounces
12 tablespoons	= ¾ cup = 6 ounces
16 tablespoons	= 1 cup = 8 ounces
2 cups	= 1 pint = 16 ounces
4 cups	= 2 pints = 1 (liquid) quart = 32 ounces
4 (liquid) quarts	= 1 gallon

MEASURING UP

Most recipes list exact amounts of the ingredients you need to use. These exact amounts, called **measurements,** are needed to get the best results.

Measurements can be given in grams, liters, pounds, ounces, cups, teaspoons, or tablespoons. When you measure ingredients, choose the right measuring tool for the ingredient and amount that you are working with.

To measure dry ingredients, such as flour and sugar, choose the right size of measuring cup for the ingredient. Spoon or scoop the ingredient lightly into the cup. Do not pack down unless the recipe so states. Level off the top with a spatula or the straight edge of a knife.

To measure liquid ingredients, choose a liquid measuring cup. Set the cup on a level surface and pour in the liquid. Check the measurement at eye level. Do not hold the cup in your hand or look down to check the measurement because either practice is likely to give you an inaccurate measure.

After filling a dry measuring cup, level off the ingredient with a straight-edge spatula or a knife. This will give you an accurate measurement.

When measuring liquid ingredients, always place the cup on a flat surface and check the measurement at eye level.

If you want to double a recipe, it is a good idea to write the doubled measurements on a piece of paper so that you do not forget to double any one ingredient. Measure all ingredients ahead of time, and then check your recipe a second time before you mix the ingredients to be sure that you have doubled all ingredients.

To cut a recipe in half, you need to understand measurement equivalents. Suppose a recipe calls for a tablespoon of sugar. If you know that one tablespoon equals three teaspoons, then you will know how much sugar to add. One-half of three teaspoons or one and one-half teaspoons equal one-half tablespoon.

Sometimes a recipe calls for an ingredient that you do not have on hand. Many cookbooks have a special section that lists substitutes for ingredients. Remember, when you use one ingredient in place of another, the end result may be a little different. For instance, margarine can be used in place of butter, but the taste of the product may be slightly different.

METRIC MEASUREMENTS

Measuring with the metric system is easy. It is less confusing because all of its measurements are based on the number ten. For example:

100 millileters = 1 cup
1,000 milliliters = 1 liter

To use metric measurements, use metric measuring tools. Metric measuring cups come in a set of 50 ml, 125 ml and 250 ml sizes. Liquid measures are available in 250 ml, 500 ml, and 1,000 ml. Small measures (spoons) are also available in sizes 1 ml, 2 ml, 5 ml, 15 ml and 25 ml. A metric scale is used to measure grams and kilograms of ingredients.

SAFETY IN THE KITCHEN

A kitchen that is clean, neat, and safe makes work more enjoyable. In that kind of kitchen, you can work more efficiently. You can also avoid accidents and keep food safe to eat.

Most kitchen accidents happen when cooks are in a hurry, when they are careless, or when they misuse their equipment. The accidents that usually occur are cuts and burns, spills, and electric shocks. As you work in the kitchen, keep safety in mind. Develop safe work habits to reduce your chances of an accident.

PREVENTING CUTS

To prevent cuts, do the following:

1. Be careful when you handle knives. Never pick up a knife by the blade. Always hold the handle and keep the blade pointing away from your body. As you cut food, cut down and away from yourself. Use a cutting board to protect the counter, and keep your fingers away from the blade.
2. Never soak knives. Wash, rinse, and dry knives right away. Do not wash in the dishwasher unless the handle is heat and moisture resistant.
3. Store knives in a knife rack or a separate container. Do not store them loose in a drawer.
4. Sweep up broken glass right away and wrap it in newspaper before you throw it away. Never pick up pieces with bare fingers. Instead, use two or three damp paper towels to pick up small pieces of glass.
5. When opening cans, cut off the lids completely and throw them away.

When cutting food, cut down and away from yourself. Use a cutting board to protect the counter, and keep your fingers away from the blade.

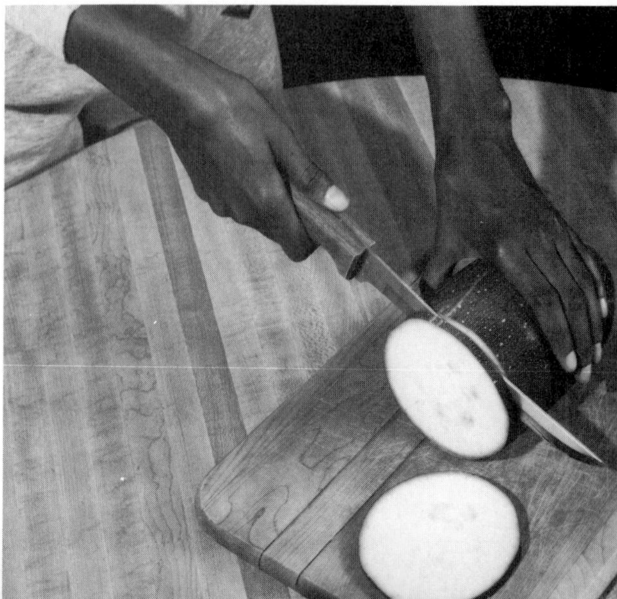

PREVENTING FALLS AND SPILLS

To prevent falls and spills, do the following:

1. Use pot holders to lift containers with hot handles or to remove lids from pans.
2. Clean up spills right away to prevent someone slipping on the food.
3. Use a firm stepstool to reach for objects in high places.
4. Secure rugs with nonskid backing.

PREVENTING BURNS

To prevent burns, do the following:

1. Turn pan handles away from the outer edge of the range to prevent pans from being knocked off the range.
2. When uncovering a pan, make sure you lift the lid away from your body to cause the steam to rise away from your face.
3. Use pot holders to handle hot utensils.
4. Avoid loose garments and long sleeves that could easily catch on fire.
5. Keep long hair pulled back and away from any flame.
6. Unplug a heated appliance right after use and allow it to cool before you clean and store it.
7. Never try to put out a grease fire with water. Use a fire extinguisher or smother the flame with salt or baking soda.

PREVENTING ELECTRIC SHOCKS

To prevent electric shocks, do the following:

1. Turn off the appliance before you disconnect it from a wall outlet. When disconnecting it, always pull the plug and not the cord.
2. Keep electric cords in good repair. Do not use cords that are frayed.
3. Never immerse an appliance in water unless it is unplugged and labeled "immersible." You can damage the appliance and create a safety hazard.
4. Never handle switches or appliance controls with wet hands. Keep water away from electrical appliances and their cords.

KITCHEN FIRST AID

The most common kitchen injuries are cuts and burns. When you cut yourself, it is important to control the bleeding and prevent infection. If the cut is small, wash it with soap and water. Then apply a mild **antiseptic** that will help prevent infection. Cover the cut with a bandage, and keep the wound dry while it heals. Deep cuts are more serious and should be treated by a doctor.

A burn is a painful experience. The basic rule is to keep the burned area away from direct contact with air. To relieve the pain, run cold water over the burn. Or you can apply ice wrapped in a clean cloth to the burned area. Keep the burned area cold until it no longer hurts. See a doctor for serious burns, especially if the skin is broken.

FOOD SAFETY

Have you ever had an upset stomach or stomach cramps? You may have thought you had a small case of the flu. Perhaps you did, but it is also quite possible that you had food poisoning, also known as **food-borne disease.** Experts say that 2 million cases of food-borne disease occur in the United States each year. Food contaminated with harmful bacteria does not always have an odor or an off flavor. Thus, many people are not aware of the real cause of their illness.

It is important for you to learn how to handle food so that it does not spoil or become contaminated. Most foods will perish, which means that they will spoil if they are not stored properly. There are two keys to storing food so that it will not spoil.

One key is temperature, and the other is time. When foods, such as meats, poultry, and dairy products, are kept at temperatures where bacteria can multiply, food spoilage can occur. It has been said life starts at 40 and ends at 140. This is a good concept to keep in mind when you store food. Room temperature is an ideal temperature for bacterial growth. The longer food is kept at room temperature, the greater chances are for food to spoil. So keep perishable food below 40° F. to prevent bacterial growth. Once food is being cooked, get it to a temperature above 140° F. Then to assure the stopping of bacterial growth, keep food at this temperature until you are ready to serve it. Also, keep cold foods cold or refrigerated until you are ready to serve them. This will involve special plans when you prepare sack lunches, picnics, and outdoor camping events.

Perishable food should be stored in the refrigerator as soon as possible. Avoid leaving food at room temperature for more than an hour and store leftover foods right after meals.

BACTERIA THAT CAUSE FOOD POISONING

There are four kinds of bacteria that cause food poisoning. They are (1) Staphylococcus aureus (Staph), (2) Salmonella, (3) Clostridium perfringens, and (4) Clostridium botulinum. A chart on page 348 describes the causes and symptoms of these diseases.

SANITATION IN THE HOME

Sanitation in the home can prevent food-borne illness. It means keeping bacteria out of food through personal hygiene and proper food-handling procedures. It also means keeping the food at the proper temperatures so bacteria already present do not have a chance to multiply.

Bacteria enters food in two ways. Some bacteria are naturally in the food when you buy it. Other bacteria get into food because of careless handling when it is prepared and served. To eliminate harmful bacteria in your food, use personal hygiene and keep foods at the right temperature.

Personal hygiene means keeping yourself clean so you do not pass along harmful bacteria to food you are handling. It is always important to scrub your hands with soap and hot water before you handle any food. Have a separate towel with which to dry your hands. Do not use the same towel to wipe dishes and counters as you do to wipe your hands. And always use a separate spoon to taste foods and to stir foods.

By following safety and sanitation principles each time you cook, taking the time to arrange and organize your work space, and learning to use kitchen tools and equipment, you can become a master in your own kitchen laboratory.

FOOD-BORNE ILLNESSES—CAUSE AND PREVENTION

Illness and Cause	Kind of Bacteria	Symptoms	Prevention
Salmonellosis. Caused by eating contaminated food or by coming in contact with a carrier.	*Salmonella.* Carried by insects, rodents, and pets, especially turtles, birds, dogs, and cats. Can live and grow in human digestive tract, causing disturbances. Grow and multiply at temperatures between 15°C and 52°C (60°F and 125°F).	Severe headache, followed by vomiting, diarrhea, abdominal cramps, and fever. Infants, elderly, and persons with low resistance most suseptible. Severe infections cause high fever and may even cause death.	• Wash raw foods thoroughly. • Keep hot foods hot—temperatures above 60°C (140°F) destroy bacteria. • Keep cold foods cold—temperatures below 4°C (40°F) do not kill bacteria but keep them from multiplying. • Keep hands, counters, and utensils clean. This stops spread and growth of salmonella.
Perfringens poisoning. Caused by eating food contaminated with abnormally large amounts of bacteria. Likely to occur when large amounts of food are not handled properly. This happens relatively often at large dinners not prepared by professional cooks, such as church suppers, community dinners.	*Clostridium perfringens.* Spore-forming bacteria grow in absence of oxygen. Spores are everywhere—in food, soil, dust, and sewage. Found in human intestinal tract and in warm-blooded animals. Cooking temperatures kill bacteria but not spores. Surviving bacteria continue to grow in cooked food if not kept at right temperatures.	Nausea without vomiting; diarrhea; acute inflamation of stomach and intestines.	• Serve cooked food immediately or keep at temperatures above 60°C (140°F) until ready to serve. • Serve cold food immediately or keep refrigerated at temperatures below 4°C (40°F) until ready to serve. • To store cooked meat, refrigerate promptly.
Staphylococcal poisoning. Caused by eating food containing the toxin.	*Staphyloccocus aureus.* Transmitted by food handlers who carry bacteria. These bacteria are fairly resistant to heat. They grow in food and produce a toxin that is extremely resistant to heat. Bacteria grow fastest and produce most toxin at temperatures between 15°C and 52°C (60°F and 125°F).	Vomiting, diarrhea, prostration (tired feeling), abdominal cramps. Generally mild and often attributed to other causes.	• Bacteria growth stopped by keeping hot foods above 60°C (140°F) and cold foods below 4°C (40°F). • Toxin is destroyed by boiling for several hours or heating food in pressure cooker at 116°C (240°F) for 30 minutes. • Cleanliness prevents spread of bacteria.
Botulism. Caused by eating food containing the toxin.	*Clostridium botulinum.* Spore-forming bacteria that grow and produce a deadly toxin. Bacteria are found in soil and water. Spores are harmless but extremely heat resistant. In absence of oxygen, as in a sealed container, and with low-acid foods present, spores germinate. If canned food is not properly processed, bacteria produce toxin in sealed container. They can also produce toxin in improperly prepared or stored low acid foods.	Double vision; inability to swallow; speech difficulty; progressive paralysis of respiratory system. About 65 percent of people who get botulism in the United States die. Most cases caused by improper home-canning methods.	• In home-canning, low-acid foods must be processed in pressure canner to destroy spores. Toxin is destroyed by boiling for 10 or 20 minutes; time required depends on kind of food. • Never taste or eat food from a can that is bulging, damaged, or leaking. Never eat food that does not look or smell normal. Destroy such food so children and animals cannot get to it.

WORDS TO REMEMBER

American Gas Association (AGA)
antiseptic
food-borne disease
measurements
portable appliances
recipe
Underwriters Laboratories (UL)
work centers
work flow
work triangle

CHECKING YOUR UNDERSTANDING

1. What are the three main work centers of a work triangle? What items should be stored at each center? Name two other centers that can be included in a kitchen if space permits.
2. Explain the difference between the work triangle and the work flow. How can a small work triangle help the cook be more efficient?
3. What are the major appliances in the kitchen? How do they differ from the small appliances? Why should more thought and comparison be given when buying large appliances.
4. What safety precautions should a person take when working in the kitchen? What types of accidents occur most often in the kitchen?
5. List four kinds of bacteria that cause food poisoning. How can food poisoning be prevented?

APPLYING YOUR UNDERSTANDING

1. Collect pictures of different kitchens. Analyze the work triangle and the various work centers in each. Which kitchens seem most efficient? Which ones have the best storage arrangements? Create a plan for your "dream kitchen."
2. Visit a store that sells major appliances. Choose one type of appliance and compare the purchase price and operating cost of the most costly and least costly models. What special features does the best model have? What do the energy guide labels on the appliances tell you.
3. Make a list of all the tools in your home or school kitchen. Note where they are stored and how often they are used. Suggest ways to improve the organization of the kitchen.
4. Practice doubling and dividing recipes. Choose three recipes and identify the parts of the recipes. Then double and divide the ingredients in half.
5. Develop a lesson to teach children about food and safety in the kitchen.

Chapter 26 FOOD PREPARATION

Has this ever happened to you?

Sam, Terry's older brother, has come over to ask for some help from his mom and sister.

"Mom, I really need to do something special for my friends. They have had me over to their apartments for dinner several times. I want to invite them to my place and fix a nice meal, but I don't know where to begin," Sam said. "You make fixing a meal look so easy. Can you help me find an easy way to make an inexpensive meal?"

"We can begin by deciding on the menu and recipes that you will be using," suggested Sam's mother. "A slow cooking stew that could be started early on the day of the party is one idea. You could use a cheap cut of meat and serve the stew with a simple salad and cornbread. However, it's probably a good idea if Terry and I went over the recipes to be sure that you understand how each one is put together."

"Mom, Sam probably doesn't even know the difference between sauteeing, simmering, and boiling," chided Terry.

"Like I said, I need to start with the basics," agreed Sam. "Do you think there's hope for me?"

"Sure there is," smiled his mother. "With a few lessons and some easy-to-prepare menus, you'll be serving gourmet meals in no time!"

What makes a good cook? Have you ever wished you had more cooking skills?

Do you think that everyone can learn the skills needed to become a good cook?

After reading this chapter, you will be able to

- understand the importance of choosing the correct method for preparing fruits, vegetables, protein foods, dairy foods, and grain products to bring out their best flavor, color, and texture;
- explain how to prepare food to conserve the most nutrients for the food dollar;
- define terms commonly used in recipes;
- select the correct method for cooking fruits, vegetables, protein foods, dairy foods, and grain products.

Do you have a science lab in your home? You probably do but do not know it. In many ways, your home kitchen is like a science lab. In the kitchen, chemicals (foods) are heated, cooled, mixed, and dissolved. Scientific formulas—or recipes—tell you what materials you need and how to use them. One wrong step may turn the entire "experiment" into a failure.

Cooking means heating food to the proper temperature so that certain pleasant changes take place in the food. If too much heat is used, however, the food can burn or scorch. If not enough heat is used, the food may be partly raw.

For best results learn the difference between boiling and simmering. Boiling means the bubbles in the liquid rise up continuously and break the surface of the liquid. Simmering means the bubbles come up to the surface slowly but do not break the surface.

COOKING METHODS

You can use several different methods for cooking. These include cooking in liquid or in moist heat, cooking in dry heat, cooking in fat, and cooking in a microwave oven.

COOKING IN LIQUID OR MOIST HEAT

The difference between cooking in liquid and moist heat is the amount of liquid used. If you are cooking in liquid, you cover the food with liquid. Examples of this type of cooking are boiling, simmering, braising, stewing, and poaching.

To **boil** means to cook in liquid at a temperature high enough so that the liquid bubbles. The bubbles rise to the surface and break.

To **simmer** means to cook in liquid at a temperature below boiling. Tiny bubbles form slowly on the bottom or sides of the pan. They break before they reach the surface.

Braising and stewing are two ways to simmer foods. Braised foods are cooked slowly in a small amount of liquid in a covered pot. Stewed foods are cut into small pieces, covered with liquid, and simmered in a large pot. The pot may or may not be covered.

Delicate foods like fish and eggs can be **poached.** To poach, cook the food in hot or simmering liquid. There should be enough liquid in the pan so the food can float. Handle the food carefully so it keeps its shape.

Cooking in moist heat means using little or no liquid in a pan with a tight-fitting lid. The food cooks in liquid and steam created during the cooking process. A lid is needed to keep the steam in the pan. Steaming, cooking in plastic bags, and cooking in a pressure cooker are methods of cooking with moist heat.

Some foods, such as vegetables and fish, taste especially good when they are **steamed.** To steam food, place it on a rack or in a basket. Then put the rack or basket in a deep pot with a small amount of water. The water should not touch the food or the rack. Cover the pot, and bring the water to a boil. The steam from the water cooks the food.

Many kinds of foods are cooked in moist heat or liquid. Less tender cuts of meat and poultry need the moisture to make them moist and tender. Starchy vegetables and grains such as potatoes and rice need large amounts of liquid because the starch absorbs liquid as it cooks.

Effect on Nutrients

Cooking in liquid or moist heat greatly affects water-soluble vitamins and minerals. It pulls these nutrients out of the food. The more liquid in the pan, the more nutrients it draws out. Longer cooking and higher temperatures also mean greater loss of nutrients.

Foods cooked in steam tend to lose the least amount of nutrients because the food is not actually in the water. The food is suspended above the water, which boils to create steam to cook the food.

COOKING IN DRY HEAT

Cooking in dry heat means to cook food uncovered without any liquid or fat added. This method includes cooking in the broiler and oven and on an outdoor grill. As food cooks in dry heat, fat drips away. The food has a crispy crust and is moist and tender on the inside.

The most common terms used in oven cookery are baking and roasting. Baking means to cook in an oven. Foods such as cookies, breads, pies, cakes, and casseroles are baked.

Roasting also means to cook in an oven. But the term often refers to cooking meats or poultry in the oven. The meat or poultry may rest on the pan bottom or on a rack. A thermometer can be used to determine how well done, or cooked, the meat is.

Food is **broiled** in the broiling unit. Food is placed on a broiling pan, which is placed directly under the heat source (element or gas flame).

Roasts and poultry can be basted with juices, seasoned broth, or special sauces. Basting helps to keep food from drying out while cooking. To baste, spoon or brush liquid on the food several times while the food is cooking.

Only tender cuts of meat, poultry, and fish can be cooked in dry heat. Foods with little or no fat, such as lean fish, must be brushed (or basted) with fat or sauce to keep them from drying out.

Effect on Nutrients

Some nutrients are lost in juices that drip from meat and poultry. If the food is overcooked, the protein can become tough, dry, and difficult to digest.

Fat drips away as meat and poultry cook in dry heat. That means fewer calories in the food. If you are watching your weight, you may prefer a dry-heat method for cooking.

COOKING IN FAT

Food that is **deep-fat fried** is cooked in hot fat until it is brown. Cooking in fat is usually called frying or grilling. Either solid fat or oil can be used for frying. You can deep-fat fry, panbroil, panfry, or sauté. The main difference is in the amount of fat used.

When you deep-fat fry (French fry), there should be enough fat for the food to float. The fat should be hot enough to cook the food quickly before the fat can soak into the food. Use a deep-fat thermometer to check the temperature of the fat before you add the food. If there is moisture on the surface of the food, use paper towels to pat the food dry before it is placed in the hot fat. Moisture can cause hot fat to splatter. This can cause a painful burn. Often food is dredged or breaded before it is deep-fat fried.

When you **panbroil,** there is little or no fat used. As fat melts from the food, it is poured off. Panbroiling refers only to preparing meat in an uncovered skillet.

Panfrying or sautéing is done in a skillet. You use only a small amount of fat to cover the bottom of the pan and heat it before you add the food. The food cooks slowly until done. You can panfry any food that cooks quickly such as eggs, poultry, tender cuts of meat, and fish.

When you sauté, only a small amount of fat is used. You cook the food slowly until done but not brown.

Fats and oils have a smoking point. The smoking point is the temperature at which fats and oils begin to break down and give off smoke. Nutrients are destroyed and an off-flavor develops. The fats and oils should not be used for further cooking. Use low or medium heat to keep fat from reaching the smoking point.

Effect on Nutrients

Some nutrients are lost when juices drip from the food. Fried foods soak up fat. The more fat in the pan and the longer they cook, the more fat the foods soak up. Added fat means added calories.

PREPARING AND SERVING FRUITS

The easiest way to serve fresh fruits is to wash them and place them in a bowl or basket. Whole fresh fruits served with cheese make a great dessert.

Low acid fruits such as apples, bananas, peaches, pears and avocados will turn brown when exposed to air. If using these fruits in a salad, coat them with lemon juice, to prevent discoloration, after you have cut them and before you add them to the salad.

Fruits with thin skins, such as apples, pears, and peaches, do not require peeling. But sometimes you may want to serve them without their skins. Apples and pears can be peeled with a paring knife or vegetable peeler.

The way a fruit is cooked will determine whether it will be soft or firm. Fruit cooked in a light syrup will hold its shape better. For instance, this method is used to cook pears. Pears cooked in water will become soft and break apart. If sugar is added, the pears will hold their shape. On the other hand, if you are making applesauce, you want the apples to be soft, so the sugar is added after the apples have been cooked. When cooking fruit, cook gently with as little water as possible. This will help retain nutrients.

Fresh fruit added to baked goods will give the batter an interesting texture and flavor with the bonus of extra nutrition. You might try using berries, sliced apples, or bananas in muffins or cookies for a different twist to your favorite recipes.

Peaches will peel better if they are blanched first. To blanch peaches, dip them into boiling water for a few seconds. Drain them and peel away the skins. To blanch tomatoes dip them in boiling water for 10 seconds before peeling.

PREPARING AND SERVING VEGETABLES

Vegetables are versatile. They can be served raw or cooked in many different ways. Raw vegetables can be served with dips and sauces. Most salads are made with raw vegetables. You can cook vegetables by steaming, boiling, frying, baking, broiling, or deep-fat frying. Vegetables can be creamed, scalloped, or added to casseroles, soups, and stews.

Vegetables will need to be washed, and most will need some peeling or trimming before they are used. After cleaning and trimming vegetables, you can cut them into slices, strips, chunks, or cubes. It is best to cut vegetables just before you are ready to cook or serve them to preserve nutrients.

The color of some vegetables is affected by how they are cooked. For instance, green vegetables such as broccoli and green beans can change from a bright green to a dull olive color depending on what temperature is used to cook them and what acids are present during cooking. You can prevent this color change by cooking green vegetables quickly. Use a small amount of rapidly boiling water. Add the vegetables and cook until they are fork tender. Leave the pan lid off for the first few minutes of cooking. Then cover until the vegetables are done. Serve immediately. If they are left in the covered pan, they will continue to cook and turn olive green.

Red vegetables such as red cabbage may turn purple or blue during cooking. You can prevent this change by adding a small amount of acid (vinegar or cream of tartar) to the cooking water. Red vegetables are usually cooked with a small amount of water in a covered pan.

HOW TO COOK VEGETABLES

Cooked vegetables taste best when they retain their color, flavor, texture, and nutritional value. The basic guides for cooking vegetables are:

- Use as little water as possible to conserve flavor and nutrients which are lost in water during cooking.
- Depending on the recipe, try to cook vegetables in large pieces. This also prevents loss of flavor and nutrients.
- Keep cooking time short. Cook just until the vegetable is fork-tender (firm, but tender). Overcooking can destroy nutrients.
- In general use moderate heat. High heat destroys many vitamins.

There are many ways to cook vegetables so that they are both nutritious and tasty. Vegetables can be boiled or steamed. They can also be baked. Baking takes a longer time than boiling and steaming. Broiling, braising, stir-frying, and deep-fat frying are other methods used to cook vegetables.

MICROWAVE MAGIC

Sharpen your cooking skills and save time in the kitchen by cooking your favorite foods in a microwave oven. Not only will it reduce the cooking time and save on nutritional value, but it will also make cleanup a breeze!

Fruits and Vegetables

Because fruits are naturally juicy, the microwave preserves most of the water-soluble nutrients such as vitamin C. You can also defrost fruit in the microwave. Be sure to remove any metal or foil from the package and place the frozen fruit in a casserole. Be sure to check the cooking time and break the fruit up with a fork.

Microwave cooking is a good way to cook vegetables. The vegetables will stay crisp, yet tender, and keep their bright colors and most of their nutrient value. Nutritionists say that many microwaved vegetables lose fewer water-soluble vitamins than when cooked conventionally. This is due to a shorter cooking time and to using less water during the microwave process.

Protein Sources

Some meats can be microwave cooked with good results. If a beef cut is cooked in the microwave for over fifteen minutes, the fat will have time to rise to the surface and start browning naturally. Otherwise, for smaller, thin cuts of meat, toppings and coatings can be used to make the meat turn brown. Less tender cuts of meat, such as chuck, will need a longer microwave time at a lower power level to get good results.

Poultry can be cooked quickly in the microwave with moist, tender results. Since the outside of the meat will not brown you may want to cook poultry in a sauce or brush it with a browning agent to make it look more attractive. When prepared just plain, microwaved chicken is good for salads and casseroles.

Fish and shellfish are naturals to cook in the microwave. They will stay tender with little cooking to preserve their delicate flavor and texture. You will microwave cook many seafoods, especially the meatier types, just until the meat is flaky when it is poked with a fork, or fork tender.

Eggs will microwave quickly, and since they are a delicate food, they will toughen when overcooked. For best results, egg yolks and whites should be mixed together when microwaved, such as scrambled eggs. Do not cook eggs in the shell in the microwave oven.

Grain Products

The microwave can make some aspects of bread baking simpler, such as using it to defrost yeast doughs or to speed the rising process. However, breads baked in the microwave will not brown. Cereals can be prepared with ease in the microwave with good results. Pasta and rice will take just about as long to cook in the microwave as on the range top.

PREPARING AND SERVING PROTEIN SOURCES

Meat, poultry, fish, and eggs are the best sources of high-quality protein. Protein dishes are the most costly part of your food budget.

MEAT

The best way to cook meat depends on the tenderness and size of the cut. There are two main cooking methods: dry heat and moist heat. Dry-heat methods are best for tender cuts. Dry-heat methods include roasting, broiling, panbroiling, and panfrying. Less tender cuts should usually be cooked by a moist-heat method. The slow, moist heat helps to tenderize these cuts. Moist-heat methods include braising and cooking in liquid.

Meat shrinks as it cooks. It loses juices and becomes smaller in size. By carefully following directions for cooking meats, you can cut down on the amount of shrinkage. The meat will also be more moist and tasty.

Temperature is an important factor in cooking meat. High temperatures cause more juices to be lost. Therefore, shrinkage is greater.

POULTRY

Most poultry can be cooked using either dry- or moist-heat cooking methods. Dry-heat methods include frying, broiling, and roasting. Moist-heat methods include braising and stewing.

If you are going to stuff poultry, do so just before you cook it. If you try to get a head start on the meal by stuffing poultry early in the day, the warm stuffing provides just the right conditions for bacteria to grow. This can cause food poisoning. You can prepare stuffing in advance and store it in the refrigerator until you are ready to cook the bird.

FISH AND SHELLFISH

There are many ways to prepare fish and shellfish. You can use most of the methods used to cook meats. The most important thing to remember is that fish cooks quickly. When overcooked, fish becomes tough and dry, and the flavor is spoiled.

The texture of fish is an important guide to doneness. You can tell when fish is cooked by testing it with a fork. Press a fork against the thickest part of the cooked fish. If it starts to flake apart, it is done.

Meat thermometers are the best way to check the doneness of larger pieces of meat. The tip of the thermometer should be centered in the cut. For accurate reading the thermometer should not touch a bone or rest in fat.

EGGS

When you cook eggs, use low heat to keep them tender. If you use high heat or overcook the eggs, they become tough.

Eggs can be prepared five ways: cooked in the shell, fried, scrambled, poached, and baked. Eggs are useful in general cooking. Many recipes call for them to thicken custards, puddings, and sauces. Popovers and souffles depend on eggs for leavening. Meat loaf recipes rely on eggs to help bind ingredients together. Many dried foods are dipped first in beaten eggs and then in crumbs before they are fried. Sometimes a beaten egg is brushed on top of breads and cookies to give the baked product a shiny appearance and crust. Eggs are frequently used as a garnish for salads or plates of food.

PREPARING AND SERVING DAIRY PRODUCTS

The term dairy product includes both milk and milk products such as yogurt, sour cream, cheese, and ice cream. These are used in many ways. Milk can be served either plain or flavored with syrups, powders, or fruit. Milk can also be the basis for many soups, sauces, and desserts. Yogurt and cheese are eaten plain or used in cooking. Cream and sour cream are used in many recipes. Ice cream by itself is a good dessert. It can also be used with other foods to make frozen desserts and beverages.

Milk is a basic ingredient in a variety of recipes. When cooking with milk, three things can happen to cause a failure. A skin can form, the milk can curdle, or the milk can stick to the pan and scorch. Always cook milk over a low heat and stir constantly.

Cheese is another versatile food, which can be eaten plain, with fruit or crackers, or used in cooking as a main dish or as an ingredient. When cooking with cheese, remember that cheese will get stringy and tough if overcooked. Cheese has a low melting point. It is usually cut into pieces when used in cooking. Generally, recipes will call for cheese to be sliced, cubed, or grated.

When adding grated cheese to a sauce, wait until the last few minutes of cooking. When cheese is used as a topping for a casserole, it should be added during the last part of the cooking time.

When cooking milk or milk products, always use low heat and stir the milk to prevent scorching and a skin to form on the surface of the milk.

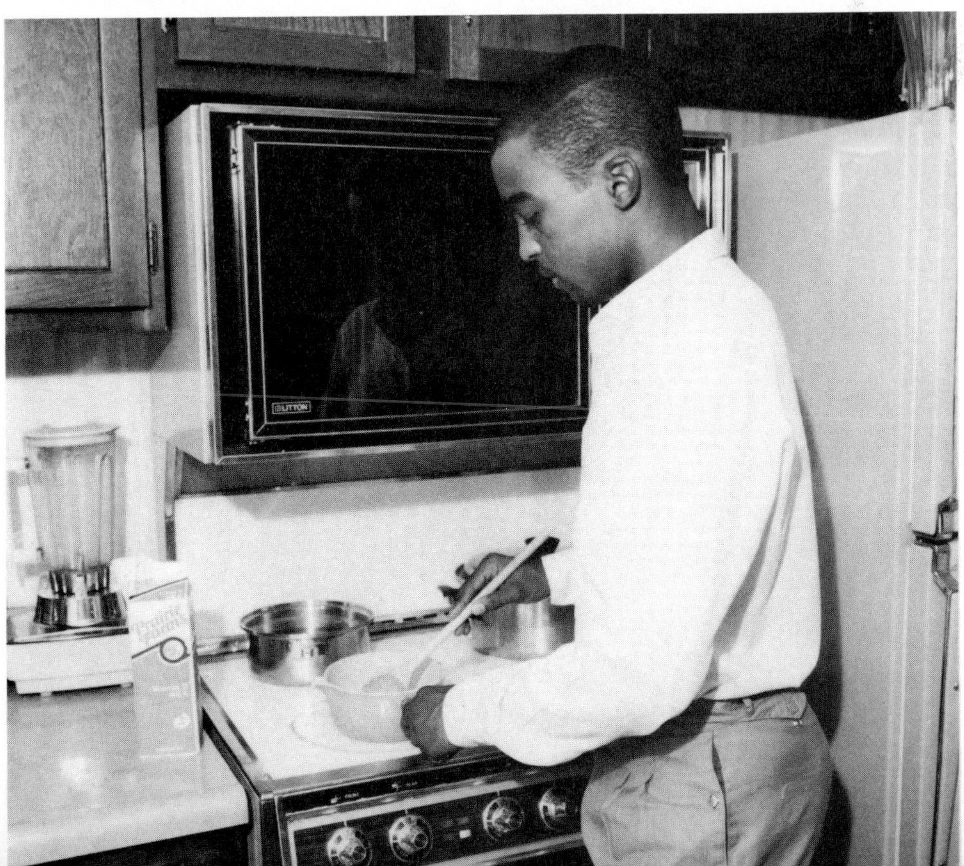

PREPARING AND SERVING GRAIN PRODUCTS

Grain products are used in many baked goods such as quick breads and yeast breads. However, other important grain products we often eat include pasta, rice, and cooked cereals. There are certain cooking techniques for you to learn when you prepare any grain product.

When you prepare bread products, they will be referred to as batters and doughs. These words describe the consistency or thickness of the flour mixtures.

Products such as pancakes and muffins are made from batters. Yeast breads and biscuits are made from doughs. Doughs are much thicker than batters.

QUICK BREADS

Quick breads are made with baking soda, baking powder, steam, air, or a combination of these leavening agents. Quick breads include muffins, biscuits, pancakes, and waffles. Also nut breads and some coffee cakes are quick breads. Quick bread describes the method that you will use to make these products. They are mixed quickly, just to moisten the ingredients. Usually the dry ingredients are combined in one bowl and the moist liquid ingredients are mixed in another bowl. You will make a "well" in the center of the dry mixture and pour the liquid mixture into it. Mix all ingredients together quickly. The batter will look lumpy, and you may think it is not mixed enough. But overmixing will cause the product to be tough with large holds or "tunnels" forming when it is cooked.

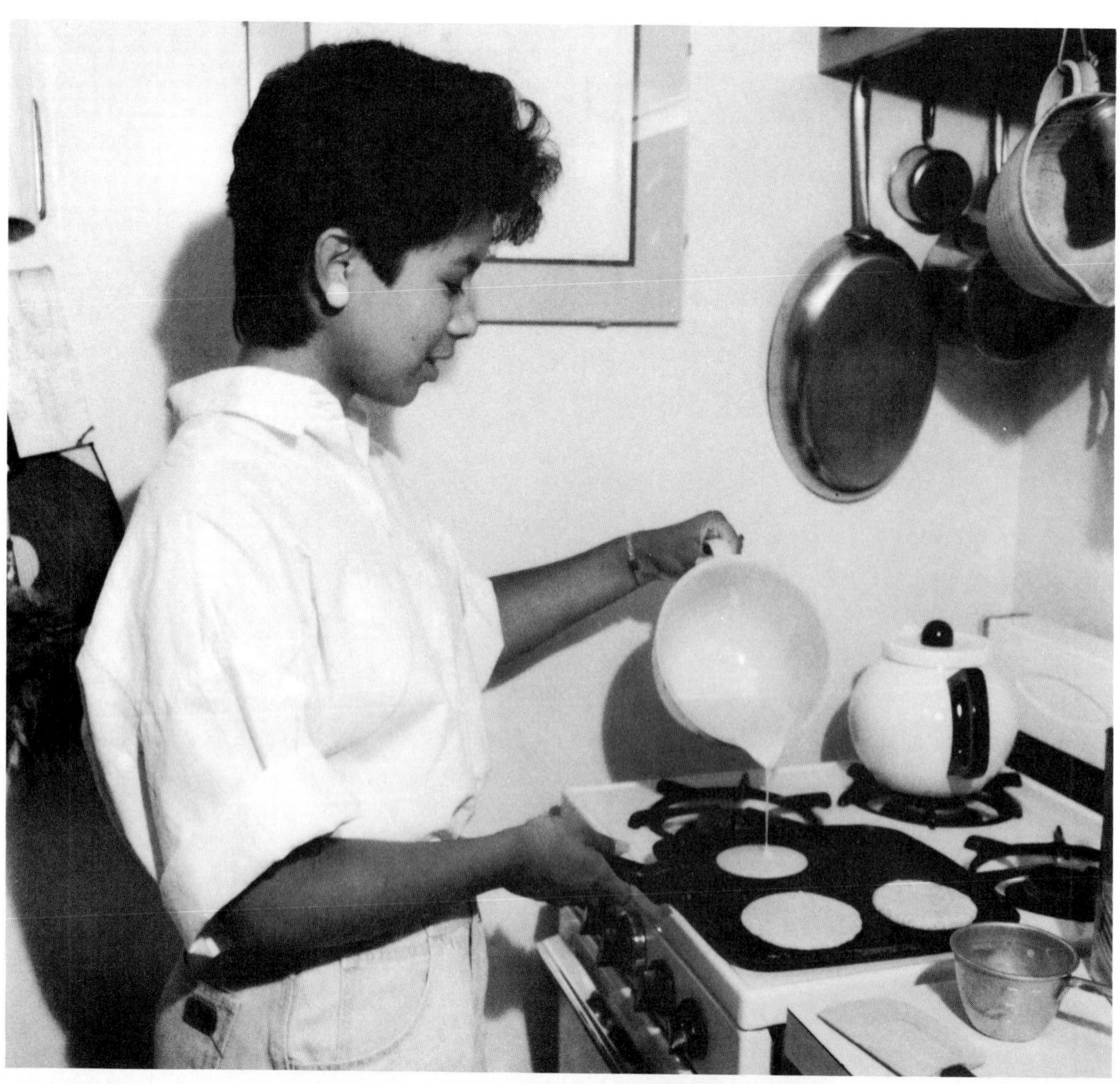

YEAST BREADS

The basic ingredient of yeast breads is yeast, which is the leavening. You can make plain yeast breads, dinner rolls, or specialty breads. Usually a yeast bread will include yeast, sugar, flour, liquid, shortening, and salt. Each of these ingredients performs a special (chemical) job.

Today there are many convenience products that make baking homemade bread much faster. There are brown-and-serve breads, mixes, frozen dough, and refrigerated doughs.

CEREALS

Nothing is more satisfying on a chilly morning than a steaming bowl of hot cereal. Cooked cereals should be smooth and creamy. When cereals are cooked, the starch granules absorb water or other liquid, which causes the granules to expand. To prevent lumps, you need to make sure that all the granules swell evenly so they will not stick together in clumps of uncooked cereal.

Usually, you will stir the dry cereal slowly into rapidly boiling water. Stirring and the bubbling, boiling water keep the granules apart until they have begun to swell. After all the cereal has been added to the boiling water, the heat should be lowered and the mixture cooked according to package directions. At the end of the cooking time, all the water should be absorbed, and the cooked cereal will be smooth.

PASTA

You will want to use large amounts of boiling water when you cook pasta. Use a large, deep pot so you will be able to have enough water. Heat the water to a rapid boil, add a little salt, and add the pasta. The bubbling, boiling water will keep the pasta pieces apart. Stir gently once or twice during cooking. The cooking time for pasta depends on the size and shape of the pieces.

RICE

The most important thing to remember when cooking rice is that it should be tender and fluffy. To help make rice cook perfectly, be sure to measure accurately and watch the cooking time carefully. Rice, like cereal, absorbs water and expands as it cooks. Always check the package for specific cooking directions.

Pasta should be cooked al denter or "to the bite." Simply take a sample of pasta out of the pot, cool it quickly under cold running water and bite into it. The pasta should be cooked through (no hard, white center), but still firm and chewy.

Review CHAPTER 26

WORDS TO REMEMBER

boil
braising
broiled
deep-fat fried
panbroil
panfrying
poached
roasting
simmer
steamed

CHECKING YOUR UNDERSTANDING

1. List the three basic methods for cooking food. Explain what happens to nutrients when each method is used.
2. Describe the procedure to follow when cooking vegetables to retain their color and texture.
3. What cuts of meat are considered tender and what cuts are considered to be less tender? How should tender cuts of meat be cooked? Less tender cuts?
4. List five different ways that eggs can be prepared for breakfast. Name other ways that eggs are used in recipes and explain their function in the recipe.
5. What types of leavening agents are used for quick breads? Name four food products that are quick breads.

APPLYING YOUR UNDERSTANDING

1. List the fruits currently in plentiful supply in your area. How would you prepare them to serve as accompaniments to main dishes? What main dish would you serve with each? Make up a display showing some of your ideas.
2. Prepare two hard-cooked eggs. Remove from hot water. Place one immediately in cold water to cool. Let the other cool at room temperature. Use the eggs for a snack or sandwich, or slice them for a salad. How did the two eggs differ? Was there any difference in flavor? Which did you prefer? Why?
3. Select your favorite baked product—cake, cookie, or pie. Research the history. Prepare a five-minute talk to give in class.
4. Search for six recipes combining pasta, grits, or rice with a high-quality protein such as chicken or fish. Make up a menu for each.

Chapter 27

MEALS IN MINUTES

Has this ever happened to you?

"Tonight it's my turn to fix dinner," moaned Jason on his way home from school.

"So what's the big deal?" asked Lisa, his good friend and next-door neighbor.

"Well, it wouldn't be so bad, but mom is on a diet, dad doesn't get home till late, and Andrew went to the dentist today, so he won't be able to chew very well. I have no idea what to fix," stated Jason.

"Why don't you fix a chowder soup and main-dish salad for dinner," suggested Lisa. "You could keep the soup warm for your dad, it would be easy for Andrew to eat. A salad would be low in calories for your mom's diet."

"That's a terrific idea," Jason happily replied. "Would you serve anything else?"

"I think I would fix some sourdough bread and maybe some fruit and cheese for dessert," said Lisa. "And, Jason, the best part about it is that it won't take you very long to prepare the meal!"

Have you ever prepared a meal for an entire family? What special considerations did you have to make?

Why are people interested in timesaving recipes and menu suggestions?

After reading this chapter, you will be able to

- evaluate the pros and cons of microwave cooking;
- use the proper procedures to cook with a microwave oven;
- identify and evaluate timesaving small appliances;
- know methods to preserve food at home;
- plan and cook fast, creative meals on a budget.

The right meal for those times when there is "no time to cook" can mean different things to different people. Some want a simple dish or meal they can pop into the oven and forget for an hour or so while they tend to other things. Others want a meal that can be put together, cooked, and served in minutes. In this chapter you will explore some of the timesaving and economical appliances and foods from which to choose.

SPECIALIZED APPLIANCES

When saving time in the kitchen is a priority, one of the best ways is to make good use of equipment and appliances. The microwave oven, a blender, and a toaster oven are a few pieces of kitchen equipment that can make the cook's work faster, more energy efficient, and, hopefully, tastier.

MICROWAVE COOKING

Microwave ovens are very popular because they can defrost, warm, cook, and reheat food much faster than conventional cooking methods. For instance, one baked potato, cooks in about four minutes in a microwave oven. A potato baked in a conventional oven takes forty-five to sixty minutes.

In a microwave oven, the microwaves are distributed throughout the inside of the oven. When microwaves enter the food, they cause the molecules in the food to rub against each other. The movement creates friction, and the friction creates heat. This heat cooks the food. The process is very fast. Depending on the food being cooked, it may cook two to ten times faster than by conventional methods.

With microwave cooking, the oven does not become hot. Because microwaves are a form of energy that is not hot, a microwave oven stays cool and food spills do not burn onto the oven. Dishes also stay cool when cooking times are short. If you cook foods for long periods of time, the dishes will become hot, because the hot foods transfer heat to the cooking dish.

In some cases, food cooked in a microwave oven is more nutritious. Vegetables retain more nutrients because the cooking time is shorter and little or no water is needed.

Not all foods can be prepared satisfactorily in a microwave oven because it cooks so fast. Baked goods such as cookies, as well as broiled steaks or chops cook better in a conventional oven.

Many different materials can be used as "cooking utensils" in a microwave oven. You can use paper towels, paper plates, waxed paper, glass, plastic wrap, and some plastic dishes. Microwaves can pass through these types of materials to cook the food.

Metal pans should not be used in most microwave ovens. This is because metal reflects microwaves. The microwaves will bounce off the pan instead of being transmitted to the food.

With the help of time-saving appliances and the use of simple recipes, you can create your own fast food dishes in minutes.

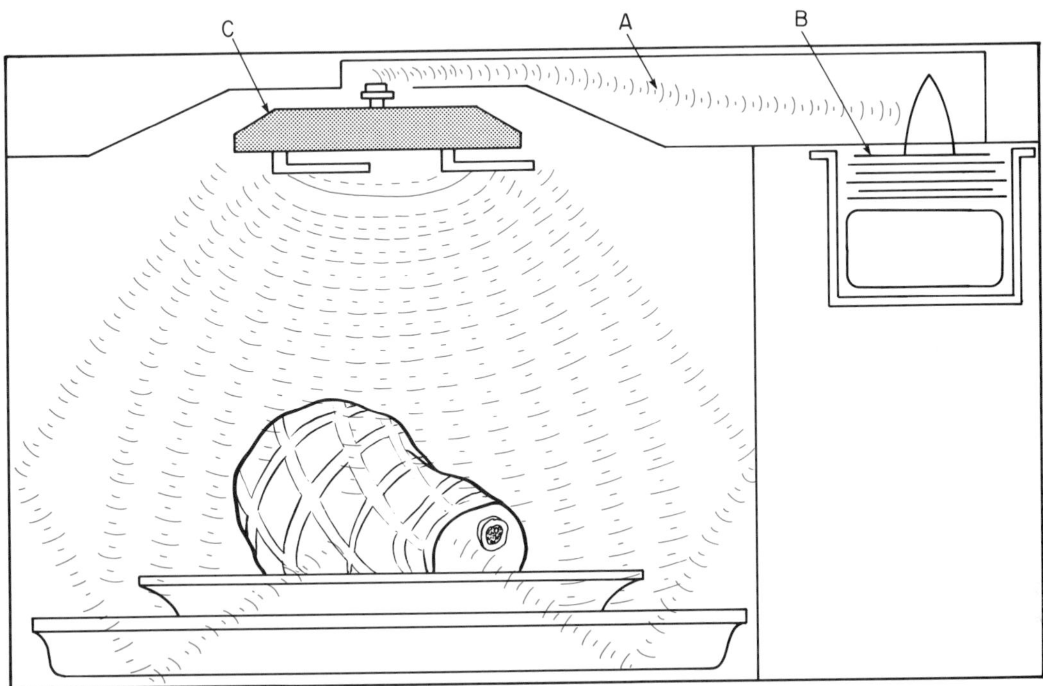

A microwave oven cooks with tiny waves of energy called microwaves (A). These are generated by a special magnetron tube (B), that is electronically and magnetically controlled (C).

You may not need to purchase special microwave cookware. Paper towels, paper plates, waxed paper, glass, plastic wrap, and some plastic dishes can be used in the microwave oven.

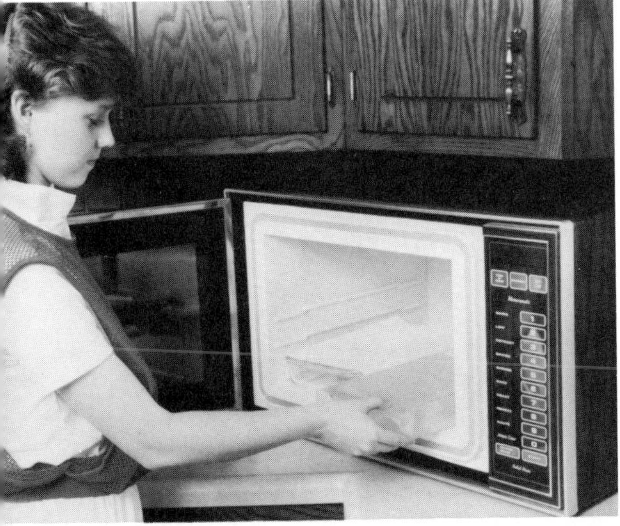

Microwave Techniques

When you cook in the microwave oven, several special techniques are important to remember. For instance, there are two kinds of cooking time—microwave time and standing time.

Microwave Time

Microwave time is the actual time food cooks with microwave energy. Most recipes will give a range of microwave time. Microwave time is affected by the following:

1. size of the food
2. shape of the food
3. original temperature of the food
4. density of the food
5. amount of food to be cooked
6. moisture content of the food
7. fat and sugar content of the food
8. cooking utensil material
9. power level used.

Small, thin pieces of food at room temperature will cook faster in the microwave oven than thick chunks from the refrigerator. A food such as bread, which is porous and less dense, will cook faster than a thick roast. The larger the food load in the microwave oven, the longer the cooking time. Dry foods will cook faster than moist foods. Fat and sugar molecules absorb microwaves quickly and will cook faster than foods that are higher in water content.

Some microwave oven models will have variable power levels. They will have different power settings for cooking, defrosting, reheating, and warming foods. Read the owner's manual.

Standing Time

When the microwave time is finished, the food continues to cook until it cools slightly. This cooking is called **standing time.** It is important to plan for standing time; otherwise, foods may become overcooked.

When using the microwave oven be sure to allow for standing time, to prevent foods from overcooking. Standing time is the time food continues to cook when the microwave time is finished.

Cooking Methods

When you cook in the microwave, you will need to use many of the same methods you would if you were cooking on a conventional range. For instance, you will need to stir and turn foods occasionally. Stirring and turning foods during microwave cooking time helps equalize the heat in the food. You will get more evenly cooked food if this procedure is used.

BLENDERS

Meal preparation can be a snap if you put your blender to work for you. At the flick of a switch, this versatile kitchen helper trims minutes from cooking jobs, for it can take the place of a meat grinder, grater, shredder, and sieve. Some of the culinary jobs your blender can perform in seconds are

1. crumb bread and crackers;
2. grate hard cheese, nuts, and chocolate;
3. shred semisolid cheese, cooked meat, crisp fruit, and vegetables;
4. puree soft fruit and vegetables;
5. mix and refresh juices;
6. mix powdered milk;
7. smooth lumpy gravy and sauces;
8. blend instant pudding, pancake, and popover batters;
9. mix salad dressings.

A blender works very fast. Even at the lowest speed, seconds can make a tremendous difference in the texture of the final product.

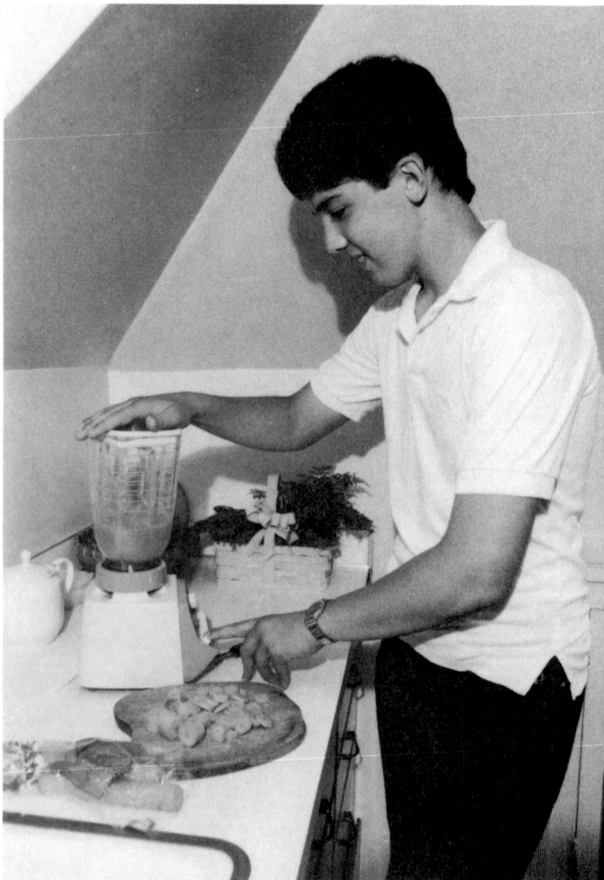

Keep your blender handy where you can use it whenever there is a timesaving job to do. To make the best use of your blender, here are some basic rules to use:

1. Cut fresh fruits and vegetables, cooked meats, fish, or seafood into one-half to one-inch pieces before chopping.
2. Cut firm cheeses in one-half-inch pieces. Cube and soften cream cheese before blending with liquid ingredients.
3. Place liquid ingredients into the blender container first unless the recipe directs otherwise.
4. Add large amounts of foods such as cracker crumbs or raw vegetables in several small batches. It is easier to control the fineness of the pieces and, at the same time, it does not overtax the blender's motor.

TOASTER OVEN

Although a toaster oven is smaller than a conventional oven, a toaster oven is capable of baking and broiling many of your favorite foods—just in smaller quantities. The small toaster oven operates when plugged into a wall outlet, while a conventional oven requires special wiring to handle the higher wattage. Thus, the toaster oven will save energy, and it will not heat up your kitchen as much.

The toaster oven is perfect for baking potatoes, reheating pizza, and making toast. It can also heat a small casserole, bake a few cookies, or broil a small chop.

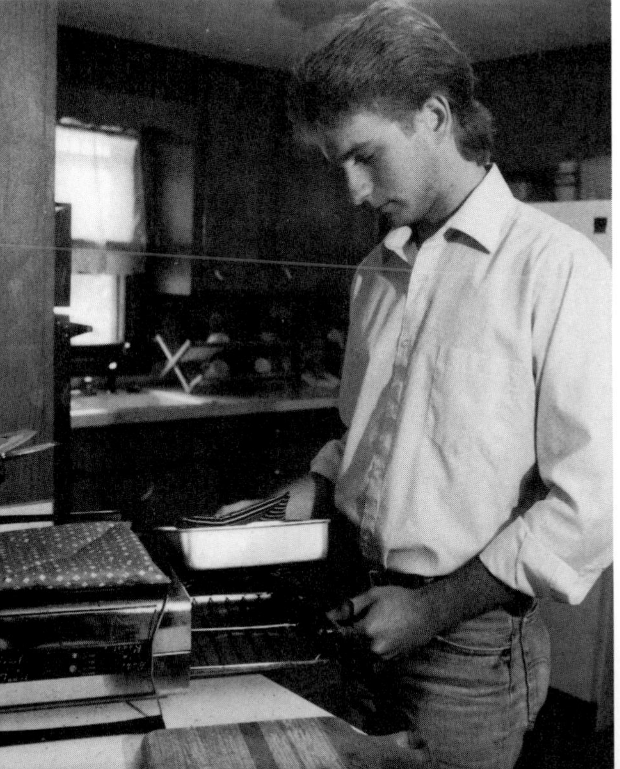

Save energy costs by baking items in a toaster oven.

FOOD PRESERVATION

Food preservation is done to keep food from spoiling for a fairly long time. The three methods used to preserve food at home are canning, freezing, and drying. For the best results, choose fully ripe, top quality fruits and vegetables.

USDA pamphlets, available from county extension offices, can provide basic, up to date information for canning, freezing, and drying foods.

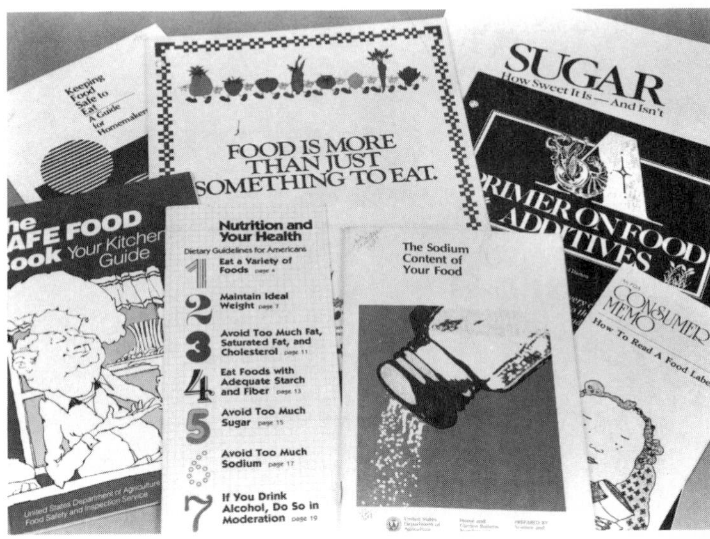

CANNING

Canning is a process that heats food to temperatures of 100°C (212°F.) or above in boiling water for a specific length of time.

Before you start to can, you should read the canning procedures with care. Your canning directions will give you exact processing times. The food is first prepared according to the recipe and then put into sterilized jars or cans.

Canning can be time-consuming and requires special equipment. You must follow instructions with care. If you take shortcuts, food may become contaminated, causing food poisoning.

Canning is a good way to make jams, jellies, and pickles. When special decorative canning jars are used for these products, they make attractive gifts. When stored in a dry, cool place, canned food will keep up to a year.

A SNACKER'S DELIGHT

For a quick energy pickup after work or school, or for an impromptu get-together, try some of these nutritious snacks to satisfy your hunger and impress your guests.

Overstuffed celery is an easy, crunchy snack. Wash and trim six to eight short celery ribs, leaving the tops on. Chill and stuff with any of the following combinations:

- *Blue cheese and walnuts.* Combine one cup creamed cottage cheese, one-third cup crumbled blue cheese, one-third cup chopped walnuts, and one-half teaspoon Worcestershire sauce.
- *Chili-cheese.* Combine one cup creamed cottage cheese, one finely chopped green onion, two teaspoons chili powder, and one-fourth teaspoon garlic salt.
- *Lemon-cheese.* Combine one cup creamed cottage cheese, one-fourth cup chopped fresh celery leaves, grated peel of one lemon, and one-half teaspoon salt.

For a taste of Mexico, try whipping up a bowl of guacamole dip. With the help of a blender, a dip such as this only takes a few seconds. In the blender container, put two tablespoons lemon juice, one-fourth teaspoon salt, one small tomato (peeled and cut in pieces), one-fourth medium onion, two to three canned green chilies (seeded), and two ripe avocados (halved, seeded, peeled, and cut in cubes). Blend all the ingredients until smooth. Serve dips with thinly sliced vegetables such as carrots, zucchini, cauliflower, and broccoli for extra nutrition.

Make a speedy cheese-fruit snack by piercing a cube of sharp cheese and a grape, mandarin-orange section, or pineapple chunk with a cocktail stick.

Stuffed tomatoes are another easy snack you can make. Hollow out cherry tomatoes and fill them with whipped cream cheese seasoned to taste with drained prepared horseradish, salt, and pepper.

Fruit spikes are refreshing and fast to make. Using long wooden picks, push a chunk of pineapple, a strawberry, and two seedless grapes on each pick. Insert picks in a bowl of crushed ice to serve.

FREEZING

Freezing food can be easy and economical if you have enough freezer space available. Fruits and vegetables keep more color, flavor, and texture than canned or dried fruits and vegetables.

Vegetables should be blanched before they are frozen. **Blanching** helps to prevent spoilage. You blanch vegetables by placing them in boiling water or steam for a short time. They are then plunged into cold water to stop the food from overcooking. Food is then packaged and frozen.

Label frozen food with contents and freezing date. Keep frozen fruits and vegetables only eight to twelve months.

DRYING

One of the oldest methods used to preserve food is drying. Drying is a process that circulates warm air around the food. The moisture is drawn from the food, which helps prevent spoilage.

In areas where the climate is warm and sunny, food is dried outdoors. If you do not have the advantage of free energy from the sun to dry food, you can use an electrical food **dehydrator.** Dehydrators are appliances that provide a controlled drying atmosphere. Some foods that dry especially well are grapes, apricots, apples, bananas, pears, onions, peas, and zucchini.

SEASONING

Seasoning and flavoring can be one of the simplest and most creative ways to add excitement to foods. Just a dash of spice can turn a plain dish into a real taste treat. Seasonings include spices, herbs, blends, vegetable seasonings, seeds, flavor enhancers, mustards, vinegars, and extracts.

USING SEASONINGS

The rule of thumb for using spices is "A little bit goes a long way." It is much better to have the option to add more flavor if you think a recipe needs it after the first taste. Start with 1 ml (one-fourth teaspoon) for every four servings if you are not using a recipe.

Here are some other tips to keep in mind when you are "going creative" with spices:

1. Dried herbs are stronger than fresh ones, because dried herbs are more concentrated.
2. To release the flavor of fresh or whole leaf herbs, crush them before using.
3. Add seasonings to uncooked dressing several hours in advance for the flavor to develop.
4. Dishes that require long-cooking times should be seasoned near the end of the cooking time. This prevents the flavors of the seasoning from being lost.

STORAGE

Age does not improve seasonings. Herbs and spices dry out and lose their flavor, color, and aroma. They should be stored in tightly sealed containers away from heat and moisture. Sunlight can also affect some seasonings.

Seasonings tend to lose flavor easily and should be kept as fresh as possible. Date each container as you buy it. To test for freshness, rub a bit of the spice or herb between your palms and smell the aroma. If there is no aroma, it is time to replenish the supply.

HOT AND COLD MEALS

When you are caught in the what-should-I-fixfor-dinner panic, turn to a main dish such as a hearty soup, sandwich, or a main-dish salad. One of these selections can be the core of your meal. Then round out your menu with a side-dish salad, vegetable, bread, or dessert.

When time is real short, take advantage of the convenience of canned soups. You can mix canned soup with other ingredients, or you can mix several canned soups and add a dash of your own seasoning to create a special recipe from store-bought soups. For instance, add barley to beef broth for a hearty beef and barley soup. Or make a speedy clam chowder by mixing a ten-and-threefourths-ounce can of cream of celery soup, one soup can of milk, one seven-ounce can of clams (drained), one tablespoon thinly sliced green onion, one-half chopped tomato, and one-fourth teaspoon lemon juice in a saucepan and heat to serving temperature.

Stews are a way you can take the sting out of a skimpy food budget. You simply buy low-cost meat cuts and stretch them with a bounty of vegetables. A stew topped with your own homemade or storebought biscuits makes a hearty meal.

SANDWICHES

You can make sandwiches creatively by varying breads, fillings, or spreads. By cutting sandwiches in different ways, they can become the garnish. For instance, tiny, toasted triangles of cheese sandwiches can be made to garnish an egg dish. They would add color contrast and texture to the finished egg dish.

Begin by opening a can of soup, add your favorite ingredients and seasonings, and turn it into a custom-made thick and hearty meal.

SALADS

Salads are a natural for creative touches with vegetables and fruits. A salad can begin a meal or be the meal itself. It can also be the most laborintensive part of the meal to prepare. You can save preparation time by making use of labor-saving appliances to chop vegetables, slice meat and cheese, and blend dressings. If you are going to make a salad for a crowd, why not let them help? Organize your salad ingredients on a counter top or table, and make a salad bar where everyone can make their own combination.

When you set up your salad bar, make the food look inviting with tempting textures and colors. Offer lots of variety. Salads can be made with anything from fruit to pasta. Include tasty toppings for greens, like corn chips (for a Mexican-style salad) and croutons, plus a choice of dressings. Set out a large tray of assorted cold cuts and cheeses so guests can fix a chef's salad.

FINISHING TOUCHES

You eat with your eyes first, and you may turn down the best-cooked food if it does not look good. Eye appeal is so important that a restaurant will generally not serve a dish that is not garnished in some small way.

GARNISHES

Garnishes are an edible decoration that add color and variety to food to make it look more appetizing. Many times you can garnish any dish with foods commonly found in the kitchen. For instance, baked fish as the main dish can become more interesting by adding a small bunch of parsley, a lemon wedge, or a slice of tomato on the serving plate.

A garnish should be selected to complement the food you are preparing. It should accent the flavor and color of the recipe.

When you plan to cook an appetizer, soup, sandwich, or a dessert, try to think how the food will look when it is served. Then decide what effect you want to create with a garnish. The finished recipe will look complete and be appetizing—a true work of art. Below are some suggestions:

1. *Scallion fan.* Trim the root end from the scallion. Make several lengthwise slits along the white portion, rotating the bulb each time you cut. Crisp in ice water. Cut off the green portion one inch above the curls.

2. *Radish rose.* Radishes can be cut into a number of flowers, the simplest of which is the rose. To make the rose, cut the root end off a radish. Using a sharp paring knife, make four vertical cuts around the circumference, almost down to the stem. Make a second row of cuts inside the first. Place in ice water to crisp.

3. *Lily.* Slice a large turnip into very thin rounds (the thinner the round, the easier it will be to coax into a petal). Roll each round into a cone, place an ear of miniature corn in the center for the stamen, and fasten with a toothpick. Crisp the completed flower in ice water.

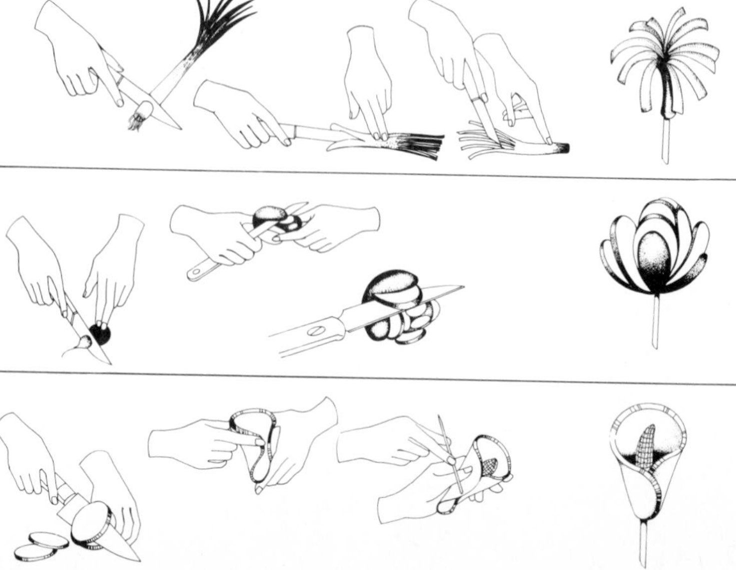

Follow these steps to create attractive garnishes. Then, experiment to develop your own ideas.

WORDS TO REMEMBER

blanching
canning
dehydrator
garnishes
food preservation
standing time

CHECKING YOUR UNDERSTANDING

1. Explain the difference between microwave time and standing time. What will happen if a cook does not account for standing time when using the microwave oven?
2. What types of food preservation methods can be done at home? What specialized equipment is needed for drying food?
3. How does the knowledge of seasonings help the cook? What tips should be kept in mind when using seasonings? Describe the correct storage methods for seasonings.
4. Identify a main-dish soup or salad that could be served for dinner. What foods could accompany the dish so that the meal would be nutritionally balanced?
5. Name four garnishes that can be added to food. With what food would you serve the garnishes? How do the garnishes contribute to the overall appearance of the meal?

APPLYING YOUR UNDERSTANDING

1. Demonstrate to the class a food product that uses the microwave oven, a blender, or a toaster oven. How does the appliance save food preparation time? What other benefits can you see by using the appliance? If you did not have this appliance, how would you prepare the food?
2. Look in your kitchen cupboard and identify three cooking utensils that can be used in the microwave oven. Locate a pan that cannot be used in the microwave and explain why.
3. Compare a similar type of food that has been preserved by canning, drying, and freezing. Compare the taste, texture, and appearance of the food. Which food preservation method do you like best?
4. Look through magazines for dishes with different garnishes. Collect the pictures and prepare a montage showing the types of garnishes used.

Chapter 28

DINING AT HOME AND AWAY

Has this ever happened to you?

Linda and Mark were representing their HERO Student Leadership group at a local Chamber of Commerce dinner meeting. Things were going pretty well, as Mark remembered to put his napkin on his lap and to use the flatware on the outside first. Linda was enjoying her talk with Mrs. White, the owner of a local store.

Suddenly, Mark became quite ill at ease. The entrée was a quarter of roast chicken. He remembered something about eating chicken, but couldn't remember quite what he was to do. He looked around at the other diners. "Were they going to use their forks or their fingers?" he wondered.

Linda was so interested in her talk with Mrs. White that she was hardly eating. But she, too, started eyeing the chicken with apprehension.

Mark whispered to her, "Should we use a fork or just pick up the chicken?" Linda picked up her fork and began to cut the meat away from the bone.

Have you ever wondered what pieces of flatware to use at a dinner?

Why is it important to use good manners when eating at home or dining out?

After reading this chapter, you will be able to

- describe how to set a table for buffet or table service;
- evaluate and choose foods that are appropriate for outdoor cooking;
- demonstrate the behavior expected of a guest in a restaurant or in someone's home.

Having friends over for a backyard barbecue, planning a backpack trip, or celebrating a special event with a sit-down dinner are a few ways that people enjoy food in the midst of family and friends. Whatever style you like, the rules of meal management, good etiquette, and nutrition can turn your dinner or party into enjoyable experience.

ENTERTAINING AT HOME

Entertaining at home can mean asking a few friends over for an impromptu meal or planning a dinner party for a holiday or special event. If the event is unplanned, you might simply serve a beverage or a light snack. But when you want to serve a whole meal, you will need to plan with more care.

PLANNING A DINNER PARTY

The first step in planning a dinner party is to decide on the menu. Select a menu that is suited to the tastes of your guests, your budget, the time and skills you have for food preparation, and your kitchen equipment. Make a special effort to serve food attractively and to set a colorful, appealing table.

If you plan your dinner around a theme, such as Italian night or Mexican fiesta, you probably will want to serve ethnic foods. To establish the theme, design the centerpiece and table settings to reflect the theme. Even if you do not have a theme for your meal, carefully plan how you will create a relaxing, pleasing mood. Soft music, matching napkins and tablecloth, a centerpiece, pleasant conversation, and good food work together to set the mood for a pleasant meal.

Types of Table Service

Once you have planned your menu, decide what type of meal service would be appropriate. Choose a style that is convenient, easy for you to do, and that will make your guests feel at ease.

Food can be served to guests by having them pick up their own plates and food at a serving table, called **buffet service.** Or food can be served to the people at the table, which is called **table service.**

There are five kinds of table service that are popular in this country. They include:

1. *Family or country style.* Table service is informal and simplified, because people serve themselves from common serving dishes. The serving dishes are passed at the table so that individuals can serve themselves.
2. *Plate service.* This service requires no serving dishes, because the food is placed on the plates in the kitchen and served directly to the person.
3. *Modified English service.* This service requires the host or hostess to serve from serving dishes at the table.
4. *Compromise service.* Part of the meal, such as the appetizer, salad, and dessert, is served using plate service, while the main course is served using modified English service.
5. *Formal service.* This service usually involves several courses and many plates. It is more often used by restaurants and hotels for banquets.

The table service that you choose should suit the event, the menu, the number of people you plan to serve, and the time available to serve and eat the meal. Be sure to consider the comfort of your guests, too, so that each one feels at ease and enjoys herself or himself.

What type of table service is being used to serve the food?

RULES FOR SERVING AND CLEARING

Rules for serving and clearing have been made to save time and avoid confusion. When using family service, set the plates and **flatware** (knives, forks, spoons, and so forth) at each place before you announce the meal. When the food is ready, fill the serving dishes in the kitchen and place them on the table with the serving pieces set beside them. After people are seated, begin passing the serving dishes. Avoid confusion by passing the dishes in a clockwise fashion. It is customary for the dessert and, in some cases, the beverages to be brought to the table after the dishes used for the main meal have been cleared.

For any style of service, remove the dishes from the table after the main course. First, take away all the serving dishes. Then, remove the used dishes and flatware from each person's place. Use your left hand to remove the dinnerware and flatware. Then transfer them to your right hand. Use your left hand again to remove the salad plate and place it on top of the dinner plate. Remove any remaining dishes with your left hand and carry the dishes to the kitchen or put them on a serving cart until all the places have been cleared. Refrigerate all leftover food as soon as possible.

PLANNING A BUFFET

A buffet is the easiest way to serve a meal to a large group of friends. Buffets can be simple or elegant. Menus can be planned economically around seasonal foods. Since the food will be on display, think of foods that look attractive and vary in color, texture, and taste.

The simplest approach is to prepare food ahead of time and then warm it up just before serving. Or, you might plan a menu in which foods can stay warm using a crock pot, or you might plan to serve only cold foods.

When you are setting up a buffet, set the serving dishes in the order in which they will be eaten. Appetizers would be first, followed by salads, main dishes, vegetables, rolls, and butter. The flatware may be rolled up in the napkins to make it easier for the guests to pick them up.

Setting the Table

When planning to serve guests at the table, use the type of table service that is best for you. For table service you will need about twenty inches (50 cm) for each person. This is often referred to as a cover. The dishes and flatware you place on the table depend on the menu you have planned.

Study the diagrams below. Choose the flatware you will need and place them in the order in which they will be used from the outside in toward the plate. On the right side of the plate, place the knife, with the blade turned in, all the spoons needed, the beverage glass, and the cup. On the left side, place the forks, tines up. The salad plate, bread and butter plate, and sauce dish are also placed on the left, along with the napkin. Both the plates and flatware should be about one inch from the edge of the table.

PLANNING A PARTY

Use this handy checklist to plan and organize a party. Then you can relax and enjoy your guests when the party begins.

3 to 4 Weeks Ahead

_______ Decide on a theme for your party.

_______ Set the date and time of the party.

_______ Get permission and set budget.

_______ Make guest list.

2 Weeks Ahead

_______ Invite guests. Give RSVP phone number.

_______ List any items that you will need to borrow.

_______ Plan menu.

_______ Make a shopping list.

_______ Purchase decorations and any prizes.

1 Week Ahead

_______ Buy foods and drinks.

_______ Prepare foods that can be frozen.

_______ Notify neighbors of the party.

_______ Pick up borrowed items.

_______ Ask a friend to help with some party tasks, if necessary.

2 Days Ahead

_______ Chop and measure foods, such as nuts or chopped vegetables, that may be refrigerated in plastic bags.

_______ Prepare food that may be refrigerated and stored in serving dishes.

1 Day Ahead

_______ Clean house.

_______ Remove frozen foods to thaw overnight in the refrigerator.

Day of the Party

_______ Decorate the room.

_______ Set table.

_______ Prepare food and beverage.

Party Time

_______ Greet guests.

_______ Introduce guests to new people.

After the Party

_______ Clean up.

_______ Return borrowed items promptly.

_______ Evaluate the success of the party.

OUTDOOR COOKING

If you are the type of person who thinks that food always tastes twice as good when it is eaten outdoors, you may want to entertain outdoors and cook food on a grill.

COOKING ON A GRILL

Cooking on a grill over an open fire is called **barbecuing.** Whether you use a simple hibachi, a gas or electric grill, or a charcoal or wood fire, keep your menu simple, especially if it is your first attempt to grill food.

Grilling is a cooking skill that takes practice. Vegetables, breads, and even desserts can be cooked this way. A beginning cook may want to begin with one food, such as meat, and then add the others as skills increase.

You will need the following equipment for cooking over an open fire: long-handled tongs, forks, spatula, and basting brush, along with a sharp knife, cutting board, and asbestos mitts. Heavy duty foil can be used to hold the food if the metal of the gridiron is spaced too far apart. Food mixtures, such as fish and vegetables, can also be cooked in foil packets on the grill over the hot coals.

Plan to light your fire thirty-five to forty-five minutes before cooking if you plan to use charcoal or wood. Take safety precautions and follow the directions on the charcoal package when lighting the fire. If you are using a gas or electric grill, follow the directions that come with the equipment.

Any tender cut of meat, as well as fish or poultry, can be grilled. Less tender meats can be marinated to tenderize them before they are grilled. As you gain experience, you might try kabobs of meats and vegetables roasted together on skewers.

Since grilling is dry heat, basting with barbecue sauce will keep the meat moist as well as give it a new flavor. To avoid fat fires, trim all excess fat from the meat. In the case of poultry, remove the skin and baste the meat with a sauce. Grease or oil the grill in order to keep the meat from sticking to it. If you use foil, poke holes to drain the fat. Small pieces of meat should be placed no closer than three to five inches from the fire. Whole roasts or poultry should be placed on a spit and turned for slow, even cooking.

As you gain outdoor cooking skills, you may want to try new dishes, such as roasted corn, baked potatoes, or whole fresh fruits. Consult one of the many cookbooks written for outdoor cooking for ideas for other exciting foods to cook over a grill.

BACKPACKING AND CAMPSITE COOKING

Backpacking calls for meals that are simple, healthful, and high in energy, as well as lightweight and nonperishable. Camping allows a little more flexibility, but refrigeration is usually limited.

Prepare backpacking meals by dividing food into portions and wrapping them tightly in small, heavyweight plastic bags. Foods can be portioned out for each day or by meals and labeled. Use dehydrated or dried foods such as egg and milk powder, instant potato, air-dried vegetables and fruits, and freeze-dried meals.

Plan meals that require only warming or very little cooking and can be served with a cup, bowl, and spoon. Usually the water available needs treatment so be sure to include water-treatment tablets in your supplies.

If you were this hiker, what foods would you pack in your backpack?

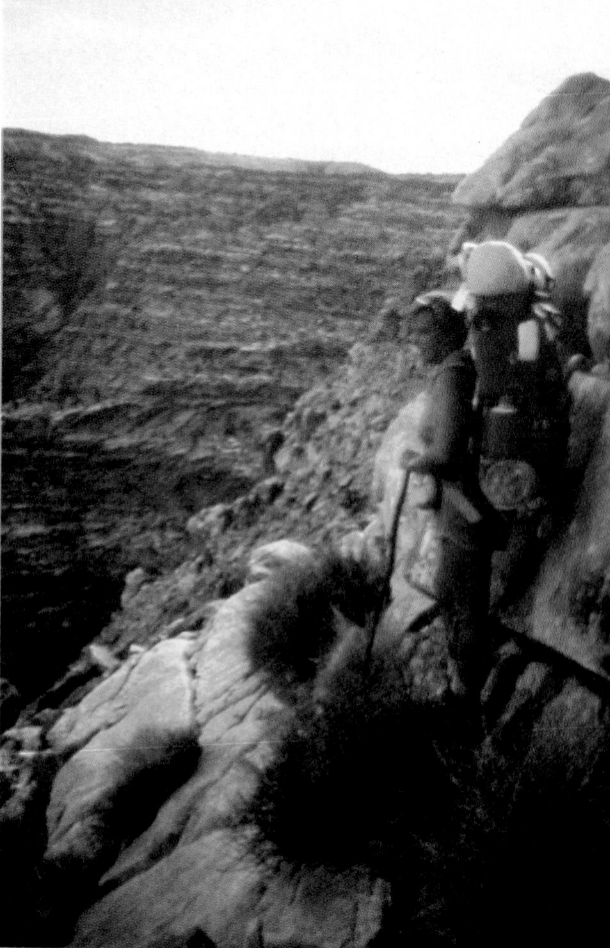

Careers
A BRIEF LOOK

FOODS AND NUTRITION

If you are searching for a career where there are opportunities to grow, you might want to get a job in the foods and nutrition field. As more and more people eat meals away from home, choose convenience foods, and yet are concerned about their diet and health, careers in this field continue to grow. There is a job for you in this field if you want it.

The jobs in this field fall into three broad areas: food service, food processing, and home economics. Such careers include those in schools, colleges, hospitals, research labs, and the media.

To prepare for the jobs in this area, you might consider being a waiter or waitress, a diet aide in a hospital, or a cook in a day-care center. If food technology appeals to you, be sure to get a strong background in science, physics, and chemistry. And if writing comes easily to you, use your skills and submit articles about nutrition, restaurants, and food products to the school newspaper.

Entry Level Jobs
Waiter/waitress
Food demonstrator
Assistant cook
Dishwashing machine operator
Fast food worker
Supermarket worker

Jobs That Require More Training
Executive chef
Meat cutter
Kitchen supervisor
Dining room supervisor
Purchasing agent
Assistant restaurant manager
Food production manager
Merchandising supervisor

Jobs That Require an Advanced Degree
Dietitian
Food service director
Director of recipe development
Food writer
Food technologist
Personnel director
Food inspector
Food stylist
Extension home economist
Nutrition counselor

For more information, contact:

Science and Education Administration
United States Department of Agriculture
Hyattsville, Maryland 20782

The American Dietetic Association
430 North Michigan Avenue
Chicago, Illinois 60611

American Home Economics Association
2010 Massachusetts Avenue
Washington, D.C. 20036

National Restaurant Association
1 IBM Plaza
Chicago, Illinois 60611

Camping

The meals you plan for a camping trip should include a variety of foods that are easy to prepare and should supply all the nutrients you need.

One-skillet or one-pot dinners, filling soups and meals that can be grilled are all good choices for camping.

As you plan your meals, consider the following:

1. the number and ages of people who will be eating the meals;
2. the number of days and meals needed;
3. the type of equipment available for cooking, storage, and refrigeration.

DINING OUT

It is said that one out of every three meals is eaten away from home. There are many reasons why people eat out. They range from the lack of time to prepare meals to business needs or to a desire to celebrate an event or to enjoy the luxury of service.

TYPES OF RESTAURANTS

There are many different kinds of restaurants. They offer you a variety of foods, service, and prices.

Fast-food restaurants serve a limited menu and offer quick service at reasonable prices. Service is quick because you choose food from a posted menu and give the order to a clerk at the central serving area. The food is placed on a tray and given to you to carry to a nearby table.

Family restaurants offer a greater variety of food than fast-food chains. With the exception of cafeterias, some steak houses, and delicatessens, food is served at the table. Prices vary, depending on the quality of the food and the extent of the service. Some family restaurants, such as steak houses, specialize in one kind of food, but most offer a variety of foods.

A luxury restaurant is the place to go if you want a meal prepared to order and served at a leisurely pace. Many such restaurants require that a reservation be made in advance. When you call for a reservation, give your name, the size of party, and the time you would like to be seated at a table. Be sure to arrive promptly, because most reservations are held for only ten minutes after the agreed time.

ORDERING

When you look at a menu board that lists choices and prices, deciding what you want to order is fairly simple. But using a menu can pose some problems if you are not familiar with that restaurant's menu. As you enter a restaurant, you can ask to see a menu before you are seated to be sure that the type of food you want is served and that the prices are within your budget.

When you are presented with a menu, read over the entire menu. The **entrée** is the main dish. A salad bar may offer soup, cheese, bread or rolls, fruit, and sometimes a dessert. Foods can be ordered separately or **à la carte** if you do not want all the foods on a full menu. Also foods can sometimes be substituted or prepared without oils or salt if you are on a special diet.

TIPPING

A tip is a payment for service. In most sit-down restaurants a tip of 15 to 20 percent of the bill before taxes is expected. The size of the tip is related to the quality of the service. If you get very good service, you may wish to tip more than 20 percent or less if service was poor. You may include the tip as part of payment by a credit card or leave money on the table where it can be easily found.

MINDING YOUR MANNERS

Good manners are nothing more than being considerate of other people, not only those in your party, but others in the restaurant or at your home. Some guidelines are the following:

1. Wait until the host/hostess begins before starting to eat your food.
2. Sit up straight with your feet on the floor.
3. Put your napkin on your lap.
4. Keep your elbows off the table.
5. Ask for food to be passed, rather than reaching in front of others.
6. Do not talk and chew food at the same time.
7. Cut food into small pieces and chew them slowly.
8. Keep conversation pleasant; avoid arguments.
9. If you spill anything, wipe it up quickly with your napkin.
10. Talk quietly.

A place setting is planned so that you will use the flatware on the outside first. If you are in doubt, follow the lead of the hostess. Use the utensil that is most comfortable—forks for most foods and spoons for puddings, soups, and cereal. Using the wrong utensil is not a disaster. Being courteous and relaxed is more important than being too concerned with the mechanics of eating.

WORDS TO REMEMBER

à la carte
barbecuing
buffet service
entrée
flatware
plate service
table service

CHECKING YOUR UNDERSTANDING

1. When planning a menu for a dinner party, what should be taken into consideration? What factors should be considered when deciding on the type of table service to use?
2. Describe the difference between a buffet and table service. When serving a large crowd, what type of service would be easier? Explain.
3. Demonstrate or draw a diagram of a place setting and an arrangement for a buffet table.
4. Why are good time management skills necessary when cooking food on an outdoor grill?
5. Describe what is meant by ordering an entrée à la carte from a restaurant menu.

APPLYING YOUR UNDERSTANDING

1. Choose a type of table service and show how to set and clear the table correctly.
2. Plan a menu, a supply list, and a time schedule for a meal to be prepared outdoors.
3. Demonstrate how to order a meal from a menu, how to pay a bill, and how to calculate the tip.
4. Prepare and present two skits, one demonstrating good manners at the dinner table, the other, poor manners. Explain the basis of good manners.

Unit 6
HOUSING

Unit 6 will help you to understand some of the challenges you will face in finding and managing a home of your own.

Your first task will be to find a home that will fit your needs. Chapter 29 will help you to become familiar with types and functions of housing and how you can finance your home.

In chapter 30, you will learn ways to evaluate the various aspects of the home you have chosen. Learning to use furniture, accessories, and equipment to personalize your home is the focus of chapter 31. Finally, learning how to manage and care for your home is covered in chapter 32.

Chapter 29

A HOME TO FIT YOUR NEEDS

Has this ever happened to you?

Abby answered the phone on the first ring, anxious to hear how moving day had gone for her sister Macy.

Macy, however, was furious. "Abby, you won't believe what that Mr. Finney did to me," she raged. "He wouldn't give me my security deposit back on the apartment. I was counting on that money to buy things for my new place. Boy, do I feel cheated!"

"I don't understand," said Abby. "I thought Mr. Finney had to give it back to you when you moved out. Why didn't he?"

"Oh, he was really being picky," answered Macy. "First he said the oven wasn't clean. That was true, but it wasn't clean when I moved in either. Then he said there were stains on the carpet. When Dottie was my roommate, she spilled makeup on the carpet in her room—but that wasn't my fault!"

"I guess he figures he'll have to get the carpet cleaned," said Abby. "Was that all?"

"No, he complained because the hall light fixture was gone," Macy said. "Bill broke it one night when he was fooling around at a party I had. And Mr. Finney noticed the crayon marks on the kitchen wall. You remember the night you and I babysat with Keith and he did that? I never could get them off."

"I know how disappointed you are not to get your deposit back," said Abby. "But there really were quite a few things wrong in the apartment. I'm sure Mr. Finney will have to use that money to fix the place up before someone else moves in."

Have you ever known someone who did not get a security deposit back?

What can renters do to ensure they will get their security deposits back when they move out?

After reading this chapter, you will be able to

- recognize factors to be considered in making housing decisions;
- identify and describe the various types of housing;
- understand the procedures and responsibilities of renting and buying a home;
- compare and contrast moving yourself with hiring a commercial mover.

Housing is the setting for private living. Your home will reflect you as well as your goals and values. Whether you have a home that fits your needs depends on your resources and how you manage them.

Because of the influence that housing plays on your life, it is important to use the management process to choose housing. By identifying your goals and values for your home, you can make plans and decisions that will help you achieve what you want.

A comfortable and decent home can help build good family relationships. One that is near work, school and shopping makes life easier to manage.

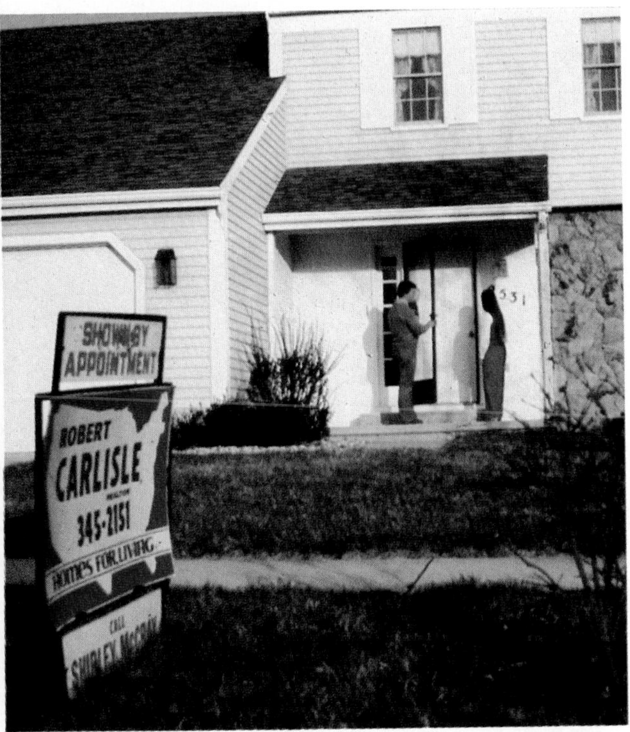

FUNCTIONS OF HOUSING

Housing is the dwelling in which people live. But this definition does not explain the many functions or special purposes that housing fills. At the most basic level, housing provides shelter from the elements. In a home, you are physically protected from extreme heat or cold, rain, snow, wind, and other bad weather. Housing also shields family members from rodents, insects, snakes, and animals. Locked doors and windows help safeguard people from vandals and thieves.

Housing provides the setting for family members to be together and share activities. It is also a place for singles and family members to bring friends and enjoy fellowship with others. A home can provide persons living in it with a feeling of belonging. Housing gives a sense of being part of a neighborhood or community.

Housing is often the setting where people seek fulfillment or self-satisfaction. They express themselves by having a room or area in which to pursue hobbies or special interests.

Of course, not all housing will serve these functions for all families. Basically, housing functions help people to meet their wants and needs. While people share the same human needs, how they meet them varies.

Personal space within a home is used for self-expression. What does this room tell you about the person who lives here?

MAKING HOUSING DECISIONS

Which home will best fit you and your family's needs? Each person or family is unique and looks for different qualities in housing. The first step in finding a home to fit your needs is to consider what kind of life you wish to live.

GOALS AND VALUES

The home you choose should fit your activities and interests. If you are a person who enjoys home-centered activities, your housing needs will be different from those of a person who merely eats and sleeps at home. A close look at the activities you enjoy, your values, and your life-style is the first step in thinking about housing.

HOUSING NEEDS

The needs of those who will live in the home should be considered in choosing housing. How many people will be in the household? Housing needs for a single person living alone will differ from those of a married couple with three children. How many bedrooms will be needed? If several friends share housing, will they want their own rooms? Will there be room for everyone to eat together?

How old are the people who will live in the housing? Stairs may be a danger for both toddlers and elderly people. A home that was comfortable when children were young may seem small when they become teenagers.

Simple or elaborate housing? City, suburban or country living? Weigh the advantages of each before making your decision.

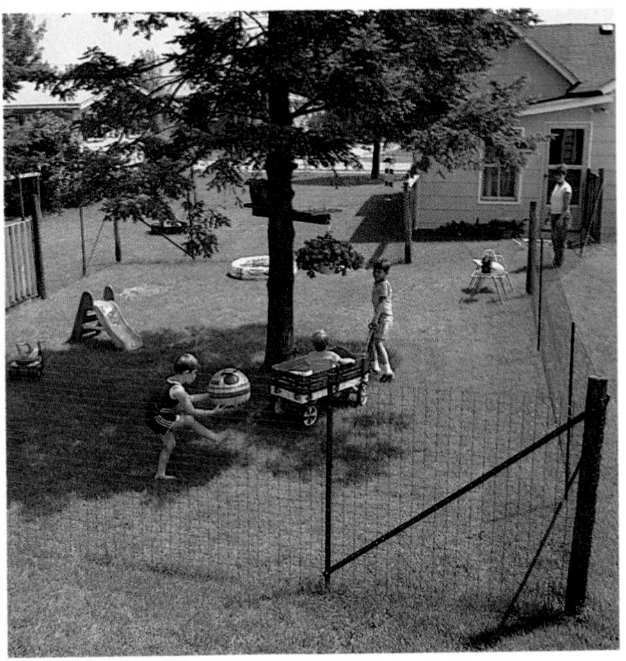

When selecting housing, the special needs of all family members should be considered. A family with young children may prefer a fenced backyard, while an elderly couple may choose a single story home.

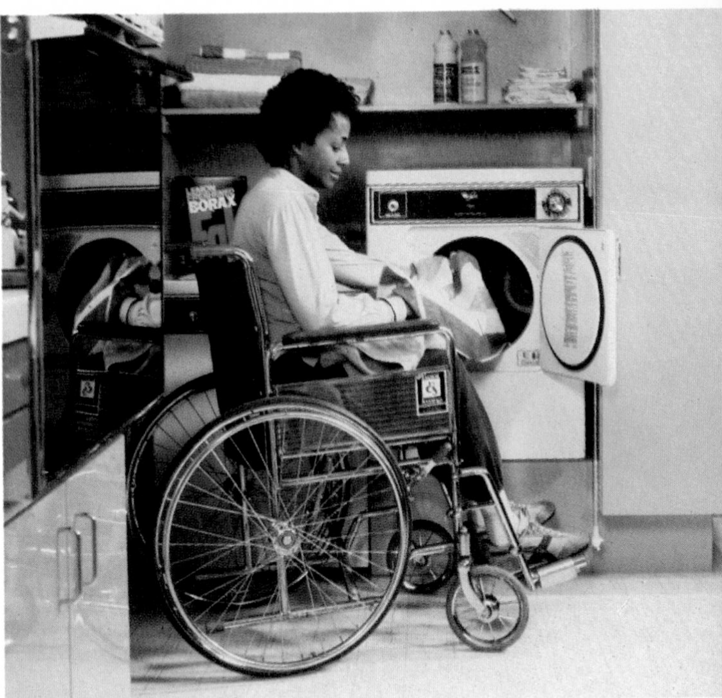

Notice how the raised dryer makes it easier for a person in a wheelchair to do the laundry.

Sometimes families have handicapped members or others with special housing needs. A person in a wheelchair needs housing on one floor unless there is an elevator. Halls must be wide. Ramps at the entrances would be essential.

A blind person would need enough room to get around easily. A person in a walker or on crutches would also need extra room.

Besides the extra space, there may be special changes needed to make the housing suitable for a handicapped person. Storage may need to be lowered in kitchens or bathrooms. Closets may have to be altered so clothes can be reached. Bathtubs and toilets may need grab bars or other special aids. Housing features are vital in whether a handicapped person can live independently or must rely on others for help in everyday living.

RESOURCES

Next, you need to consider your resources. How much can you afford to pay for rent or to buy housing? One guideline suggests people can afford to pay about one-third of their monthly income for housing. However, today's high housing costs may mean lower-income families must spend an even higher percentage on housing, leaving less money to meet other needs.

Another resource to consider in making housing choices is the knowledge and skills you have. Do you want an apartment or house that is ready to live in? Or do you enjoy fixing things up? Many times, skills and knowledge can be used in place of money to make housing fit your needs and to add a personal touch.

Relatives and friends may be another resource when you are setting up your first home. Parents may give you furniture or other items they no longer use. Other relatives or friends may give or loan household goods to help you get started. Many first-time home buyers borrow a part of their down payment from family members.

AVAILABILITY OF HOUSING

The community where you live will determine, to some extent, the type of housing you select. You may have decided a three-bedroom apartment on the ground floor is what you and two friends need. When you start to look, you find there are no three bedroom apartments available in your area at any price. You may feel a condominium or a town house would be right for you, but there may be none for sale where you want to live. Therefore, you may find your housing choices limited by what is for rent or sale in your location.

Remember that the rent per month on mortgage payment will not be your only housing expense. Home furnishings, insurance, taxes and utilities all add to the housing budget.

TYPES OF HOUSING

There are two major types of housing: multiple-family units and single-family units. Either type can be rented or purchased. The location of a housing unit is called its **site.**

MULTIPLE-FAMILY UNITS

Multiple-family units are those housing structures that have space for more than one household. They are usually cheaper to build per unit than single-family units because they require less land.

Multiple-family units come in many forms. They can be small two-unit buildings or large complexes. Complexes often have tennis courts or swimming pools. Multiple-family units can range from the deluxe to the spartan, and costs vary accordingly.

You can either rent multiple-family units from a landlord or purchase a unit. Two types of ownership plans, cooperatives and condominiums, are described below. You cannot tell from the outside of a building or complex whether it contains cooperatives, condominiums, or rental units.

Rental Apartments

Rental apartment buildings are probably the most common type of multiple-family units. People of all ages and family types live in them. Some enjoy the freedom from repairs and upkeep of apartment living. Others move frequently and do not want to bother with buying and selling homes. Some people are never able to save enough money for a down payment on a home. Others simply do not want the work that is part of owning a home. Renting an apartment is one way of trying out a new location before buying.

When you leave your family home for the first time, you will probably rent an apartment, either by yourself or with friends. You may choose a furnished apartment because it requires no major money outlay for furniture. Renting an unfurnished apartment saves rental money but also means you must own or rent your own furniture.

Cooperatives

Cooperative apartments, or co-ops, are owned rather than rented. A nonprofit corporation is formed and shares of stock are issued. With the money from the stock, a building is purchased. A person who buys stock becomes a co-op member and has the right to live in one of the units in the building. The larger the living unit, the more stock a person must buy. However, the owner does not buy an apartment, but rather owns a part of the corporation that owns the building.

The board of directors and its officers and committees manage the co-op. In large co-ops, a manager or agent is hired to run the building. In addition to buying shares in the corporation, co-op members pay a monthly fee. This fee covers building management, security, upkeep, and repairs.

When co-op owners want to sell, they sell their shares, not the housing units. Buyers usually must be approved by the co-op board of directors.

Because a co-op is a democracy, each owner must be willing to go along with the group. When disagreements occur, the majority of members rules. A person who buys into a co-op must be willing to get along with other owners.

Condominiums

Condominiums, or condos, are another form of multiple-family units. Individuals or families buy their own units in a building or complex. The land and any leisure facilities are owned and kept up by all owners.

A home-owners' association governs the use of the common areas. Each owner has a vote in the

The housing market is spiced with a variety of multiple family units including apartments, condominiums, town homes and cooperatives.

group. A monthly fee paid to the association covers lawn care, snow removal, driveway and sidewalk repair, outside painting, and other needed upkeep and repair. In large condo complexes, the home-owners' group may hire a manager.

The condo units are the property of their owners and can be altered or sold without the permission of the other owners. Condo owners have the freedom to decorate or remodel their units as they wish.

Condominiums and cooperatives are popular with many people because they combine the freedom of apartment living with the advantages of home ownership.

Town Houses and Duplexes

Town houses and duplexes are cheaper to build than houses because they need less land. However, they can look like single-family homes and offer some of the benefits of them.

Town houses are built in rows, with units sharing side walls but having their own front and back walls. Each unit has front and back doors and yards, and usually has living space on three levels. Some town houses differ in color, roof line, and exterior finish from the units next door.

There can be more space and privacy in town houses than in apartments. Noise from others is heard only through the side walls rather than from all directions. The three-story floor plan makes the unit seem more like a detached home than an apartment.

A duplex is housing for two families. Each unit has front and back doors, and may be one or two stories. Duplexes offer the most privacy of any type of multiple-family unit because the two units share only one wall.

Town houses and duplexes can be owned or rented. They can be sold as condominiums with each owner buying a unit and sharing the land jointly. Or each buyer may own the unit and the land on which it stands. Sometimes a family owns a duplex, lives in one unit, and rents out the other.

Town homes are gaining in popularity, especially in cities where land is scarce. The exterior styling of the group gives each unit a distinctive appearance.

SINGLE-FAMILY UNITS

A single-family unit is one detached dwelling, which usually has a plot of land around it. Single-family homes generally have the most privacy and space. They come in many sizes, styles, and designs with a variety of features and costs.

Mobile Homes

Mobile homes are an increasingly popular type of single-family home. They are portable dwellings built for year-around living. A mobile home is towed to a site by truck where it is set up and connected to utilities. Most mobile homes remain on their original sites. They are often placed on concrete foundations and landscaped as permanent buildings. Mobile home owners do not move any more often than others of similar age and family size.

Mobile homes are at least nine meters (twenty-nine feet) long and three meters (ten feet) wide, though most are larger. Double wides, which are made up of two or more units, are towed separately and joined into one dwelling on the site. These provide more floor space than many small detached homes. Most mobile homes come completely furnished.

Mobile homes offer you the versatility of being able to be towed to the prepared home site. However, mobile homes depreciate in value and are usually sold for less than they were bought for.

Most mobile homes are found in mobile home parks. Some parks provide small lots with few services or facilities. Other parks, which charge higher rents, have larger lots, landscaping, leisure facilities, and service activities.

If you wish to place your mobile home on a lot that is not in a mobile home park, check the local laws. Some governments require mobile homes be set up only in parks. Others have strict laws for mobile homes located on their own lots.

Detached Houses

Detached houses range from new to decades old. Most that are rented or sold have been lived in before. In general, an older home sells for less than a new home of similar size and quality. However, an older home may cost more to live in. It may need more repairs and upkeep than a newer one.

The cost of a home is affected by how it is built. Manufactured housing is factory built and then shipped to the site where it is placed on a permanent foundation. Savings result from the production line process, which also saves time. Housing parts, such as roof and floor trusses and wall panels, can be built at the factory and sold as a package to the builder. There is no measuring and cutting lumber when the house is erected at the site.

Modular or sectional homes are the most complete form of manufactured housing. Homes are shipped from the factory in sections, which are called modules. These are bolted together at the site to form a house. When a module leaves the factory, it is almost complete. Exterior siding, windows, and doors are in place, and the roof may be already shingled. Interiors can be carpeted, wallpapered, and painted. Kitchen and bathroom cabinets, fixtures, and appliances are usually hung after the house is set up.

A traditionally built dwelling is called a *stick-built* house. It is built board by board and brick by brick at the site. This type of construction lets a home be more personalized, but it is also more costly.

Larger houses, whether stick-built or manufactured, cost more than smaller ones. While quality construction can add to cost, an expensive house is not necessarily of good quality. What to look for in a dwelling is discussed in the next chapter.

Literally overnight you can see a modular home erected on the home site. Sections are produced in the factory, then shipped and bolted together at the site. This saves the home buyer time and money.

FINANCING A HOME

How you finance a home is an important decision. There are advantages and disadvantages in either renting or buying. In the end, your choice depends on two factors—what is important to you and what you can afford.

One advantage of renting is the freedom from upkeep and repair. Renters are able to move relatively easily. There is no need for a large sum of money for a down payment, and monthly housing costs are fixed.

Home ownership is one way for a family to build financial security.

On the other hand, buying a home is a source of personal pride and satisfaction. It can promote a feeling of belonging to the community. Owners are free to make changes to the property as they wish. When housing prices rise, a home is a protection against inflation. Home ownership also has tax advantages.

The weight you give to each benefit or limitation depends on your values. Some people save and sacrifice for many years to buy a home. Others with money for a down payment like the freedom of renting. The higher your income and the longer you stay in a home, the greater the financial advantages of owning a home. However, the choice you make must be one that is personally and economically satisfying to you.

RENTING A HOME

In the United States, renters make up about one-third of the population. Renters are also known as **tenants.** The first step in renting a home is to locate a unit in which you wish to live.

Finding a unit to rent is usually easier than finding one to buy. As a renter, you do not have to worry about the quality of construction, the condition of the building, or tying up savings in a twenty- or thirty-year mortgage. On the other hand, any housing you rent should be in fairly good shape because owners sometimes are slow to make repairs.

In looking for housing in a strange city or town, you should first buy a map with a street directory. Locate schools, churches, bus routes, and shopping areas. Try to find the neighborhoods in which you would like to live. If possible, drive around the areas you have chosen and look for rental signs.

Most people begin their search for rental housing by checking the newspaper classified ads. Many people find rental units by word of mouth through personal networks. Let your friends or fellow employees at work know you are looking for a place to rent.

In larger cities where rental units are few and hard to find, there are agencies to help renters locate housing. Real estate agents can also help you to find rental units. A flat fee, a month's rent, or a percentage of a year's rent may be charged for these services. For your protection, do not pay any fee until after housing has been found for you.

In some cities, rents are controlled by the local government. This means owners cannot raise rents more than a certain amount each year. When rents are controlled, owners sometimes charge *key money.* The renter has to pay a sum of money for the right to rent the unit.

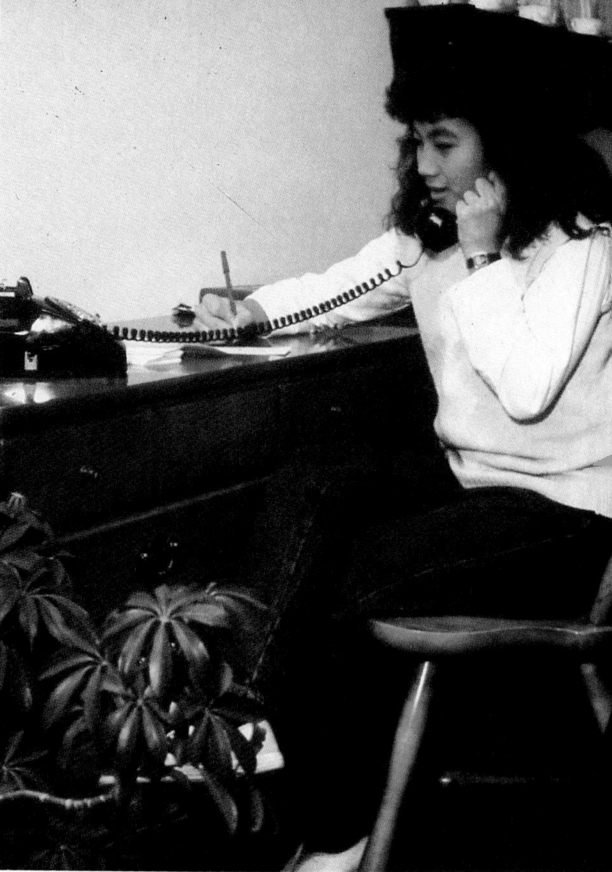

Get to the real estate section ahead of time, make the call first, and be the first in line to see the rental—that's what is involved in obtaining a good rental.

It is against the law for an owner to discriminate against a prospective tenant because of race, creed, color, or national origin. Discrimination can be shown in several ways. The owner can simply refuse to rent the unit or make the rent fee too high. The owner also may charge fees for services given free to other tenants.

If you feel you have been discriminated against, check with the local human rights commission or fair housing office. It will help to find out if discrimination has occurred. If so, it will work to solve the problem and get you the housing you want. A lawyer can also advise you in discrimination cases.

Security Deposits and Leases

When you choose to rent a dwelling, the owner may require a **security deposit.** This is a payment, often equal to a month's rent, that protects the owner against any damage you do to the rental unit. If the unit is clean and in good repair when you leave it, you should get your money back promptly. In some places, owners are required to pay interest on money they hold.

When a prospective tenant comes to an agreement with the owner, they enter into a legal contract. This contract may be informal, made between the two on an oral basis. Usually the tenant signs a **lease** or a written contract. A lease lists the conditions to be met by both parties.

Leases provide protection for both the owner and tenant. The tenant is guaranteed a rental unit for a certain length of time, often one year, for a certain price. Rents cannot usually be raised while a lease is in effect.

The owner receives protection through a list of conditions the tenant must meet. Owners have the right to know how many people will be living in the unit. There may be a fee if rent is not paid on time. The lease spells out who must pay for water, fuel, and other utilities. Leases may restrict guests, pets, or children.

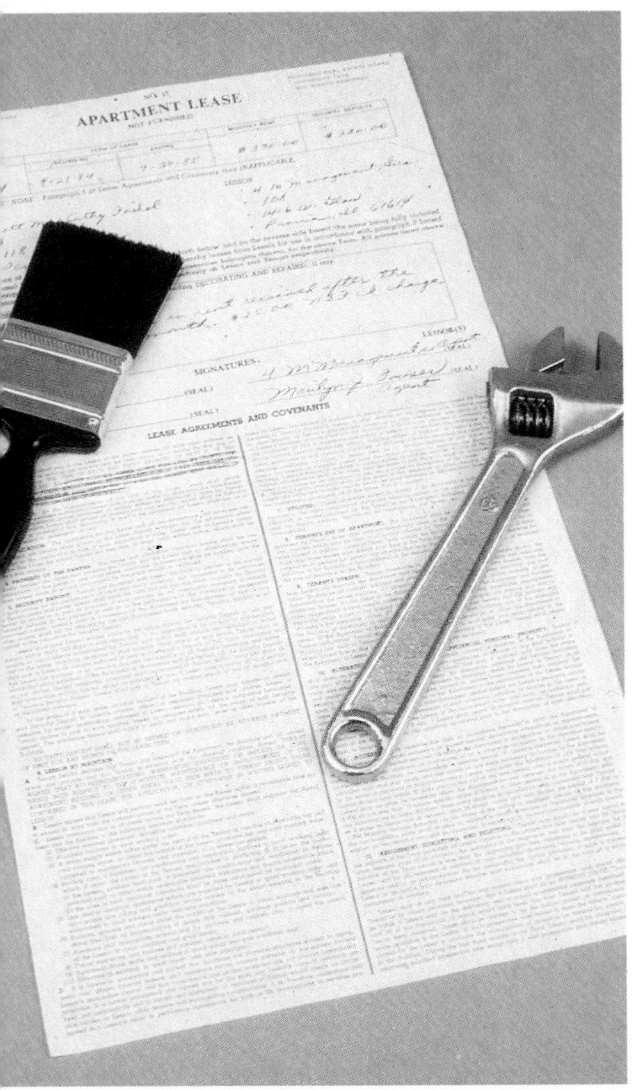

The tenant must usually leave the unit in its original condition. The lease may require that if you paint, you must repaint the original color before you leave. Bookshelves you attach to walls or locks you put on doors may become the owner's when you move.

It is important that tenants read their leases and know what they have agreed to do. They should never sign a blank lease. Special attention should be paid to typed in entries.

As long as a lease is in effect, the tenant is responsible for the rent, even after leaving the unit. Some leases allow tenants to **sublet** the unit to another person or family. The original tenant still leases the housing and is responsible for the rent but can rent the unit to someone else.

If an owner says repairs or redecorating will be done to a unit you want to rent, have that written into your lease before you sign it. An owner may show you through a unit and say that certain repairs or changes will be made. For your protection, write these agreements in the lease in ink and have the owner initial each of them. Then if there is any conflict about what is to be done, the lease shows what the agreement was.

Renting housing and signing a lease or other written agreement are serious steps. You become legally responsible for the conditions of the lease. If you do not live up to them, you can be taken to court.

Rights and Responsibilities of Tenants

As a tenant, you are responsible for paying your rent on time and keeping your dwelling in good condition. You are legally obligated to pay if the housing is not in the same state when you leave as when you moved in. You need the owner's permission before making decorating or structural changes. It may be useful to get the permission in writing.

When you rent, you expect the owner to provide a safe and sanitary dwelling in good repair. The owner is usually in charge of insect extermination, lawn care, snow removal, garbage collection, plumbing and appliance repair, and security. Public areas such as hallways should be kept in good repair. As a tenant, you can expect repairs and upkeep to be done promptly and well.

If the landlord promises to paint the kitchen and repair the leaky faucet, be sure that it is stated in the lease. A verbal agreement does not give you any legal redress.

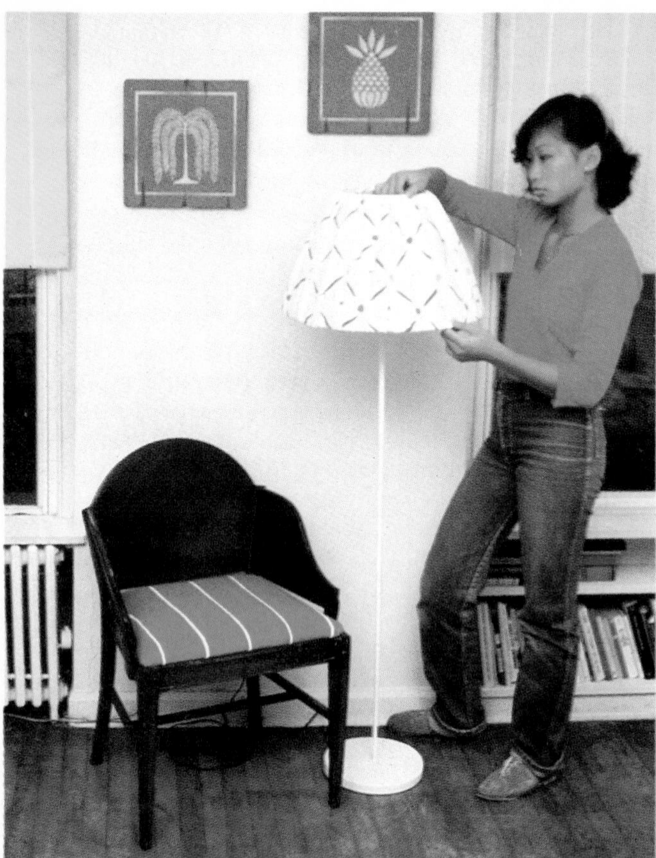

Before making decorative or structural changes be sure to get the owner's permission. Any shelving that you install could become the owner's property.

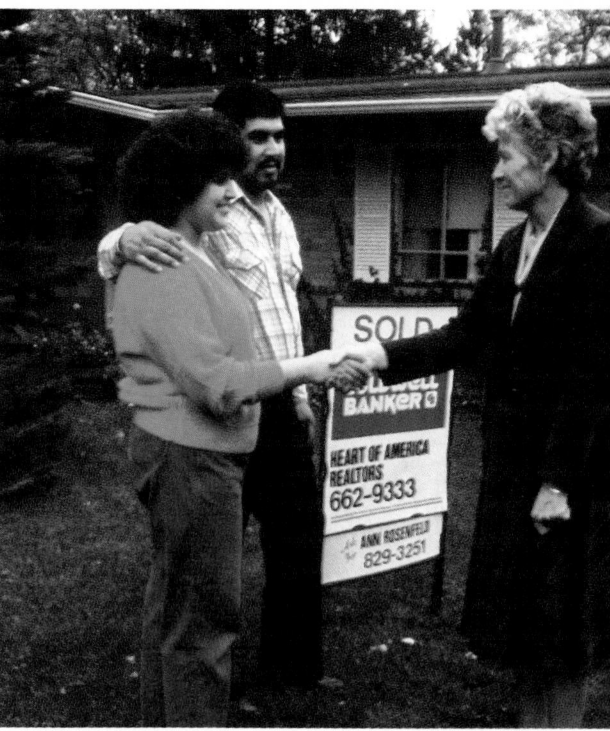

Real estate agents earn a percentage of the selling price of a home. These services may well be worth it when you consider the time involved in taking care of financial, legal, and ownership transactions.

BUYING A HOME

A home is probably the most expensive purchase most people make in their lives. For first-time buyers, it can be a confusing and stressful experience. Being familiar with the process of buying a home and having the help of qualified people can make the experience easier.

Many home buyers and sellers use a real estate agent to help in the process. Such agents know what is on the market, the price levels in the area, and the process of transferring ownership. Such expert help is valuable to those who are buying and selling real estate.

Some people buy and sell homes without the help of a real estate agent. This saves them money, thus reducing the price of the home. However, the help of a lawyer and other financial experts becomes more important to make sure the contracts are legal and proper. Extra time is required to make the arrangements, file papers, and see all the needed people.

Transferring Property

When you have decided on a house to buy, there are many steps to complete to transfer ownership of the property. First, you and the seller must come to an agreement on the price and the conditions of the sale. These conditions may include items such as

1. the day you wish to move in;
2. the condition of the property (if any improvements are to be made before the sale);
3. whether any inspections, such as termite or structural, are to be made;
4. what personal property, such as drapes or appliances, will remain in the home when the owner moves.

If you are buying a condominium or shares in a cooperative, it is important to read the legal documents for the development. These include the master deed, the bylaws, the budget, and the management contract. A lawyer can explain what your rights and responsibilities will be. You should agree to buy a condo or co-op only if you can accept the restrictions outlined.

As a buyer, you will need to arrange financing, which is discussed more fully in the next section. The lender will appraise the home to determine its worth, because the amount of your loan will be based on that value. A credit check will be run to see if you are financially dependable.

The **title** is the legal document proving the owner's right to the property. There will be a title search to find out whether the owner indeed has the right to sell the home. This is usually done by a lawyer and involves looking at the records of all previous sales.

The final step in the transfer of ownership is the closing or settlement. You and the seller, or your representatives, meet to carry out the transfer. The **deed** is the written document that passes ownership. It is signed, given to you as the new owner, and recorded with the county/state government. If you borrowed money from a lender to buy the house, that lender will hold the deed until the money is paid back. At the closing all remaining financial arrangements are handled.

Financial Arrangements

Most buyers borrow part of the price of the home they purchase. Thus, the first step in financing a home is to figure out how much money you can pay and how much you can borrow.

You will be required to make a **down payment,** which is a cash payment of a part of the cost of the home. The rest of the cost is borrowed from a lender and is called a **mortgage.** A payment plan will be set up to repay the loan. Each monthly payment will include part of the principal, or the amount borrowed, as well as the interest, the charge for borrowing the money. In the early years of a mortgage, most of each payment covers interest costs, while in the later years, more and more goes toward principal.

A mortgage loan officer can help you figure costs and give you an idea of how much money you can borrow. Sometimes the amount of the loan is based on your monthly income.

There are two main types of mortgages, though there are many variations of the two types. One general kind is called a conventional mortgage. The interest rate and the payment size remain the same during the loan. This type of mortgage usually covers 70 to 80 percent of the cost of the home and lasts from fifteen to thirty years.

The second general type of mortgage is called an adjustable rate mortgage. These mortgages can last up to forty years and usually cover 75 to 90 percent of the cost of a home.

The interest on an adjustable rate mortgage varies with economic conditions. This means the monthly payment varies with interest rates. There are many ways adjustable mortgages can be written. If you are interested in one of these mortgages, you need to be certain you understand the terms of the loan. The government has rules that limit how often changes in payment size can be made and the amount the payment can change.

When interest rates are low and stable, conventional mortgages are common. In times of high or rapidly changing interest rates, conventional mortgages are not profitable. Thus, adjustable rate mortgages may be the only ones available.

For any mortgage there are basic questions to consider:

1. How much and when will you have to pay?
2. When and how will payments change?
3. Will payments vary in ways you cannot anticipate?
4. Do you expect your income to be enough to cover all the payments?

For most people, a mortgage with set payments is easiest to understand. With adjustable rate mortgages, borrowers need to know when increases will occur so they can plan ways to meet them. To protect yourself with a variable-interest-rate mortgage, be sure there is a limit on payment or rate increases.

Interest rates vary from one institution to another. Therefore, shop around, compare interest rates, and compare the costs of conventional and adjustable rate mortgage.

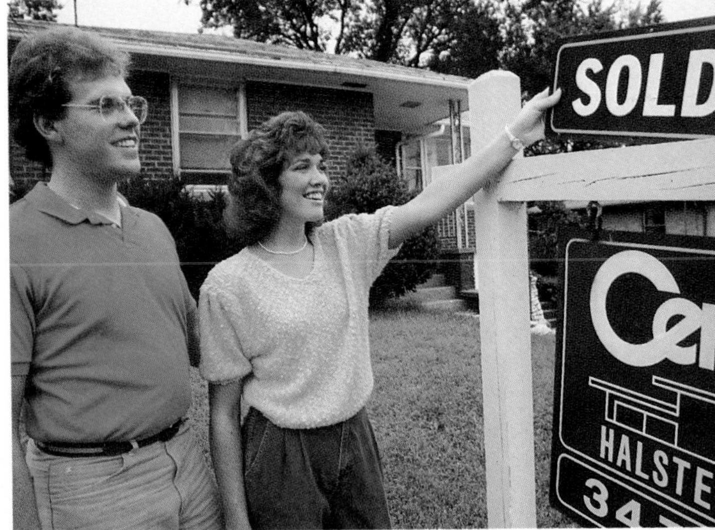

Comparison shopping for mortgages is just as important as for any other large purchase. Most mortgages are written by savings and loan associations. However, commercial banks, mutual savings banks, and mortgage banking companies issue mortgages. Credit unions, state housing finance authorities, or insurance companies are other sources. When buyers are aware of the sources of mortgages and the terms offered, they can choose the contract that best fits their situations.

Settlement and Ongoing Costs

The down payment may be the largest sum of money you pay at closing time. However, there are other settlement costs to pay.

There may be fees that the lender charges to make and process the loan. The house appraisal, the credit report, the title search, inspections, and other fees and charges will need to be paid.

Some lenders handle paying the taxes and insurance on the home rather than having the homeowner pay them directly. They collect money from the buyer in advance and save it to cover these costs.

The lender is required by federal law to provide the buyer with the amount of the closing costs before the day of settlement.

There are also other expenses involved in buying a home. First are moving costs. Hookup charges for a telephone and deposits to utility companies may have to be paid. You may want to buy appliances and furniture for your new home. Most first-time home owners need many items such as garbage cans, snow shovels, and lawn mowers. Unexpected costs in getting settled in a new home almost always occur.

Home owners have to plan and budget their money for the regular expenses involved in owning a home. Property taxes and insurance bills come due at least yearly. There may be special assessments for sewers, street lights, or sidewalks. A reserve fund is useful when upkeep and repairs are needed.

MOVING

When you move, you end or transfer certain services. These are taken care of in advance. Your telephone and utilities, such as water, gas, and electricity, need to be discontinued. Trash service and newspaper delivery will no longer be needed at your old address. Leave your new address at the post office so it can forward your mail. Notify magazine publishers, insurance agents, credit card companies, tax bureaus, and financial agencies of your change of address.

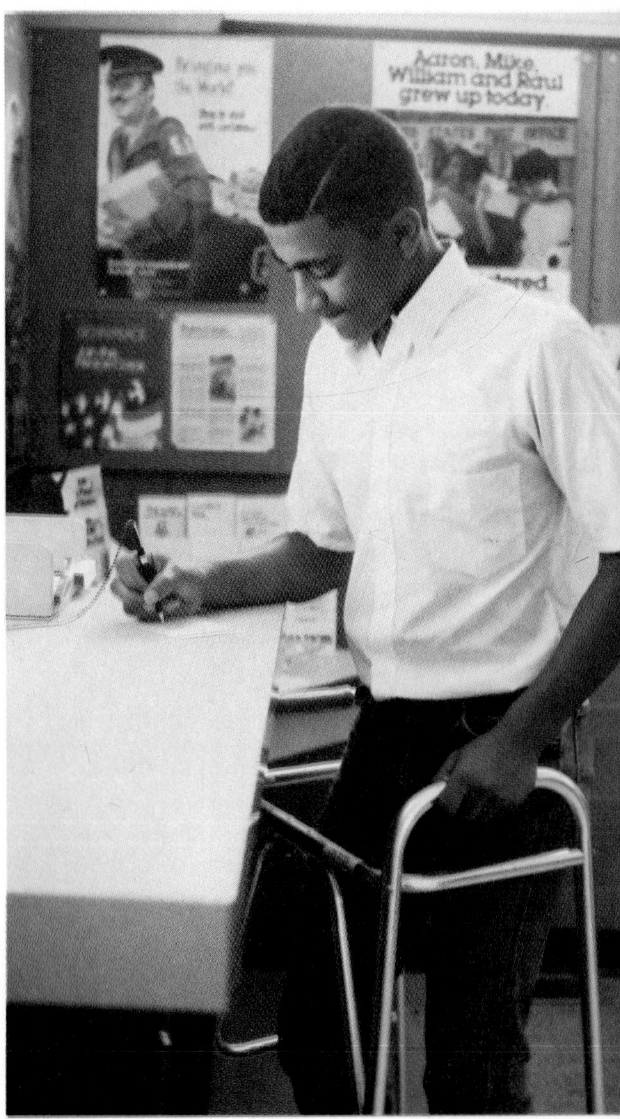

Six weeks in advance is not too early to notify magazines, cable T.V., landlords, DMV, and the telephone company of your intent to move and new address.

DO-IT-YOURSELF MOVING

Many people move themselves. It is usually more convenient and less expensive than hiring a mover. Do-it-yourselfers rent or borrow a trailer or truck to haul household goods.

By packing and loading your own goods, you will know it is done the way you wish. You will need to collect a good supply of cardboard boxes and newspapers to wrap and pad your breakables. The more padding you use, the safer your breakables will be.

You can plan your moving date so that you move out and in at times you choose. You know where your goods are at all times. Moving yourself may cut costs in half when moving long distances.

COMMERCAL MOVERS

If you hire someone to move you, it is helpful to have several firms make bids. They will give you an idea of the costs involved. You can also get a feeling for how well the company will care for your possessions.

The cost is based on the weight and bulk of your goods, the distance to your new home, and the extra services you want. These services include packing and unpacking. When you compare bids, be sure to compare similar services. If you are moving within a city, you will usually be charged a flat fee per hour for workers and a truck.

Two weeks in advance start packing books, dishes, glasses and out-of-season clothing. Pack them in sturdy boxes, tape them tightly closed, and label with a felt pen.

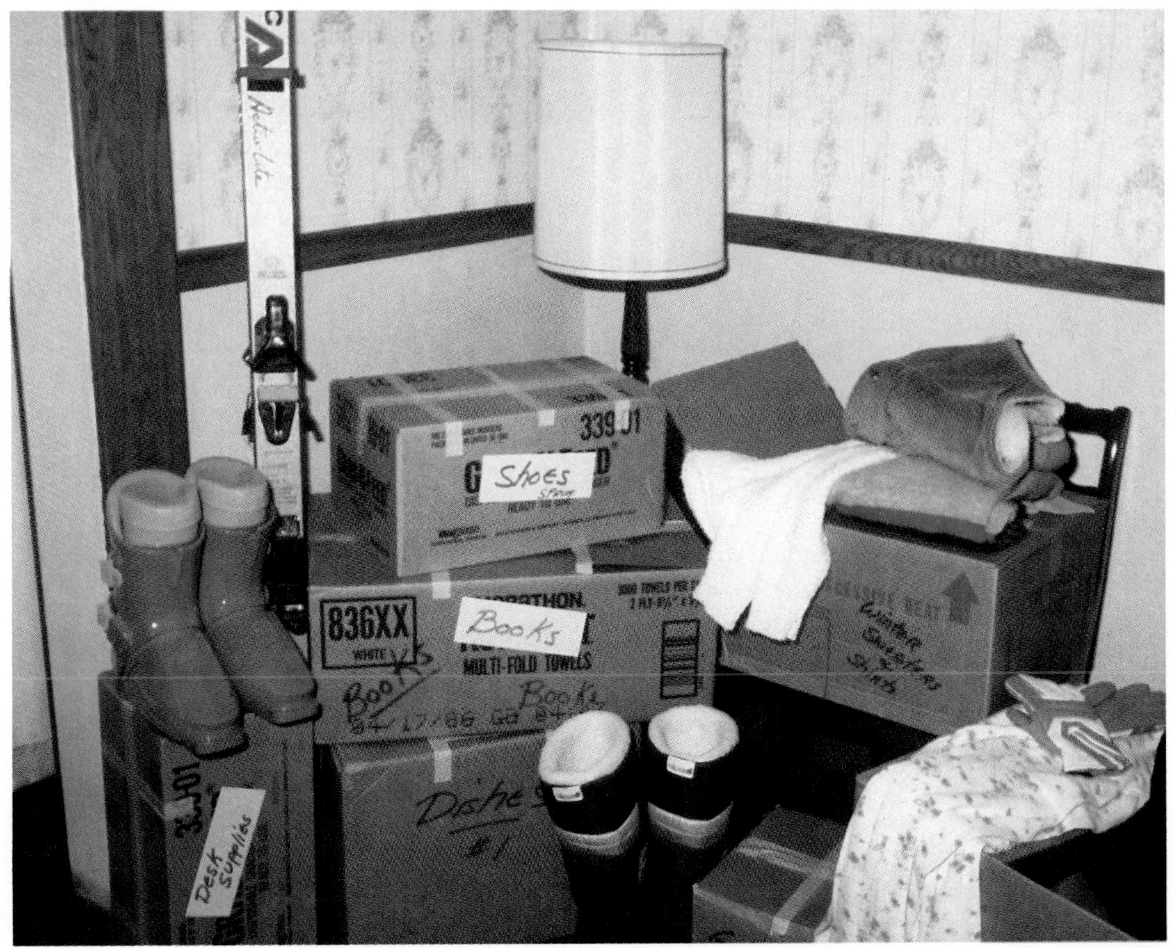

Managing Your Life

USING THE WANT ADS

The want ads in your local newspaper are a major source of information about the housing market in your community. It can be helpful to begin reading the want ads several weeks before you actually want to look for housing. Then, when you are ready to find a new home, you will have the knowledge to proceed. Knowing how to use the want ads can help you manage your search for a home.

- *Information about the market.* The general categories of the want ads can give you an idea of the types of housing available in your area. For example, there may be listings for mobile homes; mobile home lots to rent; rooms, apartments, and homes to share; unfurnished and furnished apartments; homes for rent; condominiums and cooperatives; duplexes for sale or rent; and detached homes for sale.
- *Learning the vocabulary.* The want ads will help you learn the vocabulary of housing. You will need to become familiar with the abbreviations used in the want ads. For example, would you know that "2 br, 1 ½ ba twnhs, W/D in bsmt, att. gar., sec., new cpt." describes a two bedroom, one and one-half bath townhouse with a washer and dryer in the basement, an attached garage, security services, and new carpet?
- *Price ranges.* Whether you are renting or buying, the want ads can give you an idea of the price ranges available in your area. How much is the rent for two apartments? What seems to be the average sale price of a three bedroom house? What extras and features are offered in the more expensive housing? You can use this information to compare the cost of the kind of housing you want with your resources.
- *Addresses of available units.* Before you begin looking at specific housing units, use the want ads to get a feel for where certain priced housing is located in your city or town. You may decide to choose a neighborhood and focus on finding a home there.
- *Professional help.* Through the want ads, you can discover how much housing is offered through real estate firms and how much is for rent or sale by owners. You can choose whether or not you want help in locating housing.
- *Timing.* Sunday is usually the day when the paper contains the most real estate ads. If you have been reading the want ads regularly, you will know what day's paper has the most or best ads.
- *Advertise for what you want.* If you have decided exactly the type of rental unit you want, you may wish to advertise. You can place an advertisement under "Housing Wanted" and describe exactly what you are looking for. By using the classified ads in both ways—reading others' ads and inserting your own—you increase your chances of finding what you want.

WORDS TO REMEMBER

condominium
cooperative apartments
deed
down payment
lease
mortgage
site
security deposit
sublet
tenant
title

CHECKING YOUR UNDERSTANDING

1. What function of housing seems most important to you? Describe at least three features in a dwelling that would help meet this function.
2. Describe resources you would have in finding and establishing a home to fit your needs.
3. Compare and contrast the characteristics of cooperative apartments and condominiums.
4. Compare and contrast the rights and responsibilities of tenants with those of owners of rental property.
5. In general, describe the steps involved in buying a home. What are the two main types of mortgages? Besides the down payment, what are some other costs involved in owning a home?

APPLYING YOUR UNDERSTANDING

1. The Rivers family consists of Bill and Margaret Rivers, Bill's mother, who is in a wheelchair, fifteen-year-old Dale, who enjoys all kinds of sports, and ten-year-old Tony, who takes piano and drum lessons. Margaret Rivers runs an upholstery business in the home. The family does not go out often but enjoys watching television, playing games, and working puzzles together. Describe a home that would meet some of the goals, values, and needs of the Rivers family.
2. Imagine you are a real estate agent. Prepare a brochure to give to clients explaining the differences and similarities in rental apartments, cooperatives, condominiums, town houses, and duplexes. How do these types of housing differ from mobile homes and detached houses? In your brochure, describe the kind of help you could give people looking for each type of housing.
3. Interview a home renter and a home owner. Find out why they have financed their homes as they have. What are the advantages or disadvantages that they see in their arrangements? Do they anticipate changing in the future? Compare your answers to those of your classmates. Discuss the similarities and differences in your findings.
4. Assume you are ready to move into a college dorm or an apartment with friends. What items will you take or leave? Make a plan for moving your possessions. How will you pack them? Haul them? Estimate how much it will cost.

Chapter 30

CHOOSING AND EVALUATING HOUSING

Has this ever happened to you?

Martin opened his locker one Friday morning. "Hey Beth," he called across the hall. "You won't believe what happened at home last night. My parents are talking about moving!"

"You're kidding," said Beth. "Is one of them changing jobs or something? Are they going to move before you graduate? Surely they won't make you take your last semester at a different school."

"No, I get to stay here and finish," answered Martin. "And they aren't changing jobs. But dad says they are tired of driving so far to get to work. They carpool about forty minutes each way now. They are talking about some condos that would be five minutes from my mom's job and about two minutes from dad's. Mom could take the bus to work and I think dad could even walk in good weather."

"It sounds like a major change to me," commented Beth.

"You're right about that!" said Martin. "They keep talking about the convenience of the condos. All I can think about is how close all the neighbors would be and how noisy it is where those condos are—there's an interstate highway pretty close and lots of businesses."

Do you know someone whose family has moved to a location more convenient to work?

What are some factors to consider in choosing a location for a home?

After reading this chapter, you will be able to

- analyze how effectively space is used in a home in floor plans and in storage areas;
- understand features to look for in the efficient use of energy and water in a home;
- recognize factors that contribute to a safe, secure, and well-maintained home;
- identify several aspects of location to consider in choosing a home;
- describe ways to adapt a home to your needs.

There are many things to think about in deciding whether housing is suitable or a good buy. Most of the topics discussed in this chapter apply to all types of housing, ranging from rental apartments to detached homes. Whether you are renting or buying, you will be happier in your housing choices when you know what to look for.

SPACE

Perhaps the most basic factor in choosing housing is the use of space. The amount of space you need or want is a personal matter. Minimum standards set by the government suggest at least one room per person. Many people prefer as much space as they can afford to buy or rent. However, too much space can be a burden to heat, cool, maintain, and repair.

Take a tape measure along and check room measurements before signing a lease. A place that appears spacious may be overcrowded once your furniture arrives.

People look for housing that will be large enough for their possessions and furniture. If three children are to share a bedroom, they need enough room for their beds. A large sofa may not go through a narrow entry hall. Think about your belongings and how they will fill the available space.

How usable is the space? Can it be used in different ways if your needs and wants change? This may be more important for buyers because renters can move more easily when their needs change.

FLOOR PLANS

A **floor plan** is an illustration of the layout of a room or dwelling. A full-house floor plan shows where the rooms are placed. Other plans may show more detail. For example, a plan of a room layout may include electrical outlets, plumbing, windows, and furniture placement. In choosing housing, the full-house floor plan is an important factor to consider.

The actual layout of rooms in a home affects how well it works for you. The size and shape of rooms in relation to each other are important. Even small inconveniences can annoy you over days and months of everyday life.

There are two major things to consider in deciding whether the floor plan of a housing unit will fit your needs. These are the layout of the space zones and the traffic patterns.

Space Zones

The space in a well-designed home is divided into three **zones,** or areas. These are the work zone, the living zone, and the sleeping zone. Ideally, the zones should be separate from each other. It is even better if you cannot see activities in one zone from the others. It is also helpful if you can move from one zone to another without going through the third.

The work zone includes the garage, entryway, kitchen, and laundry area. You will do many chores in the work zone. These chores are easier to manage if the rooms are grouped in one place. This zone is usually the noisiest area in the home.

The living zone is generally the living, dining, and family rooms. This zone provides space for games, TV, talking, and other social activities. You can be with other family members and your guests in the living zone.

Identify the three space zones in the picture below. Why would you consider this a good arrangement?

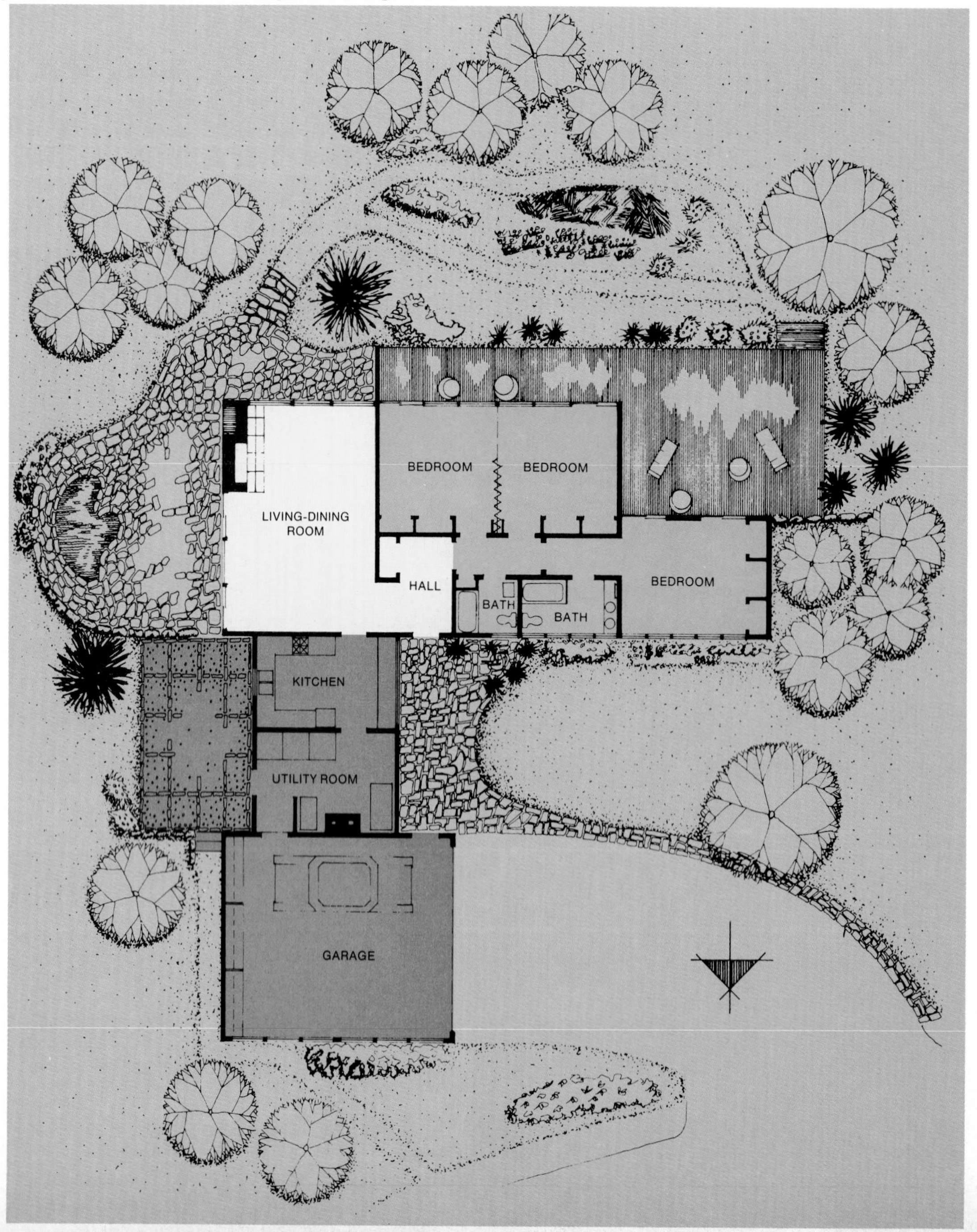

The bedrooms and bathrooms make up the sleeping zone. This zone is usually buffered from other zones by stairs, hallways, or closets. They help cut noise that might keep sleepers awake. A multistoried home with the bedrooms on a separate floor provides the best noise control for the sleeping zone.

The sleeping zone is the setting for sleeping, resting, grooming, and dressing. It also is the place for your private activities, such as work on hobbies, studying, reading, or listening to music.

If you are looking at multiple-family housing, check the floor plan of the entire building. Avoid a plan that has the bedrooms of your unit near the living or work areas of another. Noise from the other unit can disturb you as you sleep next door or upstairs or downstairs.

People vary in the amount of space they wish in each zone. You may want a floor plan with lots of space in the work zone, while others prefer more in the sleeping zone. People who entertain often may look for a large living zone. Your values and life-style will guide you in how to divide space among the three zones in your home.

Traffic Patterns

The paths you follow as you move about a home are called **traffic patterns.** Patterns begin at the doors to the housing unit. The best patterns allow access to every room without going through another room. When you enter the home, you should be able to reach all three zones without disturbing activities in other parts of the unit.

There are four types of traffic patterns to consider. These are patterns for work, family life, service, and guests.

Work traffic patterns center in the kitchen. A clear path to the stove, refrigerator, sink, and eating area makes cooking easier. Cross traffic through the kitchen causes confusion. Therefore, a dead-end kitchen is best to work in. A kitchen that is near the laundry, the entrance doors, and children's play areas is convenient.

Family life traffic patterns depend on the habits of family members. People walking through the home should not distract those who are busy. Traffic through the living zone may disturb televison watching, conversation, or other activities. Students need study areas away from heavy traffic.

Service traffic patterns are those used by persons who offer service to the home. If repairmen or delivery people walk through your home doing their jobs, they will cause extra work for you. A floor plan that gives them access to the part of the home they will work in can avoid this.

Traffic patterns for guests are simply those they follow after they enter the house. Is there easy access to a coat closet, bathroom, and the living area? An entryway that contains a coat closet can be helpful when guests arrive.

Good traffic patterns and organization of space zones are the keys to a good floor plan. Finding a home floor plan to suit your needs is a big step in ensuring the home functions well for you.

The first step to insure that a home will function for you is to analyze the floor plans. Efficient traffic patterns and organization of space zones are the keys to a good floor plan.

Managing Your Life

ENERGY SAVING IDEAS

Because energy costs are a major part of housing expenses, most people want to manage their energy use to save money. The following suggestions can help you reduce the use of energy in your home.

• Buy energy efficient appliances. The efficiency of home appliances, such as refrigerators, hot water heaters, clothes dryers, and ovens, is a measure of how little energy they waste in doing a job. The higher the efficiency, the less energy used and the lower the cost. Look for efficiency ratings on appliances that range from seven to twelve.

Often appliances and equipment with high energy efficiency ratings are more expensive to buy than others. However, because they cost less to operate, they are cheaper to own in the long run.

• Control thermostat settings. Reducing the work load on heating and cooling systems can save energy. When the thermostat is set at 20° C (68° F.) and the outside temperature is almost 43° C (110° F.), the air conditioner will have to work hard. Even the most efficient unit will use a lot of energy. Reducing the work load on appliances and equipment will lower costs. This is why thermostat settings of 20° C (68° F.) in winter and 27° C (80° F.) for summer are suggested.

• Insulate. **Insulation** is a material that does not conduct heat or cold. In hot weather, insulation holds cool air in the home. In winter, heat is retained when there is enough insulation. Insulated walls and attics can help lower utility costs. The amount of insulation needed depends on the climate where the home is located.

Good insulation on appliances and equipment can help save energy. Ovens, clothes dryers, hot water heaters, refrigerators, and freezers that are well insulated will run more effectively.

• Use energy only when needed. Turn off the television, radio, and lights when no one is using them. Use the dishwasher only when it is full because it takes the same amount of energy to run it whether it is full or half full. Save laundry until you have complete loads for the washer and dryer.

• Use weatherstripping and caulking. A great deal of air enters and leaves a home around doors and windows, even when they are closed. Use weatherstripping or caulk around the inside or outside of window or door frames. Fill cracks between the frames and the walls. This will help hold in heat during the winter and cool air during the summer.

• Invest in storm windows and doors. Storm windows and doors are another way to decrease the air flow around windows and doors. Stretching clear plastic over windows instead of buying storm windows is a cheaper way to cut heat loss.

STORAGE

Having enough storage in a home is very desirable. Every room needs some kind of storage for the items used there. A list of your possessions and those of other members of your family will show you the need for storage in your home.

In looking at housing units, note the storage space. Will there be enough room for your possessions? Is the storage space easy to use? Older dwellings and housing in multiple-family units often have less storage. The smaller the housing unit, the more important is having enough easy-access storage. Therefore, it is vital to carefully look at the storage areas before renting or buying.

Types of Storage

Storage can be either built-in or freestanding. There are pros and cons to both types.

Built-in storage is attached permanently to walls, floors, or ceilings. Types of built-ins are closets, shelves, cabinets, and racks of all kinds. Built-ins make the most use of space in a small area. However, you cannot move most built-ins easily. They have limited use in a room because they cannot be easily changed. Some units are hard to convert to other uses when storage needs change.

Freestanding units add flexibility to storage. These units are not attached to the home and include cabinets, chests of drawers, office filing cabinets, trunks, and chests. Other types are china cabinets, shelf units, storage racks, wardrobe closets, and hutches. Freestanding storage tends to take up more floor space than built-ins. However, it can be moved where needed and used in many ways.

A desk made from a plank and two file cabinets combines as a storage and study area.

Location of Storage

You will find storage most usable when it is located where stored items are used. Do bedrooms have closets for clothing and other personal items? Are there closets for outdoor clothing near entrances? Can towels be stored in or near bathrooms and bedding near bedrooms?

Is there enough space in the kitchen for storing dishes, equipment, small appliances, and food. Most people also need a storage area for bicycles, sports equipment, lawn and garden tools, trunks, boxes, and off-season clothes. Garages, attics, or basements provide space for storing these kinds of items. Multiple-family units often have a storage area where lockers or cages are provided. Each unit has access to one of these storage spaces. The temperature in these areas may need consideration when choosing what to store. Candles may melt in the heat of an attic while paint may freeze in an unheated garage or basement.

Making a Storage Plan

Organizing and planning storage can be very helpful when space is limited. Ask yourself what needs to be stored, where it is used and how often, and where it can best be stored.

The top priority in planning storage is given to items used most often. The dishes and pans used for each meal should be stored in the nearest space possible. Clothes, makeup, or accessories worn often should be easy to find. Store little-used items on top shelves or at the back of deep cupboards or closets.

Items are most usable when stored near their point of first use. Small kitchen appliances can be stored near the place where mixing and baking are done. Soaps and bleaches are most handy near the laundry area. Important papers may be kept near the desk or area where family business is done.

Storage that is flexible is helpful when planning. Adjustable shelves, vertical dividers, and pegboards are examples of storage that can be changed to meet new needs. Adjustable shelves can be set the ideal height for the books, linen, or china stored in them.

Often furniture can be bought for two purposes. A coffee or end table may have storage space underneath. Some beds have storage in the headboards and drawers under the mattresses. When storage space is limited, dual-purpose furniture can be a good buy.

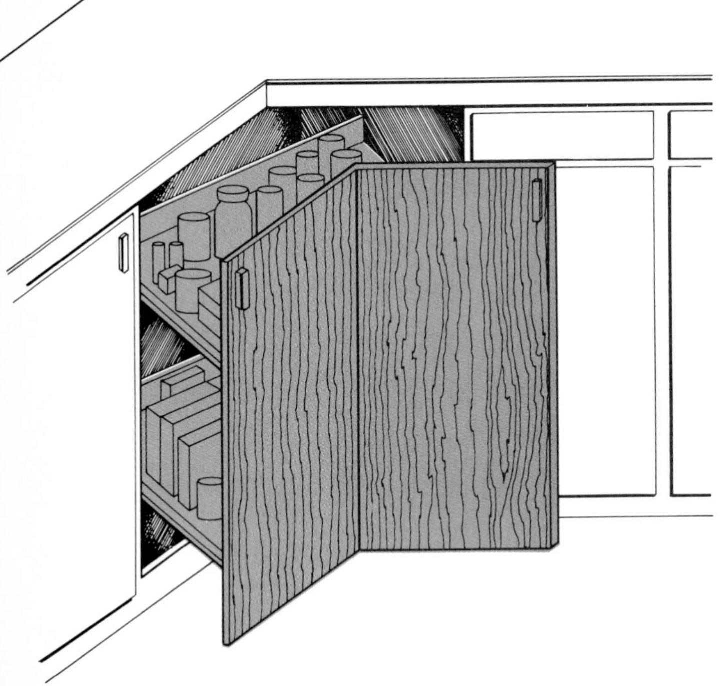

Install revolving shelfs and pullout sliding trays to maximize hard to reach storage space.

There are many devices available to help organize storage. Turntables, racks, drawer dividers, and stackable bins are some examples.

Lack of good storage space can cause irritation. When looking at housing, compare the storage in different units. Storage problems can be solved or eased by freestanding storage units, dual-use furniture, and storage devices.

ENERGY AND WATER USE

Modern living calls for the easy use of energy and water. Electricity runs appliances and lights the home. Heating and cooling may be fueled by electricity, oil, gas, wood, or solar power. Some appliances are run by gas. Water is needed for cleaning, cooking, and sanitation.

Both renters and home owners need to be concerned about utility costs. If you are interested in a home, you may ask to look at the utility bills of the former occupant. This can give you an idea of energy costs.

If you are a home owner, you will want to hold down costs during the years you own the home. An energy-efficient home is worth 5 percent to 9 percent more at resale than a less efficient one.

As a renter, you may have meters for your unit and pay directly for the utilities you use. In some older units, utilities are included in the rent. Increased costs lead to higher rents.

Dual purpose furniture can eliminate clutter and expand storage capabilities.

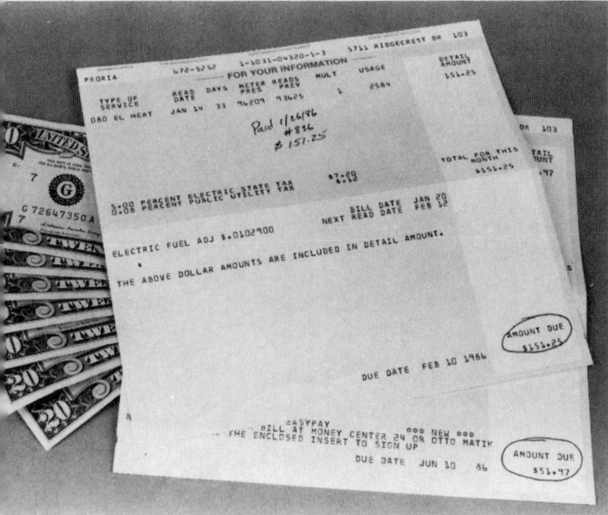

Before renting a place ask to see the past utility bills. Compare the cost and efficiency of the utilities.

HEATING AND COOLING

Good heating and cooling equipment mean comfort for those who live in the unit. The best systems use little energy and are quiet, clean, and effective.

The temperature of a home is usually controlled by a thermostat. A thermostat in every room means you can control the temperature in each room. Rooms you seldom use may not need as much heating or cooling as rooms used more often.

Some rental apartments do not contain thermostats because the temperature is controlled by the owner. This is usually not as desirable as being able to set the temperature in your own unit.

The location of windows in your home can play a big role in heating and cooling. If you live in a cold climate, windows on the north often let in wind and cold air. Curtains and shades can help insulate against the winter weather.

The winter sun, however, can help heat your home if you open shades and drapes in the morning. Windows on the south are especially useful in getting heat from the low winter sun. When the sun moves away from the windows, pulling the shades and drapes helps hold the heat inside.

In warm sunny climates, windows on the east, south, and west can cause a house to become hot and stuffy. Shades can be pulled and drapes closed to prevent the sun from overheating the home. They can be opened when the sun no longer shines on the windows.

Awnings, blinds, and sun-control film can help reduce the sun that enters glass areas. Plants, trees, bushes, and roof overhangs also cut down on heat. Check to see what else can be done to keep out the sun's heat.

Heating Systems

There are several kinds of heating systems. Some are gravity warm air, forced warm air, circulating hot water, steam heat, radiant electrical heat, heat pumps, wood-burning stoves, and solar systems.

Each heating system has good and bad points. For example, forced-warm-air systems can often be noisy and the blower may stir up dirt and dust. A hot water system is usually economical while radiant electrical heat is expensive, but clean and quiet. Heat pumps and solar systems are costly to install but cheaper to run. Wood is less safe than other fuels because wood tars build up in chimneys and frequently catch fire.

Most heating systems have filters to remove dust and dirt from the air. These filters must be cleaned or replaced when they become dirty. A dirty filter wastes heat and may cause the system to overheat.

Heating and cooling systems of a home require the most energy to operate. Therefore, learn to operate, maintain, and take measures to conserve energy with these two systems.

Gas and oil fired furnaces have burners to ignite the fuel. These have a pilot light that may need relighting sometimes. There are fuel shut-off valves so you can turn off the gas or oil when it is not needed. It is necessary to know how to light the pilot light and shut off the fuel if you have a burner on your furnace.

Heating systems run more cheaply when they are serviced each year. An adjustment can save up to 10 percent on fuel use.

Cooling Systems

Newer homes in many parts of the country are cooled by central air conditioning. Air is cooled and filtered in one outdoor unit and blown throughout the house.

You may use room air conditioners when there is no central system. These units are set in windows and cool the air they pull in from outside. They are bought according to the size of the area to be cooled. Older housing may not be wired for air conditioners. It may also have odd-sized windows that cannot hold room coolers. Air conditioners have filters that need cleaning often and must be replaced when worn out.

Fans can also be used in cooling. Cool air is drawn into the home while hot air is forced out. Attic fans remove hot air that builds up under the roof. They are especially useful in warm climates that have cool nights. The night air can be pulled in to replace air heated in the warmth of the day.

ELECTRICAL SYSTEMS

The first step in checking the electrical system is to find out if it can carry enough power for your needs. Electric current enters the home through a service panel. Power can be turned off completely by the main switch. From the service panel, electricity flows through the home on circuits. Heavy duty appliances, like ranges and dryers, usually have their own circuits. Separate circuits supply power for lights, outlets, and other appliances.

Electric current is measured in **amperes.** The number of amperes that can safely enter the home is marked on the service box. For most families one hundred amperes is the minimum needed. The ideal is two hundred amperes. Some older homes have only thirty-to-sixty-ampere capacities and need rewiring.

One way to check whether there is enough power coming into the home is to turn on all the lights. Then turn on a major appliance like the furnace or oven. If the lights dim, there is not enough power available.

If an overload draws too much power into the home, the service panel shuts off the current. This protects the home. Too much power carried on inadequate wiring is very dangerous and can cause fires. The load needs to be reduced before the power is turned back on.

The type of service panel determines how the power is turned off and on. A circuit breaker is a metal box with switches or buttons for each circuit. When an overload on a circuit occurs the switch turns off or the button pops out, cutting off power. You restart the power by flipping the switch or pushing in the button.

A fuse box contains fuses for each circuit. These fuses blow out during a power overload. A new fuse is needed to turn on the power again. New fuses should be for the same amperage as those they replace. If there is a fuse box in your home, it is wise to keep a supply of fuses on hand. A chart showing what each circuit breaker or fuse controls is helpful.

Check the number of wall outlets. Double or triple plugs in an outlet may mean there are not enough outlets available.

The electrical system is probably most important to those who are thinking of buying an older home. It may be wise to have an electrician look at the wiring before you agree to buy. Then you will know if repairs will have to be made soon and can plan for them.

Learn how to restart the circuit breaker or replace a fuse before an overload occurs.

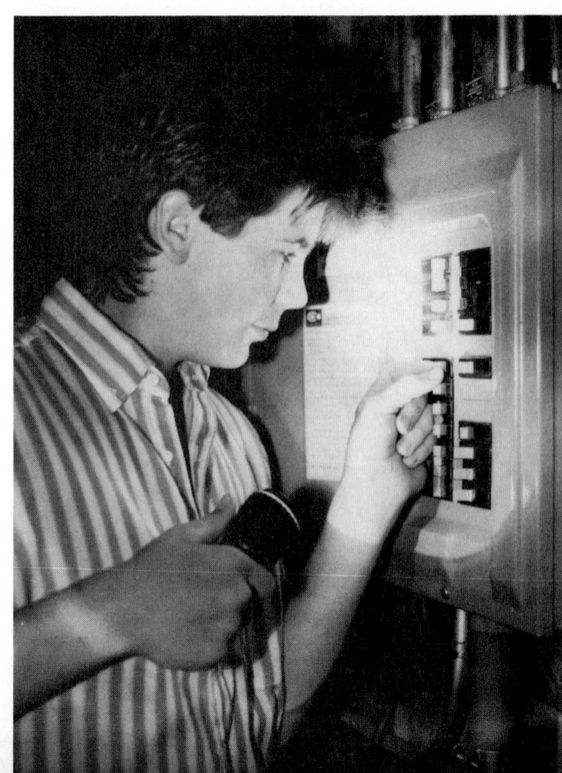

PLUMBING

The plumbing system carries water in and out of your home. It should carry water to fixtures without leaking, making noise, reducing pressure, or giving any color or taste to the water. A good supply of safe water is important to health.

Can the water system deliver enough water? To check water pressure, turn on the sink and bathtub faucets and flush the toilet. If the flow in the sink or tub slows down, there may be a pressure problem.

See if any of the faucets leak. In a day, the amount of water leaked can be more than that used. If the faucet leaks hot water, you will pay to heat the wasted water.

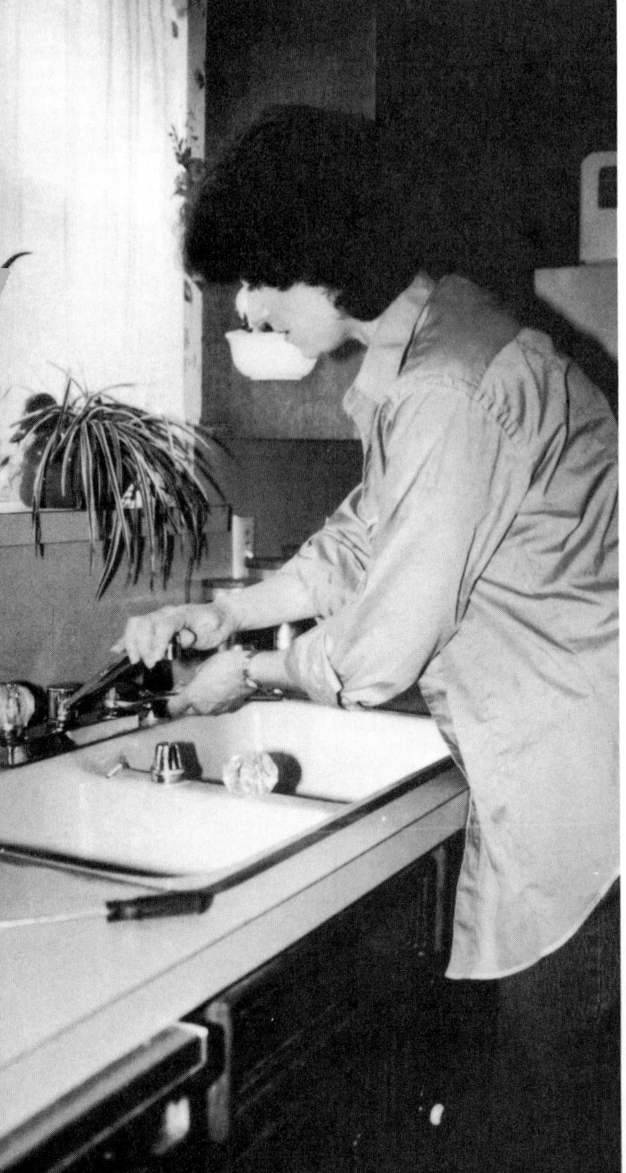

A noisy water heater is a sign of mineral buildup inside. Check the heater to find out if it is run by gas, oil, or electricity. How fast will it reheat water? How large is it? A 115 to 150 liter (thirty to forty gallon) heater will serve two people. A 190 liter (fifty gallon) is needed for most families. Good heaters last about ten years.

If you are considering a home with a water well, check it carefully. It may be wise to have the water's purity tested. You can check the pump and pressure storage tank by running the water for about fifteen minutes. The well may not be too good if the water gets cloudy and the pressure changes.

If you are renting, you will not usually be responsible for repairs to heating and cooling equipment or the electrical and plumbing systems. However, your comfort depends on whether the systems work well. If something needs repair, you will have to wait for the owner to fix it. This may mean a time of inconvenience until the repairs are made.

SAFETY AND SECURITY

One of the functions of housing is to keep you safe and secure. Dwellings vary in how well they protect those in them. There are a few simple items to look at when checking the security of a home.

First, is there lighting outdoors. There should be lights near the place where you and your guests will park your cars. Are there lights in the halls, stairs, and entryways in a multiple-family unit? In a detached home, is there enough lighting by doors? Good lighting will help you feel more at ease when coming and going at night.

Next, check the locks on doors and windows. If all doors and windows are locked, the chances of a break-in are reduced. Almost half of all home thefts occurs when a home is not locked. The best kinds of locks are those that have the word "dead" in their name. Any lock that takes a key to lock is safer than one locked by slamming the door.

Having a locksmith put new locks on the doors as soon as you move in helps protect you. Otherwise, you do not know who may have keys to fit your doors. This may be more important for those who live in rental units.

You can do your part to conserve water by fixing leaky faucets, installing water saving devices, and taking shorter showers.

Improve your security and increase your sense of safety by installing home security devices.

Another safety feature is a door chain. This lets you open the door a crack to talk to a stranger before opening the door completely. However, the screws can be easily ripped out of a chain guard. Therefore, it should not be the only lock on your door. A peephole in the door is even better because you can look at the person at the door without opening it.

Good locks are no protection if doors are flimsy. Solid doors provide more security as well as better insulation. Many thieves have gotten in homes by breaking glass in doors and reaching inside to unlock them.

Sliding glass doors to yards, patios, or balconies are very vulnerable. You can put a block of wood or a broom handle cut to fit on the inside to brace the door shut. This will help secure the door.

In multiple-family units, find out about any special security measures. Is there a security guard or check-in gate? Mirrors in elevators or at hallway corners help you see if anyone is there. The laundry room may be a trouble spot. It is safer if kept locked and each tenant given a key.

If you are worried about theft in a neighborhood or multiple-family complex, check with the police. They can tell you about the crime rates in the areas in which you are interested.

CONDITION OF THE HOME

The condition of the home and the quality of its construction are other factors to think about. A well-built and maintained home will be easier and less expensive to manage and care for.

There are construction standards set for housing. City, county, and state building codes govern local building. Government agencies require certain construction standards before they will insure or guarantee a housing loan. Thus, you can expect housing to meet certain minimum standards.

However, home defects are a leading cause of consumer complaints. Therefore, you should make a thorough inspection of the dwelling before you agree to buy or rent it. Ask the real estate agent or owner as many questions about the condition of the home as you can.

Termites or rotted wood in any part of the home is a serious flaw. The most costly defects to repair are a wet basement or crawl space, a leaky roof, a cracked foundation, and problems in the plumbing, wiring, and heating/cooling systems.

LOCATION

Where should your home be located? A home's value is affected by its location. Think about the kind of life you lead when trying to find a location for a home. A home that is near work, schools, shopping, and entertainment saves time, energy, and money. You may not be able to find a perfect location, but at least you can look for one that fits your family's needs.

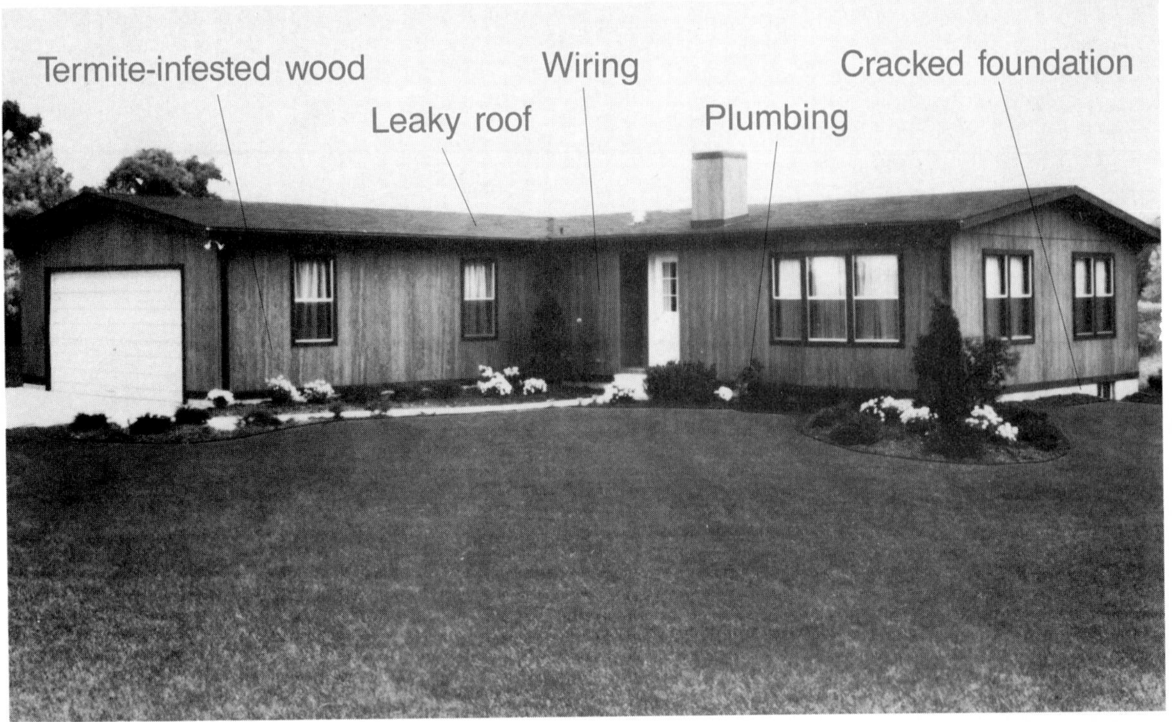

Carefully inspect for potential problems such as a leaky roof, cracked foundation, or inadequate plumbing and wiring before agreeing to rent or buy a dwelling.

NEIGHBORHOOD

A neighborhood includes the people who live near each other and their housing. The neighborhood you choose will affect your life.

There are three ways the choice of a neighborhood will affect you. First, it will affect your budget. Most housing in a neighborhood is similar in price. Choose an area that fits your pocketbook.

Second, you will be influencd by the life-style of the neighborhood and how you get along with others living there. Many people like to live among their peers. A young, newly married couple may be unhappy living in an apartment building filled with retired couples or families with older children. On the other hand, you may enjoy neighbors of varying ages and interests.

Third, if you are buying a home, the neighborhood will affect the future resale value of your unit. Check the condition of homes in an older neighborhood. Avoid a neighborhood where property is not well kept.

Remember that the neighborhood not only affects your satisfaction with the living area, but also resale value.

NOISE

People have only just begun to learn how damaging noise can be. Noise is stressful or unwanted sound. It can be irritating and distracting. High noise levels can damage hearing and health. How noisy is the location you have chosen?

Noise is more of a problem in multiple-family units than in single-family homes. When looking at an apartment or condo, listen for voices in neighboring units. Can you hear the radio, television, or toilet being flushed next door? Send people into the next room and see how loudly they have to talk before being heard where you are.

Carpeting, heavy drapes, and wall hangings can help reduce unwanted sounds. How much sound-absorbing material is there in the unit?

Shrubbery around a building serves as a noise barrier. Units on the first floor of a well-landscaped multiple-family complex are often quieter than those on higher floors. Solid fences, trees, and other plantings can muffle noise in a single-family home as well.

COMMUNITY SERVICES

What services does the community provide the area where you would like to live? You want a home where law enforcement and fire protection are nearby. How long will it take the police, sheriff, or fire fighters to get to your home when they are needed? Where is the nearest fire hydrant or other source of water for fighting fires?

Find out what kind of medical facilities are available. Are doctors, hospitals, and dentists nearby? Or will you have to travel long distances for treatment? Older people and those with children may prefer to live close to medical care.

Discover what kind of public transportation the area offers. Will you be able to take busses, trains, or trolleys to work or other places? How close do they come to the home you have chosen? How much are fares?

How is garbage collection handled? Some cities provide trash pickup. In other places, private companies collect it. People handle their own disposal in rural areas and smaller communities.

Parks and recreational facilities nearby are an asset. You will be better able to attend or take part in activities you enjoy. Multiple-family units with tennis courts, swimming pools, and other facilities are especially convenient for those who enjoy these activities.

ADAPTING A HOME TO YOUR NEEDS

Every home you look at will have its good and bad points. Finding housing you will enjoy living in means looking for those things that are most important to you. It may also mean being willing and able to adapt a home to meet your needs.

Changes can range from the simple to the complex. A new coat of paint on bedroom walls will cost a little in terms of money and hours of work. Remodeling the kitchen may take weeks and cost much. The money, time, and skills you have will decide the kinds of changes you can make. In rental units, changes are governed by the lease.

Sometimes, small rooms are a drawback. The use of mirrors and color can help to make a room look bigger. A wall of mirrors makes a room look twice as large. A light color or monochromatic color scheme makes a room look larger.

Browse through decorating books and magazines for inexpensive and easy to do ideas for adapting a living space to meet your needs.

Both sunlight and indoor lighting will make rooms seem larger. Therefore, take advantage of windows and glass doors and skylights to give the feeling of space. Controlling indoor light to provide brightness and shadows gives a feeling of distance and openness.

Keeping rooms uncluttered is another simple way to make rooms seem bigger. A room crowded with furniture will look small. Because the furniture limits the traffic flow, the room will also "live" small.

If too much noise is a drawback in a home, sound-deadening materials can be added. Carpet is probably the best one you can buy. Cork or heavy fabric on walls also helps cut noise.

When children share a bedroom, a desk or set of shelves for each may prevent fighting. A room divider of fabric, beads, or other material can give each child some privacy.

If you have guests often, but do not have an extra bedroom, a sofa that makes into a bed will be useful. Guests can then sleep in the living area. Other dual-purpose furniture is useful when space is limited.

When you have a handicapped family member or one with other special needs, you may have to make more extensive adaptations in your home. Carpeting may have to be removed so that a person in a wheelchair can get around. Special guardrails and seats may be needed in showers or bathtubs. Drawers may need to be built into undercounter storage space.

Identifying the weaknesses in a home and thinking of creative ways to overcome them can be a challenge. However, the effort is worth it if the changes make the home more livable. Basic flaws in construction, energy efficiency, use of space, and other factors discussed in this chapter present greater problems. They will probably require a great deal of effort and money to correct. Being able to avoid housing with basic flaws and to adapt the home you have picked are two important steps in making good housing choices.

This family has creatively divided the children's bedroom area into sleep and play areas.

WORDS TO REMEMBER

ampere
floor plan
insulation
traffic patterns
zones

CHECKING YOUR UNDERSTANDING

1. Of the four types of traffic patterns in a home, which would be the most important in choosing a dwelling? Least important? Explain your choices.
2. What are some things to consider in making a storage plan for a home? What influence would the type of storage and its location have on a plan? List some items in a home to be stored. What kinds of storage would you need to keep the items where they are first used?
3. Describe different heating and cooling systems and the good and bad points of each. Which system do you prefer and why?
4. What are some of the possible consequences if the plumbing system in a home is not in good condition? How would you identify potential trouble spots?
5. Describe the various security devices with which you are familiar. Which ones provide the most safety? How can you protect your home while you are away from it?

APPLYING YOUR UNDERSTANDING

1. Examine a floor plan for a housing unit. Identify the three space zones. How effective is the traffic pattern through the home? List the good and bad points of the floor plan. Would you like to live in the unit? Why or why not?
2. Locate the service panel in your home, school, or some other building. Is it a circuit breaker or a fuse box? With expert supervision, identify as many circuits as you can. Find out how to turn off the power at the main switch. How do you restart the current after a power overload has caused it to shut off?
3. Arrange to tour a home that is for sale in your community. Before you go, identify at least five potential trouble spots to check in judging the condition of the house. Plan what you will look for in these areas. After touring the home, write a report listing any problems or potential problems you saw. Which of the possible trouble spots did you consider most important? Why?
4. What community services are available in your area? Work with your classmates to develop a complete list. Which services would you want to live near? Are there some you would not want to be close to? How are these services paid for?

Chapter 31

MAKING YOUR HOUSE A HOME

Has this ever happened to you?

Josie hurriedly pushed the buttons on the telephone. She was anxious to talk to Shelly. "Guess what I found today?" she asked when Shelly answered. "I was poking around in my grandmother's attic trying to see if there was anything we could use when we get our apartment. You won't believe the treasures Gran's got stored up there. And she says we can have whatever we want!"

"Come on, tell me," said Shelly.

"First off, there's an old brass bedframe," said Josie. "It needs polishing badly, but I think it will look great when it's cleaned up. I found a couple of old dressers that are really beat up. I couldn't tell whether they could be refinished or not, but we might be able to paint them if the wood doesn't look too good."

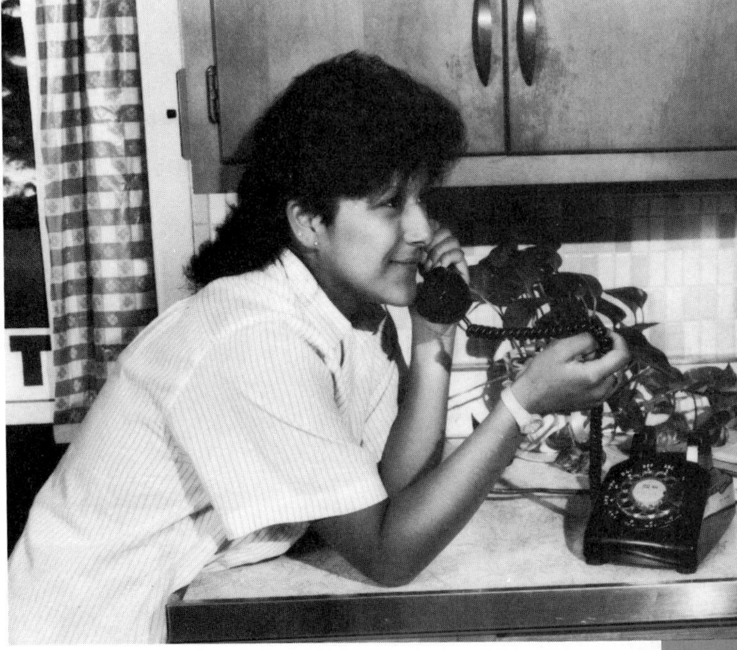

"I don't know the first thing about refinishing, but I've done some painting around here," said Shelly. "They might be pretty in some bright colors."

"There's a wooden rocking chair in good shape and an old sofa that looks awful, but I think it's still sturdy," said Josie. "We'd have to have a slipcover or reupholster it though. Do you know anything about that?"

"Well, I helped my mom reupholster a chair last summer," said Shelly. "She can tell us if the sofa is worth fixing up. I'm really getting excited—we've got half the furniture we need for our apartment already."

Have you ever fixed up an old piece of furniture so it could be used?

What are some sources of furnishings and furniture for someone setting up housekeeping for the first time?

After reading this chapter, you will be able to

- compare and contrast the different kinds of wall coverings, floor coverings, and window treatments;
- identify kinds and functions of lighting;
- describe types of furniture and features to look for when choosing furniture;
- discuss design principles as applied to furniture arrangement and accessories placement;
- recognize costs involved in owning, operating, and repairing appliances.

How you plan the interior of your home will depend on your resources. One important resource is money. Furnishings for a home are costly. Most people setting up housekeeping for the first time cannot afford to buy all new furnishings. Furnished apartments help some people solve this problem. Others turn to rental furniture to fill an unfurnished dwelling. Still others buy only a few basic furnishings for comfort and convenience, and add more items later.

Making use of secondhand finds will not only save you money but make your decorating especially personalized, lively and creative.

Of all the design elements, color is the easiest to change. This can be done with a quick paint job, addition of accent pieces or using coordinating wall coverings and fabrics.

INTERIOR FEATURES

Interior features are important in decorating your home. These include walls, ceilings, floors, windows, and lighting. They provide the setting for your furnishings, accessories, and equipment.

WALLS AND CEILINGS

The walls and ceilings are the largest surfaces in a room. Clean walls with a finish you like and that blend with your furnishings are ideal.

However, walls are not always in the best condition. You may wish to paint them or cover them with new wallpaper. They may be soiled beyond cleaning. Your choice of a new wall finish will depend on the current finish, the condition of the wall, and your budget and tastes.

Painting is the easiest and cheapest way to redo a wall. Paint can be put on smooth or textured walls and is an easy do-it-yourself project. Because paint comes in shades and tints of all colors, you can choose a hue to blend with your furnishings.

Wallpaper is another common wall covering. It comes in a wide range of colors, patterns, and textures. Wallpaper is usually more costly than paint, so you may want to use it only on one or two walls of a room to add interest. Rough or cracked walls can be disguised by wallpaper. (Painting and wallpapering are discussed further in chapter 32).

Paneling is found in the family room or den in some homes. As the name implies, it is put up in panels, which are usually made of plywood. Paneling is easy to clean and care for. However, it is costly to put up and is considered permanent.

Brick, stone, and ceramic tile walls are other permanent wall treatments. They, too, are costly to put up but easy to care for.

FLOOR COVERINGS

The floor coverings in a home affect how comfortable the floor is to walk and stand on, and how easy it is to keep clean. Patterns, tweeds, and small designs hide dirt and footprints best. Soil shows most on very light or very dark colors. Medium tones disguise soil. There are three basic types of floor coverings: resilient, nonresilient, and rugs and carpets.

Area rugs add color and excitement, yet can be picked up for easy cleaning. A heavy patterned rug will tend not to show the dirt.

Resilient Coverings

Resilient covering is a dense, nonabsorbent flooring that "gives." The resilience provides sound control and helps prevent denting. You will also find it more comfortable to stand on than harder flooring. Resilient coverings are water resistant and are made from asphalt, vinyl, rubber, or cork. Asphalt is the least durable and stains easily. Vinyl lasts well and is easy to care for.

Resilient flooring comes in sheets or tiles. Sheets are good in a room with lots of moisture, such as a bath, entry hall, or laundry area. The flooring can be put down so there are no seams through which water can seep to cause damage to the floor beneath.

Nonresilient Coverings

Nonresilient or "hard" floor treatments are attractive and last well. Some examples of this kind of flooring are wood, brick, stone, or tile. Wood flooring is a favorite with many people because of its beauty.

Hard-surface flooring is often used in special areas such as an entry hall. It is very durable but costly. You will find hard flooring uncomfortable to stand on for long periods of time. It also offers little noise control.

Rugs and Carpets

Rugs and carpets are popular floor coverings. They are comfortable to walk on and give some sound control. You can care for rugs and carpeting easily with a vacuum cleaner.

Rugs are cut to less than room size and finished with bound edges. They are bought by size. Room-sized rugs cover most of the floor of a room. They blend the warmth and comfort of the rug with the beauty of the flooring underneath. You can turn them for even wear or move them to other rooms in the home when needed.

Area rugs come in a variety of sizes but do not cover a whole room. They can be used in many ways—to provide interest, to cover high-traffic areas, or to set off parts of a room. If you use area rugs on hard or resilient flooring, they will need a rubberized backing to prevent slipping and falls.

Carpeting covers the whole floor. It is bought by the meter or yard, cut to exact room size, and fastened in place. It cannot be moved. Areas with heavy traffic often show wear first.

Rugs and carpets are a special kind of fabric woven with three yarns. The third yarn forms the **pile,** the soft fibers coming up from the base. Hundreds of short yarns are fastened side by side into the backing made of the other two yarns. This is what makes rugs and carpets more expensive than other kinds of fabric.

The density and kind of pile affects quality and wear. When the pile is dense, that is, the yarns are close together, the carpet will look fuller and wear longer. You can fold back a corner of the carpet to check pile density. Carpets that show lots of backing when bent are of poorer quality.

Pile can be looped, looped and twisted, or cut. Cut pile gives a plush velvet look. A twisted, looped pile is most durable. Pile with level yarns is easy to clean and wears well.

The fiber the rug or carpet is made of also affects quality and wear. Nylon is the most common fiber used. It is durable and easy to keep up, though you may find static electricity is a problem. Acrylic is a synthetic fiber that is not as durable as nylon. Therefore, it is used in low-traffic areas.

Kitchen carpet is often made from olefin because it resists stain and is easy to keep clean.

Wool is strong, resilient, expensive, and wears well. Although soil and stain resistant, it must be mothproofed. Olefin is used in kitchen and outdoor carpet because it resists soil and stain. It is nonabsorbent and easy to maintain.

Rugs and carpets are sometimes made of rayon, cotton, sisal, straw, and hemp. Used mostly in area rugs, these fibers usually do not wear well. However, the rugs are often low in price.

WINDOW TREATMENTS

The treatment you give to windows can affect the looks of a room. Window coverings can range from simple curtains to elaborate drapes or shades. In some rooms, windows are part of the background while in others they are a focal point.

Window coverings control the natural light coming in the window. They soften incoming light, making the light dimmer and the shadows not as dark. They also give privacy from the neighbors.

Although you usually can't change the type of windows, you can select an arrangement of curtains, shutters, draperies, or shades that will make the most of what you have.

Insulation in summer and winter can be provided by window coverings. If sunlight and heat enter the window, you may want a heavy, sun-blocking covering. In cold climates, windows in the north and east may need coverings that stop cold drafts.

The best window treatments blend with the rest of the furnishings. They are the right size for the window and the room. The style of the covering goes with the decor of the room and its furnishings.

These full, ruffled curtains are single priscillas that meet in the center. What type of furnishings are they best used with?

The window treatments in this room combines two different types of window coverings—draperies and sheer curtains.

Curtains and Drapes

Curtains have a pocket hem, or casing, at the top through which a rod passes. They usually cannot be open or closed. There are three main types of curtains—glass, cafe, and priscillas.

Glass curtains get their name because they hang next to the window or glass. They are panels of material gathered on the curtain rod that hang in straight, full folds. You can use glass curtains alone or with drapes.

Cafe curtains are tiered with one tier covering the lower part of the window. There may be a valance, which is a narrow strip of fabric, or a second tier across the top of the window.

Priscillas are ruffled, tie-back curtains. They may crisscross on double rods or hang on one rod and meet in the middle.

Drapes are pleated and hooked onto a rod. Panel drapes hang on both sides of the window and do not move. Traverse or draw drapes are movable. You can pull them back as side panels or draw them together to cover the entire window. Heavy drapes are sometimes used over sheer glass curtains or sheer drapes. The sheer fabric allows light to enter but gives some privacy during the day. The heavier drapes provide privacy at night when pulled.

The fabric you choose makes a great deal of difference in how the window looks. The fabric should fold and drape well. Draperies are usually made of heavier fabric than curtains. The finished width of the bottom of the curtain or drape should be two to three times the width of the window. Anything smaller will look skimpy and will not be attractive.

Many curtains and drapes are lined. Linings protect against fading and wear. A fragile or loosely woven fabric needs a lining to give it body. The added weight of the lining helps curtains fold and drape well. The linings help drapes to screen out light and improve insulation.

Shades and Blinds

Shades and blinds are very good at light control and in insulating windows. While mostly used with drapes or curtains, some decorative shades and blinds are used alone as window coverings.

Roller shades are made of plastic or coated fabric, which hangs from a roller. If you choose opaque shades, they will totally block outside light. Soft, diffused light comes through translucent shades. Roller shades are usually easy to care for and not costly to buy. Appliqués, decals, and decorative painting on the shades make them an attractive addition to a window.

Roman and Austrian shades are made of fabric and are pulled up with cords. The fabric hangs flat when the shade is down. When you raise a Roman shade, it folds into horizontal pleats. As Austrian shades are raised, the material gathers to form graceful scallops.

Blinds are made of slats supported by tapes. You can open or close them or roll them up and down. Blinds control the light while still letting air in through the window. Wood, metal, or plastic can be used to make blinds.

LIGHTING

The lighting system in your home adds to natural light during the day and is the only source of light at night. Good lighting is often taken for granted in a home. However, poor lighting can cause eyestrain, headaches, fatigue, and accidents. Therefore, good lighting is important in your home.

Lighting can be built-in or portable. Built-in lighting is set in the ceiling or behind panels. It gives good light distribution in a room and saves space because it does not take up floor or tabletop areas.

You can unplug portable lighting and move it from room to room or to a new home. Table, pole, swag, or floor lamps are portable lighting. It is flexible and can be adapted to your special needs.

Lighting can be used to create a mood, accent a room feature, or dramatize a background. Explain the function of each of the lights in the picture below.

Kinds of Lighting

General lighting is a low level of light in a room. It gives enough light for you to move about safely to do household chores. One light fixture or lamp may supply enough general light for a room. Rooms in the work zone need more general light because of the many activities done there.

Local lighting is focused in a specific area. It is also known as task lighting because it is used when you do a task in a certain place. Local lighting helps prevent eyestrain while reading, studying, or working at a sink or work table.

Accent lighting creates a center of interest in a room. It is used to highlight furnishings or accessories.

General, local, and accent lighting can be either built-in or portable. General lighting is often built-in while local and accent lighting are portable.

There are two kinds of bulbs used in lighting systems. Incandescent bulbs are most common in homes. They contain fine filments in a glass bulb. Incandescent bulbs are made in many shapes and sizes and can be clear or frosted. They are less costly than fluorescent bulbs and give more light from a smaller space.

Fluorescent bulbs contain mercury vapor sealed in long tubes. They give off less heat, use less energy, and last longer than incandescent bulbs. However, the light is not as flattering to the skin and may change a color completely.

Light bulbs are sized in **watts,** a measure of the electrical current used by the bulb. When bulbs of the same kind are compared, the one with the higher wattage gives off more light. A fluorescent light gives off three to four times as much light as an incandescent one of the same wattage.

Functions of Lighting

Lighting serves several functions in the home. The most important one is to give a safe comfortable level for your activities. Lighting that is bright enough will prevent eyestrain and allow you to work longer.

Adequate light prevents accidents, especially in new settings. Lights that can be turned on from your bed help you to avoid accidents in the dark. Lights turned on at the doorway to a room or at the top and bottom of stairs may prevent you from falling. Switches inside the home to turn on outdoor lights or lights in a garage or carport are safety measures.

Another use of lighting is to set the mood of your home. Soft lighting gives a quiet, restful feeling. Bright light seems more businesslike. A small area of light seems personal and intimate. Large brightly lit rooms are not as personal.

A final use of lighting is to add to the decor. The lamps themselves can add beauty to your rooms. Made from a variety of materials in many colors and styles, lamps can match or accent furnishings and accessories.

Replace incandescent bulbs with fluorescent lighting in work areas such as the kitchen and garage. It gives off three to four times more light for the same wattage.

Be sure that light switches are easily accessible near the entrance to the house and to each room.

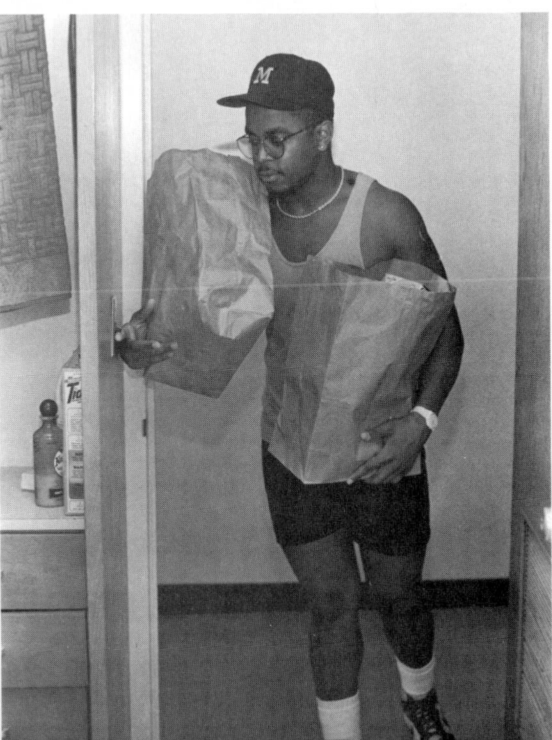

DECORATING ON A BUDGET

Furnishing and decorating your first home may be a challenge if you do not have much money. You may need to use your knowledge and skill instead of money to make an attractive home for yourself. Given below are some ideas for decorating on a budget.

• Make improvised furniture. Some people make furniture for their homes from simple building materials. Bricks or cement blocks can be used with boards to form shelves. A door can be placed on top of two filing cabinets to make a desk. Attaching legs to a door creates a dining or coffee table. A discarded telephone cable spool can be finished and used as a table. Improvised furniture is usually cheap. However, it takes time to find suitable materials and some skill to put them together.

• Attend garage, rummage, and estate sales. Such sales can be good sources of household items such as used furniture, accessories, curtains, lamps, rugs, and kitchen utensils. You may need to attend sales over several months to find all the items you need.

• Use color lavishly. Bright cheerful colors can draw attention away from old, utilitarian furnishings. Paint, slipcovers, and accessories such as pillows, mats, and tablecloths are ways to add color to a home.

• Decorate with everyday items. Use attractive greeting cards to form a decorative grouping on a wall. You can buy cheap frames or mats with which to mount them.

Posters are colorful, attractive, and relatively cheap. You may be able to get scenic posters free or at cost from a travel agency or airline.

Use bottles and cans to decorate with. A set of various sized cans covered with fabric, yarn, or old stamps can make attractive holders for pencils, paper clips, rubber bands, plants, and other household items. Decorated bottles can be used as candle holders or vases.

Use your collection(s) to decorate your home. Shells, rocks, coins, or stamps can be mounted and displayed. If you collect angels, pigs, stuffed animals, or other items, you can use them to add interest and personality to your home.

Hanging baskets and utensils on kitchen walls provide decoration and save storage space. Glass jars filled with nuts, dried beans, rice, cereal, or pasta look attractive on kitchen counters.

Plants add interest and color to a home. Many plants are started from leaves or rootings that you can get from family or friends. Avocado pits, carrot tops, and sweet potatoes sprout attractive greenery when soaked in water. Developing a "green thumb" is one way to get attractive accessories with a small investment of money.

FURNITURE

Furniture is expensive. You will be more satisfied with your purchases if you plan what you need, want, and can afford and then shop carefully.

If you are like most people, when you shop for furniture, you will look for the following:

1. *Good value for the money.* The most costly furniture is not always the best buy. If you shop carefully, you can find quality at a fair price.
2. *Usefulness and comfort.* Even the most beautiful furniture is not a good buy if you do not use it because it is uncomfortable. Furniture that can be put to more than one use increases flexibility.
3. *Durability.* Furniture is used in everyday living. If it is durable, it will last even with hard wear.
4. *Beauty.* Because furniture will be the major decoration in your rooms, each piece should be attractive. Good design and pleasing colors increase the beauty of your rooms. Furniture should go well with other furnishings.
5. *Pieces that reflect your taste.* You want to like the furniture you buy and have it show your personality.

Quality wood furniture can be bought unfinished. You add the stain and finish that matches the other furnishings in your home.

TYPES OF FURNITURE

Furniture can be bought in many places. Comparing brands, construction, appearance, and cost in a variety of stores will help you learn what is right for you.

Most new furniture comes completely finished and assembled. You can move it into a room and use it. New furniture is made in many materials and styles, and comes in a wide range of prices.

To save money, you can buy new unfinished furniture and finish it yourself. You can stain and varnish it to bring out the beauty of the wood. Or you may choose a simpler task and paint the furniture.

Another type of furniture is known as knock-down. It comes in a box and can be put together with a few simple tools.

A good used piece of furniture is often better than a brand new but cheap piece. You can usually find used furniture for about 25 percent of what a similar new piece would cost. In figuring the total price, remember to add the cost of hauling it home, cleaning it up, and doing any needed repairs or refinishing. Look at used furniture closely because you normally cannot return it.

Because used upholstered furniture may have insects in the stuffing, use extra caution before buying it. Unless you are skilled in upholstery, having a piece recovered may cost more than buying a new one would.

EVALUATING FURNITURE QUALITY

Furniture should be built well enough to perform its functions. Both materials and construction are vital to its long life. There are many materials used to make furniture. Each material has quality features you can look at and judge. However, there are a few general features to check on all furniture.

Does the furniture wobble? Try to rock the piece by putting your hand on its surface. Legs should be rock solid. Tall pieces of furniture may have levelers for uneven floors.

Do all movable parts move smoothly and easily? Are knobs, pulls, and handles easy to hold and firmly attached? Is the back finished the same as the top and sides if the furniture is to stand away from the wall?

Wood is the most common material used in furniture. Hardwoods, such as maple and oak, are strong, hard to dent, and wear well. Pine and cedar are known as softwoods and are not as desirable or as costly as the hardwoods. In general, the heavier the piece of furniture, the better the quality of the wood used.

Because hardwood is costly, a veneer of hardwood is often used over softwood. **Veneer** is a thin sheet of wood glued on another piece of wood to improve appearance. Veneered surfaces can be damaged by water and are not suitable for long, hard use. If you are looking at furniture with a veneer, check how well the veneer has been glued to the underlying wood.

Furniture should be pleasing to the eye as well as durable. Check for signs of quality before you purchase.

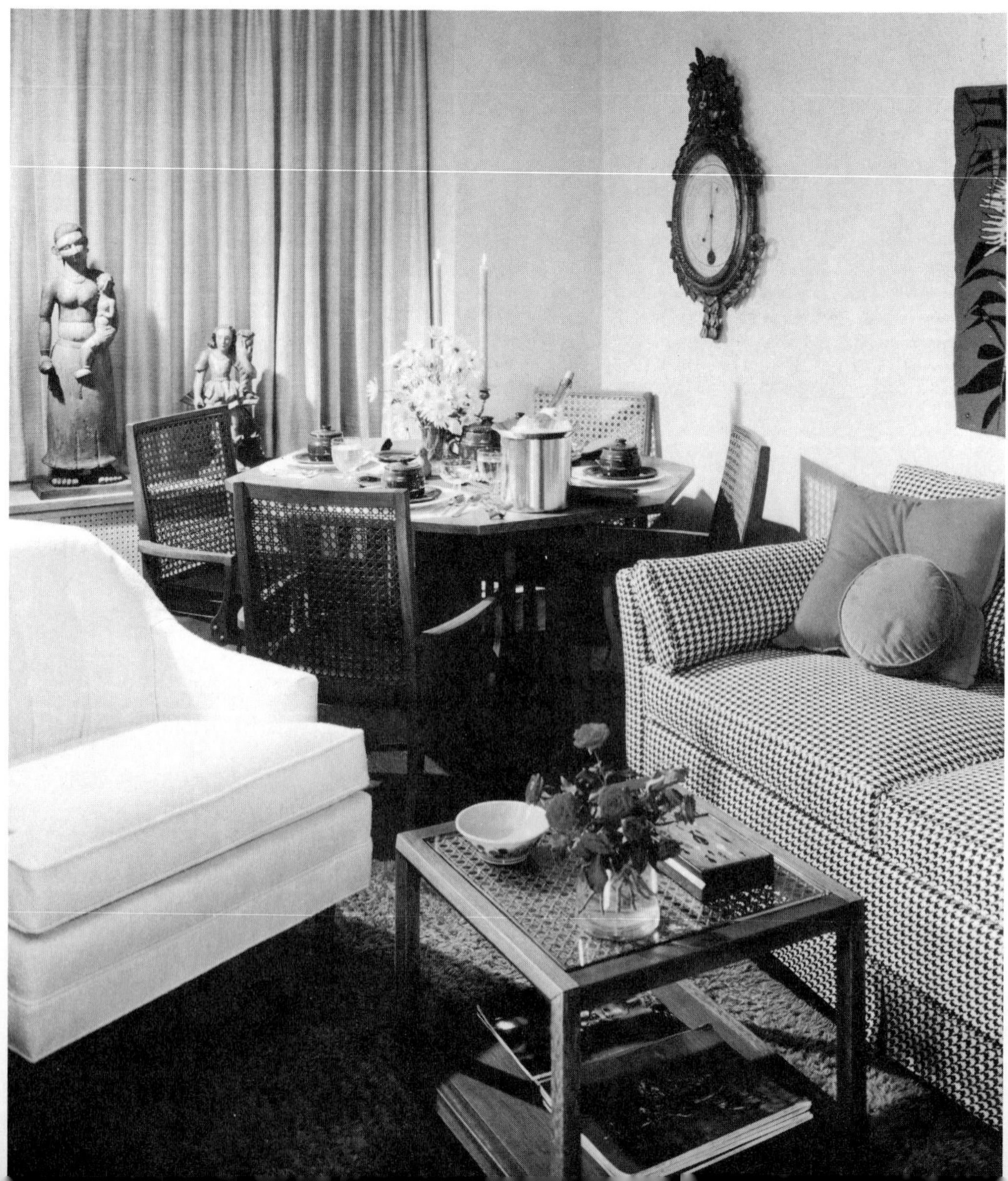

One indicator of quality is how the pieces of wood are joined. Joints should be snuggly fitted with no space visible. The strongest joints are formed when two or more pieces of wood are cut and interlocked with each other. Joints can also be glued but excess glue should be removed. A reinforcing corner block can be added for extra strength. Screws hold wood together better than nails.

In some cheap furniture, wood is joined by staples, nails, or glue alone. These types of joints are usually not very strong.

Check the finish of all parts of the furniture. All wood should be smooth to the touch. A quality outside finish will be clear, deep, and rich. The inside need not be finished like the outside. Stored items will not snag or scratch as long as the inside is sanded smooth and stained or waxed.

The backs of good quality furniture are sanded smooth and stained. They are usually attached to the frame with screws and, for added strength, supported and fastened across the bottom as well.

The back on this chest is neither sanded nor stained, nor is it fastened across the bottom. Notice the split wood. A back that overlaps the side and is either nailed or stapled on is another indication of poor quality.

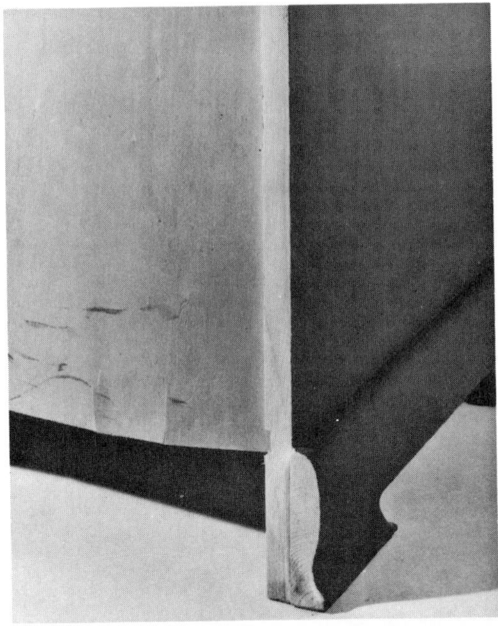

Drawers in quality furniture will be constructed with well-cut, well-fitted dovetail joints, as shown here.

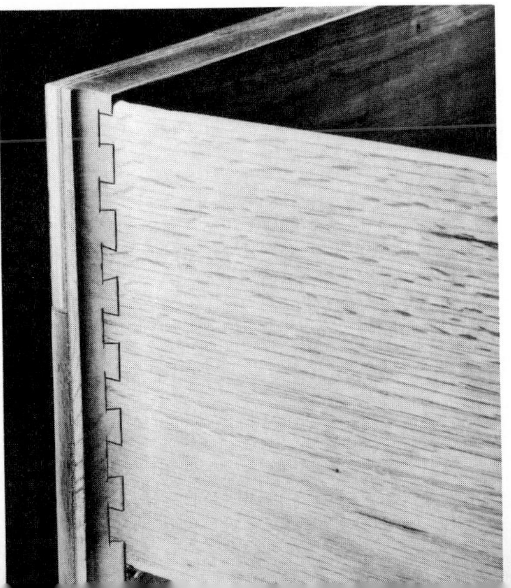

Here is an example of "budget" construction. The joints are merely stapled together—a sure sign that they aren't very sturdy. Notice, too, that the sides are rough—they haven't even been sanded.

Upholstered furniture is covered with permanent padding. Such furniture has a strong wooden frame. A webbing is stretched over the back and seat. Springs and padding are added, and the outside is covered with fabric.

A good hardwood frame is the most vital part of the furniture. The life of the furniture will also depend on the springs used. Coil springs are fastened to steel bands or the webbing in the base or back. They are used in large pieces of furniture and are more costly. Zigzag springs are made of heavy-gauged steel wire. They are used in smaller, lightweight furniture. In general, more springs mean more comfort and support.

The fabric used to cover upholstered furniture affects its wear. Tightly woven heavy fabrics wear quite well. Fabrics of a loose weave tend to snag, stretch, or sag. Vinyl is an often used nonwoven fabric. It is easy to clean but can be sticky in hot weather. Expensive furniture may be covered with leather.

Look for quality in the fabric cover. Are patterns centered and matched? Do seams, cording, hems, and pleats hang smoothly and evenly? Are cushion covers smooth and well fitted? A zipper in a pillow cover provides a tighter, smoother fit. Reversible cushions add life to the fabric.

Other kinds of furniture may be made from chrome, wrought iron, aluminum, glass, or wicker. Whatever kind of furniture you choose, buying quality pieces that look nice and will wear well will help you be happy with your purchases.

This love seat was chosen for its durability. The dark colored fabric is tightly woven Herculon that has been treated with a stain and soil resistant finish.

FURNITURE ARRANGEMENT

There are three basic goals in arranging furniture in a room. The first is to set up an arrangement that is attractive to look at. The second goal is to group the furniture to suit your living needs, and finally, to produce a room comfortable to be in.

Planning ahead will help you find an attractive, comfortable, and convenient arrangement. A plan is a good way to try out different arrangements without moving heavy furniture. Prepare a scale floor plan of the room. Cut out shapes to represent the furniture you will place in the room and arrange them on the floor plan. Trying out several arrangements can help you find one that will be right for you.

Draw a floor plan of a room and sketch the furniture to scale. Use this as a guide to plan work space, traffic flow and room arrangements before actually moving the furniture.

Applying Design Principles

The design principles you studied in chapter 15 can be used to create an attractive room. The most important design features to use to arrange furniture are emphasis and balance.

Use emphasis to create a center of interest in the room. This may be a special piece of furniture or a feature of the room. Fireplaces, picture or bay windows, or paneled walls may be stressed. When you have chosen a center of interest, arrange the furniture to accent it.

Balance in a room appeals to a sense of order and harmony. To create balance, draw an imaginary line through the center of interest. Then place objects equally on both sides of the line. Formal or informal balance can be used depending on your tastes.

Another part of balance includes weight. Large heavy pieces of furniture are balanced when spread throughout the room. In planning a room arrangement, place large pieces first. When these are in balance, plan where smaller pieces will go.

Convenience and Comfort

A beautifully arranged room also needs to be usable. You can plan the furniture arrangement around the habits and activities of those who use the room. What activities are carried out most often in the room? How can the room be arranged so you can do these activities in comfort and convenience?

If the room is used mostly for visiting, arrange the furniture into compact groupings. Sitting beside or across from each other promotes conversation. A room used for reading needs comfortable seating, good lighting, and shelves to store books. Watching television requires seating with a good view of the set and lighting to reduce glare.

A good arrangement also considers traffic through the room. Start at the entrance to the room. Are there paths to other doors? Is there access to bookshelves or storage? Can you get to windows to open them or care for plants? A traffic lane of forty-five centimeters (thirty inches) allows room to move easily between items.

Also think about space needed to use furniture when you arrange it in a room. Unless the edge of the tabletop is forty-five centimeters (thirty inches) away from the wall, when you are sitting at the table, you will not be able to move back your chair to rise. In front of a dresser, one hundred centimeters (forty inches) are needed for you and an open drawer. At least fifty-five centimeters (twenty-two inches) are needed to make a bed easily. Arranging furniture to give enough space to use it makes a room more convenient.

You can create interesting and attractive focal points with a fireplace, bookcase, piece of art, shelving unit, or textured wall hanging.

An arrangement such as this is ideal for a one-room apartment. The table can serve as a game or dining table. The chairs can easily be turned toward the "living" end of the room when extra seating is needed.

ACCESSORIES

Accessories provide the final touches to a room. They add interest and are a means of self-expression. Well-chosen pieces are in harmony with the room, its colors, and furnishings, and they give a feeling of unity. You may select some accessories because they have special meaning to you. Others you chose because of their usefulness or their beauty.

Functional accessories are those that have a useful purpose in the room. These are items such as lamps, pillows, clocks, mirrors, vases, ash trays, or screens. In choosing functional accessories, look for attractive, truly useful ones. Will pillows add to your comfort? Does the clock keep good time? How much light does the lamp give?

Decorative accessories are chosen for their beauty alone. Artwork, china, pottery, crafts, flowers, and plants are examples of this type of accessory.

Accent pieces or accessories can be used to create a mood, add color, or serve as a display of collectible items.

APPLIANCES

Most homes today have four or five major appliances. These save time and energy in running a home. The most common are the range, refrigerator, clothes washer, clothes dryer, and dishwasher. Other examples are trash compactors, food disposals, freezers, and microwave ovens.

In choosing an appliance, think about your family's needs and size. How large an appliance do you need? Is there enough space in your home for it? Allow room for servicing and ventilation. Are doors, stairs, halls, or entryways large enough for the appliance to pass through before it is set up? What fuel will you use? If your home contains both gas and electric hookups, you can choose the fuel you want.

Major appliances are coming in new smaller packages. The microwave that fits under-the-cabinet, the stackable washer/dryer and the under-the-counter refrigerator/freezer may be small on size but they are big on features.

APPLIANCE COSTS

The costs of owning appliances are purchasing, running, and servicing them. Appliances come in a range of prices based on a variety of features. If you choose a "bottom line," or low-cost, appliance, it will do the basic task for which it was made. It will have no extra conveniences and may not offer you any choices in operation. A more expensive, or "top of the line," model may have many extras like programmed cycles. It usually will offer you many choices.

Whichever "end" of the product line you buy, look for quality construction. Do doors close firmly? Are there sturdy shelves and drawers that slide out easily? Are finishes and materials durable and easy to clean? An appliance will be easier to use if its design matches your height and physical condition.

The cost of operating the appliance depends on how energy efficient it is and how often you use it. Those that use a lot of energy are more costly to run. Energy-efficient appliances may have higher price tags but cost less over their lifetimes because of lower fuel costs.

Many special features on appliances use extra energy. The more automatic the machine is, the more it costs to buy and run. For example, frost-free refrigerators and freezers cost more to operate than those you defrost yourself.

Appliance Repair

If an appliance breaks down, get a firm estimate of cost in writing before repair work begins. In some cases, it may be better to buy new equipment than to repair old. Unless you know what repairs will cost, you cannot make a wise choice. Repair costs depend on the parts needed, the labor time needed, and the travel time needed for the service person to reach your home.

Most appliances come with a guarantee or warranty. The warranty protects you against defects in quality and workmanship in the product. It should cover the appliance for a reasonable length of time. A thirty-to-sixty day warranty is not very useful because the appliance should not break down in that amount of time.

Find out exactly what is covered under the warranty. Most of the cost of repairs is labor. Will labor be covered? Some parts may be guaranteed longer than others. Be sure to keep your warranty and sales slip for future use.

Some companies offer **service contracts** to cover repair costs after the guarantee expires. You purchase a contract that insures you against the breakdown of the appliance. The contract costs so much per year. If something breaks down that is covered by it, the work is done with no charge.

Check the details of the service contract carefully before you buy it. What repairs and services are covered? Will the contract cover the appliance if you move it to another home? The yearly fee for the contract may be more than a repair bill would be. The appliance might need to break down two or more times in a year for the contract to be a good buy for you.

A service contract can be purchased for most major appliances but check details of the contract carefully before purchasing it.

WORDS TO REMEMBER

carpeting	drapes	rugs	veneer
curtains	pile	service contract	watt

CHECKING YOUR UNDERSTANDING

1. Describe the good and bad points of three types of wall coverings. If cost were no object, which would you prefer to have in your home? Why?
2. What would be some possible window treatments for kitchen windows that face south and west? Explain the reasons for your suggestions.
3. What are the differences between general, local, and accent lighting? Describe a use of each type of lighting.
4. Describe some items used as accessories in home decoration. Identify whether each is a functional or decorative accessory.

APPLYING YOUR UNDERSTANDING

1. Assume you are ready to move into your first apartment. It has two unfurnished rooms plus a kitchenette that contains a range and refrigerator. Your savings are small because you have just started to work. Plan furnishings for the apartment and identify what pieces you will get, where you will get them, and how you will pay for them.
2. Imagine you are an interior decorator who is planning the floor coverings for a new home. What coverings would you choose for the entry hall, the living area, the kitchen, the bedrooms, and the bath? Explain the reasons for your choices.
3. List at least five places in your community where furniture can be bought. What kinds of furniture are sold in each place? What would be the pros and cons of shopping for furniture in each? Where would you like to shop for furniture for your home? Compare the advantages and disadvantages of buying new, used, or other types of furniture.
4. How would you arrange furniture in a room to create both emphasis and balance? Make a plan for the arrangement of furniture in a 3 m × 4.6 m (10 ft. × 15 ft.) room, using a sofa, two chairs, two end tables, and accessories of your choice. Identify the center of interest and whether your plan uses formal or informal balance. What else did you consider in making the plan?
5. Imagine you have just bought a new refrigerator and range and a used washer and dryer for the home you have rented. You paid cash for the washer and dryer at a garage sale but bought the refrigerator and range on credit from the appliance store. Describe some of the costs of owning these appliances.

Chapter 32

CARING FOR YOUR HOME

Has this ever happened to you?

Sally adjusted her sling and mentally braced herself as she went to her first class on Monday morning. Sure enough, as she walked through the door, the teasing began.

Chad was laughing. "Who did you meet up with in a dark alley?" he asked.

"Oh, Sally," said Mary, "what in the world happened to your arm?"

"I broke my arm Saturday. It really isn't all that big of a deal, but I have to wear this cast for about three weeks. Who wants to be the first to sign it?" asked Sally.

"Oh, let me be first," said Mary. "But how did you break your arm?"

"You won't believe this," said Sally as her friends began signing her cast. "My little brother Tim left some of his cars and trucks on the stairs. I came flying down them to answer the phone and didn't bother to turn on the light. I stepped on a jeep and the next thing I knew I was on the floor in the hall. Talk about something that hurt! It isn't an experience I want to repeat too soon!"

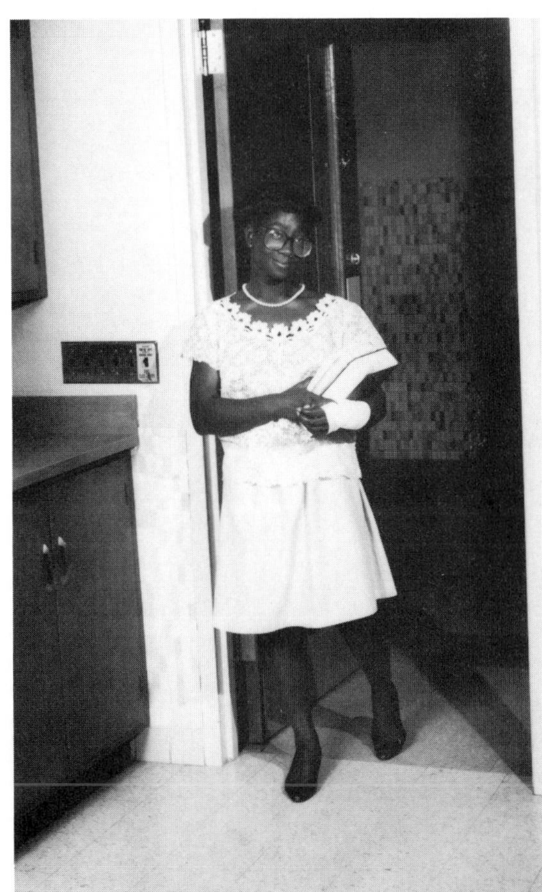

Have you ever had a bad injury from an accident at home?

What are some ways to make your home safer and prevent accidents?

After reading this chapter, you will be able to

- list ways to prevent home accidents;
- describe causes of home fires and the various kinds of smoke detectors and fire extinguishers;
- explain the importance of insurance in protecting your property and possessions;
- list tools, equipment, and supplies that make organizing and doing house cleaning easier;
- identify tools and equipment needed for home repairs, painting, and wallpapering.

A well cared for home is a pleasure to live in. It makes a safe, healthful, and attractive setting for your life. Caring for your home means making it safe from accidents and fires. It means protecting your home and possessions with insurance. A clean home is a healthful place in which to live. Finally, caring for your home means keeping it in good repair and making improvements as they are needed.

HOME SAFETY

Nearly as many people are injured in their homes as at work and in traffic accidents combined. However, with care and effort, your home can be a safe place to live.

ACCIDENT PREVENTION

Most injuries received in the home are the result of some type of accident. Working to stop accidents can help do away with these injuries.

Falls

The most common type of home accident is a fall. Small children need to be watched closely when they play on porches or near open windows. If you look where you are going, do not hurry, and think about what you are doing, you will rarely fall.

Safe habits include promptly wiping up water and grease spots on floors and putting away toys or boxes rather than setting them on the stairs. You can also help prevent falls by keeping extension cords out of a room's traffic pattern and taking care of torn or loose places in floor coverings.

A sturdy handrail for each flight of stairs makes their use safer. Stairs that are covered with carpet or rubber mats are less slippery and less apt to cause falls.

Ladders are often needed for home care or repair. However, unless you use them carefully, they can cause falls. Check to see if the ladder is stable before climbing it. To be safe, climb only until your shoulders are even with the top rung. Keep both feet on the ladder and one hand free to hold on with. Face the ladder as you climb up and down. Wood ladders left outside will rot, so checking their safety is very important.

Injuries from falls are highest during the fall and winter. Wet leaves, water, sleet, snow, or ice on steps and sidewalks are a danger.

Electrical Injuries

The unsafe use of electricity and electrical tools also causes injuries in the home. When you replace worn cords and plugs, you help prevent shocks. Grasp the plug, not the cord, when pulling the plug from an outlet.

A three-pronged grounding plug is found on many major appliances and hand tools. It gives you added protection against shock. It should only be plugged into a grounded three-pronged outlet. You can hire an electrician to change a two-pronged outlet to a three-pronged one if needed.

Roommates can work together and share in the responsibility of providing a safe, clean environment.

You can help to prevent falls by wiping up spills immediately, attaching nonskid objects on rugs, and keeping extension cords and speaker wires out of the room's traffic pattern.

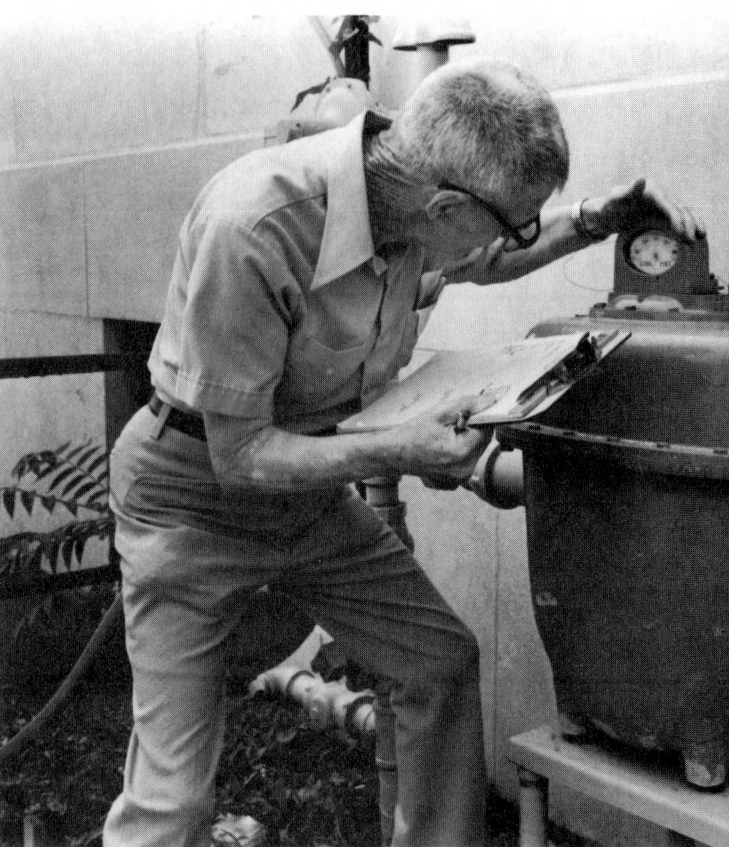

If you suspect a gas leak or need to have a pilot relit, call the gas company. They will send a service representative to your home.

Extension cords are handy to have but can be a hazard. If you use an extension cord, its wire size should be the same as the equipment to which it will carry current. Ordinary cords are not meant to be used with appliances or power tools. Some appliance plugs will not fit into the outlets of small extension cords. This protects you from using a cord that is not large enough to safely carry the current needed for the appliance.

When an extension cord is needed, use only one, for power is lost when a series of cords are strung together. Avoid using cords except as a short-term measure.

Any electrical device you use in a damp spot or near water is a hazard. Water is a good conductor of electricity and can carry severe shocks. Therefore, be sure your hands are dry when using electrical equipment. Water can cause electrical short circuits, so use care when you are cleaning equipment. In addition, keep small appliances away from tubs and sinks.

If you feel even the slightest shock, turn off the power and unplug the equipment. Use it again only when you have found and fixed the cause of the shock. Turn off the electricity at the service panel to replace switches or outlets.

Other Hazards

Some appliances are fueled with gas, which can also be a danger. Be sure gas appliances are set up by an expert service person to prevent leaks from the gas lines. If you smell the odor of gas, open the windows. Call the gas company right away and ask what further measures to take. A lighted match, a pilot light, or an open flame near a gas leak could cause an explosion or fire or both.

Many dangerous materials are stored in a home. Cleaning supplies, insect sprays, paints, and medicines can all be poisonous if you do not use them carefully. Medicine chests and storage cupboards that are locked or have child-proof latches keep young children from drinking or eating household poisons. Store such materials in their own bottles so you will have the directions for using them properly.

Use cleaning supplies only as directed. Mixing two or more products may form and release poisonous fumes that make you ill.

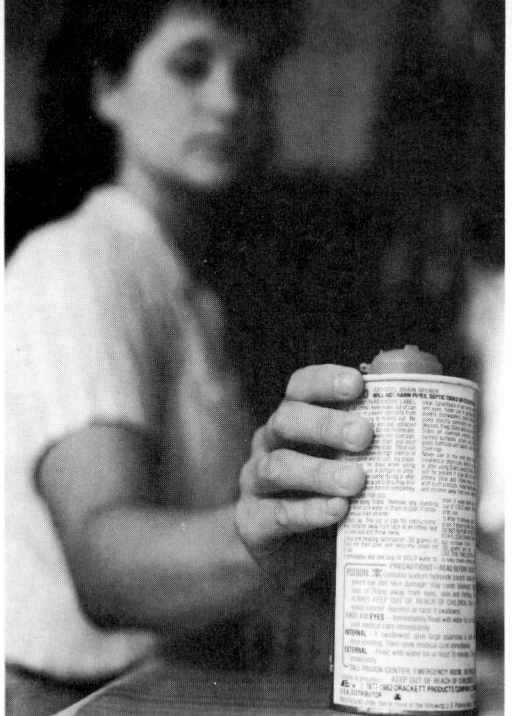

Read directions and take heed of warning labels that appear on household cleaning supplies, insect sprays, paints and medicines.

More deaths from guns occur in the home than in the hunting field, on a firing range, and all other places combined. If you have guns at home, keep them unloaded and away from children.

Some hobbies such as woodworking require care and safety measures. Avoid wearing jewelry and loose-fitting clothing that might get caught in the moving parts of power tools. Gloves can protect your hands from rough or caustic materials that might cut or burn you. Safety glasses, bought at a hardware or drug store, protect your eyes from flying objects.

Use care with power tools and equipment. Tools with sharp edges are dangerous if not used in the right way. These include lawn mowers, snow blowers, electric drills, saws, and shredders.

If you have a garage, open the door before you start the car motor. In a closed garage, carbon monoxide in the exhaust gases can be deadly. If the garage is attached to the house the carbon monoxide can enter your home as well.

The bathroom is probably the most dangerous room in your home. If you keep hot water in the taps below 45° C (115° F), the chance of burns is reduced. Shower and tub doors made of clear plastic or tempered glass are much safer than those made of plate glass. If tempered glass breaks, it crumbles into small pieces with no sharp edges. Grab bars and no-skid stickers on the bottom of tubs and shower stalls can prevent falls. Rubberized mats help make wet tile floors safer.

FIRE SAFETY

Fire safety is vital to home care. Fires can start anywhere, but more than one-third start in the living room. The kitchen, basement, and bedrooms are other common places where fires start.

The first rule when a fire occurs is to get out of your home—*fast.* Do not take time to call the fire department, pick up valuables, or try to put out the fire yourself. A well-rehearsed escape plan will help you know what to do in case of fire.

Most home fires occur between 12:00 P.M. and 6:00 A.M. Nighttime fires are the most serious because you are asleep and your discovery of the fire is delayed. Therefore, every bedroom needs two escape routes—the normal one and an emergency exit, such as a window.

A basic fire safety rule is to sleep with your bedroom door closed. A closed door delays the gases and fire and, thus, gives you a few more minutes to escape.

Most fire deaths are caused by deadly smoke and gas. Gases from the fire can easily reach the bedrooms and cause death before the flames travel that far. Because the gases rise, you are in the most danger if you are on the top floor.

In high-rise multiple-family buildings, check the fire escapes. Find the nearest exits to your living unit. Find out if there is a sprinkler system in case of fire. If so, how is it turned on?

Causes of Fires

Home fires have many causes. Some start because combustible items are set or stored too close to fires. For example, some cleaning chemicals can burn or even blow up. If you store them near a pilot light or stove, they may catch fire.

Cluttered halls and storage spaces can cause fires. Oily, greasy rags, and other trash can catch fire by themselves. Keeping all storage areas neat and clean is one step to prevent fires.

In the kitchen, you should keep curtains, towels, potholders, and utensils away from the range. Remove spilled food promptly from the range and oven. Hot grease is very flammable.

Starting a small fire with a flammable liquid can cause a home fire. Use care in starting fires in fireplaces or barbeque grills.

A fire can start with faulty heating or electrical equipment. Be sure not to overload cords and circuits. Faulty appliances can be a fire hazard. New electrical equipment made in the United States is inspected by the Underwriters Laboratory (UL). The American Gas Association (AGA) checks gas appliances. A product that is safe to use has either a UL or an AGA seal. If you choose a product with one of these seals, you can feel certain it will not cause fires.

Smoke Detectors

The sooner you discover a fire, the faster you can get to safety. Property damage is also reduced when the fire is found early. One way to be warned about fires quickly is to put up a smoke detector on the ceiling or wall of your home. It will sound an alarm when there are smoke particles in the air around the detector.

Detectors are powered by a battery. The battery lasts about a year and signals with a gentle, periodic beep when it runs down. A test button on the alarm lets you test to see if it is working.

There are two kinds of smoke detectors sold for home use. An **ionization detector** is quick to warn of a fast-burning blaze, such as burning paper or flammable liquids. **Photoelectric** models detect slow-smoldering fires. An example of this type of fire is a cigarette dropped on bedding or upholstered furniture.

To be really safe, you should put up both kinds of detectors. If you are going to put up only one detector, the photoelectric one is the best choice. The reason for this choice is because smoldering fires are more common in homes and cause more deaths and injuries.

Install smoke detectors in your home and check batteries regularly. A smoke detection unit located near the kitchen and bathrooms can give you ample warning if a fire breaks out.

Fire Extinguishers

Fire extinguishers can be used to put out small fires. Water is useful in putting out wood, paper, or cloth fires. However, water will spread a fire fed on flammable liquids such as gasoline or grease. If you use water on an electrical fire, you could get a deadly shock. Therefore, it probably is safest for you to use a fire extinguisher. It can put out all kinds of fires.

A **dry chemical extinguisher** uses a powder that coats the burning surface and smothers the fire. You can refill it yourself at home after use. The extinguisher has a gauge on it to show if it is properly charged. Check your unit every few months to see whether it is holding its charge.

A **carbon dioxide extinguisher** smothers the fire with carbon dioxide, a heavy gas. It can only be refilled by a firm that does that kind of work. Therefore, it is less practical for home use.

You should keep a fire extinguisher where it is most apt to be used. The kitchen, bedroom, basement workshop, or a central closet are good places to store one. Be sure all members of your household know how to use it.

INSURANCE

The loss of your possessions through fire, theft, or other means is more often than not a financial hardship. Few people have the money to replace all of the items lost. One way to care for your home is to insure it against such losses. Insurance can help prevent such financial hardships.

Whether you are a home owner or a renter, you can buy insurance to protect yourself. A basic renter's policy is the same as home-owner's policy except there is no coverage on the dwelling. That is carried by the building's owner.

If you are a home owner, the holder of the mortgage will require that you carry insurance on your home. You may pay for your insurance through a special account held by the mortgage holder. Some firms let you make your own insurance payments. In these cases, the insurance company tells the mortgage holder if you fail to make payments on the policy. Most mortgage holders think a home is adequately insured if it is covered for at least 80 percent of its replacement cost.

The cost of a policy will depend on the amount of coverage for which you ask. The more dangers you insure against, the more the policy will cost. The condition of the home itself may affect the price of the policy.

Most policies have limits set on the loss of valuable items like jewelry, furs, coin collections, or paintings. These items can be covered with extra insurance called *endorsements* or *floaters*.

Keep an up-to-date inventory of household belongings and document them with photographs in case everything is lost due to a fire, flood or robbery.

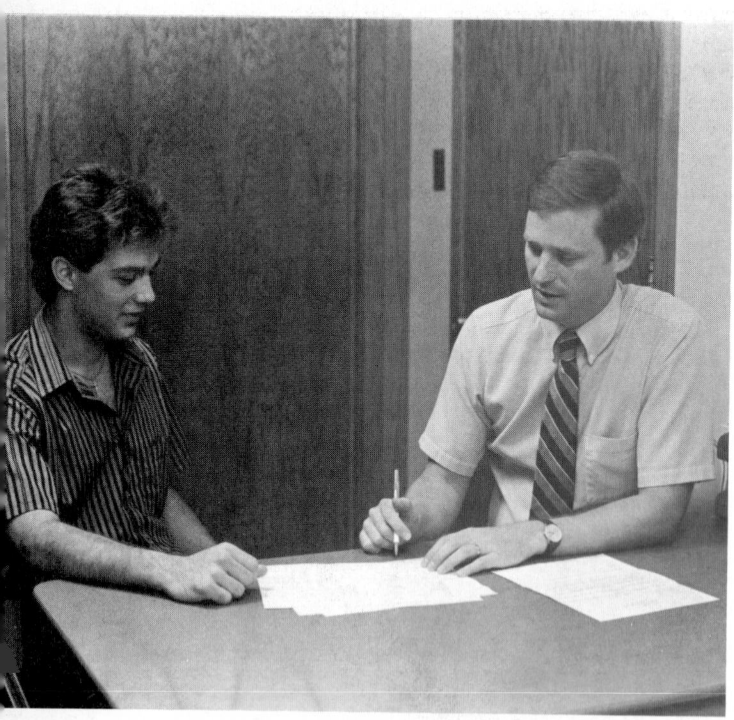

A reliable insurance agent can advise you on the types and amount of homeowner's or renter's insurance that you should carry.

CLEANING YOUR HOME

Keeping your home neat and clean is an important part of home care. Your home's upkeep affects how it looks, its efficiency, and how easy it is to live in.

How neat and clean your home is depends on what is important to you. If you value order and appearance, you may keep your home neat and clean. Or, you may want to spend less time on home care because you have other activities you value more.

Health and safety require some effort on your part. Garbage will draw disease-bearing insects, mice, and rats. Trash can be a fire hazard. Fresh air is needed to keep family members healthy.

If your home is neat, it will be more livable than if it is messy. Clothes kept in neatly arranged drawers or closets are always ready for you to wear. Hobby and work tools are easy to find and use when stored close to work areas.

Cleaning can also be vital to the life of your possessions. Dust and dirt can shorten the life of household items. If you clean regularly, you can help prevent wear and tear to furnishings.

Cleaning tools and supplies that have been organized in a portable tray or bin make it easy to move from one room to another.

TOOLS, EQUIPMENT, AND SUPPLIES

Cleaning is easy when you have tools, equipment, and supplies you need. Using the best tool or product for each task will cut the time needed to do it. In addition, the task is more apt to be done well.

Loose dirt is made up of dust, hair, fur, loose fibers, or ashes. A broom and dust pan, a wet mop, or a dust mop can be used to pick up loose dirt on bare floors. A soft-bristled hand brush is good when you clean upholstery. When dusting furniture by hand, use a soft lint-free cloth. A polish or wax on the cloth will help pick up loose dirt.

Probably the best way to pick up loose dirt is with a vacuum cleaner. A canister vacuum sucks up dirt. You can dust or clean wood floors, upholstery, furniture, and draperies with a canister cleaner.

A hand carpet sweeper or electric broom can pick up loose dirt from a lightly soiled carpet. An upright vacuum cleaner is useful to clean a carpet that is more heavily soiled.

Another type of soil to be cleaned is water-soluble dirt. Examples are mud, juices, and sugary or starchy foods. Because these soils will dissolve in water, they are usually easy to clean. However, they can stain and become hard to get up if not treated right away.

The use of soaps and detergents helps in cleaning water-soluble soil. Soaps are made from natural substances, while detergents are made from synthetic products. Both help water to dissolve dirt and wash it away.

Other soils are oil and grease based and are harder to clean. If not cleaned up right away, oil and grease can cause lasting stains. Detergents cut grease better than soaps do. Cleaning products with an acid such as ammonia can be used on grease. Some cleaning fluids are fat solvents, which means they dissolve grease or oil. These products are often flammable and must be used with care.

Other kinds of household soil are tarnish or corrosion. These are chemical reactions on metal surfaces. You will need to polish dishes or items of silver, chrome, or brass to keep their shine. Iron metals rust easily and will have rust spots to clean up.

Some cleaning products use a chemical action to clean up tarnish and corrosion. Abrasives such as steel wool, silver polish, or scouring powder rub or scrape away dirt.

After cleaning, you can use a wax or polish to protect surfaces from soil and wear. Floor wax guards resilient or hard-surface floors from scuffs and scratches. Choose a wax made for the material of the floor being treated. Furniture polishes come in aerosol sprays, creamy liquids, or solid pastes. They clean, seal, and protect wood. Multi-purpose cleaning waxes are used on counters, appliances, paneling, tile, and plastic items.

There are a number of cleaning products on the market. Many are used for special chores. However, a few multi-purpose products may be all you need to keep your home as clean as you wish.

Prolong the life of carpeting and upholstered furniture by cleaning it regularly with a vacuum cleaner and its attachments.

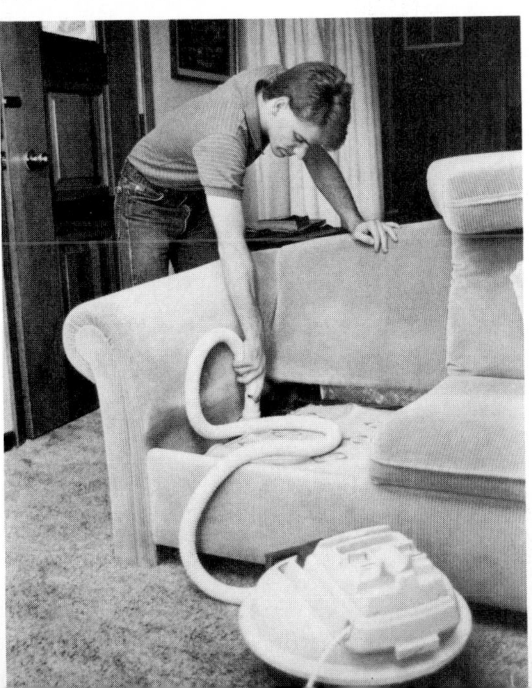

Many cleaning products are available to clean, wax and protect surfaces. Select the ones suitable for the material that you will be cleaning.

Careers
A BRIEF LOOK

HOUSING

To build, decorate, furnish, and care for homes are major industries in this country. There are many careers in the housing area that may appeal to you. Do you enjoy being in or creating comfortable, well-functioning, attractive homes? Do you have an eye for beauty and design? Do you have good mechanical skills? Do you like to make or sell things? If you have any of these interests or skills, you may find a career in one of the housing fields rewarding.

Entry Level Jobs
Lawn-care worker
House cleaner
Painter
Paperhanger
Housing maintenance worker
Housing management aide
Social director of a mobile home park
Salesperson for:
- Paint
- Wallpaper
- Furniture
- Window coverings
- Carpets and rugs
- Resilient and nonresilient flooring
- Appliances
- Housing accessories
- Mobile homes
- Construction materials

Jobs That Require Training
Real estate agent
Bricklayer
Carpenter
Mason
Dry-waller
Insulation worker
Plasterer
Plumber
Roofer
Tile setter
Land developer
Drafter
Surveyor
Floor-covering installer
Electrician
Insurance agent
Property manager
Appliance repairer
Upholsterer
Furniture refinisher and/or repairer
Mobile home park owner or manager

Jobs That Require a College Degree
Architect
Engineer
Mortgage banker
Interior designer
Kitchen designer
Landscape designer
Appraiser
Land-use planner

For information on apprenticeship programs in the construction trades, contact the Bureau of Apprenticeship and Training in the U.S. Department of Labor. For other housing careers, read the newspaper want ads, or write to:

National Association of Real Estate Appraisers
8715 Via De Commercio
Scottsdale, Arizona 85258

American Furniture Manufacturer
P.O. Box HP-7
High Point, North Carolina 27261

MANAGING CLEANING TASKS

Keeping your home clean is an ongoing series of tasks. Some jobs need to be done daily. Other tasks need to be done once or twice a week, depending on how an area is used and the amount of dirt in the air. Some tasks may be done once or twice a month or year.

How often some chores are done depends on your values. You may want to dust furniture twice a week. Someone else may dust only once every two weeks. Another person may wash windows once a month while you may choose to wash them only twice a year. However, those who do not clean often find that dirt accumulated for a long time is hard to remove.

In managing cleaning tasks, think about how often you wish to do each chore. Plan a routine or schedule to do chores regularly. This can help you keep your home clean and neat.

Make up a plan to fit your work habits. Some people like to set aside a few hours or a day to clean everything at once. Others break the tasks into smaller groups. For example, they may choose to clean a room a day.

A complete plan will list the tasks to be done. It will note who is to do the job and how often. Such a plan can help all family members know their roles in keeping the home clean. It also can help them fit the cleaning chores into their daily schedules. A written plan serves as a reminder not to forget cleaning tasks.

Most furnishings and appliances come with cleaning directions. If you follow them, you will keep the item in the best condition. All cleaning products come with directions for use. Read labels closely and follow the suggestions given.

The need to clean can be cut down by your choice of furnishings. Items that are simple in design with few parts are easier to clean. Furniture with ledges, ornate carvings, and moldings catches dust. Furnishings should either sit flush on the floor or be high enough to clean under. Shiny surfaces show fingerprints, water spots, and dust while dull surfaces hide them.

Fibers in curtains and upholstery that do not absorb dirt, or are treated to resist soil and stain are easy to care for. Patterns are simpler to keep up than plain surfaces. Medium-toned colors hide dust or dirt that settles on their surfaces.

Resilient or hard-surfaced floors are usually easier to clean than carpeting. Loose dirt sits on top of the floor until swept or mopped. Dirt can become embedded in carpets, making them very hard for you to clean. Shampooing soiled carpets is more effort than mopping tile or hard-surfaced floors. Having resilient or hard-surfaced flooring in rooms with heavy use may save time and effort in cleaning.

Cleaning tasks become less of a burden when divided among all those living in the home. When all family members help clean, they have the satisfaction of knowing they have done their part to help care for their home.

Your choice of furnishings and accessories will influence the amount of cleaning. Compare the difficulty of cleaning the items on the right to the ease of cleaning the items on the left.

Even small children can be taught to help with household chores. Learning to pick up their toys and clothes and tidy their rooms teaches responsibility.

In colder climates, replace screens with storm windows and doors for added insulation.

HOME REPAIRS

Whether you rent or own your home, there will be items that need to be fixed. Being able to do simple repairs yourself will save money and give you a sense of achievement.

Many people learn to do their own repairs. Some people are mechanically minded. They can often figure out how to fix items. Others take classes to learn how to make repairs. A do-it-yourself book with drawings and directions can be useful in caring for your home.

When you set up your first home, buy tools and supplies as you need them. Then they will be on hand for future jobs. Most home repairs take a basic set of tools. Pliers, wrenches, saws, screwdrivers, and a hammer are essentials. There are many other tools used for special purposes. Be sure tools are strong enough and of a quality to do the jobs in your home.

Some basic supplies are also used in home repair. Oil, grease, sandpaper, steel wool, glues, and cements are useful to have on hand. A variety of sizes of screws, nails, bolts, tacks, nuts, and washers will ensure you have what you need.

There will be many times when you will not have the tools or skills to make repairs. An expert will be needed for the job.

Finding a skilled repair person may be hard. The best method is to ask friends and neighbors for the names of persons who have worked for them. A person or firm that has done good work for others will probably do good work for you as well.

It will cost less if you take the item to a repair shop, rather than have the service person come to your home. If the job is a large one, it may be wise to get a cost estimate from two or more firms. Then you can compare the costs before choosing who will make the repair.

Do not try to fix products still under warranty. Your doing so will cancel the manufacturer's obligation to fix the product.

SIMPLE HOME REPAIRS

Learning to make simple home repairs can save you money. You will be able to fix some things without hiring someone to do the work for you.

- *Clogged drains.* A drain becomes clogged when grease, hair, or other solids stop the flow of water through it. Pouring boiling water down the drain can sometimes restore water flow. A plunger may be needed to clear the drain. Fill the sink with enough water to cover the plunger cup and fit the plunger over the drain opening. Pump the plunger up and down with vigor to loosen the plug in the drain. Commercial drain cleaners may be able to dissolve stubborn blockages. Be sure to read and follow the directions on the container closely because drain cleaners are strong chemicals that can be harmful if used incorrectly. Do not use a drain cleaner before using a plunger because, if the chemical splashed on your face, it could cause a serious injury.
- *Replacing an electrical plug.* An appliance or light cord with a worn or damaged plug is a fire hazard. Take the plug from the outlet and cut the electrical cord about 5 cm (2 in.) above the worn out plug. This will remove the frayed ends of the old wires. For lamps and small appliances, you can use a clamp plug. First, slit the cord about 6 mm (1/4 in.) between the wires. Open the clamp, slip the cord into the plug as far as it will go, and close the clamp. For a heavier cord and major appliance, you will need to use a heavy duty plug. Instructions are included on the package.
- *Replacing a wall switch.* A wall switch may be worn out if the light fails to work when the switch is turned on. Before beginning work on the switch, test the lamp and its bulb in another outlet. If the lamp still does not work, unscrew the fuse or trip the circuit breaker to shut off power to the switch. Remove the plate covering the switch, pull out the switch, and unscrew the wires. Attach the wires of a new switch in the same positions you found the wires on the old switch. Turn the circuit power back on and test the new switch. If the light still does not work, have an electrician check the wiring.
- *Repairing water leaks.* When a pipe leaks, the first step is to shut off the water supply to the pipe. Dry the area around the leak and use steel wool to remove any rust or scale from the pipe. Electrical tape wrapped around the pipe will seal small leaks. If the leak is at a threaded joint, gently tighten the joint. An epoxy compound can be put on the joint to help seal it. A pipe clamp, bolted over a rubber pad, can stop larger leaks.
- *Patching a screen.* Buy a piece of aluminum screening at least 50 mm (2 in.) larger than the rip or hole in the screen. Remove four wires from each edge of the patch. Bend the unwoven wires at a right angle and push them through the damaged screen. Bend the wires even with the screen to hold the patch in place.

HOME IMPROVEMENTS

Home improvements range from the simple to the complex. Many people do their own painting and wallpapering. Large projects usually require the help of experts.

PAINTING

Painting is one of the simplest ways to change and improve the looks of a home. Fresh paint covers spots and stains. A new color can make a room look brand new. Painting is the least costly way to change the looks of walls and ceilings.

There are two basic types of paint. Water-based paint is also called **latex. Alkyd** paints are oil based.

You can thin latex paints with water. You will be able to wipe up fresh spots and splatters with a wet rag. Your brushes and rollers will come clean in water. Latex paint is ideal for use on walls because it can be put on with a roller and dries quickly with little odor.

You must thin oil-based paints with a solvent such as turpentine or gasoline. You will also need to use the solvent in clean up. Oil-based paints give off fumes and take longer to dry than latex. A brush should be used to apply them. Alkyd paint stands up to scrubbing better than latex. Thus, it is better for areas of hard use such as kitchens or bathrooms.

Both types of paint come in three finishes. A flat finish has no gloss, or shine. It is not very durable so grease and scrubbing can harm it.

A high-gloss finish is tough and shiny. Easy to clean, it is often used on woodwork. However, it makes surface bumps and dents easy to see and can cause glare. A semigloss finish is between a flat and high-gloss finish. It has a little shine, resists grease stains, and is fairly easy to clean.

Figure how many square meters (or feet) of area you will be painting. Use the figures given on the paint can to decide how much paint you will need. Clerks in the paint store will help you decide how much paint to buy.

A certain amount of equipment is needed to paint. A mixing paddle is used to stir the paint. A brush with natural hog bristles works best with oil-based paint. However, use a roller, or foam rubber or nylon brush with latex paint. Natural bristles soak up the water in latex paint and become limp. The more split ends on a brush, the better it will paint. A good quality brush will hold more paint and take less effort to use.

Rollers with a medium nap are best for painting walls. A short nap is used for wood trim, while a long nap is good for brick or cement. The roller should fit into a roller pan, which holds the paint.

A fresh coat of paint can transform a dark, drab room into a light, clean, airy space.

Masking tape or a paint guard protects the edges of wood trim as you paint. They can also be used where one color meets another. The floor and furniture should be covered with plastic drop cloths or old sheets before you paint to prevent drip and spatter marks.

After you buy the paint and equipment, the next step is to prepare the walls. Cracks and nail holes can be filled with patching plaster. When the plaster dries, sand it smooth. Scrape and sand any areas where the paint has peeled. Wash the surface with a detergent and let it dry. Paint will peel if you put it on a dirty or greasy surface.

Finally, move furniture to the center of the room and cover it to protect it from splatters. Open and stir the paint well, and you are ready to start. The time and money spent in painting will bring a fresh look to the rooms of your home.

WALLPAPERING

Wallpaper comes in many designs, colors, and textures. While more costly than paint, it adds richness, variety, and texture to a room.

Wallpaper is actually made of many materials besides paper. Vinyl, foil, burlap, fabric, or cork can be used in wallpaper. Vinyl is popular because it is easy to wash and resists stains and fading. It is stronger than paper, so it is easier for you to handle when it is wet with paste.

Many wallpapers come in prepasted form. The paste is already on the back of the paper, which you dip in water before hanging.

Wallpaper comes in standard rolls that are 3.2 sq. m (36 sq. ft.). In hanging the paper, there is always some waste in matching patterns, cutting, and trimming. Therefore, only about 2.4 sq. m (30 sq. ft.) of actual wall space will be covered by a roll. Wallpaper is usually sold in double or triple rolls. Information in wallpaper sample books will help you figure how many rolls you need to paper a room. A large design will take more wallpaper in order to match the pattern.

A paste bucket and brush, and a paste table are needed to hang wallpaper. If the wallpaper is prepasted, you will need a water tray to wet the paste. A smoothing brush smooths the paper on the wall. A plumb line and chalk will help you get the wallpaper up straight.

You can press the seams flat between strips of wallpaper with a seam roller, and you can wipe away the excess paste from the seam with a sponge. A trimming knife and straight edge cut away excess paper at the ceiling, baseboards, and around doors and windows.

Before you begin to wallpaper, study the directions you have received. Putting up wallpaper takes time and patience. Following directions will help make any job you do easier and more satisfactory.

Textured or washable wall coverings with matching coordinating fabrics gives you the flexibility of adding floral, striped, bold or subdued patterns to a room.

WORDS TO REMEMBER

alkyd
carbon dioxide fire extinguisher
dry chemical fire extinguisher
ionization smoke detector
latex
photoelectric smoke detector

CHECKING YOUR UNDERSTANDING

1. Make a list of the causes of falls in the home. Which causes are the result of human error? Which are the result of furnishings or other items in the home? What might people do to reduce their chances of a fall? What could you do to make your home a safer place?
2. Describe ways to keep an active curious two-year-old child safe from household poisons.
3. Explain why the bathroom is thought to be the most dangerous room in a home. How could you make it safer?
4. Discuss why property insurance is vital in protecting your home and possessions.
5. List the basic tools and supplies you would need to make simple home repairs.
6. You want to paint a bedroom that is 3 × 3 m (10 × 10 ft.). The ceiling is 2.1 m (7 ft.) high. There is a door into the room and one small window. If 1 liter (1 qt.) of paint covers about 9 sq. m (100 sq. ft.), how much paint would be needed to paint the room?

APPLYING YOUR UNDERSTANDING

1. With your classmates, develop an electrical safety checklist that could be used to judge the safety of a building. Using the list you developed, conduct an electrical safety check at home, school, or in another building. How safe was the building you checked? How could any hazards you found be corrected? How complete was your list? Suggest changes to make the checklist more useful.
2. Make a plan for getting out of your home in case of fire. How would people get out of each room in an emergency? Tell your plan to all family members and hold a fire drill at home. How successful was the drill? How well did your plan work? Make improvements if needed.
3. Pretend you are living in a two-bedroom apartment. List all the cleaning chores you would do to keep it clean. Decide how often you would do each task. Make a chart that you could use to carry out your cleaning plan. What tools, equipment, and supplies would you need to do these jobs? Make a list of the types of cleaning products you would buy to keep the apartment clean. What tools and equipment would you buy?

Appendix

PERCENTAGE OF U.S. RDA

This chart shows what percentage of the U.S. RDA you need for your age and sex.

Most people do not need 100 percent of the U.S. RDA for every nutrient. Use of 100 percent of the U.S. RDA as a nutritional goal is in no way dangerous. However, it may lead to needless changes in your diet and to spending more money on food than is necessary. It may also cause you unwarranted concern about nutrient shortages in your day's food choices. On the other hand, at certain stages of the life cycle, some people need more than 100 percent of certain nutrients.

For your daily nutritional goal, select the appropriate amounts of nutrients shown in this table. For example, the recommended amount of calcium for a 16-year-old male or female is 120 percent of the U.S. RDA. Therefore, daily food choices by 16-year-olds should provide 120 percent or more of the U.S. RDA for calcium, rather than 100 percent.

Age	Food Energy[1]	Protein[2]	Vitamin A	Vitamin C	Thiamine	Riboflavin	Niacin[3]	Calcium	Iron
Years	*Calories*	*Percent of U.S. Recommended Daily Allowance*							
Child:									
1-3	1300	35	40	70	50	50	30	80	85
4-6	1800	50	50	70	60	65	35	80	60
7-10	2400	55	70	70	80	75	50	80	60
Male:									
11-14	2800	70	100	75	95	90	55	120	100
15-18	3000	85	100	75	100	110	55	120	100
19-22	3000	85	100	75	100	110	60	80	60
23-50	2700	90	100	75	95	95	45	80	60
51+	2400	90	100	75	80	90	35	80	60
Female:									
11-14	2400	70	80	75	80	80	45	120	100
15-18	2100	75	80	75	75	85	30	120	100
19-22	2100	75	80	75	75	85	35	80	100
23-50	2000	75	80	75	70	75	30	80	100
51+	1800	75	80	75	70	65	25	80	60
Pregnant	+300[4]	+50[4]	100	100	+20[4]	+20[4]	35	120	100+
Nursing	+500[4]	+35[4]	120	135	+20[4]	+30[4]	35	120	100

[1]Calorie needs differ depending on body composition and size, age, and activity of the person.
[2]U.S. RDA of 65 grams is used for this table. In labeling, a U.S. RDA of 45 grams is used for foods providing high-quality protein, such as milk, meat, and eggs.
[3]The percentage of the U.S. RDA shown for niacin will provide the RDA for niacin if the RDA for protein is met. Some niacin is derived in the body from tryptophan, an amino acid present in protein.
[4]To be added to the percentage for the girl or woman of the appropriate age.

Source: *Nutrition Labeling, Tools for Its Use,* Agriculture Information Bulletin No. 382, U.S. Department of Agriculture, 1975.

TABLE OF FOOD VALUES

MILK GROUP	Amount	Calories	Carbohydrates (g)	Fat (g)	Protein (g)	Calcium (mg)	Iron (mg)	Vitamin A (IU)	Thiamine (mg)	Riboflavin (mg)	Niacin (mg)	Vitamin C (mg)
Cheese, American, process	1 oz/28 g	105	Tr	9	6	174	.1	340	.01	.10	Tr	0
Cheese, Cheddar	1 oz/28 g	115	Tr	9	7	204	.2	300	.01	.11	Tr	0
Cheese, cottage, creamed	½ c/120 ml	117	.1	5	14	67.5	.15	185	.025	.185	.135	Tr
Cheese, cottage, dry	½ c/120 ml	62.5	.5	Tr	12.5	23	.15	20	.02	.10	.1	0
Cheese, cream	1 oz/28 g	100	.2	10	2	23	.3	400	Tr	.06	Tr	0
Chocolate milk	1 c/240 ml	210	26	8	8	280	.6	300	.09	.41	.3	2
Cream, heavy	1 T/15 ml	80	.1	6	Tr	10	Tr	220	Tr	.02	Tr	Tr
Cream, light	1 T/15 ml	30	1	3	Tr	14	Tr	110	Tr	.02	Tr	Tr
Cream, sour	1 T/15 ml	25	1	3	Tr	14	Tr	90	Tr	.02	Tr	Tr
Ice cream 16% fat	½ c/120 ml	175	16	12	2	75.5	.05	445	.02	.14	.5	5
Milk	1 c/240 ml	150	11	8	8	291	.1	310	.09	.4	.2	2
Milk, low fat 2%	1 c/240 ml	121	12	5	8	297	.1	500	.1	.4	.2	2
Milk, skim	1 c/240 ml	85	12	Tr	8	302	.1	500	.09	.34	.2	2
Yogurt, fruit	1 c/240 ml	230	42	3	10	343	.2	120	.08	.4	.2	21
Yogurt, plain, skim milk	1 c/240 ml	125	17	Tr	13	452	.2	20	.11	.53	.3	2
Yogurt, plain, whole milk	1 c/240 ml	140	11	7	8	274	.1	280	.07	.32	.2	1

TABLE OF FOOD VALUES (Continued)

MEAT, POULTRY, EGGS, FISH, AND LEGUMES GROUP	Amount	Cal- ories	Car- bohy- drates (g)	Fat (g)	Pro- tein (g)	Cal- cium (mg)	Iron (mg)	Vita- min A (IU)	Thia- mine (mg)	Ribo- flavin (mg)	Nia- cin (mg)	Vita- min C (mg)
Beef, lean (roasted)	3 oz/85 g	165	0	7	25	11	3.2	10	.06	.19	4.5	—
Beef, hamburger, 21% fat	3 oz/85 g	235	0	17	20	9	2.6	30	.07	.17	4.4	—
Chicken (broiled)	3 oz/85 g	115	0	3	20	8	1.4	80	.05	.16	7.4	—
Chicken (fried)	3 oz/85 g	160	1	5	26	9	1.3	70	.04	.17	11.6	—
Eggs (hard cooked)	1	80	1	6	6	28	1	260	.04	.13	Tr	0
Fish, bluefish (baked)	3½ oz/100g	135	0	4	22	25	0.6	40	.09	.08	31.6	—
Ham, boiled	1 oz/28 g	65	0	5	5	3	.8	0	.12	.04	.7	—
Kidney beans (red beans)	1 c/240 ml	230	42	1	15	74	4.6	10	.13	.10	1.5	—
Lamb shoulder (roasted)	3 oz/85 g	285	0	18	23	9	1.0	—	.11	.2	4.0	—
Lentils	1 c/240 ml	210	39	Tr	16	50	4.2	40	.14	.12	1.2	0
Peanut butter	2 T/30 ml	190	6	16	8	20	.6	0	.04	.04	4.8	0
Peas, dried, split	1 c/240 ml	230	42	1	16	22	3.4	80	.3	.18	1.8	—
Pork (roast)	3 oz/85 g	310	0	20	26	9	2.6	0	.46	.21	4.1	—
Sardines	3 oz/85 g	175	0	9	20	372	2.5	190	.02	.17	4.6	—
Tuna, canned in oil	3 oz/85 g	170	0	7	24	7	1.6	70	.04	.1	10.1	—
Turkey, dark meat (roasted)	3 oz/85 g	175	0	7	26	—	2.0	—	.03	.2	3.6	—
Veal cutlet	3 oz/85 g	185	0	9	23	9	2.7	—	.06	.21	4.6	—

TABLE OF FOOD VALUES (Continued)

FRUITS AND VEGETABLES GROUP	Amount	Calories	Carbohydrates (g)	Fat (g)	Protein (g)	Calcium (mg)	Iron (mg)	Vitamin A (IU)	Thiamine (mg)	Riboflavin (mg)	Niacin (mg)	Vitamin C (mg)
Apple	1 (2¾″/63 mm)	80	20	1	Tr	10	.4	120	.04	.03	.1	6
Apricots	3 med	55	14	Tr	1	18	.5	2,890	.03	.04	.6	11
Banana	1 med	100	26	Tr	2	10	.8	230	.06	.07	.8	12
Beans, green	1 c/240 ml	30	7	Tr	2	63	.8	680	.07	.11	.6	15
Bean sprouts	1 c/240 ml	35	7	Tr	4	20	1.4	20	.14	.14	.8	20
Blueberries	1 c/240 ml	90	22	1	1	22	1.5	150	.04	.09	.7	20
Broccoli	1 c/240 ml	40	7	Tr	5	136	1.2	3,880	.14	.31	1.2	140
Cabbage, shredded	1 c/240 ml	15	4	Tr	1	34	.03	90	.04	.04	.2	33
Cabbage, red, shredded, raw	1 c/240 ml	20	5	Tr	1	29	.6	30	.06	.04	.3	43
Cantaloupe	½ melon	80	20	Tr	2	38	1.1	9,240	.11	.08	1.6	90
Carrots	1	30	7	Tr	1	27	.5	7,930	.04	.04	.4	6
Celery, raw	3 stalks	15	6	Tr	Tr	48	.3	330	.03	.03	.3	12
Corn, sweet kernels	1 c/240 ml	130	31	1	5	5	.3	580	.15	.10	2.5	8
Cranberry sauce	½ c/120 ml	202.5	52	Tr	.5	8.5	.3	30	.015	.015	.5	3
Dates	10	220	58	Tr	2	47	2.4	40	.07	.08	1.8	0
Grapefruit juice[a]	¼ c/60 ml	25	6	Tr	.25	6	.05	5	.01	.01	.1	24
Grapes, seedless	10	81	9	Tr	Tr	6	.2	50	.03	.02	.2	2
Lettuce, iceberg	¼ head	17.5	2.6	Tr	.8	18	.45	297	.05	.05	.3	5
Mustard greens	1 c/240 ml	30	6	1	3	193	2.5	8,120	.11	.20	.8	67
Onions, boiled	½ c/120 ml	30	7	Tr	1.5	25	.4	Tr	.03	.03	.2	7.5
Orange	1 (3″/76 mm)	65	16	Tr	1	54	.5	260	.13	.05	.5	66
Orange juice[a]	¼ c/60 ml	30	7.25	Tr	.5	6.25	.1	135	.05	.001	.22	30
Peaches, peeled	1 (2½″/63 mm)	40	10	Tr	1	9	.5	1,330	.02	.05	1.0	7
Pear, Bartlett	1 (2½″/63 mm)	100	25	1	1	13	.5	30	.03	.07	.2	7
Peas, green, frozen	1 c/240 ml	110	19	Tr	.8	30	2.3	960	.43	.14	2.7	21
Pepper, green sweet, raw	1 med	15	4	Tr	1	7	.5	310	.06	.06	.4	94
Pineapple, cubed	1 c/240 ml	80	21	Tr	1	26	.5	110	.14	.05	.3	26
Potato, baked	1 med	145	33	Tr	4	14	1.1	Tr	.15	.07	2.7	31
Potatoes, French fried	10 pieces	155	18	7	2	9	.7	Tr	.07	.04	1.8	12
Prunes, dried	4 med	110	29	Tr	1	22	1.7	690	.04	.07	.7	1
Raisins (snack package)	½ oz/14 g	40	11	Tr	Tr	9	.5	Tr	.02	.01	.1	Tr
Spinach	1 c/240 ml	40	6	1	5	167	4	14,580	.13	.25	.9	50
Tomatoes, canned	1 c/240 ml	50	10	Tr	2	14	1.2	2,170	.12	.07	1.7	41
Tomato, raw	1 med	25	6	Tr	1	16	.6	1,110	.07	.05	.9	28
Tomato juice	6 oz/170 g	35	8	Tr	2	13	1.6	1,460	.09	.05	1.5	29

Note: Although ice cream is a good source of calcium, it also contains many calories, and may lead to weight problems.
Key: Tr—Nutrient present in trace amounts. [a] Made from concentrate.

TABLE OF FOOD VALUES (Continued)

BREAD AND CEREALS GROUP	Amount	Calories	Carbohydrates (g)	Fat (g)	Protein (g)	Calcium (mg)	Iron (mg)	Vitamin A (IU)	Thiamine (mg)	Riboflavin (mg)	Niacin (mg)	Vitamin C (mg)
Bread, white enriched	1 slice	70	13	1	2	21	.6	Tr	.08	.06	.8	Tr
Bread, whole wheat	1 slice	65	14	1	3	24	.8	0	.07	.03	.8	Tr
Bread, pumpernickel (⅔% rye)	1 slice	80	17	Tr	3	27	.8	0	.09	.07	.6	0
Corn flakes, fortified (25% RDA)	1 c/240 ml	95	21	Tr	2	V	V	V	V	V	V	13
Crackers, saltines	4	50	8	1	1	2	.5	0	.05	.05	.4	0
Egg noodles, enriched	1 c/240 ml	200	37	2	7	16	1.4	110	.22	.13	1.9	0
Pasta, enriched, (macaroni cooked, etc.)	1 c/240 ml	190	39	1	7	14	1.4	0	.23	.13	1.8	0
Rice, instant, enriched	1 c/240 ml	180	40	Tr	4	5	1.3	0	.21	V	1.7	0
Rice, enriched	1 c/240 ml	185	41	Tr	4	33	1.4	0	.19	.02	2.1	0
Rice, puffed, whole grain	1 c/240 ml	60	13	Tr	1	3	.3	0	.07	.01	.7	0
Wheat, farina, quick	1 c/240 ml	105	22	Tr	3	147	V	0	.12	.07	1	0
Wheat flakes, fortified, 25% U.S. RDA	¾ c/180 ml	105	24	Tr	3	12	4.8	1,320	.40	.45	5.3	16
Wheat, puffed, whole grain	1 c/240 ml	55	12	Tr	2	4	.6	0	.08	.03	1.2	0
Wheat, shredded, whole grain	1 large biscuit	90	20	1	2	11	.9	0	.06	.03	1.1	0
Wheat, whole grain cereal	1 c/240 ml	110	23	1	4	17	1.2	0	.15	.05	1.5	0

TABLE OF FOOD VALUES (Continued)

OTHER	Amount	Calories	Carbohydrates (g)	Fat (g)	Protein (g)	Calcium (mg)	Iron (mg)	Vitamin A (IU)	Thiamine (mg)	Riboflavin (mg)	Niacin (mg)	Vitamin C (mg)
Bacon, fried crisp	2 slices	85	Tr	8	4	2	.5	0	.08	.05	.8	—
Butter	1 T/14 g	100	Tr	12	Tr	3	Tr	430	Tr	Tr	Tr	0
Doughnuts, glazed	1	205	22	11	3	16	.6	25	.1	.1	.8	0
Honey	1 T/21 g	65	17	0	Tr	1	.1	0	Tr	.01	.1	Tr
Margarine, regular	1 T/15 g	100	Tr	12	Tr	3	Tr	470	Tr	Tr	Tr	0
Mayonnaise	1 T/15 ml	100	Tr	11	Tr	3	.1	40	Tr	.01	Tr	—
Nuts, peanuts, salted	1 c/240 ml	840	27	72	37	107	3	—	.46	.19	24.8	0
Nuts, walnuts	1 c/240 ml	785	19	74	26	Tr	7.5	380	.28	.14	.9	—
Oil, corn	1 T/15 ml	120	0	14	0	0	0	—	0	0	0	0
Pizza, cheese	1 slice	145	22	4	6	86	1.1	230	.16	.18	1.6	4
Popcorn, plain	1 c/240 ml	25	5	Tr	1	1	.2	—	—	.01	.1	0
Salad dressing, Italian	1 T/15 ml	85	1	9	Tr	2	Tr	Tr	Tr	Tr	Tr	—
Salad dressing, Italian low calorie	1 T/15 ml	10	Tr	1	Tr	Tr	Tr	Tr	Tr	Tr	Tr	—
Seeds, sunflower	½ c/120 g	405	14.5	34.5	17.5	87	5.15	35	1.42	.17	3.9	—
Sugar	1 T/12 g	45	12	0	0	0	Tr	0	0	0	0	0

Note: All fruits and vegetables fresh unless noted. Vegetables fresh cooked unless noted.
Key: [a] Made from concentrate. Tr—Nutrient present in trace amounts. V—Varies by brand; consult label.

PATTERN SIZES

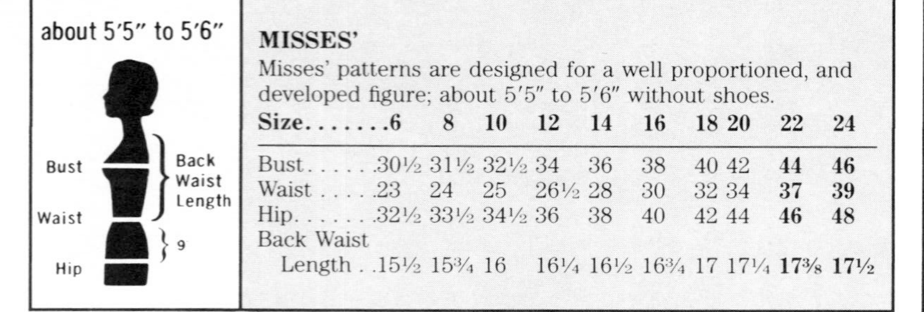

about 5′5″ to 5′6″

MISSES'

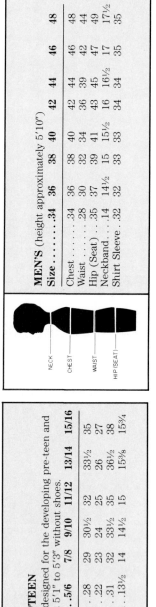

Misses' patterns are designed for a well proportioned, and developed figure; about 5′5″ to 5′6″ without shoes.

Size	6	8	10	12	14	16	18	20	**22**	**24**
Bust	30½	31½	32½	34	36	38	40	42	**44**	**46**
Waist	23	24	25	26½	28	30	32	34	**37**	**39**
Hip	32½	33½	34½	36	38	40	42	44	**46**	**48**
Back Waist Length	15½	15¾	16	16¼	16½	16¾	17	17¼	**17⅜**	**17½**

about 5′2″ to 5′3″

MISS PETITE

This new size range is designed for the shorter Miss figure; about 5′2″ to 5′3″ without shoes.

Size	6mp	8mp	10mp	12mp	14mp	16mp
Bust	30½	31½	32½	34	36	38
Waist	23½	24½	25½	27	28½	30½
Hip	32½	33½	34½	36	38	40
Back Waist Length	14½	14¾	15	15¼	15½	15¾

about 5′2″ to 5′3″

HALF-SIZE

Half-size patterns are for a fully developed figure with a short backwaist length. Waist and hip are larger in proportion to bust than other figure types; about 5′2″ to 5′3″ without shoes.

Size	10½	12½	14½	16½	18½	20½	22½	24½
Bust	33	35	37	39	41	43	45	47
Waist	27	29	31	33	35	37½	40	42½
Hip	35	37	39	41	43	45½	48	50½
Back Waist Length	15	15¼	15½	15¾	15⅞	16	16⅛	16¼

about 5′1″ to 5′3″

YOUNG JUNIOR/TEEN

This size range is designed for the developing pre-teen and teen figures; about 5′1″ to 5′3″ without shoes.

Size	5/6	7/8	9/10	11/12	13/14	15/16
Bust	28	29	30½	32	33½	35
Waist	22	23	24	25	26	27
Hip	31	32	33½	35	36½	38
Back Waist Length	13½	14	14½	15	15⅜	15¾

about 5′4″ to 5′5″

JUNIOR

Junior patterns are designed for a well proportioned, shorter waisted figure; about 5′4″ to 5′5″ without shoes.

Size	5	7	9	11	13	15
Bust	30	31	32	33½	35	37
Waist	22½	23½	24½	25½	27	29
Hip	32	33	34	35½	37	39
Back Waist Length	15	15¼	15½	15¾	16	16¼

about 5′ to 5′1″

JUNIOR PETITE

Junior Petite patterns are designed for a well proportioned, petite figure; about 5′ to 5′1″ without shoes.

Size	3jp	5jp	7jp	9jp	11jp	13jp
Bust	30	31	32	33	34	35
Waist	22	23	24	25	26	27
Hip	31	32	33	34	35	36
Back Waist Length	14	14¼	14½	14¾	15	15¼

about 5′5″ to 5′6″

WOMEN'S

Women's patterns are designed for the larger, more fully mature figure; about 5′5″ to 5′6″ without shoes.

Size	38	40	42	44	46	48	50
Bust	42	44	46	48	50	52	54
Waist	35	37	39	41½	44	46½	49
Hip	44	46	48	50	52	54	56
Back Waist Length	17¼	17⅜	17½	17⅝	17¾	17⅞	18

NECK / CHEST / WAIST / HIP (SEAT)

MEN'S (height approximately 5′10″)

Size	34	36	38	40	42	44	46	48
Chest	34	36	38	40	42	44	46	48
Waist	28	30	32	34	36	39	42	44
Hip (Seat)	35	37	39	41	43	45	47	49
Neckband	14	14½	15	15½	16	16½	17	17½
Shirt Sleeve	32	32	33	33	34	34	35	35

Glossary

Achromatic: Without color; in color language, black, white, and gray are neutral or achromatic colors. (15)

Adjustments: Changes in length and width that can be made on the pattern tissue before the garment is cut out. (19)

Adoption: A civil procedure in which an adult becomes legally responsible for a child who is not biologically related. (7)

Adversarial divorce: A dissolution of a marriage in which one partner is blamed for the marital breakdown. (6)

À la carte (ah la CART): Foods listed and priced individually on a menu. (28)

Alkyd: Oil-based paint. (32)

Alterations: Complicated changes in a pattern that affect the contours of a garment. (19)

American Gas Association (AGA) Seal: A seal found on all gas appliances tested by the American Gas Association laboratories. (25)

Amniocentesis: A medical diagnostic procedure during which the doctor removes and analyzes a sample of the fluid from the amniotic sac. (8)

Amniotic sac: A membrane bag of fluid which holds and supports the fetus during pregnancy. (8)

Ampere: A measure of electrical current. (30)

Analogous: In color language, colors that are next to each other on the color wheel. (15)

Annual percentage yield: The number of dollars each $100 will earn if left in an account for one year. (11)

Annuity: A contract with an insurance firm. You pay the company a given amount of money, and in return, you get income based on the amount of money invested, the interest that has built up, and your life expectancy. (13)

Annuity rate (yield): The amount of income obtainable for each $1,000 put into the annuity. (13)

Antiseptic: A mild substance that will help prevent infection. (25)

Arbitration: The settlement of a dispute by a person or group chosen to listen to both sides and make judgement. (14)

Assembly line: A way of organizing sewing methods to do as much sewing and then as much pressing as possible at one time. (20)

Assets: What you own. (10)

Backstitch: A strong hand stitch used to mend machine-stitched seams and to fasten thread ends securely. (18)

Balance: The way the internal spaces of a design work together. (15)

Ball and socket: The two halves of a snap. If the edges of the garment overlap, the ball part is always sewn to the underside of the top layers. (18)

Beneficiary: The person the policyholder names to get the money (face value) after his or her death. You may name more than one beneficiary. (13)

Blanching: The process of placing food in boiling water or steam for a short time and then plunging it into cold water to stop the food from overcooking. (27)

Blended family: A family formed when a couple with children from previous families marry. (4)

Boil: To cook in liquid at a temperature high enough so that the liquid bubbles. (26)

Boutique: A type of specialty store that carries high-fashion or unique clothes. (17)

Braise: A method of cooking food slowly in a small amount of liquid in a covered pan. (26)

Broil: Food that is placed directly under the heat source (element or gas flame). (26)

Buffet service: A type of meal service in which the food and dishes are arranged on a serving table and people help themselves. (28)

Calendering: A finishing technique that smooths the fabric and improves its luster by passing it between two heated rollers. (16)

Calorie: A term used to measure energy or heat. One calorie is the amount of heat required to raise the temperature of 1 kilogram of water by 1°C. (21)

Canceled check: A check for which a bank made payment with money from your checking account. (11)

Canning: A food preservation method in which food is heated to a temperature of 100° C. (212° F.) or above, in boiling water for a specific amount of time. (27)

Carbohydrate: An important source of food energy, made up of the elements carbon, hydrogen, and oxygen. (21)

Carbon dioxide fire extinguisher: A device that smothers a fire with (carbon dioxide) gas. (32)

Carpeting: A woven fabric floor covering that covers the entire floor. (31)

Cash value or cash surrender: The value of a policy a policyholder gets if he or she stops premium payments before the policy's maturity date. It is also the loan value of a policy and usually referred to as the savings. (13)

Checking account: Lets you transfer money by check or electronically, from your account to another person or firm. (11)

Cholesterol: A fatlike substance used by the body to make the necessary chemicals and to aid in digestion. (21)

Chromosome: A part of a body cell that sets and passes on hereditary traits. (8)

Classic: A traditional style that stays in fashion for a long time. (17)

Classification: Organizing items or ideas according to their traits. (9)

Clip: A small cut in the seam allowance of an inside curve. Clipping makes it possible for the seam allowance to lie flat when the seam is pressed. (20)

Clique: Groups of three-to-eight people who exclude others from the group. (3)

C.O.D.: An abbreviation for the cash-on-delivery way of payment. (17)

Communication: Sharing messages or ideas with other people. It can be either verbal or nonverbal. (2)

Comparison shopping: The process of getting facts about a product or service before you buy it. (14)

Complementary: In color language, the two colors opposite each other on the color wheel. (15)

Complete proteins: High quality proteins that contain the eight essential amino acids. (21)

Compound interest: Figured on the principal and the accumulated interest. (11)

Concepts: Ideas. (9)

Condominiums: Multiple-family housing owned in which each unit is owned individually with common areas owned jointly. (29)

Consignment shop: A type of shop that sells used clothes and takes a percentage of the selling price. (17)

Consumer credit: Credit used by individuals and families. (12)

Cooperative apartments: Multiple-family housing owned by a nonprofit corporation whose shareholders have a right to live in the building. (29)

Couple family: A family that does not have children living in the home. (4)

Courtship: A dating relationship in which the couple is serious about each other and think of a future together. (3)

Credit: An arrangement by which you receive money, goods, or services now and pay for it later. (11)

Credit bureau: A clearinghouse for consumer information. Its purpose is to collect, keep, and pass along facts about consumer financial transactions. (12)

Credit card: A plastic card identifying you as approved for a predetermined amount of credit by the issuer of the card. (12)

Credit history: A record of how you have handled credit in the past. (12)

Credit rating: How a potential lender of sales or cash credit rates you as a credit risk. (12)

Crowd: A loosely knit group of peers. (3)

Cured meat: Meat that has been treated with preservatives, such as salt, nitrates, wood smoke, spices, chemicals, and sugar to help preserve it and give it a special flavor and color. (24)

Curtains: Window coverings that have a casing at the top through which a rod passes. (31)

Custodial child care: Programs that provide safe physical care for a child but have no planned activities for physical, social, or intellectual growth. (7)

Cut of meat: A portion of meat cut away from the animal carcass. Meat cuts are based on the muscle and bone structure and on the appropriate method to cook the meat. (24)

Daily Food Guide: A guide compiled by nutritionists to help people make wise food choices. It divides food into five groups according to the nutrients they contain and lists the number and size of servings needed daily from each group. (22)

Darning: A network of stitches used to fill in a hole. (18)

Decision making: The process of making choices from among options. (1)

Deductible: The amount of an insurance claim that must be paid by the insured. The insurance firm is responsible for the balance. (13)

Deed: The written document that passes ownership of property. (29)

Deep fat fry: Food that is cooked in hot fat until it is brown. (26)

Dehydrator: An appliance that provides a controlled drying atmosphere for the drying of foods. (27)

Delustering: Process of treating fibers or fabric chemically to reduce their gloss. (16)

Designer ease: The amount of room built into a garment to make it look the way the designer intended. This type of ease is in addition to minimum ease. (19)

Development: A change in body function or skill. (8)

Developmental tasks: The skills, knowledge, and attitudes needed to succeed in each stage of life. (1)

Developmental child care: Programs that promote the child's physical, social, and intellectual growth. (7)

Dietary Guidelines: Established by the U.S. government as recommendations for people to improve their health by changing their eating habits. (22)

Directional stitching: To stitch in the same direction as the grain of the fabric. (20)

Discipline: To train or develop through teaching and guidance. (9)

Divorce: The legal ending or dissolution of a marriage. It changes the legal rights and duties between a man and a woman. (6)

Dope: The liquid formed when natural materials or chemicals are combined to create manufactured fibers. (16)

Down payment: A part of the cost of an item that you must give to a store. The store will then hold the item for you until you pay the rest of the money; a cash payment of a part of the cost of buying a home. (17) (29)

Drapes: Window coverings that are pleated and hooked onto a rod. (31)

Drive time: In radio, the morning and afternoon hours when many people drive to and from work by car. (14)

Dry chemical fire extinguisher: A device that uses a powder to coat a burning surface and smother the fire. (32)

Easestitching: A technique used to join a larger garment part to a slightly smaller one. (20)

Edgestitching: Topstitching done close to a seamline or garment edge. (20)

Elaboration: A process used to teach a child language in which the adult repeats what the child says and adds to (or elaborates on) it. (9)

Embryo: The fertilized egg during the second to tenth week of pregnancy. (8)

Empathy: The ability to see the world through another person's eyes. (2)

Enclosed seam: A seam that is hidden between layers of fabric. (20)

Engagement: A commitment to marry. (6)

Enriched: When nutrients lost in processing have been replaced. (23)

Entrée (AHN-tray): The main dish in a meal. (28)

Entrepreneurs: People who own and operate their own businesses. (5)

Entry level job: Job that requires little, if any, skill, schooling, or experience to do. (5)

Environment: The physical surroundings. (8)

Evaluation: The process of judging or measuring performance. (1)

Extended family: Several generations of relatives living together. (4)

Face value: The amount paid to a beneficiary after the policyholder's death. It is also the amount paid to the policyholder when a policy matures (the end of a certain time period). (13)

Fad: A fashion that is popular for a very short time. (17)

Family: Two or more people related to each other by blood, marriage, or adoption. (4)

Family life cycle: The changes and development that a family experiences over the years. (4)

Fashion cycle: A slow, recurring change in fashion. (17)

Fat-soluble vitamin: A vitamin that dissolves in fat such as vitamins A, D, E, and K. (21)

Fetus: The unborn child. (8)

Figure type: Size ranges based on body contours and proportions. (19)

Filament: A fiber long enough to be measured in yards or meters. (16)

Finance charge: A statement that includes the interest charge plus any other costs for the loan, such as credit investigation fee, life insurance (if asked for), service fees, and handling charges. (12)

Financial plan: A personal financial road map—a guide to help you reach your financial goals. (11)

First impression: An image someone forms about another person when they meet for the first time. (18)

Fixed expense: A fixed amount of money paid each week, month, quarter, or year. (11)

Flat construction: A sewing method where as many details as possible are done on each garment part while it is still flat. (20)

Flatware: The knives, forks, spoons, and other eating and serving pieces used by diners. (28)

Flexible expense: A payment that varies in amount and payment due date. (11)

Floor plan: An illustration of the layout of a room or dwelling. (30)

Food additives: Substances that are added to foods during processing. (23)

Food-borne disease: Food poisoning caused by various bacteria in food. (25)

Food preservation: A process, such as canning, freezing, or drying foods, that keeps foods from spoiling for a fairly long time. (27)

Friend: Someone with whom you are on familiar and good terms. (3)

Fusible: An interfacing that is applied with a combination of heat, steam, and pressure. (19)

Garnishes: An edible decoration that adds color and variety to foods to make them look more appealing. (27)

Gene: A part of a chromosome that holds the specific message for a particular inherited trait. Each gene has a definite location on the chromosome. (8)

Generic: The name given to a group of manufactured fibers that have the same chemical composition. (16)

Generic foods: Food products with no brand name. (23)

Goal: An objective for which you are willing to make an effort to achieve. (1)

Grading: The process of trimming each seam allowance to a different width. (20)

Grain perfect: When the crosswise and lengthwise yarns of a fabric are at right angles to each other. (19)

Grounds for divorce: Marital "crimes," such as cruelty, desertion, or adultery, which are the basis of an adversarial divorce. (6)

Growth: A change in body size or weight. (8)

Hand: The way a fabric feels and how well it drapes. (19)

Heredity: Those traits you inherit from your parents. (1)

Hierarchy: An arrangement of persons, things, or ideas based on their level of importance. (14)

Homogenize: To break up fat particles so that they are uniformly small and evenly suspended in the milk. (24)

Hormones: Chemicals that cause the body to grow and mature. (1)

Hue: The name given to a specific color or pigment, such as red, purple, or blue. (15)

Image ad: An ad designed to appeal to your fantasies, to make a fashion statement, or to promote a store's or manufacturer's name. (14)

Imitation foods: Foods made to resemble natural foods in taste, texture, and appearance. (23)

Income: The money you have to pay expenses, save, and invest. (10)

Incomplete protein: Protein lacking one or more essential amino acids. (21)

Installment credit: Usually involves a printed contract, may need a down payment or trade-in, and requires the balance to be paid in equal payments for a certain time period. The finance charge is determined by the amount of money financed and the length of the payment period. (12)

Insulation: A material that does not conduct heat or cold air. (30)

Insurance: Financial protection against the risks, mishaps, and uncertainties of life. These include a major illness, an accident, a disability, an early death, theft, or a natural disaster. (13)

Insurance policy: A legal contract between the policyholder (the insured) and the insurance firm. (13)

Intensity: The brightness or dullness of color. (15)

Interest: The fee charged or paid for the use of money. (11)

Interfacing: An extra layer of fabric that adds shape and strength to areas of the garment that are subject to extra stress. (19)

Ionized smoke detector: A device that best detects a fast burning fire such as burning paper or flammable liquids. (32)

Iron: Removing wrinkles from fabric by sliding a warm or hot iron back and forth over it. (18)

Latex: Water-based paint. (32)

Leader: Someone who guides or influences a group. (2)

Lease: A written legal contract between an owner and a tenant listing the conditions to be met by both parties. (29)

Legumes: Seeds that grow in a pod, such as kidney beans and peas. (24)

Liability insurance: Applies to people and property. If judged liable (at fault) for an accident, you are legally bound to pay for the bodily harm and property damage incurred. (13)

Machine baste: To use long machine stitches to hold the fabric in place only until the permanent seam is stitched. (20)

Management: The process of reaching goals through the effective use of human and material resources. (1)

Marbling: Flecks or veins of fat distributed in meat. (24)

Meal management: The process of planning, selecting, and serving meals that contribute to a healthful, balanced diet. (22)

Meal pattern: Habits or schedules that one has for eating. (22)

Measurements: Exact amounts of ingredients given in a recipe. (25)

Menu: A list of dishes to be served at a meal. (22)

Mercerization: A process that adds luster to a fiber and improves its ability to absorb dyes. (19)

Metabolism: The body's ability to burn calories. (22)

Minimum balance checking account: An account in which if you keep a required amount of money at all times, you pay no service charges. (11)

Minimum ease: The extra room needed in a garment to let the body move. (19)

Modeling: Demonstrating actions or being an example for others to follow. (9)

Money management: Financially being in control of your money. (10)

Monochromatic: Using only one color; a variety of shades, tints, textures, and intensities may be used. (15)

Mortgage: Money borrowed to finance purchase of a home. (29)

Mutual expectations: When both people in a relationship expect the relationship to head in the same way or toward the same purpose. (2)

Napping: A finishing technique that uses wire brushes to give the fabric a soft, fuzzy surface. (16)

Needs: Things that are essential for survival. (1)

Net earnings: Your total earnings less all deductions. (10)

Network: A system of relationships in which you are involved. (5)

Networking: Working with others in your network to achieve personal goals. (5)

Net worth: The total current cash value of your assets less your liabilities. (10)

No-fault divorce: A dissolution of a marriage that is not blamed on either partner. (6)

Notch: A small wedge of fabric that is cut from the seam allowance on an outside curve. Notching makes it possible for the seam allowance to lie flat when the seam is pressed. (20)

Notions: Things such as buttons, zippers, snaps, seam tapes, hooks and eyes, and elastic used to finish a garment. (19)

Nuclear family: A family with two parents and their children who live together. (4)

Nurture: To promote or influence development or growth. (7)

Nutrient density: The ratio of nutrients in food to the number of calories. (22)

Nutrients: Substances found in foods that supply the body with nourishment and energy. (21)

Object permanance: Understanding that objects exist out of sight. (9)

Open dating: A system of date coding food products. (23)

Osteoporosis: A thinning of the bones due to a lack of calcium over a period of years. (21)

Outlet store: A type of store that sells only the items made by the manufacturer that owns it. (17)

Panbroil: Method of preparing meat in an uncovered skillet by pouring off fat as it melts from the food. (26)

Panfry: Method of cooking food in a skillet using only a small amount of fat to cover the bottom of the pan. (26)

Parenthood: Being the natural mother or father of a child. (7)

Parenting: Skills in caring for and nurturing a child whether or not you are the natural parent of the child. (7)

Pasteurize: To heat a fluid to a given temperature for a period of time in order to kill harmful bacteria. (24)

Payroll deduction plan: A private agreement between you and your employer. It allows the deduction of a set amount from your earnings to be put in the savings and/or investment plan(s) you choose. (11)

Peers: People of the same age. (3)

Peer group: Group of people of the same or similar age. (3)

Peer pressure: The influence that a group exerts on its members to get them to conform to the values and standards of the group. (14)

Perishable: Food that spoils easily unless it is kept at the correct temperature. (23)

Photoelectric smoke detector: A device that best identifies a slow smoldering fire, such as a fire in upholstered furniture. (32)

Pile: The soft fibers coming up from the base in a rug or carpet. (31)

Placenta: The organ that nourishes the fetus during pregnancy. (8)

Placket: A slit in a garment that forms a closure. (19)

Ply: The number of individual strands of fibers that make up a yarn. (16)

Poached: Cooking delicate foods, like fish and eggs, in hot or simmering liquid. Enough liquid in the pan is used so that the food can float. (26)

Portable appliances: Small electrical appliances that can be moved from one place to another. (25)

Premium: The price or cost of the insurance, or what you pay for a policy's protection. (13)

Prenatal: Before birth. (8)

Press: To remove wrinkles by picking the iron up and putting it back down on the fabric in an overlapping pattern. (18)

Press cloth: A piece of lightweight fabric that is placed between the iron and the fashion fabric. It protects the fabric from shine and iron marks. (18)

Prime time: In television, the early evening hours when families turn on their TV sets. (14)

Private label: A store label put on clothes or other merchandise made by a manufacturer exclusively for a particular store. (17)

Produce: Fresh fruits and vegetables. (24)

Property settlement: A division of possessions in a divorce. (6)

Proportion: The relationship of two or more spaces to each other and to the total shape or appearance of an object. (15)

Rancidity: Having a bad smell or taste, caused by the breakdown of fats in foods. (24)

Rapport: Being comfortable and at ease with someone else. (2)

Recipe: A list of ingredients and instructions for mixing them. (25)

Regular or single payment charge account: An account where you pay the bill in full within the certain time period, usually ten to thirty days after the billing date. (12)

Refined: The processing of grain that results in removal of parts of the kernel and the destruction of many nutrients. (24)

Resources: Human and material sources of support or supply for use in reaching goals. (1)

Respect: Accepting and appreciating the other person as a person in his or her own right. (2)

Resume: A listing of your personal information, school record, and work experience. (5)

Revolving charge account: An account that enables you to make partial payment rather than payment in full. The business sets the maximum amount of credit you may use. You agree to make a stated monthly minimum payment plus a finance charge on the unpaid balance. (12)

Reweaving: A method of mending small holes and tears by using yarns from the inside parts of a garment. (18)

Roasting: To cook meat or poultry in an oven so that the food rests on the pan bottom or on a rack. (26)

Role: A position or part you play in a relationship. (2)

Rugs: Woven fabric floor coverings cut to less than room size and finished with bound edges. (31)

Rule of 72: A formula to find roughly the number of years it will take for money to double. Divide 72 by the rate of compound interest that the savings and/or investments earn. (11)

Safe deposit box: One of a group of locked, metal boxes in a vault at your bank. (10)

Saturated fats: Fats that are found in foods of animal origin, that contain more hydrogen, and that are solid at room temperature. (21)

Savings account: Lets you save money (deposits plus earned interest) for future use. (11)

Seam finish: Any treatment that stops the fabric from fraying on the inside of a garment. (20)

Seasonal: The time when fruits and vegetables naturally ripen and are ready for harvesting. (24)

Security deposits: A payment made by the tenant that protects the owner against any damage done to a rental unit. (29)

Self-concept: How you feel about yourself. (1)

Selvage: The smooth edge along the length of woven fabric. (16)

Seriation: Putting items in order. (9)

Service contract: A type of insurance that protects you against the breakdown of an appliance. (31)

Shade: A color that is darkened by the addition of black. (15)

Shank: The stem on a button that provides the space to make room for the layers of fabric that surround a buttonhole. Shanks can be built-in to the button or they can be created out of thread when the button is attached. (18)

Siblings: Brothers and sisters. (4)

Simmer: To cook food in liquid at a temperature below boiling. (26)

Simple interest: Figured on only the principal or amount of money involved. (11)

Single-parent family: A family led, or headed by one parent. (4)

Site: The location of a housing unit. (29)

Sizing: The process of adding starches or resins to fabric for extra body. (16)

Spouse: A husband or wife. (6)

Standard of identity: A list of key ingredients and the minimum amount of each to be included in a product. (23)

Standing time: The time food continues to cook after the microwave power has been turned off. (27)

Staple: A fiber short enough to be measured in inches or centimeters. (16)

Statement of earnings: An itemized explanation of earnings and deductions. (10)

Staystitching: A line of stitches that stops curved or bias edges from stretching out of shape as they are handled. (20)

Steamed: Food that is placed on a rack or in a basket in a deep pot with a small amount of water. (26)

Sublet: When an original tenant rents a leased unit to another person. (29)

Synthetic: A fiber created from chemicals. (16)

System: A logical, orderly way to do something. (18)

Tax-deferred: The interest that builds up tax free until you redeem a U.S. savings bond or take money out of an IRA and so forth. (13)

Tenant: A person who rents property. (29)

Thrift shop: A type of store that sells secondhand or used clothes and household items. (17)

Tint: A color that is lightened by the addition of white. (15)

Title: The legal document proving the owner's right to the property. (29)

Topstitching: Stitching that appears on the outside of the garment. (20)

Trade name: The name assigned to a generic fiber made by a particular manufacturer. Manufacturers cannot use each other's trade names. (16)

Traffic patterns: The paths people follow as they move about a home. (30)

Trend: A gradual change in a style or a way of wearing clothes. (17)

Triadic: A color scheme using any three colors that are an equal distance apart on the color wheel. (15)

Trimming: The process of cutting off part of the seam allowance so that it is a narrower width. (20)

Trust: Being able to rely and depend on another person. (2)

Twist: The ways plies are put together to form a yarn. (16)

Umbilical cord: A tubelike organ that attaches the fetus to the placenta. (8)

Understitching: An extra row of stitching that prevents a facing or layer of fabric from rolling to the outside of a garment. (20)

Underwriters Laboratories (UL) Seal: A seal found on all electrical equipment, appliances, and materials showing that the units have been laboratory tested and approved safe. (25)

Unit construction: A sewing method where garments are done in small parts, or units, and then the units are joined together. (20)

Unit pricing: The cost per unit of measure, such as kilogram or pound, or other convenient unit. (23)

Universal Product Code: A small block of ten bars with some numbers to one side printed on a label. The block is a code that can be read by a computerized scanner which can identify the item to produce a receipt and a record for inventory. (23)

Unsaturated fats: Fats that are found in fish and plants, that are liquid at room temperature, and that contain less hydrogen. (21)

Value: The lightness or darkness of a color. (15)

Values: Personal ideals and principles about what makes life important and worthwhile. (1)

Veneer: A thin sheet of wood glued over another piece of wood to improve appearance. (31)

Vested right: The claim for benefits you earn under the provisions of a firm's pension plan. Generally, your claim is determined by the number of years of eligible employment. (13)

W-2 form: Itemizes for a one year period the total earnings, the amount withheld for taxes, and the amount withheld for Social Security. (10)

Wants: Things you desire to make life more enjoyable. (1)

Warp: The threads that run lengthwise on a loom or a piece of fabric. (16)

Warranty: A printed guarantee by the manufacturer or store that a product or service will meet certain standards. (14)

Water-soluble vitamins: Vitamins that dissolve in water, such as the B vitamins and vitamin C.

Watt: A measure of electrical current used by a light bulb. (31)

Wedding: The ceremony symbolizing the public commitment of two people to each other in marriage. (6)

Woof (Weft): In weaving, the crosswise threads on a loom or a piece of fabric. In knitting, a type of fabric knit with only one yarn. (16)

Work centers: Centers in the kitchen that include appliances, equipment, and enough work space and storage area for the work done there. (25)

Work flow: The path traveled among work centers in normal food preparation. (25)

Work triangle: The imaginary triangle established among the three work centers in the kitchen. (25)

Zones: Areas in a house. Most homes have three zones—the work zone, the living zone, and the sleeping zone. (30)

Index

Listening, 32

N

O

P

Q

R

S

Abbott Laboratories, 55
American Sheep Producers Council, Inc., 211
Apple Computers, 129
Armstrong World Industries, 387

Bannon, Lynn/St. Francis Hospital, Peoria, IL, 174
Better Homes and Gardens/Meredith Corporation, 421
Black & Decker, 341
Boy Scouts of America, 113
Brown, William, 238
Burlington Coat Factory/Carroll, 198
Burlington Industries, 220

Caldwell, Barbara, 24, 60, 95, 104, 110
Cannon, Brian, 84, 202
Carroll, Todd, 16, 28, 41, 70, 82, 92, 140, 167, 172, 181, 196, 208, 224, 226, 237, 251, 257, 262, 265, 296, 321, 335, 346, 350, 361, 370, 380, 396, 411, 427
Casual Corner/Gaffney, 259
Caterpillar Credit Union/Gaffney, 170
Corning Glass Works, 75
Croscill Home Furnishings, 414
Cy DeCosse, Inc., Copyright © 1984, 258

Dana Corporation, 71
Del Monte Kitchens, 306
Dusenbery, Eric, 206

Esser, Stephan, 351, 355, 357, 358, 359, 364, 365, 367, 392, 397, 404

Featherly, Janet, 21
Fishel, Scott, 51, 114, 120, 131, 141, 142, 143, 158, 186, 189, 229, 231, 233, 244, 275, 315, 317, 353, 382, 385, 386
Fleetwood Enterprises, 85
Florida Department of Tourism, 42

G.E. Lighting/Vance Roth, 412, 416, 417
GNC Store/Gaffney, 327
Gaffney, James B., 31, 34, 44, 47, 56, 57, 62, 65, 79, 87, 89, 96, 100, 103, 108, 116, 155, 183, 228, 229, 232, 311, 326, 393, 422, 428, 436
Gerber Products, Inc., 117
Godfather's Pizza/Gaffney, 303

Haas Cabinet Company, 414
Henley, Butch/American Hiking Society, 374
Hobie Cat/Craig Fineman, 281
House Beautiful's Home Decorating, 420

Illinois State University, 38, 83

Jenkins, Mike, 161, 362

King, Lis, 412, 423, 424, 439
Kee, Vicky, 19, 23, 24, 43, 46, 96

Lee, Robert II, 323
Levi Strauss & Co., 226

Management Housing Institute, 221
Man-Made Fiber Producers Association, Inc., 211
Manual High School/Carroll, 204
Manufactured Housing Institute, 407
The Maytag Company, 424
McElwee, Robert, 20, 22, 24, 30, 37, 43, 51, 73, 84, 93, 112, 115, 150, 184, 190, 209, 225, 234, 287, 308, 381, 406, 413, 417, 419, 425, 429, 431, 432, 433, 435
Merete Shopping—Norway, 235
Michigan Bean Commission, 289

National Dairy Council, 294
National Pork Producers Council, 304

Pillsbury Nutrition Program, 306
Purcell, Liz, 15, 66, 69, 125, 195, 199, 201, 203, 276, 279, 379

Rubbermaid, Inc., 103

Simpson, David, 74, 388
The Softness Group, 228
Solar Power Corporation, 382
Sports 'n' Spokes/Paralyzed Veterans of America, 105
Stephen's Institute, 197
Sunkist Growers, 292

3M Corporation, 71
Trillium/Wolinsky, 211

United States Department of Agriculture, 284

Village Plantation/Gaffney, 327

Welsh, Mark, 99, 252, 429
West Bend Company, 341
Western Wood Producers Association, 409
Whirlpool Corporation, 64, 297, 298, 299, 340, 383
Windowshade Manufacturers Association, 423
Wright, Ann, 18, 29, 39, 52, 84, 102, 159, 234, 242, 318, 405

Zehr, Duane, 18, 24, 33, 35, 48, 54, 77, 94, 95, 99, 119, 126, 130, 131, 139, 144, 157, 158, 160, 173, 179, 182, 185, 186, 188, 190, 201, 217, 218, 219, 231, 253, 261, 266, 267, 280, 283, 284, 288, 291, 292, 309, 311, 312, 315, 323, 324, 325, 329, 353, 365, 389, 391, 403, 408, 415, 430, 436